PEOPLES AND CULTURES OF AFRICA

AN ANTHROPOLOGICAL READER

EDITED AND WITH
SECTIONAL INTRODUCTIONS BY
ELLIOTT P. SKINNER

PUBLISHED FOR
THE AMERICAN MUSEUM OF NATURAL HISTORY
THE DOUBLEDAY / NATURAL HISTORY PRESS
GARDEN CITY, NEW YORK
1973

ISBN: 0-385-08349-1 Paperback
        0-385-08345-9 Trade
Library of Congress Catalog Card Number 72–77003

PEOPLES AND CULTURES
OF AFRICA

The Natural History Press, publisher for The American Museum of Natural History, is a division of Doubleday & Company, Inc. Directed by a joint editorial board made up of members of the staff of both the Museum and Doubleday, the Natural History Press publishes books in all branches of the life and earth sciences, including anthropology and astronomy. The Natural History Press has its editorial offices at Doubleday & Company, Inc., 277 Park Avenue, New York, New York 10017, and its business offices at 501 Franklin Avenue, Garden City, New York 11530.

ELLIOTT P. SKINNER received his doctorate from Columbia University in 1955. He has been a lecturer on African Affairs at the Foreign Service Institute of the Department of State, and from 1966 to 1969 he served as United States Ambassador to Upper Volta.

Dr. Skinner is currently Professor of Anthropology at Columbia University, where he specializes in African ethnology. He is the author of scores of articles; and his books include: *THE MOSSI OF UPPER VOLTA* and *A GLORIOUS AGE IN AFRICA*.

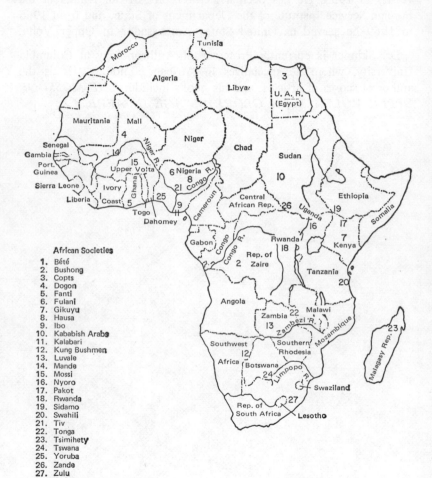

African Societies

1. Bété
2. Bushong
3. Copts
4. Dogon
5. Fanti
6. Fulani
7. Gikuyu
8. Hausa
9. Ibo
10. Kababish Arabs
11. Kalabari
12. Kung Bushmen
13. Luvale
14. Mande
15. Mossi
16. Nyoro
17. Pakot
18. Rwanda
19. Sidamo
20. Swahili
21. Tiv
22. Tonga
23. Tsimihety
24. Tswana
25. Yoruba
26. Zande
27. Zulu

Preface

Africa is very much like a mirror, and African scholarship often reveals more about the scholar than about the continent whose cultures and societies he seeks to describe. Indeed, the very shape of Africa, a question mark, is sphinx-like in its challenge to all scholars to find the proper key to an understanding of its rich diversity and complexity. This collection of readings on Africa, then, reflects not only my interests and attitudes as the editor, but also my hopes that the articles will contribute to a better understanding of a continent and peoples too often misunderstood and maligned.

The reader was designed for the student and laymen interested in obtaining an overview of Africa, its peoples and their traditional cultures and societies. Today, many of these cultures and societies are being transformed quite rapidly, but unless we know the nature of traditional Africa, it is difficult to understand the changes now taking place there. The approach is anthropological, since for historical as well as methodological reasons, anthropologists have been more active than other scholars in collecting and analyzing data on all aspects of human behavior in African societies. Interestingly enough, even the anthropologists could not provide all the data desired, so appropriate articles from other disciplines were chosen. This enabled me to provide articles dealing with the origin of man and culture in Africa as well as with the normally ignored fields of architecture, music, and poetry. Of course, given the limitations of space and resources, certain aspects of African cultures, especially the plastic arts, have not received the deserved treatment, and a number of illustrations in the articles have been eliminated. Nevertheless, an attempt was made to compensate for this either in the choice of articles or by retaining those illustrations without which the meaning of the articles would be distorted.

The choice of articles for any reader is always fraught with difficulty, since articles that meet one criterion often fail to meet others. One difficulty was that good articles on all aspects of African life were not available, and some areas of Africa were not well represented in the literature. As a result, I included one original article in this reader, and translations of two excellent articles which have only appeared in French and German periodicals. I am now satisfied that the geographical distribution of societies treated is quite good, and believe that for the first time, an article from the African island of Madagascar has been included in a book of readings on Africa.

My final concern was to choose articles that are theoretically sound and ethnographically interesting, but not deprecatory. Contemporary African peoples are concerned that the language and tone used to portray the customs of Africa too often emphasize (and perhaps invent) the bizarre and exotic; that the African man therefore loses his commonality with all mankind. I had more difficulty finding such acceptable articles than one would suspect. All the articles that were finally selected, however, did meet most of the criteria, although a few of them do have outdated theoretical and linguistic conventions. Fortunately, Africans and younger non-African scholars are now proving that the differences in African societies and cultures can be described to show their wide diversity without resorting to quaint or exotic language.

It is a truism that no book of readings is the work of its collector despite the amount of care and attention he puts into compiling the material. Thus, thanks must be given, above all, to the authors whose works are included in this book and to the publishers who gave the necessary permissions to have these articles and excerpts reprinted. Special thanks are due to my friend and colleague, Dr. Alexander Alland, for his original article in this volume and to Mrs. Vera C. Chimene and Mrs. Marguerite Chesbrough for their help in translation. I am grateful to the many students in the Department of Anthropology at Columbia University who did much of the research involved in securing articles to be considered, and to the personnel of both the Anthropology Department and of Columbia University's Urban Center for reproducing them. Miss Nora Stevenson is thanked for her unstinting help in preparing this manuscript for publication. I, alone, bear responsibility for selecting the articles and for any shortcomings in the preparation of the manuscript.

Contents

PART III
AFRICAN SOCIAL INSTITUTIONS

PART IV
AFRICAN POLITICAL INSTITUTIONS

PART V
AFRICAN AESTHETICS AND RECREATION

Contents

PART VI
AFRICAN BELIEFS AND RELIGIONS

PART I

Basic Characteristics
of Africa and Its People

Introduction

Africa provides the setting for one of the most intriguing interplays of ecology, biology, and culture in the history of man. As Lucile Carlson shows in her chapter, the African setting is itself unique. The second largest continent in the world, Africa is the most tropical of them all. It boasts the world's largest desert, the Sahara, and some of the largest expanses of tropical rain forests. Yet, the most common landscape of Africa is the savanna or veld. Certain low-lying parts of the Sahara have the highest temperatures in the world, but there is perpetual ice and snow upon the high mountains in the East African equatorial region. These contrasts in landscape and climate have had an effect on the soils of Africa and on its dependent flora and fauna. Innumerable species of plants inhabit the African continent, and the East African plains are host to the largest surviving herds of wild animals in the entire world.

Given its tropical climate and its rich fauna, Africa appears to be the logical place for the evolution of man, himself a tropical animal. Indeed Charles Darwin speculated long ago that it was to Africa, and not to some garden of Eden in the Near East or the Far East, that man should look for the origin of his kind, especially since man's nearest biological relatives lived in tropical Africa. Darwin's views were ignored, not only because of the paucity of paleontological research in Africa, but also because the intellectual prejudices of the time led scholars to reject the notion that something good or new could "come out of Africa." Thanks in part to a lucky find and hardheadedness, Dr. Robert Broom and Dr. Raymond Dart forced the world to accept the possibility that a Southern man-ape, the Australopithecines, represented something new in nature, and probably a significant step in primate evolution that led to man.

Dr. and Mrs. L. S. B. Leakey have provided a great deal of evidence that Africa was not only a crucible of human evolution, but that this biological process was accompanied by a cultural one, the production of stone tools. This means that quite early man's evolution ceased to be a function of genetic change alone, but also depended upon his ability to invade and adapt to specific ecological niches with the use of tools and possibly with the help of language. J. Desmond Clark shows in his chapter that certain tool assemblages were associated with specific types of early hominids, and attributed the persistence of both human types and tool types to satisfactory adaptations to ecological conditions. However, since human biological and cultural evolution continued both inside and outside Africa, the peoples, cultures, and languages in Africa became more heterogeneous over a period of time.

The diversity of physical types of man, languages, and cultures in Africa has challenged the taxonomic abilities of scholars interested in physical anthropology, linguistics, culture/history, and culture/evolution. The efforts of these scholars were made more difficult by their penchant or need to account for or to justify European domination of the world. They developed rigid classificatory and evolutionary systems in which race, language, and culture were often inseparably linked, and where Caucasoids and their attributes ranked first. Thus the most Caucasoid peoples of Africa were held to spread the more "civilized" Semitic languages, and were the invariable immigrants who brought civilization to Africa. Contradictions in the biological, linguistic, or cultural data were resolved by attributing traits to populations which they do not have, or considering them blends of the stereotyped "Negro" and "Caucasoid" physical types: "proto-Hamites," "Hamites," or "Half Hamites." Confusion was often compounded when the Hamites, once considered the original Negroid sons of Noah, were later said to be Dark Mediterranean Caucasoids such as the Egyptians.

Recent work in physical anthropology, archaeology, and linguistics has led scholars to abandon rigid categorizations, especially those linking race, language, and culture. Instead, they are more attentive to dynamic factors such as history, migration, adaptation to ecological niches, and genetic exchange and drift in their efforts to understand the peoples of Africa and their culture/history. Alexander Alland reviews for us in his article the many classifications of the populations of Africa, and indicates the criteria used. Like Jean Hiernaux, he prefers a genetic rather than a gross morphological or even phenotypic approach, paying a great deal of attention to adaptive genetic mechanisms operating within ecological zones over periods of time. This approach precludes the division of Africa's population into the traditional "races" and emphasizes the genetic characteristics of small inter-breeding populations. These discrete populations rather than the large "races" are to Alland the significant biological and socio-cultural entities in Africa.

The modern classification of African languages appears to support the equally new work being done in physical anthropology. Greenberg's classification of African languages on strictly linguistic terms, without the prism of "race" and "culture," resolved many problems created by the earlier extra-linguistic analyses of African languages. He found that the more than eight hundred African languages were members of four major linguistic groups; that the presence or absence of related languages in one area or their scattering over wide distant areas indicated the migration, gradual drift, or isolation of their speakers. Greenberg also found a few instances, such as among the Khoisan-speakers, where there was a correlation between biology, language, and culture, but here the reasons were clearly historical. On the other hand, he found agricultural "Negroids" speaking putative "Afro-Asiatic" languages, and "Caucasoid" herders speaking "Niger-Congo" (now Congo-Kordofanian) languages heretofore associated only with the "Negroid" groups. In other words, Greenberg demonstrated for Africa what is palpably true for other continents, that there is no necessary correlation between race, language, and culture; that populations change languages and culture as a function of historical factors.

If the biological and linguistic characteristics of the African peoples have been subjected to distortions, the same is true of their culture/history. Here the blatant racism has only been moderated by the use of scientific terminology and biblical exegesis, or appeals to "unknown" culture-heroes who brought civilization to Africa. Most often the dark European "Egyptians" or pastoralist "Hamites" were the alleged "culture-bearers" or civilizers of Africa. Ignored were the well-known facts that no nomadic population had ever been known to found states but, to the contrary, often took them over or destroyed them. Overlooked also was the evidence that the Egyptian corridor from time immemorial has been inhabited by, or penetrated by, biologically complex populations. Wrigley, addressing himself to Professor C. G. Seligman's notion that either the "Semites" or "Hamites" brought civilization to Africa, suggested that the "Negroid" populations of Africa participated in the agricultural revolution which laid the basis of newer types of socio-cultural systems. He believes that the prehistory of Africa shows a continuous indigenous development rather than a succession of external cultural impacts. Moreover, he suggests that the "Caucasoid" types cannot be invoked as the *deus ex machina* to account for complex societies of Africa since they, like the "Negroid" types, have been present in parts of Africa from the remotest times.

From such a basic introduction to the "lands and peoples" of Africa, we are better equipped to understand and appreciate the articles that follow.

1. African Landscapes

Africa is the second largest continent in the world, 11,635,000 square miles in area. It straddles four hemispheres, for both the Prime Meridian and the Equator pass over it. In the Gulf of Guinea, below the great African hump, the two lines cross, the Prime Meridian bisecting the bulge, the Equator the continent. Africa extends 37° N and 35° S of the Equator and is the most tropical of the continents.

It is a part of the great "World Island," that vast block of land made up of Eurasia and Africa, and is barely separated from Europe at Gibraltar, and from Asia at Suez. In fact, Africa and Asia were joined by the thread of land across which the Suez Canal now passes until the canal was dug and opened in A.D. 1869. Because of this, Africa is a part of three worlds—Middle Eastern, Mediterranean, and African.

Its interior is difficult of access. Littoral plains abut against plateaus onto which there are no easy routes because the rivers fall to the sea, or the plains merge into the immensity of the Sahara. Once the interior has been attained, it is still a hard land that repulses conquest—hot and humid, or hot and dry, or swinging climatically from extremes of drought to equal extremes of moisture. Huge rifts rend the surface, forming a system of valleys that cuts across well over half of the north-south length of the continent: East Africa was almost split apart from the rest of the continent in the geologic past.

There are mountains in Africa that are capped with eternal snow, one (Mount Kenya) whose flanks touch the Equator. The climates of Africa, therefore, range from some of the hottest on earth to some that, because of altitude, are polar in character. It holds the world's greatest desert, and the most impenetrable swamp. Henry M.

SOURCE: Lucile Carlson, "African Landscapes," Chap. 1 of *Africa's Lands and Nations* by Lucile Carlson. Copyright © 1967, McGraw-Hill, pp. 3–24. Reprinted by permission of the author and publisher.

Stanley opened up the unknown interior of "Darkest Africa," by tracing the course of the Congo River, less than 4 decades before Robert Falcon Scott was pushing across the snows toward the South Pole in Antarctica.

PATTERNS OF RELIEF AND RIVERS

Africa is a block plateau of notable extent, with edging escarpments whose abrupt fronts, dissected by streams and notched with ravines, resemble angular mountains when viewed from the sea. Once the summits of the escarpments are reached, broad and relatively flat uplands stretch away in many directions. Prominences rise upon the plateau surface, some very high. These are apt to be volcanic in structure or capped by lava. Notable among the interior mountains of nonvolcanic origin, however, is Mount Ruwenzori lying along the rift valley (see Glossary). Some are more like hills, and are likely to be remnants left during periods of intense erosion.

The African plateau has several times been lifted en masse, and as often undergone peneplanation (see Glossary, peneplain). It is a very rigid piece of the earth's crust on which tectonic forces have had little effect. The relatively flat lying rock strata that form the basement of the continent are, therefore, little crumpled. Only in the extreme northwest in the Atlas Mountains and in the extreme south in the Cape highlands has extensive folding occurred. In some places warping has left gently undulating surfaces, as in parts of the Sahara; volcanic activity, fairly widespread and yet extremely localized, has constructed mountains whose bold features stand out conspicuously within the landscape. Lava flows were associated with the formation of the central Saharan domes, and the resistant igneous rocks that represent the formerly molten deposits stand up as grotesque and tortured landforms in this arid region. Volcanic activity was associated with the rifting of the East African plateau (see Glossary). The volcanoes thus formed rise as majestic mountains—Kilimanjaro, Kenya, Elgon, the Mufumbiro cluster, and others; a double range of volcanoes forms the linear highlands that run diagonally southwest-northeast through the Cameroons.

The plateau extends without interruption from the bounding escarpments of South Africa northward to the northern Sahara, and from the Guinea coast to Somaliland. The folded regions in the south and northwest lie outside of the plateau.

Since Africa is a plateau, the continent generally stands high with the margins dropping as escarpments to the sea. Some of the most rugged mountains in Africa mark the plateau or rift edges, such as the Drakensberg and Ruwenzori. In general, the plateau rises from the west and north toward the east and south. The eastern and southern portions of the upland stand highest—Abyssinia and north-ward along the Red Sea coast and south, and all of the plateau south of the Congo basin; portions of the ranges of the Guinea lands and the central Saharan massifs also rise high in parts.

Between and among the higher blocks lie wide basins. The central portion of the plateau, cradling the Congo basin, is one such de-pression. It is separated from the basinlike surface of South Africa by the Benguela swell; in the north, the Congo and Chad basins are separated by the Ubangi-Chari upland, the water divide between Congo and Chad drainage.

THE SAHARA

The Ubangi-Chari swell slopes northward into the Sahara, a vast desert that persists without interruption from one side of the con-tinent to the other through a band of 20° of latitude. It stretches away, a remarkably flat surface averaging from 600 to 2,000 feet in elevation but with mountainlike masses rising above the plateau platform here and there, and basins occurring as shallow, intervening lowlands. Underneath lies the African shield, as rigid and resistant here as elsewhere.

Relief in the Sahara has been controlled both by tectonic and erosion factors, and by the rigidity of the rock base. The mountains —Ahaggar, Tibesti, Ouenat, Aïr, Adrar des Iforas—are structural domes, formed by a combination of warping and symmetrical local uplift due to pressure, and volcanic activity. The latter was particu-larly important, and the rocks testify that these massifs are essen-tially eroded lava plateaus; volcanic necks, lava flows, and craters crown the domed surfaces of the ancient structures. Subsequent erosion carved the broad slopes into series of wide encircling low-lands and inward-facing scarps and plateaus rimming the domes, and of barren and forbidding sandstone and rock plateaus that sweep, in places, nearly to the base of the Sahara Atlas. The massifs and their "halos" of erosional forms make up the principal features of the central Sahara. The Tibesti plateau rises the highest; its greatest eminence, Emi Kusi, a still active volcano, mounts to over 11,000 feet elevation.

Surrounding and separating the domes are the *ergs* and *regs* (see Glossary), the sand and gravel surfaces that cover a large part of the central Sahara. The greatest of the sand deserts, the Oriental and Occidental *ergs,* are the immense alluvial fans of rivers: the Grand Erg Oriental of the ancient Irharhar River that flowed northward from the Ahaggar to lose itself in the depression of the shotts (see Glossary) Melghir and Djerid, the Grand Erg Occidental of the several rivers that flow down the slopes of the Southern Atlas, jointly depositing their alluviums in a series of fans that together form the huge western dune desert of the Erg Occidental, the Erg Iguidi formed by the Daoura River, and the *ergs* Raoui and Chech deposited by the Saoura River.

More forbidding and less known than the central portions, the western Sahara is an immense waste where few transportation lines cross and few oases are found. Structurally it is simple, dominated by the northeast-southwest trending arch of the Yetti-Eglab that is bounded, as in the case of the central Saharan plateaus, by the eroded slopes of the dome. Broad lowlands and rugged escarpments face toward the anticline (see Glossary). At the base of these eroded slopes are two longitudinal synclines (see Glossary), the Tindouf lowland between the Yetti-Eglab arch and the arch of the Anti-Atlas, and the broad depression of the Djouf that blends into the flat and barren Azaouad and Tanezrouft. To the south and east of this syncline lie the Aouker dome and the Adrar des Iforas. The Yetti-Eglab arch stretches westward, as the Mauritanian upland, to the borders of the Atlantic.

Like the western portion of the desert, the eastern Sahara, extending from the Tibesti to the Red Sea ranges, is an immense, little traveled waste except where the Nile River makes possible the long oasis confined within the valley bottom. The strata here are generally flat lying, with slight uplift toward the east in the Arabian-Nubian deserts beyond the Nile; northward, from the Ouenat dome, the Libyan desert slopes gradually down toward the Mediterranean so that eroded scarps face inward and south. In the far north, the scarps of Marmarica mark the edge of the Libyan plateau and, at the foot of the escarpment, lie the Quattara depression and the famed oasis and desert entrepôt (see Glossary) of Siwa.

THE GREAT RIFT VALLEY

More spectacular, possibly, than any of the foregoing features are those associated with the eastern plateau, namely, the great rift valleys with their elongate grabens (see Glossary) and associated lofty mountains and volcanoes, and the sagging plateau that lies between the western and eastern rifts and within which lies equatorial Lake Victoria (see Glossary).

The upland surface of East Africa is high, edged by escarpments that may present long slopes or resemble bold, serrate mountains. The upland is a broad, level to undulating plateau interrupted here and there by hills and volcanoes, the latter isolated and impressive features. Deep ravines slash through the whole.

Horizontal force of one kind or another caused the formation of the East African rifts, which are a part of a greater rift system with links continuous in a generally north-south direction, across one-sixth of the earth's circumference from the Sea of Galilee–Jordan River –Red Sea depression to and beyond the coastline of Mozambique.

The rift occupied by the Red Sea is intermediary between the Asian and African sectors, and represents a faulted block of the earth's crust. It is bordered by the steep escarpments of the Arabian plateau on the east, and the edges of the Nubian and Abyssinian plateaus on the west. In the north, the Red Sea rift divides to send spurs along the two sides of Sinai Peninsula; in the south, also it bifurcates, one stem being represented in the southwest-northeast trench of the Gulf of Aden, which is depressed between the precipitous plateau margins of southern Arabia and northern Somalia, the second and more impressive branch striking south and slightly to the west. The latter begins as a wide funnel top between the bisected parts of the Ethiopian massif and narrows to a furrowlike graben about halfway through the massif. The main strike of fracture faulting continues, interruptedly and generally southward, as an eastern branch across the uplands of Kenya and into Tanganyika. In Tanganyika the clear trace of rifting becomes partially lost, but is picked up again somewhat farther south as it recurves to meet the western rift. The latter arcuately outlines the western margin of the Nyanza basin, which therefore occupies a cradled position between the eastern and western rifts. Lake Victoria lies in a gentle dip in the center of this saucerlike upland.

South of the point of juncture the line of faulting passes south to southeast through the cleft of the Lake Nyasa graben, across Malawi and Mozambique to disappear under the ocean waters.

PATTERNING OF CLIMATE, VEGETATION, AND SOILS

Every day of the year, the vertical rays of the sun fall on some part of Africa. There is no landmass on earth that proportionately receives an equivalent amount of sunshine because there is no other continent that is so "symmetrically located"[1] relative to latitude. Most of Africa lies within the tropics; only the extreme northern and southern tips are extratropical. These sectors, subtropical, extend poleward from the Equator far enough to come under the influence of the westerly winds and their accompanying disturbances during the low sun period.

As Africa is a plateau standing moderately above sea level, altitude introduces modifications: the equatorial African lands that lie over and near the Equator, averaging generally between 1,000 and 2,000 feet elevation, are neither so hot nor so humid as are the South American tropics with comparable distances from the Equator. However, where mountains stand athwart winds that are drawn in from the sea onto the continent, as along the Guinea coast, rainfall averages are so high that South America can show no equivalent readings. In South America the equatorial basin lowlands are the wettest lands; in Africa, coasts backed by mountainous highlands receive the highest rainfall. Great mountain systems, that act so effectively as climatic divides in North and South America and in Eurasia, are absent in Africa, and transitional zones of climate are characteristic.

Pressure, Wind, and Climate: Mechanics of Seasonality

Night is the "winter" of tropical Africa. In other words, diurnal ranges of temperature are greater than seasonal ranges. Temperatures are warm the year around, and except as elevations intervene or cold currents send in cooling effects to produce asymmetry, tem-

[1] Glenn T. Trewartha, *The Earth's Problem Climates,* Madison, Wis.: The University of Wisconsin Press, 1961, p. 91.

peratures vary smoothly and transitionally across Africa from the Equator north and south. Belts of climate likewise match outward from the Equator (except in East Africa), the equatorial rainy zone merging into wet and dry tropics which in turn pass into tropical deserts, dry subtropics, and in the southeast, humid subtropics. The basic character of African climate is derived from latitude; varying elevation and trend of the landforms, differentials in continental bulk, proximity to Eurasia, and ocean currents impose the modifications.

The year-round high incidence of sunshine, low pressures, and vigorous convection make the equatorial zone hot and humid. Contrariwise, because the anticylonic effects of the subtropical high pressure belts north and south of the equatorial areas likewise persist the year around, extensive areas of Africa both north and south of the Equator are desert. Africa is the only continent that feels the effects of the subtropical anticyclonic, high pressure belts in both hemispheres. Transitional between the belts of moisture and drought are the tropical wet and dry lands, or the tropical savannas whose climates derive from the movement inward of the bordering belts at reciprocal seasons: during the high sun period, when the humid equatorial zone with its organized disturbances and high humidity is pulled in, these tropics are wet; they are dry when the sun, shining vertically in the opposite hemisphere, pulls the desert across the land. The alternating seasons are as absolute in character as are the migrating belts that set the climatic frame.

The trade winds, or the tropical easterlies, blow toward the Equator out of the subtropical high pressure belts. Anticyclonic in their source regions, warm, and blowing toward equatorial lands, they are by nature drying winds. Poleward out of the subtropical highs move the westerlies, away from warm tropical regions toward cooler zones, by their very nature moist winds. Dominating a zone 30° or more of latitude in width in each hemisphere, the westerlies alternate their influence seasonally with the arid tropics over intervening areas, producing another wet and dry climate known as the dry subtropical or Mediterranean. In Africa this occurs in the extreme northwest and southwest. The alternating wet and dry periods of these subtropics occur at seasons directly opposite to those of the tropical wet and dry lands, so that the Mediterranean lands have wet winters and dry summers.

GRADATIONS OF TEMPERATURE

Plotting actual seasonal temperatures on maps will bring out several significant factors. It is notable that in the broad belt between 10° S and 23½° N, there are no stations that record average monthly temperatures below 64.4° F except on the East African plateaus. Nairobi, Kenya (altitude 5,450 feet, latitude 1.17° S) may be taken as a typical plateau station. Here, in July and August, the average temperature falls to 62.9 and 63.7° F respectively; on the Abyssinian plateau where elevations reach to above 8,000 feet, the whole temperature curve is thrown several degrees lower than in a lowland area in the same latitude.

North and south of this middle, high temperature zone there are no cold seasons, although both the deserts and uplands have weather during the low sun period that can be called cool. Winters throughout Africa, if the term winter can be applied here as distinct from summers (the high sun period), are to be defined in terms of moisture, not temperature, although with distance from the Equator seasonal temperature differences become greater. Contrasts in temperature between the daylight and nighttime hours may make sensible temperatures (see Glossary) seem extreme: in humid lands the diurnal range, although normally low, can be greater than the annual; in dry lands temperatures tend to drop rapidly at night due to radiation cooling, sometimes many degrees within a short time.

These effects of changing humidity conditions, elevation and trend of uplands, situation—marine or inland, windward or leeward—and currents bring an asymmetry into thermal and other elements of climatic distribution in Africa. The contrary effects of cold and warm currents produce a lower thermal curve on west side littorals, where cold currents moving toward the Equator lower temperatures in all months of the year, than on the East coast, where equatorial currents are warming and moistening. The effects of currents upon temperatures are most noticeable right along the coast and in latitudes where cold currents parallel the shore; inland, after a distance of a few miles, the influence of the currents plays out. Warm currents touching warm coasts have only slight temperature effects in tropical lands.

Temperature contrasts between lowlands and uplands in those regions of Africa that have humid climates are sharp and considerable, with consequent greater periodicity of seasons and lower humidity on the plateaus. The Lake Victoria plateau, bisected by the Equator, is equatorial in neither temperature nor moisture; it falls within the wet and dry climate, and the drought-resistant character of the acacia grass and bush savannas reflect the semiaridity and lowered temperatures. This contrasts sharply with conditions throughout most of the Congo basin and the Guinea coast in like latitudes; desert laps along all sides of the green-crested Ethiopian plateau.

Generalized maps bring out only the broad thermal contrasts between the equatorial and tropical lowlands and the uplands of the same latitudes. They do not show the gradations that occur with ascent, as along the slopes of Ruwenzori, Kenya, Kilimanjaro, and Elgon where climates pass from equatorial or tropical through a series that terminates in polarlike zones of bare rock and sometimes glaciers. Nor do generalized maps define the pattern of windward, rainy slopes and semiarid to arid lee slopes that occurs in crossing some mountains, as the Atlas from the seaward north to the Saharan south. Such maps do not prepare one for the quick appearance of semiarid vegetation as one departs from the equatorial Congo River basin, as at Yangambi or Kisangani and drives by car, north and east, into the bush savanna of Parc de la Garamba. The savanna seems to appear too soon and too close to the Equator. One is unprepared, after studying a generalized climatic map, for the chill and gusty winds that blow across the plateau veld of South Africa in July and August, at latitudes just beyond the Tropic of Capricorn. One expects the Congo basin to be distressingly hot and humid at all times; but such is not the case because the plateau character of the basin, lifting the basin to a 1,000 to 2,000 foot elevation, ameliorates the equatorial effects. Also not discernible on these maps are the contrasts in daytime temperatures between the equatorial and desert lands: daytime temperatures in the rainy tropics are not so high as are those of the central Sahara, 15° or 20° from the Equator, where, in the afternoon, the mercury can climb to 122° F in the shade, and where average daytime temperatures are not much below this extreme figure. By contrast, people have perished in snowstorms on the Algerian plateaus just north of the Sahara.

PATTERNS OF MOISTURE DISTRIBUTION

Humidity and precipitation follow conditions of temperature, pressure, and winds.

The trade winds are the most persistent winds of Africa. Blowing diagonally from the northeast and southeast out of the cells of subtropical high pressure toward the low pressure belt engirdling the Equator, the trades help to sustain the great tropical deserts that cover a good two-fifths of the continent. Meager rainfall, excessive aridity of the air, and excessive evapotranspiration are characteristic. There is no rainfall in the Sahara except from passing storms, always unpredictable in time, which may drop abundant showers occasionally over limited localities. There is no season of rainfall, no assurance even that rain will fall during the course of a given year except along the fringes where traces of rain may be seasonally predicted at the height of the rainy periods in the adjacent wet and dry lands. There are desert stations that record the passage of several years without rainfall; whatever falls is negligible. It is the heights that draw most of the moisture from the atmosphere in the deserts. But even this usually fails, and desert rivers are ephemeral in the extreme, some merely leaving scars from the past to recall a former more humid era. Such a river is the Irharhar.

Evaporation is high, because in addition to great heat, relative humidity is low. At Tamanrasset in the Ahaggar, relative humidity varies between 4 and 21 percent; while in contrast, relative humidity in New York City varies between 65 and 72 percent.

CLIMATIC PATTERN

The realm of the rainy tropics extends across a belt that is irregular and asymmetric and varies in width from about 4 to 10° of latitude on either side of the Equator; outliers extend along sections of the Guinea coast. Within the basin of the Congo River, the ever near vertical rays of the sun, heating the earth, creating low pressures, and generating convection provide the requisites for intensified moisture conditions despite the small frontage on the ocean. Heat, high humidity, and year-round rainfall obtain across wide sectors, giving rise to an abundant verdure in most places where conditions of equatoriality occur. These are the equatorial rain forests. The rainy tropics are nature's greenhouse. Although rainfall in central Africa does not compare with the amounts spilled seasonally upon sections of the monsoon lands of Asia, nevertheless the constancy of precipitation and the conditions of high humidity create an environment that is "conservatory" in character. The warm humid air has an earthy scent.

The equatorial climate terminates abruptly in the east along the base of the East African plateau, and is almost absent in East Africa even along the low coast. Only on the lowlands of the eastern Madagascar shore does the wet tropical climate really prevail. West of the East African plateau, the symmetry of the equatorial belt of the interior becomes less marked as the Atlantic shore is approached: the equatorial zone recedes toward the north, especially along the south and markedly along the coast, compressing the span of tropical wet climate to about half the width that it had in the interior basin. The isohyets (see Glossary) bend northward so that along the Gulf of Guinea the sectors of heaviest rainfall and the most marked development of equatorial climate occur north of the Equator. This is Africa's rainiest sector.

The rainfall of the tropical wet regions results less from the mechanics of local heating and convection, however, than from winds that originate outside of but penetrate into the equatorial zones. Two circulations of air of contrasting characteristics dominate the Congo basin. One is a southwesterly flow of surface air, present at all seasons, that originates over the South Atlantic Ocean and above the cool Benguela Current off the southwestern coast of Africa. Maritime in its source, it is a humid air current about 3,000 to 4,500 feet in depth that flows into the equatorial zone of low pressure with relative ease. Above these southwesterly maritime air masses blow the tropical easterlies, both from the southeast and the northeast, the latter affecting especially the lands lying in the latitudes north of 5° N. These trades extend down to the surface of the earth, where they flow contrary to the movement of air currents from the southwest along a zone of convergence that fluctuates greatly, changing its position not only with the seasons but "aperiodically as well. Seemingly, the stream of southwesterly maritime air varies considerably in thickness and also in vertical structure, and as a consequence its weather does as well."

There is a wide divergence of opinion as to the functions of the easterly and westerly circulations in Congo weather and also of the relative significance of the Atlantic and Indian Oceans

> as moisture sources of this region . . . . Jeandidier and Rainteau . . . look upon the southwesterlies as providing much the greater part of the precipitable moisture, [and state the view that] weather in the Congo Basin depends largely upon the vertical

depth and the extent of penetration by the southwest current. Even as far east as Uganda on the East African Plateau the equatorial westerlies appear to play an important role in the precipitation processes. . . . When the westerly flow is weak or absent, rainfall on the western part of the East African Plateau in equatorial latitudes is below normal.

According to Rainteau, the eastern plateau and associated mountains exert a blocking effect upon the southeast trades so that there is no significant contribution of moisture to the Congo basin from the Indian Ocean except "along the corridor" between the Ethiopian and Kenyan highlands, along which small amounts are carried to the interior. Locally the tropical southeasterlies are called monsoons.[2]

Despite the constant high humidity, rainfall in most areas is relatively moderate, although torrential in character. However, where elevations stand in the path of winds drawn in from the sea, as in the Gulf of Guinea, rainfall may exceed 400 inches a year, as in the Cameroon Mountains; Monrovia averages 198.48 inches annually. In these and other instances, topography puts the "orographic squeeze"[3] (see Glossary) on the humid monsoonal air masses, causing excessive amounts of moisture to fall.

As distance from the equator increases, marked periodicity of rainfall sets in, and the climate becomes tropical wet and dry. Because these tropics merge on one side with rainy, forested lands and on the other with arid, barren lands, conditions within the realm are transitional. The rainfall pattern ranges from a wet and dry cycle that does not have a really dry season but only one that is less wet and is therefore modified wet tropical as at Lagos, to one where seasons are nearly equal in length as at Kano, to near desert as at Timbuktu, where for 5 months no rain falls and for 4 more months only traces of rain appear. In the southern part of the continent the pattern is much the same, going from a long rainy and short dry season on the equatorial side to a long dry and short rainy season on the desert margin. The belt from Bujumbura to Elizabethville to Bulawayo might be taken as illustrative. The extreme conditions of the two bordering climates typify the seasons in the wet and dry regions: during the months of drought, desert conditions obtain and out of the

[2] Ibid., pp. 111–12.
[3] Joseph E. Spencer, *Asia, East by South,* New York: John Wiley & Sons, Inc., 1954, p. 49.

Sahara the harmattan blows; during the wet period, humid heat and rain are characteristic. Colors change from brown to green, and back to brown with the seasons.

These are the savanna lands. Except along streams, the dry periods impairs the growth of tree vegetation other than such drought resistant types as acacias and bush savanna. Tropical grass is characteristic of this zone. It varies from thick elephant grass that grows to heights of 10 and 12 feet on the equatorial edges to low clump steppe along the dry side.

These lands of varying savannas stretch in a horseshoe-shaped belt across what are known as the Sudan, the plateau of East Africa, and, southward, the veld, a broad but ill-defined and irregular region extending almost from sea to sea along the southern side of the equatorial rain forests. The zone of savanna is broader in the south than in the north, the more rapid advance toward aridity along the north being due to the greater bulk of the African continent here.

Outward from the deserts and their poleward steppelike fringes are the dry subtropical, or Mediterranean lands, like the wet and dry tropics intermediate between arid and humid belts, the latter in this case being that of the westerlies. Since the Mediterranean lands partake of the characteristics of the bordering zones at alternate seasons, summers are clear, bright, and dry as the desert takes over while winters bring rain as the fringes of the moist westerlies drop across the area.

Only two small sectors of Africa are dry subtropical, the tip of Cape Province in the southwest, and the coastal sectors of the Atlas lands in the northwest. Vegetation is drought resistant because it must endure through a long dry period: the olive tree with its deep taproot, the cork oak with its evaporation resistant bark, and bush (known as maqui and including a large group of sagelike and dwarf plants) live through the dry seasons.

Winters are cool, not cold, and as might be expected, temperature contrasts heighten inland with cooler winter and warmer summer temperatures. Rainfall is moderate, ranging from about 15 to 27 inches. The rainfall pattern is typified in the regimes of Cape Town and Casablanca, at opposite ends of Africa and in different hemispheres and therefore with the wet season in one coming at the time of the dry season in the other.

Most of South Africa, except the southwest corner of Mediterranean climate and the humid southeast, is steppe or desert. The humid eastern coast of the south (the Natal coast) comprises the African humid subtropics. The warm Mozambique Current washes along this shore, reflecting its influence in both temperature and moisture. Rainfall, while not excessively high, is enough to support a tropical palm and bush vegetation, and this subtropical Natal coast is sometimes called "the palm belt" in South Africa.

The eastern side of the plateau of the south is more moist than the western two-thirds of the upland in the same latitude, owing to the indrawn humid air from the Indian Ocean. Although the veld lands show the same seasonality in rainfall as do those of the Natal coast, year-round precipitation with a summer maximum, the plateau is semicontinental in climate and vegetation. This means that winters are colder and drier, summers are warm, and temperature ranges are greater than along the coast. This semicontinentality becomes more marked westward as aridity increases.

One other feature of African climate should be mentioned before leaving moisture. This is the effect of the monsoon control upon winds and rainfall in certain parts of Africa. By the monsoon effect is meant that alternation of wind direction controlled by the differential pressures set up seasonally on land and over adjacent seas: during the low sun period north of the Equator, a high pressure center that represents a movement inward of the permanent high pressure belt found in the southern part of the North Atlantic forms over the northern desert and fends off moisture-laden winds from the sea; at the same season, a large center of low pressure forms from approximately the Equator southward. Air moves from the northern high, which is most pronounced in the northwest, mostly south across the Sahara, pulled into the areas of lower pressures off the coast of Guinea and Africa south of the Equator. This southward pull of air across the desert from the dominant high in the north is responsible for the disagreeable harmattans, previously referred to—hot, searing, dusty winds that blow out of the Sahara southward.

During the northern high sun period, opposite conditions of pressure obtain across the northern half of Africa: the dominant Asian low, centered over the Indus valley, extends westward into northern Africa. The effect is to accentuate, along those areas where indrawn winds flow across the coast, the humid conditions brought on by the movement inward of the equatorial belt with its convectional rains. The Guinea coast and the Ethiopian highlands feel strong effects from this summer monsoon.

Preliminary to an analysis of the causes for excessive or meager rainfall we must bear in mind the seasonal patterns of atmospheric circulation over Africa. Except in southern Africa a "marked seasonal reversal of surface winds is conspicuous"—southerly winds when the sun is in the Northern Hemisphere, northerly winds when the sun is south of the Equator. Locally these are called the northeast and the southeast monsoons. "However, the seasonal wind reversal is scarcely the result of differential heating of land and water, but instead represents only a normal migration of pressure and wind systems following the course of the sun. The somewhat elusive and diffuse zone of wind discontinuity and confluence separating the two monsoons is the well-known ITC"[4] (see Glossary).

The major controls of climate in West Africa are the seasonal movements of two air masses: tropical continental air that moves down from the Sahara between November and late April reaching its most southerly extent (5 to 7° N) in January; and tropical maritime air that migrates inland from the west and southwest, beginning in May, to about 17° N along the coast and 21° N inland at the time of its greatest extent (in July or August). Since during the winter months highest pressures lie over the northern Sahara and decrease southward across West Africa, the winds are out of the Sahara, northeasterly or easterly, and are warm and dry. During the summer season the opposite condition obtains: highest pressures are offshore and along the shores, and decrease toward the interior of the desert. Winds drawn in from the sea bring moisture.

The two air masses meet along a front, the maritime air, because of its cooler temperatures and greater density, wedging under the continental air. Rains occur where the wedge of moist maritime air reaches heights of 3,000 feet or more. The front migrates—advances or retreats—with the seasons, and also with daily variations in the depth of the wedge; precipitation seems to be related to these diurnal and seasonal changes. Because dry air overlies the moist, the front itself is not a rain producer; rather, a belt of doldrums develops, the weather is clear with few clouds, and winds are persistently gentle.

Thus in West Africa the front acts to screen out rain rather than

4 Trewartha, op. cit., pp. 123–24.

to generate it. The tropical easterlies, which originate in the Indian Ocean and most of the time overlie the two alternating air masses discussed above, may at times produce line squalls because they are moist.

Orographic precipitation is particularly heavy where uplands run athwart the winds from the sea. This accounts for the excessive rainfall averages in the southwest (Guinea, Sierra Leone, and Liberia especially), and in southeast Nigeria and the highlands of the Cameroons. On the other hand, those lands that lie in the rain shadow of the uplands are drier than would otherwise be the case, as in central Ivory Coast and the coastal sectors of eastern Ghana, Togo, and Dahomey. A further effect of the highlands upon climate is to decrease the overall average temperatures in the upland areas and to increase the daily temperature ranges.

In East Africa "the northerly flow is made up of two unlike air streams, a drier one that has traveled across Egypt and the Sudan, and a more humid one originating in much the same region but which in moving around the eastern side of the Arabian high has had a sea track of modest length. In the equinoctial transition seasons, between the retreat of one monsoon and the advance of the other, winds are fickle and more easterly. Above the surface monsoons the winds of higher altitudes are dominantly from the east.

"In addition to the northerly and southerly surface currents there are also occasional invasions of moist unstable westerlies representing Congo air which probably originated in the South Atlantic" (see beginning of section on Climatic Pattern earlier in this chapter).

Over most of East Africa there is a deficiency of rainfall despite the incidence of the two monsoons. Reasons for this differ among East African meteorologists, but most agree that the origin of the water deficiency is found in not one but several causes. "There is general agreement that both monsoons are divergent and subsident over extensive areas; . . . the surface air flow . . . likewise is not of great depth," in places "too shallow to surmount the escarpment and reach the plateau. . . . In addition, these shallow monsoon currents are capped by another current moving from a somewhat different direction, usually easterly, in which moisture content is low but variable and lapse rates weak and even inverted" in consequence of which, if clouds do form in the lower moister air strata they are "unable to develop and expand in the dry and stable easterly air aloft."

A further element conducive to moderate rainfall in East Africa, states Trewartha:

> is the strongly meridional flow characteristic of both monsoons over the land. The southeasterly current, the moister of the two, has had a long trajectory across the Indian Ocean before reaching the African coast, but the drier northerly monsoon has a much more meridional than zonal track both over the ocean and the adjoining land. But along the coast and over the land the southerly monsoon likewise becomes strongly meridional, so that at times it is nearly parallel to the coast or even offshore. The result is a much smaller transport of moisture from ocean to land than would be true if the air flow were more nearly normal to the coast while the lifting effect of the eastward-facing plateau escarpment is greatly minimized. It is significant in this respect that it is during the transition seasons between the two monsoons, when the air movement is more zonal and from the east, that rainfall reaches its maximum.[5]

In southern Africa climates and seasons reflect the controls imposed by the great planetary pressure and wind belts except as relief and altitude introduce modifications. Isohyets representing annual rainfall, from the Equator to about 20° S latitude, trend generally east and west; precipitation is greater near the Equator and declines southward, and shows a high maximum during the high sun period. "This expresses the operation of latitudinally migrating zonal controls such as the ITC wind systems, and associated disturbance belts." South of about 20° S the trend of the isohyets is transverse to the east-west direction farther north, running generally north-south and parallel with the coast. Rainfall decreases from east to west, the 16-inch isohyet approximately bisecting the southern sector.

> This contrasting meridional alignment of the isohyets south of about 20° S reflects the waning effect on rainfall of zonal tropical controls, and the rapid taking over of subtropical anticyclones and westerly flow, with drought-producing controls in the form of a stable anticyclone and cold waters prevailing on the west side, and weaker subsidence, a warm current and more numerous disturbances, chiefly of westerly origin, on the east.

[5] Ibid., pp. 124–26.

An exception to the prevailing aridity on the west side is to be found in the extreme southwest, where, in the vicinity of the elevated Cape, cold-season cyclonic-orographic rains produce a limited area of Mediterranean climate.[6]

AFRICA'S WATER PROBLEMS

Water problems in Africa swing to extremes, regionally and seasonally, from excess water owing to too persistent rainfall and high humidity, or the flooding of rivers to too little water as a result of low rainfall and high evaporation, to a harsh swinging from one extreme to the other, seasonally, in the wet and dry lands. Only in the humid and dry subtropical parts can the continent be described as not being plagued by a water problem, and even in the Mediterranean lands, irrigation is a necessity for the most part, so the water problem is not absent.

In places where subsurface conditions, aridity, and excessive evaporation have caused salts to accumulate in the upper layers of the soil, a region may have not only the problem of irrigating the land but, because of irrigation, also that of drawing off the salty vadose (see Glossary) waters at depths so that they will not accumulate. In parts of North Africa, for example, impervious layers of subsurface clay cause water to be retained at depths varying from 8 to 10 feet. Deep drainage ditches must be dug to draw off these salt-impregnated waters, at the same time that irrigation water is needed to provide moisture at the surface. Nature is lavish—and harsh—in Africa and often both at one and the same time and place. These two features of irrigation and drainage in the African environment accentuate the difficulty of development.

Although swamps undoubtedly cover far wider regions and a greater proportion of the equatorial lands in South America than they do in Africa, along riverine areas of equatorial Africa where lowlands extend away from stream edges, swamps nevertheless stretch outward for miles and miles beneath the tree vegetation. Such inundated lands are a major problem along sections of the Nile River, in the upper Niger delta, and along the Congo River and its tributary streams and lakes. Only fishing peoples occupy these wetlands in the Congo basin: their houses stand precariously along the riverfront, hemmed in on three sides by marshes, on tiny islets of moist land

[6] Ibid., p. 138.

standing but slightly above the water in the midst of these murky swamps. The all-pervading humidity and heat, the ever-present moisture underfoot, and the thick dark drapery of vegetation overhead and all around make these swamp forests extremely dismal and unhealthful. Mangrove swamps make useless large sections of the Guinea coast and the delta lands that build up along the sea, as in the delta area between Port Harcourt and the historic old slaving port of Bonny.

At the opposite extreme are the dry lands. It has already been noted that deserts alone cover two-fifths of Africa, and if the steppelands are included in these water-starved lands, three-fifths of the continent is arid to semiarid. The problem here is to find enough water to irrigate the land, to grow pastures, and to support life. Where rivers like the Nile send their waters from equatorial headstreams across the width of the desert, or, like the Niger, intrude along the arid fringe, or like the Atlas streams rush, short but swiftly, down the Saharan side from moister heights to water the thirsty land, or where man-made pipes conduct water across miles of arid surface to irrigate such garden spots as Marrakech watered from the distant Atlas, the land is blessed, and with painstaking work flowers and produces.

Where such obvious means are absent, where will the water be obtained to sustain life?

It may be concealed in the porous dunes of sand that billow across the surfaces of the *ergs,* to be tapped by plant roots or by shallow digging, as in the Saharan Suf. Or it may lie deep beneath the surface in the rocks, to be laboriously drawn up from 50 to 100 or more feet by rope and leather bucket, by man or animal or, if modern technology has reached the reservoir, by diesel motor from thousands of feet below the surface. This is occurring in some places in both the Algerian and Libyan deserts in association with oil development. Or water may be trapped between layers of rock—porous rocks that make good reservoirs when resting on impervious layers—and seep out as springs at the base of the reservoir; then oases will be found along the base of the rocks adjacent to the springs, as at Egyptian Siwa situated at the foot of the Marmarica escarpment. Or diligent, persevering men may hollow out cisterns on the surface, the rocks to serve as catchments for the rain that occasionally may fall, or build barrages across wadis to dam the waters of flash floods originating farther upstream. The Algerian Mozabites do this.

Man taxes his ingenuity to meet the challenge of sustaining life in the midst of aridity. A look at the map of the deserts, however, indicates the measure of success that man has had in his efforts to conquer the arid places. The oases are few, far between, and small. Each green spot, set alone and apart, is a haven of security against the cruel lack or insufficiency of water and a harsh, relentless sun. Entire caravans have been known to perish for lack of water.

Modern science and engineering are trying to utilize a small fraction of the desert by impounding water that originates outside of the desert, as in the case of the High and Sennar dams on the Nile, or along the Orange and other rivers. But were the acres reclaimed by such perennial irrigation projects plotted on the breadth of the African arid and semidesert lands, they would look minute in contrast to the area of the water-deficient expanses of the Sahara, the Namib and Kalahari deserts, and the steppes. Their importance, however, can scarcely be calculated.

Water Balance. The amount of rain that falls is not the sole determinant of how well the water needs of any given region are being met. Also involved is the area's potential rate of evapotranspiration: by placing one against the other, a "water balance" is determined from which the water needs can be calculated. This is not a direct or simple process.

Thornthwaite introduced the idea of potential evapotranspiration as a method of climatic classification; from his studies, others have followed. He defined evapotranspiration as "the combined evaporation from the soil surfaces and transpiration from plants," therefore "the reserve of precipitation." The process of evapotranspiration is accomplished by the combination of vaporization by the sun and of the "sink strength (attractive power)" of the atmosphere. The effect of the sun upon vaporization is translated through isolation (sunshine), length of the daylight period, and temperature; that of atmosphere in wind and atmospheric turbulence, and relative humidity. The effectiveness of evapotranspiration depends upon the completeness or incompleteness of the vegetation cover, and upon the moisture that is available.[7]

On the basis of water balance, a possible 36 percent of Africa may be characterized as humid; of the remainder, about 16 percent is true desert, 26 percent arid, and 22 percent semiarid. In other

[7] C. W. Thornthwaite, "An Approach toward a Rational Classification of Climate," *Geographical Review,* Vol. XXXVIII, No. 1, p. 55, Jan. 1948.

words, nearly two-thirds of Africa is plagued during all or part of the year by a moisture deficiency. Where seasons are based on moisture variation, as throughout most of Africa, the seasonal distribution sets limits on the crops that can be cultivated: those plants that require a growing period that is longer than the season of rains can be cultivated only under irrigation. Where seasonal changes are marked not only by moisture differences but also by temperature change and by a winter maximum of precipitation, as in the northern and southern Mediterranean extremities, evaporation is less critical, and the rainfall, although less than in the tropical lands, will be more effective. In other words, it requires less rain to grow crops in lands of winter rain than in those where rain falls during the warm season and consequently have a higher evaporation rate.

The cultivation mosaic that prevails is greatly influenced by natural conditions of the habitat, reflecting in no small measure the precipitation-evapotranspiration factor. New techniques of cultivation and the stabilization of the water supply through irrigation can, in places and at times, better the water balance even as poor methods may accentuate the rate of moisture loss. How best to procure the maximum good out of this coefficient is a problem for scientific agriculture to solve. In the extensive regions where a deficiency of water exists, there is also greater variability and seasonal fluctuation. Since an accentuation of low moisture conditions in these normally moisture-deficient regions is almost invariably accompanied by high temperatures, thereby raising the rate of evapotranspiration, crop yields show a like fluctuation. Only where irrigation is practiced on a broad scale, as in the Nile valley, can crop yields be held steady in the arid and semiarid lands; only then will yields consistently rise to above continental averages.

SOILS

African soils generally show a remarkably belted distribution closely coincident with climatic and vegetation belts. Since climate, vegetation, and soil impact upon each other, and in the case of soil and vegetation, are basically interdependent, our study of African soils will be largely an interpretation of soils from this viewpoint. This means that we will be speaking largely in generalizations that hold for wide sweeps of territory. As soon as one begins to do detailed soil analyses within small areas, however, this method will break down, because in addition to climate and vegetation, a number of other things such as topography, use and misuse by man, drainage conditions, parent rock material, insects, and animal life have their effects and often create wide soil differences within small areas. Leaching is another basic process, operative especially in humid areas, that affects the soil horizons. In some climates it operates slowly, in others rapidly, but in all places it has a similar effect—soaking out the mineral substances and leaving the soil more or less infertile depending upon the amount, rate, and continuousness of the leaching process. And yet a comparison of the climatic, vegetation, and soil maps of Africa will reveal that vegetation follows climate, and soil follows vegetation (and climate). The process of soil formation is slow. It has operated under all conditions of climate, and throughout all eras of time.

Laterization, which sometimes is applied blanketlike to all humid soils from the equator into the humid subtropics, is by no means so generally prevalent as this. Laterites develop under conditions of tropically hot temperatures and high rainfall, as do also red loams. Both have their red color because of a residual iron constituent. This characteristic of color is so widespread and striking that it has been accepted as "a universal and essential characteristic of laterites. It is always present (also) in red loams."[8] Both soil types occur in Africa. It is perhaps unwise to say, therefore, that the laterites are the soils of the tropical and equatorial zones of Africa. Rather it is better to use terms cautiously, and to speak of characteristics, instead, until further research clarifies the exact types.

Most tropical soils, although deep, wear out rapidly, losing both fertility and structure when continuously cultivated, because cultivation places a greater strain upon soil than does natural growth, luxuriant though the latter may be. Even where tropical lands have a profuse floral complex, and much humus is therefore added to the soil, soils are leached and infertile because the rapidity of decomposition, caused by the persistency of the rains and heat, does not permit the humus to accumulate in the surface horizon. If the organic material could remain for a long time undisturbed, and if the profuse plant association persisted, the soils would be rich because the plants would so continuously feed a supply of organic materials into the soil that they would maintain a supply of the soluble elements, and

[8] H. L. Shantz and C. F. Marbut, *The Vegetation and Soils of Africa,* New York: American Geophysical Society, Res. Series 13, 1923, pp. 125–26.

also support bacteria. However, once the plant cover is removed by burning and clearing for cultivation, the meager residue of organic and inorganic solubles depletes much more rapidly than it does in temperate latitudes. It takes only a few years for a soil that formerly supported a towering three-storied rain forest, whose highest species may have reached 175 to 200 feet, to become exhausted.

Across all the equatorial and wet and dry tropical lands of Africa, the problem of how to preserve soil fertility and structure is insistent. The Africans solved it by engaging in a type of shifting cultivation that is an excellent adaptation to soil conditions as they naturally exist. Two years of cultivation (generally four croppings) will wear out a tropical soil and break down the structure. To counter this, the migratory cultivators practice long periods of fallowing—to restore a vegetation cover that will once more provide humus, and that can be burned to contribute potash, at the beginning at least. The long fallow also allows the roots of trees time to penetrate deeply into the soil and bring up fertilizing chemicals from the zones of alluviation. Shifting cultivation is practiced throughout all of the equatorial and wet and dry tropical lands of Africa. Although a soil preserving technique, it is highly destructive of vegetation.

Overlooking the wasteful aspects of vegetation destruction and/or deterioration, the method of migratory cultivation is suitable where population pressure is not great; but when large populations begin to press on the land, making impossible the long fallow and continuous clearing of new lands, the system becomes impractical and precarious. Cultivation techniques whereby fertility is maintained or restored by shorter periods of fallowing, or fertilization must then be substituted. Fertilization comprises the use of commercial fertilizers, composting, green or animal manuring, cover cropping, crop rotation, or the adoption of integrated farming that involves animal rearing as well as cultivation. Most humid African soils need to be protected and restored.

To prescribe and to practice are, however, two different things, because success depends also upon the solution of many other problems. Plant a leguminous fallow (green manure) and permit animals to graze upon this land? In many parts of the continent animal rearing awaits control of the tsetse fly, a scourge across hundreds of thousands of square miles of African savannas and forests where other environmental conditions would favor animal keeping. Add commercial fertilizer? It is too expensive for most small cultivators.

All African soils are good for short periods of cultivation and long fallow, but as agriculture intensifies, soil analyses and changed techniques are needed. Not only must a right system be used, but also the right soil for the right plant culture. It is a slow process to experiment with soil usage under varying conditions of climate, cropping, and fallowing. . . . It is likely that integrated farming, with animals and the restorative manures, in combination with other remedies will be needed to provide the answer to this problem of soil and agriculture in tropical and equatorial Africa.

The problems incident to soils in arid and semiarid lands are completely different from those of the humid hot lands. In deserts, the first need is to obtain water to use the soil at all. Generally, desert soils are relatively rich in inorganic minerals because scant moisture and high evaporation tend to concentrate salts near the surface. An excess of these chemicals may even be harmful. Humus is low, and absent in many parts. Erosion, both by running water and wind, is another problem of immense proportions. When soil and water are properly handled, however, the deserts produce abundantly.

NATURAL FAUNA

Africa has the greatest and most varied reserve of natural fauna on earth, and the combination of African wildlife and the untamed environment that is their habitat leaves an impression of immensity and grandeur. The setting is primeval, and everything is on a grand scale: the animals graze across the vast plains of the savannas, in the valleys of the mighty rifts, up the slopes of mountains and rock faults—profuse in variety and numerous.

A century ago extratropical America was also a vast natural conservatory of wildlife, but with the filling in of the land by humans and with man's encroachment upon the haunts of the wildlife, the picture changed. The herds of bison that had thundered over the plains, supplying meat and furs and horns for the Indians without diminishment, disappeared almost to the point of extinction.

But for the setting aside of reserves for the preservation of the fauna decades ago, Africa would have followed the same way to the near extinction of the faunal species. The wanton killing began later in Africa because the European hunter with his gun did not get into the interior of the continent until the latter years of the nineteenth century, or the destruction of game would have been greater. However, in those parts where he did penetrate Africa at an earlier date, the indigenous animal life was all but exterminated, as in the Maghrib where the Romans wiped out the animals of Mediterranean lands, and when no more were available there, transported wild beasts from below the Sahara for the spectacles in the arenas. The pressure of the native Africans upon faunal life before the advent of the European (as in America) was not so great but that natural replacement was sufficient to replenish the herds; but as "the great hunters" and traders began their trophy-killing, hunting by Africans —who wanted to get in on the profits that this rich booty brought —also increased.

Although game reserves and "controlled areas" have been set aside, they have not eliminated illegal hunting and poaching; both are problems. The two most serious forms of poaching are the killing of animals for the traffic in trophies such as ivory, rhino horn, and leopard skins, and commercialized meat hunting. Whereas petty poaching makes only small inroads on the game because the number killed is small, poaching for trophies and commercial meat constitutes a genuine threat to faunal populations. Further, the practice of trophy-hunting takes the "trophy," and leaves the carcass of the animal to rot where it was killed—or, possibly, leaves the animal to die a slow, agonizing death. The circling of vultures indicates the spot of such killings. Clearing of the land for safe occupation, especially in the past, also made great inroads on the reserves of wildlife.

Why is man so destructive of this treasury of wildlife that is so quickly destroyed, so difficult to replenish, and impossible to replace once it is gone? The above is only one side of the wildlife picture; crop damage and conveying contagion are another. Intruding on the farmlands, trampling and tearing up their crops, killing and carrying off their livestock, spreading disease, the natural fauna represent a destructive force that must be held in check. Crop destruction by some marauding mammals, such as elephants and hippos, is considerable; elephants are particularly destructive. Plundering by lions results in considerable loss of livestock; baboons and monkeys are pests.

The wild game are also carriers of disease, the herds constituting "reservoirs of infection"; in the various stages of development of ticks and insects, birds, bats, animals, reptiles, and even amphibians play host to many species of these arachnids (see Glossary) and insects that infest extensive areas of Africa and to a greater degree than on any other continent; various sorts of tick fever result from the bite. The fur, feathers, and hides of the wild creatures serve as admirable places for germ carriers to hide and be transported, and the arachnids and insects thus transferred may communicate diseases not only to other animals but also to human beings.

Thus, although the wildlife in their natural habitat may create scenes of haunting beauty, men, cohabiting Africa with the animals, must protect themselves and their property from them.

Nevertheless, this rich faunal heritage should be preserved. Some species are already extinct; some strains have been so decimated that extinction is a possibility; all African wildlife has numerically declined as compared with the prolific populations that existed a century and a half ago, and as the balance that nature created is upset by further changes in the proportions of the faunal population and in the vegetation, the imbalance thus induced may lead naturally to an ungovernable decimation of some species and the ungovernable multiplication of others. Out of this an entirely new faunal complex could emerge. Sanctuaries where the fauna are allowed to live unrestricted and unmolested within an environment natural to their habits are now the only means by which the complex developed by Nature can be maintained; control over population numbers and ratios is also affected by the setting up of reserves.

GLOSSARY

ANTICLINE—arched strata that dip in opposite directions from a common axis.

ARACHNIDS—large class of Arthropoda which includes scorpions, spiders, mites, and ticks.

EAST AFRICAN PLATEAU—also known as the Lake plateau, the Lake Victoria plateau, or the Nyanza plateau.

ENTREPÔT—a port where goods are warehoused and from which they are again redistributed.

ERG—term used in the Sahara, but applicable elsewhere, for sand desert.

GRABEN—depression produced by subsidence of a strip between normal faults; downthrow along faults.

ISOHYET—line connecting places receiving equal amounts of rainfall.

ITC—Intertropical Convergence Zone.

LAKE VICTORIA—sometimes called Victoria Nyanza.

OROGRAPHIC SQUEEZE—rainfall wrung out as a result of air cooling due to ascent over topographic barriers.

PENEPLAIN—land surface worn down to almost a plain.

REG—gravel desert.

RIFT VALLEY—valley produced by subsidence of a strip bounded by two parallel rifts; an elongated valley formed by the depression of a block of the earth's crust between two faults or fault zones of approximately parallel strike, a graben.

SENSIBLE TEMPERATURE—sensation of temperature that the body feels.

SHOTT—closed basin occupied by shallow saline lakes.

SYNCLINE—rock fold in which strata dip inward from both sides toward axis.

VADOSE WATER—suspended water; subsurface water above the zone of saturation.

2. The Prehistoric Origins of African Culture

Remarkable and exciting discoveries that have been made in Africa during the last five years suggest that it was here that tool-making first appeared in the geological record, and that it was then carried to other continents by hominid forms, the discovery of which has necessitated completely new thinking about the biological development of Man. In the same way the discovery, undreamed of twenty years ago, of urban centers in the Near East, dating to as early as the eighth millennium B.C., is providing unique details of life in early Neolithic times and is causing prehistorians to look back ever further into the past, almost to the close of the last glacial, for the first signs of the domestication of plants and animals and of settled village life.

Such discoveries are fundamental to the study of the origins and growth of social and economic life, and increasing use is being made of the archaeological record by the cultural anthropologist and ethno-historian, although there is still in places a lingering tendency to consider that prehistory has nothing to offer the student of present-day culture. The success of collaboration between anthropologists, linguists, historians and archaeologists has, however, already been amply demonstrated in several African countries—for example in Uganda[1] and Northern[2] and Southern[3] Rhodesia. Indeed, the archaeologist is now an indispensable part of any co-operative project to reconstruct the history of a pre-literate population.

SOURCE: J. Desmond Clark, "The Prehistoric Origins of African Culture," *The Journal of African History*, Vol. V, No. 2, 1964, p. 161–83. Reprinted by permission of the author and publisher.

[1] M. Posnansky, "Some archaeological aspects of the ethno-history of Uganda," in G. Mortelmans (editor), *Actes du IVe Congrès Panafricain de Préhistoire* (Leopoldville, 1959), Tervuren (1962), pp. 375–80.

[2] B. M. Fagan, "The Iron Age sequence in the Southern Province of Northern Rhodesia." *Journal of African History* (1963), IV, pp. 2, 157–77.

[3] E. T. Stokes (editor), "Historians in tropical Africa," in *Proceedings of the Leverhulme Intercollegiate History Conference* (Salisbury, 1960). Salisbury, Southern Rhodesia (1962).

While it is now obvious that archaeology can provide some of the best source material for the reconstruction of cultural antecedents, population movements, and even of the origins of some social and religious practices on a factual basis, it is the new ways in which the archaeologist is using his data that render the results and potential so valuable. Today the archaeologist relies heavily on the help of his colleagues in many disciplines, particularly on those in the natural sciences. This, together with the precision resulting from improved field techniques and more meticulous observation and analysis, is providing an increasing quantity of solid scientific data, and permitting radical reassessment in their interpretation. The absolute dating techniques now available have revolutionized chronologies, just as the more accurate knowledge of past environments has imparted new and vital significance to cultural remains, and permitted a deeper appreciation of the importance of the inseparable relationship there has always been between environment, culture and biological adaptation.

In addition to the close collaboration between palaeo-ecologist, physical anthropologist and prehistorian, the cultural anthropologist and ethnographer are drawn upon for help in the interpretation of the cultural evidence. Thus, on the one hand, primate behavior studies are important as a basis for the reconstruction of life in Australopithecine times; on the other hand, ecological studies of present-day Bantu agriculturalists are a vital necessity for the interpretation of early Iron Age cultures in southern Africa, and it is necessary to study the whole continuous process of culture change in prehistoric times on a continental scale if we are to try to understand it at the regional level.

The earliest evidence of culture in the world occurs at the unique site at the Olduvai Gorge, the discovery of which is due to Dr. and Mrs. L. S. B. Leakey (as also is so much of our knowledge of the earliest history of man the tool-maker). Olduvai Gorge is situated in northern Tanganyika in the Eastern Rift, and cuts through some 300 feet of old lake sediments of Lower and Middle Pleistocene age. These beds are dated relatively in respect of the fossil faunas and cultural remains they contain, and absolutely by the potassium/argon method.[4] Bed I is between 1½ and 2 million years old, and

[4] L. S. B. Leakey, *Olduvai Gorge* (Cambridge, 1951). L. S. B. Leakey, J. F. Evernden and G. H. Curtis, "The age of Bed I, Olduvai Gorge, Tanganyika," *Nature* (1961), CXCI, p. 478.

indisputable evidence of cultural activity has been found from top to bottom within it. The tool-makers camped round the edge of shallow open water near small lakes, and formed temporary camps on the mud flats exposed by seasonal fluctuations of the water level of the kind that can be seen at many of the Rift Valley lakes today. The surfaces on which the artifacts occur appear to have been covered fairly rapidly by falls of volcanic tuffs from the adjacent Ngorongoro crater.[5] The skill and patience with which these occupation areas have been uncovered have permitted the making of floor plans that show beyond any question the artificial nature of the accumulations. On these floors stones and bones are concentrated in quantity, and many of them have been artificially broken.[6] Many stones occur which, though unworked, are not natural in the area and can only have been carried in, while many others have been intentionally flaked, and bashing stones, choppers, cores, flakes and small chunks, some utilized and occasionally retouched, occur inextricably mixed with the smashed bones of a number of different species of animal.[7] Long bones and other bones have been broken to extract the marrow, and some of them show unmistakable marks of having been smashed with a rounded blunt object. The most famous of these floors is that in the upper part of Bed I, on which were lying the remains of the Australopithecine *Zinjan-thropus boisei.* Here the Leakeys found a concentration of highly comminuted bone some 15 feet in diameter, with larger bones on the periphery and a mass of worked stone in and among the bone. The remains represented several different antelopes, pig, tortoise, catfish, a snake, and several other small animals. A high proportion of the pig and antelope remains are from immature creatures.[8] The most characteristic forms of tool are a chopper flaked from two directions to form an irregular and usually wide-angled cutting or chopping edge, made on a lava pebble or chunk of quartz, and a sharp flake for cutting.

The other floors are similar, but of especial interest is one only a foot or so above the lava on which the beds rest. Here the stone

[5] R. L. Hay, "Stratigraphy of Beds I through IV, Olduvai Gorge, Tanganyika," *Science* (1963), CXXXIX, pp. 829–33.

[6] L. S. B. Leakey, "A new fossil skull from Olduvai," *Nature* (1959), CLXXXIV, pp. 491–93. "Recent discoveries at Olduvai Gorge," *Nature* (1960), CLXXXVIII, pp. 1050–51. "New finds at Olduvai Gorge," *Nature* (1961), CLXXXIX, pp. 649–50.

[7] J. D. Clark, "Sites yielding Hominid remains in Bed I, Olduvai Gorge," *Nature* (1961), CLXXXIX, pp. 903–4.

[8] L. S. B. Leakey, Ibid. (6a).

tools are, on an average, a good deal smaller, but they are associated
with various accumulations of natural stones. It is very difficult to see
how these could have gotten to their present position, resting on the
clay, except by having been carried there. There is certainly one,
and perhaps two, concentrations in rough semicircles, and several
stones rest one upon the other as if they had been purposely piled
up.[9]

These occupation floors represent the home bases—the living
quarters—of early tool-making hominids who were in part carnivo-
rous, obtaining their meat by hunting and scavenging. It is probable,
however, on the analogy of modern hunter-gatherers, that quite 75
per cent of their food was vegetable, and, in this connection, the
pebble chopper may have been developed as a tool for sharpening
sticks for digging.

Recent geological assessment of the climatic conditions under
which Bed I was formed shows that the environment must have been
very like that of the Serengeti Plains today, that is to say, semi-arid
grass and parkland, with shallow pans and lakes, and forest relicts on
the slopes of the adjacent volcanic masses. The relatively sparse
scatter of occupation debris suggests that Lower Pleistocene hominids rarely stayed long in one place.

Artifacts of comparable age and form have been found at a few
other sites, notably at Ain Hanech in Algeria, at Casablanca in
Morocco, in the Albertine Rift, and at Kanam on the Kavirondo
Gulf of Lake Victoria (which yielded also an enigmatic hominid
jaw fragment), as well as in residual gravels in river and marine
high terraces. It would seem that if it is indeed in the East African
tectonic region that tool-making first developed, it was not very long
before such a fundamental advance in technology spread widely
throughout and beyond the continent (Fig. 2–1).

No hominid more advanced than the Australopithecines is known
from any of these Lower Pleistocene sediments. They are well
represented by over 300 fossil remains. Two forms are known—a
slenderer type (*Australopithecus africanus*), and a more heavily
built type (*A. robustus,* known also as *Paranthropus*). Their membership of the family of the Hominidae is unquestionable on the
evidence of their brains, teeth and jaw patterns, and because of their
bipedalism and their possession of hands adapted to tool-using.

[9] L. S. B. Leakey, "Adventures in the search for man," *National Geographic
Magazine,* Jan. 1963, pp. 132–52.

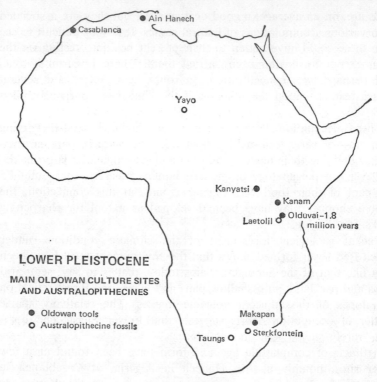

Figure 2–1. Distribution of Lower Pleistocene Culture and
Australopithecines

Lightly built and only some 4 feet 6 inches tall, they were nevertheless able to run fast and had arms adapted to throwing.[10] In the
small size of the brain and the massiveness of the face, however,
they resembled the apes, with the result that they are sometimes
known as the "Man-Apes." Napier's[11] study of the hand from the
pre-Zinjanthropus horizon at FLK NNI in Bed I at Olduvai shows
that though primitive, it is intermediate between the hands of apes
and of man, and would have been capable of clumsy tool-making.

    The artifacts in the Bed I living-sites show that there can be little

[10] S. L. Washburn, "Tools and human evolution," *Scientific American*
(1960), CCIII, pp. 3, 1–15.
[11] J. R. Napier and J. S. Weiner, "Olduvai Gorge and human origins,"
Antiquity (1962), XXXVI, pp. 41–47.

doubt that the East African Australopithecines were working stone for use as tools. Indeed, their Pliocene ancestors had been using tools for millions of years. The hand is the best proof of this, though another is the extreme simplicity of the technique involved in making the tools, and we must expect that at the end of the Lower Pleistocene certainly more than one form of hominid was living that was capable of making—and did make—tools.

There is no indication that the Australopithecine tool-makers lived in large groups. The small areas of the living-places rather suggest that there were unlikely to have been more than a dozen or so individuals in the band. While they seem to have been incapable of killing large animals, the concentrations of bones in the Transvaal caves (if they are indeed, as Dart claims, the food debris of the Australopithecines) would argue that they were, none the less, resourceful hunters and scavengers of medium- and small-sized animals. No doubt, also, they made capital of the necessity for the game to seek the only available surface water during the dry season, which was in the deep limestone caves where they were ambushed and slaughtered. For this some co-operation between members of the group must have been essential and, since the young were dependent on the adults for longer than were the young of apes,[12] regular sharing of food is also implicit.

Many find it difficult to accept the wholesale manufacture of bone tools claimed for the Australopithecines by Dart in his "Osteodontokeratic Culture," and consider that most of this material represents food debris.[13] These caves have, nevertheless, provided fairly good, though rare, evidence of the utilization of bone, as has also one of the Olduvai floors. The most impressive of these bone tools are fragments of long bones that show shallow, high polished groovings.

Why did stone tool-making first begin in the savanna? The answer is believed to lie in economic and social necessity. The African savanna is an environment with a long dry season in which a small and very defenseless hominid, forced to protect its hunting territory and ill-equipped biologically for digging or meat-eating, had to find some way to supplement the sources of vegetable foods that would dwindle under times of climatic deterioration. It is believed that this

[12] R. A. Dart, "The infancy of Australopithecines," *Robert Broom Commemorative Volume* (Johannesburg, 1948), pp. 143–52.

[13] R. A. Dart, "The Osteodontokeratic culture of *Australopithecus prometheus*," Memoir No. 10 (1957), Transvaal Museum, Pretoria.

was one of the primary reasons why these early hominids turned to meat-eating, just as baboons sometimes do today. The use of some kind of sharp cutting tool to open the skin of an antelope, or of a bashing tool to break open long bones or the shell of a tortoise, or of a sharp tool to point a stick for digging, would have meant a regular and substantial increase in the quantity and variety of food available. The hominids would also have found these tools useful for defense.

Australopithecines have been found in South and East Africa, and now in Chad, as well as in the Far East, so that it is reasonable to suppose that tool-making, this most fundamental of human inventions, spread with remarkable rapidity.

Africa abounds with pebble tools, but the earlier claim that most of these are of Lower Pleistocene age remains as yet largely unsubstantiated, and it is probable that many of these industries belong to the earlier Middle, rather than to the Lower Pleistocene. For knowledge of the cultural pattern of these times we again rely most heavily on Olduvai, for this site preserves a unique evolutionary sequence of developing stages up to the earlier part of the Upper Pleistocene. But there are now several other sites, equally well dated, though without such a long stratigraphy (Fig. 2–2). By the beginning of the second glaciation in the northern hemisphere, there is substantial evidence that tool-making had spread throughout all the semi-arid regions of the continent and had overflowed into other parts of the Old World. The artifacts are still predominantly choppers, chopping tools and worked flakes, but they are now more shapely, show greater variety, and are generally more skillfully made, though still remaining remarkably crude in appearance. They represent the earliest stages of what is known as the Chelles-Acheul or Handax culture, the latter name being derived from the commonest type of tool, roughly the shape of a hand when seen in silhouette, though the earliest examples are very crude and rare.

An evolved pebble culture of this time occurs outside Africa in the Jordan valley.[14] Closely related forms may be seen in the industries from the Choukoutien Cave near Peking and from South-East Asia. In Europe also it has been claimed that a pebble culture occurs with Heidelberg man at Mauer in Germany. In Africa, Europe, the Near East, and India, the Handax culture passed through remark-

[14] M. Stekelis, "Recent discoveries in the Jordan valley," *South African Journal of Science* (1963), LIX, pp. 3, 77–80.

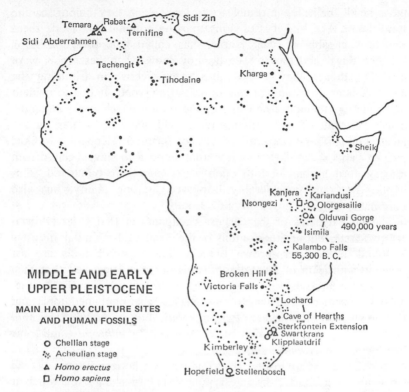

Figure 2-2. Distribution of Middle and early Upper Pleistocene Culture
(Chellian and Acheulian) and hominids

ably similar evolutionary stages, and it seems probable that the
populations of those continents were not as isolated as was at first
supposed and that changes in culture as well as in the genotype were
the outcome of free movement, exchange and intercommunication.

What do these early Handax cultures look like? The living-sites
stratified at the base of Bed II at the Olduvai Gorge, which are now
believed to date to about one million years ago, show that important
changes had taken place since Bed I times. The accumulations of
tools are much more extensive and there are generally many more
artifacts. There are choppers, polyhedral stones and utilized flakes in
quantity, together with a few pear-shaped, handax-like forms. But
perhaps the most significant tool is a small flake or chunk that shows
careful retouching to form notches and scraping edges. Some of

these small, delicate, informal tools look as if they belong to the Later Stone Age, and it is obvious that the hominid that made them was fully capable of what Napier has called "the precision grip" between finger and thumb. We do not know what these tools were used for, though they would have been effective in trimming the meat off bone, in cleaning skins or in paring wood. It is also evident that hunting techniques had undergone important changes, and now it was very often large animals that provided the major part of the meat supply. These consisted of extinct forms of elephant, giraffids, and ox- and sheep-like creatures that appear to have been driven into swampy ground or into open water and there butchered. This implies not only considerably improved hunting ability, but also reasonably efficient group organization.[15]

The only remains of the earliest occupants of Bed II at Olduvai are two teeth, but at Sterkfontein in the Transvaal a similar industry is found in the later, brown breccia. These pebble tools are associated with teeth of *Australopithecus,* but it is suggested that they were really made by an early form of *Homo erectus.* The somewhat later and adjacent site of Swartkrans also contained tools and the large Australopithecine *Paranthropus,* but in addition another hominid is present, previously known as *Telanthropus* and now identified with *Homo erectus.*[16]

About mid-way up in Bed II at Olduvai is a horizon known as "the Chellean III horizon," the latest potassium/argon date for which is 490,000 years. Handaxes made by a stone technique are now much more common, though the pebble chopper still predominates. All the other types of tool occur, and there are now steep core-scraper forms besides, though full details have not yet been published. Associated with this cultural stage, Leakey found the greater part of a skull cap which falls within the pattern of the Pithecanthropoids, or *Homo erectus,* as this stock is now called. The Chellean III skull differs, however, in having a larger cranial capacity, and in anticipating in some measure the Rhodesioid type of man. There can be no doubt that the cultural, physical and intellectual developments that had taken place since Australopithecine times are inextricably

[15] L. S. B. Leakey, "Recent discoveries at Olduvai Gorge, Tanganyika," *Nature* (1958), CLXXXI, pp. 1099–103. S. Cole, *The Prehistory of East Africa* (Macmillan, New York, 1963).

[16] J. T. Robinson and R. J. Mason, "Australopithecines and artifacts at Sterkfontein," *South African Archaeological Bulletin* (1962), XVII, pp. 66, 87–125.

interconnected, and the rapidity of the biological change could not have occurred without culture.

With this level at Olduvai we can correlate a "Chellean" (Clacto-Abevillian) stage from an early marine level at Sidi Abderrahman, near Casablanca, as well as the lakeside site of Ternifine on the Algerian plateau. Here there is a somewhat more developed stone industry, and the usual bone debris from meals, together with three well-preserved jaws and a parietal bone. Arambourg has described these as belonging to an African Pithecanthropoid stock which he has named *Atlanthropus*. Thus the African representatives of this "palaeo-anthropoid" level would be contemporary with those from China and south-east Asia.

The second half of the Handax culture—the Acheulian—was a time of population movement into areas where no signs of earlier occupation by man have yet been found, and it was probably a period of population increase also. The extreme richness of Africa in the stone tools of this time points to the very favorable environment in which the Acheulian was practiced. It may be inferred, though it has not yet been proved, that with the advances of the polar ice-sheets in the second and third glacials, and during the Great Interglacial, there was a more temperate environment over most of the African continent, so that many areas now desert became favorable for settlement. This was also a time of great proliferation of species among the antelopes, pigs and other African mammals, so that it is to be expected that man was also quick to take advantage of the opportunities now available to him.

The Acheulian populations were, however, still confined to the savanna and, as rainfall and temperature permitted, to the drier parts of the continent. It was only later that the tropical forest zone became permanently occupied. Moreover, man was still virtually confined in his choice of living quarters to waterside sites, probably because he had evolved no efficient means of carrying water supplies for any distance. Even more important than the richness of the stone industries of this period is the existence of a number of stratigraphically sealed and dated camping-sites, from which we can gain some idea of the manner of living of the people. Most of these occupation sites belong to later Acheulian times, from perhaps 150–50,000 years ago. There are several sites of this kind: in East Africa, at Olorgesailie, Kariandusi and Isimila; in Rhodesia, at Broken Hill and Kalambo Falls; in South Africa, at Kimberley and the Cave of Hearths; while in North Africa there are caves at Casablanca and Rabat, fossil spring sites in Egypt and the Maghrib, to mention but a few.

Acheulian man still concentrated on killing large animals, and he seems to have been much better equipped to do so than his predecessors. The handaxes are now really fine examples of the stoneworker's craft. They were made by what is known as the cylinder hammer technique, which enabled thinner and flatter flakes to be removed, and the result was more shapely tools with straight cutting edges. Another cutting tool is known as a "cleaver," and is often U-shaped and ax-like. Balls of stone, different types of steep core-scrapers, and many varieties of small scraping and cutting tools also form an integral part of any Acheulian industry. There was already selection of raw material: the tougher, harder rocks were used for the heavy cutting and chopping tools, while the fine-grained, homogeneous rocks, capable of producing a sharp but relatively brittle edge, were used for the small tools. This must reflect differences in activity.

Some four or five variations in the cultural pattern can now be seen, though as yet no regional specialization is discernible.[17] Sometimes industries consist of high percentages of large cutting tools and low percentages of other forms. Elsewhere the large cutting tools may be completely absent (as at Hope Fountain). At yet other sites there are roughly equal percentages of both large and small tools, or industries occur with high percentages of heavy equipment —choppers, picks, core-scrapers and the like. Finally, there are the mining-sites, where the raw materials were worked up from cobbles, boulders or outcrops. This again shows that Acheulian man engaged in a number of different activities for which he used different stone tools.

Analysis of floor plans and artifact percentages, and the relationships of artifacts to each other and to the other associated material —bones, wood, natural stones that have been carried in, etc.—is helping to distinguish which groups of tools may be associated with butchering, or with hunting, with food getting, with vegetable foods and so on. But it will need a number of careful analyses before we have any data that can be considered reliable.

[17] M. R. Kleindienst, "Variability within the Late Acheulian assemblage in East Africa," *South African Archaeological Bulletin* (1961), xvi, 62, pp. 35–48. "Components of the East African Acheulian assemblage: an analytical approach," in G. Mortelmans (editor), *Actes du IVᵉ Congrès Panafricain de Préhistoire* (Leopoldville, 1959), Tervuren (1962), pp. 81–112.

The sizes of the camp-sites in the open also vary—from a few feet across at Broken Hill to as much as 30 feet or more in diameter at Olorgesailie or Kalambo. In a site of this size, there will often be concentrated a large number of tools of the same kind. If the tools were all made at once, it is difficult to see the reason for such quantities; but if the site were reoccupied seasonally over several years, this profusion presents no particular problem. The same forms and profusion of tools characterize the Acheulian wherever it occurs. There is very little difference between the industries at the Cape, in Rhodesia, East Africa, the Sahara, Egypt or Peninsular India, except in the raw materials used. The reason for this is as yet not fully understood though it probably results from the Handax makers being confined largely to one type of country, namely the savanna, and to the great length of time (about 2 million years) involved. This slow development of technical ability and food-gathering practices is in turn directly related to the evolution of the genotype.

As yet, the physical type of Acheulian man is imperfectly known, whether in Africa or elsewhere, but responses to adaption and to changes in environment appear to have produced, by genetic modification from a Pithecanthropoid ancestor, several forms. One of these must have approached the massive-browed Rhodesian man of southern Africa, another was an evolved *Atlanthropus* in Maghrib, and yet a third was a *sapiens*-like stock, such as is represented by the smooth-browed Kanjera crania from Kavirondo.

It was not until the very end of Acheulian times in Africa that man became a regular user of fire. There are some three or four sites where evidence of fire is preserved, and all these probably date to between 50,000 and 60,000 years ago. One such site is at the Kalambo Falls, where charred logs and charcoals occur, and where man used fire to aid in sharpening sticks for digging, to shape clubs, or to make edges on knife-like tools of wood.

Thus fire-making, first known from second glacial times in the Far East, does not appear to have spread universally in Africa before the end of Acheulian times some 50–60,000 years ago, presumably because there was no need for it before. But now the climate became cooler and wetter, bringing about a considerable readjustment in the vegetation patterns and in the distribution of animal and human populations. Under a lowering of temperature of between 4° and 5° C., coinciding with the earlier part of the last glaciation in Europe, higher-living forest species replaced lowland tropical forest down to 600–900 meters below their present altitude range in sub-Saharan Africa, and a Mediterranean flora spread southwards to the southern borders of the Sahara.[18] With the vastly increased potential for food getting, technical development, and living conditions made possible by a regular use of fire, man now spread into country which he had not previously occupied—the now most favorable but formerly forest-covered regions of Equatoria. Here the routes of migration into the Congo basin and the West African rain forest must have lain along the grass-covered interfluves, and man was better able to avail himself of the opportunities offered by, on the one hand, the savanna and, on the other, the forest galleries in the adjacent valleys.

This was a time of considerable population movement and of cultural experiment. It saw the fairly rapid disappearance of the old traditional forms of tool—the handax and the cleaver—in the higher rainfall, more heavily tree-covered parts of the continent. Here there developed many heavy chopping tools and smaller denticulated artifacts that are believed to have been associated with woodworking. This complex became dominant throughout the Congo and West Africa, spreading into East Africa west of the Eastern Rift and into south-east Africa down to Natal. It is known as the Sangoan culture. Elsewhere in southern and eastern Africa, in regions favorable for the preservation of the traditional type of habitat, the old handax tradition lingered on. This is known as the Fauresmith complex, and it is associated with pans and grasslands and an abundant ungulate and large-animal fauna (Fig. 2–3).

For the first time man now began to occupy caves and rock shelters as regular homes, for, with his control of fire, these provided safe and more comfortable living-quarters. Furthermore, because of the regulation of the seasonal movements of the bands and the use of efficient carrying devices, he could now afford to stay in one place for much longer. Whereas the Australopithecines with their limited technology must very quickly have exhausted the sources of food available to them, the Acheulian and, later, the Sangoan and Fauresmith peoples, who were becoming steadily more proficient and inventive in their methods of food getting, were able

---

[18] E. M. van Zinderen Bakker, "Early man and his environments in southern Africa: Palaeobotanical studies," *South African Journal of Science* (1963), LIX, pp. 7, 332–40.

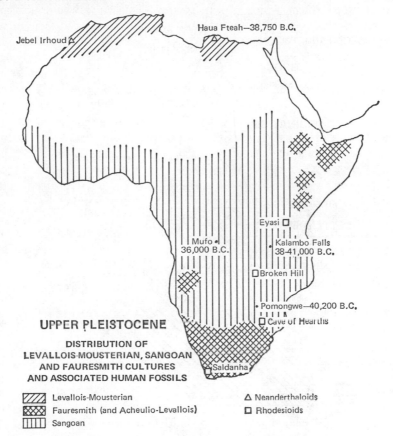

Figure 2–3. Distribution of early Upper Pleistocene Culture and hominids (Fauresmith, Sangoan, etc.)

to exploit the available resources with ever-increasing efficiency. Increase in the size of the band, more permanent residence, and ability to live in a greater variety of habitats, previously unfavorable, must have been the inevitable concomitant of increasing technical skill and mental ability, and at this time, as the distribution maps show, there were few parts of the continent where man did not penetrate. Figure 2–4 is an attempt to show the interrelationship of environment, genotype and culture through time, and their effect on the prehistoric societies of Africa.

After the disappearance of the Acheulian culture from North

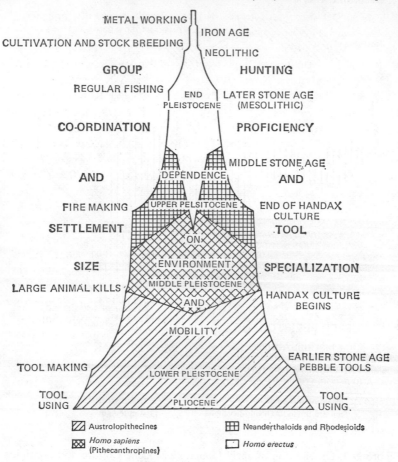

Figure 2–4. Diagrammatic presentation of the inter-relationship of environment, genotype and culture through time and their effect on the prehistoric societies of Africa

Africa, which was contemporary with encroaching desertification, there appear, from Cyrenaica to Morocco, flake industries that are closely similar to those from the Levantine coast and the Near East generally. These are known culturally as Levallois-Mousterian and they are associated with a Neanderthal physical type. From the magnificent site of Haua Fteah in Cyrenaica, and from the newly discovered site at Jebel Irhoud in Morocco, we know that the

Levallois-Mousterian people were cave dwellers, competent fire-users, and specialized in making light cutting, scraping and piercing tools from fine, thin flakes.

It is an intriguing problem whether these industries and the associated Neanderthal men were the outcome of migration into Africa from the Near East or Europe, or whether they were an autochthonous evolution from the Acheulian. The evidence is equivocal. The Kanjera type of man, if he is accurately dated, could have been ancestral to both the Neanderthal and the *sapiens* forms in Africa and, so far as the industry is concerned, the prepared-core technique is also present in the late Acheulian in North Africa. Any movement could, therefore, equally well have been out of Africa as into it. On the other hand, the closer similarities with the Near East rather than with sub-Saharan Africa, and the appearance of some representatives of the Palaeoarctic fauna in North Africa, suggest that the culture and the human stock could also be intrusive. At present the evidence is, it would seem, if anything weighted in favor of the latter alternative.

Whatever the answer, it is from this time onwards that culture in North Africa becomes differentiated from that south of the Sahara, though influences spread at favorable times in both directions (Fig. 2–5). In the Maghrib the Levallois-Mousterian evolved into a culture—known as the Aterian—specializing in the use of tanged flakes and points, while further east and as far south as the Horn the more generalized Levallois-Mousterian pattern was preserved. The Levallois-Mousterian was largely contemporary with the savanna-living Sangoan and the Fauresmith populations of the grasslands south of the Sahara, thus making the Neanderthalers of the north contemporary with the Rhodesian physical type in the south. This last represents the extreme development of the heavy-browed stock, and it is known from as far apart as Broken Hill and the Cape, where it represents the makers of a late Rhodesian Sangoan (or Proto-Stillbay, since these are now known to be the same thing) and of the Cape Fauresmith.

In the earlier part of the Middle Stone Age, the Rhodesioid type began to be replaced by the more efficient *Homo sapiens* forms as a result of natural selection. The Middle Stone Age proper evolved from the Sangoan and Fauresmith after about 35,000 B.C. and ended about 8–10,000 B.C. There has for long been a tendency in Europe to refer to Africa after the end of the Middle Pleistocene as a

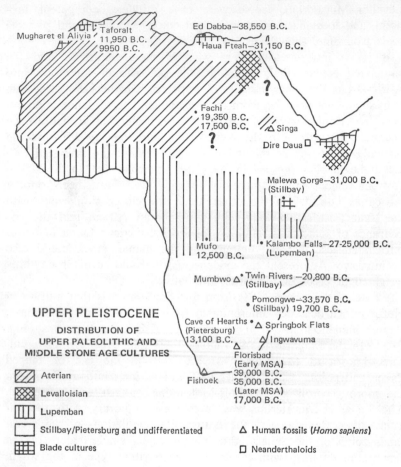

Figure 2–5. Distribution of the Aterian, Lupemban and Stillbay/Pietersburg

cultural backwater. This was based initially on the fact that the earliest *sapiens* stock in Europe is associated with what we know as blade and burin, or Upper Palaeolithic, industries, which rather abruptly replaced the Neanderthal populations and the Mousterian culture there about 35,000 B.C. In Africa the prepared-core technique, Mousterian if you like, continued for a further 25,000 years, and by inference drawn from the European associations it was, therefore, considered that in Africa the Middle Stone Age was made by late surviving Neanderthalers. Radiocarbon and later discoveries show that this is not the case, and there is no evidence of any such time lag in the genotype as had been postulated. The reason for the survival of the prepared-core tradition is obviously that it was the most efficient for producing the specialized equipment that was required by a hunting people in tropical and sub-tropical environments.

These Middle Stone Age cultures, as they are known in sub-Saharan terminology, though based essentially on the prepared core and faceted flake, differ in fact considerably in the nature of their end-products, so that a number of distinct variants can be identified and directly related to environmental specialization. Thus we find the Stillbay and Pietersburg variants in the savanna and grasslands of south and east Africa concentrating on light cutting, piercing and projectile tools of stone, while in the Congo forests, for example, the contemporary form, known as Lupemban, contains many ax and chopping elements and magnificent lanceolate knives or stabbing points. Whereas the tanged point was the speciality of the Aterian population, the foliate form in many varieties was that favored south of the Sahara.

During the African Middle Stone Age there is the same evidence as in Europe for the appearance of religious beliefs. This is shown by the careful burial of the dead. Simultaneously there appear signs of an aesthetic sense in the use of paint and ornamentation. It would seem, therefore, that it was primarily the contrasting environments of glacial and tropical Africa that were responsible for the basic differences in the stone cultures.

Upper Palaeolithic blade and burin industries are found in two parts of Africa—on the Mediterranean littoral and in the East African Rift. The first appearance of Upper Palaeolithic culture in Cyrenaica[19] has been dated to between 38 and 31,000 B.C.[20] It is considered that this may also be the time of its earliest appearance in East Africa, though most of the evidence there, as

[19] A much earlier blade industry occurs in the lower levels of the Haua Fteah cave, and is probably of an age with similar industries from the Levantine coast, where they are named Amudian and intercalate with a final stage of regional Acheulian known as Jabroudian. It is not known at present whether these early blade industries represent the ancestral form from which the Upper Palaeolithic of the Near East is derived, since they are followed in both regions by the Levallois-Mousterian.

[20] E. S. Deevey, et al. (editors), *Radiocarbon* (1963), v, pp. 37, 170–72.

also in north-west Africa, belongs to later times. There can be little doubt that these industries are intrusive from the Levant, being introduced presumably by an early *Homo sapiens* stock which must inevitably have hybridized with the existing populations. No human fossils of this culture stage are as yet known, so it is not possible at present to say whether the makers could have been the ancestors of the Erythriote and Mediterranean longheads. There is quite a possibility that this might have been so, for in East Africa, certainly, the later blade and burin industries were the work of populations of this physical type, largely identified today with the Hamites.

The close of the Pleistocene about 8000 B.C. was preceded by a cooler and wetter climate of some 2000 years duration, during which there were two immigrations of Caucasoid stock into North Africa, the one of Cromagnon type, bringing the Oranian culture to the Maghrib and the other, probably of Mediterranean type, bringing the Et Tera culture to Cyrenaica. At the same time there appears evidence of blade and burin industries in the Horn, while the Aterian populations of the Maghrib were able to move down as far as the southern and eastern Sahara and the Nile. These contacts resulted, for example, in the Congo with the final Middle Stone Age, in the appearance of tanged projectile heads, and in South Africa and Rhodesia in the appearance of new forms of tool made on blades. Similarly, the bifacial foliate points of the later Aterian, the transverse arrowheads and heavy lunate forms of the Mesolithic, and the bifaced ax element of the Neolithic are probably the result of diffusion northward from the Lupemban and Tshitolian of Equatoria. This was the second major period of cultural readjustment in Africa.

The wet phase known as the Makalian that followed the end of the Pleistocene, which lasted from about 5500 to 2500 B.C., similarly permitted free exchange between Mediterranean and Negroid populations that had both moved into the Sahara with the advance of the Mediterranean flora and the improved water supplies (Fig. 2–6). It is from this time that waterside habitats take on new significance. The sea coasts, rivers and lakes were now exploited for their food sources as never before, and it was the permanent food supply provided by the fish, shellfish and other water foods that enabled man to remain permanently in occupation of areas where previously he had been only a seasonal visitor. The wide distribution of, for example, the bone harpoon, the gouge and

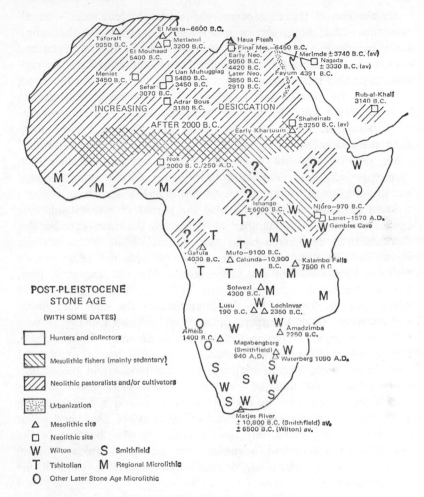

Figure 2–6. Distribution of Culture in post-Pleistocene times

other traits of a waterside culture throughout the southern Sahara, the Nile and the Central African lakes, shows the rapidity with which the indigenous populations in such favorable localities took the opportunity to improve their economy.[21] It is useful to keep in mind this facility for readjustment when considering the change-over from a stone-using to a metal-working economy.

[21] J. de Heinzelin, "Ishango," *Scientific American* (1962), CCVI, pp. 6, 105–16.

By the end of the Pleistocene, the Bush physical stock was already present in South Africa and it may be postulated that, similarly, by selective processes, the Negroid and Erythriote types had also made their appearance, though the earliest known fossils representing these types are no older than the Mesolithic or the Later Stone Age. Because of their blood group relationships, the Bushman and the Negro must be derived from the same African ancestral stock. However, only in the case of the Erythriote or Proto-Hamite does there seem to be any close tie between culture and physical stock, and it was not so much race as cultural specialization springing from long adaptation to different habitats that dictated the distribution of culture forms in the post-Pleistocene.

Since the Later Stone Age is also the period of greatest adaptive specialization, a large number of distinctive cultures can be distinguished. In the Congo basin the cultures of the plateaus differ markedly from those of the forests, though both are fairly certain to have been made by an unspecialized Negroid ancestral type. Markedly different again are those in the Albertine Rift or the Kenya Rift. In South Africa the Smithfield of the high veld, using various forms of end-scrapers made from indurated shale, is very different from the crescent-like microliths of the Wilton culture, though both were made by Bushmen and both had a number of traits in common. This specialization of equipment and the greater use that was now made of quite small animals for food is likely to have been stimulated by population increase and a corresponding reduction in the size of the hunting territory of the band. This in turn, however, could only have become possible because of the spread of new technical advances—the bow and arrow, poison, barbed fish-spears and other devices—that raised the yield of the hunting territory.

Food production and domestication first make their appearance in the continent in the later half of the sixth or early fifth millennium B.C. in Egypt. This is, therefore, later than the beginnings of cultivation (of wheat and barley) and of animal domestication in the Near East, and there can be little doubt that in the first instance Africa derived its knowledge of these things from immigrants into the Nile Valley.[22] It took, however, a surprisingly

[22] J. D. Clark, "The spread of food production in sub-Saharan Africa," *Journal of African History* (1962), 111, pp. 2, 211–28.

short time for the new economy to spread across North Africa. It was present in Cyrenaica by 5000 B.C. and throughout much of the Sahara by 3500–3000 B.C. Neolithic culture is unknown south of the Sahara, however, until later, and in fact it never succeeded at all in replacing the Mesolithic, collecting, way of life throughout most of the sub-continent.

What is the reason for this cultural lag? In part it must have been geographic. But it was also, and probably more importantly, economic. Cereal crops and domestic stock in the rich environment of tropical Africa were not the necessities for permanent village life that they were in the arid and semi-arid regions in which they were first developed. This would be especially so if the primary importance of livestock was already then, as it is today in Africa, an expression of wealth rather than a source of food. The abundant vegetable and animal resources of the tropical savanna and forests provided all that was needed to maintain the Mesolithic populations at much the same level of subsistence as did the crops and stock of the Neolithic farmers, and probably with less expenditure of labor.

It was not until the Sahara began to dry up after 2500 B.C., and the consequent overgrazing forced some of the Neolithic populations there to move southwards into what is now the Sudan belt, that any serious attempt at farming could have been made, though "vegecultural" practices round the forest margins had probably been in use for some considerable time before that. Barley and wheat, however, are winter rainfall crops, and can barely be grown in the tropics successfully except under irrigation. The high plateau in Ethiopia is one of the exceptions, but in other parts there must of necessity have been much experimentation with local potential domesticates from ±2000 B.C. onwards. Thus several indigenous food crops were developed—rice in Guinea, sorghum and *Pennisetum* in the Sudan, tef and *Eleusine* in those parts of Ethiopia where wheat and barley were not established. This experimentation may also have stimulated the cultivation on the forest fringes of the indigenous *Dioscoreas* and of *Ensete*.

We find Neolithic cultivators in northern Nigeria, the makers of the Nok culture, between 2000 B.C. and A.D. 200, when stone began to be replaced by metal for essential tools. Neolithic pastoralists also reached Ethiopia and the Kenya Rift about 2000

B.C., and in the latter region they were not replaced by Bantu immigrants until after the sixteenth century A.D. The only other part where Neolithic industries are known, though they are all believed to be late, is the Congo basin. The whole of the rest of southern Africa remained in the collecting stage. The reason why it did so must be due, as well as to the richness of the wild food resources, to the generally inefficient equipment of Neolithic man for clearing forest and closed woodland and his inability to maintain himself in large enough communities. It was, therefore, not until the population explosion that precipitated the Bantu movements around the beginning of the Christian era that any fundamental change in the economy was feasible. What made this possible, even then, was the development of iron-working—the iron ax and spear—and, no doubt, also the introduction of the Asian food plants.

The many investigations that are going on today are steadily tracing the history of the spread of Negroid and Bantu culture into the sub-continent, and in another decade it is certain that a firm chronology will have become available. We can already trace the spread down the Central African lakes of the earliest Iron Age immigrants, the makers of the Dimple-based and Channelled ware pottery, the earliest date for which is A.D. 100 from Machili in eastern Barotseland. We know that the copper mines of Katanga were being worked and the products traded widely by the eighth century A.D.; that central Angola had been occupied by metal-users a century earlier; that trade was coming up the lower Zambezi at the same time; that by A.D. 300 there were agriculturalists living at Zimbabwe, and that by A.D. 1100 there was a flourishing center at Mapungubwe (Bambandyanalo) on the Limpopo. At the beginning of the sixteenth century these earlier Iron Age cultivators were joined by other more efficiently organized groups establishing powerful political confederacies, and the process of absorption of the older populations was speeded up.

One point that needs stressing here, however, is that the coming of the Iron Age mixed farmers was not, as is all too often supposed, necessarily coincident with the disappearance of the old hunting-collecting populations. Such apparent anomalies as a Bush-Hottentot physical stock with a Negroid culture, as is found at Mapungubwe or at Inyanga and a number of other places, is surely the result of some of the old hunting populations having changed their economy. In the same way the historic Cape Hottentots were a Stone Age people who had acquired stock and become pastoralists. Moreover, from the skeletal remains from Northern Rhodesia and Nyasaland it can be seen that the Late Stone Age population was already Negroid in a number of its physical characteristics, and in the Bergdama and Hadza we can probably see surviving examples of two of the Later Stone Age populations of Equatoria.

It is, therefore, probably true to say that the origins of the older Bantu populations of these countries are most likely to be found in the Stone Age, though of course the present populations must be the results of subsequent modification by hybridization with small groups of immigrants. The fundamental change is not so much in the population as in the economy, though there is of course ample evidence to prove immigration and replacement in a number of cases. The caves and rock shelters were gradually abandoned as pressures dictated, that is, by all except the unadjustable minority of the hunting populations, and the inhabitants now settled in open villages, planted crops and herded stock. Hybridization completed the transformation that economic expediency had begun.

There is increasing proof to show that this was the pattern in many of the southern and central parts of Africa following the coming of the first groups of iron-using immigrants. The consequence is to emphasize the continuity of African culture, and to show the need to study both the prehistoric populations and their culture, since here lies the clue to the understanding of the present.

ADDENDUM

At the time of correcting the proofs of this paper Dr. L. S. B. Leakey has just announced that the Pre-Zinjanthropus fossils from Bed I and new fossils from the lower part of Bed II at the Olduvai Gorge together represent a new species, *Homo habilis* (so called for his toolmaking ability), whose characteristics, it is claimed, fall outside the range of Australopithecine variability. This implies, therefore, that the species *Homo* had become genetically differentiated from the *Australopithecinae* at a time anterior to the deposition of Bed I rather than posterior to this time. If this is so it would also seem unlikely that *Homo erectus* represents a stage of human evolution directly ancestral to modern man. Some lively controversy can be expected when the full details of the new discovery are made available.

SUMMARY

The paper traces the beginnings of human culture in Africa, its evolution and spread, and shows the feedback relationship that exists between biological evolution and culture. It is demonstrated how environment is the most important factor in producing variability at the food-gathering level, and the present-day regional differences in culture are shown to have been in existence for some 40,000 years. The history of the introduction and spread of domestication is summarized, and evidence is adduced to indicate that the diffusion of Iron Age economy in southern Africa was due as much to adaptation as to immigration, thus demonstrating a real and traceable continuity up to the present day.

ALEXANDER ALLAND, JR.

3. *Human Biological Diversity in Africa*

Modern man and his predecessors, the *Australopithecinae, Homo erectus,* and the Neanderthaloids, have all occupied Africa, and it is probable that the fossil line leading to modern man first arose there about four million years ago. Early man, limited in economic activity to hunting and gathering, spread over the eastern and northern savannas and later penetrated the forest zones, where he encountered a new set of environmental challenges. The expansion of populations across the continent led to biological differentiation. Each environmental zone undoubtedly exerted its own specific selective pressures, but such factors as genetic drift, based on random variation and gene flow from adjacent populations, also contributed to genetic change. While isolation, particularly of small populations, produced biological and cultural diversity, new population shifts, migrations, and conquests tended to reshuffle genes in a process of never-ending recombination. The result is a continent populated by groups speaking a wide variety of languages, separated, in differing degrees, both ethnically and genetically.

Anthropologists have attempted to make sense of the biological side of human diversity through two rather different approaches. The first, rather static in nature, attempts to classify existing population, or groups of populations, into categories that are traditionally known as racial or subracial. The second, to be discussed below, attempts to unravel the dynamic aspect of human variation in order to understand the process of ongoing human evolution.

In accordance with the first approach and beginning with what appear to be the most genetically distant groups, Africa is divided racially among Bushmanoids, Caucasoids, and Negroids (some classify Pygmies as a separate race: Negrillo). These major divisions are subdivided into what are supposed to be smaller biological clusters. The physical criteria for these are usually refinements in

SOURCE: Dr. Alland's article was commissioned expressly for this volume.

degree of skin tone, hair texture, body build, height, facial features, and cephalic index. Such a system is superficial at best because it ignores a wide range of genetic traits such as blood groups which, while invisible, are equally valid markers of genetic similarity or diversity among populations. In most cases, the evidence that such African subgroups are legitimate biologically is questionable. In fact, these subclassifications are frequently drawn from linguistic or ethnic classifications with the assumption that such cultural distinctions reflect, even produce, genetic isolation.

Phenotypic and genotypic differences occur both within and between populations. If single traits or small clusters are considered, and if intermediate populations are ignored, certain rather clear geographic patterns emerge. Forest people tend to be shorter than those who inhabit the savanna or the desert. The gene for sickle-cell anemia reaches high proportions among agricultural populations of West Africa. Dark skin occurs with greater frequency south of the Sahara than in the Mediterranean littoral. Thus, real biological differences have played their part in the attempts of anthropologists to delineate subgroupings on the African continent. The problem with these classifications, however, rests on frequent confusion of biological and cultural criteria.[1]

Ashley Montagu, himself highly critical of the concept of race as a valid biological concept, has nevertheless attempted to divide African population clusters on the basis of a quasi-cultural, quasi-biological system. For Montagu the African subdivisions are as follows: *Caucasoid:* North African Hamites consisting of Arabs and Berbers as well as more southerly peoples who speak Hamitic languages. The Mediterranean Berbers occupy Cyrenaica, Tripolitania, Tunisia, and Algeria, and are together often referred to as the Libyans. Other Berber groups include the Atlantic Berbers of Morocco, such as the Kabyles and the West Saharan Berbers. The Tuaregs, the Tebu of East Sahara, the Fula or Fulani of Nigeria, and the extinct Guanche of the Canary Islands are all classed as Hamites. This subdivision is clearly cultural and linguistic, since the Northern Hamites tend to be rather more Caucasoid in appearance and to form a somewhat more homogeneous type than the Eastern Minites who have, in most cases, a greater Negroid admixture. . . .

---

[1] Five classifications of Africa showing how cultural and linguistic factors have influenced biological typologies (after Hiernaux, pp. 97–98).

CHART I

Seligman 1935

I Caucasoids 1. Semites
               2. Hamites   A. Orientals (Egyptians, Nubians, Somalis, and most Ethiopians)
                                       B. Northern (Berbers, Tuaregs, Tebu, Fulani)

II Negroids   1. Negroes   A. True Negroes (Guinea, Senegal, and Central Sudan)
                                       B. Groups in region of Upper Congo, Nile, Uele, and Ubangi rivers (Zande, Bongo)
               2. Negrillos   C. Dama
               3. Khoisan
               4. Negro-Samites A. Half Hamites (Masai, Nandi, Suk, Turkana)
                                       B. Nilotes a) Upper Nile (Luba, Lendu)
                                               b) Middle Nile (Shilluk, Anuak, Acholi, Lango)
                                               c) Nile Basin (Dinka, Nuer)
                                      C. Bantus a) eastern
                                                 b) central
                                               c) western

Von Eickstedt 1937

I Negroids   1. Euro-Africans A. Ethiopians
                                       B. Indomelanesians
               2. Cafro-malgaches A. Sudanese
                                       B. Nilotes
                                       C. Cafrides
               3. Paleomelan-   D. Paleonigritos
                   nesoids, Australians, Papuans
               4. Pygmies   A. Banboutu
                                       B. Negritos

II Mongoloids 1. Subnigritos   A. Khoisan

Vallois 1944

I Sub-Saharan
  Africans 1. Ethiopians   A. Abyssinians, Somalis, Nubians
                                       B. Mixed Ethiopians x MelanoAfricans (Masai, Nandi, Suk)
                                       C. Mixed Ethiopians x MelanoAfricans x Arabs (Fulani)
               2. MelanoAfricans A. Sudanese
                                       B. Guineans
                                       C. Congolese
                                       D. Nilotes
                                       E. South Africans
               3. Negrillos
               4. Khoisan

CHART I (cont.)

Biassuti 1959

I Group of subequatorial   1. Ethiopians (Oromo, Masai, Tutsi)
   races of mixed origins   2. Saharans (Tebu)
II Group of primary   1. Australoids
   equatorial races   2. Negroids
                                 A. Negroes   a) Sudanese
                                            b) Nilotes
                                            c) Cafres
                                            d) Savanna
                                            e) Twa
                                          f) Andamanese
                                          g) Aeta-Semang
                             B. Pygmies
                             C. Khoisan

Garn 1961

I Sub-Saharan Africa   1. East Africans
                               2. Sudanese
                               3. Forest Negroes
                               4. Bantus
                               5. African Pygmies
                               6. Khoisan

The Eastern Hamites for their part comprise the ancient and modern Egyptians, now much mixed with Semitic-speaking (Arabic) elements, the Nubians, Beja, Galla, Somali, Danakil, and most Ethiopians (Montagu 1960:456).

Negroid: Under this division Montagu includes not only Black African populations but also the Bushmen and Hottentots, as well as a group which he terms "Half Hamites" or "Nilo Hamites." Again, these groups are recognized more as cultural than as biological entities. In reference to the "Hamites," for example, Montagu states: ". . . Hamitic is a linguistic and not a physical category" (Montagu 1960:421). Montagu divides the Black Africans into "True Negroes," "Forest Negroes," "Nilotic Negroes," "Half Hamites," "Negrollos" (Pygmies), and the "Bantu-speaking Negroes."

According to Montagu the "True" Negroes are distributed mainly in West Africa, ranging from the mouth of the Senegal River to the south as far as parts of the Cameroons and the Congo. They are characterized by the following traits: black skin, woolly hair, broad and flat nose, average height (five feet, eight inches), full and often everted lips, moderately long head, considerable prognathism, strong body build, relatively long armed and long-legged (Montagu 1960:421).

The "Forest" Negroes, for their part, are shorter than the above type, with more everted lips, short legs but long arms, very prominent lower face, and high cheekbones. Their distribution overlaps that of the "True" Negroes extending from the Senegal River in the west, to the Sudan, Uganda and Northern Rhodesia in the east, and down to Angola.

In contrast, the "Nilotic" Negroes are limited to the Sudan and the upper Nile Valley. They are tall and slim with very dark skin. Their heads are fairly long and noses range from broad to narrow. Montagu suggests that the Nilotes are mixed populations of "True" or "Forest" Negroes and "Hamites."

The group that Montagu calls the "Half Hamites" or "Nilo Hamites" are found in East Africa, particularly in Kenya and Uganda. He considers them to be hybrids of "True" Negroes and "Hamites." Their skin color is prescribed as ranging from light to very dark and their noses are also variable from broad to thin. Lips are not everted and facial prognathism is slight. The Half Hamites are tall, but not as tall as the Nilotes.

Montagu has a separated classification for the "Bantu-speaking Negroes" who are widely distributed over the lower two thirds of black Africa. He frankly admits that his criteria for this group are primarily linguistic, since these people are highly variable in physical type.

Montagu believes that the group he calls the "Bushmen," were once widely distributed in Africa but are now limited to Southern Angola and the Kalahari Desert, are very short people (1.58m., or five feet, two inches). Their skin is light, and their arms and legs are long in relation to trunk. Hair texture is distinctive, with tightly coiled spirals known as peppercorns. Heads are fairly broad and the face is usually angular or only slightly prognathous. Noses are short and very broad, and while lips are fleshy, they are not as fleshy as in Negro populations. The Bushmen are held to be related to the Hottentots, a herding people believed by Montagu to be a hybrid between Negro or Hamitic populations and Bushmen.

The Pygmies form the last subgroup of Montagu's Negroid division. They are found in the tropical rain forests of the Congo and part of the Cameroons. The Pygmy is very short (four feet, eight and one-half inches), has a short trunk, short legs, and long arms. The skin and hair though frequently very dark include reddish or reddish-yellow and yellowish-brown shades. The head is mesocephalic, the face short and broad. The nose is very flat and broad, the wings of the nostrils being both broad and overhanging at the tip. The eyes tend to be prominent and the upper jaw prognathous (Montagu 1960:431–34).

In a recent attempt at racial classification, Carlton Coon (1965) divides Africa's inhabitants into *Pygmies* (a group he views as ancestral to the Negro), *Bushmen* (or Capoids), *Berbers, Arabs,* and *"proper Negroes."* He declares: "By 'proper Negroes' we mean those peoples of Africa who are neither Pygmies nor Bushmen, Berbers, Arabs, or any of the clinal populations with a readily visible Caucasoid racial element. We mean the West Africans, some of the East Africans, and most of the Bantu . . ." (p. 122).

Coon states that the Negro racial characteristics include tightly coiled black hair; black or dark brown skin color; black or dark brown eyes with pigmented spots in the sclera; pigmented lips and gums; a dolichocephalic or mesocephalic head, with a prominent occiput; broad nose; large, often prominent eyeballs; full and everted lips; highly variable nasal bridge form and prognathism; small ears with intricate antihelical patterns, broad shoulders; narrow hips; long arms; relatively long distal portions of the limbs (Coon 1965:123–24).

As is readily apparent there is considerable disagreement between Coon and Montagu. Coon emphasizes the uniformity of Negro populations throughout black Africa, while Montagu splits this group into a series of subpopulations. Moreover, while Coon's racial divisions are purely biological, Montagu's are based on a combination of mixed biological and cultural criteria. While Montagu includes Bushmen under Negro groups (he is unique in this respect among physical anthropologists), Coon makes a basic distinction between "proper Negroes" and Bushmen. Finally, while Coon argues for real biological divisions ("races"), the thrust of Montagu's argument is that although biological diversity exists, no clear-cut divisions can be made between human groups above the level of the population.

Tobias' (1966) approach to the study of Africa's populations is qualitatively different from those of Montagu and Coon. He is primarily interested in blood groups and reports a considerable genetic and ecological diversity in Africa south of the Sahara. For example, he notes that the phenotypes of the ABO system in sub-

Saharan populations vary widely, ". . . with phenotype A ranging from 6.0 in 50 Pygmoid Boni of Somaliland to 54.2 in 22 Bantu Himba from Angola . . . while the B phenotype ranges from 0 in the Bantu Nyungwe and the small Angolan Himba sample, to 46 in a sample of Kenyan Swahili and 50 in the Pygmoid Boni . . ." Tobias (1966:117). Rh_0 is noted as high in all black African populations, but it ranges from 45.3 percent to 80.5 percent.

Tobias states that in African populations the M and N in the MNS group are listed as about equal in frequency. Henshaw is present in all tested populations with a range from 2.0 in Cape Malays, 2.7 in Bushmen, 10.5 in Hottentots, and 11.8 in a sample of Tanganyikan Iraqw. Note that only the latter is a "Negro" African population. The Kell-Cellano blood group is found in low percentages in most African populations with relatively high scores for Bushmen and southernmost Bantu-speaking groups (around 10 percent). The Diego factor is not found in black Africans, and the distribution of Lutheran compares with Caucasians. Of interest is that it is not found in either Bushmen or Hottentots. Clearly, Tobias' data do not lend themselves to a facile classification into the traditional "races" of Africa.

The most recent study of diversity in Africa (limited to sub-Saharan populations) is *La Diversité-Humaine en Afrique Subsaharienne* by Jean Hiernaux (1968).

Hiernaux has gathered genetic and anthropometric data on 460 populations. Using the method of *matrix analysis,* he has attempted to derive population clusters (those which are more alike than different) and to account for genetic diversity in Africa through a review of environmental-genetic correlations, as well as such historical factors as migrations and conquests. Of the 460 societies, only 101 were adequately documented in relation to physical traits for purposes of analysis. Twenty-five constellations resulted, of which twenty-three had only two populations; forty-nine could not be grouped at all. Such results make a hash of most classificatory schemes, and Hiernaux is prepared to throw them all out.

First of all Hiernaux believes that cluster analysis is the only objective way to derive groupings within species on a higher level than the population, for it determines mathematically which groups, if any, are naturally alike. That is to say, the distance between the members of any cluster must be smaller than the distance between clusters. Hiernaux's results tend to put the entire concept of "race" into doubt as a classificatory device, since it is designed to establish groupings on the level between the population and the species. His African data show that the traditional "racial" classification just does not work except in the most minimal terms. This is not to say that genetic variation does not exist; only that it falls into a vast series of continuums. Furthermore, because the continuums for different traits are distributed differentially, no single order can be derived from the data.

Secondly, Hiernaux believes that anthropometric data and particular individual traits should be studied in relation to sets of genetic, environmental, and historical factors. With this dynamic rather than static approach it would be readily seen that some traits show a clinal distribution. That is, they display a regular gradient in the frequency and/or expression of a trait across geographic space. Clines may reflect gene flow from a region of high gene frequency to a region of low gene frequency (or vice versa) through intermediate populations. They may also reflect the differential effects of selection on populations located along an environmental gradient.

In an attempt to unravel the effects of natural selection on anthropometric and single gene traits, Hiernaux performed statistical correlations between six climatic variables and the following physical characteristics: stature, weight, height seated, length of superior extremities, biacromial diameter, iliac diameter, transverse thoracic diameter, sagittal thoracic diameter, calf circumference, head length, head width, cephalic index, total facial height, bizygomatic diameter, facial index, nose height, nose width, nasal index, ABO frequencies, RH system frequencies, frequency of the gene L^m of the MN system, gene frequencies of abnormal hemoglobins Hb^S and Hb^C, frequencies of arcs, whorls, and loops in fingerprints. The climatic factors tested were mean annual rainfall, average humidity in the most humid months, average humidity in the least humid months, maximum daily temperature in the warmest months, maximum daily temperature in the coolest months, and altitude. In addition, each of the six climatic variables was run against all the others. The analysis suggests high correlations between humidity and maximal temperature in the warmest months, and Hiernaux considers humidity to be a major factor acting in these correlations.

Hiernaux suggests that anthropometric characters are more often related to humidity than to temperature. It is not that temperature is

CHART II

Coefficients of correlation of four anthropometric traits
with the range of humidity and the range of temperature

	N	range of humidity	range of temperature
Stature	312	0.48	0.30
Head length	190	−0.29	−0.32
Bizygomatic diameter	160	−0.22	−0.39
Nasal index	122	−0.12	−0.34

less important than humidity in sub-Saharan Africa. For example, humidity and temperature are both related to stature, seated height, width of head, and width of nose, while relative weight, billic diameter, and nasal height are related only to humidity. But, among climatic factors studied, atmospheric humidity appears to be a more important selective agent than temperature. Moreover, there is no character that is tied solely to temperature (Hiernaux 1968:91).

According to Hiernaux ABO frequencies in African populations are unrelated to the climatic factors tested. The sample of populations for which adequate data on the MN system was available is too small for judgment; the same was true for the Rh group. Hb^S is related to malarial distribution as noted by other scholars. Hb^C is not related to climate, but its low frequency on the coast and its rather high frequency on the Voltaic plateau suggest either that some environmental factor is operating or that the gene originated in that geographic zone.

Hiernaux summarizes his findings on African populations as follows:

"The multiplicity of migrations and gene flow suggested by ethnohistory and prehistory has been presented through an analysis of the geographic distribution of anthropological characters. These distributions reveal the influence of multiple factors which have marked the biological history of African populations. They depend upon the degree of initial contrast between gene frequencies, on the force of natural selection, and upon the flow of time. Only a trace of recent and major events emerges, and this is revealed sometimes by one character and sometimes by another. For example, the influence of a genetic center outside of Africa is suggested in central Ethiopia by the frequencies of R_o and L^M. The trace of major gene flow which covers sub-Saharan Africa from north to south appears to be marked by the distribution of fingerprint patterns. The distribution of stature and of the indices of the head and face suggest genetic exchanges between the equatorial forest and the zones which surround it. The latter is clear because the relations between these characters are not effaced by the partial correlations with climate which is held constant.

"Finally, though the analysis presented here cannot serve as evidence of genetic drift, the intervention of the latter in the diversity studied is highly probable" (Hiernaux 1968:96; translation mine).

It would appear from Hiernaux's work that diversity in Africa is due to a wide range of factors, including selection, draft, migration, and interbreeding. These factors have affected different populations in different ways, and if we are to understand the patterns we must look at the historical interplay of genetic, social, cultural, and environmental forces. For example, until very recent times, most of the world's populations depended upon hunting and gathering for their subsistence. Hunting and gathering populations tend to be small and to some extent migratory, since they are forced to seek out new game areas as old ones are depleted. When climatic change occurs which affects the distribution of game animals, hunters must shift along with the game.

On the other hand, when the game supply is good, such groups will expand their numbers rapidly. But since there appears to be a rather small optimum number for a hunting people they tend to divide into new bands as they grow. Of course marriage occurs between bands, but as successful groups expand they may move farther and farther away from each other. Such a spread fosters genetic as well as geographic distance.

Herding populations as well as farming ones, particularly those dependent upon slash and burn agriculture, tend to follow a pattern of slow movement and splitting. In Africa, where much of the land is underpopulated, the best and simplest solution to the population problem has been migration and pioneering. The astonishingly rapid expansion of Bantu-speaking peoples from a nodal area in West Africa into most of East and South Africa in only a few hundred years is an example of such movement and expansion. Here again, when the migrating populations are small, genetic drift is likely to occur, for the sample of genes found in the gene pool of a small migrating group is not likely to be equivalent to the gene pool of its parental population. Small populations *in situ* suffer frequent depletion through disease, wars, and other disasters. Groups of this sort have a rather good statistical chance of diverging genetically by accident. And once such random change has occurred, selection begins to operate again on the new gene pools. They may then diverge even further because local selection pressures are frequently different and because selection works on existing gene pools. If these are different, initial divergences are likely to be enlarged (c.f. Gajdusek 1964).

One example of natural selection that occurred in Africa and which appears to have had a profound influence upon the indigenous population is that known as sickle-cell anemia. The mutant allele S is a recessive; that is, sickle-cell anemia will occur only if an individual has a homozygous or double dose, one gene donated by the father and the other by the mother. If this occurs, the individual suffers from severe anemia and may die, thus leaving no or few offspring. In contrast, an individual who is heterozygous (who carried a single dose) is a carrier but does not display the major symptoms of the disease. Under most environmental conditions a heterozygous carrier and a homozygous normal individual have about the same selective advantage over the sickler. But in areas in which *Falcaparum malaria* is endemic the heterozygous carrier has an advantage over the other two genotypes. The heterozygote's hemoglobin differs sufficiently from the normal type to produce a poor environment for the malaria parasite which passes part of its life cycle in the red blood cell. Thus, the heterozygote is resistant to malaria. This phenomenon, known as adaptive polymorphism, accounts for the high frequency of the Hb^S gene in parts of Africa and is an example of natural selection in action.

Other traits may also be implicated in the complicated process of accommodation to the natural environment. Such factors as skin color, stature, and hair texture may well reflect adaptive adjustments, but the genetic structure of these traits is much more complicated than that of sickle-cell anemia. They are polygenetic; that is, more than a single set of genes is responsible for their expression, and this makes analysis very complicated. Nonetheless, such authors as Coon, Garn, and Birdsell (1950) have suggested that high surface to weight ratio (tall, thin individuals) is an adaptation to heat, particularly dry heat. Such an adaptation is used as an explanation of the distribution of tall, thin individuals among the Nilotic peoples in East Africa. The same authors have suggested that black skin is an adaptation to intense sunlight, although Coon, in his most recent publication on race (1965), suggests that it is an adaptation to the cool, damp environment of the tropical rain forest. Woolly hair, so characteristic of black African populations, is seen also as a possible insulator, providing protection from the sun.

For the same reason or set of reasons, dark skin may have been the original condition for *Homo sapiens,* with light skins developing later in evolution. Such a change could occur as a result of drift, but the regular skin color clines suggest that natural selection may have been responsible for the process. Peter Post (personal communication) suggests that melanin pigment is cold sensitive. Thus, individuals who carry low melanin are somewhat more resistant to frost bite than are dark individuals. On the other hand, it is well known that dark skins are more resistant to sunburn than light ones. Unfortunately, most hypotheses about skin color are highly speculative. Little is really known at present about the adaptive significance of skin color, and we now have exactly contrary hypotheses about its selective value.

There are many gaps in our knowledge about the factors making for biological diversity in Africa, or in the rest of the world, for that matter. A great deal of research needs to be done. Nevertheless, the data that we have at present from Africa and the rest of the world suggests that *Homo sapiens* (modern man) is a single, continuous, widely distributed species grouped in local populations. These local populations exhibit variations produced by genetic and environmental factors. The variation is continuous from population to population, with different genetic traits having their specific genetic distributions.

JOSEPH H. GREENBERG

4. African Languages

Africa, particularly that part which lies south of the Sahara, is characterized by a great multiplicity of languages. In the absence of a generally accepted method for distinguishing between dialect and language no exact figure can be given. On any reasonable criterion, however, the number of distinct languages is well above 800. One source mentions 248 as the number of languages in Nigeria alone. Many of these languages have only a small number of speakers, but others are widespread and spoken by millions—including both native speakers and those for whom the languages function as an auxiliary means of communication. Even before the period of intensive European contact, such languages as Swahili in East Africa and Hausa in West Africa were widely employed as lingua francas (languages used in common by multilingual groups). In spite of their great diversity, the languages of Africa fall into a small number of stocks of apparently distinct origin. The four major stocks are Afroasiatic, Niger-Congo (formerly known as West Sudanic, and including Bantu), Sudanic, and Click (former Bushman, including Hottentot, and two languages of East Africa).

Although the four major African stocks cannot be shown to have a single origin, there are some linguistic characteristics shared by large numbers of African languages which are infrequent or nonexistent elsewhere and help mark off Africa as a linguistic area. Tone, the existence of systems of nominal classification, and verbal derivations are discussed below. Vowel systems are generally simple without umlauted vowels or other modifications except nasalization, which is fairly common. Outside of most Afroasiatic languages, syllables are usually open, that is, end only in vowels. The initial sequences of nasal plus voiced stop are common, such as *mb-* and *nd-*.

SOURCE: Joseph H. Greenberg, "African Languages," *Collier's Encyclopedia,* Vol. I, © 1970, Crowell-Collier Educational Corporation, pp. 243–47. Reprinted by permission of the author and publisher.

Besides clicks, the labiovelars consisting of simultaneous labial and velar closures (*kp* and *gb*) and imploded stops involving an inrushing instead of expulsion of air are common and are seldom found outside Africa. The tonal systems usually involve two or three significant pitch-levels, unlike such languages as Chinese which use rises, falls, and other contours. Many semantic idioms are likewise found throughout most of Africa, such as the phrase "mouth of the house" for "door," "children of the hand" for "fingers," and in general the use of the term "child" as a diminutive.

During the nineteenth century, with the opening up of interior Africa to Europeans, substantial linguistic information regarding Africa, particularly the southern portion, became available for the first time. This led to the pioneer attempts at over-all classification by such investigators as R. Lepsius, F. Müller and R. N. Cust. In the first two decades of the twentieth century, chiefly through the efforts of C. Meinhof and D. Westermann, the former a Bantu specialist, the latter a student of the languages of the Sudan, a widely used general classification of African languages emerged. According to this scheme, the languages of the continent were divided into five families: Semitic, Hamitic, Sudanic, Bantu, and Bushman. These were distributed in general from north to south in that order. The first two families were presumed originally to have been spoken by Caucasoids, the second pair by Negroids, while the last was the language of the Bushman race. Although widely accepted for a time, this classification had obvious weaknesses and has now been superseded. Its major defects were the following. 1) As Westermann himself demonstrated, Bantu is related to the large Western Sudanic group of languages in a family to which the languages of the East Sudan do not in general belong. 2) Semitic likewise is not independent, but is related to Hamitic. As M. Cohen and others have indicated, Hamitic is not a valid unit within this larger group but simply the name traditionally applied to all non-Semitic branches. 3) Of the various proposals made by Meinhof regarding the Hamitic status of a number of languages (e.g., Fulani, Hottentot, Masai), almost all are generally admitted now to be incorrect. Only Hausa, to which a large number of languages in the Chad area should be added to form a Chad subgroup, can be considered to be Hamitic and therefore a branch of Afroasiatic (formerly Hamito-Semitic). The result of these over-all modifications is the system set forth in this article.

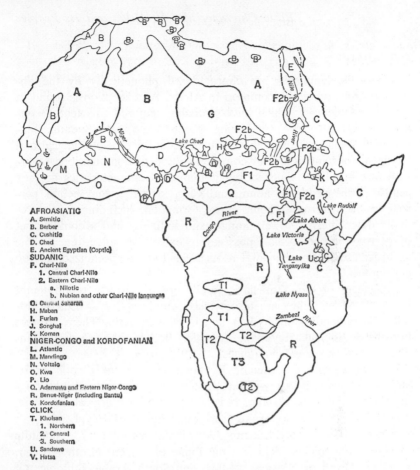

AFROASIATIC
A. Semitic
B. Berber
C. Cushitic
D. Chad
E. Ancient Egyptian (Coptic)
SUDANIC
F. Chari-Nile
  1. Central Chari-Nile
  2. Eastern Chari-Nile
    a. Nilotic
    b. Nubian and other Chari-Nile languages
G. Central Saharan
H. Maban
I. Furian
J. Songhai
K. Koman
NIGER-CONGO and KORDOFANIAN
L. Atlantic
M. Mandingo
N. Voltaic
O. Kwa
P. Ijo
Q. Adamawa and Eastern Niger-Congo
R. Benue-Niger (including Bantu)
S. Kordofanian
CLICK
T. Khoisan
  1. Northern
  2. Central
  3. Southern
U. Sandawe
V. Hatsa

Figure 4–1. The approximate distribution of the main native language groups of Africa is shown on the map. Although the number of different languages is very high (perhaps more than 800), all native languages derive from four basic stocks. These stocks are represented by the shaded and unshaded portions of the map. Key letters indicate divisions of the main stocks and are placed in localities where interrelated languages are spoken. European and European colonial languages, which often serve as a common language between language groups, are not included in this presentation. The dotted line at E shows the area where Ancient Egyptian was spoken, but the present language is Arabic. Certain other distributions, too minute to be shown on the map, include complex variations in the Sudanic languages; pockets of Sulani in the Atlantic subgroup of Niger-Congo (L) found as far east as Lake Chad; and Bantu (R) encroachments on the territory of the Click-speakers.

AFROASIATIC

Afroasiatic languages are characterized phonetically by the absence of tone, otherwise common in Africa. An exception is found in the Chad languages, which have probably acquired this feature under the influence of neighboring Niger-Congo and Sudanic languages. We may note also the frequent occurrence of pharyngeal and laryngeal consonants and of complex consonant combinations otherwise rare in Africa. Outstanding grammatical characteristics are sex gender in the pronoun, noun, and verb, including the second person; varied patterns of noun plural formation, including partial reduplication, internal vowel change, and suffixing; and a complex set of derived verbal forms (passive, reflexive, causative, etc.). The exclusive use of triconsonantal roots seems to be a specialized Semitic development.

Languages of the Afroasiatic family are exclusively predominant in North Africa. They are also widely found in East Africa (Ethiopia, Somaliland, Tanganyika) and in western Asia. There are five branches: Ancient Egyptian, Semitic, Berber, the Cushitic languages, and the Chad languages.

Ancient Egyptian. Ancient Egyptian (known as Coptic in its later stages when it was written alphabetically) is now extinct, having been replaced by Arabic. It is still used as a liturgical language, however, by the Monophysite Christian Church of Egypt.

Semitic. Semitic divides into Akkadian (now extinct), Canaanite (Hebrew, Phoenician including the Punic of ancient North Africa), Aramaic, North or classical Arabic, and South Arabic-Ethiopic. Of these, classical Arabic was carried across all of North Africa and up the Nile Valley into the Sudan by the Muslim invasions of the early Middle Ages. It is now spoken in a wide variety of locally differing dialects. Arabic is the native language of some Negroid groups, e.g., the Shuwa of the Lake Chad region, and is used as a lingua franca by the racially Negro people of Wadai and Darfur east of Lake Chad.

The other Semitic languages of Africa belong to the Ethiopian division and are most closely akin to the South Arabic languages of the Sabaean and Minaean inscriptions. These languages came into Africa by a not easily datable migration from southern Arabia, well before the beginning of the Christian era. The Ethiopian Semitic languages fall into two groups. The northern includes the extinct Ge'ez (classical Ethiopic), Tigre, and Tigrinya. The southern contains the Gurage dialects; Harari, the local language of the city of Harar; and most importantly, Amharic, now the standard language of Ethiopia with nearly six million speakers.

Berber. Berber, formerly spoken in all of North Africa except Egypt and in the Canary Islands, now survives mainly in the western part of this area and among the Tuareg nomads of the Sahara. Ancient Berber inscriptions are found in an alphabet which is probably of Carthaginian origin, a system of writing still in use among the contemporary Tuareg.

Cushitic. Cushitic, spoken in East Africa, consists of five branches: a northern or Beja group; an eastern group which includes the important Somali, Galla, Saho-Afar, and Sidamo languages; a central group spoken by the Agau peoples, who have been largely Semiticized culturally and linguistically; a western group consisting of Kaffa and numerous other small linguistic communities in southwestern Ethiopia and adjoining regions; and a small southern group consisting of a few languages of minor importance, such as the Iraku (Iraqw) of Tanganyika.

Chad Languages. The Chad languages, a very large substock, are distributed chiefly in the northern region of Nigeria, in Niger, and eastward into Cameroon and the Republic of Chad. By far the most important Chad language is Hausa (Haoussa), which has well over six million native speakers. It is the dominant language of the northern region of Nigeria and the most widely used auxiliary language of West Africa. It possesses a literature written in an adaptation of the Arabic alphabet. Other Chadic languages include Bolewa, Angas, Ankwe, Tangale, Bura, Margi, Higi, Mandara, Musgu, Mubi, Sokoro, and Kotoko-Buduma.

NIGER-CONGO

The Niger-Congo languages, the largest linguistic stock of Negro Africa, are generally tonal. A conspicuous feature of the grammatical structure is a set of noun classes, marked by separate affixes for the singular and plural. As with the sex gender systems of many European languages, in many of the languages adjectives and pronouns agree in class with the noun to which they refer. However, as contrasted with sex gender languages which have at most three categories—masculine, feminine, and neuter—the number of classes is large and sex is not a basis of distinction among them. For example, human beings belong in one class, animals in another, trees (along with other items not easily classifiable) in another, while some of the classes have no discernible basis of meaning classification.

The Niger-Congo languages may be tentatively divided into eight substocks. From west to east we have: an Atlantic subfamily, Mandingo, Voltaic, Kwa, Benue-Niger (including Bantu), Ijo, Adamawa, and an Eastern subfamily.

The Atlantic Subfamily. The Atlantic subfamily consists of languages spoken primarily in the Republic of Senegal, the Republic of Guinea, Portuguese Guinea, and Sierra Leone. Among the languages in this group are Wolof, the local language of Dakar, also spoken elsewhere in the Republic of Senegal; the Temne of Sierra Leone; and Fulani, a language with some millions of speakers who have migrated as far east as Wadai beyond Lake Chad.

Mandingo. The Mandingo languages are found immediately to the east of the main body of Atlantic languages, chiefly in the upper valley of the Niger and in Sierra Leone and Liberia. Important languages of the Mandingo group are Mende in Liberia, and Malinke, Bambara, and Dyula in Mali (formerly French Sudan). Dyula is widespread as a commercial lingua franca. Smaller scattered communities of speakers of Mandingo languages are found as far east as northeastern Nigeria.

Voltaic. The Voltaic or Gur substock is dominant in the Upper Volta and the northern territories of Ghana. Among the languages included here are More, the language of the indigenous Mossi kingdom; Dagomba; and Dogon. The Senufo languages farther west are probably to be considered a subgroup of the Voltaic languages.

Kwa. The Kwa languages have a large west-east extension bounded by the Gulf of Guinea on the south. In the extreme west, the inclusion of the Kru group of Liberia is doubtful. The Kwa substock includes such important languages as the Akan group in the Republic of the Ivory Coast and in Ghana; Fõ, the language of the aboriginal state of Dahomey; and Gã, the local language of Accra, the capital of Ghana. In Nigeria the two chief languages of the southern part of the country, Yoruba and Ibo, are Kwa languages. Also included are Nupe and Bini, the latter the language of Benin, the celebrated art center.

Benue-Niger. The Benue-Niger substock contains the vast Bantu group of languages as a division. Bantu languages are spoken to the partial or complete exclusion of other stocks in most of the Congo basin, in the Portuguese colonies of Angola and Mozambique, in the territory comprising the Federation of Rhodesia and Nyasaland, and (together with Click languages) in the Republic of South Africa and its territories.

The most important Bantu language is Swahili, with approximately eight million native speakers. In addition Swahili is spoken as a second auxiliary language in almost all of East Africa and even in the eastern part of the former Belgian Congo, where it is known as Kingwana. There is a traditional literature of considerable proportions, written in an adaptation of the Arabic alphabet. Other important Bantu languages with estimated numbers of speakers are Zulu (2,500,000), Xhosa (2,400,000), Pedi (700,000), Sotho (600,-000), and Chwana or Tswana (500,000) in the Republic of South Africa; Makua (1,000,000), Thonga (800,000), and Shitswa (500,-000), in Mozambique; Nyanja (400,000) in Nyasaland; Shona (1,500,000) and Bemba (500,000) in the Rhodesias; Kikuyu (700,-000) in Kenya; Luganda (1,000,000), the chief language of Uganda; Nyaruanda (5,000,000) and Rundi (1,500,000) of Ruanda-Urundi; Umbundu (1,700,000) and Kimbundu (1,000,000) in Angola; and the four chief languages of the former Belgian Congo, Luba (3,400,-000), Kikongo (1,200,000), Lingala (700,000), and Mongo-Nkundu (500,000). The non-Bantu languages of the Benue-Niger substock, often called semi-Bantu, are spoken in central and eastern Nigeria and Cameroon. Among these may be mentioned Tiv, Jukun, and Efik.

The Ijo language of the central coastal area of southern Nigeria appears to form a separate group of the Niger-Congo stock. The Adamawa substock consists of a number of relatively little-known languages in east central Nigeria and the neighboring Cameroons. The Eastern substock extends north of the Bantu line in the Niger-Congo divide area as far east as the Republic of the Sudan (formerly Anglo-Egyptian Sudan). Important languages in this branch include Zande, Panda, and Sango, the last a widespread lingua franca.

The Niger-Congo languages are probably related to the Kordofanian languages, a far smaller group, spoken in some of the Nuba hills of Kordofan in the Republic of the Sudan.

SUDANIC

The Sudanic languages are in general tonal. There are no divisions into noun classes, but some of the languages have a division into two sex genders. The nouns sometimes exhibit a system of cases. The verb in some of the languages has a complicated set of verbal derivatives. This family contains most of the languages spoken by Negroes not belonging to the Niger-Congo group.

Chari-Nile. The chief substock is that of the Chari-Nile languages (formerly called Macro-Sudanic). The Chari-Nile languages in turn have two major divisions, Eastern Chari-Nile and Central Chari-Nile, as well as a number of languages that must be classed separately. The Eastern Chari-Nile division includes the Nubian dialects of the Nile Valley and of the Kordofan Land plateau and Darfur to the west, and the Nilotic group: Western Nilotic (Shilluk, Dinka, Nuer, Lango), Eastern Nilotic (Masai, Bari, Turkana, Lotuho) and Southern Nilotic (Nandi-Suk). The last two are sometimes classed together as Nilo-Hamitic. The Central Chari-Nile division includes Mangbetu of the former Belgian Congo and the Sara-Bagirmi languages of the Republic of Chad. A medieval Christian literature exists in Nile Nubian, the language being written in an alphabet derived from Coptic.

Saharan. Another important branch of Sudanic consists of the Saharan languages. Among these are Kanuri, the language of the aboriginal kingdom of Bornu near Lake Chad, and the Teda and Daza languages of the eastern Sahara.

Other Sudanic Languages. In the Republic of the Sudan, the Maban languages of Wadai as well as Furian, the dominant language of Darfur, form further small branches of the Sudanic family. It seems likely that both Songhai, the language of a medieval Negro empire with its capital at Timbuktu, and the small Koman group of the Sudan-Ethiopian border areas are also Sudanic. In general, the Sudanic languages are distributed over a very extensive territory north and east of the Niger-Congo languages.

CLICK LANGUAGES

This family has three substocks. The largest is the Khoisan division of South Africa, which in turn falls into three groups: northern, central, and southern. The Khoisan languages are spoken by

Bushmen and Hottentots; Hottentot belongs to the central branch of the Khoisan division. The other two divisions of the Click languages consist of the Sandawe and Hatsa languages of Tanganyika, far to the north of the Khoisan substock.

The Click languages are characterized by the implosive, "click" sounds not used anywhere else in the world outside Africa as parts of words analogous to ordinary consonant-sounds. They are confined to these languages and a few Bantu languages which have borrowed them from Khoisan speakers. Sandawe and some of the central Khoisan languages, including Hottentot, have sex gender.

OTHER AFRICAN LANGUAGES

In addition to the four major groups described here, the languages of the island of Madagascar are Malayo-Polynesian and distinct from those of the African mainland. Meroitic, formerly spoken near the confluence of the Blue and White Nile, was written in an alphabet based on Egyptian hieroglyphs; we cannot connect it with any other language on the basis of present knowledge.

The European colonization of the last few centuries has resulted in one distinctly African language of European origin, Afrikaans, which has developed along distinctive lines from its Dutch origin so that it must be considered a separate language. English is the first language of the descendants of the Negro settlers from the United States who founded the Republic of Liberia. A creole language based on pidgin English is the language of Freetown in Sierra Leone founded by repatriated slaves in the nineteenth century.

LANGUAGE, RACE, AND HISTORY

There is no necessary correlation between race and language, since a people can adopt the language of a different race or, on the other hand, retain their language in spite of thoroughgoing physical modification by another race. In Africa, as elsewhere, there is only an imperfect correlation between racial and linguistic classification. The strongest agreement is between the speakers of Click languages and the Bushman-Hottentot race. This only holds in full for the large Khoisan branch of the family. Even here, a Negroid group, the Bergdama, speaks a Hottentot language. The Pygmies apparently have no distinct language of their own but have adopted Niger-Congo or Sudanic modes of speech from their Negro neighbors.

Otherwise these two families of language are spoken exclusively by racially Negroid people. Afroasiatic languages are spoken both by Caucasian and Negro peoples. The Cushites and Ethiopian Semites are often classed as Caucasoids. The Egyptians, Berbers, and remaining Semitic people are indisputably Caucasian, while the Chad speakers are Negroid. On this evidence it seems probable that Afroasiatic languages were originally spoken by Caucasians and in some instances taken over by Negroes.

Several important conclusions can be reached regarding the history of Africa from the classification and distribution of languages. The large Bantu movement which eventually covered the southern third of Africa must have begun in relatively recent times, not much more than two thousand years ago, from the area in which the most closely related languages of the Benue-Niger substock are at present spoken in east central Nigeria. This is in accord with other types of evidence which show that this very large area was only recently occupied by Negroes, and that the preceding peoples were Pygmoids and Bushmanoids. Another significant conclusion is that the Afroasiatic family must have originated in Africa, where all branches except Semitic are exclusively found. The Semites then must have migrated, probably at first to Arabia from East Africa, a movement later reversed by the Ethiopian Semites.

Much work remains to be done correlating details of African language distributions with archaeological and documentary historical evidence. Likewise much can be done by the study of the distribution of specific words of culture-historical import, for example, terms for domestic plants and animals. Many terms have penetrated from the Mediterranean cultural area via the Sudan or the Nile to West and East Africa. Thus the Hausa word for "gold," *zinariya,* is ultimately from Latin *denarius,* a gold coin, having reached Hausa via Berber. Again, Arabic influences correlate with the spread of Islam as a religion, while the effects of European contact have also left linguistic traces, for example, the Portuguese terms for the domestic pig and for manioc, the latter brought from South America.

5. Speculations on the Economic Prehistory of Africa

Apart from relatively late Semitic influence . . . the civilizations of Africa are the civilizations of the Hamites, its history the record of these peoples and of their interaction with the two other African stocks, the Negro and the Bushman, whether this influence was exerted by highly civilized Egyptians or by such wider pastoralists as are represented at the present day by the Beja and Somali. . . .The incoming Hamites were pastoral "Europeans"—arriving wave after wave—better armed as well as quicker witted than the dark agricultural Negroes.

These propositions, taken from the late Professor C. G. Seligman's *Races of Africa,* are perhaps the most notorious expression of the racialist interpretation which dominated studies of the African past during the first half of the twentieth century. It is deplorable that they should have been allowed to appear in the third, posthumous edition, issued in 1957 with the blessing of most of Britain's leading Africanists and clearly intended to serve as the standard British textbook on African ethnology. The idea of negro Africa as savagery modified by the influence of European or quasi-European intruders is clearly no more than an extrapolation from the situation that has existed in very recent times; and sufficient knowledge has been accumulated to make it no longer legitimate to theorize *in vacuo* about "waves" of invasion. Although tropical Africa has certainly received major cultural imports from time to time, the archaeological record suggests, on the whole, continuous indigenous development rather than a succession of external impacts; and the palaeontological record makes it clear that people of caucasoid type, so far from being invaders, were resident, at least in East Africa, from the remotest times with which we need concern ourselves.

The point to which I would draw attention here, however, is that

SOURCE: Christopher Wrigley, "Speculations on the Economic Prehistory of Africa," *Journal of African History,* Vol. 1, No. 2, 1960, pp. 189–203. Reprinted by permission of the author and publisher.

the negroes were described as "agricultural." Nor was Seligman alone in conceding the most important of human arts to the dim-witted aboriginals. Stuhlmann had assigned the introduction of cultivation to the earlier, negro waves of immigration from Asia.[1] Baumann's "palaeonigritic" peoples were likewise cultivators.[2] It is at first sight surprising that writers who were so firmly convinced that tropical Africa owed all the rudiments of civilization to foreigners should have been prepared to admit that it possessed the basis of all civilized life before it came under the influence of caucasoid intruders. Part of the explanation, no doubt, lies in the deep-rooted north European upper-class prejudice which made it easy to associate tillers of the soil with inferior status and capacity. A more important point, however, is that in Seligman's day the historic significance of the development of agriculture had not yet been fully appreciated. It was even commonly believed that hoe-cultivation was the oldest of all forms of economy.[3] Given this premise, there was no problem. In so far as the question was discussed at all, it was merely assumed that the negroes had brought their hoe-culture with them from their supposed homeland somewhere in Asia, whence they had emigrated before the evolution of the superior white race and of its superior plough-culture.

But with the progress of prehistoric archaeology in the Middle East during the inter-war years a new picture was taking shape. Gordon Childe, especially, taught us[4] to believe that the emergence of a food-producing economy was the great divide in human history; that this change took place in the Middle East quite abruptly in the fifth or sixth millennium B.C.; that it was closely linked with a number of other technical innovations, notably pottery and polished stone implements; and that this "neolithic" complex was subsequently diffused to other areas of the world. Now in Africa south of the Sahara assemblages of the classical neolithic type have been found only in Ethiopia[5] and Kenya[6], and unequivocal evidence for the practice

---

[1] *Beiträge zur Kulturgeschichte von Ostafrika* (Berlin, 1909), pp. 824–28.

[2] H. Baumann and D. Westermann, *Les Peuples et les Civilisations de l'Afrique* (Paris, 1948).

[3] See for instance M. Weber, *General Economic History* (London, 1923), p. 1.

[4] V. Gordon Childe, *New Light on the Most Ancient East* (London, 1934); *What Happened in History* (Harmondsworth, 1942).

[5] G. Bailloud, "La Préhistoire de l'Ethiopie," in M. Albospeyre and others, *Mer Rouge—Afrique Orientale* (Paris, 1959), p. 24.

[6] L. S. B. Leakey, *The Stone Age Cultures of Kenya Colony* (Cambridge, 1931); Sonia Cole, *The Prehistory of East Africa* (Harmondsworth, 1954).

of agriculture is lacking except in Iron Age sites. There is thus a consensus of opinion among archaeologists, not only that the agriculture of tropical Africa derives from the example of the Middle East, but also that in this part of the world Middle Eastern influence was feeble and belated. On this point, Alimen's summing up may be taken as representative.

> La profonde révolution de l'économie humaine qu'est le Néolithique, apportant l'agriculture et la domestication, ne se marque vraiment que dans l'Afrique septentrionale, la seule à vrai dire qui, comme l'Europe, soit assez facile à cultiver. Dans de nombreuses portions d'Afrique, les conditions désertiques ou tropicales ont été, pour les premiers cultivateurs, un trop grave handicap. . . . La civilisation néolithique apparait donc comme étrangère au continent africain, où elle pénètre par le N.[7]

Childe's concept of the "neolithic revolution," followed at the close of the fourth millennium by the "urban revolution," was too obviously inspired by the nineteenth-century (and especially the Marxist) scheme of sharply defined historical stages to carry complete conviction; and recent discoveries have made rather drastic modifications necessary. In the first place, the date of the transition to agriculture has been pushed further and further back into the past, until the excavations at Jericho have brought it back to the eighth millennium at least.[8] Moreover, this first Jericho, which came into existence four thousand years or more before the "urban revolution," was already, by any ordinary standard, a town. Secondly, the neolithic complex has tended to disintegrate. Pottery, for example, which was formerly regarded as an integral part of the complex, has turned up in non-neolithic contexts in the Ertebølle culture of northern Europe, in the Khartoum mesolithic[9] and in the upper Capsian of Kenya.[10]

Meanwhile, the idea of agriculture as a relatively late and revolutionary development in human history has been opposed from a

[7] H. Alimen, *Préhistoire de l'Afrique* (Paris, 1955), 496–97. This statement is not free from ambiguity, and I have therefore left it in the original rather than use the English translation by A. H. Brodrick, *The Prehistory of Africa* (London, 1957), p. 427.

[8] K. M. Kenyon, *Digging up Jericho* (London, 1957).

[9] A. J. Arkell, *Early Khartoum* (London, 1949).

[10] Leakey, op. cit., p. 103.

quite different quarter. The arguments of American ethnobotanists such as Ames, Anderson and Sauer[11] have made almost no impact on prehistorical thinking in Britain, which is virtually monopolized by archaeology. They nevertheless appear to deserve very serious consideration. Most of the world's crop plants were already in use by 3000 B.C., some of them in highly evolved forms which imply a very long prior history. Nor is it likely that the main staples of modern agriculture were the first to be developed, for in out-of-the-way places there are still to be found a number of inferior crop plants, such as "Job's tears" and the grain amaranths, which would hardly have been taken into use when wheat or rice or maize was already available. The botanical evidence, in fact, points to the conclusion that the flowering of the neolithic economy in the Middle East was preceded by a long period of rudimentary and experimental agriculture, the beginnings of which may go back well into the Pleistocene epoch. Nor were these beginnings necessarily in the Middle East, or concerned with cereals. Sauer believes that tropical gardening, based on the propagation of fruit and tuber plants, is ancestral to the sowing of field crops, and that its origins lie in south-east Asia.

Professor G. P. Murdock has now applied similar botanical arguments to the problem of the origins of agriculture in tropical Africa. Pointing out that the crop plants of this region are quite different from those of the Middle East, and that many of them—notably the millets (*Sorghum vulgare, Eleusine coracana* and *Pennisetum typhoides*), simsim (*Sesamum orientale*), certain pulses (*Vigna sinensis, Cajanus cajan*) and the Guinea yam (*Dioscorea cayenensis*)—are certainly or probably indigenous, he makes the forthright assertion that agriculture was initiated in the upper Niger area by the ancestors of the Mande-speaking peoples about 5000 B.C., and that they took this step independently of, though somewhat later than, the peoples of south-western Asia.[12]

For such precision of date and place there does not appear to be any adequate justification. Nor is it, on the whole, likely that the starting-point of African agriculture was in the western Sudan. Murdock's main argument for this choice is based on plant distribution:

[11] Oakes Ames, *Economic Annuals and Human Culture* (Cambridge, 1939); Edgar Anderson, *Plants, Man and Life* (Boston, 1952); Carl O. Sauer, *Agricultural Origins and Dispersals* (New York, 1952).

[12] *Africa: Its Peoples and Their Culture History* (New York, 1959), pp. 64ff.

certain crops, such as fonio (*Digitaria exilis*) are peculiar to West Africa. But this hardly proves his point, for such plants might well have been added by West Africans to the stock of cultigens which they had received, or brought with them, from the east. We might even turn the argument about, and ask why, if sorghum and pearl millet spread from west to east, fonio should have failed to accompany them. A secondary argument, founded on the wide extension of the "Nigritic," or Niger-Congo language-family, and especially of its Mande branch, is even less convincing. The dispersion of Mande languages can more plausibly be attributed to empire-building and trading activities at a very much later date. The Sudanic language-family, centered on the upper Nile area, has ramifications hardly less wide than those of Niger-Congo; and it is in the region of the eastern Sudan and western Ethiopia that the birthplace of most African crop plants is probably to be sought. Botanists have long regarded Ethiopia as a major center of agricultural evolution—not merely, as Murdock suggests, because this was the only part of tropical Africa to be visited by Vavilov, but because its wide range of soils and climates makes it ideally suited to plant variation and ennoblement.

Whereas criticisms may be made of his more specific hypotheses, Murdock's main contention, that the antiquity of African agriculture is much greater than archaeologists have been willing to concede, is surely well founded. Not only is the continent the original home of a large number of cultivated plants, but some at least of these species have proliferated into a great many different races and varieties,[13] clearly indicating a history that cannot reasonably be fitted into the two-thousand-year span of the African Iron Age. Many of them, moreover, recur in India; and, again, the number of Indian varieties, as well as their concentration in the interior of the sub-continent, suggests that their introduction cannot have been at all recent. The most concrete evidence, however, comes from the study of the cotton plant.

The cultivated cottons of the Old World belong to two species, *Gossypium herbaceum* and *G. arboreum*. The latter, which is fairly certainly the more recently evolved, is known to have been woven at Mohenjodaro in the third millennium B.C. Varieties of the older *herbaceum* species are widely distributed in northern Africa, Persia

[13] See J. D. Snowden, *The Cultivated Races of Sorghum* (London, 1936).

and central Asia, but until recently its original center was believed to have been in or near southern Arabia. It is well established that the wild ancestor of the true cottons was *G. anomalum,* a desert shrub which grows only on the fringes of the Sahara and the Kalahari. Between this plant and the most primitive cultivated plants, however, there is a morphological as well as a geographical gap. Sir Joseph Hutchinson (to whom I am indebted for much patient tuition on this subject) argued that the former could be filled only by *G. herbaceum* race *africanum,* a crude but lint-bearing cotton which is found growing wild in a belt running across southern Africa from Ngamiland to Mozambique.[14] The geographical gap remained, and could be bridged only by one of two very improbable hypotheses. Either, as Hutchinson himself suggested, seeds of the wild *africanum* were gathered and taken home by Arabian seafarers, who must therefore be supposed to have reached southern Africa at least as early as 3000 B.C. Or cotton spread northwards across East Africa under cultivation, so that agriculture must be supposed to have been practiced in *southern* Africa at an equally early date. Now, however, an alternative theory has been proposed. It is suggested that a primitive *herbaceum,* ancestral both to the *africanum* race and to the known cultivated cottons, was developed in south-west Ethiopia.[15] However this may be, the combined evidence from cotton genetics and Indian archaeology leaves no reasonable escape from the conclusion that cotton was being cultivated in Africa before 3000 B.C.—and probably long before, since the plant had to undergo considerable evolutionary change before being used in the Indus Valley civilization. Further, although cotton may have been grown for its oil long before its lint was spun, it is not likely to have been among the first African plants to be domesticated.

The theory of the high antiquity of African agriculture receives additional support—more nebulous perhaps, but also, in my view, convincing—from the linguistic configuration of the continent. The languages of tropical Africa are legion, and, apart from Bantu, there are no large groups having an indisputable common descent. Nevertheless, on the most widely accepted view, the great majority of languages do belong to three main stocks: the Hamito-Semitic family,

[14] J. B. Hutchinson, "Evidence on the origin of the Old World Cottons," *Heredity* (1954), p. VIII.

[15] G. Edward Nicholson, "The Production, History, Uses and Relationships of Cottons in Ethiopia," *Economic Botany* (1960), XIV, p. 3.

including the Chadic and Cushitic groups; the Niger-Congo family, comprising most of the languages of West Africa together with Bantu; and the Sudanic family, occupying most of north-central Africa.[16] The Hamito-Semitic family extends over north Africa and western Asia, but the other two stocks are confined within, and clearly indigenous to, the regions south of the Sahara.[17] This configuration seems to me to be radically inconsistent with the view that until about two thousand years ago these regions were inhabited only by a few primitive hunters. Are we to suppose that peoples equipped with a knowledge of metallurgy and agriculture, and presumably multiplying and expanding with great rapidity, would everywhere have adopted the speech of the scanty groups of aboriginals whom they found in the land? Common sense forbids, and so does analogy. On the contrary, many of the surviving independent hunters—such as the Pygmies, the Ndorobo and the Bergdama—speak the language of their agricultural or pastoral neighbors. Yet, if the first cultivators did not thus lose their language, the orthodox conception of African prehistory cannot be reconciled with the range of African linguistic variation. What we should expect, if agriculture were a recent innovation, would be a wide network of closely related languages. This is just what we do find in the Bantu third of Africa, but elsewhere we are confronted by wide networks of languages that are only very remotely related. The more ambitious claims of glottochronology may or may not command conviction, but on no reasonable concept of relative linguistic distance can a period of less than several millennia be allotted to the differentiation which has taken place within the Niger-Congo and Sudanic stocks. And it seems at least a plausible assumption that this differentiation accompanied the spread of an agricultural economy.

Against these arguments are arrayed the negative inferences from archaeology. In the first place, there is the rarity in tropical Africa of assemblages that are strictly comparable with those of Middle Eastern and European neolithic sites. It is, however, not true that neolithic tools are absent, for the characteristic ground stone axe has been

[16] J. H. Greenberg, *Studies in African Linguistic Classification* (New Haven, 1955). We learn from Murdock (op. cit. 14) that Greenberg now tentatively includes in the Sudanic family most of the minor groups which he formerly classed as independent.

[17] Bantu has been related, by one student or another, to nearly every language-family of the Old World, except Indo-European. These theories, however, are sheer fantasy.

found sporadically in almost every part of the continent. It is admittedly possible, even probable, that neither these implements nor the more elaborate neolithic assemblages of Ethiopia and Kenya belong to a period which antedates the Iron Age by any very wide margin. On the other hand, although polished stone tools and the cultivation of the soil are so closely linked in the minds of archaeologists that the term "neolithic" has virtually come to *mean* "food-producing," there is in reality no universal or necessary connection between these two techniques. Even in the last century, many thoroughly agricultural African tribes did not use either iron or stone hoes. Moreover, in the equipment of "neolithic" Jericho there was an "almost complete lack . . . of picks or hoes for working the soil."[18] An agriculture sufficiently advanced to support a town of perhaps three thousand people was apparently carried on by means of the stone-weighted digging-stick, such as was used by many prehistoric African peoples who have not been accorded neolithic status.

A much more serious difficulty is the absence of direct evidence for agriculture, in the form of actual grains or of grain-impressions on potsherds. For this reason Arkell has rejected the view that the authors of his Khartoum mesolithic culture were agriculturalists, even though their equipment included not only pottery but also large numbers of grinding stones. He assumes that the sole function of the latter was the preparation of ochre, with which indeed many of them were stained. It is not for a layman to dispute this conclusion. Yet I am inclined to think that it should not weigh decisively against the botanical and linguistic evidence for the great antiquity of African agriculture.

To affirm that the cultivation of the soil has a long history in tropical Africa, however, is not necessarily to affirm, as Murdock does, that it had no historical connection with developments in the Middle East. The fact that the Middle Eastern crops do not occur in negro Africa is not in itself conclusive, for in few parts of negro Africa can they be grown with satisfactory results. As cultivating peoples moved southwards they might have discarded wheat and barley in favor of tropical grasses better suited to their new environment, much as in northern Europe these plants were partially displaced by oats and rye.[19] A variant on this would be a theory of "stimulus diffusion":

18 Kenyon, op. cit., p. 57.
19 The analogy is not exact, however, for oats and rye were themselves originally Middle Eastern plants.

a tenuous culture-contact might have induced the peoples south of the Sahara to seek out and utilize their own cultivable grasses.

The case for the derivation of tropical African agriculture from the Middle East would be strengthened if it could be shown that the pottery associated with the Khartoum mesolithic and with the Upper Capsian of Kenya was, or could have been, similarly derivative. This is largely a matter of dating, and here, unfortunately, we are in an area of complete uncertainty. The neolithic site of Shaheinab in the Sudan has been dated by radio-carbon to c. 3300 B.C.; and McBurney suggests that the Khartoum mesolithic preceded it by no more than five hundred years, so making it possible to attribute the earliest Sudanese pottery to the influence of neolithic Egypt (Fayum, c. 4400 B.C.).[20] This short dating, however, seems hardly reconcilable with the marked climatic change which Arkell showed to have occurred in the interval. In Kenya, the Upper Capsian culture belongs to the latter part of the Gamblian pluvial, which Leakey equated with the last glaciation of Europe. This correlation has been seriously questioned, and a considerably lower date has been postulated for the Kenya Capsian.[21] Yet it is difficult to reduce the chronology sufficiently for the purpose now in view, for the Elmenteitan culture, which succeeded the Capsian after an interval, and which produced *fine* pottery, has been dated by the varve method to about 5000 B.C.[22] On balance, therefore, it still seems likely that pottery was being made in parts of tropical Africa before it was being made in Egypt, and at least as early as it was being made anywhere in the Middle East.

On the other hand, there are indications of a different kind which tend to support the diffusionist hypothesis. I have elsewhere adduced evidence for the former presence in Uganda of myth and ritual which have Middle Eastern and Aegean affinities and which, in my view, clearly go back to the very beginnings of agricultural civilization.[23] And the first Jericho seems to be linked to the lacustrine region of central Africa by its beehive huts and, more specifically, by the curious custom of removing the jawbones of the dead.[24]

[20] C. B. M. McBurney, *The Stone Age of Northern Africa* (Harmondsworth, 1960), p. 244.

[21] F. E. Zeuner, *Dating the Past* (London, 4th ed., 1958), pp. 249ff. Alimen, op. cit., pp. 249–50. McBurney, op. cit., pp. 59–60.

[22] Alimen, op. cit., p. 251.

[23] C. C. Wrigley, "Kimera," *Uganda Journal* (1959), xxiii, p. 38.

[24] Kenyon, op. cit., p. 62. Cf. J. Roscoe, *The Baganda* (London, 1911), p. 109.

The whole question of diffusion and independent development in relation to agriculture seems to need re-examination. I believe, indeed, that the basic idea of putting seeds (or tubers) back into the ground was a genuine and unique invention. For it is hard to accept that man should have lived on the earth for tens of thousands of years, during which this idea occurred to no one, and that it should then have occurred to several people independently at what was, prehistorically speaking, almost the same moment. On the other hand, we have to account for the existence in different parts of the world of agricultural systems based on entirely different sets of cultigens and showing no definite trace of historical connection. These considerations can be reconciled by accepting both the antiquity and the gradualness of agricultural development. The first crucial step having been taken, there ensued, not a revolutionary change in the ways of human life, but a period of several thousand years, in which, over steadily widening areas of the world, people were practicing a very rudimentary and part-time agriculture, collecting seeds of all kinds and sometimes re-sowing them. Eventually, in each region, certain of the plants so assisted became productive enough to be used to the exclusion of all others, and to provide the main instead of the subsidiary source of food. The period of collection and experimentation then came to an end, and regular agriculture began.

It is even conceivable that, in this limited sense, the agriculture of tropical Africa is original and that of the Middle East derivative. For this there can be no kind of proof, but certain general considerations may be adduced. It was formerly supposed that agriculture arose in the Middle East as a response to a shift in the storm-track, the Saharan or Arabian hunters deciding that as the game supply was giving out they had better go down into the valley and grow wheat instead. It is not difficult to see the essential implausibility of this theory. The Industrial Revolution may indeed be looked on as a response to the challenge presented by rapid population growth and, indirectly, by exhaustion of the timber supply. But it could have been carried out only by a society that was already exceptionally wealthy, well organized and technically proficient. And in the same way it is likely that agriculture was initiated by a culturally advanced people living in a favorable setting; it was probably not cultivation but irrigation that was forced on the peoples of Egypt and western Asia by an increasingly unpropitious climate.

Now, if a high chronology can be accepted for the Khartoum

mesolithic and the Kenya Capsian, we have in tropical Africa, at the relevant period, societies of high technical capacity, proved by their pottery to have attained the sedentary condition which is the basic pre-condition of agriculture. And from the ecological aspect I must take issue with Alimen's condition that, apart from its northern fringe, the African continent was ill-suited to cultivators. Much the greater part of Africa is neither desert nor jungle, and its wide savannas, with their easily worked soils and rapid vegetation growth, surely provided an environment that was *better* suited to a primitive agriculture than either the arid sub-tropics or the cold dark forests of the temperate zone. It is true that tropical soils are mostly poor and that agriculture did not possess here the rich potentialities that belonged to it in some other regions. But those potentialities were realized only by a long effort of adaptation, organization and invention. The agricultural systems of tropical Africa remained primitive precisely because they were in the first place so easily established.

Besides the agriculture of the savannas, there is also the fundamentally different system which prevails in the forest and woodland zone of Africa. And whereas Murdock claims an independent and ancient origin for the former, he believes the latter to be exotic and relatively recent. Some of the most important of the forest-zone crops are undoubtedly native to south-east Asia: the banana or plantain, at least two species of yam (*Dioscorea alata* and *D. esculenta*)[25] and taro or cocoyam (*Colocasia antiquorum*), as well as sugar-cane. Murdock's view is that the forests of west and central Africa could not have been effectively occupied by cultivating peoples until after the introduction of these "Malaysian" plants, an event which he dates, mainly on lexicostatistical grounds, to the first centuries of the Christian era. The manner of their coming he describes as follows.[26]

People of southern Borneo, having become active in maritime trade, made their way round the shores of the Indian Ocean and arrived on the East African coast. Thence some of them set out to colonize Madagascar, where their language is still spoken. Meanwhile their crop plants had been adopted by the Cushitic peoples who were already practicing the savanna type of agriculture both in

---

[25] *D. bulbifera* is often added to this list, but the attribution of certain African yams to this Asiatic species is not certain.

[26] Op. cit., pp. 207ff.

Kenya and in Uganda. From Uganda they were transmitted to the central and western Sudan. Thus equipped, the West African culti- vators began to move into the Guinea forest zone. One tribe, how- ever, whose language formed the Bantu sub-sub-sub-group of the Niger-Congo family, advanced into the Congo basin, eventually emerging on to the savanna to occupy most of central and south- eastern Africa. Here, however, a problem arises. During their sojourn in the forests the Bantu had inevitably lost their savanna crops. How then did they re-acquire them? Answer: some of them went first to Uganda, where they borrowed sorghum and eleusine millet from the Cushites and passed them on, together with monarchical institutions, to their brethren in the Congo, who were then able to press on with the occupation of the lands to the east and the south.

This account is almost entirely conjectural, unnecessarily compli- cated and intrinsically improbable. These drought-hating plants would have had great difficulty in crossing the arid wilderness of east- ern Kenya. It would be much better, as well as simpler, to bring them straight across the ocean to Madagascar, where an Indonesian in- vasion is attested by the incontrovertible testimony of language, and then to ferry them over to the Zambezi valley, whence they could spread without difficulty over central and west Africa. In addition, the assumption that tropical gardening, the cultivation of fruits and tubers, began in Africa only with the advent of the Malaysian plants is very much open to question. It is evident that the Indonesians did not themselves colonize the mainland in any numbers, or they would have left definite ethnic and linguistic traces of their presence. Their crops must therefore have been adopted and diffused by the indigenous population. This is unlikely to have happened, at any rate with the speed with which it must have happened, unless the aborigines had already been familiar with a similar form of agricul- ture. Now Murdock's main reason for selecting a more northerly and roundabout route is his belief that archaeology denies the existence at this time of any kind of agriculture southward of northern Tanganyika, and, secondly, his total and literal acceptance of Green- berg's theory of the derivation of the Bantu languages from the Niger- Congo family. As to the second, the recent work of Bantu linguists in England suggests that, while the ultimate derivation of Bantu from Niger-Congo may be accepted, there was nevertheless a secondary fanning-out of Bantu peoples from a dispersal area situated toward the south-center of their present sphere. As to the first argument, the evidence is not unambiguous. There are definite traces of a prehistoric "vegeculture" in central and south-central Africa, though it has been suggested that its practitioners, in spite of their wholly lithic equipment, may have been contemporary with iron-using peoples.[27] The botanical evidence points in the same direction. Not all the forest-zone crops of Africa are exotics. The "Kaffir potato" (*Coleus spp.*) and the Guinea yam are undoubtedly native; and in central as well as west Africa there are a number of other yam species which are found both in wild and in cultivated forms.[28] These, being of inferior quality, are now rarely used. But they exist, and their existence shows that some sort of forest gardening could have been and probably was practiced before the coming of the banana and the Asiatic yams. It is also perhaps significant that in a great number of languages, distributed across the continent from Tanganyika to Guinea, the word for "yam" contains the element *ku*.[29] This element is undoubtedly indigenous, being identical with a common West African verb meaning "to dig." In Bantu languages it occurs in a variety of compound forms, which cannot be derived from a single ancestor. In central and east Africa, therefore, the use of these words, and of the plant they denote, must have preceded the migrations of the Bantu. Thus it appears that the Malaysian plants, though very valuable acquisitions, did not have quite the revolutionary significance that Murdock has assigned to them, that there was already an ancient province of yam culture, extending over the whole forest and woodland zone of Africa.

Whatever may be said about agriculture, it is quite certain that animal husbandry did *not* develop independently in Africa south of the Sahara where the fauna does not and did not include possible ancestors of the domestic cow, sheep or goat. As to the time and manner of their coming there is very little direct evidence. Sheep and goats were present at Shaheinab in the late fourth millennium,[30] cattle and

---

[27] J. Desmond Clark, *The Prehistory of Southern Africa* (Harmondsworth, 1959), pp. 191–96.

[28] See articles in the *Revue Internationale de Botanique Appliquée et d'Agriculture Tropicale* by A. Chevalier, xxxii (1952), H. Jaques-Felix, xxxvii (1947), and A. Walker, p. xxxii (1952).

[29] E.g. Mende, Nalu, Avatime *ku;* Teke, Chagga, Kikuyu *-kwa;* Kamba *-kwatsi;* Taveta *-likwa;* Mabea *nankwa;* Zigua *-kudumbe;* Ruanda *-tuku;* perhaps Bemba *-rungwa,* Shambala, Luba *-lungu* (< *-rukwa, -luku?*). See D. Westerman, *Die Westlichen Sudansprachen* (Berlin, 1927), p. 233 and H. H. Johnston, *A Comparative Study of the Bantu and Semi Bantu Languages* (London, 1923), ii, p. 421.

[30] A. J. Arkell, *Shaheinab* (London, 1953), p. 17.

sheep in the Kenya Neolithic, probably not much later. Domestic animals are not attested archaeologically in other areas until quite recent times, but it seems highly improbable that, having crossed the main geographical barrier, they should not soon have spread over the remainder of the continent. The original route of entry almost certainly led from Egypt by way of the Nile Valley. The other route sometimes suggested, from Arabia across the Horn, is ruled out by the absence of all but the most primitive cultures in south Arabia until the first millennium B.C.[31] and in Somalia until the Christian era.[32] Moreover the word for "cow," in a great variety of Sudanese and East African languages, can be referred to the Nubian form, *ti*.[33]

Murdock makes in this connection an extremely important and original point. Stock-keeping in Africa is by no means co-extensive with the practice of milking. In West Africa, notably, cattle are milked only by the Fulani and in areas of Fulani influence. From this he infers that the Nubians borrowed cattle from Egypt "without the associated milking complex."[34] The argument might, I think, be taken further: the Nubians acquired cattle before the practice of milking had begun. It is noteworthy that the unmilked cattle of the West African forest zone and pockets of central Africa are dwarf shorthorns of the species *Bos brachyceros*.[35] Their distribution in the least accessible parts of the continent (where they have lived long enough to acquire immunity from trypanosomiasis) implies that they were among the first, if not the first, arrivals. Yet *Bos brachyceros* is generally believed to have been evolved later than the humpless longhorn, *Bos primigenius,* and to have reached Egypt only in early dynastic times. These assumptions, however, may need revision. The first cattle to reach north-west Europe, in the third

[31] G. Caton Thompson, *The Tombs and Moon Temple of Hureidha* (London, 1944).

[32] J. Desmond Clark, *The Prehistoric Cultures of the Horn of Africa* (Cambridge, 1954).

[33] E.g. Moru-Madi *ti;* Interlacustrine Bantu *-te;* Mbugu *dee;* Temein *nteng;* Shilluk *dyang;* Nandi *tany,* pl. *tic;* Merarit *te.* The numerous West African forms in *ni* perhaps have the same origin. These data were kindly supplied to me by Professor A. N. Tucker and Miss Bryan, who are not responsible for the linguistic and other inferences drawn.

[34] Op. cit., pp. 19, 44.

[35] J. Boettger, *Die Afrikanische Haustiere* (Jena, 1958); Colonial Office, *The Indigenous Cattle of the British Dependent Territories in Africa* (London, 1957).

millennium, were shorthorns, said to bear a close resemblance to those of West Africa.[36] Moreover, in association with the pre-neolithic Sebilian culture of upper Egypt there are bones both of *primigenius* and of *brachyceros* cattle.[37] The Sebilians are assumed to have been a purely hunting people and the bones to be those of wild animals. But is it not possible that they were in fact the domesticators of cattle, and that tropical Africa acquired its first stock from this source in the fifth millennium or earlier?

It has generally been believed hitherto that the pastoral and agricultural economies of Africa were originally quite distinct; that pastoralism was a racial characteristic (Baumann, for instance, used cattle-herding as irrefragable evidence for the presence of his Eastern Hamites); and even, absurdly, that the pastoralists were responsible for the transmission of the elements of higher culture to the Negro peoples and for the original construction of complex political systems. Murdock's argument, as he sees, completes the work of destruction that Greenberg began when he severed the supposed link between a pastoral economy and Hamitic forms of speech. The extensive dairying of such peoples as the Fulani, the Masai and the Herero, so far from being an original trait, must be a secondary and comparatively recent development. Cattle, in Africa as elsewhere, must have been originally the property of agricultural peoples.

The innovation, moreover, was a disastrous one. The fourth chapter of Genesis is an impudent libel, for Abel, not Cain, has always been the killer. It is one of Murdock's chief achievements to have seen the herdsmen of Africa, from the Masai to the Hilalian Arabs, for the destructive barbarians that they were—chief disturbers of the peace of the continent, and, we may add, chief spoliators of its soil.

Up to the end of the Egyptian Neolithic we have assumed that tropical Africa was in tenuous contact with Egypt and, through Egypt, with western Asia. In the case of agriculture and pottery, contact is only probable, and the direction of movement uncertain. In the case of domestic animals neither the fact of contact nor its orientation can be in any doubt. Toward the end of the fourth millennium, however, the general picture undergoes a sharp, and for tropical Africa a disastrous, change. Just at the time when the northern

[36] D. Hill, "The Origins of West African Cattle," *Ibadan* (1957), no. 1.

[37] Alimen, op. cit., p. 126; D. M. A. Bate in A. J. Arkell, *Early Khartoum*, pp. 272–73.

peoples were constructing urban civilizations, characterized by large-scale social organization, metallurgy and writing, it seems that insuperable geographical obstacles arose to sunder them from the peoples of the south. For tropical Africa had no bronze or copper age; and, although this deficiency might possibly be accounted for by the scarcity of the relevant mineral deposits, the most likely inference is that between the fourth and the first millennium it was totally out of contact with the north. This period of isolation, in the post-Makalian dry phase, was probably the most crucial in the whole long history of the region. It was then that it fell decisively behind North Africa and most of Eurasia, and acquired that character of technical and cultural backwardness which even the advent of the Iron Age could not entirely alter.

The technique of iron-working did succeed in crossing the Sahara without any very undue time-lag, reaching Nigeria shortly before and south central Africa shortly after the time of Christ. There seems little reason to doubt that the mediators of this technique were the people of Meroe in upper Nubia. It is, however, doubtful whether it spread directly southward into central Africa. The tribes of the southern Sudan, who might have been expected to have experienced the earliest and most intensive influences of Nile Valley civilization, notoriously remained among the most primitive, from the point of view of material culture, in the entire continent; and it seems that the swamps of the Bahr-al-Ghazal and the arid steppes lying between the upper Nile and the mountains of Ethiopia long acted as a barrier to the passage of iron-age cultures, which were forced to penetrate southward by a more devious route.

The immensity of the area covered by the closely related group of Bantu languages calls out for explanation. Behind these vast and evidently quite recent movements there must have been a powerful dynamic. Murdock's theory, that the dynamic was provided by the acquisition of bananas, fails to account for the Bantu penetration of large areas in which the banana could have been of little or no use; and his solution of this difficulty is too involved to be readily accepted. Moreover, it could be valid only on the assumption that the banana reached central Africa from the north-west, and that it entered a land which was previously devoid of crops. I have argued, however, that bananas arrived first in south-east Africa, which is certainly not the homeland of the Bantu, and that they were adopted by people who were already cultivators. If these things are so, it might be a reasonable hypothesis that the acquisition of bananas by the Bantu when some of them were already settled in the latitude of the Zambezi might have produced important secondary migrations into favorable areas, but we must still look elsewhere for the asset which enabled the first Bantu-speakers to impose themselves and their language on these pre-existent agricultural societies. I do not see what that asset could have been unless it were the iron spear. Plausible *a priori,* this theory finds support in the fact that the early iron-using Nok culture impinges on the central Benue valley, which Greenberg has selected as the probable homeland of the Bantu.[38] Thus I see these people, not as agriculturalists spreading out over a virtually empty land, but as a dominant minority, specialized to hunting with the spear, constantly attracting new adherents (as many east and central African traditions actually affirm) by their fabulous prestige as suppliers of meat, constantly throwing off new bands of migratory adventurers, until the whole southern sub-continent was iron-using and Bantu-speaking.

This story, however, is probably an over-simplification, for it is necessary also to account for the distinction, clearly visible in the archaeological record of southern Africa, between the peaceful, un-stratified society of its Iron Age A and the complex warlike states that succeeded them.[39] It is possible that there were two "waves" of Bantu immigration, or that the Bantu civilization of Rhodesia underwent a profound internal change as the result of the development of the gold trade. There are, however, some indications, especially from the associated pottery, that the "A" cultures derived from the north-east, perhaps ultimately from the "Azanian" coast, and were therefore not Bantu.[40] If so, the later Bantu ascendancy would be attributed, not to metallurgy as such, but to the military organization and ethos which arose from the full exploitation of the iron spear.

The coming of iron technology must indeed have brought about far-reaching changes in every branch of African life. But if there is any substance in the arguments presented in this paper there can be no warrant for the common assumption that it made for a complete break with the past, and that the history of Africa is virtually coter-

[38] Greenberg, op. cit., p. 116.
[39] J. Desmond Clark, *The Prehistory of Southern Africa;* R. F. H. Summers; *Inyanga* (Cambridge, 1957).
[40] Murdock, op. cit., p. 210.

minous with the Iron Age—as is implied, for example, in Mr. Basil Davidson's recent book.[41]

The orthodox picture of African prehistory presents, indeed, a curiously unconformable appearance. Up to a point, the record is one of extraordinary continuity. From the first chipped pebbles to the cultures of almost modern times there is unbroken linear evolution —with one possible interruption represented by the blade-using cultures of late pluvial times. Even the Kenya Neolithic shows clear links with what had gone before. But as we approach the threshold of history this continuity is abruptly shattered. The whole of Africa's enormous past is bundled off into the Kalahari with the Bushmen, and the stage is cleared for the enactment of a new story with a new cast. First, we are told, the Negro appears from nowhere and takes possession of the land. Later, a ghostly horde of civilized Hamites, having apparently no connection with the "proto-Hamites" long resident in the land, marches across eastern Africa, constructing roads and terraces and irrigation systems and founding elaborate political systems.[42] These then disappear into the mists from which they came, and their civilizations fade into the light of common Bantu day.

All this is very odd. There is really no need to make a mystery of the emergence of "the Negro." The various physical traits which make up this concept were presumably gradual deviations, for the most part environmentally determined, from the less specialized forms of *Homo sapiens* which occupied Africa in the pluvial epoch. (Though not visible in the archaeological record until perhaps ten thousand years ago, this evolutionary trend may have begun much earlier in the forest zone, where evidence is lacking.) Nor is there anything specially mysterious about the outburst of engineering activity that clearly took place in many parts of east and central Africa between 500 and 1500 A.D. It was the product of iron tools and of the political organization associated with the iron spear—both, I have suggested, brought thither from the west. Nor, again, need we be puzzled by the disintegration of most of the Bantu states and the dereliction of their works, or attribute these disasters to that *diabolus ex machina,* the slave trade. A "dark age," after all, is a familiar historical phenomenon, signifying merely that organization

[41] *Old Africa Rediscovered* (London, 1959).
[42] Cole, op. cit., 275ff. Cf. H. A. Wieschoff, *The Zimbabwe-Monomotapa Culture* (Wisconsin, 1941).

has broken down. The cause of the breakdown here was undoubtedly again the iron spear. It is not for nothing that Ogun, god of smiths, is also god of war. Unlike Bronze Age kingdoms, whose rulers could easily monopolize the raw materials of military power, the kingdoms of the Early Iron Age are almost necessarily ephemeral, for in these conditions every young man can say with Archilochus, *mutatis mutandis:* "My spear wins bread, my spear wins Thracian wine." Where this is said, the center cannot hold. The sackers of cities soon gain ascendancy over the builders. Nor was there here an active commerce such as made the dark age of post-Mycenean Greece a relatively brief interlude. Indeed, the misfortune of most parts of eastern Africa was not that they had to endure the slave trade but that they had no trade at all. Where commercial possibilities did exist, as on the coast and in the region of the Rhodesian gold-field, Bantu civilization was exceptionally vigorous and long-sustained.

PART II
Ecology, Economy, and Habitation

Introduction

The peoples of Africa provide us with excellent examples of the techniques used by man to obtain food and shelter under varying ecological conditions. The !Kung (Bushman), Batwa (Pygmy), Ndorobo, Sandawe, and Hadza have used hunting and gathering techniques in adapting to desert, forest, and savanna. The Luvale practice hunting and fishing in savannas and rivers. The Bozo of Mali specialize as fishermen on the Niger river, the Buduma on Lake Chad, and such peoples as the Ebrie on the coastal lagoons of the Ivory Coast. In contrast, the pastoral Nuer, Fulani, Pakot, Masai, Somali, and Kababish adapt to savanna and desert-like ecological zones. The more numerous agricultural African peoples such as the Tiv, Mossi, Hausa, Baganda, Swazi, BaKongo, and Ibo utilize the relatively dry savanna areas as well as the wet rain forests. Not only did these populations possess various technical inventories and cultivate different crops, but they had many different types of social organizations and economically related ritual practices.

These data from Africa show clearly that the adaptation of populations to varying ecological zones is a function of environment, technical inventories, social organizations, and ritual practices. Moreover, there is a general interrelationship of all of these factors in societies of various types and complexities. John Marshall shows that while the !Kung have a simple technology, they possess a detailed knowledge of the water resources, vegetable products, and behavior of the game animals in their environment. Moreover, they have the type of social organization that makes the exploitation of these resources possible, and values such as reciprocity which are important to their survival. Similarly, the Luvale know a great deal about the various animal species in their environment and developed quite efficient techniques for hunting and fishing. Their organized social relations and rituals are undoubtedly efficacious in their quest for food.

The ability of the Kababish Arabs to utilize the relatively difficult semi-desert environment for their flocks and herds is as much a function of their knowledge of the seasons and the natural resources as of their social organization for doing the necessary work. Asad believes that failure to mobilize the necessary manpower to move the animals in transhumance cycles or to keep enough animals to weather drought or disease could have spelled disaster for the Kababish. Like Asad, Schneider insists that the herding practices of such East African cattle-keeping peoples as the Pakot are not "mystical" but quite "practical." He acknowledges the importance of cattle in the social and ceremonial lives of the East African peoples but demonstrates that the cattle are ultimately used for meat, an important element of their diets.

Agriculture, rather than either hunting-gathering or herding, is the most important economic activity of African peoples. As we saw in the last section, the Africans are believed to have ennobled a large variety of indigenous plants. They later made extensive use of such Southeastern Asian crops as bananas and plantains, and New World cultigens such as maize, peanuts, cocoa, and cassava, among others. The spread of agricultural techniques in Africa was accompanied by demographic increase, land shortages in the savannas and velds, and the invasions by agricultural peoples of the more difficult semi-desert and rain forest areas. Morgan shows admirably the inter-relationship of farming practices, settlement patterns, and population density among the peoples of Southeastern Nigeria. Land shortage influenced the types of crops grown, changed the pattern of "shifting" agriculture, affected family relations, stimulated out-migration, and facilitated the subsequent development of cash-cropping.

The view of anthropologists that agriculture is often the necessary basis for the development of complex societies finds ready confirmation in Africa. The civilizations of ancient Egypt and Ethiopia had a demonstrable agricultural base, but without the ability to procure the products of agricultural peoples the empires of Ghana, Mali, and Songhay, which depended a great deal on trade, could never have survived in their desert-like environments. The article "West African Economic Systems" shows the types of both simple and complex economies that could develop from an agricultural base. Populations in this region of Africa produced not only crops for subsistence, but supported ruling classes and traded surpluses in markets to merchants, artisans, and craftsmen. Some West African economies with their guilds, journeymen, master craftsmen, credit facilities, multiple currencies, and long-range traders linking small-scale societies and complex ones had all the characteristics of the economies of feudal states.

Africa's tropical environment more than the economics or politics of its peoples appears to have influenced the types of shelters and dwellings that developed there. Glück believes that the main function of African architecture was to provide shelter, since Africans spent most of their time outdoors rather than in habitations. He approaches African architecture from a developmental standpoint, showing how, on the basis of an original simple hut design, the Africans developed different house types and shelters to cope with ecological conditions and to meet their social needs. The twelve basic types of structures that emerged range from the rather simple domed hut of the Batwa and !Kung peoples to the elaborate dry-stone structures of Zimbabwe. Glück's article does betray a number of older biases. Perhaps the absence of ready data or ideological predilections did not permit him to include in his typologies the fascinating pit-carved churches in Ethiopia, and the temple complexes of Egypt. Without doubt these structures, too, represent the architectural activities of African peoples.

JOHN MARSHALL

6. Hunting Among the Kalahari Bushmen

A people, small of stature, few in numbers, calling themselves "!Kung," but who are called "Bushmen" by others, live today in a tremendous depression, half-a-continent wide and sunken in the southern African plateau—by name, the Kalahari Desert Basin. They live on the huge floor of this Basin, near one of its imperceptible sides. It is an open land—large to the point of vagueness, under a limitless sky. There is a word used frequently by the other inhabitants of this Basin—mostly black-skinned peoples—to define the different cultural groups now living there. The word is "nation." One speaks of the Herero nation, the Chuana nations, the Okavango nations. To follow this usage, one would speak of the !Kung nation of *Nyae Nyae*—one among several Bushmen nations. [The prefix, (!), indicates one of the so-called "clicks" that mark the speech of the Bushmen. Distinction is made between four classes of "click": the dental (/), lateral (//), palatal (≠), and alveolar (!)—ED.]

But "nation" is a new word, recently arisen in the vocabulary of a country whose people are struggling to define themselves in present times. The !Kung, who know who they are, do not yet need it. For, besides !Kung, which they use rarely, they call themselves *Dzu/oassi*. *Dzu/oassi* can be interpreted as "the people" in opposition to "the animals," for example, or as "the perfect people," or, indeed, as "the only people."

Unlike other nations, the Bushmen practice no agriculture, domesticate no animals. They are hunting and gathering peoples. But all the nations—Bushmen, Bantu and white alike—who live in the Kalahari Basin must face its exigencies, for this sand-filled depression is distantly rimmed by mountains, and the mountains catch most of

SOURCE: John Marshall, "Hunting Among the Kalahari Bushmen," *Natural History,* Vol. 67, 1958, pp. 291–309, 376–95. Reprinted by permission of the author and publisher. © 1958 The American Museum of Natural History.

the clouds that might otherwise bring rain. The rain that does fall is sucked into the sand, so that there is little surface water and much of the Kalahari Basin is true desert.

Although true desert, the Kalahari is not a bare place: the face of the sand is hidden. Much of the desert is clothed with stalwart, similar bushes, most of them thorned. In places, dry forests grow slowly: the trees stand apart and the air between them is strangely still on days of wind. Grass covers the sand: in sweeps on the dry plains, in glens in the bush; grass grows on dunes gathered long ago by patient wind, and in the silent valleys, called *omuramba*'s. In a younger, greener time that has come and gone since man first lived in southern Africa, these valleys once flowed—draining water from the high edges into the Basin. Now the sand has wandered into these valleys also.

There are four seasons in the Kalahari, two are brief. Winter begins in May and lasts through September. It is a healthful season. Of the foods available to gatherers in winter, roots are the most abundant. The earth is dry: the days are warm and clear, but cold in the shade; the nights are chill. Temperatures sink to 20° F. and below when the night wind turns, blowing from the antarctic south. On some hazeless nights, when the empty air seems insufficient protection from the cold of space, the morning ground will be wet with heavy dew. However, the smoke from a thousand African veld fires often thickens the skies of noon, reddens the setting sun and keeps the nights warmer and the earth dry.

At the end of September, clouds begin to tower in the afternoons. They wear over the desert from the east and are usually gone by morning. But should they encounter the right conditions, the local rains that fall from these clouds—the "little rains"—bring the spring of the year. This is the sudden season of thunderstorms. The storms are like gods walking in the desert, each attending to a narrow path with violence and rain. In the quiet, after their passing, many plants bloom—small flowers and edible greens.

Spring is also the season of heat. Myriads of flies, the year's crop, now hatch. The heat increases toward summer and, although clouds continue to form early in the afternoon, often no rain falls. November and December pass in heat and privation for the people. Temperatures rise above 100° F. not long after the brief dawn, as the sun mounts, close and huge, bringing the heat of day. Many of the blooms of the "little rains" wither in November, as do many young greens. The roots have sent their substance into vines; now the loose skins of the roots lie collapsed around inedible fiber. Spring means blooming of plants, but spring is ardent and quickly over: many of the desert's flowers have only a few days in which to flourish.

Late in December or early in January the rains of summer—the "big rains"—begin. This is the season of water. Water collects in the hollows of the land; it seeps into the pans, changing them into shallow lakes; it melts the baked clay in the *omuramba* bottoms, and turns the Kalahari green.

This is the season when two nuts, the *tsi* and the *mangetti*—the most important and abundant of the wild desert foods—begin to mature. By March, the *mangetti* forests sound with the falling nuts. Beside the summer storms—when water piles up uselessly on the reverberating earth—days on end are cloudy and, sometimes, a fine mist falls over parts of the northern Kalahari through the day and into the night. Now, the people eat many fruits. In the deeps of green thickets, ponderous flowers droop on slender vines. Spring and summer, the times of bounty, are also the seasons of disease.

By the end of April, the afternoon skies begin to clear, the air dries, the wind seeks. It is autumn. In April, the *tsi* nuts ripen and the pods split, turning out their brown wealth. The many desert roots cease their activity and become firm and full, safe in themselves for the winter and in a state most suitable for food. The desert pales. Day and night, water evaporates from the pans; first becoming a film, then less than a film, with only the damp clay glistening. One noon, the clay begins to wrinkle in the sun. By June, the earth is dry: the land is fast and quietly held by winter.

Such would be a perfect round of seasons. In the periods of drought that have come every few years in the recent past, however, there have been no such perfect seasons and all living things have, of necessity, fastened tenaciously to the drying earth and held on. Even in normal years, the weather is unbalanced: large areas of the Kalahari may be flooded, while others receive a sprinkling of rain in what amounts to drought conditions. In this land, and through these seasons, the !Kung nation lives.

The area in which the !Kung now live is called *Nyae Nyae*. How long they have lived there is not known. At one time, Bushmen lived throughout Africa from as far north as Angola and Tanganyika to, southward, the Cape of Good Hope. This was a time when few peoples shared that part of the continent. In southern Africa, beside the many Bushmen nations, there were Hottentots and pre-Bantu Negroes—some of whom were hunters and some of whom practiced agriculture. In the distances between the nations grew years of peace.

About five centuries ago, larger, stronger, Bantu-speaking peoples, who had cattle to pasture, entered southern Africa from the north. They came in two prongs, like the horns of a bull, prodding down the eastern and western highlands. In search of grazing land, these Bantus were themselves driven south by defeat in wars then current on the plains of East Africa. The established peoples of the south—the Bushmen, the Hottentots and pre-Bantus—were dislocated by this push and began to move, themselves. This flux has yet to come completely to rest.

In such disturbed times, the Bushmen fare ill. They are not, and probably were not ever, a warlike people. Their society is not constructed for war, their culture dampens war. Yet, now, wars and battles began to scatter across the land, as groups of people—large and small, Bantu armies, itinerant raiders, the remnants of tiny nations and the dispossessed—marched and wandered in their search of conquest or safe distant places.

Some Bushmen nations were driven into pockets in the hills, where they died slowly. Some stayed on their land and were decimated and made slaves. Some resisted and, as one who spoke of his people told me: "We were soldiers in those days." Their armies changed into marauder bands that sometimes fought and often ran. Of these, the Heikum were an example—an embittered, scattered nation of travelers on the then uncertain grasslands of South West Africa. When, at last, white and black met,—raiding one another for cattle across the Fish River—and the time of the Zulu and the Voortrekker was near, the classic period of the Bushmen was over.

The area called *Nyae Nyae* lies on the border between South West Africa and Bechuanaland. It covers about 10,000 square miles, between 18°55′ and 21°0′ South latitude and 19°50′ to 21°25′ East longitude. In the center of this area is a ring of *kalk* pans. *Nyae Nyae* is actually the name the !Kung gave to this ring of pans, although I have applied it to the whole area occupied by the !Kung nation.

There is game round these pans and, in small groups, everywhere in *Nyae Nyae*. Wild roots grow in the bush that shrouds much of the territory. There is *tsi* in the south, while *mangetti* forests crowd along the crests of white sand dunes in the south and east, and spread over the north. Their nuts drop abundantly to the ground every year. There are ten permanent waterholes—some clustered around the ring of the pans, the others set like infrequent jewels in a low limestone ridge along the eastern border. During the rains, small pans and hollows hold embroidered pools. Hollow trees also catch water and keep it until it turns brown, while several kinds of water roots can be counted on all year.

Until recently, few came and none but Bushmen stayed for long in *Nyae Nyae,* for there is not enough water to attract pastoral peoples, and the soils are not the best for crops. The !Kung say: "We have always been here, drinking the *Nyae Nyae* waters." Perhaps this "always" began at about the time when the western Bantu horn was moving southward through Ovamboland. All one can say for sure is that they came, possibly seeking sanctuary in the empty spaces of the Kalahari, found, in *Nyae Nyae,* a quiet place, and stayed. In *Nyae Nyae,* the !Kung have since lived on unchanged—replacing only their bone arrow-points with metal ones, made from the nails and wire that filtered into the desert after the Europeans' entry into South West Africa.

The !Kung nation cannot so live for much longer. Already their last lands are being occupied by the Herero nation—Bantu-speakers —who say: "The Bushmen are like our children. We feel obligated to care for them." It seems likely that, in a few years, these lands will be farmed by white people. Then, if the past of other Bushmen is any omen, some !Kung will become farm laborers, some will contract syphilis, some will die and some will breed. Few will marry.

So much for the little history and the brief geography. How do the !Kung live in *Nyae Nyae?* Human ecology is the study of the relationship between man and his natural environment. In such a relationship, two directions of cause and effect are implied. These two directions may be understood by two terms—adaption and control. Adaption means the effect wrought by the environment upon the body or the culture of man. Control is the effect wrought upon the environment by man, his body and his culture. In the one case, man conforms to the environment. In the other, man conforms the environment to his needs.

There is no ecological situation where either adaptation or control prevails to the exclusion of the other, for the fact of man's presence changes an environment, and the most effective technology, the most developed society, are—in part—responses to an environment. Every ecological relationship is a welter of compromise. Yet, there are extremes. If we take Western technological culture as one extreme —with control prevailing and America the exponent—the !Kung might be considered the opposite extreme, for the !Kung control their environment scarcely at all.

To the !Kung, in their environment, there are available a certain number of natural resources, in a certain geographical pattern. There are also available a certain number of !Kung. They have a culture. Living within their culture, they are able to exploit their environment. The first aspect of this ecological relationship is the fairly obvious relationship between !Kung technology and environment.

With considerable empirical knowledge, the !Kung have arrived at workable solutions to the problems of subsistence. By means of their technology, they have managed to satisfy their basic needs and their many wants of life (at least, they satisfied them until they were exposed to the wealth of white men). The fact that their population is limited because of their technology is one result of this adaptation—of which infanticide is an occasional expression. That they live to all intents and purposes from day to day—having no real measure of surplus in the form of stored crops and beasts ready to slaughter—is another indication that the !Kung have largely adapted to their environment. But the contrasting fact that the !Kung live in *Nyae Nyae* as easily as they do also indicates some measure of environmental control.

The more complex aspects of the !Kung ecological relationship exist in areas other than their simple technology. That the !Kung are able to exploit their environment with a certain degree of efficiency is due in some measure to the structure of their society. Thus, the second aspect of the ecological relationship is this one: the relationship between a certain number of natural resources, arranged in a certain environment, and a society that has developed in the presence of these resources and whose members are dependent on them.

Of course, their society did not come into being because the !Kung needed it to exploit their environment, nor is that society shaped only in accordance with environmental dictates. Indeed, some elements of !Kung society seem to exist in spite of the environment.

There is reason to believe that their society has not basically changed through periods when there was more water, more game, and probably more *veldkos*—the wild vegetable products of the land, gathered by the women of the bands—in South Africa, although this point might be debated on grounds that the !Kung depended more on hunting in previous periods. But it is that aspect of !Kung social structure, the functioning of which clearly seems to facilitate exploitation of their environment by means of their technology, that we shall discuss. These manifestations appear primarily adaptive in nature, although control is also discernible.

There are about 1,000 !Kung—gathered into 28 bands—who build their ephemeral camps, or *werft's*, separately in an area of 10,000 square miles. The houses in the *werft's* are of grass, pressed over a framework of sticks, making small quarter-shells, with their backs to the prevailing wind. Gossamer things, made of the same grass that sways and crowds against their doors, they are positioned in a loose pattern according to their occupants' kinship, and all are held—finally—by the headman, who builds his shelter under the tallest tree.

From a little distance, when the sound of voices is lost on the wind, one would not know a *werft* was near. The people never return to the same *werft*—preferring to build anew and saying it would not be safe from the spirits of the dead, or sanitary, to do so. Perhaps, also, they find it sad to see the little houses toppling, day by day, into the grass of the new year.

As a starting point, labor among the !Kung is divided between two basic subsistence activities—hunting game and gathering *veldkos*. Men hunt, because their bodies are better suited to the chase. Women gather, because they could not leave their children for the long periods of hunting that men both enjoy and endure.

Women's work—the technology of gathering—is simple and adaptable: the tools are easily acquired, the methods quickly learned. The constant necessity to provide and the almost daily edge of effort slowly bends the !Kung women, who are slender-armed and do this monotonous work to the end of their lives. All roots—a major food—are gathered in identical fashion. The implement for this is a digging stick—made usually by a woman's husband from any of a number of hardwoods: the bark is peeled from a branch, a point is whittled sharp. Women, squatting, dig narrow holes in the earth with these sticks, and tug until the root they have reached comes free. Berries are picked—high ones jostled down with sticks and sought for carefully among the grass stems. Nuts are collected on the ground.

Small animals, such as tortoises and even grasshoppers, are sometimes captured by the women and brought home in the evening —such small creatures are also considered *veldkos*. The women, too, will kill snakes, even puff adders. When they see a puff adder, they gather around it in a little crowd, their high laughter tinkling while they drop large, heavy things on its flat head.

Averaged over a year, women gather on four or five days of each week—the number of days depending on the season. In the long days of wilting between the October spring and the January summer, food is scarce and the women may go out every day into the failing veld, leaving their *werft* early in the morning and returning late in the afternoon. All that a woman gathers belongs to her alone, and of course is shared with her family She feeds her husband, her children and often a visitor or two, at her own hearth. No formal instruction is practiced among the !Kung, with the possible exception of certain kinds of religious teaching and what might be called an occasional hunting school. Learning to gather comes from the children's observation of the more experienced women. Girls soon learn to recognize more than a hundred kinds of edible plants that grow in *Nyae Nyae,* as well as the seasons and places in which these plants grow. They learn to see tiny, shriveled root vines coiled around thorns in the thickets and, in the process, develop fine powers of observation. Possibly complementary to this lack of formal instruction, no formal pressure is exerted on young people to take up adult roles. Girls, if they wish, accompany their mothers on gathering trips. If they do not, they rarely feel guilty. A girl usually begins to feel responsible soon after she marries, which is often before puberty. But only when she has children of her own does a woman see the world through the eyes of a provider.

Hunting is the work of men. !Kung hunters range the land, seeking the agile game. The men walk rapidly, never lowering their eyes, making sure of the awkward ground with their dextrous feet. They glance swiftly over the distances of the country and, with their good vision and knowledge of what to look for, see any moving thing. As girls learn gathering, boys learn most of hunting on their own. They hunt little birds in the grass around the *werft* houses.

They impale beetles with tiny arrows shot from toy bows. Tracking, which is the most difficult part of hunting, is learned last of all. Hunters must be able to recognize the spoor of one wounded wildebeest out of a herd of fifty, and follow that track across desert ground which is almost as hard as stone.

The usual techniques of hunting are well adapted to the Kalahari terrain and, except on rare occasions, do not change—no matter what the animal may be. The !Kung hunt an eland and a duiker in the same manner; the idea is to get to the animal just as quickly as possible. The hunters feel that the longer they creep and wait, the more time the animal will have to decide what to do. I have seen a man, using this principle, run crouched across a perfectly open flat, with grass no higher than his knees, and come within twenty yards of a wildebeest who was watching him all the time. Of course the men use cover when they can, but they use it quickly and deftly, keeping on their feet and running bent and bunched so that their arms will not wave and attract unnecessary attention. Although their arrows are true and straight, they are unfeathered and therefore not very accurate. At fifty yards, a !Kung hunter can only feel sure of hitting a kudu somewhere.

Among the less frequently used techniques of hunting are trapping, the use of blinds built near the pans (manned at night during the rains), and a technique of running down fat elands in the dry season when, what with the heat and exertion, the portly animals suffer a kind of stroke and have to take to the shade to recover. There, puffing and dizzy, the exhausted elands can be butchered by the deep-breathing hunters.

The trap is a spring-pole snare, of which exists a small version for birds and a larger version for small bucks. Such trapping is usually practiced only by young boys, and even they seem to do it rarely, so that what could amount to an important food source is neglected by the !Kung. The men would rather be gone after the big game, absorbed in the heat and chance of hunting, than to be squatting around the edges of the pans, making little guises with sticks and string into which guinea fowl invariably fall.

The technology of hunting is the most complex in !Kung culture, and the most involved aspect of that technology is their amazing poison. Without it, the little unfeathered arrows, driven by a light bow, would be useless against big game. With the poison, a !Kung hunter could kill an elephant although, perhaps fortunately, for both, the two seldom encounter one another.

There are four kinds of poison—a root (which is rarely used), two grubs and the pod of a tree. One of the two kinds of grub is the larva of an unidentified beetle that lives in a bush; the other is the larva of a beetle that lives in certain Murula trees, identified as *Diamphidia simplex*. This identity, however, is complicated by the presence of still a third beetle, a parasitic one that apparently lives on the grubs of *Diamphidia simplex,* so that it is not now clear *which* is the poisonous grub. The Bushmen are aware of the parasite and feel that its grub does contain poison. They say it "runs around and runs away." They may be speaking of the beetle, for it is difficult to imagine a grub running, and the grub may be so similar to the young *Diamphidia* that the !Kung simply confuse the two. Lastly, still a fourth insect—smaller, and hairy—said to become easily inflamed, is occasionally encountered among the grubs. It is possible that this is the insect that has a poisonous larva: in any case, somewhere in the community is a poisonous grub, and how the Bushmen found it we have no idea.

Assuming *Diamphidia* to be the poison-bearer, its cycle is somewhat as follows: the beetle lays its eggs in the Murula tree leaves. Hatching in the rains, the grubs migrate down the trunk, progressing through a number of growth stages. Finally, they make their cocoons under the ground near the tree. In these cocoons, they struggle through metamorphosis and emerge as small, bravely-colored beetles in the New Year's rains, providing the Bushmen have not already dug them up. The hunters know the particular trees frequented by the beetles and make expeditions to them at least twice a year to replenish their supply. Then the grubs are dug up, and used on the spot or kept in their cocoons, depending on the man's needs.

The poisoning of !Kung arrows is a long process, with a number of variations. The most common poison is a mixture of the grub and the previously mentioned tree-pod. The grubs are crushed and the pod is warmed until its contents melt slightly and can be crushed with the grubs. This mixture is thinned with the copious spit which results from chewing any of a variety of barks and is then smeared on the foreshaft of the arrow—but cleaned immaculately off the point, for the slightest prick, the least bit of poison getting in such a wound, would cause death.

Depending on where the poisoned arrow hits, a small buck can die in a morning, a man in a few hours, a giraffe in four to five days. There is nothing that can be done for a man, short of amputating a limb or immediately excising the wound and cutting the nearby flesh to let the blood drain. Yet, the poison has no effect upon the game's meat. One can even eat the mixture with relative impunity: it must enter the bloodstream directly to be deadly.

As subsistence activities, the men's and women's roles—hunting and gathering—are of unequal weight. Almost eighty per cent of the people's food is *veldkos,* more abundant than game in *Nyae Nyae,* and far more easily acquired. If from one summer to the next, a man kills twelve antelope, he feels he has had a good year.

But, despite its relatively minor subsistence value, hunting is extremely important in !Kung culture. It has developed its body of technology, acquired a large tradition of beliefs, fostered a wealth of knowledge, and become both the measure of a man's ability and a test of his readiness to marry. Part of the explanation may come from the passion in hunting. Like their fires, the tales of hunting burn brightly for the !Kung in the night, warming their memories. Of equal or greater significance is the !Kung craving for meat and undoubtedly for protein. Unlike the sharing of *veldkos,* limited to the nuclear family, a complex system of distribution insures that everyone in the *werft* will get a share of all game killed. This is done, they say, simply to prevent jealousy and the inevitable renunciations that go with it. The !Kung declare "We are a jealous people" and they try to keep jealousy at a minimum, for they fear it.

Still another aspect of hunting—perhaps the most important in terms of subsistence—is the by-products it provides. Sinew is used for thongs and bowstrings, horn makes spoons and small containers: most needed of all are the skins—converted into bags and nets for carrying, and into clothes. Men wear only a breech-clout. Women wear modesty aprons, often one in front and one behind, as well as a piece of soft skin, clasped between their buttocks and thighs, when menstruating. Both men and women wear *kaross*'s. The *kaross,* or skin cloak, is the most important garment and everyone tries to have one. If a man has only one *kaross,* and he is a good man, he will give it to his wife and do without —for, to a woman, a *kaross* is essential. In it, she is modest. In it, she carries the roots she has gathered in the day and the baby who must go where she goes. Her *kaross* is her warmth at night, her softness on the cold ground. It breaks the blind wind and roofs away the narrow rain.

Ten permanent waterholes, as we have seen, occur in two areas— around the ring of pans in the east center of *Nyae Nyae,* and along the eastern border. To the west, beyond the limit of the pans, there is no water in the long dry seasons. Around each permanent waterhole, the *veldkos* near enough to be gathered in a day are considered by the !Kung to be an integral part of that waterhole. This means that such a waterhole includes both the water itself and all the *veldkos* within a circle with a radius of some four miles. This area might be called a certain waterhole's "district," taking its name from the waterhole. When a man mentions a waterhole, he usually has such a district in mind.

Yet neither the *veldkos* in these districts nor the *veldkos* scattered between the districts, nor the game, which wanders, constitute the main food resources of *Nyae Nyae.* Instead, these are the *mangetti* and *tsi* nuts. Both are found only far from permanent water. Distance becomes more significant when one thinks not only of miles—but of time, footsteps, heat and carrying capacity. From the nearest western water, it is about twenty miles to a *mangetti* forest. The distance between *tsi* and the closest water is about seven miles. The people calculate their marching ability at about ten miles a day, with women and children, although men can make forty if necessary. They gather food as they travel, for a day of traveling is just like any other day, with children and old people to be provided for.

In order to exploit the environment successfully, with their limited technological equipment, the !Kung must move from place to place. The calendar of their movements is revealing. In winter, the people are forced to remain near the waterholes, gathering in districts and making occasional trips to places where enough water-roots can be dug to support them for several days. When the "little rains" of spring come to *Nyae Nyae,* the land usually relents somewhat. Some of the small western and northern pans fill, and a hollow *mangetti* tree may have collected some water. The people, who keep track of conditions throughout *Nyae Nyae* from the reports of hunters and visitors, try to get to the *mangetti* forests as soon as possible, and bring back as many nuts as they can carry.

The "big rains" open the land. People travel to distant places and remove to the *mangetti* forests until autumn, when the *tsi* ripens. Then they remain in the *tsi* areas till the *tsi* nuts are exhausted—which sometimes happens before the small annual waters have evaporated—and finally make their way back to their permanent waterholes.

In such a transient life, the importance of light belongings—and of ostrich eggshells for carrying water and skin bags for food—is evident. With carrying bags and ostrich eggshells, the people can bring water to food and food to water. Partly because of their life of motion, the !Kung do not accumulate heavy wealth. Infanticide is uncommon among the !Kung, but one of the various reasons for the practice is that a woman may feel she cannot carry another child when the band moves. Then, the baby is born into a tiny grave near the *werft,* and the grave is closed.

That the !Kung live in small bands, flexible in their composition and spread widely over their Kalahari world, is owing in good part to their environment and to the technological means by which they cope with it. But the effect of the environment, carrying through the technology, penetrates the structure of the bands themselves and influences the way in which the !Kung distribute themselves around their resources.

The headman of each band is considered to "own" a waterhole. What he is considered to "own," is both the water and the *veldkos* of the district. The ground itself is described as *chi dole,* worthless. Headmanship is hereditary, the headman being the oldest son of the previous headman although, if the male line is cut off for a generation, headmanship is passed through the eldest daughter to her eldest son. But headmanship is different from leadership, which is not hereditary. Leadership depends heavily on a man's character, his hunting prowess, and especially his ability to focus people's opinions. Usually headman and leader are the same person but, should a headman be too young—perhaps still in his mother's womb—or very old, a band will have a separate leader.

Theoretically, the right to refuse water to members of another band belongs to the headman, although we never saw this done nor did we ever hear of such a thing. Neither leadership nor headmanship implies any overt coercive power over the other members of a band. Only as a sort of coagulation of group opinion can headmen or leaders exert a control—which, even then, is not final. The leader, being the kind of person to whom others come when decisions must be made, is often an arbiter, in quarrels, a focal point in discussion of plans, a comfort to the bereaved and a strength for those in doubt.

The functions of headman, as headman, are of a different nature. In order to take up residence with a band, a person must have certain ties of kin with members of the band. Such a person may live with his own parents or siblings, or with his wife's parents or siblings. It is a wide choice, providing for flexibility—but within limits. There are, of course, exceptions, and visitors from other bands are never denied, but possession of some kinship tie seems to be a general requirement for residence which, if violated, would subject the violator to criticism by the band.

Short of fighting, all the !Kung can do to control the actions of individuals is to criticize. But this is apparently enough. A man, expelled from his band, *might* be able to survive alone in the desert—with luck, he might even manage for years. If he could persuade his family to come with him, they might survive together even more easily, for the family is the basic subsistence unit. But freshly gone, he would be an outlaw and, in time, become a stranger to his people. This would be an unthinkable horror to a !Kung! The worst dream might be to see the fires flickering in the *werft* at midnight and be unable to go to them. All the people we knew could tell us of only one time when such a departure from the group occurred: and the man had gone insane, had murdered and then run raving into the veld. There he had lived for a little while in a hole, then died.

It is in connection with the need to live widely spread over the land that the !Kung headman's functions are peculiar. There is one essential qualification to headmanship in addition to heredity. A headman cannot leave his waterhole to join another band and still remain a headman, for he, in his person, does not possess headmanship. It is only when a person is *born* headman, and in association with his waterhole, that he assumes the full authority of headmanship. We have seen that headmen were considered to "own" the water and *veldkos* of a district. I believe this association is another way of expressing what the !Kung mean by "own": the headman is the symbol of a place.

In the same manner that a headman "owns" a district, he also "owns" other geographical features of the country. These include pans that fill during the rains, *veldkos* areas, baobab trees, and —most important—*mangetti* trees that hold water in their trunks, and *tsi* areas. It is these "owned" features, and the direction from the waterhole in which they lie, that define a territory. Since, as we have seen, *mangetti*'s and *tsi* are the most important !Kung resources, they are the main determinants of a direction.

But animals are *not* owned. Neatly bounded sections of the countryside are *not* owned. A territory, therefore can best be defined as the combination of a permanent waterhole and a direction: the !Kung so define it by the word "side." One headman's territory is said to be on this "side."

Just as the Kalahari's scant resources of food and water are distributed in accordance with a geographical pattern, the !Kung bands are distributed in accordance with both a geographical and a social pattern. Natural resources are the focal points in the geographical pattern of band distribution: headmen are the focal points in the social pattern. In a sense, headmen tie together the two patterns, the concept of headmanship being the embodiment of a certain quantity of resources in a person around whom a band can take shape and operate. Because of their kin ties with a headman, the people living round him, clustering their *skerms* around his and moving with him over his territory, feel right in being where they are.

The headman receives no special privileges. He is no more wealthy than other men. If he is a leader, he may assume responsibility and speak out. But as headman, he need not speak, for headmanship is a silent office and while the headman lives— by his waterhole or out somewhere on his territory with his band —he serves his whole purpose.

Most of the permanent waterholes have two !Kung bands associated with them, and the *tsi* areas are likewise shared by bands from the same and different waterholes. Such sharing may come about because two brothers (only one of whom may be the true headman) live together and feel they possess joint claims. It may come about through the passage of time, which confuses genealogies and lets claims, once tenuous, become firm through usage. The !Kung are a people of present tense, living—in their minds as well as with their bodies—from day to day. If the waterholes were not shared, some bands would be without permanent water.

Not all !Kung territories are of equal value in terms of food and water. Some people have *mangetti* nuts, some have *tsi,* and some have both. There is mild wealth, and gentle poverty in *Nyae Nyae.* Territories also change in value year by year. The rains may fail in some parts of *Nyae Nyae,* and fall in others. In normal years, *mangetti*'s in the north may become available earlier in the season than those of the western forests. Because of the flexibility of band composition, the bands gathering *mangetti*'s in such a favored area are enlarged by people who would otherwise have to wait.

This is usually a temporary situation, the newcomers having more the status of guests than members of the bands. Often, whole bands —headman and all—will visit kin in this manner. During years of dessication, the fact that a person has several choices of bands in which to live becomes vital to him—he can move from a hopeless place to perhaps a better one.

By such means, balance works out between the desert's resources and the numbers and distribution of !Kung who exploit them. No one district or *mangetti* forest could support more than a limited number of people. Only certain people possess the necessary kinship qualifications to join a band. The flexibility of their composition enables bands to swell during lean years, while the concept of association, through a headman, to a district and a territory provides for the distribution of people throughout the barren land.

If a band were confined strictly to one territory, or could use the resources of another territory only over the bodies of the band that lived there, there would be many less *Nyae Nyae* !Kung— perhaps none at all.

The !Kung give various reasons for their preference of the territory they consider home. For some, it is where they were born. For others, it is where they spent their youth. And for some, it is where they are waiting in their old age. Hunters say they must know their territories—every pan and stretch of bush, every unusual tree—and they say that to amass such knowledge takes years. An old man we met while he was visiting for a few days from the west, said that the weather was more gentle in Debera, the place where he lived, and that, moreover, "there are no stones in Debera ground."

Early one autumn morning, blue and sweet, when dawn air was still fragile on our faces, a close !Kung friend stood beside me in /Gautcha Territory, looking across a pan that still smiled with water despite the late season. It was the pan where he had come, as a young man, to live with his bride. We were quiet, waiting for the rising sun. "/Gautcha is beautiful," he said.

7. The Role of Hunting and Fishing in Luvale Society

SYNOPSIS

The scope of hunting and fishing in Luvale economy and society is described. Both are branches of a single Luvale concept, but of contrasting importance both in their place in the economy and their status in the field of ritual. In hunting the central point is the specialist hunter whose ritualized position is described. Fishing is outlined in relation to ecology and the annual cycle of the seasons, with details of techniques, rituals associated with it, the nature of fishing rights, and its significance in a modern cash economy. The possible relationship between hunting and social structure involving virilocal marriage in a matrilineal society is considered. It is concluded that no close correlation between the two can be proved; hunting is rather a repository for certain ritual values quite independent of a given social structure.

Tradition says that before the coming of chiefs stemming from Ndalamuhitanganyi the Luvale were food gatherers, without any knowledge of agriculture. In their traditional homeland of plains, rivers and seasonal inundations both game and animals and fish are plentiful though game is in places much depleted today. Luvale knowledge of fish and fishing is exceptional; Mr. P. I. R. Maclaren, Fisheries Officer in the Game and Tsetse Control Department, who also has experience of African fisheries in Nigeria, informs me that the Luvale fishermen impressed him by a specialized knowledge of the distinctions between species of fish, greatly in advance of any other African fishermen whom he has encountered. To this I can add that they and the allied Lunda, Luchazi and Chokwe are excellent and observant field naturalists with a wide knowledge of birds and animals which embraces their ecology, habits, behavior, calls and breeding seasons. This they have turned to good account

SOURCE: C. M. N. White, "The Role of Hunting and Fishing in Luvale Society," *African Studies*, Vol. 15, No. 2, 1956, pp. 75–86. Reprinted by permission of the author and publisher.

in their diverse techniques for trapping them. Rodents which often look superficially alike each have their specific vernacular names and a youth barely in his teens will quickly and confidently point out characters to distinguish them and describe differences in their habits and habitats.

Hunting and fishing to the Luvale are branches of a single field of activity embraced by the term *unyanga*, although it is common for translation to associate this term with hunting in contrast to fishing. The latter today (and probably in the past) contributes more to the economy and diet of the Luvale than hunting. But fishing is held in less esteem and the Luvale will refer to fishing as *unyanga wauleya* or fool's hunting. In the following pages I shall deal more briefly with hunting and more fully with fishing, because of the actual importance of the latter, but at the same time endeavor to contrast features of the two types of activity which may throw some light upon the different values applied to them by the people themselves.

HUNTING

The Great Plains which form a feature of the Luvale homeland are the haunt of numbers of wildebeest (*Gorgon taurinus*). Locally common also are reedbuck (*Redunca arundinum*), red lechwe (*Onotragus lechwe*), roan antelope (*Hippotragus equinus*) and tsessebe (*Damaliscus lunatus*), but the Luvale have always eaten a variety of smaller mammals and birds as well, and evidently never found it practicable to obtain an adequate supply of animal protein from the larger game animals alone. Hence hunting may be carried out with small fiber snares, larger noose snares for larger animals, spears, bows and arrows, muzzle loading guns and game drives. Moreover women are not debarred from contributing to the supply of animal protein by their efforts, and they dig up nests of gerbils (*Tatera* spp.) on the plains. There is reason to believe that the sporadic outbreaks of bubonic plague at Balovale may be connected with this practice since these gerbils are a known reservoir of plague-carrying fleas.

But the mere catching of animals is not in itself of special significance in society. This however is otherwise with the professional hunter who has been initiated into the circle of expert hunters.

Hence if a man has had some success with bow or gun in killing larger game animals, he feels the need to seek admission to this circle. This desire for initiation springs from the fear that his success will be short-lived because the professional hunters will be jealous of his success and bring to bear supernatural powers to thwart him. Moreover it is believed that a hunter, unless he is initiated, is exposed to special dangers; human familiars of sorcerers will be especially interested in anyone who has frequent supplies of meat, and the hunter himself may fall a victim to them unless he is ritually protected. He therefore takes his bow or gun and goes to a professional hunter, leaning his gun against the shrine (*chishinga*) of the latter on arrival. The professional hunter understands the sign and takes appropriate action. First he prepares charms for the novice including special medicine in which he must wash, and magical preparation in skin bundles which will enable him to be invisible to game or will protect him from danger such as lions or familiars of sorcerers when he is out hunting. He then warns his wife that she must beware of sexual relations with other men while he takes the novice out hunting. It is noteworthy that these are very stringent. Not only must she have no relations with any lover, but she must keep away from other people and never greet anyone by a hand-clasp, lest these situations lead on to other consequences.

The hunter and the novice at this stage are symbolized as mother and child (*mama yanyanga* and *mwana wanyanga* respectively). The first action is for the hunter to make a kill, and then place the novice seated on the neck of the dead beast and mark him with its blood. This may be repeated several times after which the novice shoots a beast to show what he has learned and the trainer shoots several more. On their return to the village the hunter cooks for him the special portions (*makonda*) which are the prerogative of a learner hunter. These consist of the ears, heart and lungs.

The process of going out to hunt together may be continued for a whole year before the hunter decides that his pupil is ready to dedicate a shrine of his own. When this time is reached the trainer summons other professional hunters and a dance is held. The next morning they go and cut a pole for the shrine. Only the trees known as *mutete, musole, musese* or *mupepe* may be used. In the evening this pole is set up close to the hut of the novice; at the same time a small hut (*katunda*) is built in which the hunter's charms are kept, and which his wife must not approach or see.

In another form of the charms known as *ndele* however the wife of the hunter is the only person who may see the horn of medicine which is kept in the *katunda*. It is she who takes a little of the medicine from the horn container and daubs it on her husband before he goes out to hunt. In this form of the special observances of the hunter we have the contrast to the previous one since a woman plays an essential part in it.

In a further form of charms to ensure success the trainer prepares a carved human figure for the learner. This is kept in the *katunda* and can be animated with human blood and will then go out with its owner and round up wild animals like cattle for the hunter to kill. This is known as *unyanga wakapangula*. It can only occur if the teacher is himself a sorcerer and therefore able to hand on the art to his pupil. The villagers where he lives may suspect a hunter of having such a familiar spirit if he brings in meat lacking fat or blood, because he has had to feed his familiar. Or again if many children die in the village, the hunter may be thought to have a familiar which is feeding on human beings because of a lack of game. Such suspicions will not in any case arise where a hunter's wife is seen entering the *katundu* as described above under *ndele;* there is therefore no automatic association of hunters as a class with sorcery of familiars.

Once the rites of initiation are completed the teacher receives his pay from the pupil for services rendered. The newly qualified professional hunter takes himself a praise-name to boast of his prowess; *Kachongo luhonda-mbinga* (*Kachongo,* the twister of horns) or *Sakawaya musoji keshi mavanda* (*Sakawaya* who provides meat soup, not fish scales) are typical examples.

A professional hunter must observe various taboos to preserve his prowess, but still more important those at his village who depend upon him for meat must likewise follow certain observances with meat killed by him. They must never cut it with a hoe, only with an ax or knife; they must not mix it with other meat in the same pot and they must never hang it up under the roof poles inside a house. Any member of the village found doing such a thing would be considered to have endangered the hunter's powers and hence be liable to pay him compensation. A professional hunter is also closely linked to manifestations of displeased ancestral spirits. He himself must take care to make offerings to any ancestor who was himself a professional hunter and so ensure the ancestor's aid in his hunting.

In addition deceased professional hunters are especially prone to manifest themselves in troublesome ways to their living kin as *mahamba* whether the kin are hunters or not.[1] Of these the most common are those known in Luvale as *tambwe* or *muta kalombo, chitakai* and *chitapakasa.* Living hunters play a prominent part in the exorcism rites of such *mahamba.* The special status of a professional hunter is also emphasized in his burial rites. Whereas the Luvale in the past merely placed corpses in the bush without any grave, a hunter must be buried by other hunters in a grave dug at a place where an animal hoof print shows that an animal has passed, and rocks or lumps of gray anthill earth are heaped on the grave.

The circumstances surrounding the status of a professional hunter in the community are similar to those that are found with certain other specialists such as diviners and blacksmiths. Superficially the professional hunter appears to be a very important component in any community; yet it is clear that his actual contribution to the supply of animal protein is in no way overwhelmingly important. Fish has always been more important to the Luvale as an assured source of protein than meat, and anyone may catch and provide meat without being a specialist hunter. Nevertheless the importance of the status is stressed not only by the ritual attending it and observances to be followed by the whole community in respect of how his meat is treated, but also by the special precautions against social amnesia where hunters are concerned which take the form of the frequent appearance of hunters as *mahamba* spirits. It must also be borne in mind that the Luvale are in no sense today a people dependent on food-gathering for existence. They have for many years been an agricultural people in which food gathering has been limited to the provision of animal protein for a mixed diet. Moreover, for at least a century they have had guns and gun-powder so that the hunting of game animals during that period has been considerably easier than when it depended upon a bow and arrows. But the special status of a hunter institutionalized in the way described above goes back much further into the past, and has managed to survive as a relic of a time when the Luvale or their forebears were presumably collectors, sometime before the coming of Ndala-

[1] For a general description of the *mahamba* manifestations cf. White, *Africa,* XIX, 1949, pp. 324–31.

muhitanganyi. Perhaps here once again the Luvale addiction to ritual has enabled this status to survive although it has long ceased to be functionally important.

There is perhaps another reason why the status of the professional hunter was preserved long after hunting had ceased to be of prime importance in providing a food supply. Of all the various types of relish eaten with porridge (*shima*), game meat is perhaps more highly prized than any other, just as *shima yaukatu* or porridge without relish represents the lowest level of diet. Snares of various types depend upon an animal finding its way into them, and though skill in setting a snare is also important it is no guarantee that meat will be forthcoming. Game drives are seasonal; they depend upon long grass dry enough to fire for the Luvale type of *likazo*. Hence they are only operable for part of the year. But the professional hunter is in a different category; for he can go out at any time and obtain meat. Some periods are of course better than others. If the grass is excessively long, game can escape notice more easily; if the grass has all been burned off game may be difficult to approach, hence the emphasis on charms which will make a professional hunter invisible.

There is unfortunately little in the literature to indicate that previous accounts of other tribes have drawn a sharp line between hunting as a general part of economic organization and as a specially ritualized occupation of a few adepts, though references are found to specialist hunters of dangerous game such as elephants.[2] The Ovimbundu and Lamba have specialist initiated hunters however.[3] Richards remarks: "Hunting in former times seems to have been associated with political authority or prestige." This tempts one to seek for a connection between the function of the hunter in Luvale society and the coming of chiefs from Mwachiamvwa, especially as the motif of hunters acquiring political power occurs in several traditions of the south western Congo Basin and adjacent areas. But if hunting played a prominent practical role in Luvale economy in the past, it must have been before the coming of chiefs, at a time when the Luvale were an acephalous people, and traditionally lacking agricultural activities.

[2] Cf. e.g. Junod: *The Life of a South African Tribe*, II, p. 56.
[3] Cf. Doke: *The Lambas of Northern Rhodesia*, and Hambley: *The Ovimbundu of Angola*.

FISHING

The Luvale constantly emphasize their fishing activities in contrast to the relative lack of such activities among the Lunda, Luchazi and Chokwe. The Lunda indeed are remarkably deficient in detailed terminology for different species of fish and will fall back on the blanket title of *anshi atooka* (white fish) when at a loss for a specific name. This lack of knowledge on their part is largely determined by different environmental conditions for the Lunda live predominantly in country watered by small swift streams often near the top of the watershed, as in Mwinilunga district. In such areas fish are not abundant and there is a great lack of suitable breeding places for them. But even within these limited resources it must be observed that the Lunda have not made great efforts to catch what fish they have. The small lake Chibesha at Mwinilunga contains excellent fish but until recently local taboos caused it to be left strictly un-fished.

In the following account I have tried to give a fairly full outline of Luvale fishing for little has been put on record about it.[4] I have also taken the opportunity to make some comparisons with the data for the Unga of Lake Bwangweulu as described by V. W. Brels-ford.[5]

THE ECOLOGICAL BACKGROUND

The main Luvale area in Balovale district lies west of the Zam-bezi; it consists of large open plains intersected by belts of *Erythrophloeum* and *Burkea* woodland with palms; in the north west it rises to the watershed plain known as *Minyanya* and is broken in a north south line by several drainage depressions which form flood plains for the rivers, especially the Litapi and the Kashiji. The latter dry up extensively during the dry season. The only major perennial rivers are the Zambezi and Lungwevungu which form the eastern and southern boundaries of this area.

Rainfall occurs from mid-October to early April; the average

[4] Cf. McCulloch, *The Southern Lunda and Related Peoples*, Ethnographic Survey, 1951, pp. 55 and 61.
[5] *Fishermen of the Bangweulu Swamps*, Rhodes-Livingstone Papers, No. 12, 1946.

precipitation during this period is about 45 inches. During this time the sandy plains absorb moisture which drains into the flood plains, aided by the run-off from the watershed plain in the north. The flood reaches its height in January and February and thereafter falls steadily until the end of the dry season by when the flood plains and their lesser arms have dried up, leaving pools, some of considerable size such as Mwange "lake" on the Litapi.

Luvale fishing activities form an annual cycle correlated with this environmental background, and except at the height of the flood fish are caught throughout the year, the techniques being suitably adjusted to the changing conditions.

THE MAIN ANNUAL FISHING CYCLE

The Luvale regard their fishing cycle as beginning at the end of the year after the rain has started but before the water table has risen high enough to start filling the drainage depressions. About the end of November or early December preparations are made for the spawning run of the mud barbel (*Clarias* sp.); this run is known as *musuza*. A small affluent of a larger stream is chosen. A fence of reeds is built across it, leaving a passage in the middle; from the latter on the upstream side a circular fence is constructed into which the fish pass and from which they cannot escape. The main fence is called *jingando* and the circular enclosure *malela*. As the water arises the frogs on the plains begin to call, and when the stream fills the mud barbel come from down stream to spawn in the flooded drainage depressions. One morning the *malela* is found full of fish, and the men enter and kill the fish with spears and axes. The mud barbel have large flat skulls and must not be killed with clubs, lest, it is said, the others hear the noise and turn back.

The mud barbel killed thus are buried in a hole in the water at the bank for twenty-four hours before splitting and drying; if this is not done, it is considered that when dry the flesh breaks up easily when they are handled or made up into bundles. The spawning run of the mud barbel lasts only a few days and is followed by about two months when fishing is at its lowest ebb, as the flood rises. January and February are the two months when fish are extremely scarce and fishing at a virtual standstill.

The second major stage occurs when the flood begins to fall; fish weirs are then built across seepage streams on plains feeding into larger streams. These weirs are called *makalila* and consist of a barrage of sods of grass to block the flow; holes are left in them and on the downstream side pocket-shaped traps of matting called *vikanga* are placed, into which the fish from upstream fall as they descend with the receding flood. Fishing in *makalila* goes on in March and April. By May these seepage streams have become dry, and it is necessary to repeat the process on the larger streams.

The dam built there in a suitable shallow place is a much stronger structure of poles firmly braced and finally blocked with branches and sods. It is called *walilo*. Cylindrical basket traps are placed on the downstream side; the largest of these *likaza* or *ngombe namwana* is big enough to catch a crocodile which swims into it, and is made of withies and sticks. Smaller but similar traps are *muvuwa* made of reeds or sticks, and *likanda* made of grass or small reeds. The *walilo* is too large a structure to enable one man to build it; a number participate, each placing his individual traps at it. Fishing at these large dams lasts from May to July and during this period great numbers of people camp along the rivers and streams in temporary camps.

By August the flood has fallen so far that these weirs and dams are no longer productive; numerous pools remain, large and small. A man and his wife will fish the small pools by bailing out the water with baskets; this is called *kusuhwa*. The larger pools cannot be bailed and these are treated with fish poison, parties of men and women combining for the purpose. Further reference to this made below under Ritual. Fish poisoning takes place most commonly in September and October. The drying pools attract numerous pelicans, cormorants, herons and marabout storks, and at this time it is a race between man and the birds as to who will get the fish first. Fish poison is apparently most effective on *Tilapia* (so-called "bream"), and less so on the mud barbel. These last which are found at this time in the larger pools are killed by spearing, known as *kuwaya*. Concurrently with this, men and women may combine with conical hand traps in shallow pools, placing the trap over fish which are located. This trap is called *chongo,* and fishing thus is *kutavika*.

By November these activities have ended and the time has again come to prepare for the spawning run of the mud barbel.

Brelsford (1. c. pp. 61–62) refers to the belief that fish only move freely at Bangweulu on moonless nights, and adds that the weirs are not visited when the nights are bright. This is quite different from the Luvale area. Here the fish seem to move freely by daylight or on bright nights and there is no indication that the weir fishing is only worth while on dark nights. The spawning run of the mud barbel seems to take place at night so that the trap is found full early in the morning, but here too there is no belief or evidence that moonless nights are required. More biological data about the fish and their habits is needed before any comment on this discrepancy can be made.

Subsidiary methods of fishing

In addition to the main annual cycle of weir fishing and the other methods just described, certain additional methods of fishing are carried on. These may be listed under techniques as:

(a) *Hook and line fishing:* This is known as *kulowa* if the fisherman is fishing himself; *kuta ulovo* or *linata* if a line is left and set. Baited lines may be of a single large hook or a line with a number of hooks at intervals. Such lines are known as *linata* or *liyumbila*. In pools and lagoons the line is often tied to a bundle of reeds which is left to float freely in the water. Large mud barbel, Tiger fish (*Hydrocyon* sp.) and "Pike" (*Sarcodaces* sp.) are commonly taken thus, but "bream" are not normally taken on hooks. A variant of this but without actual hooks is *kanyangapelu:* here the fisherman has a bunch of cords baited with worms and trails them or dangles them from a canoe. Mud barbel and *musuta* (*Crenopoma* sp.) take the bait and are hauled out of the water.

(b) *Traps set in suitable places: Lunguwa* is a rough bark rope cone basket without a valve; it is used between December and February; near the bank of a small stream a fence is constructed to guide the fish and in the center is a space where the *lunguwa* is set with its closed end facing into mid stream. It is baited with cassava peelings or pounded cassava leaves. Fish are caught thus one at a time. It is very effective for "bream" (*Tilapia*).

Lizakasa is a stronger version constructed of fibrous roots and with a valve (*chilazo*) at the mouth to prevent fish emerging after they have entered. It is about three feet long but with a wide mouth and is baited and thrown into a river in a place with deep water, secured to the bank and left for a day or two. Many fish may be caught simultaneously.

Makinda are long rush traps which may run up to ten feet in length; they are only a few inches wide at the closed end but rather wider at the mouth: men or women make them, and place them on a *walilo* to catch the very small fish which might otherwise escape but they are also sometimes set by themselves in grassy inundations or in shallow or by a ford on a large river, and may be regarded as secondary to the main types of weir fishing.

(c) *Net fishing:* Net fishing is important because it can be practiced almost throughout the year; its scope is however limited because it requires considerable expanses of water either as large rivers or lakes. It follows that in some such suitable places net fishing for environmental reasons may be locally more important than the main annual cycle described above. Nets were formerly made from bark fibers but now the cords from discarded motor tires are widely used. I am not aware that any Luvale have started to make nylon nets such as are in wide use at lake Mweru and the Luapula, but net fishing is hardly so important in the Luvale scheme of fishing. Methods of net fishing are:

Kulalika (set net and leave for the night).

Kukuvulwila (driving into net by making noise with a paddle). By this technique one man in a boat selects a place where there are obviously plenty of fish; he then sets his net and by beating his paddle in the water drives the fish into the net.

Kufuta (seine-netting). This requires two canoes to draw the net. A special type of net is used in deep open waters; it has very large mesh and is known as *likokela*. The general term for a net is *lyoji;* a small type of gill net often used for setting at night is called *kalenge.*

(d) *Drag baskets:* These are used only by women; the basket is known as *liyanga* and the method of fishing as *kuswinga.* Women fish thus dragging their baskets through the water which may be waist deep. The normal method is for a party of women to fish together; each woman with a drag basket has a helper known as *swavi.* The women with the baskets form a continuous line with their baskets touching end to end; the helpers then enter the water and by the disturbance they make, drive the fish into the drag baskets. Casualties from crocodiles are by no means unknown among women fishing thus; the women with the baskets rather than their helpers seem to be the victims most often, as a crocodile comes from behind and seizes one by the leg as she bends over basket facing the helpers.

(e) *Night fishing by flares:* This is called *kumunyika;* it is done from a canoe on larger rivers, the canoe having a flare in the stern;

as the fish rise to the flame, they are speared. It is done between June and October and only on a moonless night. Certain "bream" are caught thus.

It is noteworthy that fishing is not only a male occupation; women alone use the drag baskets; men and women combine in bailing pools, in *kutavika* with *vyongo* traps and in using *makinda* traps; small girls may be seen fishing with a hand line or with *kanyangapelu*.

MAGIC AND RITUAL ASSOCIATION WITH FISHING

(a) *Fish poisoning:* The most important of the special observances are those connected with fish poisoning. Brelsford (1.c. pp. 67–68) refers to the use of fish poison at Bangweulu but does not indicate that there is any ritual about it.

Among the Luvale sexual intercourse is forbidden between the participants on a fish poisoning expedition; this is significant because men and women actually participate together in fish poisoning so that the taboo must be observed throughout the period of the expedition. At night the men and women sleep in separate shelters to ensure that no one breaks the taboo. After going to the scene of the fish poisoning the following morning, the senior member of the party strikes a blow with a hoe at the fish poison plant, and thereupon the rest of the party lie down on their backs and writhe as a symbol of the dying and wriggling fish when the poison has been put in the water. After this the party dig up the bulbs and return to their camp. On lifting the baskets of bulbs, each man must lift his own basket without help; otherwise the fish may recover from the poison. The ban on sexual relations is so strict that the party coming back to their camp with the bulbs must likewise not pass through a village lest they are contaminated by the presence of those living there who have had intercourse. No one who has had intercourse during the night may come to the camp of the fish poisoners. The next stage is to summon someone who is regarded as skilled and lucky in his casting of fish poison. He has no special title but is referred to as "one with a bitter arm". For want of a better term, I refer to him here as the "specialist". Men and women now pound the bulbs, on the ground and not in wooden mortar. The pounded cake is placed in a grass basket; now no one may eat or drink until further notice. The "specialist" enters the pool, dragging the grass basket of poison up and down calling on the fish to come. When the contents of one grass basket have been dissolved, he takes a new basket. Suddenly the first fish to be affected appears; this is called *tangu*. The "specialist" quickly recovers it and hands it to his companions who roast it for him. The "specialist" eats this fish and casts its bones back into the water. Now the rest of the party may eat and drink. Many fish now begin to rise to the surface; no one may point to them with his finger, only with his fist, lest the catch is spoiled. If they have finished collecting all the fish and do not intend going on to poison another pool, sexual relations may be resumed.

Fish-poisoning is referred to as *kusukila;* the fish poison is called *usungu*. But this is a generic term and several different plants are used. *Tephrosia* sp. is grown in villages and known in Luvale as *kahulula* but often simply called *usungu;* the leaves of this are pounded up as poison. The commonest wild species with the bulb which is pounded up and referred to in the above account is known as *chikala*. It may be transplanted to a village. The botanical name has not been ascertained. A third and very potent species whose roots are pounded up is known as *mbondo*. (Botanical name not known.) A further species, *kaveya,* has a milky latex and the whole plant and roots are pounded up. This is known to the Luchazi as *vinyota*. Other plants used are *mutandakembe* (in Luchazi *ntandakembe*), and *munyakajila* (in Luchazi *muntsato*). None of these names appears in the considerable collection of vernacular names collected by the Forestry Department of Northern Rhodesia, which serves as an invaluable source of botanical identifications. As fish poisoning is illegal, although still indulged in, no doubt there has been reluctance to reveal the names of the plants used. The above details should enable botanical determinations to be made in due course.

(b) *Fish weirs:* In the past the Luvale abstained from intercourse while working at a *walilo* weir; today this taboo is often observed only while the weir is being built, but thereafter charms may be put upon it and intercourse resumed. Individual variation in the strictness of this taboo is to be found; the Luchazi who have a similar taboo only resume intercourse after the weir has already yielded many fish. They also wash with a decoction of *mupepe,*[6] *mukula,*[7] and *munyumbe*[8] if they have an emission during a dream, before intercourse

---

[6] *Hymenocardia mollis.*
[7] *Pterocarpus angolensis.*
[8] *Isoberlinia paniculata.*

has been resumed. This agrees with Brelsford's data for the Unga.

(c) *Magical charms to ensure good fishing:* These are in widespread use and take many different forms; one or two illustrations will suffice to indicate the use of such charms. Charm for woman's drag basket: the woman cooks a few fish, calls some small children to eat them and covers the children with her drag basket while they eat. They must keep completely silent while eating. Next morning she digs a hole in the path near the village and places in it the fish bones left by the children. She adds some wood from a tree struck by lightning, some twigs of *mutete*[9] or *mupepe* and a preparation called *tambikila* (feathers or bones of a bird of uncertain identification). On this she lights a fire and places her drag basket over it. The smoke from this fire is regarded as a guarantee of a good catch. Charm for a net: the fisherman obtains the bones for the recipe by going out with his net and catching a fish which he brings home; this is cooked and eaten by him and his family. The bones are collected and the process described above is then followed and the net smoked over the fire. Charms containing wood from a tree struck by lightning, *tambikila* and tied with fibers of *pundukaina* (*Grewia flavescens*) are also fastened to the weighted side of the net. Brelsford's medicines for netting (1.c., p. 142) at Bangweulu should be compared with these for certain echoes of similar practices are found there though the details are quite different.

(d) *Invocation of ancestral spirits to aid fishing:* A fisherman at his village may come with his fish spear and a fish and leave them at his *muyombo* stick as a mark of respect to his *mukulu* (guardian ancestral spirit). His wife soon comes and takes away the fish to cook but the spear is left thus all night.

At a fishing camp a man will set up a *muyombo* stick to his guardian spirit. From time to time he puts a few fish there and asks his spirit to ensure good fishing. A man afflicted by a troublesome *lihamba* spirit makes a little mound of earth near his shelter at the fishing camp and makes offerings of meal to it before fishing; later he will put a few fish there to ensure that the *lihamba* does not adversely affect his fishing. The practice of either ritual or magic in connection with fishing in Luvale camps is not conspicuous; women frequent the fishing camps freely though they must not actually go to the *walilo* and the casual visitor might not even think of looking for charms. This is in marked contrast with the Unga of Bangweulu

---

[9] *Amblygonocarpus obtusangulus.*

as described by Brelsford. On the other hand it is noteworthy that the ritual concerned with fish poisoning which is strictly observed by the Luvale seems to have no counterpart among the Unga. There are no Luvale fishing priests such as are found at Bangweulu.

NATURE OF FISHING RIGHTS

Rights in weirs and pools suitable for poisoning are owned by individuals. These rights are acquired in the first instance simply by finding a suitable site and setting up a weir or finding a suitable pool and fishing it with poison. The Luvale political system lacks centralization and it was never considered that the fish were specifically owned by a territorial chief to whom a request must be made before a man could obtain fishing rights for a weir or pool to poison. Once a man had obtained such rights by prescription, they vested in him and his heirs and no stranger could infringe them. It is however common for persons who own such rights to give permission to a stranger to fish his pools upon a suitable return. Since a weir requires a number of men to build it, the owner of the weir invites others to participate.

There are no specific rights over areas of net fishing and any one may come and fish in a suitable place without interference. A site for the spawning run of the mud barbel is owned in the same way as a weir site by prescription; sites for the small weirs known as *makalila* are not owned as they are regarded as too ephemeral. Pools for spearing or fishing by *chongo* traps are owned. The various subsidiary types of fishing listed in the previous paragraphs may be indulged in anywhere. Drag basket fishing by women does not as such involve the ownership of any rights but the pools in which it is done are almost certain to be the property of some individual for reasons of other types of fishing there.

This division between weirs which are owned and netting grounds which are open to the public is similar to the position reported by Brelsford (1.c., Chapter 5.) for the Unga of Bangweulu, though he gives no data about pools for poisoning, spearing etc. in this connection.

The rights to tribute enjoyed by Luvale chiefs are confined to those places where the fishing place has an actual owner, that is to say the owner of a *walilo* weir, a barbel spawning run place, or a pool for spearing or fishing by *vyongo* or poison was under a traditional obligation to take an annual tribute of fish to the chief. But persons fishing in netting places or other free places without any individual rights of ownership did not take tribute to the chief from their catchers. This position appears to continue today.

From Brelsford's account it would appear that Unga chiefs had considerably wider claims to tributes of fish from those fishing in their areas; whether this was so before European administration is not clear since in arcas lacking a strong political organization the recognition of chiefs under the Native Authorities Ordinances has often greatly enhanced the standing of so-called chiefs who had previously enjoyed much less status. Comparing the position as between Luvale and Unga where fishing rights are concerned, the types of rights vested in individuals appear to be very similar in both areas, but the type of rights to tribute from fishing considerably different. Since in the Luvale area, a fisherman not under an obligation to give tribute from e.g. a netting area might nevertheless after a good catch give a chief a present of fish on account of his politeness toward the chief, it is not impossible that in Unga areas this situation was converted into a wider range of obligatory tribute once the Unga chiefs found that their position had the support of the British Administration.

The Attitude of the Luvale toward fish

As noted above the Luvale have a wide range of names for different kinds of fish; over fifty names are in common general use. It is not, however, known how many different kinds of fish actually live in the area. Brelsford reports sixty-seven different species for the Bangweulu area. Maclaren's short survey indicates about fifty and is likely to be a fair preliminary approximation.

The Unga are said to have no strong preference as between fresh and dry fish; among the Luvale there is an overwhelming preference for fresh fish. As far as I know the only fish not eaten by any Luvale is an eel-like species called *musokongo*. However many other people may have taboos affecting certain fish. A woman who has not yet had her first menstruation or who is pregnant may not eat *musuta;* in the first instance lest she has a blocked vagina, in the second lest her child be an epileptic. *Pungu* (Tiger fish) and kundu (a *Tilapia*) are also taboo to a pregnant woman. The novices at the circumcision rites are also forbidden to eat these same two fishes until their scars have healed. A leper is forbidden to eat both these fish and also *chingwele* (*Synodontis* sp.)

While no single fish is more highly rated by the Luvale than any other, there is no doubt that each individual has his own preference. In the Mweru-Bangweulu region it is commonly said that Africans prefer the oily *Bagridae* and their allies such as *Synodontis* and *Auchenoglanis,* and rate the more delicate *Cichlidae* less highly. There is no evidence to substantiate this for the Luvale.

Maclaren analyzed some catches at Balovale. In one sample caught at a barrier across the mouth of a swamp depression 39 per cent were cichlids (bream), 30 per cent mormyrids, and 15 per cent cyprinids (minnows, etc.). *Synodontis* and *Clarias* (Squeakers and mud barbel) only amounted to 11 per cent.

Until recently, African fishing, like African agriculture, was for subsistence only and there was no great surplus of fish until the industrialization of the Copperbelt provided a concentration of African population short of fish and willing to pay high prices for it. In considering the nature of Luvale weir fishing or the fishing of the barbel spawning run, this must be born in mind. As long as these fishing methods were merely to provide a man and his family with fish the amount caught was very small. But with the modern commercialization of the fish the picture is very different.

Nevertheless it is unwise to assume that overfishing in general is taking place. Maclaren considered after a visit that the areas of swampy inundation are so great that only a fraction of them is being exploited by fishing. He also pointed out that at least half the fish caught at barriers are species which never grow big, and that experience from fish farming shows that the production of fry in many species is excessive and vigorous thinning out may be beneficial. On the other hand I know from personal experience that in 1938 the Lunsongwe, a flood plain stream, was teeming with fish; soon after population came in to settle there in some numbers; weir fishing started and ten years later the Lunsongwe was almost devoid of fish. Any extensive change in this respect will not be popular for the Luvale have an intense urge for money and any interference by controlling the weirs or spawning run will appear as a threat to their economic position. However, it appears that at present the only measures of conservation necessary are a limitation of fishing to requirements for personal consumption during January and February when fish are breeding, and a prohibition of the use of fish poisons.

THE ECONOMIC SIGNIFICANCE OF FISHING

The Luvale fisheries do not of course compare with the much larger fisheries of Lakes Mweru and Bangweulu. Nevertheless they are far from being insignificant in the modern cash economy, and in particular enable the African traders who act as middlemen to be quite well off. I give some statistics for several years. The *African Affairs Report, Northern Rhodesia,* 1951, shows the following:

Price paid to fishermen at waterside £10 per ton.
Transport costs waterside to Chingola £23 per ton.
Sale price on Copperbelt £100 per ton.

It was estimated that 200 tons of fish were exported, and thus the fish traders realized £20,000, from which they would have to deduct £2,000 paid to the fishermen producers and £4,600 for transport. At this time the Luvale Native Authority levied a fish trading licence which brought their Treasury £355. In 1952 the same report estimated the Copperbelt value of the trade at over £100,000.

In 1953 the price to the fisherman producers was raised to 2*d*. per pound, and 180 tons was exported. In that year Mr. Maclaren made a survey of the fisheries and gave some valuable figures of the economics. He worked on a waterside price to the producer of 2*d*. per lb. and a Copperbelt average sale price of 2*s*. 4*d*. per lb. This gave the middleman a net profit of £225 per cent. In round figures this meant that the fisherman got £16. 6*s*. 0*d*. per ton or £3,000 for the year. The Copperbelt value was £233 per ton or £42,000 for the total value of the trade to consumers. I think that the 1952 estimate of the value of the trade as in excess of £100,000 was too optimistic, although figures are in any case only approximate, and at periods of shortage it is well known that Copperbelt prices may soar. Later in 1953 plans were made to reorganize the industry. The Native Authority made it compulsory for fish to be marketed through organized markets and sold by weight at 4*d*. per lb., of which 3*d*. went to the fisherman and 1*d*. as a cess to the Native Treasury. This reorganization went off without any difficulties and now gives the producer a better share in the value of the industry. Unfortunately no very reliable figures of the number of middlemen benefiting are available. In 1952 when the fish trading licence for middlemen was still in force, it was paid by 622 persons but many of those were not full-time traders, and merely taking a few bundles to sell to get easy money.

SOCIAL ASPECTS OF HUNTING AND FISHING

The foregoing account will serve to show how much more systematic was the exploitation of fishing than hunting even before the fisheries were drawn into the present day cash economy. It will also be noted that there is no ritualized great fisherman comparable with the specialist hunter. Ritual is not absent from fishing but plays a less prominent part in it than in hunting, and only fish poisoning can be said to have important ritual observances associated with it. I believe that fish poisoning represents a primitive element in the various techniques of fishing, since it involves no techniques requiring the use of apparatus. This would seem to support the suggestion that both in hunting and in fishing the elements involving special ritual may be relics from the past. In my recent study of Luvale social organization[10] I made brief mention, in a postscript, of Dr. Turner's paper[11] in which he associates virilocal marriage among the Mwinilunga Ndembu with hunting. He says: "The high value set on hunting out of the total constellation of economic activities; the fact that hunting was carried out most commonly by a small band of males; the co-residence of the male hunters; the association of virilocal marriage with this condition"; are structural characteristics of Ndembu society. Now I have shown that Luvale social structure partakes of similar virilocal marriage, but that hunting is of small practical significance in comparison with fishing in Luvale economy. Although Dr. Turner does not refer to the association of ritualized professional hunters, which exists among the Ndembu just as among the Luvale, it is only in the existence of this status that hunting can be said to have a special value in these societies. But the professional hunter with very similar ritual apprenticeship and subsequent observances exists among the Lamba, as well described by Doke. Yet the Lamba are not a people following virilocal marriage in the manner of the Ndembu and Luvale. Moreover the specialist hunter is a solitary hunter, not the leader of a band of hunters. He is pro-

[10] *African Studies,* 1955.
[11] *Africa,* xxv, 1955.

tected by magical means against the dangers attendant upon long solitary sojourns in the bush, and is the sterotype that so often recurs in folk tales, of the type found throughout these tribes. In these, a man comes upon a mysterious lone hunter at his shelter surrounded by meat, and far from people.

This archetypal hunter, particularly well characterized in the *Liyambi lyangongo* (great hunter of the wilderness) of Luchazi folk tales is the antithesis of co-operation between a group of related males all co-operating in hunting. The professional hunter inducted by ritual into the association of hunters is the actual realization in society of this mythical great hunter. I do not question that combined hunting activities do take place as for instance in game drives, although collective operations of this sort are much better illustrated by Luvale fishing than by hunting. Yet as we have seen fishing is in any case "fool's hunting" as the Luvale say, and is not given a special status comparable with that of the lone specialist hunter.

In all these tribes a strong element of collecting of feral protein can be traced, although it is rapidly giving place to other and domestic or commercial sources of supply today. With the Lunda, small animals, birds and honey seem to have been the dominant features of collecting; with the Luvale animals and fish; with the Luchazi animals and grasshoppers.[12] I would therefore suggest that Turner's hypothesis of the virilocal element in social structure might be tested not so much against the presence of a high value set upon hunting as against collecting of protein. But here it seems certain that adequate information would show equal importance for protein collecting in the past in uxorilocal societies. Alternatively the special status of the great hunter is a survival and not necessarily to be associated with modern social structure. Dr. Turner in his work on Ndembu social structure takes matrilineal descent for granted in that he seeks no explanation for it as a phenomenon, but virilocal marriage as an element in the structure of society which needs explanation in terms of a society of hunters. My own feeling is that at present both have to be taken as given elements in these societies, and that while social structure reflects the existence of both these principles, one is no more susceptible of immediate explanation than the other. Richards has reviewed variations in the pattern of residence as-

---

[12] The specialized Luchazi terminology for kinds of grasshoppers on this account is noteworthy and comparable to Luvale knowledge of fish.

sociated with matrilineal descent.[13] She points out that virilocal marriage in a matrilineal society is found among the Mayombe and Kongo; the similar structure in this respect among the Luvale, Ndembu and others serves to provide one more feature which associates these tribes with a culture complex extending from the lower Congo to northwestern Northern Rhodesia, in contrast to the rather different societies further south and east. If this is so, it is preferable to regard hunting not as a factor underlying social organization, but as a practice which has survived because it preserves certain ritual values. This is likewise illustrated by M. Douglas for the Lele in her essay in *African Worlds* (pp. 1–26) where the basis for ritual is a communal hunt and not the isolated specialist hunter of the Luvale and Ndembu.

[13] Some Types of Family Structure among the Central Bantu; in *African Systems of Kinship and Marriage*, pp. 207–51.

8. Seasonal Movements of the Kababish Arabs of Northern Kordofan [Sudan][1]

I

The purpose of this paper is twofold: to provide a descriptive account of the seasonal movements of the pastoral Kababish, and to stress the rational character of Kababish decisions relating to the utilization of environmental resources.

In recent years many writers have proceeded on the assumption that it is both desirable and inevitable that pastoral nomads be settled.[2] The administrative arguments in favor of this view are often clearer than the economic ones, but in any case my immediate concern here is neither to attack nor to support it. I am concerned rather to show (with special reference to the Kababish) that a pastoral nomadic economy is not necessarily an anachronism, and that the way the Kababish exploit their natural resources is in principle a rational one. To say that the Kababish are rational in the way they exploit their resources does not mean that they do not make mistakes, or that no improvements are possible in their system of resource-use. There is no system anywhere that can claim to be rational in this absolute sense. It means rather that they have certain basic economic aims (which are reasonable), that these aims raise a number of practical problems (which are recognized), and

SOURCE: Talal Asad, "Seasonal Movements of the Kababish Arabs of Northern Kordofan [Sudan]." *Sudan Notes,* Vol. 45, 1964, pp. 45–58. Reprinted by permission of the author and publisher.

[1] I wish to thank the University of Khartoum and Ford Foundation for generous assistance in financing the fieldwork on which this paper is based. I wish to thank, also, Mr. F. Rehfisch, who read early drafts of the paper and made useful suggestions for its improvement.

[2] See, for example, Mohd. Awad, "Nomadism in the Arab Lands of the Middle East," *The Problems of the Arid Zones,* UNESCO, 1962; and J. Randell, "The Potential Development of Lands Devoted to Nomadic Pastoralism," *The Effect of Nomadism on the Economic and Social Development of the People of the Sudan,* Philosophical Society of the Sudan, 1962.

that their pastoral activities and decisions are directed toward the solution of these problems in the light of the knowledge and techniques available to them.

The reason I think this needs to be stressed is that several statements have been made, representing an influential point of view, which imply that pastoral nomadism is essentially an irresponsible mode of existence. These statements range from the dogmatic assertion that "nomadism is not a natural way of life"[3]—which deserves very little comment; to the seemingly objective remark that "nomads use untamed and unimproved natural resources without any contribution to their improvement or perpetuation"[4]—which calls for the following observations:—In the first place the Kababish do contribute to the perpetuation of their natural resources (by alternate use of grazing grounds) for if they did not they could not keep animals in such numbers as they do. Secondly, if the Kababish do not actively contribute to the improvement of their natural resources it is for the simple reason that they have neither the skill nor the means to do so—no more than the traders in Kordofan have for improving the roads they use. Indeed both the individual trader and the individual Kabbashi pastoralist are using extensive communally owned resources whose improvement can only be carried out by a large government or quasi-government agency. Further, if it should prove that the Kababish remain unenthusiastic about improvements imposed from above, which involve de-stocking and restricted grazing, their attitude will be no different basically from that of the owners of any cluster of small traditional industries which are required to submit to rationalization—for the immediate loss to the many individuals is more palpable than the eventual gain in efficiency to the economy as a whole.

My point is that broad generalizations of the kind I have quoted above are not only incorrect, but serve also to perpetuate the misleading impression that pastoral nomadic economy is inherently

[3] Dr. Mihaymid, Ministry of Animal Resources, in "Discussion" following Dr. El Hadji El Nagar and Dr. Taha Baasher, "Psychomedical Aspects of Nomadism in the Sudan," *The Effect of Nomadism on the Economic and Social Development of the People of the Sudan,* Philosophical Society of the Sudan, 1962.

[4] Dr. Mustafa Baasher, "Range and Livestock Problems Facing the Settlement of Nomads," *The Effect of Nomadism on the Economic and Social Development of the People of the Sudan,* Philosophical Society of the Sudan, 1962.

primitive and destructive, and that it lacks a rational basis.[5] In fact, as I hope to show, it is nothing of the kind.

The basic economic problem facing Kababish nomads is the same as that facing individuals in any society: the use of scarce resources to achieve given ends. How the system of resource-use can be made more efficient or different ends substituted for those now in existence are subjects for legitimate discussion. But these things can only be done when the rational character of the system is first understood. And the present system of the Kababish is rational for the following reasons: (a) by choosing to be pastoralists herding appropriate kinds of livestock in a marginal environment they make use of resources that might otherwise remain idle, and (b) by organizing the use of unpromising natural resources for the maintenance of growing herds they are able to satisfy their needs and produce large numbers of surplus animals for sale. Both (a) and (b) are connected. The use of extensive but poor natural resources, and the maintenance of large herds of animals are only possible because, as we shall see, the Kababish have a dual cycle of seasonal movements. The seasonal movements are therefore to be seen as a systematic solution of a number of basic problems which Kababish pastoralism raises, rather than as an opportunistic and haphazard search for grazing and water.

The Kababish use the water and grazing at their disposal to maintain growing herds which constitute their capital. But what they seek from these herds is the maximum rate of increase in total animal numbers for enhancing social advantage, rather than the optimum rate of off-take for maximizing financial advantage. Their need for cash is limited in part because much of what they consume can be obtained directly from their animals. Their attitude in this matter was once graphically put to me by a Kabbashi in the following words: "A camel has no real price. The buying and selling of camels merely represents a rough equivalent of their value, and it goes on because people need things, not because it represents the true value of camels. One can drink camel's milk, use its hair, make it carry a

---

[5] Cf. J. Randell, ". . . the destructive exploitation of the environment . . . is an almost universal characteristic of (the nomad's) way of life." (op. cit.); and J. Berque: "Yet under (the nomadic) system, whatever care may be devoted to supplying the everyday needs of the livestock, there is no direct and conscious causal relationship between human effort and production." In Introduction to "Nomads and Nomadism in the Arid Zone," *Int. Soc. Sci. Bull.*, xi, No. 4, 1959.

load—even eat it. And with the blessing of God it multiplies under your hands. But what do you do with the bits of paper the merchant gives you? Put them in your pocket. The Arabs want these bits of paper only because the merchants want them, and the Government wants them."

Money is never used by the Kababish for productive investment. Since land is not individually owned, there is no inducement for individuals to invest in it. And unlike some other pastoral peoples .they never buy animals for breeding purposes, although sires are frequently borrowed to improve strains. But to say that the Kababish do not use money for productive investment is not to say, of course, that they do not invest productively. The withholding of animals for the purpose of natural increase is itself a form of investment.

The primary objects of cash expenditure among the Kababish are grain (bulrush millet), tea, sugar, gold and silver ornaments, and animal tax. The family's consumption of grain (together with milk the staple diet), as well as of tea and sugar, is on the whole limited. The purchase of gold and silver ornaments is merely the formation of a kind of unproductive reserve—to be translated back into cash when the need arises. Animals are therefore usually sold only to meet the cash requirements of a relatively stable level of consumption.

In the mobilization of manpower for the care of livestock it is family and kinship ties that are the important factor rather than financial ability to secure wage labor. But the existence of family and kinship ties, though it serves this purpose, has other implications which are equally important for the life of the Kababish, and in the maintenance of these ties livestock are an essential element. Indeed growing herds have considerable advantages for the Kababish other than the purely economic one: thus the more numerous the herds, the greater the measure of prestige, as well as the means of creating useful social links and fulfilling vital social obligations.[6] It is therefore this aim—the maintenance of growing herds of livestock—that provides the underlying motive for the economic life of the Kababish.

[6] Much of what has been described for the Humr of Southern Kordofan concerning the social significance of livestock applies equally to the Kababish. See I. Cunnison, "The Social Role of Cattle," *Sudan Journ. of Vet. Sci. and Animal Husb.*, I, No. 1, 1960.

II

Most of the pastoral Kababish inhabit the arid belt in northern Kordofan which lies roughly between latitudes 14° and 16° North, and longitudes 21° and 32° East. This area, approximately 48,000 square miles in extent, is administered by Dar Kababish Rural Council with its headquarters at Sodiri. A convenient territorial distinction (but one having no administrative significance) is sometimes made between western and eastern Dar Kababish lying on either side of the great Wadi al Milk. Sharing this area with the Kababish are a number of smaller groups, some pastoral nomads (e.g. Kawahla and Hawawir) and some sedentary cultivators (e.g. Kaja and Northern Nuba). The pastoral nomads number about 113,000 of whom the Kababish alone are about 70,000. The total number of cultivators is about 22,000, and they are scattered in small pockets of a few thousand each mainly in the southern portion of Dar Kababish.

Although by far the greater proportion of the Kababish have their dry season watering centers (*madamir,* sing. *damar*) within the Dar Kababish Rural Council Area, there are considerable numbers who spend the same season at watering centers outside it—to the west, in northern Darfur; to the north-west, in some of the oases in the South Libyan Desert; and to the north-east, along the lower reaches of the Wadi al Milk in Northern Province. Thus when a Kabbashi speaks of Dar Kababish he usually refers to a region larger than that of the Dar Kababish Rural Council Area.

Dar Kababish is a semi-desert region. Although deep shifting sand is not very common, most of the area is covered by loose sand. Bare rocky hills and patches of hard barren ground are also found. Much of the southern portion of the region is cut by innumerable watercourses that are flooded for brief periods during the rainy season. Evidence of erosion is most noticeable in areas with permanently settled cultivators who also keep a few animals.

Mean annual rainfall in the southern portion of Dar Kababish is around 200 mm., and in the northern portion about half this figure. Rainfall is normally confined to the three months July, August, and September. It is erratic in its incidence and intensity, especially in the north.

Thorn-trees and bushes (mainly Acacias) abound along the water-courses. Perennial tussock grasses are a common form of vegetation, especially in the vast sandy wastes of the north, and there are also considerable varieties of annual herbs and grasses. Both trees and bushes, wherever found, tend to be stunted.

The Kababish area is not therefore distinguished by an abundance of natural resources. The soil is poor, and both grazing and water are limited. Given that Kababish economy is geared to the main-tenance and increase of herds, the problem facing them is how to organize the use of natural resources at their disposal to achieve this purpose. It is worth emphasizing that Kababish economy is not strictly a subsistence one, since they export annually large numbers of animals to the outside world.[7] And this they are able to do not as the result of a mechanical adaptation to their natural environment—since they could conceivably confine themselves to certain selected places and eke out a bare substance by cultivation—but by choos-ing to make methodical use of scarce resources for the maintenance of livestock.

The Kababish keep camels, sheep, goats, cattle, donkeys, horses, dogs and chickens. Of these, camels, sheep, and goats are by far the most numerous. Horses and chickens are not very common. Cattle are found mainly in the south; donkeys and dogs everywhere.

The respective advantages of keeping camels, sheep, and goats (the major categories of livestock) are clearly distinguished by the Kababish, most of whom try to herd all three varieties. All three, of course, can be sold to obtain cash, although the market for sheep is easily the most secure. Compared with camels both sheep and goats are more prolific, the gestation period for camels being twelve months compared with six months for sheep and goats. Goats are good milkers, and because they are generally kept near the house-hold, provide a basic supply of milk for household consumption.

[7] Animal statistics on this subject are hard to come by, but some idea of the magnitude of Kababish camel exports alone may be gained by a considera-tion of the following facts: until the recent official attempts to regularize the camel trade, the Sudan exported camels to the U.A.R. to an average annual value of about £S.1,000,000. (See *Annual Foreign Trade Reports for 1952–61*, Department of Statistics, Sudan Government.) An official of the Ministry of Commerce estimated that of this total the proportion exported by Kordofan Province alone was about 40 percent. And in Kordofan Province by far the largest group of camel exporters are the Kababish.

In addition they are the readiest and cheapest source of meat on the infrequent occasions when it is eaten. Both camel- and goat-hair are said to be especially suitable for weaving into tents and rugs. But the really indispensable use of camels is of course in transport.

From the point of view of herding, goats (when they are kept separate from sheep) require least attention. They are generally driven out to pasture before sunrise, and left to graze alone, or with perhaps a child in attendance. By sunset they normally return on their own. Herding sheep is the most difficult in that it requires constant vigilance by day and by night. A considerable portion of the flock may wander off at night, especially if the animals are hungry, and become liable to attack by wild animals. During the breeding season the shepherd has to assist most rams individually to cover the fat-tailed ewes. Lambing also demands the shepherd's help and attention, and during the lambing season supplementary labor may well be required. Herding camels, in comparison, is much less exacting if sometimes more strenuous. While they are grazing, camels are much more dispersed and move more rapidly than any other livestock. When camels get lost, the search usually involves lengthy and tiring journeys. They are also more easily stolen by strangers than either sheep or goats.

The size of herds varies considerably. Technically the herd is a group of animals having its own arrangements for breeding, grazing and watering, usually in the care of two or three herders. The chief herder knows the characteristics, life history, and ancestry of each animal in his herd. For camels the maximum number in a single herd is about 150, and for sheep about 200. Goats, when they are not herded together with sheep, rarely exceed a couple of dozen to a flock.

In their ability to endure thirst, camels are of course proverbial. In the hot, dry season Kababish camels are watered about once every nine days; in the winter they need not be watered for several months. Sheep, on the other hand, are watered about once every four days in the hot, dry season, and much less frequently in the winter. Goats can survive without water for longer periods than sheep, but they are normally watered as frequently as the latter, and usually at the same time. Watering in the hot, dry season is hard work in which the normal herders must be assisted by other members of the household (including women) because the water is drawn by hand from wells.[8] In the rainy season it is much easier, and can be done by the normal herders alone as the water is available in open pools.

From the point of view of grazing, goats are least selective (they browse as well as graze), and sheep most selective (they graze only). The advantage of camels in this respect is clearly appreciated by the Kababish: because they are less selective in grazing, they can exploit a given area more efficiently than sheep, but because they are most mobile and most resilient to thirst, they can range much farther from any given water supply, and thus never need to graze a confined area bare.

The availability of water and grazing, which is so crucial in the maintenance of livestock, is subject to seasonal variations in Dar Kababish. There are three main seasons in the year: *khareef* (cool, wet season); *shita* (cold, dry season); and *saif* (hot, dry season). In *saif*, when the animals require water most frequently, the water supply is confined to certain well centers, and consequently the areas available for grazing in Dar Kababish are restricted. In *khareef*, when animals require water less frequently, the water supply is widely scattered in the form of rain pools and consequently the area available for grazing is extensive. In *shita*, when animals can do without water for considerable periods, limitation to the grazing area available is imposed not by the scarcity of water as such, but by the number of human beings accompanying them who can survive on milk as a substitute.

The problem for the Kababish under these circumstances is to try to keep the maximum number of animals under *saif* conditions in order to utilize *khareef* and *shita* potentialities efficiently. They do this by adopting separate migratory cycles for their main herds and their households—with the former moving over greater stretches of territory than the latter. The main herds, accompanied only by a few herders, have greater mobility. They can thus lighten the pressure on the restricted *saif* grazing grounds by going away early and coming back late; and they can extend the pastures available to them during late *saif* by going south to the early rains grazing in central Kordofan and Darfur, and during *shita* by going north to

[8] There is a permanent lake in the extreme south-east corner of Dar Kababish used mainly by the Kawahla, but also by the Kababish. In addition, there are five government operated bore-wells in the Rural Council Area used by the Kababish.

the desert winter pastures of Northern Province, Darfur, and the Chad Republic. The households, in turn, remain at the well centers during *saif* to provide the maximum labor when it is needed. During *khareef* they can move a relatively short distance away to the easier sources of water and grazing, thus giving the *saif* pastures a complete rest. And during mid-*khareef* they are able to meet up again with the main herds at a time and place that is advantageous to both.

In the next section I shall give a more detailed account of the seasonal migration of the Kababish which I have here outlined.

III

Toward the close of the hot, dry season in Dar Kababish, but when the rains have fallen in central Kordofan and Darfur (about May), herds of camels and sheep are driven south or south-west to take advantage of the earlier pastures there. This exodus greatly eases the laborious work of watering animals from the wells for the households that remain behind at the *madamir,* and relieves the pressure on *damar* pastures. This southward movement of the main herds is known as *shogara.*

The households are eager to move as soon as the downpours begin in Dar Kababish (about the beginning of July). The urgency in getting away from the *damar* is dictated initially not so much by the need for fresh pastures as by the desire for easy watering which the numerous rain pools afford. The hot, dry season is the most exhausting and monotonous period of the year, and in many places the water level in the wells sinks uncomfortably low toward the end of this period.

The movement of the households at the start of the rainy season is roughly in a westerly direction. The rule is that in one's migration one should skirt the *damar* lying ahead by a reasonable distance in order not to spoil it for those who usually return there. This rule is generally observed during the outward phase of the migration for the simple reason that there is little point in going through an area that has been intensively grazed throughout the long, dry season. But on the return journey, and especially in bad years, herds are sometimes driven through the *damar* grazing around a watering point at which their owners do not normally settle. However, since neither the watering point nor the grazing area around it is owned by sections of the tribe, complaints about breaking of the above rule amount to the charge of willful lack of consideration rather than that of any infringement of legal rights.

The outward movement of the households is fairly rapid. At this stage the families are mainly accompanied by flocks of goats, and sometimes by small numbers of sheep and camels which have not, for one reason or another, been sent south. Information is always obtained, before each move, about the state of water and grazing ahead. The normal practice, on the day camp is struck, is for the animals to be sent ahead early in the morning with the households following on later. The households then overtake the animals on the way and establish themselves at the new site before the latter arrive at sunset. Distances between sites at this stage vary normally between a few hours and a whole day by camel (baggage camels usually travel at between three to four miles an hour). This outward migration is known as *nashugh*.

By about the middle of the rainy season (August–September) the herds from the south return and meet up with the households in the *khareef* pastures. (News always travels quickly in Dar Kababish; both households and herders make continuous inquiries on their way to enable them to locate one another.) Hitherto the problem of finding suitable grazing and water has not been very pressing. Especially if the rainfall is plentiful, there has been a sense of abundance which has allowed the households to ignore all but the very best places. But with the sudden arrival of large numbers of animals, and the rainy season already half over, the choice of where to move has to be more carefully made. As already mentioned, neither watering points nor grazing grounds are individually or sectionally owned. Even prior occupation gives no exclusive rights of usufruct. Herds of different owners may and do frequently mingle at the rain pools and on the grazing grounds. There is, however, the courtesy custom of not allowing one's herd to stray too near someone else's tent.

Herds and households at this stage try to stay together for as long as they possibly can. The need for rapid and extensive moves on the part of the herds does not normally arise yet. This is the period when the milk yield is highest, so the households have convenient access to the surplus milk which is either drunk or made into clarified butter. In turn, women from the households can contribute toward the extra labor-requirement involved in lambing, milking, and separating the lambs from their mothers. And owners, who do not usually accompany their main herds, can examine the condition of their animals and discuss herding problems with their herders.

Large groups begin to congregate near the bigger pools, for whom generally speaking longer periods of stay are now possible. But many households make their way to the numerous smaller pools scattered about, thus making it necessary to move rather more frequently as one after another of them gets used up. The choice between frequenting the smaller or larger pools (which is also, on another level, the choice between occupying the more arid North or the less arid South) involves taking into account a number of considerations: the larger pool, while giving the assurance of a greater and more prolonged supply of water, and enabling the maintenance of direct contacts with a wider range of friends and relatives, is also more quickly fouled, results in more rapid overgrazing, increases the risk of spread of animal diseases, and is the scene of more quarrels and thefts. Muddy or foul water, incidentally, seems to worry the animals (and especially camels) more than the humans. As the water in the larger pools gets steadily more dirty and depleted, the households that insist on staying have to reconcile themselves to sending most of their animals to drink from other, more satisfactory, sources of water. They are thus separated from their herds sooner, and by greater distances, than those who are willing or able to move frequently with their animals from one place to another.

Many of the large pools used by the Kababish during the rainy season are located in north-east Darfur Province, and this increases the incidence of theft and the possibilities of conflict with such Darfurian tribes as the Meidob, Zeyadia and Berti.

When the rains are over (September–October), the households prepare to make their way back slowly to the *madamir,* and the herds (mainly camels but also sheep) move off further north west. If the year has been a good one, the camels go far out into the real desert to graze on the succulent grasses and herbs that grow there in the winter. (This vegetation, as well as the area in which it is grazed, are referred to as *jizu.*) The period of sustained or intermittent contact between these herds and the households is now over until well into the next hot, dry season. The return journey to the *damar* is known as *mota.*

Arrival at the *damar* is delayed by the households for as long as they possibly can. More households than ever now collect round the larger pools, some of which have only been completely filled up since the households passed by them during the outward phase of the migration. They stay at these pools for longer periods, sometimes weeks at a stretch. The marked reluctance to get back to the *damar* is determined as much by the desire to put off the arduous but inevitable routine of life during the hot, dry season as it is by the wish to preserve *damar* grazing.

It is when all the water in rain pools is used up that the households hasten back to the *damar*. The last part of the journey usually takes several days, with only overnight pauses. At the *damar* those that depend on impermanent wells (and these are the majority) must redig and reline them—normally several times in the course of the hot, dry season. These wells are owned, sometimes several wells to one household and sometimes one well to several households, depending on the depth of the well and the amount of water in it in relation to the available manpower and water requirement of the household. Where the water is not very plentiful several well owners may combine their individual wells to form a watering unit for their animals, taking it in turn to use all the wells together on a given day. The same procedure is adopted where several households own a single well in common.

In the few places where permanent brick-lined wells are located water is always plentiful. Although these deep wells belong to the households that first dug them (they are lined and maintained at the expense of the Rural Council), many others are allowed to make use of them with the consent of the traditional owners.

In good years the camels return from the desert grazing grounds as late as March; in bad years they return several months earlier. For the herds to return to the *madamir* means that they are now watered at them. They will therefore be within a reasonable distance from the *damar* watering point. But this may mean as much as a four-day journey away for camels, and a two-day journey away for sheep.

The general pattern of transhumance described above is subject to certain variations. Thus very few of the eastern Kababish go as far as Darfur Province, their rainy season movements are normally less extensive and their direction often south-westerly. They have fewer camels and more cattle than the western Kababish. In the northern more arid portion of west Dar Kababish the details of rainy season routes vary more from year to year, and comparatively fewer herds go very far south on the *shogara* move, although they usually stay longer in the desert pastures which lie near them. The north is believed to be healthier for sheep and camels than the south. In the relatively more abundant south-west, where the Nazir's group has its *damar,* an informal attempt is made at regulating the main grazing grounds with this group having a broad priority with respect to rain pools and pastures.

Sometimes the households and their main herds (especially camels) are attached to separate *madamir.* For example in the southwest many households watering at the deep wells in Hamrat al-Shaikh have their main herds watered at the bore well in Um Sunta about fifty miles west. Because although water from the Hamra wells is free and from the bore well it is not, if one has exceptionally large herds it is cheaper to pay for the water at the bore well than to pay for the hire of several people to draw the water from the deep Hamra wells on a daily basis. Watering at the bore well is of course quicker and less laborious than watering at the deep Hamra wells. On the other hand it suffers from the disadvantage that a mechanical breakdown at the pump may spell disaster, as happened some years ago.

It may also happen that households wishing for one reason or another to spend the hot, dry season at one of the less peripheral centers are unable to muster enough hands from within the family and unwilling or unable to hire people for the job of watering all their animals there. In such cases they will keep their herds during the hot, dry season at centers where watering is easier, and where preferably there are relatives who are able and willing to help in the watering.

In addition to the transhumance cycle there is another kind of movement in Dar Kababish which may be called migration proper. This occurs mainly, but not only, in bad years and involves the shifting of households from one *damar* to another. Sometimes the usual transhumance cycle is completed, with the household returning to its old *damar,* before the forced march to the new and more attractive *damar* is undertaken. But usually the transhumance route is itself adjusted to end up at the new *damar* (see table p. 156).

One of the main factors underlying this kind of movement is of course inadequate rainfall which results in poor *damar* pastures and scanty water supply in certain areas. But the migration is never haphazard. People normally move to one of a limited number of centers with which they are familiar. The actual choice of where to move is also to some extent determined by kinship links, with households moving to areas where relatives who will be helpful are already established.

The comparatively easy conditions in the south-west means a proportionately smaller amount of migration into and out of this area. Here the existence of deep, lined wells (in which there are personal rights of a kind) exerts a pull on households traditionally based here to return to their *madamir* after the rainy season. But for those who have temporarily come down from the north, the attractions in their traditional area still exist, if only because they

SAIF	KHAREEF	DARAD	SHITA
HOT DRY	COOL WET	WARM DRY	COLD DRY
February-June	July-September	October	November-January
HOUSEHOLDS			
At dry season well centers. Redigging and relining of wells. Heavy work watering main herds.	Move to west or north-west after first showers. Contact with main herds in mid-khareef. Fairly rapid movement between rain pools.	Separation from main herds. Exploitation of larger rain pools with extended stops.	Digging of shallow water holes. Movement back to dry-season well centers (speed depending on intensity of khareef rainfall). Move to different dry-season well centers if khareef rainfall has been poor.
MAIN HERDS			
Return from north-west in early summer to dry-season well centers. Circulating in dry-season pastures around well centers. Move to south or south-west in late summer to exploit early pastures in central Kordofan and Darfur. (Camel herds farther than sheep flocks.)	Rapid move north to exploit khareef pastures in Dar Kababish. Contact with households.	Separation from households. Slow move north-west.	Move farther north-west to exploit winter grazing in desert. (Camel herds farther than sheep flocks.)

know the pastures and rain pools of the north better. And in good years watering is easier from the short wells of the north, and animals are less exposed to contagious diseases there than in the south.

IV

In this paper I have tried to show that the exploitation of their environment by the Kababish is based on rational aims and calculations. I have described, in particular, the separate nomadic cycles of main herds and households by which they seek to achieve their basic economic objectives as efficiently as they are able.

Seen in this light it may in theory be possible to suggest how this resource-use can be made more efficient—although I have not tried to do this here. But to make sweeping generalizations about the alleged primitiveness of pastoral nomad economy as such, or the supposed economic advantage of settling nomads everywhere, does not contribute to clear thinking. In the first place it is necessary to specify whether one is referring to low level of consumption or low rate of production or high degree of wastage of natural resources or some other undesirable feature of the local economy. It may then be possible to calculate, given the natural resources of the region, the capital that can be economically invested in it, and the population to be supported, how these features can best be improved. Whether the answer to this problem lies in the improvement of pastoralism, or the establishment of agriculture or some other new industry, or perhaps in a combination of some or all of these, will depend on various considerations.[9]

In any case, it is quite false to say, as one writer has done, that in the Sudan "taken together, overpopulation of grazing lands and underexploitation of potentially cultivable land, point logically to the necessity of settling nomad populations on cultivable soil."[10] Overpopulation is a relative concept, and may call for greater capital investment rather than an absolute reduction in human numbers.

[9] For a clear and useful preliminary discussion of this topic in reference to the Sudan, see F. Barth, I. Cunnison, and N. Dyson-Hudson, "The Settlement of Nomads as a Development Policy" (in Arabic), *Sudan Society,* No. 2, 1963.

[10] J. Randell, op. cit.

And if the investment required to raise by a given proportion the output of pastoral nomads is less than that required to settle them and enable them to maintain a comparable level of output as culti- vators, the supposed economic necessity for settlement is seen to be spurious. But a full discussion of this problem lies beyond the scope of this paper.

What I want to emphasize here is that it seems to me a mistake to regard a system of resource-use such as I have described, as essentially primitive merely because the Kababish are pastoral nomads. Since I take the term "pastoralism" to mean that the economy is based on the rearing of livestock, and the term "nomad- ism" to mean that the system of resource-use involves the seasonal movement of men and animals, I would maintain that neither pastoralism nor nomadism is necessarily inconsistent with economic progress. As such it is a little difficult to understand the logic that underlies a statement such as the following:

"The course which does not recommend itself either from the view-point of the country as a whole or in view of the long-term interests of nomadic populations themselves is the creation of an artificial environment in which nomadism becomes a more attractive way of life than it is at present. Such measures retard economic, cultural and social progress and have no place in the policy of a country firmly committed to the path of modern civilization."[11]

Surely the intelligent—and humane—policy for a country "firmly committed to the path of modern civilization" is to make the pursuit of rational and productive activities by its inhabitants more at- tractive as a way of life wherever possible and not less so?

[11] J. Randell, op. cit.

HAROLD K. SCHNEIDER

9. The Subsistence Role of Cattle Among the Pakot and in East Africa[1]

One of the most notable characteristics of East African people is the behavior relating to cattle, which Herskovits has labeled the cattle-complex (1926). As he described it, the cattle-complex consists of a strong attachment to cattle, which leads to their use in areas of life to which they are foreign among other people who possess many cattle. This attachment is frequently shown in affection for and identification with these animals and dislike of killing them (ibid:256ff) except in rituals. They are associated almost universally with birth, death, and marriage ceremonies, are the chief form of wealth, the most prominent measure of power, prestige, and status, and the proper animals for feasts or ceremonies. Sex taboos are present in their handling, women being forbidden to have much to do with them, and there are special customs and taboos relating to their milk (ibid:650, 653). In Herskovits' words, ". . . it is the cattle that have become the dominant element in the cultures of these people" (ibid:653). He adds that cattle "gather about them" other cultural elements such as birth, death, marriage, and other events in such a way that the complex can be recognized wherever it exists (ibid:653). With some slight revisions and qualifications from one culture to another, this statement still holds good for East African pastoral people.

SOURCE: "The Subsistence Role of Cattle Among the Pakot and in East Africa," *American Anthropologist*, Vol. 59, No. 2, April 1957, pp. 278–300. Reprinted by permission of the author and publisher.

[1] This paper represents a revision and condensation of material presented in the writer's doctoral dissertation (1953), which contains a much fuller account of Pakot culture. Study of the Pakot was carried out during 1951–52, mainly in the Ortum area of West Suk District, Kenya, and was made possible through grants under the Fulbright Act, and from the Social Science Research Council and the Program of African Studies of Northwestern University. Thanks are due M. J. Herskovits, A. P. Merriam, R. A. Lystad, and C. W. Rowe for their valuable comments and criticisms of this paper in the various stages of its preparation. This does not indicate their endorsement of it; responsibility for its content rests with the author alone.

The cattle-complex is sometimes summarized as being chiefly an extensive religious or ritual use of cattle. Our summation of Herskovits' position shows clearly that while ritual use (but not specifically religious ritual) is recognized, the essential element of the complex is not this, but rather a kind of identification with cattle which leads to their association with ritual (and presumably religion) as well as many other things.

The cattle-complex concept has become widely used in anthropology (although the term is seldom used by British scholars), but along with the use the impression has been intentionally or unintentionally conveyed that cattle are exploited only partially for subsistence. Those who have written about East African people in comparatively recent times have all drawn different pictures of the economic role of cattle. Some, whom we will discuss, recognize great subsistence utility; others minimize it (see for example: Herskovits 1952; Huntingford 1950, 1953; Evans-Pritchard 1953; Kenya Land Commission 1934). The overall impression given by these latter is that milk production is important to subsistence but other possible subsistence functions of cattle (notably meat production and exchange for subsistence) are often not.

The purpose of this paper is, first, to attempt to show that cattle are more extensively exploited in the subsistence economy of the Pakot of Kenya than this interpretation of the cattle-complex indicates. Secondly, it will be postulated, by reference to available data, that more extensive subsistence use of cattle than is usually acknowledged is characteristic in general of East African cultures and a feature accompanying the cattle-complex.

PAKOT STOCK

The people with whom this paper is concerned are the Pakot or Suk[2] of West Suk District (west central Kenya), who number about 40,000. Two other groups, the so-called East and Kara Suk, are little known, fewer in number, and apparently similar in culture to the West Suk. The Pakot are members of the Nandi-speaking group

[2] Pakot is the plural form of the name these people apply to themselves. Suk is a word of foreign origin and generally unknown to them. To avoid unnecessary complexity, the plural will be used throughout the paper, whether the context calls for it or for the singular (Pachon).

of tribes (though heavily acculturated with Karamojong and Tur-kana) which, with the Masai, represent the southernmost branch of the Nilotic peoples, all of whom are predominantly pastoral. In addition to herding, Pakot derive subsistence from cultivation of sorghum and eleusine by means of slash and burn rain-weather farming, supplemented by some irrigation. Most Pakot seem unable to grow enough food to support themselves by agriculture alone in their often inhospitable habitat. Those who raise no crops seem unable (and sometimes unwilling) to subsist on the produce of their stock, depending on grain to supplement their diet.

A stock census, conducted in 1952 by a government livestock officer using rigorous procedures, showed that the Pakot have about 112,000 head of cattle (a reduction, he felt, from a possible total of 120,000 head before a drought of that year), 113,000 goats, and 37,000 sheep. The distribution of stock varies with habitat and circumstances. Generally speaking, people living in the plains, where agriculture is difficult and the land is suitable for stock, have larger numbers of cattle per adult man[3] than those living in and near the mountains. Some of the latter may be almost without cattle, although they usually possess numerous sheep and goats. An analysis of the stock census figures showed an average of from 10 to 20 head of cattle per adult man in the main pastoral areas, and an average of from 2 to 5 head in the more heavily agricultural areas.

The average number of sheep per adult man is only 3.4, although one district has a disproportionately high number; the average of goats is about 10.5, ranging from two to ten in the pastoral areas, and from fifteen to twenty-five in the agricultural areas (with the exception of one cattle-rich area which has an average of 13, and one agricultural area with an average of only 4).

Thus, averages of cattle tend to be higher in the plains and those of goats (using the latter term as Pakot sometimes do, to mean both goats and sheep) higher in agricultural areas.

An extensive system of terms denoting age, sex, and other charac-teristics is applied to stock (e.g., "calf beginning to take grass" *puseion*-sing.; *puselin*-pl.), those applied to cattle being somewhat more complex than for goats. Three types of stock are recognized: females, males, and castrated. In discussion of stock, the three types

---

[3] The size of herds is reckoned in terms of adult men, because the only reliable population figures pertain to them. Actually, they are the controllers of the herds even though they are technically not the owners of all stock.

must be carefully separated since they have particular roles in the economy and other aspects of culture. Cattle and goats are branded by clipping the ears, the brands indicating clan affiliation of the possessor rather than the individual owner.

Families are grouped into neighborhoods with more or less distinct boundaries, and cooperate as associations. Individual homes are scattered over the neighborhood on ridges (except in some areas in the plains where the equivalent to a neighborhood is a large compound), the only concentrations being an occasional grouping of two or three homesteads. The tendency of Pakot men is to try to stay in the same neighborhood during the year, but disease and drought force them to seek better pastures in most years. Control of the family herd is chiefly in the hands of the head of the family, even though his wife and sons may have some rights to certain of the animals. The wife and sons have much to say about how animals are used, and cases of women managing the herds after the death of the husband are not unknown. Stock are penned in the homestead at night and let out to graze in the daylight hours, during which time they are guarded by men, women, or children.

Although Pakot practices vary somewhat from those in other areas of East Africa, the essential features of the cattle-complex, as defined above, can be seen. Crops, goats, and camels, in the few instances where these occur, are not considered esthetically pleasing (*pachigh*), but the hide colors of cattle are and the horns may be. One type of animal, the *kamar,* which must be a steer, is considered to be altogether beautiful. To understand this distinction, we must realize that Pakot customarily separate the useful (*karam*) from the esthetically pleasing in any object (vide Schneider 1956). The hide colors and some horns are conceptually separated from the other aspects of cattle. This is not true of the kamar steer, which is wholly beautiful. It is with this animal that the greatest identification seems to be made. It is often decorated with bells, songs are composed about it, and it is "initiated" through a sacrificial feast similar to the one given for a young man entering adulthood. A man who owns a kamar is obligated to protect it with his life.

Other cattle are less highly esteemed than these special steers, though they may still figure in songs, folktales, and affection if they are exceptionally good animals. Even though he has no kamar, a man has a favorite steer whose name he takes as his own. There is sometimes reluctance to kill one's own steers when slaughter is required, leading to exchange arrangements that enable the use of a strange animal. Emotional attachment to cattle should not be exaggerated, though the Pakot do not display the complete lack of such feeling reported by Evans-Pritchard for the Nuer (1953:181).

Wealth is reckoned in terms of cattle, goats, and sometimes irrigated land. Cattle are by far the most valuable of goods (except for camels owned by a few Pakot in the east); the exchange rate between a steer and goat, the next most valuable thing, is about ten or fifteen to one. Few men can be considered wealthy in the Pakot view, as is seen in one informant's statement that a man with a hundred head of cattle or more is rich, one with ten is poor, and a man with no cattle is "dead." The census figures show the highest average for any area to be about 20 head. Though some men in this area must have more than 20 head, probably few have the 100 or more that would classify them as "rich."

A wealthy man is given a certain amount of deference but it is not very apparent to a non-Pakot, since they are egalitarian in philosophy and resent showing excessive deference. A wealthy man may be addressed as *echotion* and given special consideration when he attends a feast or visits a home. Government among Pakot is amorphous and lacking in clear-cut political roles; while a rich man may be accorded more attention in meetings, he does not seem to gain any dominance because of his wealth. In fact, there does not seem to be any significant correlation between wealth and political power. The culture heroes are honored more for their prowess and cunning in raiding neighboring tribes for cattle than for their wealth, and community leaders seem to be singled out largely because of their knowledge and ability or for other such reasons. Still, cattle wealth is undeniably a source of prestige and some status.

In ritual and religious life, steers are ever present. Cows and bulls are not used for such purposes, but castrated goats may act as surrogates for steers when the latter are unavailable. The principal ritual act, in the sense that it is most frequent, best attended, and most esteemed, is one that goes under various names but which we may call *"sapana-like"* after the most elaborate form, *sapana* (vide Peristiany 1951). In this ceremony a half-circle (*kerket*) is formed with the open end facing Mt. Matelo, the highest mountain in the land. (The reason for this was not discovered, though Peristiany [1951:192] said that the western plains people looked upon it as the home of the rain god, Ilat.) The initiated men are seated in the circle in order of age-set precedence, with the oldest set at the closed end and the others ranged in order down the sides. A steer is slaughtered and cut up in a prescribed fashion without removing the hide; the meat is not allowed to touch the ground, but is placed on leaves. The feast is marked by divination of the entrails, elaborate and regular distribution of the meat, and prayers, led by the elders, which relate to the chief purpose of the feast (though those in attendance may extemporaneously request prayers relating to private matters of importance to them). The women attend, but must sit by themselves away from the half-circle and are given only the head of the slain beast.

The most elaborate form of this feast, sapana, is one in which a young man, who has usually been circumcised years before, is initiated into adulthood. There is dancing and general gayety at the feast, and the guests bring milk as their share of the proceedings; the steer is the offering of the initiate's father. Milk is not consumed at the other feasts of this type—in fact it is prohibited—and there may not be dancing. In short, although the basic ritual is the same in all these feasts, the form is not as elaborate as sapana.

Nine occasions for holding the sapana-like feasts were discovered, each having its own name:

Eghpadia: signifying the release from isolation and restoration to ritual cleanliness of a warrior made ritually impure by having killed an enemy in battle.

Mis: meeting between Pakot and members of a nearby neighborhood of a neighboring tribe, signifying the establishment of peaceful relations between them.

Kinta: funeral feast in honor of a man who has recently died, at which matters relating to his estate are decided.

Kikatat: to pray for a member of the community who is seriously ill.

Kiralat: to curse a criminal or deviant by sorcery.

Achula: given by a man convicted of adultery as part of the fine, and to signify the settlement of the case and encourage re-establishment of good relations between the conflicting groups.

Sitat: given by a man convicted of some "misdemeanor" as a sort of fine.

Tatapa: given by a member of a neighborhood to discuss strategy in preparation for a legal contest.

Kerket: a feast, named after the ceremonial half-circle, given by a member of a neighborhood who requests the prayers and good will of his neighbors.

In addition to these feasts, modeled on sapana, steers are ritually employed in varying ways: at the closing ceremony of the circumcision rites, to purify children who are born in abnormal ways, as media for ordeals, and in other similar situations. It should be noted that goats also figure in rituals; they are used most often for the purification of ritually unclean persons, a role which is almost exclusive to them. These uses of cattle seem far less frequent than the sapana-like feasts.

It is logically impossible to say that the majority of cattle are butchered under ritual conditions, since only steers are normally so used and not all of those. However, a very large proportion are killed in this fashion.

Certain miscellaneous customs illustrate the pervasive influence of cattle. The food of stock has certain sacred qualities for ritual purification, although it is the grass from the goats' stomachs that is most often used in this way. Milk and ritual meat are highly esteemed foods having sacred qualities that result in a taboo against mixing them in the stomach by eating them on the same day; it is believed that to do so will cause the offender's cows to dry up. At the wedding ceremony, the bride is anointed with milk, honey, and manure.

Referring back to the cattle-complex formulation, it is clear that among the Pakot cattle have a place that conforms to the requirements of the complex. They are often affectionately regarded or identified with, are a means to prestige and status, and are the chief animals employed in special feasts and ceremonies. Various taboos surround milk, and there are certain sacred qualities associated with milk and ritual meat. There is no prohibition against women having anything to do with cattle, as is true in some East African cultures. Neither is there a prohibition against killing any but cows, but we see that most steers are killed in rituals. Herskovits emphasized the role of cattle in birth, death, and marriage ceremonies. Among the Pakot they have no special role at birth, except when it is abnormal, and death ceremonies fall within the category of sapana-like feasts. Unlike some other East African people, there is no wholesale slaughter of cattle at funerals; only the usual sacrificial animal is killed. Cattle figure most prominently in marriage, being the chief items of the bridewealth.

THE SUBSISTENCE USE OF STOCK

It is clear that the Pakot possess the cattle-complex as traditionally described. In discussing it, an attempt was made to avoid any mention of subsistence that might lead to digression from the main point. As we propose to show here, the nonsubsistence uses of cattle cannot always be clearly separated from subsistence, and many of the functions of cattle which seem to have no clear connection with subsistence, such as their use in the sapana-like feasts, are in fact inseparable from it. Put in another way, while some activities relating to cattle may be interpreted as having either a subsistence or nonsubsistence function, some have both. Our discussion of subsistence may then proceed, first, to uses in exchange; second, to consumption; and finally, to various other considerations which support some of the interpretations that will be made.

EXCHANGE

Colson (1955:77) has recently decried the emphasis on the "mystical and ritual value" of stock in East Africa, saying that they have an equal or more important role in building social ties by securing rights in persons. When an animal is given to another person for his use, certain reciprocal obligations are then established with the receiver. We can accept Colson's position and expand it by adding that cattle and goats are important capital goods among Pakot. In addition to establishing social ties, they are used in exchange for many things that are valuable economically and in other ways.

Goats and sheep are frequently used as media of exchange in trade and as valued items in gift exchange. Although British money is now widely used in Pakotland, goats are still used extensively to buy iron goods from itinerant blacksmiths, and to purchase grain. They may also be used to pay specialists for pottery and for the manufacture of headdresses. Trade goods are limited (or were up to very recent times), so it is not possible to multiply examples of this kind. Goats are also used in gift exchange, and serve to maintain good relations between lineage members, best friends, and members of a special trading partnership called *tilia,* which is discussed below, from whom various kinds of subsistence support are expected. Beyond these roles, they usually function as adjuncts to cattle, e.g., in bridewealth, and so will be mentioned again later. The position of goats in the subsistence economy seems to be based upon the fact that they are a "smaller denomination of currency" and can be exploited to acquire things which are not equivalent in value to a steer or cow. Gulliver (1951:16) has objected to the cattle-complex concept because it makes no mention of goats and sheep. He feels that among the Turkana it is a "stock-complex." While goats do not have the special role that cattle have in Pakot culture, they are of considerable importance in the subsistence economy, and this may be the point which Gulliver wished to make.

The three kinds of cattle—bulls, cows, and steers—have different roles in the subsistence economy. Steers are used as media of exchange, meat producers, and sacrificial animals. The principal role of cows is as a form of productive capital through the bearing of calves and production of milk, but they are also used in one kind of trade, tilia.

One of the more important exchange situations, known as *kipukat,* is one in which a man uses a steer to acquire grain from another man who has a surplus. The animal is sold either on the hoof or already dressed, with the latter method apparently most frequent. Today kipukat has been broadened to include the sale of steers to licensed Somali traders in return for cash or goods. The cash is used to buy ground maize or such items as sugar, shoes made of old tires, and some luxuries, including beads and wire. Hides, which are obtained from animals that are killed or die outside the sapana-like feasts, are also sold to the Somalis; although many cattle are sold each year, hides seem to be the chief source of cash income. Hides are also used in the domestic economy for such things as bed covers, and therefore constitute one of the important subsistence items derived from cattle.

Another favored use of steers is in the special tilia exchange (vide also Peristiany 1951). The institution of tilia has counterparts throughout the East African area. In contrast to other places, the Pakot variety seems to have some special features. Tilia is not a mere loaning of cattle to protect capital by spreading the risk in case of raids or loss through disease. Nor is it purely a matter of obtaining rights in persons. It is a kind of partnership between a man who desires a cow and one who wishes to acquire a steer, and is usually initiated by the person desiring the steer. As a partner, he selects a trustworthy person, who is not a clansman, from some place outside his neighborhood (with some exceptions). The reason for excluding clansmen is that they are "obligated" to loan animals to each other, and tilia is therefore unnecessary between them. The initiator gives one of his cows for the steer; the cow is then taken to the receiver's home and kept by him. The steer is used for any purpose its recipient desires, and seems usually to be exploited to obtain grain or for a sacrificial feast. The receiver of the cow cannot kill it or further dispose of it, though he now has a right to all its milk and must return a certain number of its calves to the original owner. A tilia partnership assumes many of the characteristics of clan ties. The partners support each other in disputes, exchange small gifts such as goats, beer, and ornaments, and generally assume an intimate attitude toward each other (except when one tries to cheat the other, which must be frequent according to the number of court cases involving tilia partners). However, the relationship is somewhat asymmetrical because of the greater value of the cow, so that there is a heavier obligation on its holder to give gifts. The usual procedure is for the holder of the cow to be visited by its former possessor, at which time the calves or some gifts are given up. This practice might be interpreted either as an additional payment over and above the steer, or as a share of a "dividend" from the cow's production. Whatever the case, the continued payment emphasizes the strong pecuniary considerations involved in the contract.

Tilia may be varied with circumstances. People who have mostly goats practice it with them; and in situations where cattle are used, the relinquisher of the cow may receive grain or goats instead of a steer.

The advantages of the system are clear. A man who has to give up a steer for a feast or trade may soften the impact by trading part of his rights in a cow for someone else's steer, rights in the person he deals with, and some of the cow's future production. If all goes well, he can expect eventually to replenish his loss with some of the calves returned to him. If the trade is effected when a steer is not in demand for some immediate purpose, the chief advantage is that of spreading capital so that it will not all be lost in case of warfare or disease, but some of the other advantages also accrue. The advantage of spreading the risk is present in either case, but the predominant advantage varies with the situation. The advantage to the receiver of the cow is that he gets a piece of productive capital for nonproductive capital.

No doubt one of the latent functions of tilia is the cohesiveness that it adds to Pakot society, since it binds Pakot everywhere in a complex network of rights that are related to subsistence. However, it is not the sole means to this end; clans are not contiguous, and the clan ties cross-cut and tend to unite the various neighborhoods.

An important use of cows, then, is to secure rights in persons in whom there are no rights per se; steers are also used in this manner to secure obligations. Co-operation in such subsistence acts as house building, herding, cultivation (especially irrigation), and the borrowing of milk, grain, and other goods from neighbors, is dependent on the maintenance of good relations. In addition to the mutual sharing of beer, surplus goods, and labor, co-operative ties may best be perpetuated by offering a steer for a community feast, or by the distribution of the meat of cattle killed to secure grain or which die in nonritual ways. Status may be maintained by sharing beer, grain, etc., but the supreme act, expected of everyone on a fairly regular schedule, is the sharing of meat, especially by means of a sacrificial feast.

Another important exchange role of cows, steers, and goats is in connection with bridewealth. When a man desires a wife, he must convey to her father a previously agreed-upon number of cattle and goats; to some Pakot, these latter animals are an essential part of any complete bridewealth. Though livestock are the principal content of the bridewealth, in at least one case some irrigable land was part of the contract. We do not mean to imply that Pakot women are mere slaves when we say that one of the prominent functions of the bridewealth animals is to act as payment for a capital good. Romantic love has little place in the notions of Pakot men; improvement of economic position has a large place. The bride is referred to as a "cow," and the contract is compared with tilia. (However, it is not an exact analogy since this is a trade of cows as well as other stock for a "cow," while tilia is a trade of a cow for a steer.) The affines, who receive cows when the bridewealth is distributed among them, are expected to return some of the calves to the herd of the bride and bridegroom in the same manner as in tilia.

The bride is protected from extreme exploitation by certain sanctions, chief of which is the relinquishment of his claim on the bridewealth and an additional fine to the husband if his wife should die under any circumstances before her prime. Beyond that, the woman is in fact a kind of capital in that she performs most of the basic productive labors in a household. She not only must plant, tend, and harvest the crops (receiving some help from her husband with the very heavy work), but must make shoes, weave baskets, milk the cows, and even herd them when not busy with other things. She also bears children, who are economically valuable, the girls in housework and as future sources of bridewealth, and the boys as helpers in the management of the herd. The bridewealth has other functions, such as stabilizing the marriage, but is undeniably important from the economic point of view too. One verification lies in the fact that the father-in-law does not always willingly distribute the bridewealth to his clansmen, but tries to keep all of it for himself.

A different kind of relationship exists between clansmen than between nonclansmen. Clansmen are born to certain ties and obligations; they do not have to be created through such institutions as tilia. Clansmen are expected to loan goods to each other freely, and though a strict accounting seems to be kept, the relationship is not chiefly pecuniary and no attempt is made to profiteer. If a clansman asks for a cow, no steer is demanded in return for it. The fact that cattle brands denote clan affiliation rather than individual ownership, suggests this free borrowing of goods. However, the relationship is not without economic considerations, and reciprocation ceases between clansmen if one of them fails in his duties toward the other.

Lending and borrowing is also frequent between neighbors, but this does not seem to include the free loan of cattle. If a man desires a cow from a neighbor, he must institute tilia to get it. On the other hand, a man may have several best friends who are treated like clansmen. If they desire anything it must be given to them without immediate payment, but they must be willing to reciprocate.

In summary, there is a kind of continuum in exchange relations. Between strangers there is a strict pecuniary relationship; this aspect is less marked between neighbors and tilia partners, and is least so between clansmen and best friends.

Other exchange uses of cattle may be observed, chief of which is the transfer involved in legal action. Most fines are paid in stock, and there are obvious subsistence considerations in legal action. The plaintiff is eager to get the largest fine possible, and the defendant is equally eager to make it as small as possible. The value of the defendant's herd in supporting reciprocal obligations between clansmen, neighbors, and tilia leads persons in these categories to take his side. In a sense, loss to one man in the group is a loss to all. By the same token, persons who have interests in the plaintiff give him support, for his gain is also theirs.

We may summarize this discussion of the exchange role of cattle by emphasizing that they may be used as mediums of exchange to obtain grain and other goods, to secure rights in other persons, to maintain ties that have important subsistence elements, to acquire stock, and to secure brides, who are essential to the establishment of an operating economic unit. The types of exchange observed include outright trade and gift exchange, both of which have important subsistence motivations, whatever other ends they attain.

CONSUMPTION

One immediately apparent source of nourishment from cattle is always acknowledged by those who have written about East African people, whatever their stand may be on other facets of cattle use. This is the exploitation of cows for milk. All cows and goats are milked and the milk is consumed without ritual or other complications, except in the one instance of sapana, where it is used in a ritual setting. The milk is allocated by the mother of the family at each milking. Any surplus may be saved, since sour milk is considered to be as edible as fresh and indeed is sometimes preferred. Except among a few very rich families, not enough milk is produced to provide complete support. Even when a man possesses a very large herd, the loss of production during the dry season and when cows are freshening may so reduce milk supplies as to force him to seek other ways to satisfy hunger. Because of this, people customarily live on reduced rations during part of the year and resort to buying grain to supplement the diet. It is said that cows produce at maximum only about four months of the year. Furthermore, no one seems willing to live without grain, so some is demanded even when milk production is high.

Another important source of nourishment is the blood of cattle, though it is difficult to estimate just how much is used. A couple of quarts of blood may be drawn from a living animal and mixed with milk. It may also be drunk unmixed, as it always is at ceremonial feasts, where it is drained from the carcass before the meat is taken to the ceremonial semicircle. An animal that has been bled cannot again be bled until its wound has healed and its lost blood has regenerated. A good deal of blood is produced each year, but the amount is comparatively small and it is a luxury.

In addition to the seeming lack of appreciation of the exchange role of cattle, the most frequent misunderstanding of subsistence cattle use relates to their consumption. It may be useful to begin this account by referring to an analysis of the livestock census figures for 1952. The most significant revelation was the ratios of various kinds of cattle. The analysis was possible for only one of the eleven Pakot "locations" (the name given to the political subdivisions of the reserve created by the colonial government), but observation in other areas seemed to bear it out. As would be expected, the ratio of female to male stock in the calf stage is about one to one, but in the adult stage it varies from three to six cows to one steer in various subareas of the location, with the average being about four or five cows to a steer. This suggests quite clearly that most steers are slaughtered when they reach their prime, while cows are not killed because of their value as productive capital. The fact that there is even one steer to four or five cows suggests that use of steers in consumption is governed by the need to maintain some reserve, but otherwise they are fully utilized.

The slaughter and consumption of most steers in ritual settings raises some questions about the interpretation of their subsistence role, but this ritual context is not always necessary. Cattle may be killed or may die and be consumed simply to satisfy hunger, either by direct consumption or indirectly by using the meat to get grain.

When an animal dies, it is promptly consumed (although some parts may be dried and stored), unless it is affected by a disease which is communicable to humans. Only steers are used in rituals; old bulls and cows are disposed of unceremoniously. Sheep and goats may be used in rituals, such as purification rites, or as substitutes for cattle in the sapana-like feasts. But goats and sheep are most frequently slaughtered outright and consumed. (Exceptions are the nanny goats and ewes, which are not killed as long as they bear young or give milk.) Goats may be killed to feed the family or an honored visitor, and there is a general feeling that a man is obligated to kill a goat for a mother and child who are traveling alone. Goats are most easily bought by whites in the reserve.

Some of the confusion about the slaughter of cattle for food among Pakot and in East Africa seems to have stemmed from semantic difficulties. One is sometimes confronted with the statement that these herding peoples have a prohibition against killing "cows." There is no precise English equivalent for the generic singular of "cattle" so "cow" is used, but "cow" in this sense is not meant. The Pakot mean exactly what they say when they state that you can kill bulls and steers, but you must not kill cows (unless they have lost their usefulness). The frequent butchering of steers for ritual purposes shows that this prohibition does not extend to all cattle, and it is made even clearer by the fact that there are many occasions on which cattle are slaughtered for no ritual reason whatever.

Occasions for nonceremonial slaughter of cattle are as follows: *lapai,* which is a solemn meeting to discuss the fine to be levied on a man whose wife has died; at the session, one of his steers is killed and skinned and the bulk of the meat given to his affines as part of his fine, while portions are also taken by others who are present; *kotupak,* the slaughter of a steer for a gang of prepubertal boys by a member of the neighborhood upon whom they have prevailed and who, it is said, cannot refuse; *ngorola* and *karasa,* which are two kinds of occasions for slaughter to provide sustenance for persons who are desperately ill and need the strength meat will provide; *kipukat,* previously mentioned, is the slaughter or sale of a steer for the purpose of obtaining grain. Part of the meat is kept for home consumption and part is given to neighbors. Finally, there are rare cases of outright slaughter simply to get meat for the home. There is no name for this, and ideally it is condemned since the meat is not shared with neighbors. Pakot feel that the meat should be distributed in the neighborhood, preferably in a formal feast.

There is, then, no absolute repudiation of the slaughter of cattle, even if we allow ritual slaughter as an exception. Of these many instances of nonceremonial butchering, kipukat is probably the most frequent. If we add all the occasions for killing old cows and bulls and the eating of goats and sheep and cattle that die, it is apparent that the majority of animals are made available each year for consumption outside ritual.

However, it still seems to be true that most steers are killed for some ritual, and of these the sapana-like are most frequent. The statement that East African people eat their cattle only when they die or in rituals, seems to imply that ritual consumption is uneconomic and only distantly related to subsistence ends. This is true in some cases, but it does not seem to be generally true among the Pakot.

In discussing ritual consumption, it should be emphasized that all steers killed for these feasts are eaten and a kind of subsistence act is therefore performed, whether or not it is foremost in the minds of the people. The question is whether this method of consumption is economic in the sense of being regulated to meet subsistence ends, or whether consumption is secondary. If the latter is true, then meat may conceivably be wasted. The impression given by some writers that meat consumption in rituals is not an essential component of subsistence is presumably based, at least implicitly, upon the assumption that such distribution is not governed by attitudes of conservation, that meat is wasted, and that there is a piling up of feasts. But this does not seem to be so. Clearly, some animals are killed privately to fulfill subsistence needs. Similarly, the most frequent feast seems to be the one known simply as kerket; this is not required at any special time but is held when there is a need for meat, even though ritual ends are also served by it. The other sapana-like feasts, such as the funeral, are of relatively rare occurrence. But even these fulfill a subsistence role, for presumably the decision to hold a kerket is conditioned by whether a compulsory feast such as the funeral has recently been held. The attitudes of conservation which accompany kerket are most prominently seen in the fact that it is often initiated by the community, which calls upon one of its members to give a steer as an obligation. The person selected may demur on the grounds of placing himself in economic jeopardy, but he must eventually consent in order to maintain his standing in the community. Two feasts never occur on the same day or even on adjoining days, except in unusual circumstances. Finally, the consumption of meat does not conflict with the economic use of milk, except in the sapana. Persons who consume ritually slaughtered meat may not take milk on the same day; the milk thus saved is either made available to those who have had no meat, or is eaten sour on the following day.

If meat disposal in ritual settings is in large part subject to subsistence needs, the question arises as to why animals are not simply slaughtered and distributed among members of a neighborhood. As we have seen, this is sometimes done. When a man kills an animal to buy grain, some of the meat is saved and some given to neighbors. When animals die, the meat is also passed around. Beyond this, the answer depends on three linked considerations.

The cattle-complex definition maintains, and it has been pointed out in other places in East Africa (Evans-Pritchard 1953, 1954), that cattle have a kind of mystical value as items of sacrifice. The sapana and sapana-like feasts have a strong religious element, and its fulfillment depends on the sacrificial animal. The feast seems designed to appeal to supernatural forces (perhaps Tororut, the creator, though it is not clearly indicated) and the theology seems to be that the steer appeases these forces, thus making possible the attainment of the ends prayed for. The theology is not clear, and it is complicated enough to lead to the kind of elaborate argumentation that Evans-Pritchard (1953, 1954) found necessary to explain the Nuer sacrifices of animals. Whatever the case, appeals for aid in this setting are viewed as the most powerful; although calls for aid may be made by the group outside the feast, the feast has an incomparable magical quality. All this, of course, is manifest to Pakot. But there is a latent function in that the order of Pakot life is dramatized and reinforced in the ritual. The age-sets are carefully arranged according to precedence and the meat is assigned according to quality to the various age-sets; the men of the oldest set get the best, and the women, who are set off from the men by their subordination, get the least desirable. The continual repetition of this feast reinforces the structure of Pakot society, bringing together people who normally seldom have an opportunity to gather in large groups and reimpressing them with the proper order of life.

When Pakot desire something badly—a cure for a sick person, the cursing of a thief, or alleviation of a drought—they make the strongest request in a sapana-like feast. However, the kerket variety of this feast is not called to fulfill any specific request, except perhaps to pray for the good fortune of the donor of the ox. It is held to get meat, and as a sort of insurance. Divination occurs in all these feasts in order to see what the future portends in regard to the alleviation of droughts, disease, and other ends sought by the prayers, or simply to discover if these disasters are in the offing. The divination of the kerket seems to be for this last purpose. It may also be argued that by holding the feast in this setting, a declaration is made to the supernatural that Pakot are adhering to the correct way, thus helping to insure that it will continue.

A second consideration is that Pakot attain social support by creating and maintaining a wide network of social ties. They nourish relations with clansmen who are dependable, and seek to establish associational ties with strangers through institutionalized friendships and tilia. By the same token, they maintain good relations with their neighbors in order to insure co-operation. But communal co-operation, to be placed on the most solid footing, requires the giving of beer, labor, and other such things; the sharing of meat both in the feast and outside is a means to this end. When some special desire appears which requires the co-operation of many people, it can best be attained by paying the people through this medium. In praying for someone who is ill, the donor of the feast wants the help of the supernatural force; apart from the use of the steer, it is necessary for as many people as possible to come and pray with him to get this help. The more people present, the louder the responses to the prayers and the more effective the request. In kerket, the donor merely insures future co-operation (either willingly, if he initiates the feast, or unwillingly, if it is thrust upon him), although in a sense he is paid back immediately by the prestige which the feast brings. The distribution of meat in the ritual sanctifies communal support in all things as one of the requirements of the proper Pakot life, and those who attend are placed under obligation to reciprocate. This attitude is reflected in the condemnation of private slaughter of cattle. People expect a man to share his meat with them, as they have shared with him—and indeed, as the supernatural requires.

Thirdly, communal sharing of meat is probably inevitable; although Pakot know how to prepare jerked beef and thus preserve meat for long periods without refrigeration, this does not seem an efficient method of preserving a whole steer. They complain that meat left too long in the house becomes infested with vermin and that it does not taste as good as fresh meat. Added to this, the household is frequently left empty for long periods and large quantities of meat stored there would probably attract animal and human predators. The problem of how to utilize beef most efficiently is solved by offering it to the community in a ceremonial setting. This provides the most efficient distribution (particularly in the sense that there is no fighting over the meat, as in lapai; it is doled out according to a formula), makes possible a good supply for the present, since the giver gets one leg and more to take home, and insures that meat will be forthcoming in the future by placing neighbors under an obligation to return the gift.

The consumption of meat in these rituals can therefore be seen to have both religious and secular considerations of such a nature that meat is carefully utilized to supplement the diet and at the same time insures supernatural and communal aid and helps to stabilize the society. The steer is the medium par excellence for such sacrifice and the "mystical" value attached to it derives from this role. But it is also the best meat producer of all cattle. The subsistence value of the steer in this setting is made even clearer by the fact that a feast can be held without one; a goat or even a camel can be substituted, even though these do not have the affectional or ritual status of steers.

It can be said with assurance that Pakot love meat (especially fresh), and we have seen how often it is consumed. In a medical examination of Pakot made by a European doctor,[4] the people were found to be generally quite healthy, and he felt that this was due to their well balanced diet. However, malaria and tapeworm were prevalent. The latter was most common and was presumably due to the consumption of much raw meat (the meat is cooked in the rituals, but so lightly as to have little effect on it). Pakot eagerly eat the meat of animals that die or are slaughtered. Sometimes they are glad when an animal dies, and they fight wildly over the division of meat in situations where the division is not clearly prescribed. The value of attendance at any ritual is determined on the basis of how much meat will be available, and reasons are sometimes invented for holding rituals just in order to get meat. When asked why they kill steers for rites, the reply is usually that no one will come if they do not. In talking with Pakot, it is common to hear of cases in which persons entering new neighborhoods are required to give initial feasts as a sort of payment for entry and settlement; if they refuse, they are arraigned on trumped-up

---

[4] This examination was carried out by Dr. W. H. G. Patton in April of 1945. His report is unpublished, and is in the files of the government headquarters of West Suk at Kapenguria.

charges so that they must give a sitat, which is a sapana-like feast for some minor offense. Oxen are sometimes used in ordeals arising out of litigation, and there are cases reported in which ordeals seem to have been prompted merely to get meat.

Informants say that a man has done his duty to his neighbors by giving a feast at least once a year. Since a neighborhood may consist of forty or fifty adult men (as two near the writer's camp did), it seems theoretically possible that meat is available in some ceremonial on an average of once a week. But such a statement gives a spurious impression, for Pakot do not deliberately arrange things so that meat will be available on schedule. When conservation considerations arise, feasts may not occur for long periods of time. During the seasons when milk is in short supply and there is little grain left in the stores, there is a tendency to give more careful consideration to expenditure and to utilize resources with the future more clearly in mind. Smaller amounts of grain are drawn upon daily, cattle are more frequently killed to trade for grain and are sold to traders in larger numbers, and unnecessary feasts are avoided; such feasts as initiation and circumcision are completely absent during this period. Kerkets continue and people seem particularly to choose this time to make demands on members of the community who are obligated to make this feast and can afford it, but there are also strong attempts to avoid being called upon. Since most of the meat consumed comes from animals that die or are killed outside rituals, the number of ritual feasts held will to some extent be governed by this. Finally, not all men in a community can afford to give steers for feasts.

Without better quantitative data it is impossible to say how often animals are consumed, but the process might be stated in this manner: each year a number of steers reach maturity and are in prime condition for consumption (and a number of animals die). A given neighborhood will arrange disposition as best it can, but if no animals are available, none can be killed. In the end, however, all animals are consumed, consistent with maintenance of a reservoir. Although it is impossible to determine how much meat is available to each home each day, or how much is consumed regularly, it seems obvious that among Pakot who have significant numbers of cattle, meat is a frequent item in the diet. Thus informants from areas where cattle are numerous can say that the usual meal consists of milk and mush or meat and mush.

OTHER CONSIDERATIONS

The foregoing discussion has pointed up the subsistence value of cattle. But there are considerations that further demonstrate this which cannot be dealt with in terms of the categories of exchange and consumption.

The attitude that cattle are useful economic goods is seen in the way their value is verbalized. They can be neatly ranked according to beauty, but there is a second valuation in terms of subsistence. An informant can explain that steers, and particularly kamar steers, are most beautiful, while at the same time stating that cows are the most valuable for economic reasons because they give milk and calves. This is borne out in trade, where cows are worth more than steers.

Similarly, the majority of morphemes which refer to cattle seem to be related to their economic worth. While cattle can be finely differentiated by terminology referring to sex, age, and other such considerations, goats and even crops can also be classified in this manner. In a few words, a man cannot only describe the general condition of any animal, but also of his crops. One term for cattle connotes "a calf just taking grass" and one term applied to sorghum tells that "the plants are just beginning to show the seed head."

With regard to prestige, we have noted that it is associated with large cattle holdings but is not a pure function of possession, since it is derived basically from the willingness of the owner to dispose of his cattle to help meet the needs of the community. Prestige does not go to the rich but miserly man. Pakot dislike boastful and pretentious people, especially when they brag about their wealth in stock. An exception is the *egh* or Steer Dance, in which men are allowed to brag in songs about their favorite animal or animals; those who have none worthy of praise invent them. They do not talk openly about their wealth and do not like others to know how large their holdings are. One of the strongest sanctions is magic, whether condoned by the community or not, and it is considered proper to employ it against a wealthy braggart. One informant said he would not want a herd of more than seventy or eighty head of cattle for fear his neighbors would envy him so much that they would practice magic against him. This implies, of course, that Pakot do know roughly how many cattle their neighbors have, but they seldom admit it. It is difficult for anyone to know exactly how wealthy a man is, since all are involved in the tilia relationship and have cows scattered over the tribal area.

An emotional tie can be developed with some animals, especially the prize steer, but not all Pakot have such an animal. The nature of affectional ties with cattle is seen when informants are questioned as to whether they would refuse to utilize a steer for trade or food because of attachment to him. The question is considered odd, and all say frankly that they would not do this. As one put it, even a starving person would hesitate to kill one remaining animal; if he did, and conditions improved, his neighbors would ridicule him for having been shortsighted. But he would kill the animal if all else failed. Even the prize steer is not safe, for there are instances in which men are called upon to give this animal for a feast.

So far our discussion has been centered exclusively on men's values, as most discussions of the cattle-complex probably are. It is a striking fact that Pakot women do not place as high a valuation upon cattle as do the men. One woman said she did not think cattle were beautiful at all, but that grain was beautiful. Related to this are the facts that in ritual feasts women get less meat than men (though they get meat in other ways), and are thought of as being without responsibility for their acts and so protected by the supernatural, while men are responsible for their destinies and must appeal to the supernatural through rituals. Furthermore, women have little actual control over stock, though they may nominally own cattle and control their disposition to some extent. However, it is possible for women to exercise considerable control over land and crops, and sometimes to grow a private crop to dispose of as they see fit. They are in complete charge of the family granary, from which men are excluded, and ration the grain to the rest of the family. While this situation can be interpreted as merely meaning that the cattle-complex is found in men's value systems, it also implies the subsistence valuation of animals by showing they are more prized by the men, who control and receive the most food from them.

Attitudes toward food consumption are revealing in estimating the role of stock in subsistence. Pakot feel that it is gluttonous to eat more than two foods at a meal. The usual meal consists of milk and mush (cooked ground sorghum, eleusine, or maize). During the seasons when these foods are scarce, some wild plants are also gathered and used in combination with milk, meat, and mush. Significantly, there seems to be little hunting; in this respect the Pakot resemble the Nuer, of whom Evans-Pritchard (1940:28) says they get enough meat from their herds so that they have little need to hunt. One never sees fat men. When a man gorges himself he is ridiculed and sometimes told that his downfall is assured, since he will be unused to deprivation and the first to die when food becomes scarce. Actually, most Pakot must live on a low calorie diet part of each year, as their gaunt appearance testifies, and they could not survive such periods if they were used to too much food.

This dietary attitude correlates with the taboo on mixing milk and unskinned meat, which has the effect of conserving food. The prohibition is not absolute; milk and meat are eaten together in the initiation ceremony, but this is exceptional. There is an atmosphere of celebration at the initiation feast and extravagances are allowed. In fact, the feast is only held when food supplies are large enough to allow such extravagance. In other instances this mixing is not allowed, and Pakot say that if it is done the cows will dry up. What this statement means otherwise is not clear, but it can be interpreted to mean that if supplies are not distributed wisely, milk will be taken away. When government officials ask Pakot why they will not grow tomatoes and other foods which they have been offered, they give the same reason—if they do, the cows will dry up. Pakot seem to feel that the creator established life as it is, that it is the best sort of life, and that he intended they should conform to traditional patterns if they want it to remain good. They say, "God gave us three things: cattle, sheep, and goats; if we add to these with chickens and other foreign foods, he will take one away." They grow some maize today, which they think of as analogous to sorghum, but otherwise they have had little to do with new crops or animals. Thus, they seem to think of the separation of milk and meat, which are principal foods, as part of the order of things to insure good fortune. Meat and milk are essential to the diet, but they should be eaten only singly with mush; otherwise there is extravagance which will bring retribution.

This taboo can also be interpreted to mean that the milk and meat have sacred qualities such that contamination by mixing them will cause ritual imbalance. This is Huntingford's interpretation of the same taboo among the Nandi (1950:41). Pakot say only that the cows will dry up, but the interpretation could still apply for the taboo includes only ritual meat. However, it seems that even non-ritual meat is seldom taken with milk, and whatever the ritual interpretation, the taboo aids in food conservation.

THE SUBSISTENCE USE OF CATTLE IN OTHER PARTS OF EAST AFRICA

In recent years, data from widely separated areas of East Africa indicate that the high subsistence valuation of cattle among the Pakot is not unique. In few cases is the question of subsistence dealt with directly, but the occasional direct observations on and allusions to the problem are revealing.

Sheddick, in writing of the Sotho of South Africa, says: "Their attitude toward their stock may appear to be irrational and uneconomic by European way of thinking, but their evaluation of cattle is for the most part based on practical considerations" (1953: 21). He argues that Sotho freely sell stock to traveling meat vendors when they need money, and are reluctant to kill stock mainly because they are not plentiful. The Sotho, he says, cannot be considered a part of the cattle-complex culture area because of this practical attitude toward cattle. It is clear that Sheddick feels the economic use of stock is a very important part of Sotho life.

Goodfellow, in discussing the economic systems of South and Southeast African peoples, makes it clear that cattle are utilized for subsistence, even though motives for killing them are seldom simple: "It is clear, for example, that at least until recent times, it was the custom among the cattle-owning Bantu to kill numbers of cattle at that period in the year when their flesh was most needed as food, and particularly when the people needed that extra stimulation which could be derived from the consumption of flesh" (1939:68–69). He notes that animals killed for sacrifice were eaten, and that the desires for meat and for supernatural help combined to encourage slaughter (ibid: 69). Other than desire for meat, the motives that led to slaughter were not always of ritual or subsistence origin. It is pointed out that women, who did not value cattle highly because they were allowed to have little to do with them, needed new clothing at certain times of the year and would often urge their husbands to slaughter animals for the hides (ibid: 69).

Of the Ndebele of Southern Rhodesia, Hughes and van Velsen say, "One's own cattle are only occasionally a source of meat, as few people nowadays possess sufficiently large herds to allow them to kill a beast for food when the whim takes them. Beasts killed for ritual purposes may be consumed as food, but when a beast is killed in any other way, the greater part of the meat is usually sold" (1955:58). This suggests that some ritual animals are not eaten, but otherwise shows the economic value of cattle as food and as mediums of exchange. Furthermore, the situation described is contemporary, and it is implied that in former times cattle were much more freely utilized for food.

In Northern Rhodesia we find the situation described by Colson among the Tonga (1951), where cattle are widely used to secure rights in people. In discussing the institution of cattle dispersal, Colson argues that it is "more important" than ritual uses of stock (1955:77). Although Colson does not seem to emphasize it, we might add that these relationships also provide people with a kind of security which has subsistence aspects. The particular form of cattle dispersal noted here differs from that of the Pakot, but the two systems have many functions in common.

There are few data available north of the Tonga until we get to Uganda and Kenya. For the Ankole of Uganda, Oberg has noted that the herd of the Mugabe, or king, like those of all the Hima aristocracy, was made up of cattle "which were set aside for the ancestral and *emandwa* spirits and others which served purely economic purposes" (1950:144). Wagner (1950:208) tells of an occasion for feasting among the Bantu of Kavirondo in which an "ox of splitting" is consumed. This type of feast seems comparable to the Pakot kerket.[5] Huntingford discussing the Masai, says that they eat their cattle in large numbers, and implies that this is done solely to satisfy hunger (1953:107). In his discussions of the Nandi, however, he suggests that meat consumption is unimportant (Huntingford 1950; 1953:20, 107). Like Sheddick, Gulliver (1951:16) questions the cattle-complex, but for a different reason: his studies of the Turkana and Jie have impressed him with the fact that all stock are economically important. He notes that herds are carefully manipulated to obtain meat, invest in social relationships, and the

[5] This conclusion is borne out in Gunter Wagner's recently published *The Bantu of North Kavirondo, Volume II: Economic Life,* which supports the thesis of this paper in other important details.

like (1955:41–42, 60, 131). In his discussion of the Jie, Gulliver indicates the importance of beef in the diet, though he emphasizes that ritual consumption of meat is limited to initiated males (1955: 131; 1953:158). This seems to conflict with Pakot usage, since little of the ritual meat is held back from others, even though the initiated men get most of it. In general, Gulliver's accounts of the Turkana and Jie seem very similar to the Pakot situation, but the Turkana are next-door neighbors to the Pakot and the source of many Pakot customs.

The final example in this review is that of the Nuer. Evans-Pritchard has consistently emphasized the subsistence importance of cattle, and says "the end of every beast is, in fact, the pot, so that they obtain sufficient meat to satisfy their craving and have no pressing need to hunt wild animals. . . . Except when epidemics are rife the usual occasions of eating meat are ritual and it is the festal character of the rites which gives them much of their significance in the life of the people" (1940:26–28). The import is that the ritual significance of rites is in competition with the consumption of beef, a fact which Evans-Pritchard underscores elsewhere (1953: 192). This attitude is directly comparable to that of the Pakot. However, Evans-Pritchard's position in this matter is somewhat obscured by his insistence on the fact that Nuer feel cattle are to be reserved for sacrifice, and that to slaughter animals solely for consumption could bring punishment to the killers of the animals (1953:193). Whatever the intent, this seems to be another situation in which cattle consumption is necessary for subsistence, though it often occurs in the setting of a ritual.

CONCLUSION

The purpose of this paper has been to show that cattle are more fully exploited for subsistence than has generally been acknowledged, both among Pakot and in East Africa in general. In addition to the subsistence value of milk, our examination of exchange and consumption utilization has shown that both overtly and to some degree covertly (i.e., in rituals), cattle are essential to subsistence. The fact that cattle are valued for other than subsistence reasons, and that this valuation is associated with a variety of nonsubsistence uses, does not exclude their use to support life.

Some points deserve further examination. First, it should not be assumed that other considerations than subsistence never interfere with the economic exploitation of cattle. There is commonly an attempt to serve dual ends without sacrifice of either, but this is not entirely possible. Instances where meat (or even milk and grain) is wasted because of the need to satisfy nonsubsistence needs can be found in any of these cultures. One example of this was noted among the Pakot. A man who suspected a vulture that was frequenting his locale of being possessed of an evil spirit threw a goat to it in the hope that it would be satisfied and go away. Evans-Pritchard states that the Nuer sometimes leave sacrificial animals to rot (1954:26), and Hughes and van Velsen, in the passage quoted above, suggest that sometimes the Ndebele do not eat sacrificial animals. The rhythm of consumption among Pakot resembles to some extent that found by Fortes among the Tallensi (1936:260–61). Resources are exploited most fully when they are least needed to provide energy to cultivate the crops for the next season's needs; during the growing season, food consumption is greatly lowered and people commonly eat only about one meal a day. The pattern is not identical with that of the Tallensi, since there is a continued consumption of beef or even an increase in slaughter during this time, but the resemblance illustrates the fact that subsistence considerations may be outweighed by others. Looked at one way, what we have said implies a certain "inefficiency" in the use of life-supporting goods. This does not mean to convey any criticism of Pakot standards, but rather to contrast what actually happens with what might logically be considered the most efficient use of goods. But there is no inefficiency in terms of the society's continued existence. The people have managed to survive under this system, and their consumption, irregular though it is, insures survival except in those drought and disease-ridden years when they are caught off guard. Even then, it might be argued, pastoralism is a rewarding way of life, for there is always a reservoir of cattle to be drawn on for food in extreme emergencies where a totally agricultural people might find themselves destitute.

"Waste" of goods does occur, an intentional waste which may be contrasted with the unintentional waste which occurs when disease kills large numbers of animals. But the waste is not a result of refusal to exploit cattle. In the one case, where cattle are used ritually and not consumed, the number not utilized is small; in the other case, having to do with the rhythm of consumption, the waste results from a movement toward higher standards of consumption during the time of the year when food supplies are most complete, and it is directed equally at all subsistence goods.

A second point is that the Pakot pattern seems general in East Africa only in the sense that cattle are considered legitimate subsistence resources in exchange and consumption. Variation in basic factors in other areas leads to a different working out of subsistence use. People who have greater resources than Pakot seem to be more extravagant in disposal. The point is illustrated by instances of enormous slaughter at burial ceremonies in some areas (Herskovits 1926:506). Pakot cannot afford this, and mass butchering does not occur except perhaps in the sapana, where more than one steer is occasionally offered in a single feast. Conversely, there are some regions in East Africa where the numbers of cattle are so small that they are insignificant in the subsistence economy, even when the cattle-complex is present. Middleton (1953:20) remarks that the consumption of milk is small among the Kikuyu who have few cattle. Similarly, McCulloch (1952:13) notes that the herds of the Ovimbundu of Angola are exceedingly small and cows are not even milked.

Finally, we must stress the point that this paper is not an attempt to establish a simplistic kind of subsistence determinism among Pakot. It is not argued that the desire for the best kind of subsistence support is so overwhelming that everything else must conform to it. It is possible that some Pakot could derive a better living, in terms of subsistence, by following another road than pastoralism. But they have made this choice historically, and defend it fiercely. Many of them despise agriculture, even though they have to engage in it, and others are indifferent to it. Most Pakot maintain the superiority of herding as a way of life. This, of course, is a manifestation of the cattle-complex; if subsistence were the only consideration, some would turn to other pursuits. What we maintain is merely that given pastoralism and the cattle-complex, the available potential resources are very extensively exploited; cattle are not excluded from this exploitation, but are used in conjunction with their non-subsistence uses. An ingenious balance is maintained between the various needs, a balance which seems to make possible an almost complete subsistence exploitation of cattle.

Despite the objections of Gulliver and Sheddick, the cattle-complex is present in East Africa. It is exemplified in the affection for and identification with cattle, the feeling that they are the best source of help from the supernatural, and the belief that only cattle have esthetic qualities. But the cattle-complex, as defined here, does not preclude using cattle to support life, as many have assumed. It is hoped that this paper will be a contribution to the understanding of East African cultures insofar as it clarifies this point of frequent misunderstanding and opens it to further direct examination.

W. B. MORGAN

10. Farming Practice, Settlement Pattern, and Population Density in South-eastern Nigeria[1]

In 1951 A. T. Grove read a paper before the Society on the badly eroded country of Iboland in the Eastern Region of Nigeria.[2] In conclusion he pointed to the need for further research among the Ibo, particularly in the contrasting environments of the lowlands. The following paper represents an attempt to develop such research and is based on field work from the centers of Port Harcourt and Aba in 1954. The major part of the work is concerned with conditions in Aba Division, especially in that part of it termed Aba Ngwa County, while the study made in the area north of Port Harcourt, that is in Diobu District, is used to provide a comparison.

The farmer of south-eastern Nigeria is essentially a hoe cultivator; his work has the character of gardening rather than farming, since it is small scale and permits individual attention to the plants grown. Since holdings are small a large number of people per unit area is possible upon farmed land with resulting high rural densities. However, the chief problem of the south-east is that in many parts the population densities are very much higher than the present system of land holding would appear to allow. Grove has already shown the problem in the Awka-Orlu uplands and the Udi Plateau. South of these the lower and more level regions, stretching down to the deltas of the Niger and Cross rivers and to the lagoons and bars of

SOURCE: W. B. Morgan, "Farming Practice, Settlement Pattern, and Population Density in South-eastern Nigeria," *Geographic Journal of the Royal Geographical Society,* Vol. 121, 1955, pp. 320–33. Reprinted by permission of the author and publisher.

[1] The author wishes to acknowledge the help received from District Officers, Officers of the Agricultural Department and the many Ibo cultivators interviewed in the areas concerned, and also the loan of aerial photographs by the Nigerian Survey Department.

[2] A. T. Grove, "Soil erosion and population problems in south-east Nigeria," *Geogr. J.* 117 (1951), pp. 291–306.

the firmer ground between, appear to be divided into two density zones characterized by Aba Division with 347 to the square mile and Ahoada, which includes Diobu District, with 143. It was felt therefore that an investigation of the conditions around Aba and in the area adjacent to Port Harcourt might shed some light on density problems and in particular on the carrying capacities of the lands concerned.

The normal practice among the Ngwa and Ikwerri divisions of the Ibo-speaking peoples in Aba Division and Diobu District respectively is to plant their crops in two types of land—farmland, which is the major food producer, and compound land, which serves the purpose of a kitchen garden. Farmland is divided into holdings consisting of "farms" which may be further divided into plots. Generally, holdings average less than 3 acres per family plus another ½ acre of compound land.[3] The cultivating unit is the family grouped into settlements whose pattern reflects the nature of the cultivation, since agriculture is the basis of existence. Here a contrast is immediately apparent among the Ngwa and Ikwerri. In Figure 10–1 it may be seen that the settlement pattern near Aba consists of scattered compounds entirely devoid of nucleation. The Ngwa in fact have no villages in the accepted sense. In Diobu however, while compounds rather than individual huts are still characteristic, they are normally grouped together in well-defined villages of which that of Atako (Fig. 10–2) is an excellent example. The contrast in pattern appears to be related to a contrast in the form of local authority. Among the Ngwa, compounds are larger than those of the Ikwerri and house what may be described as an extended family or *onumara*—that is, not only a man and his wife or wives and children as represented by the *ezi* or smallest unit; but his sons, their wives and their children and often brothers and cousins. Even within this unit of closely related families, each family undertakes its own farm work and, while some assistance may be given by one to another, the labor is in no sense communally performed.[4] Groups of com-

---

[3] Estimates of sizes of holdings have been made from observations in the field and from surveys made in Aba Division by Assistants of the Agricultural Department. They are no more than approximations to the truth. The size of a "family" is generally reckoned to be seven persons, *i.e.* a man, his two wives and four children.

[4] See M. M. Green, "Land tenure in an Ibo village" (1941), published for the London School of Economics and Political Science. Monographs on Social Anthropology No. 6, particularly p. 11.

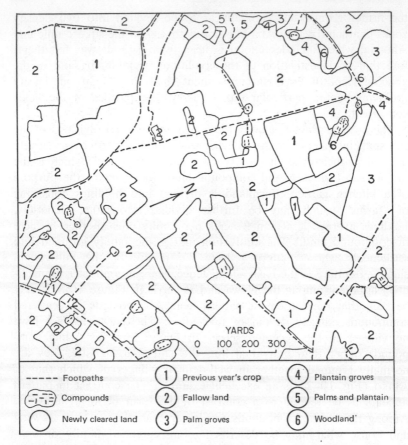

Figure 10–1. Settlement and land use in Umu Ocham, Aba

pounds inhabited by kinsfolk together form a larger unit called a "village" or *mba* in which unrelated family groups may be permitted to settle if land is available. "Village" affairs are discussed at a common meeting place. The connecting paths or *ama* are thus of vital importance in such administrative system as exists, and furthermore link the compounds for trade purposes. Their importance is stressed by the common occurrence of the word *ama* in Ibo settlement names[5] and, as will be shown, they have left an imprint

[5] Note that *Ama uku* signifies a meeting place. Similarly the fact that most settlements are founded from a common center is illustrated by the prefix *umu* or "children."

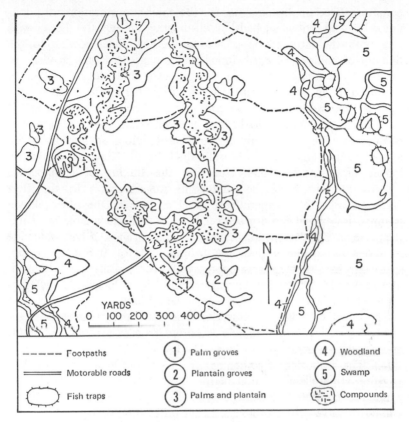

Figure 10–2. Atako's Village, Diobu District

on the agricultural pattern. The paths are vital also for water supply, since convenience with regard to agricultural land and not the location of water is the most important factor in determining the settlement site: this is so despite the scattered distribution of water, due to the porous nature of the sub-soil with its low dry season water-table, and despite the difficult descents to streams. Distances of 8 miles to water are not unknown. Each household provides itself with a clay-lined catch pit which, however, is usually too foul for drinking purposes. With the exception of location near local springs arising from the few laterite outcrops, Ngwa settlement tends to be away from streams with their steep valley slopes, steep high banks in the dry season and lack of flood-plain. This seems to be a common Nigerian phenomenon, for the chief concentrations of population are all on watersheds. Well-digging among the Ngwa was rare until the introduction of European techniques, owing to the liability of collapse of excavations and the great depths needed. In Diobu, by contrast, while the village also tends to be a kinship group, it is in effect comparable to a gathering together of the scattered *onumara* of its Ngwa counterpart. Local authority is vested in a chief who appears to have a greater control over village and compound affairs, and many agricultural activities are performed on a communal rather than an individual basis. Here the paths no longer have as their main function the linking of compounds, but radiate out from the village to the "farms." In the Port Harcourt area the comparatively level surface of the older alluvia is much lower and the dry season level of the water-table is nearer the surface. The descent to streams is less than at Aba and waterside locations are common both for fishing and for trading purposes. Thus one has the surprising contrast of evenly dispersed settlement in a region of restricted water supply and highly localized, nucleated settlement in a region offering easier conditions.

The effect of village organization and settlement pattern on agricultural practice is immediately apparent from a comparison of the cultivated area depicted in Figure 10–1 with that depicted in Figure 10–3. The scattering of settlement in the Umu Ocham area of Aba Division is paralleled by that of the small blocks of cultivated land, while the nucleated settlement type of the Diobu area is accompanied by large cohesive blocks. Land utilization among both groups of Ibo is based broadly on six types of land:

1. The village or compound area with its accompanying kitchen garden land.
2. Farmland under cultivation and various stages of fallow, bearing oil palms in addition to annual crops.
3. Oil palm groves, usually close to the village or compound, and occasionally cropped.
4. Woodland, divided into (*a*) timber and firewood reserves including a windbreak round the settlement; (*b*) sacrosanct land, *i.e.* cemetery or religious shrines; (*c*) boundary demarcation lots, of which there is a good example in the northern-eastern quarter of Figure 10–3.

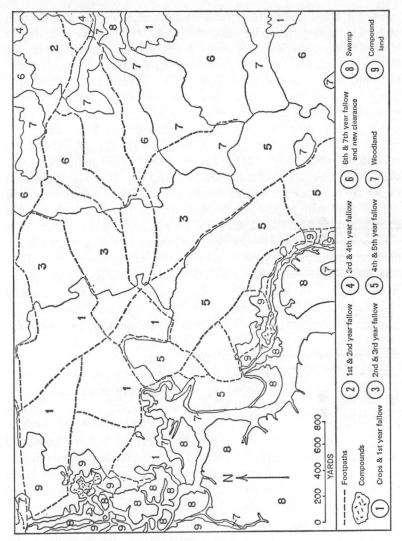

Figure 10–3.

5. Plantations, generally of oil palms, a recent innovation due to European influence.

6. Wasteland, including swamp, steep slopes and areas of infertile soils.

Of this classification farm land clearly occupies the greater part of both areas depicted, with most of it in fallow. The fallow period in Umu Ocham generally lasts three years, and in eastern Diobu six to seven years. Only a small proportion of the farmed land is therefore productive in any one year. The confusion of fallow and farmed land in Umu Ocham illustrates the effect of farming from a variety of centers and this confusion is made worse by the development of land ownership and fragmentation due to inheritance.

The greater part of the area shown in Figure 10–3, illustrating conditions in February 1951, is farmed from the village in the northwestern corner whose limits are marked by the woodland belt stretching with small breaks eastwards in a broad curve from Amadi. In Amadi village farming is restricted to the narrow riverain stretch of compound land since its people are Okrika whose main occupation is fishing. The outstanding feature of the farmland is the division into large blocks each representing two years of cultivation. The normal practice is to clear scattered patches in fallow of the sixth and seventh years. Community needs take up approximately half the area available. Since, however, there is insufficient land to continue the process of scattered clearance indefinitely, the remainder of the block must be cleared the following year and the chief and elders must advise on the equitable division of the land. Thus the pattern of cultivation pursued is one combining random clearance with the thoroughness needed by a people who must cultivate all the land locally available. The remaining blocks, therefore, consist of various two-year stages of fallow, plus a block having the previous year's planting of cassava and the first year of fallow weeds and bushes. But in Umu Ocham (Figure 10–1, depicting March conditions) only small patches of community land exist, the greater part being privately held by each compound. Private or *okpulo* land as opposed to community or *egbelu* land has always been regarded as that to which an individual or family has possessory title comparable to that of an absolute freeholder except that it cannot be permanently alienated.[6] Land may be pledged indefinitely for a loan, but it can always be redeemed without compensation for any improvements affected. With increasing shortage of land there has been a tendency for individuals to acquire private holdings in order to ensure a sufficient share of the area available. Custom has tended to weaken

[6] See T. O. Elias, "Nigerian land law and custom" (London), 1951, p. 93.

so that pledging is often virtually a sale. In addition a system of renting has developed. Community land is still divided by the decision of the elders, but scattered clearance is impossible since the blocks available are so small. Moreover, fragmentation due to division among heirs is reducing the size of holdings and of individual blocks still further. Although the figures are not available to provide a detailed comparison there is every indication that population density is higher in Umu Ocham than in Diobu and is partly responsible for the contrast in agricultural patterns.

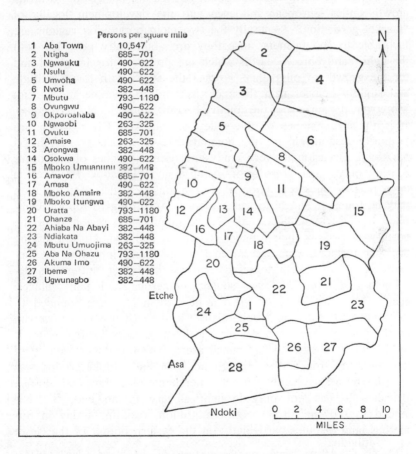

	Persons per square mile	
1	Aba Town	10,547
2	Ntigha	685—701
3	Ngwauku	490—622
4	Nsulu	490—622
5	Umvoha	490—622
6	Nvosi	382—448
7	Mbutu	793—1180
8	Ovungwu	490—622
9	Okporoahaba	490—622
10	Ngwaobi	263—325
11	Ovuku	685—701
12	Amaise	263—325
13	Arongwa	382—448
14	Osokwa	490—622
15	Mboko Umuanunu	382—448
16	Amavor	685—701
17	Amasa	490—622
18	Mboko Amaire	382—448
19	Mboko Itungwa	490—622
20	Uratta	793—1180
21	Ohanze	685—701
22	Ahiaba Na Abayi	382—448
23	Ndiakata	382—448
24	Mbutu Umuojima	263—325
25	Aba Na Ohazu	793—1180
26	Akuma Imo	490—622
27	Ibeme	382—448
28	Ugwunagbo	382—448

Figure 10–4. Distribution of population by Local Council areas in Aba Ngwa County

Figures for population density, areas of holdings and periods of fallow are difficult to obtain and of doubtful value. Nevertheless the subject is important enough to warrant the study of such material in order to obtain at least an indication of the nature of the situation. Figure 10–4 shows the distribution of population by Local Council areas in Aba Ngwa County. There are two main regions of high density: (i) the north with 931 to the square mile in Mbutu, and 685 in Ntigha and Ovukwu; (ii) Aba district with 1180 in Aba na Ohazu, 793 in Uratta and 701 in Amavor. The extremely high densities to the north-west and south of Aba are partly due to urban growth under European influence and the development locally of "market gardening." Generally the two main population regions are favorable to Ibo farmers since they are abundantly provided with the light, sandy brown earths which are preferred for farmland and for the growth of oil palms. Toward the south with lower altitude and slightly heavier rain these earths tend to become more acid. Moreover, the surface of the country becomes more highly accidented. It is the steep slopes of the valley of the Aba River which are primarily responsible for the comparatively low density of Ahiaba na Abayi. Occasionally very sandy and useless patches of soil occur bearing only spear grass as in Amaise and Ngwaobi. However, a large part of the explanation of the various densities of population may be found in the historical evidence. According to reports compiled by District Officers,[7] the Ngwa entered the region from the north-west making their founder settlement in Ngwauku and driving back the former Ibeme and mixed Ibo and Ibeme inhabitants. Other invasions of the north followed, and as these first settlements developed and more land was sought, numerous "colonial" villages, each taking the name of the parent settlement, were founded to the south and east. The Mboko district in the east was never overrun by the Ngwa, which may explain the lower density figures recorded by the three Mboko Local Council areas. The population density of the southern area and of the Etche, Asa and Ndoki groups was reduced by a slave raiding for the merchants of Bonny and Opobo. British rule has not only brought slavery to an end, but has tended to prevent further Ngwa migration, resulting today in numerous land disputes particularly on the eastern border of the Ngwa

[7] J. G. C. Allen, "Notes on the customs of the Ngwa Clan" (1934); "Supplementary reports on the Ngwa Clan."
J. Jackson, "Intelligence report on the Ngwa Clan, Aba Division."
E. J. G. Kelly, Supplementary memorandum to J. Jackson's report.

against the Ibibio. The practice of renting land has also developed, particularly on the western fringes of Mbutu Umuojima and in the lightly peopled portions of Etche, Asa and Ndoki districts where there is still land to spare. Hence the modern phenomenon of bicycle cultivators daily proceeding to their rented holdings from the crowded lands around Aba. Cultivators in the area west of Aba have holdings averaging less than 3 acres per family. In Nvosi (density 436) the average appears to be nearer 4 acres, while in Ndoki (density 148) holdings of 10 acres or more are common. Fallow periods are as low as three years in Umu Ocham, a time considered locally to be insufficient for satisfactory soil recuperation. The most common fallow period among the Ngwa, however, is five years and this is typical in Nvosi, Amaise, Mboko Itungwa and Ahiaba na Abayi. In Ndoki and the Ogwe district of Asa (density 306) seven-year fallows are usual, while in Etche (density 187) fallow periods are often of nine to fifteen years.

All the districts of Aba Ngwa County and even parts of Asa Local Council area are crowded and the central and northern portions with their short fallows and temporary migration may be described as overcrowded. An approximate calculation shows that 3 acres per family of seven with a three-year fallow means that 12 acres are needed for the family's continued support giving a density on farmed land alone of 373. Many people depend on outside resources and here one should note the movement of Ibo in search of work throughout Nigeria, many of whom remit money home. Comment by Ngwa agriculturalists suggested that five years fallow is the satisfactory minimum and the four districts already known to have this have densities of 436, 263, 490 and 382 respectively. Amaise with 263 has exceptional soil conditions so that is not typical of the region. The remainder suggest a critical density figure at approximately 382 to 490. It is interesting to compare this figure with Grove's suggestion of 300 to 400. Of the twenty-seven Local Council areas comprising Aba Ngwa County only three have lower densities than 382 and two of these have been shown to have exceptional adverse physical conditions. If Aba Ngwa County is a fair example of the lands immediately south of the Awka-Orlu highlands then there is no room here for immigration from the badly eroded parts of the latter.

One result of crowding is the development of rectilinear plot patterns, although even in areas with plentiful land there is occasionally a rectilinear tendency due to attempts to economize in the work of clearing fallow. The narrow plot frontages combined with great length indicate the importance of access to paths. Paths are often arranged in rectangular patterns at even distances apart, thus enabling easy measurement of newly cleared land by mere pacing of plot frontages for the purpose of division. One area was found to be cut by parallel paths a little over 200 yards apart. Each plot was thus 100 yards long and had approximately 9 yards of frontage giving an area of approximately one-fifth of an acre. Even on community land the scattered patches to be expected from the fragmentation of private holdings is prevalent. The distances apart of both community and private farms may be as much as 5 miles: a problem of dispersal offering serious difficulty to the introduction of European concepts of farming. The size of the plots into which the farms are divided varies. Calculation from aerial photographs and pacing in the field shows that of 75 plots in Umu Ocham the largest was 0.44 acres and the smallest was 0.07 with a mean of 0.25. In eastern Diobu, of thirty-eight plots the largest was 1.35 acres and the smallest 0.12 with a mean of 0.35. The district with the larger plots also has longer fallow periods and a lower population density.[8] With increase in the area of private land a degree of permanence in plot shape is beginning to emerge, for many of the plots near Aba have presumably reached the minimum useful size. This permanence is reflected in the common occurrence of fencing on both farm and compound land in order to protect the crops from the depredations of goats, sheep, cattle, pigs and fowls.

Crowding has brought with it the problem attached to fixing a system originally dependent on regular movement. Villages and compounds now occupy almost permanent sites. Cultivation similarly is restricted to rotation over a fixed area instead of a widespread "shifting" throughout the bush. This tendency to permanence has been encouraged by the development of a modern administrative system combined with fixed trading centers and routes. In the south of Aba Division, for example, artificial village councils or groups had to be formed in order to obtain "a workable administrative system,"[9]

[8] The indication is similar to that provided by the author's experience in Nyasaland. (W. B. Morgan, "The Lower Shire Valley of Nyasaland: a changing system of African agriculture," *Geogr. J.* 119 (1953), pp. 459–69), where it was found that increase in population density is followed firstly by a reduction in the length of fallow period and secondly by the reduction in the size of holdings by reduction in the area of each plot.

[9] Notes on the customs of the Ngwa Clan.

thus introducing a new rigidity to the old social order. Fixed paths and compound spaces have resulted in gullying. Hut foundations are often exposed and village churches and compounds undermined. Reduction in fallow period must lead eventually to lower returns per acre and possibly accelerated soil erosion. Fixed compounds must also mean fixed disposal of human excrement with a consequent danger to health. Present practice is to make cesspits on compound land which is also heaped with household refuse often making cultivation on such land possible without a fallow period. Manuring in this way is developed to the extent of heaping refuse around the trees, particularly palms and fruit trees, thus providing compound land with the richest "black" soil. In the past, plots near living quarters have become overgrown and the occupiers have been forced to move.[10]

Changing circumstances may demand changes in agricultural technique, but all suggestions for improvement must face the fact that Ibo farming practice is careful and based on long experience and that the environmental conditions offer limitations unknown to Europeans. Generally among the Ngwa and Ikwerri the men plant and tend those crops and trees needing most attention, leaving the remaining food production to the women. Thus men's crops include yams, pineapples, oil and raffia palms, coconut palms, plantains and bananas, and oranges, African pear, kola, oil bean and "vegetable leaf" trees. Women's crops are cassava, maize, cocoyams, beans, groundnuts, pumpkins, calabash, melons, okra, chillies and peppers. After careful storage seed yams are planted in April before the "former" rains, in holes dug with a special hoe, and the earth is heaped up to form mounds usually over 1 foot high and 2 feet in diameter— the spacing between plants varying from 2 feet 6 inches to 5 feet. It has been claimed that contour ridges are superior to mounds and that the latter encouraged soil erosion. However, yams need aeration, a good depth of soil and adequate drainage. Ridges would require more work to produce the same conditions and, moreover, where the quantity of the top soil available is limited, could not be made to provide the same depth of tilled earth around the plant. Cassava is

[10] On the movement of habitations in relation to oil palms and the formation of "black" soils, see also J. M. Waterston, "Observation on the influence of some ecological factors on the incidence of oil palm diseases in Nigeria," *Journal of the West Africa Institute for Oil Palm Research,* No. 1, September 1953, pp. 24–59.

interplanted in July and August before the "latter" rains and when yams have already developed a good growth. Such interplanting, which includes maize and vegetables, usually in part only of the plots, ensures not only a protective cover for the soil, but an extended period of harvest from the same piece of land. It also confers some of the benefits of crop rotation and, by including plants of variable needs, guarantees that at least one crop will succeed in the varying weather conditions. Compound land is the chief vegetable producer and is often planted to cocoyams which will produce some crop even if the rainfall is extremely low. Yams and cassava are the bases of the diet while other crops are either flavoring elements or provide some variety. Soils are carefully selected for planting and both the Ngwa and Ikwerri have their own classification.

The distinction of soil types and the recognition of the value of manuring are both evidence of careful farming. The few animals kept are allowed to graze on the fallow. Of these only goats and sheep appear to thrive. Cattle are of the dwarf trypanosomiasis-resistant variety, poor in both meat and milk yields. Grass fallows might provide increased and better quality fodder, but would entail considerable work in the suppression of encroaching shrubs and would not give the great volume of vegetable matter considered essential by the Ibo for burning before resuming cultivation. Burning supplies nutrition to the soil in the form of ash and reduces the number of insect pests. Small plots make possible individual attention to plants thus maintaining within the limits of the technique a high production per acre. Suggestions for farming on a larger scale must face the possibility of reduced production per acre in an overcrowded land. Fewer plot boundaries and the introduction of ploughlands would threaten the soil with rapid erosion from heavy showers. At Aba on 10 July 1950, 2.3 inches were recorded and on September 10, 2.8 inches. The following year 2.4 inches fell on May 5, 3.2 inches on September 2 and 3.0 inches on October 10. Occasionally rainfall totals differ considerably from normal. Whereas in 1933 106.2 inches were recorded, in 1950 there were only 60.5 inches. Concentration of the total likewise varies. The 1950 total fell in ninety-eight rainy days, *i.e.* days with more than 0.01 inches, while in 1947 94.0 inches fell in eighty-five rainy days.[11] The heavy rains

---

[11] For a diagram of rainfall reliability at Aba and discussion of rainfall reliability in Nigeria see J. C. Pugh, "Rainfall reliability in Nigeria," Proceedings of the International Geographical Congress: Commission on Periglacial Morphology and Section on Climatology (1952), pp. 36–41.

of 1955 resulted in the presence of unusually large numbers of insect pests at the time of planting, while the delayed rains of 1945 set back the maize crop and reduced the size of the yams. Two years later hot weather combined with heavier rainfall gave good returns of cassava and cocoyams, but maize again declined and so did vegetables. The 1952 fall, the heaviest for five years, gave good yams and early maize, but fostered rust among many late crops.

Despite the restrictions imposed by physical conditions and despite a conservative outlook, Ibo farmers are gradually changing their methods in response, firstly to changing social and economic circumstances, and secondly to the influence of Government Departments, particularly the Department of Agriculture. The expansion of trade has offered improved markets for palm products, the export of which from Aba Division has increased with fluctuations to a 1952 total of 39,427 tons of oil and 21,523 tons of kernels. The oil palm is the most valuable asset of the Ibo farmer since it is not only a source of cash, but provides food (in the form of fats which would otherwise be lacking with the shortage of animals), building materials and, together with the raffia palm, the staple alcoholic drink of "palm wine." Before the present large scale development of the palm oil trade, planted palms or palms on compound land were privately owned. Since the introduction of direct taxation in 1928, however, all palms must be open to fruit cutting by the whole community, generally for a period of three months in the year, in order to give everyone a means of paying tax, and thus inhibiting the establishments of palm plantations.

Cassava, and to a limited extent yams, copra, fruit and wild rubber have also become sources of cash. Cultivation of cassava has been encouraged by rising food prices with the increase in the proportion of non-agricultural population. Yams have become a rich man's food, but with the greater labor involved in their cultivation it is generally reckoned that more money may be obtained from the growth of the cheaper cassava sold in Aba Township or sent in the form of flour or *garl* to Port Harcourt and Calabar Province. The trade formerly depended chiefly on the markets of Enugu and Onitsha and was stimulated during the war by a "plant more cassava" campaign. Since the war, however, these markets have found cheaper sources of supply. The export of food from the Aba Division is balanced by the import of yams, cocoyams, fruit, fish and meat from surrounding districts. The *gari* trade has resulted in the expansion of cassava growing at the expense of yams. Other factors have also contributed to an apparent decline in yam cultivation. First, while women are keen traders and spend a proportion of their time away from the farms, men also are taking an increasing interest in trade and in transportation by bicycle competing with motor lorry traffic. In addition many men seek employment as laborers or clerks while others have probably had their attention drawn from farming by military service. There has been therefore a decreasing interest in farming among men, which has led to a decline in the production of the chief men's crop—yams. Both men and women are on the whole devoting less time to farming and therefore tending to concentrate more on cassava since it is the easiest crop to plant and tend. Moreover, cassava has become a cheap, easily transported food of increasing popularity among the major part of the employed population, has the advantage of harvest in May and June when no other fresh food is available, and is generally more productive on land with short fallows.

With regard to the cheapening of goods and the improvement of market facilities by trade the introduction of tarred road surfaces and the opening of the railway from Port Harcourt to Enugu in 1916 have had obvious effects. However, the old river routes of the Imo and Aba still compete via Opobo for palm oil traffic and are the chief means of conveying building sand and gravel. The improved facilities for export have also brought imported goods particularly cloth, metal ware, stockfish, kerosene, salt and soap. The old weaving and metal industries and the salt trade have declined. The increasing dependence on overseas markets has also made the Ibo farmers subject to world price fluctuations and wartime shortages.

Attempts directly to modify agricultural and related social conditions came first with the suppression of slave raiding, which dated from the establishment of the first consular post at Obegu in Ngwa territory in 1895 and from the Aro Expedition of 1901–2. This was followed by the acquisition of land by urban authorities, missionary societies and the Forestry Department. Although these acquisitions are small compared with the whole, nevertheless the local problems they have created have been sufficient for many Ngwa and Ikwerri farmers to place the blame for overcrowding on the authorities concerned. In Diobu compensation claims and litigation have persisted since 1913 when the chiefs sold a large part of their land to the Government for the development of Port Harcourt.

Direct interest in the agriculture of Aba Division began with experiments to improve the oil palm by the establishment in 1927 of 27 acres of experimental palm plots. In 1928 Regulation 20 enforced grading and inspection by Government agents of palm oil and kernels. The Agricultural Department followed with the issue of palm seedlings to farmers and, despite the difficulties incurred by communal culting, the encouragement of palm plantations; this was combined with the introduction of hand-operated oil presses. Experiments have been made to improve kola nut production and the growing of fruit, particularly oranges, has been fostered. During the war rubber planting and tapping boomed and the Department extended its interest to food in addition to commercial crops. This interest developed into an attempt to modify the entire agricultural system. In 1945 and 1946 an economic survey by individual sample villages was undertaken while a policy of all-round improvement in agricultural technique was laid down in Sessional Paper No. 16 of 1946 and confirmed by the Agricultural Ordinance No. 37 of 1948. In 1946 lime was issued to farmers and the construction of palm-oil mills began at Owerrinta and Azumini. There was a fear locally that the building of mills meant that the Government was going to take over the palm trees. Further post-war schemes include trials of fallow plants, of Chinese yams and rice, experiments with lime and artificial fertilizers and the establishment of Demonstration Farm Centres, Nurseries and Experimental and Demonstration Plots. The well-digging program which had been commenced before the war was intensified. Pioneer Oil Mills proposed to establish a network of mills throughout Aba Division each sited 8–10 miles from one another. This plan has been followed despite demonstrations against mill construction and opposition to the Agricultural Bill. In 1951 five mills were in production and four more building, artificial fertilizer was distributed to farmers and approximately 10,000 palm seedlings and 951 fruit trees planted, the latter encouraged by the construction of a fruit juice factory at Umuahia. Furthermore, loans were given for the establishment of plantations of oil palms and rubber, and of poultry, sheep, and pig farms.

South-eastern Nigeria faces, in regions like Aba Ngwa County, a problem of overcrowding. On the southern fringes, in regions like Ahoada, there is still land available for migrant farmers, although even this is evidently being reduced. Moreover, any attempt at a general resettlement would involve social disruption since all available farmland in the latter appears to be occupied, although farmed on more extensive lines. Farmers like the Ngwa have reacted to their new conditions by migration, by the fixing of settlement and associated farmland, by the reduction of farm size and fallow period, by changes in cropping and land tenure and even by the introduction of rules governing harvesting. The influence of world markets and the need felt to improve agricultural technique has prompted Governmental attempts to introduce further modifications, abandoning in effect the old policy of Indirect Rule. While it is true that rapid changes are disrupting the old institutions and introducing new problems which Government authorities can do much to solve, it is also evident that too rapid a promotion of new policies can also produce chaos. Similarly while the criticism can be raised that many more improvements are needed—for example, the planting of grass in all compound spaces around buildings could do much to prevent gully erosion—it is again evident that there is a danger in undertaking new methods of not fully appreciating the milieu or the results. Every improvement in agricultural technique and every increase in capital expenditure will tend to fix cultivators more and more to certain holdings. While it has been shown that the amount of movement required for farming is decreasing, it would be unwise to push the process too far by proposals involving increased expenditure on the land, until the questions raised by fixed agriculture in inter-tropical conditions have been answered.

ELLIOTT P. SKINNER

11. West African Economic Systems

I

Pre-European West Africa was by far the region of greatest indigenous economic development in sub-Saharan Africa. In contrast to
most parts of central, eastern and southern Africa, the peoples of
this part of the continent had economies which made agricultural
produce available in amounts large enough to be sold in rural and
urban markets; craft specialization often organized along the line
of craft guilds, whose members manufactured goods to be sold in
these markets; different kinds of currencies which were nearly always convertible one to another and, later, to European denomina-
tions of values; and elaborate trading systems, external as well as
internal. Goods produced in even the smallest West African societies
were circulated in local markets, and from there were funnelled to
urban market centers, and ultimately by porters, caravans, and
boats, to the large Sudanese emporiums from which they could be
shipped to Mediterranean areas in exchange for foreign products.

The economic unity of West Africa has not received the recognition it merits. Scholars have known that such towns as Kano, Timbuktu and others had large markets, but they have too often considered the other areas of West Africa as an economic wasteland.
What they have not realized is that the markets of the larger societies
could not exist without those of the smaller ones. The economic
systems of pre-colonial West Africa must therefore be seen within
the context of a West African economic unit, in which the more
highly developed economies were intimately tied to the less developed ones.

According to Bovill and Cornevin, the Carthaginians and the

SOURCE: Elliot P. Skinner, "West African Economic Systems," pp. 77–97,
Economic Transition in Africa, M. J. Herskovits and M. Harwitz, editors,
Northwestern University Press, 1964. Reprinted by permission of the publisher.

Romans had important commercial relations with northern Africa, and knew something about the economic resources of those lands south of the Sahara.[1] Sub-Saharan produce such as Moroccan leather and Sudanese gold continued to filter into North Africa during the early years of the Christian epoch. But it was only with the coming of the Arabs to West Africa in the eighth century that many Mediterranean peoples learned about such cities as Kombi, Mali, Djenne, Timbuktu, Gao, and Kano, the sources of much of their gold, ivory, skins, kola nuts, and slaves. Even then, the Arab merchants who participated in and often controlled this trade zealously barred others from taking part in it. "Consequently, Europe remained in almost complete ignorance of what lay beyond the coastal belt of North Africa. . . . All that Europe knew of the interior of Africa was that it concealed countries of immense wealth."[2] The nature of the wealth of the Sudan at this time can be judged from the story that in the fourteenth century Mansa Musa took thousands of pounds of gold dust with him to Cairo and Mecca, and that in early sixteenth-century Timbuktu "divers manuscripts or written books out of Barbary . . . are sold for more money than other merchandise."[3] With time, many of the trading cities lost a great deal of their influence, and many of the old caravan routes became unknown. Nevertheless, extant sources, used in conjuction with data from the still existing West African traditional economies, provide a good idea of the economic systems of this area just prior to European conquest.

The physical environment of West Africa provided some of the major pre-conditions for the development of a complex of economic systems. West Africa is a well-defined region. The two million or more square miles that make it up are drained by the internal systems of Lake Chad and by the tributaries of such rivers as the Senegal, the Voltas and the Niger, all of which flow into the Atlantic. Because of relatively heavy rainfall, its coastal plain is narrow, heavily forested and swampy. From this plain the land rises gently to a plateau, 500 to 1,000 feet high in places, and extending some 600 to 700 miles inland. Rainfall varies from 180 inches to fifteen and less as we move in a northerly direction. The vegetation reflects this pattern

[1] E. W. Bovill, 1958, pp. 17ff., 31ff.; R. Cornevin, 1956, pp. 64ff.
[2] E. W. Bovill, op. cit., p. 12.
[3] Ibid., p. 127.

of rainfall, changing successively from evergreen to deciduous forests with grass to Sudanese-type savannas, and fading to scrubby desert.

The nature of the soil has always been influenced by this pattern of rainfall. Lateritic soils, characteristic of the coastal plains, were formed primarily by heavy precipitation and severe climate. The savanna red and red-brown soils are the commonest in West Africa. They are fairly fertile, but have lost most of their lime because of leaching in torrential rains. In the Sudan–Sahel region, soils range from dark brown in regions of heaviest precipitation, to a fairly fertile chestnut brown where it is drier. Mineral deposits are scattered throughout the entire area, and the Africans have long exploited deposits of iron, copper, tin, rock salt, saline earths and gold, in addition to panning the rivers for alluvial gold. It has been estimated that about one million square miles of this variegated environment which is West Africa was, and is still, capable of supporting human habitation, and providing the basic conditions for the elaboration of human societies with complex cultures.[4]

II

West African peoples were basically farmers. Agriculture, or more technically horticulture, is old in this area, and at least one scholar has suggested that West Africa was one of the world centers of plant domestication.[5] The shifting cultivators of the rain forest produced such staple root crops as yams, taro or cocoyams, various kinds of cultivated bananas, varieties of both wet rice and dry rice, and such vegetables as okra, peas, gourds, fluted pumpkins, and beans, among other things. In addition, they harvested the products of such cultivated or protected trees and bushes as the kola tree, okee, tamarind, pepper bushes, red sorrel, and oil and raffia palms. With the discovery of the New World, the West Africans in the forest region and, to some extent, those in the savanna region, adopted maize, manioc, peanuts, sweet potatoes, and many other crops.[6] The savanna peoples were also shifting cultivators, but they specialized in the production of cereals. These included varieties of pearl millet, sorghum, fonio,

[4] D. S. Stamp, 1953, pp. 270–78.
[5] G. P. Murdock, 1959, p. 67.
[6] W. O. Jones, 1960.

and both wet rice and dry rice. Maize was later introduced in some areas. The savanna peoples also cultivated many varieties of root crops, tubers, vines, gourds, legumes, and leaf and stalk vegetables. In addition, they cultivated cotton and indigo, two crops which played an important role in their specialized economies. They collected the produce of such cultivated and protected trees and bushes as the shea-butter, locust bean, and hemp-leaved hibiscus.[7]

Animal husbandry was very important in the northern parts of West Africa, but it also played a role in the economies of several cultures to the south. Cattle were particularly valued by the Fulani people for their milk and butter, and among the many non-Fulani populations, for their meat and skins. The tsetse fly prevented herding by the West Africans in the forest zones, permitting them to keep only a variety of immune dwarf cattle. Goats and sheep, being more immune to the tsetse, had a wider distribution in West Africa, and were valued by their meat and skins. Chickens, ducks, bees, and the half-wild guinea fowl were also tended. Pigs had a limited distribution, and were not eaten in many areas, including those where Islam had not penetrated. Horses were limited to the northern part of the savanna region because of their high susceptibility to the tsetse fly. Here they were used as prestige animals, and in warfare. Donkeys had a wider distribution, not only because of a higher toleration for the trypanosomes, but also because of their utility as beasts of burden.

Hunting and fishing were part-time activities. Elephants provided the ivory so valued in some African societies and in the Mediterranean lands. The numerous other animals in this region were often hunted for their meat as well as for their skins. Specialization in fishing was limited to some riverine, coastal, and lacustrine populations, who traded dried and smoked fish into distant inland areas.

Agricultural production was basic to the development of the economies in West Africa, as it was for other areas. There were no cases of chronic land shortage. "Farm tenure" gave most persons the right to some land, and social pressures in many societies often dictated that they cultivate it. Every Dahomean was a farmer; no matter what his occupation, whether craftsman or not, he cultivated a plot of ground.[8] Symbolically, not even the Dahomean king himself was able to hold himself "exempt from the command to participate

[7] B. F. Johnston, 1958.
[8] M. J. Herskovits, 1938, Vol. I, p. 49.

in the cooperative labor of farming."[9] Farming was said by all Tiv to be their "great work," and provided most of the imagery and metaphor of labor.[10] Even the trade-minded populations of Djenne, Bamako, and Sansanding believed that "working the soil is the only noble profession."[11] The Mossi of the Upper Volta declare, "The hoe is the work of mankind." Similar attitudes toward food production can be found reported in the monographs dealing with most of the populations of West Africa.

The basic unit of agricultural production was the extended family. True, in most societies individuals were allowed, even encouraged, to produce commodities for their own use, but usually only after they had fulfilled their obligations to their kinsmen.[12] Nevertheless it appeared to be true for the Nupe, among others, that the extended family afforded "the only means of cultivating a large variety of both useful and profitable crops."[13] The actual amount of food produced by these units differed from society to society, and often depended upon the crops grown and whether or not there was crop specialization. Regardless of the society, however, the extended family apparently produced enough food to allow some of it to be disposed of in the market place.

The extended family which found that it could not produce enough foodstuff for itself or for sale often made use of larger cooperative units. A Dahomean had recourse to a cooperative working group known as the *dopkwe* when his fields were "too extensive to permit them to be hoed by his own labor and the labor of those whose services he has at his disposal."[14] The Nupe used a larger cooperative unit called the *egbe* for agricultural production when, for various reasons, the extended family was insufficient, or "simply because its ambitious program demands larger cooperation than is at its disposal."[15] The Jukun employed a cooperative unit similar to the *egbe* for the production of surplus food, part of which they sold "in exchange for clothes."[16] The informal cooperative work group

[9] Ibid., p. 30.
[10] L. and P. Bohannan, 1953, p. 51.
[11] V. Pacques, 1954, p. 63.
[12] Elliott P. Skinner, 1960, p. 383; cf. also S. F. Nadel, 1942, p. 241; R. E. Bradbury, 1957, p. 23.
[13] S. F. Nadel, 1942, p. 246; cf. M. J. Herskovits, 1938, I, p. 31; L. and P. Bohannan, 1953, p. 51.
[14] M. J. Herskovits, 1938, I, p. 72.
[15] S. F. Nadel, 1942, p. 248.
[16] C. K. Meek, 1931, pp. 409–10.

among the Mossi, the *sosose,* also served the same function, that is, the production of agricultural commodities, some of which were often sold in the markets.

III

In many of the more highly developed societies, surplus agricultural products were produced by serfs and slaves. Much of what was grown by them was used to feed the personnel of royal or nobles' houses, and to entertain guests, but a large portion was sold locally or traded to passing merchants or caravans. In Dahomey, there was a class of men known as the *gletanu* (great cultivators) who even produced crops especially for sale to middlewomen. The farms of these men, cultivated by their relatives and slaves, comprised areas of from 15 to 25 kilometers in length and several kilometers in breadth, and specialized in the raising of some single food staple such as millet, maize, or yams. In some exceptional cases, all three crops were grown by the same planter.[17] The Yoruba also used slaves for the specialized production of foodstuffs for resale in the markets. Talbot reports that a large number of Yoruba slaves "remained out in the suburbs, where they farmed huge plantations, in consequence of which food supplies were remarkably cheap and plentiful."[18]

Whether or not this economic specialization among the Yoruba and the Dahomeans was a response to European contact on the coast is unknown, but the fact that it also developed indigenously is seen by its appearance in Djenne, in the Sudan. Here the large merchants kept slaves in the rural districts to produce the foodstuffs so necessary for the survival of desert-surrounded Timbuktu. Thus we have in West Africa several levels of food production: subsistence crops, from which surplus food was taken to be sold in the markets; production for the nobility, some of which was also drawn off for sale; and specialized production for the markets.

Few West African societies were without craftsmen, who manufactured goods for local consumption and for external sale. Craftsmanship in the smaller groupings, such as the Ewe, Tiv, Katab, Lobi,

[17] M. J. Herskovits, 1938, I, p. 55.
[18] P. A. Talbot, 1926, III, p. 699.

Gurunsi, Birom, Ga and Tallensi was ancillary to farming and, except for the fact that craftsmen often belonged to the same lineage, was unorganized. For example, Manoukian tells us that

> The main handicrafts practiced by the Ewe are spinning, weaving, pottery-making, and black-smithing. With very few exceptions these are all part-time occupations, being combined with farming or trading. There does not seem to have been at any time any considerable development of economic specialization, comparable with that which obtained in Ashanti and Dahomey.[19]

Nevertheless, it was as true for the Ewe as for the other societies that part of the manufactured goods of even these smaller societies was eventually diffused into the larger market centers.[20]

Specialized production of manufactured goods for sale was more characteristic of the large state societies of the Guinea Coast and of the Sudan. The craftsmen and artisans here produced all manner of goods, and had highly developed social and economic organizations which facilitated production and dissemination. The Ashanti wove cotton cloth and dyed it; they also made barkcloth, pottery, numerous types of carved wooden objects and utensils, and produced many metal objects and articles, some of them by the cire-perdue process. Significantly, the *adwumfo*, or goldsmiths who played an important role in the economy of Ashanti, "were in the olden days an honoured class; they formed a sort of brotherhood and were privileged to wear gold ornaments, otherwise restricted to kings and their wives, and greater chiefs." The art was retained in certain families.[21]

The craftsmen and artisans of Dahomey and Benin produced a greater variety of manufactured goods, and were more highly organized, than in Ashanti. This fits in with other evidence that they were more highly developed than Ashanti as concerns trade and commerce. Most of the more important craft groups in Dahomey lived in special quarters. The jewellers had their own quarters; the iron-workers who made agricultural implements and weapons were organized into "forges," each of which had its houses and workshops in

[19] M. Manoukian, 1952, p. 17
[20] Ibid., p. 19.
[21] M. Manoukian, 1950, pp. 20–21.

a separate part of a town, or in a separate village. The weavers had special quarters where their looms were located; and the potters had their centers in those areas where the best clay was found.[22] Similarly, most of the "important crafts of the Benin kingdom were in the hands of special ward-guilds in Benin City. There were guilds of blacksmiths and brass-smiths, wood and ivory carvers (one group), leather workers, weavers of special embroidered cloth, drum-makers, locksmiths, etc."[23] Both in Dahomey and Benin the craft guildsmen were also members of specific families. In contrast to the smaller societies, however, guild heads, and therefore family heads, were able to control the production of goods, fix prices and also punish guildsmen who violated guild rules. The Benin ruler went even further. He granted some of the guilds virtual monopolies over certain products, but retained the products of such guilds as the brass-smiths and ivory carvers for himself.[24]

Craft guild production and guild organization reached their greatest development among the Nupe of Central Nigeria, and possibly also among the Hausa. There were iron ore miners and blacksmiths, brass and silver smiths, glassmakers, weavers, potters, bead workers, masons, wood workers and carpenters.[25] In contrast to Dahomey and Benin, however, not all who produced certain craft goods were members of guilds or had to join them. The guilds themselves, like most African craft guilds, were composed of members of the same families, but they were open to anyone who formally applied for admission and went through an apprenticeship. Some of these guilds, like that of the blacksmith, were found all over Nupe, and were controlled by chiefs who were often agents of the ruler. On the local level, they were fairly autonomous, setting their own standards of production. The other types of guilds in Nupe appear to have functioned on a slightly different basis. For example, the head of the bead workers treated his guildsmen as though they were journeymen. He procured work for them, supervised their work, and paid them out of the money he received. Most of the guildsmen of Nupe, however, were bound to their guilds and were controlled by a leader who was often admitted to the King's council. Nadel felt that the craftsmen of Nupe were "the king's craftsmen" and that their or-

22 M. J. Herskovits, 1938, I, pp. 44–50; II, p. 354.
23 R. E. Bradbury, 1957, p. 26; cf. Talbot, op. cit., II, p. 308.
24 R. E. Bradbury, ibid., pp. 26, 34–35.
25 S. F. Nadel, 1942, p. 257.

ganization presented a picture "closely resembling the organization of craft guilds of Imperial Rome and the Middle Ages."[26]

The Kano *Chronicle* suggests that in Hausa country there were guilds of blacksmiths, brewers, miners, salt workers, and even medicine makers, archers, minstrels and dancers, long before the arrival of the Hausa invaders.[27] By the time Clapperton and Barth arrived in Kano several centuries later, there were crafts and more guilds in existence. It appears that these, like those in Nupe, Benin and Dahomey, also occupied separate sections of the city.[28] Kano was especially well-known for its leather work and cloth production; in addition, the people of this important trading center also worked iron, silver and brass, and there were potters, glass workers, bead makers and wood carvers.[29] But the industry that impressed Barth most of all was the production of cotton cloth. He enumerated and described about twenty different types of cloth made in Kano and other towns. In terms of the amount of cloth produced Barth had this to say:

> In taking a general view of the subject, I think myself justified in estimating the whole produce of this manufacture, as far as it is sold abroad, at the very least at about 3,000,000,000 [cowries]; and how great this national wealth is will be understood by my readers when they know that, with from fifty to sixty thousand kurdi,[30] or from four to five pounds sterling a year, a whole family may live in that country with ease . . . [moreover] this industry is not carried on here, as in Europe, in immense establishments, degrading man to the meanest condition of life, but . . . it gives employment and support to families without compelling them to sacrifice their domestic habits.[31]

The societies north and west of Hausa did not produce as much manufactured goods as those in Nigeria; nor were their craft guilds as complex. An interesting aspect of most of these craft guilds was

26 Ibid., pp. 257–94, *passim.*
27 H. R. Palmer, 1908, pp. 62–65.
28 D. Denham and H. Clapperton, 1826, Section II, p. 53.
29 Ibid., pp. 54–56; H. Barth, 1859, I, p. 512.
30 Barth used the term kurdi for cowries. The exchange value of this currency was 2,500 cowries for one Spanish or Austrian dollar.
31 H. Barth, 1859, I, pp. 511–12.

that their members were often not respected, and occupied subordinate social positions. Rouch called Songhoi specialists in iron working, carpentering and canoe building, in weaving, leather working and pottery making "artisan castes."[32] The slipper makers, smiths, masons, tailors, and leather workers of nearby Timbuktu were said to have belonged to a "sort of guild system of hereditary crafts." Nevertheless, this guild system did not prevent the elaboration of the crafts, since some guildsmen employed slaves and serfs to work for them. Some of the smiths here even specialized in working only one metal, such as silver or gold; other smiths worked all types of metals.[33]

The people of Djenne showed "vestiges of a division into corporations" when visited by Dubois in the 1890s. The crafts found here were not too different from those in the other areas of the Sudan. These were also honored professions, however, and the craft guild leaders were "among those personages of the town who deliberate and control public affairs."[34] In contrast, similar craftsmen along the river Niger at Bougouni and Bamako were held in low esteem and known by an "injurious sobriquet, Nyamamkala."[35] The nearby Senufo of the Ivory Coast apparently came from the Niger area, bringing with them similar notions about the inferior social position of craftsmen. Their most important crafts were carpentry, weaving, smithing, and jewel making. The production of all of these "caste guilds" was controlled by the elder of each family involved.[36] In Senegal, craft guilds whose members were considered as belonging to a low social stratum were well organized. Their work was supervised by their leading men, "with whom the bur [king] dealt when he had any matter concerning their groups."[37] Similar guilds were found in neighboring Sierra Leone, Guinea, and Liberia. Among some of the groups in Liberia, however, the guilds extended far beyond the local communities, including "those practicing the same handicraft, regardless of clan or tribal affiliations."[38]

[32] J. Rouch, 1954, pp. 23–25.
[33] H. Miner, 1953, pp. 52–54.
[34] F. Dubois, 1899, p. 196.
[35] V. Pacques, 1954, p. 63.
[36] B. Holas, 1957, p. 70.
[37] D. P. Gamble, 1957, pp. 57ff.
[38] G. Schwab, 1947, p. 121.

IV

Markets were ubiquitous in West Africa. There were a few regions where aboriginal markets were absent—in parts of Liberia, southwestern Ivory Coast, and in certain portions of the plateau regions of Nigeria. Nevertheless, even here people engaged in trade, and benefited from the markets of contiguous areas. The markets served as local exchange points or nodes, and trade was the vascular system unifying all of West Africa, moving products to and from local markets, larger market centers, and still larger centers.

Important features of all the markets in the smaller West African societies and in the rural areas of the larger entities were their cyclical periodicities. These markets were held every three, four, five, eight, or even sixteen days. Within a circumscribed area covered by a cycle, not more than one market was held on any one day, so that the people within the area had the opportunity to visit every market in turn. Small local markets, held daily, made it possible to buy food and other staples in small amounts on the days when the larger ones were "closed." Another feature of markets was the segregation of vendors or merchants according to the product sold.

The first Europeans to arrive at the lower Niger River in the eastern coast of West Africa reported that they saw Ibo traders from inland bringing yams, cows, goats and sheep for trading with such coastal peoples as the Ijaw in exchange for salt.[39] Nothing much is known, however, about the early markets in this region until they appeared full-blown with the manilla currencies during the height of the slave trade.[40] We know, however, that the Nupe traders brought goods from Kano and points north to Onitsha in exchange for such forest products as palm oil.[41] Yoruba markets had periodicities of four, eight, and even sixteen days. Those in the larger urban areas were held every day and even during the evening. Large numbers of women traders sold specific types of goods, leaving other types for sale by men. There was barter in these markets, but cowries, manillas, and iron bars were also used as currencies to buy such

[39] P. A. Talbot, 1926, I, p. 184.
[40] K. O. Diké, 1956, pp. 42–43.
[41] S. F. Nadel, 1942, p. 319.

goods as live animals, cooked foods, cereals, salt, fish, palm oil and palm wine, cotton cloth clothes, pottery, soap, slaves, jewelry made of iron, brass and copper, weapons and implements made of iron.[42]

The rural trading centers of the neighboring Edo had a periodicity of four days, and formed a cycle of feeder markets which supplied the capital, Benin, and large towns outside the kingdom. There were two large markets at Benin, alternating daily. The types of goods sold here were probably no different from those among the Yoruba. A visitor to the Benin market in 1589 reported,

> Pepper and elephant teeth, oyle of palme, cloth made of cotton woll very curiously woven, and cloth made of the barke of palme trees were procured in exchange for cloth both linen and wollen, iron works of sundry sorts, Manillos or bracelets of copper, glass beades and Corrall. . . . They have good store of soap and it smelleth like beaten vilets—Also many pretie fine mats and baskets that they make, and spoones of elephants' teeth very curiously wrought with divers proportions of foules and beasts made upon them.[43]

These Edo people traded goods with Ibo and the Yoruba, and also with some unidentified "Dry Land" peoples from the hills behind Addamugu or Abela who "brought horses to them."[44] Yoruba trade to Nupe, Hausa and Dahomey was highly organized by "trade chiefs" who "furthered the commercial interests of their towns, settled disputes at the markets, and made rules and regulations to ensure just prices and safeguard the standards of workmanship in crafts."[45]

The markets of Dahomey reached their height during the period of the slave trade, but like the markets of neighboring countries they maintained their African characteristics despite European influences. Herskovits reported three types in this country—small roadside stands which opened daily, large wholesale markets for the sale of agricultural products, and retail markets which served as the major instruments for the circulation of all types of goods. The larger markets met every four days, and constituted market cycles.

[42] P. A. Talbot, op. cit., III, pp. 920–46.
[43] Quoted in P. A. Talbot, 1926, III, pp. 159–60.
[44] Ibid., p. 172.
[45] S. O. Biobaku, 1952, p. 38.

The wholesale markets were run by the *gletanu*, the specialized farmers, who might send agents to neighboring retail markets to determine the resale price of their products before setting the proper discount for the middlewomen who brought their goods. There was little barter in Dahomean markets; the people here used cowrie shells as currency. In some markets, prices were set by the first arrivals, and as the late comers followed suit there was no haggling. Some of the associations of market women established prices for the products they sold, and punished vendors who violated the set price. Many of the craft guilds, such as the iron workers, wood carvers and jewellers, permitted their members to haggle over the prices of their products.[46] Dahomey traded a great deal with the early Europeans; it also had fairly extensive indigenous foreign trade. Herskovits reports that Dahomeans traded agricultural products and salt both east and west. Some of their goods did go north to Kumasi, Sansanne Mango and Kandi, important caravan terminals for both Timbuktu and Kano. They imported large quantities of leather products from Kano along the same route.[47]

The Ewe people of what is now Ghana and Togo had small daily markets. These were held in most villages, whose women and children exchanged or bought foodstuffs and such products as soap, pottery, yarn and firewood for domestic use. Large markets were held every four days in the larger towns, which formed part of a market cycle. Such larger markets were patronized by Ewe from neighboring towns and villages, and by professional traders from Dahomey and Hausa country. The Ewe used both barter and cowrie shell currency in their small and larger markets. Foodstuffs were sold at fixed prices; in contrast, buyers and sellers of livestock and articles of craftmanship, such as pottery, mats, and cloth always haggled, especially foreign traders.[48]

The markets of the societies in the middle zone between the eastern coast of West Africa and the Hausa states in the north were important centers of exchange and trade in the period prior to European incursion. The Tiv of central Nigeria had "five-day" cycle markets. The smaller units in the cycle dealt mainly in local produce, but there was always one large one which served as a hub.

[46] M. J. Herskovits, 1938, I, pp. 51–62, *passim;* cf. ibid., 1952a, pp. 217–20, 347.
[47] M. J. Herskovits, 1938, I, p. 108; ibid., 1936, pp. 16–22.
[48] M. Manoukian, 1952, pp. 19–20.

Tiv conducted most of their small-scale commercial transactions by means of barter, occasionally using both rods and *tugudu* cloth as currency and as a standard for value. Their producers and middle-men brought their goods to the larger hub markets for resale to other Tiv, Hausa, Ibo, Jukun and Nupe merchants.[49]

Nupe country, which lay northeast of Tiv, was likened to "one big market." Nadel tells us that "the complexity of Nupe economics and . . . the far-reaching specialization of Nupe production . . . expresses itself most forcibly in the wide scope of trade and market-ing."[50] The smaller markets were held every five days and also formed cycles. In the very small villages, markets were deserted on off days, but in the larger villages restricted trade in foodstuffs was carried on. Bida, the market center of Nupe, had six centers, three main day markets close to the three royal houses, two small day markets (one near the west gate of the town, and one in the "stranger's quarters"), and one night market which, according to Nadel, usually had ten times the attendance of even the largest of the village markets, and possessed all manner of goods. There were also many small shops throughout the town.

Nupe men and women traders usually sold different types of goods. Some vendors specialized in one product, or in several products which were usually sold together; others sold a little of all types of goods. Cowries were a universal currency, and little or no barter took place. Fixed prices were charged for most merchandise. Never-theless, the Nupe saw to it that the prices of goods corresponded "closely to variations in supply and demand, above all, to seasonal fluctuations." They also made sure "that distance between area of production and market, and the additional labour and loss of time involved in transport, enter into the calculation of price and profit."[51] Many of the Nupe merchants were members of market guilds. Market guildsmen had booths where they acted as brokers, selling goods for client-traders on a commission basis. Their elected head-man, who was confirmed by the king, was paid a fee. He inspected the goods in the caravans when they arrived at the market. He reported to the ruler in order to ascertain his wishes before placing the goods on sale in the market place. Once the guild-master re-ceived this permission, he then guaranteed to all guild members

---

[49] L. and P. Bohannan, 1953, p. 53; P. J. Bohannan, 1959, pp. 491ff.
[50] S. F. Nadel, 1942, p. 319.
[51] Ibid., loc. cit.

equal access to the goods, and sought to avoid unsound competition among them. He also tried to insure business integrity on the part of trader and broker alike.[52]

V

The list of the traditional trade routes which passed through Nupe country, and moved in all directions, reveals the complexity of the trade of these people. Nupe traders, traveling along these routes, tapped the "small circle of inter-village exchange which form no less part of the comprehensive marketing scheme of the country" than did the larger markets. They also visited the "relay stations" where, according to Nadel, people brought specific types of goods for trade. The palm oil, kola nuts, other forest products and goods they collected from Nupe were taken to Hausa country to be exchanged for trans-Saharan products, cloth from Kano, and potash from Bornu. These they brought back south, sending them to the Yoruba, Ibo and Tiv. Such traders, unlike craftsmen and market brokers, belonged to the larger fraternity of Nupe traders who formed colonies, especially in the larger towns in northern Nigeria and surrounding regions.[53]

Hausa markets were the most important in all of the eastern edge of the western Sudan. In the rural communities they were held in accordance with cycles of four days.[54] Clapperton found them filled with beef, mutton, fowls, gussub, beans, Indian corn and other products.[55] Markets in the larger towns met every day. Each was divided into sections where goods of various sorts, and occasionally slaves, were sold. Clapperton tells us that merchants came to these markets from "all parts of Africa, from the Mediterranean and the Mountains of the Moon, and from Sennar and Ashanti."[56] These merchants were reportedly quite fair in their dealings. If a purchase was later found to be defective, the broker or the seller was obliged by the laws of the market to refund the price paid for it. On the other hand, the merchants were very aware of the principles of

[52] S. F. Nadel, 1942, p. 330.
[53] Ibid., p. 320.
[54] M. F. Smith, 1959, p. 20.
[55] D. Denham and H. Clapperton, 1826, Section II, p. 18.
[56] Ibid., p. 50.

TABLE I

Volume, Value, Type, Source and Destination of Goods in Kano Market, 1851

Product	Volume	Value	Source and Destination
Cloth	300 camel-loads per year	60 million cowries	Kano area to Timbuktu. *Comment:* According to Barth, this cloth was shipped as far North as Myrzuk, Ghat, and Tripoli; to the East as far as Bornu; and to the South and South-east to the Igbara, Igbo and Adamawa.
Nuts, Kola	500 ass-loads per year	200,000 cowries per ass-load; total: 80–100 million cowries	From Forest zone for shipment North to Sudan Zone. *Comment:* One-half value was profit.
Natron	20,000 loads per year	(?)	From Bornu to Nupe and Nyffi. *Comment:* Transit tax of 500 cowries per load, giving 10 million cowries carried by horses, asses and oxen.
Salt	1,000 camel-loads per year	50–80 million cowries	Salt merchants from Desert bought Kano merchandise with their money.
Ivory	100 "kantars" per year	75–100,000 cowries per kantar	Not an important trade item. *Comment:* Lowest price per kantar was "thirty dollars, or 75,000 cowries."
Silk, Coarse	3–400 camel-loads per year	200,000 cowries each, or 70 million cowries	From Tripoli by way of Ghadames.

Product	Volume	Value	Source and Destination
Cloth, Woolen	(?)	15 million cowries	
Calicoes and Prints, Bleached and Unbleached (From Manchester)	(?)	Over 40 million cowries	Cloth comes through Ghadames, but some of it often dyed and re-imported.
Sugar	100 camel-loads per year	12 million cowries	
Paper, Wrapping	(?)	5 million cowries	Probably from France, "Trés lune" trade-mark.
Needles and Looking Glasses	(?)	8 million cowries	Needles with emblem of a pig. Formerly came from Nuremberg, but lately from Leghorn. *Comment:* Needles sold for one cowrie each. Barth sold 1,000 for 600 cowries.
Blades, Sword	50,000 per year	50 million	Most blades sold out of the country to neighboring groups.
Silks, French (called "hattaya")	(?)	20 million cowries	Imported and re-imported to Yoruba country and Gonja.
Clothes, Arab	(?)	60 million cowries	From Tunis and Egypt, but some of it from Leghorn.
Beads	(?)	50 million cowries	
Frankincense, Rose Oil, Spices, Cloves	(?)	55 million cowries	Many of these luxury items for princes.
Copper and Zinc	70 loads per year	15–20 million cowries	From Tripoli and Darfur
Leather Products, such as Sandals		15 million cowries	
Slaves	5,000 per year	150–200 million cowries	Sold mainly to American slave dealers. American produce found in Nupe markets.

supply and demand, and held goods out of the market when prices fell, in order to obtain later higher prices. Currency in these markets was the *cowry,* but silver and other media were convertible.

An outstanding aspect of the Hausa country markets was the great volume of trade that passed through them. Barth described the Kano market in the following terms. "Here a caravan from Gonja arriving with the desired kolanut . . . or a caravan laden with natron, starting for Nupe, or a troop of Asbenawa going off with their salt for the neighboring towns, or some Arabs leading their camels, heavily laden with the luxuries of the North and East."[57] Due mainly to Barth's reportorial skill we have some data on the value, volume, type, source and destination of goods which passed through the Kano market in 1851.[58]

Barth estimated that over £80,000 worth of bulk merchandise passed through Kano market alone in any one year; and this without taking into account the petty trade.[59] Not all of this trade was in the hands of the Hausa, but so famous were Hausa traders in this part of West Africa that the name Hausa became synonymous with trader. Hausa traders visited Tiv, Nupe, Ibo, and probably Yoruba and Edo. In addition, they went to such Nigerian societies as the Katab, Jaba, Kagaro, Pyem, Jukun, the Kanuri, Bornu and even Bargirimi. They moved westward to Dendi in northern Dahomey; Tilho has given us a précis of their activities:

> The Dendi have a little of everything, the Zaberma [Songhoi] have only livestock and potash. The Bengou people have only salt, the inhabitants of Ilo foodstuffs which they produce, and the Hausa the cotton cloth which they weave. As it is, the Zaberma go to Bengou to sell their livestock in exchange for salt which they carry to Ilo. At Ilo they meet the Hausa who bring cotton cloth there to exchange and thereby procure merchandise, part of which they sell afterwards to the Dendi. Then the Zaberma and the Dendi go to Kani where they meet people from Togoland with whom they exchange their merchandise for kola nuts, which are then sent off to Sokoto.[60]

[57] H. Barth, I, 1859, p. 498.
[58] Ibid., pp. 507–25.
[59] H. Barth, 1859, vol. I, pp. 498–512.
[60] Ned Noll, 1960, pp. 402–3.

Hausa traders also went to Gao, Zinder and Dori in the country of the Songhoi, to Ouagadougou, Kaya and Tenkodogo in Mossi country, and to the markets of Salaga in the country which is now Ghana. Here they competed with traders who were involved in another trading complex—that between the western coastal and forest zones of West Africa, and the Sudanese emporiums along the Niger River to the north.

Few data exist about the traditional markets in the western coastal region, except those in the former Gold Coast. A report of 1602 tells us that in this area,

> Everie towne hath market daies specially appointed, upon the which you find more to bee bought than upon other daies, and everie towne hath his market upon such a day, as the others have it not, and so everie one differeth upon their daies, and when their market daies come, they have two daies market one after the other, wherein the principall boores or countrie people come from divers places to traffique with the ships. They have their Sunday also, but on that they doe nothing. The inhabitants of the seaside, come also to the market with their wares, which they buy of the Netherlands, as linen cloth, knives, ground corals, looking glasses, pinnes, arme rings, and fish, which their husbands have gotton in the sea, whereof the women buy much, and carrie them to other townes within the land, to get some profit by them, so that the fish which is taken in the sea, is carried at least an hundred or two miles up into the land.

The principal traders in these markets were women described as "very nimble about their businesse." Apparently linen cloth and gold were used as currency, since, according to most reports, the people in the coastal regions of the Gold Coast refused to accept or to use cowries.[61]

Information on the markets in the forest zone of the western part of West Africa is very sparse. This area was famous for its trade, because it was a primary source of kola nuts. Binger, in 1892, stated that in parts of the Ivory Coast a secret society had control over the trade in this commodity, and tried to prevent the Dioula and other Sudanese merchants from gaining access to the areas of produc-

[61] Pieter de Marees [1602], from F. Wolfson, 1958, pp. 55–56.

tion.[62] However, when Ollone traveled in northern Liberia about two decades later, he found the trade well organized and, in meeting places near each village, he found "bales of kola nuts, well packed as though for a long journey, with marks painted on them, perhaps those of their owners or of the consignee."[63] Chevalier found in one Guerze village of the Ivory Coast a Monday market where, "1,500 buyers and sellers gathered . . . and about 100 charges of kolas and 20 charges of rubber were exchanged there for salt, cloth, iron, copper." At Nzo, two thousand individuals, men and women, came there each week from a radius of more than 70 kilometers to exchange about 100 charges of kolas.[64] Kola nuts and other forest products found their way to Niger river towns such as Bamako, Djenne, Timbuktu, and finally across the desert.[65] Goods that came to these markets in return were traded down to the coast and even in Liberia.[66] The Kwahu people of the forest region of eastern Akim, in what is now Ghana, took their kola nuts to Kumasi, Kintampo and especially to Salaga.[67]

Salaga had a unique role in the economic structure of West Africa. In contrast to Bida in Nupe, which acted as a staging center for goods going to Kano, and Djenne, which played a similar role for Timbuktu, Salaga traded with both areas. It was strictly a traders' town. Its life depended upon trade, and in contrast to Kumasi, cowries, gold and cloth were accepted here as currency, while those persons without currency could barter. It had a daily market where one encountered

> the Mosi with his cattle, sheep and slaves . . . the natives of Dagomba, Sansanne Mango, and the many small countries on the interior with cattle, sheep, ivory, skins of wild animals, the various products of their countries, principally clothes, basket-work, mats, &c.; traders from Lagos with coast produce; the leather workers, basket and mat makers, saddle and pannier makers, water sellers, women selling various kinds of food; the whole presents a very animated though exceedingly hot scene.[68]

[62] L. G. Binger, 1892, I, pp. 142–43.
[63] L. G. Ollone, 1901, p. 309.
[64] A. Chevalier, 1909, pp. 26–27.
[65] E. W. Bovill, 1958, pp. 240–41.
[66] G. Schwab, 1947, p. 121.
[67] R. L. T. Lonsdale [1882], from F. Wolfson, 1958, p. 185.
[68] Ibid., loc. cit.

Salaga's real trade, however, was conducted outside of the market: "One may stroll for two hours in and out of the various streets before having seen the whole of the business which is carried on."[69] In its heyday, 10,000 persons entered Salaga every day, and in season many caravans of from 200 to 500 and 600 persons arrived and left for such places as Sokoto, Kano, Sansanne Mango, Salfara, Hombori and Timbuktu. These caravans were themselves "moving markets, buying and selling everywhere along the road."[70]

The caravans which went north through Mossi country often traded in the rural markets, which had periodicities of three days and were members of market cycles. The caravaneers either bought or sold goods here for cowries, or bartered them against other products. The larger Mossi market centers were open every day and afforded the merchants a wider variety of goods, since they were the collecting points for products from many of the rural markets. From Mossi country, many of these caravans went northward to Dori, at whose markets they met Hausa caravans going north to Gao, then turning east to Timbuktu. Other caravans of Dioula came north from Kong and the kola markets, heading for the Niger river towns of Bamako, Segou, Djenne and Timbuktu.[71]

Djenne, the staging area for goods from the southern and western parts of West Africa to Timbuktu, was as much a trading center as it was a market. Dubois declared that,

> Instead of confining her trade to the market-place, as in the case of other towns, Jenne cries "Commerce! Commerce!" at every step. . . . She sends her merchandise to the sea-coast; and when the first Europeans trading between Benin and Cape Palamas asked where the gold and produce offered for sale came from, the natives answered "from Jenne." Her name was thus given to the Gulf of Guinea, and indirectly, to an English coin, the guinea, so called because the first pieces were struck from gold coming from there.[72]

Whether Dubois is correct about the origin of the word Guinea or whether this is simply folk etymology, he did report that he saw virgin gold in the warehouses of Djenne as well as such exotic prod-

69 V. S. Gouldsbury [1897], from F. Wolfson, 1958, p. 169.
70 R. L. T. Lonsdale [1882], from F. Wolfson, 1958, p. 184.
71 P. L. Monteil, 1894, p. 91.
72 F. Dubois, 1899, pp. 89, 182.

ucts as packets of ostrich feathers, civet musk, lead, marble, anti-mony. In addition, there were the local commodities, especially kola nuts and foodstuffs.

The merchants at Djenne appear to have organized their trade quite efficiently. Her inhabitants,

> organized "business firms" in the European sense of the word, which were provided with a routine and staff similar to our own. They established representatives in important centers and opened branches at Timbuktu. They sent out travelling agents who received percentages of the business they accomplished, and were, in fact, none other than "commercial travellers." The staff was composed of relatives and slaves, or free men who were obliged to earn their living.[73]

One merchant, when queried by Dubois as to how this commission-agents' system worked, replied: "We trust our merchandise to people who have no goods; they sell it for us throughout the country, and part of the profit is theirs. If they have the will they can become merchants in their turn."[74] These merchants shipped their goods up and down the river in boats measuring between fifty-eight and sixty-five feet long by ten feet wide. They were capable of carrying as much as twenty to thirty tons. According to Dubois, to convey the same load by land would have necessitated a caravan of a thousand porters, or two hundred camels, or three hundred bullocks.[75] Rene Caillie reported that he "frequently" saw flotillas of sixty to eighty such boats laden with various kinds of produce, making the passage between Djenne and Timbuktu.[76]

The two daily markets of Timbuktu, the Big Market and the Little Market, dealt mainly in provisions, household and personal articles for its inhabitants. Much of the trading there was in the hands of craftsmen and lower class persons. Serfs and slaves bought goods for their noble masters, who neither went to the market, nor allowed their women folk to go there.[77] There was little or no

[73] F. Dubois, 1899, p. 174.
[74] Ibid., p. 195.
[75] Ibid., p. 177.
[76] R. Caillie, 1830, II, p. 9.
[77] H. Miner, 1953, p. 66.

barter, cowries and gold being the media of exchange used. These
two currencies fluctuated one against the other, especially during
famines. At such times cowries were more important than gold
because of the

> greater practicality of cowries for small market transactions and
> hence the greater demand for them under conditions of
> famine inflated prices. On the one known occasion when the
> cowrie value of gold did not decline during a famine—that of
> 1738—the evidence is positive that it was the shortage of gold
> which kept its value up.[78]

Haggling was common, and commerce was conducted on a basis of
mutual suspicion. In contrast to Kano, the motto here might well
have been *caveat emptor*. Perhaps this mutual suspicion reflects the
fact that Timbuktu was a place where the economic practices and
attitudes characteristic of West Africa came into contact with those
of the Mediterranean world. For to paraphrase an old Sudanese
saying: "Timbuktu was the place where the camels from across the
desert met the canoes, donkeys and porters from Black Africa."

Almost the whole life of the city of Timbuktu was based upon
foreign commerce. Caillie found the ten to twelve thousand people
there nearly all "involved in trade."[79] The goods that came from
innumerable West African producers to Timbuktu were sent to two
areas. One portion, destined for the

> towns and nomadic tribes of the Sahara, consisted principally
> of matters of alimentation, such as millet, rice, karite butter,
> manioc, peanuts, honey, kola nuts, neta, baobab flour,
> monkey bread, tamarinds, onions and tobacco (cheaper and
> inferior to that of Tuat), dried fish, and in addition, soap,
> iron, antimony, cotton, straw hats, potteries, and calabashes.
> The other portion was specially allotted to Morocco, Tuat, and
> Ghadames, and comprised gold, ivory, ostrich plumes, raw
> leather, wax, incense, civet musk, indigo, gum, etc., and a few
> slaves.[80]

[78] H. Miner, 1953, pp. 48–49.
[79] R. Caillie, 1830, II, p. 56.
[80] F. Dubois, 1899, pp. 283–84.

The goods that came across the desert from the salt mines and the Mediterranean area destined for diffusion throughout West Africa came along two main roads from the north, one from Morocco, and the other from Ghadames, which was linked to Egypt. Apparently two large salt caravans a year arrived in Timbuktu from the mines of Taodeni. The number of camel-loads of salt varied from year to year, but according to Dubois, about 50,000 to 60,000 loads entered the city annually. The other caravans brought such Mediterranean products as red cloth, looking-glasses, cutlery, tobacco, bleached and unbleached calico, firearms, scissors, needles, silk, seed pearls for embroidery, large pearls for necklaces, amber, coral, spices (mainly cloves), sugar, coffee, tea, perfumes, teapots, cups, snuff-boxes, dates, carpets, fezzes, burnouses, caftans, in addition to other commodities.[81]

VI

The coming of the Europeans had an important effect on West African economies. Some of the coastal states developed large commercial centers but often did so at the expense of the smaller societies, whose populations were sold into chattel slavery. The abolition of slavery coincided with the desire of the Europeans to explore the interior of Africa, and capture the Saharan trade for themselves. What surprised many of the travelers who went there was the scale of the economies of societies relatively untouched by the slave trade. Mungo Park's reaction to Segou is an example: "The view of this extensive city; the numerous canoes upon the river; the crowded population, and the cultivated state of the surrounding country, formed altogether a prospect of civilization and magnificence, which I little expected to find in the bosom of Africa."[82] Wherever he and the other travelers went inland; they encountered "Commerce! Commerce!" Barth, Caillie, Clapperton and Monteil all compared the interior of Africa with contemporary Europe, and advocated trade with this region. Unfortunately for the advocates of liberal trading policies, who saw in the establishment of commercial relations between Africa and Europe excellent profits for all the groups concerned, the industrial system of Europe, which had now

[81] F. Dubois, 1899, pp. 270–301 *passim;* H. Barth, 1853, I, p. 66.
[82] M. Park, 1799, I, p. 196.

made the slave trade obsolete, demanded "controlled markets."[83] The scramble for markets in Africa took place in the latter half of the nineteenth century, and soon most of West Africa was under European rule. Its economies became subservient to those of the metropolitan countries.

European controls left in their wake economies geared to those of the metropolitan countries. Yet, in the hinterland, the markets continue their periodicities, traders roam as if frontiers did not exist, or try to escape them, and money changers, often using traditional currencies that no longer exist as units, convert francs of various vintages into different types of pounds, and even dollars. A few West African states have moved to recreate an economic unity of West Africa, but they cannot revive the caravan trails which directed goods across the Sahara. Salt and manufactured goods now come more easily by sea. Nevertheless, should the oil in the Sahara pass into African hands, it may stimulate the economies of many of the interior countries of West Africa which, though once brilliant, have since been by-passed by roads and railroads whose only goal is the sea.

[83] K. O. Diké, 1956, chapters ix and xi.

12. African Architecture

The concept "architecture" in art-historical thinking is generally limited to buildings of stone or brick and to larger wooden structures (out of hewn logs); in other words, to more durable materials and to forms which require considerable mastery for controlling and shaping the materials used.

Yet one forgets that simple huts of less durable materials are also the models of architecture which every culture has used at one time or another and without which all later developments remain unintelligible.

Moreover, at simple levels of cultural organization, the construction of a house is always the most expensive item in material culture and, without the conscious knowledge of the builders, reveals in its form aspects of their feeling for beauty. Besides, a simple hut, just because it is expendable, is a relatively stable trait-complex, and is firmly rooted in the culture of the group that produces it. Further, precisely because of this characteristic, the indigenous architecture is an element of culture which, with all possible variations, remains basically similar in all its forms. This means that characteristic hut forms almost always have a substantially larger range of distribution than other, mobile, elements of culture. . . .

As far as African building techniques are concerned one can say that man is the measure of all things. Form and dimension are, to a large extent, still determined by the size of the adult human body whose physical needs are served by these structures. But where this architecture served a special purpose, it was to express political rather than religious concepts: it was used to represent the power of the ruler.

In its developmental history the hut is not living space; rather

SOURCE: Translated by Vera C. Chimene and Marguerite Chesbrough from Julius F. Glück, "Afrikanische Architektur," *Tribus*, Neue Folge, VI, 1956 (Stuttgart: Linden-Museum, 1957), pp. 65–82. Reprinted by permission of Dr. Julius F. Glück and the editors of *Tribus*.

it is sleeping space and, if need be, a shelter from the effects of climate. After man became sedentary he also took fire, provisions, and small domestic animals into the hut. The fact that it was not really a dwelling is already confirmed by the over-all absence of windows. Light has access only through the door. The original first hut was conceived for recumbent sleeping, or at most for a seated human, but not for the standing one. Hence the spatial dimensioning of this early architecture most closely approached our concept of "bedroom."

Viewed formally, African architecture reveals a certain amount of diversity in floor plans and roof forms that can be classified in terms of an historical process:

1. The dome-shaped food-gatherer's hut, built on a circular floor plan.
2. The conical-roofed cultivator's hut, built on a circular floor plan.
3. The West African gable-roofed hut, built on a rectangular floor plan.
4. The rectangular pile-built house.
5. The pyramidal-roofed hut, built on a square floor plan.

These five types can be considered to have been invented by Pygmies and Negroes. The following forms reveal ancient influences from other cultures:

6. The flat-roofed adobe cubicle, built on a rectangular floor plan.
7. The "castles" and Musgu adobe cones.
8. The trench dwellings.
9. The impluvium.
10. The dome-shaped shepherd's hut.
11. The characteristic East African hut types.
12. The Rhodesian stone structures.

1. The Pygmy's hut bears witness to the fact that at the beginning man built his dwellings on a circular floor plan well suited to his idiosyncratic biology and his experience. He, himself, does not have corners, and he used materials which a simple culture can control. The Pygmies employed sticks and leaves, materials which

are bendable and also naturally lend themselves to curved shapes. Building this hut is exclusively the women's task. Such a division of labor seems to have been universal in man's early history. Traces of this concept can still be seen in our highly developed culture where the kitchen and the bedroom are still considered to be the woman's domain. The Pygmy hut is a slight, not very durable structure, and does not always shelter its inhabitants from the frightful rains. Its average height is 1.5 meters with a diameter of 2 to 4 meters, so the entire area under roof can be considered to have an area of 12.5 square meters. The hut is large enough only for members of the nuclear family: parents and children. The hut's diameter varies depending on the size of the family. The Pygmy woman takes the possibility of expansion into consideration when she cuts the sticks; in this sense the huts are "made to measure." The hut can be widened by adding bedroom niches for older children as the need arises.[1]

This expedient architecture—a hut can be erected in one or two days—conforms to a way of life in which small groups range within a definite area, the women gathering while the men hunt. The whole group seldom stays longer than two weeks in any one place, moving off to better hunting grounds.

If we disregard the various windscreens which the Pygmies also used, it can be said that their beehive or conical hut is the origin of architecture—and this not only in Africa. Since this early period, the problem of curvature as a construction principle has never left mankind.

2. Nomadic early man had first to become a sedentary cultivator before he could develop a different form for his dwelling. In contrast to the Pygmies, most of the Negroes attained this stage of development. They retained the circular or oval floor plan, and built on it a cylindrical structure with walls made of a stick-frame which they covered with mats or, more usually, coated with clay. The roof of this hut is conical, its diameter 3 to 5 meters, creating an area of from 7 square meters to not more than 20 square meters. The peak of the roof rises up to a height of 4 to 5 meters above the ground. But even this type of hut is not very durable and can seldom withstand the considerable climatic stresses for more than three to five years.

[1] P. Schebesta, *Bambuti* (Leipzig: 1932); P. Schebesta, *Die Bambuti-Pygmäen von Ituri,* II (Brussels: 1937), 138–35; W. Immenroth, *Kultur und Umwelt der Kleinwüchsigen in Afrika, Studien für Völkerkunde,* VI (Leipzig: 1933), 61ff.

These types of huts cannot be built solely by women. The men do the planning and erect the frame of the hut while the women do the clay plastering. Because of the larger size and the greater diversity of materials used, the construction of these huts is also beyond the capability of one single nuclear family. Hence, they depend upon the help of men and women of the entire co-resident group. This close connection between architecture and society is already evident even on such a simple level.

The concept of the conical roof in construction reached its climax in the more complex cultures in the elaborate forms of round and vertical towers. Nowhere has the African attempted this except in the unique case of Zimbabwe. He kept to the horizontal level and, in terms of his needs as a cultivator, found an adequate solution—the compound. Huts are placed fairly close to one another at not-too-wide intervals and the irregular, but most often circular, area closed off with a fence, a stone wall, or a live hedge. The number of huts on the premises is determined by the wealth of the lineage as well as the number of people who are members of it. For example, among the Mofu living in the Mandara Mountains of North Cameroon, there are compounds of four to eight huts in an area of about 250 square meters. But there are also compounds of as many as twenty huts distributed in an area of 1800 square meters. Some buildings serve as barns for small or young domestic animals or as cook houses; others as women's quarters, and for storing peanuts, millet, etc.[2] Practically speaking, the possibility for expansion is unlimited, and creates no new problems either from a technical or from an aesthetic point of view. Typically, these huts have a diameter of from three to five meters with a living area not exceeding twenty square meters.

Since this conical-roofed hut is closely bound up with the development of agriculture as a way of life in Africa, its wide distribution must have arisen during the wide dispersion of population during the Neolithic era of this continent. It is found in central Sahara among the Tubbu-Teda of the Tibesti Mountains when they are sedentary[3]; but, above all, in the Sudan from the Atlantic in the west to the Nilotic areas in the region of the White Nile. But it is also found in Ethiopia from whence it spread south and was adopted by the Pare and the Dschagga; and to the Congo and

[2] J. Beguin *et al., L'Habitat au Cameroun* (Paris: 1952), p. 18.
[3] Garcia, "Moeurs et coutumes des Teda du Tou," *Bulletin institut d'études centrafricaines,* No. 10 (Paris: 1955).

Zambezi, as well as Angola. Thus the conical-roofed hut is found in all those parts of Africa which we can assume was inhabited by an autochthonous Negro population.

3. In professional literature the rectangular gable-roofed hut is contrasted with the cylindrical house type already mentioned, with the former rightly considered to be characteristic of West Africa. We find it especially in the coastal areas of upper and lower Guinea, thus from the Bissago Islands, through Nigeria, down to the Congo estuary. Typically, the rectangular gable-roofed hut is not larger than the round hut: four to five meters in diameter encompassing a living area of approximately twenty square meters. Its occurrence exclusively in the tropical virgin forest is significant and probably dates from the period when Negroes started colonizing areas formerly inhabited solely by Pygmies. It is not known just when this took place, but considering everything, it must have occurred long after the development of the conical-roofed cylindric hut and at a time when the Negro, having become a sedentary cultivator, was seeking more arable land and was about to establish symbiotic relations with the Pygmy hunters to obtain the much desired meat. The rectangular ground plan is no doubt an expedient trait—stemming from the rationality always common to migrants. Moreover, the material necessary for this type of structure was available in ample quantities in these heavily forested areas.

It is noteworthy that nowhere is the rectangular gabled-roofed hut grouped into compounds. This might be because the virgin tropical forest imposes limitations. On the other hand, the rectangular shape can be easily partitioned. Rarely used is the technically easy enlargement of this hut by lengthening the rectangle. It is only used for the huts belonging to secret societies where the many members and their dependents all lend their hands to the task.[4]

The basic difference between the conical-roofed hut and the gable-roofed hut is, of course, the system of *pillars* which they have to support the beam.

The turtle-roofed hut is also built on this principle. Therefore it should be considered to be a variation of the gable-roofed hut. Here the beam is bent and supported by two pillars, the peak of the roof being roughly over the hut's center. This type of hut has a living area of not more than twenty square meters. It is found

[4] A. Mansfeld, *Urwalddokumente* (Berlin: 1908), pp. 23–33.

along the bend of the Congo River, especially among the Kundu and the Mongo.

4. The pile-built hut, so well described by Leo Frobenius, can be found along the upper Kasai, along the Senegal, in the lagoons of the Ivory Coast and Dahomey, and in the Niger delta.[5] The fact that they are found in swampy areas or in areas prone to flooding proves that this type of pile-built structure with a platform is a local variation—conditioned by environment—of the rectangular gable-roofed house.

5. A noteworthy expression of African architecture is the square hut with the pyramid roof. We find it in Angola where, however, it is interspersed with the round conical-roofed houses and the rectangular gable-roofed houses.[6] We find it in the Congo and a special version of it in the grasslands of the Cameroons. In its most ancient version, such as it occurs in Angola, it reveals, through building technique as well as in its size, an unmistakable correlation with the conical-roofed hut and with the gable-roofed hut.

On the other hand, from every point of view, the pyramidal-roofed hut of the Cameroons Grasslands is a notable form. The appearance of its façade is aesthetically pleasing due to the use of vertical surface as architectural components. But even here the living area does not exceed the 20 square meters with sides measuring 3×3 to 4×4 meters. However, the peak of the roof rises up to a height of from 8 to 20 meters above the ground. Houses with sides measuring about 3 meters have walls 3 to 3.5 meters high, on top of which is set a 5- to 7-meter-high roof. The houses belonging to chiefs and to secret societies are even more impressive, with sides measuring 7×7 meters to 8×8 meters, a height of 6 to 7 meters on top of which a 12 to 14 meter roof is set.[7] Inside, these huts have a lateral separation, a kind of ceiling, resting on top of the walls. This is a round wickerwork cover extending, at its widest, about 2 meters over the square wall structure. At 2-meter intervals this extension is supported by wooden pillars. These pillars consist of medium-sized posts on which figures are carved. It is obvious that structures of such size and complexity can only be built by skilled artisans such as are found among the Bamileke, who do have such skilled carpenters and thatchers. They use flexible

[5] L. Frobenius, *Kulturgeschichte Afrikas* (Zürich: 1954), p. 214f.
[6] H. Baumann, *Lunda* (Berlin: 1935).
[7] J. Beguin *et al.*, *L'Habitat au Cameroun*, p. 77.

raffia palm leaves and stalks as building material, prefabricating the components of the house where they find this material. They then take it to, and assemble it at, the site chosen for the house. Claycoating of the walls, inside and out, is largely done by women.

The true roof consists of four woven triangles lashed together. A second ceiling, smaller than the first one, is installed horizontally some distance below the peak of the roof frame. The whole is then covered with a system of rafters and templets waterproofed with a straw covering. With this system the builders in fact erect a double or false roof, thus demonstrating that they can go beyond the strict techniques of building, motivated by a concern with aesthetic appearance of their work for which the concept of *architecture,* in the full sense, is valid. The particulars of the structures built by the Grassland peoples can be summed up as follows:

    a. They make use of the vertical dimension.
    b. Sculpture is a functional part of their architecture.
    c. The living area can be greater than fifty square meters.
    d. The true pyramidal-roof structure is covered and enlarged by a "false" roof.

Thus the Bamileke house represents the peak of African building styles. It is obviously of relatively recent inception, originating perhaps 400 or 500 years ago. It stems not only from the conical-roofed hut and from the gable-roofed hut, but also from the flat-roofed cubicle, since it has a ceiling separating the living area from the roof area.

6. The frequently used, flat-roofed adobe-brick square or rectangular house did not originate in Negro Africa. For thousands of years this has been the typical building style in those areas around the Mediterranean where lumber had become scarce. However, in Italy as well as in Syria, the round conical-roofed hut of dry-laid stonework and of adobe has been established as being the forerunner of the adobe square house.[8] The scarceness of wood can, therefore, not be the reason. Rather the rectangular floor plan and pillars lead to the conclusion that wood of sufficient length had been used at one time to build it. Then, later, as wood became scarce, clay,

[8] E. Gabriel and C. Rathjens, "Die nordsyrischen Bienenkorbhäuser," *Tribus,* Neue Folge, IV–VII (1956).

which had been used only for filling and thickening purposes, became the structural material. From this the dried adobe brick evolved.

It has been found, not only in Africa but in other areas of the world as well, that the distribution of the adobe square house coincides with the spread of the plow. It is indigenous among the Berbers, in the Nile regions, and in Ethiopia.

In Black Africa it is found, without the plow, among the Guang of inland Ghana. The splinter populations of Central Togo know the adobe square house; it is found along the Volta River and along the bend of the Niger River among the Bambara and the Bozo. This type of architecture attained its peak, however, in the cities of the Sudan: in Zinder, Sokoto, Kano, Bida, etc.

Although the living area of this windowless square house still remains within the customary 20 square meters and the 3×4 or 4×4 meter dimensions, its interior can be enhanced considerably. Indeed, much attention is given to this possibility. The structure can be extended by means of alignment and superposition without too many technical difficulties, provided there is sufficient manpower at hand. For this reason, there are African settlements which even we can regard as being true cities, where tens of thousands of people lived long before the advent of European colonization.

This adobe-brick architecture underwent a very interesting development when, starting in the ninth century A.D., Islam spread toward the southern part of the African continent. The Moslem built his mosques on the principle of the adobe-brick square house, but he enlarged the size in all directions. He added conical-shaped columns at regular intervals along the outside, thus subdividing the surface and giving it a third dimension not unlike what has been done through our Gothic use of buttresses.

The adobe square house reached the Sudan from North Africa during different periods, starting from about the last centuries before the Christian era. According to the latest research among the Sao, the legendary "builders of walled-in settlements"[9] in the areas around Lake Chad, it appears that the lost wax process of casting brass and bronze is associated with this type of architecture.

7. This flat-roofed adobe house has had its influence over the older African conical-roofed hut, particularly in the Sudan, and this has brought about interesting results.

Among the Nankanse, Bobo, Senufo, Tamberma, Sissala, and

[9] J. P. Lebeuf and A. M. Detourbet, *La civilisation du Tchad* (Paris: 1950).

some of the Grunshi and Lobi groups, the conical-roofed hut compound became linked adobe-brick forts with flat roofs through the replacement of the original stone wall or hedge enclosures with adobe-brick walls supporting protruding half cylinders. These agglomerations look like medieval castles in miniature. Just the same, the available living space remains modest: vertically it does not exceed five meters. The living area is the combined space of the different huts and the center is an inner courtyard.[10] When one sees these imposing architectural structures one easily forgets that these "castles" are just the dwellings of extended families of cultivators.

Another equally interesting result of the combined architectural styles of the square house and the conical-roofed hut is the adobe conical houses of the Musgu in the Lake Chad area. Here, too, the circular floor plan of the conical-roofed hut has been retained. But it is the conical-roof form and not the cylindrical wall that determines the shape of the whole structure. It is approximately five meters high, dome shaped, and covered with arrow-like reinforcements, making it one of the most aesthetically satisfying achievements of African architecture. With a three- to five-meter diameter, this hut also does not possess a living area of more than twenty square meters.

In general, several of these adobe cones are grouped together into compounds. Sometimes there are as many as fifteen of them arranged in a circular pattern linked by an adobe wall. In recent times this rather laborious building method is falling more and more into disuse.[11]

8. The subterranean pit dwelling, or "cruciform cellar-vault" (Kreuzkellergewölbe) as Leo Frobenius named it,[12] constitutes a special form of housing. Originally it was formed by tunneling under cliffs, and was done by sedentary cultivators who obviously felt the need for security. Exhibiting similarities with the adobe-brick square house, it also diffused into the Sudan from the Berber areas of North Africa. Its dimensions are the same as those of the smaller huts. Some are built on the square and others on the circular floor plan. Such structures call for fairly large expenditures

[10] Smend, "Eine Reise durch die Nordostecke von Togo," *Globus*, XCII (1907), 245–50, 265–69.
[11] J. Beguin *et al.*, *L'Habitat au Cameroun*, p. 34ff.
[12] L. Frobenius, *Kulturgeschichte Afrikas*, p. 212f.

of labor which can only be undertaken by sedentary agrarian groups.

9. A close relative of the adobe square house, although it has the addition of a veranda, is the *impluvium,* a house built around a four-cornered inner court with an inwardly inclined roof and a pit to catch rain water. It is found among the Yoruba and in Benin, where the palaces of the rulers and the aristocrats were built in this form. From Benin City this form diffused to Banum and Tikar in the Grasslands and to the Ekoi in the forest area of Cameroons. A historical connection of this form with the Roman colonization of North Africa should not be overlooked.

This method of building is pure adobe architecture; only the roof structure and the door frames are made of wood. But here again the Africans did not see fit to increase the house size despite the influences of ancient high cultures.[13] The building was usually three meters high with the now familiar floor space. The means of expansion remained that of grouping several impluvia into compounds behind an enclosing wall whose height was determined by the social and political rank of the owner. Whereas the walls of the ruler's compound were seven adobe-bricks high, those of the aristocrats were five bricks high and for the common man only three bricks high. The bricks themselves were about twenty inches in height.[14]

The inwardly inclined roof of the impluvium forms a gallery all the way around the courtyard and is subdivided by partitions. The interior walls of the house are polished with a certain kind of leaves which give the clay a soft sheen.

The aristocratic inhabitants of Benin covered the gallery pillars of their houses with ornamental bronze plaques. The walls of certain rooms were decorated with clay reliefs painted yellow, black, and red. Thus here too is another example of architecture combined with plastic art. Elsewhere besides Benin these gallery pillars were also covered with ornamental carvings.

Since the destruction of Benin in 1897, the impluvium has gradually disappeared, giving way to the so-called colonial or Brazilian form, a classic European style with numerous windows and elaborate stucco work. An example of this building style is the palace of the

---

[13] Obviously a better reason for this seeming contradiction is that the impluvium was an indigenous development. Ed.

[14] Ling Roth, *Great Benin* (Halifax: 1903), p. 178.

chief of Itsekiri. Interestingly enough, not one single sketch was made prior to erecting this building. Its main entrance is even decorated with two concrete soldiers.[15] Today the large cities of the Yoruba as well as of others have already reached the architectural stage of building with poured concrete.

10. It is one of the contradictory traits of Africa that peoples who were quite capable of creating powerful political states, as did the Mossi, the Hausa and Fulbe in the Sudan and also the Hima-Tussi in East Africa, started with the conical-roofed hut and have retained it even to the present. The Zulus and their related peoples use it, and the Barotse in . . . [Zambia], the Bayas and Wute in the Cameroons, as well as the herding peoples of Ethiopia. The *pontok* of the Herero and the Hottentots, as well as the huts of the Masai, belongs to the same house type.

This second type of conical-roof hut has no historical link with the Pygmy hut, and diffused in a huge arc from the western Sudan [eastward] around the rain forest to East and South Africa—those parts of the continent where large-scale cattle herding is possible. In fact, this beehive or conical-roofed hut serves as the overnight shelter of the nomadic herders. The floor plan remains circular or oval, the height varies from 1.5 meters to 5 meters with a 3 to 5 meter diameter, resulting once again in the 20 square meter living area. Typically, the materials used are sticks for the framework covered with hides, as among the Masai. It can also be covered with reeds or grass. Where the herding population has remained isolated and not mixed with other peoples, the huts are built by women. Where, however, they have established themselves as rulers over sedentary cultivators, the huts are built by the men and are usually larger. The princes among the Kisiba of Tanganyika have huts as large as 12 meters in diameter providing a living area of over 100 square meters.[16]

The reasons for the similarities of this hut to the Pygmy hut—floor plan and shape but not building method—are not historical but rather psychological. In both cases the life-style of nomadic man and the materials available have led to the similarity in architecture.

11. East Africa, even though different in many ways from the western part of the continent, has only two historically independent

15 U. Beier, "The Palace of the Ogogas in Ikerre," *Nigeria*, No. 44 (Lagos: 1954), 304ff.

16 H. Rehse, *Kiziba, Land und Leute* (Stuttgart: 1910).

architectural styles: the free-standing gable-roofed hut of the Swahili on the coast and the original *tembe*.

The gable-roofed hut has the same dimensions and shape as the West African hut. It has obviously been influenced by the association over many centuries of the local people with Arabs and Persians.

The tembe[17] is a completely isolated and different type of hut, unknown everywhere else in Africa. It is found in the hinterland of Tanganyika where peoples of great linguistic diversity have settled. These are the Rangi, Nyamesi, Hehe, Bena, Sango, Iraku (Iraqu), and Fiomi (Goroa). The tembe is not really a solitary hut with a rectangular floor plan and a lean-to roof sloping toward the rear of the building. Rather, it defines a compound where two, three, or even four tembes are grouped into a right-angle pattern to enclose a courtyard. Typically the tembe hut is two meters high and not more than three meters wide; but its length can be as much as twenty to one hundred meters. Consequently, it has a living area of several hundred square meters. This is significant verification of the fact that it must cater to the needs of a group larger than one single nuclear family. Moreover, even though the construction method is simple, many hands are needed to make a house so large.

Size is not the only peculiarity of the tembe hut; the Isansu (Izanu), Iramba, Tatoga, Sandawe, Mbugwe, and Fiomi place it, partially or completely, underground. The half sunken hut rises approximately 1.5 meters above the ground in front, though in the rear it is only .5 meter above ground level. Moreover, the roof is slightly raised at the center so that it slopes down on three sides. In front, the roof is extended forward to form a veranda and is supported by pillars.

The inside is deepened by .6 to .8 meters so that one may stand erect in the front part of the hut. Among the Fiomi there is a 20-to-30-meter-long trench (crawlway) in the rear of the tembe which can be reached by means of a 2-meter-deep vertical manhole. The trench leads into a cylindrical chamber measuring about 10 to 20 square meters. This chamber has a vertical airduct camouflaged with branches, tree trunks, and a light layer of earth.

The tembe hut which is entirely underground, such as is found especially among the Iraku, is sunk in a hole three meters deep in

---

[17] O. Baumann, *Durch Massailand zur Nilquelle* (Berlin: 1894), p. 176.

an area of ten to twenty square meters excavated out of the lateritic earth. It might be square, triangular, or irregular in shape. At ground level it is covered with palm-tree branches, layers of sorghum stalks, and clay. The entrance is dug on a slant.[18]

When we consider that conical-roofed huts have survived sporadically in the middle of Iraku (indeed they might even be located inside a tembe hut) and when we consider further that during the course of the last century this area was subjected again and again to armed attacks, as for instance from the Masai, and when we consider the tribulations suffered, we can understand why the tembe must have developed during that period. Nevertheless, its shape and size as well as the flat-roof arrangement reveal signs of influence from outside of Africa. The style is reminiscent of those of Arab traders who have, since the beginning of the Christian era, had an ever increasing influence on East Africa. The necessity to build so extensively and to exceed by a considerable margin, the customary twenty square meters, no doubt is to be explained by fear of attack. People banded together in concentrated groups in order to stage a common defense. The tembe system continued to diffuse widely until the European conquest at the end of the last century at a time when the power of the Arabs was then at its height.

The tembe must have originated toward the beginning of the Christian era. This does not necessarily place the origin of other trench dwellings in the same era, especially the pit dwellings found farther south in Rhodesia (Zimbabwe) and which today are taken for abandoned "slave pits," dating from approximately A.D. 1000, and associated with the kingdom of Monomotapa.[19]

12. *Dry-stone masonry* is not necessarily an indication of high culture. We find stonework associated with the conical-roofed huts of the Northern Cameroons mountain peoples and also in the Volta basin, this is, in those areas where stones are conveniently found. But in these areas stonework has no significance as far as the architecture is concerned.

Such is not the case with the Abyssinian house with the flat roof and stone walls, and with the large ruins of Zimbabwe and in Angola. The use of stone in the Nile valley does not call for an

[18] F. von Luschan, "Beiträge zur Ethnographie des abflusslosen Gebietes in Deutsch-Ost-Afrika," in Werther, *Die mittleren Hochländer des nördlichen Deutsch-Ost-Afrika* (Berlin: 1898), pp. 323–85.
[19] L. Frobenius, *Erythräa* (Berlin: 1931), p. 251ff.

explanation, but it is surprising in Rhodesia, particularly in the case of its famous ruin of Zimbabwe. One pertinent fact is that the stone structures of Zimbabwe are roofless. They are huge ellipsoidal circumvallations with fifty to eighty meter diameters and a height of eleven meters. The base of the wall is about five meters wide and the top three meters. The materials used are blocks of broken granite in the shape of large bricks. This wall has three openings to the interior. The main entrance has the raised sill customary with most types of African huts, and steps on both sides. An interior wall runs almost parallel to the eastern outer wall, creating a 1.5-to-3-meter-wide corridor which at one point expands into a kind of pouch containing a conical, 11-meter-high structure. A second structure, similar to the one in the pouch, is found close to the center of the walled in area. The largest of these two towers is approximately eight meters in diameter.[20]

Thanks to the research by Caton-Thompson, we know that Zimbabwe ("lofty house") dates from the time of the European middle ages, around A.D. 1000.[21] Its sumptuous appearance can be explained by its function as a place for ritual sacrifice to the rain gods. It is probable that this style of building with stone has disseminated from Abyssinia, along the ancient migratory track of the East African rift valley. Of course, the sedentary populations were also instrumental in its propagation. In two important papers H. Baumann stresses the connection between the Rhodesian stone works and the stone tombs of the Mbundu area. The coincidental use of flat stone slabs for ornamentation in palm rib, fishbone, and chevron design is convincing. But, of even greater architectural significance is the fact that the Mbundu city of Bailundo had, as late as 1850, a thick dry-stone wall as well as stone steps.[22] The traditional trade activities between the Rhodesian kingdom of Monomotapa and Angola by way of the extinct kingdom of Butua-Torwa constitute a logical explanation for the spread of this stonework style to the west, into Angola, at a time which must be placed

[20] Ibid.
[21] G. Caton-Thompson, *The Zimbabwe Culture* (Oxford: 1931); P. Schebesta, "Die Zimbabwe-Kultur in Afrika," *Anthropos,* XXI (1926), 484–545; H. von Sicard, "Ngoma Lungundu—eine afrikanische Bundeslade," *Studia Ethnographica Upsaliensia,* V (Uppsala, 1952).
[22] H. Baumann, "Steingräber und Steinbauten in Angola," *Koloniale Völkerkunde, Beiträge zur Kolonialforschung,* I (Berlin: 1943), 44–55.

before the emergence of the Jaga in the sixteenth century A.D.[23]

In summary, African architecture seems to be surprisingly varied at first glance. However, if we take the size of the continent into consideration, as well as the fact that the dominant house types are the conical-roofed hut, the gable-roofed hut, the pyramidal-roofed hut, the flat-roofed adobe square house, and the herder's domed hut, the variety of types somehow appears not to be so vast.

The differences lie primarily in floor plan and roof shape. On the other hand, there appear to be two general dimensions which are seldom exceeded: one, the ever recurring twenty-square-meter living area, and the other, the height of the roof, which, when seen in cross section, varies between four and six meters.

This characteristic style is conditioned by the tradition of having one-room single-story dwellings as well as the renunciation of timber construction. The problem of expansion was normally solved horizontally by means of the compound. In the case of royal or princely residences or palaces, this principle led to an agglomeration of as many as fifty to eighty separate huts; and the latrines were not forgotten either.

Such agglomerations were invariably fenced in and thereby given a unified appearance. Seen in the light of this tradition, Zimbabwe becomes an oversized fence, and therefore an intrinsic example of African architecture.

In those cases where building went beyond strict functional necessity, and embellishments were put on, the ornamental parts sometimes continued to have a structural function. When they were purely ornamental, they were still used in a sensible way. We find this mainly in the Sudan and along its southern borders, where clay reliefs decorate the rooms not only in Benin and Dahomey, but also among the Dogon, the Senufo, and other peoples. Polychrome wall paintings, in contrast, are used everywhere where clay coating is used.

The fact that, with the exception of Zimbabwe, there is a total absence of sacramental building in Africa might at first seem strange. But in Africa, as in all other culture areas, sacred buildings took their inspiration from the architectural model of the secular rulers.

[23] H. Baumann, "Die Frage der Steinbauten und Steingräber in Angola," *Paideuma,* VI (1956), 118–51.

PART III
African Social Institutions

Introduction

African societies are based upon numerous systems of kinship and descent and exhibit a wide variety of social institutions and beliefs marking the major periods and crises in life (*rites de passage*). In most African societies membership in a specific kin and descent group often determines a person's status and role, his rights, duties, and obligations. The semantic structure of Tsimihety kinship included in this section is especially interesting because it is clearly congruent with kin behavior which emphasizes the seniority of elders over juniors, of males over females, and recognizes patterns of authority and precedence. The Tsimihety are patrilineal in that they normally trace descent through the male line. But like many more African peoples than is ordinarily recognized, these people of Madagascar also acknowledge the significance of the mother's patrilineage. They not only live with their mother's brother when induced to do so either because of economic or other reasons, but they also can be ritually and sociologically absorbed into these patrilineages.

The varying roles of African descent groups in securing spouses for their members are clearly seen by comparing the Tsimihety with the Kikuyu and Mossi, whose social institutions are also described in this section. Whereas among the Tsimihety a man's father or the man himself pays the "bride-price" (the transfer of goods and services that legitimizes most African marriages), this duty falls to the corporate lineage groups among both Kikuyu and Mossi. Kenyatta's description of the marriage system of the Kikuyu is somewhat of a classic, since he describes this institution from the "inside," so to speak. His spirited defense of the bride-price and his idealized view of Kikuyu polygyny, married life, and attitudes toward children reveal aspects of African social life that at one time escaped attention.

The processes by which African societies socialize the young and teach them adult roles and values run the gamut from informal instruction to rather formal "bush schools" and initiation ceremonies. Dupire describes the rather unceremonious upbringing of the Fulani Bororo girl. This is in sharp contrast to the training of girls in other African societies such as among the Kikuyu or in the Sandawe bush schools of the Mende of Sierra Leone. Vansina's description of the initiation rituals of the Bushong shows in great detail how young boys are transformed into men. They are not only taught the history and customs of their society, and their rights and duties, but they also learn valuable lessons about the important relations between men and women. Almost all the possible future difficulties of life are presented to the Bushong youth in microcosm so that they can learn what adulthood means.

The transition from youth to adulthood in most societies is marked by tension and conflict. Even the Fulani girl, who according to Dupire leads a carefree youth, looks forward to marriage and adulthood with some trepidation. Marriage and adulthood for her not only mean leaving home, but starting a new way of life in which she often competes for status and material goods in her husband's polygynous family. The problem for the Mossi boy, especially the first son, is fraught with grave difficulties. In many cases custom dictates that he spend his early life with his mother's brother. He is usually well treated here, but he has only "residual rights" to the land and property of his mother's brother, and is expected to return home before marriage. Once at home, the youth finds that he has difficulty obtaining a wife and cannot become sociologically adult until the demise of his father. This custom creates tension and guilt feelings between father and son so that at the death of a father, a son goes to great lengths to propitiate his father's ghost.

The age organizations found in many African societies function to provide their members with good company as well as to perform certain tasks for the society. In some cases the age sets are simply composed of persons, whether young or old, male or female, who are initiated during the same period. In contrast, the age-grade is usually a stage in the development of persons whether as herders, hunters, warriors, elders, or priests. Hamer shows how the Sidamo use their rather "baroque" *Lau* system to order sociologically defined categories of "young men" and "old men." Political, judicial, military, and ritual roles are assigned to men on the basis of well-defined generational classes.

The belief that there is a relationship between physical illness and poor social relations noted in numerous African societies is clearly seen among both the Tiv and the Bunyoro. The concept of disease is not foreign to the Tiv, but, as Price-Williams declares, they do not regard "illness" or "disease" as a completely separate category distinct from the misfortunes of life. The result is that the Tiv attach as much attention to restoring relations with their living and dead kinsmen as to taking specific medicines. When, as it inevitably happens, "death arrives," many African peoples do not attribute its occurrence to chance or to the exigencies of life. Beattie tells us that the Bunyoro almost always attribute death to sorcerers, ghosts, or other malevolent non-human agents. Thus many of the rituals that take place at African burials and funerals are as much designed to get rid of the body and placate its spirit as to reduce tensions and restore harmony within these societies.

PETER J. WILSON

13. Tsimihety Kinship and Descent[1]

Though the Tsimihety tribe is the subject of three monographs by
Molet (1953, 1956, 1959) and a number of papers by various authors
(e.g. Mattei, 1938; Magnes, 1953), its social structure has not yet
been adequately described. Indeed, there is no adequate account of
the social structure of any Malagasy group, although Ottino's (1963)
analysis of aspects of Vezo social structure is very illuminating. The
primary aim of this paper therefore is to describe two of the major
features of Tsimihety social structure—kinship and descent. As there
are facets of Tsimihety kinship and descent that have some bearing on
recent discussion of these topics, a secondary aim is to contribute, in a
minor way, to that discussion.

Since the Tsimihety have not been described in English I begin with
a brief descriptive profile.

I. THE TSIMIHETY

There are approximately 400,000 people who identify themselves
as Tsimihety (cf. Kent, 1962:41). They live more or less con-
tiguously in north-central Madagascar between approximately 14–
16°S. and 47° 50′–50° E., an area of about 178,000 sq. km.
with a population density of roughly 5.65 (Molet, 1959:27–28).
A relatively large number of Malagasy who identify themselves with
other "tribes" live among the Tsimihety. These include Sakalava,

SOURCE: Peter J. Wilson, "Tsimihety Kinship and Descent," *Africa*, Vol.
XXXVII, No. 2, April 1967, pp. 133–53. Reprinted by permission of the author
and publisher.

[1] Field-work was carried out in Madagascar from 1962 to 1963 and was
financially supported by grant number G24143 from the National Science
Foundation, to whom grateful acknowledgment is made. I am grateful to Louis
Molet, Aidan Southall, and Harold Conklin for reading this paper and for their
helpful comments. I also wish to acknowledge with thanks a grant from the
Department of Anthropology, Yale University, to cover the extra cost of printing this article.

Tankarana, Betsimisaraka, Merina, Betsileo, Sihanaka, Makoa, and Antemoro, with relatively few individuals from other groups. The area in which the Tsimihety live is bordered by Sakalava to the west, Betsimisaraka to the east, Sihanaka to the south, and the uninhabited Massif de Tsaratanana to the north. The Tsimihety have been especially notable for their expansion, both demographic and geographic, which has been increasing in momentum over the past sixty years. This has come about partly through natural increase, partly through the cultural absorption of other Malagasy and partly, perhaps, through relatively increasing efficiency of census taking (for a detailed description of Tsimihety expansion see Molet, 1959).

Although distinguished by a name, there is no political or social basis whereby the Tsimihety can be defined as a tribe. There is no hierarchical organization, political or social, that would facilitate the mobilization of all Tsimihety for a specific purpose, no common ancestor posited in genealogies or in a mythology, and no pretence of unity achieved through the idiom of kinship, clanship, or marriage alliance. When the Merina conquered the area under Radama I in 1823 they met no resistance, each village submitting or withdrawing to the hills, but not combining with other villages. A similar pattern seems to have existed during the time of the *marofelana* or endemic raiding (*c.* 1880). Villages did not combine in face of attacks, but retreated to caves in the hills. And the same lack of political unity was evident during the French settlement of the area in 1896 (cf. Magnes, 1953:15).

The origins of the Tsimihety are known in general outline though it is difficult to get agreement on specific points. All Tsimihety affirm that their ancestors came from the east, principally from the coastal area around Mananara and Maroantsetra. Some Tsimihety still bury their dead in tombs located in these areas. The first major migration from the east can be roughly timed as taking place in the latter half of the seventeenth century on the basis of genealogies and certain historical incidents (cf. Grandidier, 1908:iv. 1. 196) A second major component of Tsimihety are descendants of Sakalava ancestors who were of west-coast origin. Probably as late as the arrival of Radama I in the region, the central and western area of the Tsimihety as far as the Sofia River, was occupied by Sakalava. Tsimihety today speak of the former authority of Sakalava *mpanjaka* (princes) in the area and particular reference is made to the *Zafinimena* and *Zafinifotsy* "kingdoms." A number of *foko* (see below) today identify themselves as *zafinimena* or *zafinifotsy,* and in one area centering on the village of Maringibato, the *zafinifotsy* recognize a *mpanjaka.* However, they call themselves Tsimihety, not Sakalava. A third major component in Tsimihety are of Sihanaka origin, known as Antevongo,[2] who were fugitives from coastal Betsimisaraka. Because of the ease with which Tsimihety are able to assimilate non-Tsimihety, they probably include large numbers of people whose ancestors were members of most of the other Malagasy groups. It is only against the Merina that there are specific rules preventing assimilation and intermarriage, though today the stringency of these prohibitions has been considerably mollified.

In view of the absence of an ideological and an empirical unity at the sociological and political level, I prefer not to describe the Tsimihety as a tribe, or even as "a society." Nevertheless, the term Tsimihety has some meaning with respect to a number of people, and it is this that I shall try to explain. It may be translated as "those who do not cut their hair." In fact Tsimihety people do cut their hair, but the term is said to commemorate the fact that, when the Sakalava ruled the region and one of their *mpanjaka* died, a number of people refused to cut their hair as a sign of mourning and thereby signified that they did not recognize the authority of the Sakalava. These people were termed Tsimihety—presumably by the Sakalava. As they were probably the immigrants from the east coast, this signification of the term is quite plausible. A second, less widespread but equally revealing explanation is that during the time of endemic raiding the raiders did not hesitate to kill the men, but spared the women. Since women did not cut their hair the men allowed their hair to grow in order to be mistaken for women and thereby save their lives.

The term Tsimihety is used to identify people to each other and in contrast with people who can be characterized as significantly different. However, all people with whom a Tsimihety comes into contact are Malagasy (except of course the occasional non-Malagasy such as a French personnel) and are basically the same. The key

---

[2] Grandidier (1908:iv. 1. 226) suggests the origin of the Antevongo from Fenerive and Vohilava, i.e. the east coast, which would place them with Betsimisaraka rather than Sihanaka.

differences are not biological or even political, but are summed up by differences of *fomba*—of cultural practices. Tsimihety have certain *fomba* that may be absent from, or differ from the *fomba* of other Malagasy. That they have no chiefs, for example, whereas the Sakalava and the Merina do, is a Tsimihety *fomba*. So also is the Tsimihety dialect, the use of natural rock shelters for tombs rather than man-made tombs, the payment of a bride-price (*moletry*), the design of a house, the method of growing rice, a distinctive woman's hairstyle, the conduct of a funeral, the holding of a feast called *mamahanzaza* when a husband and wife have had ten children. Many *fomba Tsimihety* are of course the same as other Malagasy peoples' customs, but it is the idea of a commonly held and practiced culture observed by some people and not others, that constitutes Tsimihety.

All Tsimihety with whom I raised the question agreed that the region known as Androna was their heartland. This did not mean that there were more Tsimihety and fewer members of other cultural groups living there (the region around the town of Befandriana has a higher percentage of Tsimihety). Nor did it mean that there was any closer form of integration among people living in the area. It referred solely to the fact that it was believed that in Androna *fomba Tsimihety* were practiced most consistently and authentically by the people living there. It was in this region that I carried out my field-work.

Tsimihety grow both wet and dry rice, but nowhere reach the efficiency achieved by the plateau peoples in their rice agriculture. Rice is the staple food, with manioc and corn regarded, with some disdain, as famine breakers. Vegetables are sometimes grown in small garden plots, most often tended by women, but not exclusively so. All Tsimihety aspire to keep large numbers of cattle of the humped zebu variety. Cattle fulfil prestige and aesthetic longings, are traded, rustled, used to draw carts, to prepare rice fields, in bride-price payments, and in ritual sacrifices. Meat is eaten only on the occasion of a sacrifice or celebration, and very few people milk their cows. Chickens, ducks, and geese are raised and eaten and occasionally pigs are kept. Fish are obtained from streams, rice fields, and are brought from the west by pedlars in various stages of preservation. Fruits, principally tree fruits, are gathered, and in some villages cultivated. Soon after the French began their administration they tried to get Tsimihety to grow certain crops for cash, such as coffee, vanilla, kapok, raphia, peanuts, cloves, and groundnuts, which would in turn allow the French to collect taxes. Though grown today in suitable areas they are not cultivated in any quantity except by non-Tsimihety (principally Betsileo and Merina) living in the area. Tsimihety people have shown little inclination toward becoming dependent on a cash economy and prefer to produce principally to meet their own needs, and not those of an outside government. The same is true today of the Tsimihety attitude to the Malagasy Government. Of the above-mentioned cash crops, raphia, present before the arrival of the French and indigenous to Madagascar, is the only one extensively cultivated since it provides a basic raw material for the Tsimihety, corresponding in its wide range of uses with the bamboo in other areas. It is used for building houses, making furniture, mats, clothing and other woven items, thatching, utensils, and implements.

Tsimihety live in small villages of between 20 and 100 inhabitants. There are a few villages with as many as 1,000 people, but these are relics of the earlier French policy of amalgamation of neighboring villages to facilitate administration. Some of these large villages have remained administrative centers. It is also not uncommon to come upon isolated homesteads where a man, his wife, and children are living, often some distance from the nearest village. Houses are arranged in parallel rows running north-west to south-east, bisecting the path of the sun with the doorway facing west— away from the direction whence the ancestors came. The house itself is rectangular in plan, built of sun-dried mud caked over a framework of raphia palm with a thatch roof. It is usually made up of three separate structures, a sleeping and reception hut, a kitchen immediately behind the sleeping hut which is also used for eating, and a granary located on the periphery of the village where danger from fire is less. Some houses have a hearth and no separate kitchen. The most common household consists of a man, his wife, and their children and/or his children by another woman.

Any description of the Tsimihety, as of any Malagasy cultural group, must make mention of the set of beliefs and practices centering upon the ancestors, which is the focus and heart of Tsimihety, and Malagasy, culture. Ancestors are influential on the course of daily life, are mediators between the earthly and the supernatural, are part and parcel of life itself as a temporal extension of the present. The supreme satisfaction in life is the knowledge that one will become an ancestor, a satisfaction achieved through children, even though becoming an ancestor ultimately means death. The same term—*dady*—is used for grandparents and for those already dead, but within living memory. Ancestors within the framework of the social structure are not thought of as "dead and gone" but as a social status which is continuous with the status system of the living. They dwell in the vast cave-tombs set high in the hills that carve up the region of Androna. Until an ancestor takes his rightful place in these tombs he cannot be happy, and will therefore be a constant threat to the living. In the tomb he is set alongside those of his own generation and arranged in a genealogical order with respect to other inhabitants of the tomb. It is the responsibility of his immediate descendants to place him in the tomb. Thus the birth of a child, especially a son, assures a parent of the status of ancestor.

II. TSIMIHETY KINSHIP

So many of a Tsimihety individual's social relationship are with people he classifies as kin, and so many of the things that an individual does are with similarly classified people, that a description of Tsimihety kinship is fundamental to any sort of understanding of Tsimihety people and culture. In the analysis of kinship it is helpful to separate the semantic structure of the kinship terminology from the sociological structure of the behavior associated with kinship. In the semantic structure we are concerned with the meanings of words to the people who use them, in so far as these can be ascertained or deduced, and with the relationship of the words to each other in terms of the classificatory system of which they form a part. The semantic structure of a kinship terminology is common to the speech community. The sociological structure concerns the identification and status of people toward each other in a behavioral setting, as they act and react with each other, thereby systematizing the rights and duties of individuals with respect to each other. Modes of conduct are correlated with this sociological structure.

The word *havana* may be glossed in English as kin, kinship, kinsman, relative, relatedness. Its primary referent is to people between whom there is a genealogical relationship. It is extended metaphorically to describe people related to each other in any way resembling a kinship relationship. Thus two people who behave familiarly and intimately, such as neighbors, may come to identify themselves to each other and outsiders as *havana*. Similarly anyone who is brought into a relationship with another person in a manner analogous to a kinship relationship, such as an adoptee, or an "in-law," may be identified as *havana*. By analogy with relationships among people any relationship observed among other living things may be described as *havana*. This, however, does not concern us here. By contrast, a non-relative is a stranger, a *vahiny*.

The term *havana* describes a class of any and all kinsmen. It may be qualified by a number of terms each denoting a relative, genealogical distance of relationship: *havana andrazambe* may be glossed as "very distant kin," those with whom a relationship could only be established by tracing back through very distant ancestors (*razana*=ancestor); *havana lavidavitra* may be glossed as "distant kin"; *havana akaiky* as "close kin." Thus the term *havana* denotes a super-class of any and all kin, and when qualified makes only general distinctions. When the word is used it establishes a basic identity. A person who is *havana* is not *vahiny*. In social situations such a person can be trusted, can exercise certain claims to hospitality, or is obliged to offer the same. Any two people identified as *havana* are potentially in a status position which they can define with precision by plotting genealogical links. A common situation in Tsimihety provides an example of the sociology of *havana*. On arrival in a strange village a Tsimihety may establish that he is *havana* with one or more of the inhabitants. This is enough to determine in which house he will sleep and from whom he will receive food and share company. If the new arrival is a *vahiny* he will receive only the minimum hospitality on an impersonal basis and will be expected to be quickly on his way.

Havana or kin may be further specified by a number of terms each denoting a class of kin. These terms are set forth below, together with a description of the more closely related kinsmen and an English gloss (the method used is that set out by Lounsbury, 1964).

Term	Gloss	Class
dadilahy	grandfather	FF, MF; FFB, FMB, MFB, MMB, FFF, MMF; FFFBs, etc.
dadivavy (synonym: *baba*)	grandmother	FM, MM; FFS, FMS, MFS, MMS, FFM, MMM; FFFBd, etc.
ray	father	F.
ray-be	father's brother	FB; FMSs, FFBs, FMBs, FFSs; FFFBss, etc., when older than father.
ray-hely (synonym: *iada*)	father's brother	Same, when younger than father.
reny	mother	M.
reny-be	mother's sister	MS; MMSd, MFBd, MMBd, MFSd, MMMSdd, etc., when older than mother.
reny-hely (synonym: *niny*)	mother's sister	Same, when younger than mother.
zama-be	senior uncle	MB; MMSs, MFBS, MMBs, MFSs; MMMSds, etc., when older than mother.
zama-hely	junior uncle	Same, when younger than mother.
angovavy-be	senior aunt	FS; FMSd, FFBd, FMBd, FFSd; FFFBsd, etc., when older than father.
angovavy-hely	junior aunt	Same, when younger than father.
rahalahy zoky (synonym: *rokilahy*)	elder brother	B; MSs, FBs; MMSds, FFBss, MFBds, FMSss, MMBds, FFSss, MFSds, FMBss; MMMSdds, etc., when older than male EGO.
rahalahy zandry	younger brother	Same, when younger than a male EGO.
anadahy zoky	elder brother	Same, when older than a female EGO.
anadahy zandry	younger brother	Same, when younger than a female EGO.

Term	Gloss	Class
rahavavy zoky (synonym: *rokivavy*)	elder sister	S; MSd, FBd, MMSdd, FFBsd, MFBdd, FMSsd, MMMBdd, FFSsd, MFSdd, FMBsd; MMMSddd, etc., when older than a female EGO.
rahavavy zandry	younger sister	Same, when younger than a female EGO.
anabavy zoky	elder sister	Same, when older than a male EGO.
anabavy zandry	younger sister	Same, when younger than a male EGO.
zanakalahy[3]	son	s; Bs; MSss, FBss, MBss, FSss; MMSdss, etc., male speaking; but s; Ss; MSds, FBds, MBds, FSds; MMSdds, etc., female speaking.
zanakavavy[4]	daughter	d; Bd; MSsd, FBsd, MBsd, FSsd; MMSdsd, etc., male speaking; but d; Sd; MSdd, FBdd, MBdd, FSdd; MMSdd, etc., female speaking.
asidilahy	nephew	Ss; MSds, FBds, MBds, FSds; MMSdds, etc., male speaking; but Bs; MSss, FBss, MBss, FSss; MMSdds, etc., female speaking.
asidivavy	niece	Sd; MSdd; FBdd, MBdd, FSdd; MMSddd, etc., male speaking; but Bd; MSsd, FBsd, MBsd, FSsd; MMSdsd, etc., female speaking.
zafilahy	grandson	ss; ds; Bss, Bds, Sss, Sds; FBsss; sss, dds, etc.
zafivavy	granddaughter	sd, dd; Bsd, Bdd, Ssd, Sdd; FBssd; ssd, ddd, etc.

Key: F=father, M=mother, B=brother, S=sister, s=son, d=daughter

[3] A first-born son is termed *talañolo lahy:* a youngest son is termed *faralahy.*
[4] A first-born daughter is termed *talañolo vaiavy:* a youngest daughter is termed *faravavy.*

These terms denote all genealogically linked kin regarded by the Tsimihety as consanguineally related.[5] The semantic structure of the terminology may be described by determining the features common to the terms. These features are particular dimensions of genealogical kinship systematically arranged. As such they are the basis not only of the semantic structure, but also of the more general cognitive structure of kinship so that the dimensions of the semantic structure may coincide with the sociological organization of kinship, at least to some extent. And, as Lounsbury has pointed out, an analysis of linguistic usage may point to the social and cultural realities behind the semantics and reveal "a few underlying *principles of classification* whose effects are far-reaching" (Lounsbury, 1964:1091).

We shall therefore define each of the terms by its component features:

dadilahy: this kin type comprises all males (symbolized ♂) of the second ascending generation and above (symbolized G^{2+}) who are kin to a propositus (symbolized K): ♂.G^{2+}.K.

[5] The terms denoting affinals are:

rafozana	HF, HM, WF, WM
soja-lahy	HF, WF
soja-vavy	HM, WM
zama-hely	FSH
iada-hely	MSH
[*zena*] [*angovavy*]	MBW
niny hely	FBW
nama (ko) *vady (ko)*	(my) wife/husband
rañao	WS, HS, BW
valilahy	WB, HB, SH
vinanto lahy	dS
vinanto vavy	sW

So far as I can tell, Tsimihety regard affinals (*mpihavana*) as "like kin" but not as kin. Parents' siblings' spouses only are denoted by terms used in the kinship terminology. It is tempting to postulate institutionalized sibling set marriages on the basis of the above terms, but I have no evidence for this. Conduct between affinals is characteristically ambivalent: respect of junior to senior is the most clear-cut observable attitude and there is an institutionalized joking relationship between siblings in law of the same sex. Both sororate and levirate are to be found, but they are not obligatory and are utilized by individuals usually only when the situation is mutually convenient to those concerned. However, my understanding of the complex of Tsimihety marriage and affinity is at present too incomplete for me to venture more than a footnote. It is hoped to remedy this and other deficiences by further fieldwork.

dadivavy: comprises all females (symbolized ♀) of the second ascending generation and above who are kin to a propositus: ♀.G^{2+}.K.

The reciprocals of these two terms are:

zafilahy: comprises all males of the second descending generation and below (symbolized G_{2-}) who are kin to a propositus: ♂.G_{2-}.K.

zafivavy: comprises all females of the second generation and below who are kin to a propositus: ♀.G_{2-}.K.

ray: comprises the primary relative, a male of the first ascending generation father to a propositus: ♂.G^{1}.K.

ray-be: comprises all males older (symbolized A^{+}) than the same sex first linking relative (symbolized $L=$) of the first ascending generation kin to a propositus: ♂.A^{+}.$L{=}G^{1}$.K.

ray hely: comprises all males younger (symbolized A^{-}) than the same sex first linking relative of the first ascending generation kin to a propositus: ♂.A^{-}.$L{=}.G^{1}$.K.

reny: comprises the primary relative, a female of the first ascending generation who is mother to the propositus: ♀.G^{1}.K.

reny-be: comprises all females older than the first linking relative of the same sex of the first ascending generation kin to a propositus: ♀.A^{+}.$L{=}.G^{1}$.K.

reny-hely: comprises all females younger than the first linking relative of the same sex of the first ascending generation kin to a propositus: ♀.A^{-}.$L{=}.G^{1}$.K.

The reciprocals of these terms are:

zanakalahy: comprises all males of the first descending generation for whom the sex of the last linking relative is the same as that of the speaker (symbolized $l=$), kin to a propositus: ♂.G_{1}.$l{=}$.K.

zanakavavy: comprises all females of the first descending generation for whom the sex of the last linking relative is the same as that of the speaker (symbolized $l=$), kin to a propositus: ♀.G_{1}.$l{=}$.K.

zama-be: comprises all males older than the first link of opposite sex (symbolized $L{\neq}$) of the first ascending generation kin to a propositus: ♂.A^{+}.$L{\neq}.G^{1}$.K.

zama-hely: comprises all males younger than the first link of opposite sex of the first ascending generation kin to a propositus: ♂.A⁻.L≠.G¹.K.

angovavy-be: comprises all females older than the first link of opposite sex of the first ascending generation kin to a propositus: ♀.A⁺.L≠.G¹.K.

angovavy hely: comprises all females younger than the first link of opposite sex of the first ascending generation kin to a propositus: ♀.A⁻.L≠.G¹.K.

The reciprocals of these terms are:

asidilahy: comprises all males of the first descending generation for whom the sex of the last linking relative is opposite to that of the speaker (symbolized l≠), kin to a propositus: ♂.G₁.l≠.K.

asidivavy: comprises all females of the first descending generation for whom the sex of the last link is opposite to that of the speaker (symbolized l≠), kin to a propositus: ♀.G₁.l≠.K.

rahalahy zoky: comprises all males older than, of the same sex (symbolized P=) as, of the same generation as, and kin to a propositus: ♂.A⁺.P=.G⁰.K.

rahalahy zandry: comprises all males younger than, of the same sex as, of the same generation as, and kin to a propositus: ♂.A⁻.P=.G⁰.K.

anadahy zoky: comprises all males older than, of opposite sex to, of the same generation as, and kin to a propositus: ♂.A⁺.P≠.G⁰.K.

anadahy zandry: comprises all males younger than, of opposite sex to, of the same generation as, and kin to a propositus: ♂.A⁻.P≠.G⁰.K.

rahavavy zoky: comprises all females older than, of the same sex as, of the same generation as, and kin to a propositus: ♀.A⁺.P=.G⁰.K.

rahavavy zandry: comprises all females younger than, of the same sex as, of the same generation as, and kin to a propositus: ♀.A⁻.P=.G⁰.K.

anabavy zoky: comprises all females older than, of the opposite sex to, of the same generation as, and kin to a propositus: ♀.A⁺.P≠.G⁰.K.

anabavy zandry: comprises all females younger than, of the opposite sex to, of the same generation as, and kin to a propositus:
♀ $.A^-.P\neq.G^0.K.$

The major features of the semantic structure of Tsimihety kinship
terminology are the distinctions based on generation with relative
age and sex. Also noteworthy is the bifurcation of terms in adjacent
generations. Generation and sex differentiation are also prominent
features of the sociological structure of the kinship system. In the
conduct of social relationships the *values* of priority, precedence,
and authority are placed on the distinctions of generation, sex,
and relative age, although these values are no part of the semantic
structure. Certain generalizations about these values may be made
which describe a basis of the structure of behavior among kin,
and in a more general sense among all Tsimihety, and which are
indicated in the semantic structure.

1. Members of the same sex who are of a senior generation
   have priority and precedence in any social context.
1a. A senior member of the same sex of the same generation
   has priority and precedence over a junior member.
2. Males have priority and precedence over females in any context
   in which they act together.
2a. A male has priority and precedence over a female of the
   same generation irrespective of relative age.
3. Authority in social relationships rests with the senior, male
   identity.

From such general propositions, or sociological rules, can be derived a number of specific rules relevant to specific forms of social
interaction among the Tsimihety. To give but a few examples: the
youngest person present should carry the burden of his or her
seniors. Men walk in front of women. The final decision on matters
of family discipline rests with the senior male of the particular
group of kinsmen involved. Men eat before women; senior males
eat before junior males.

There is, however, another way in which the kinship terminology
must be considered as a dimension of the sociological structure of
kinship, namely in the sense of the use of the terms as words in
sociological contexts, where language is also behavior. As such they
are labels that establish the identity of the two or more poles of

a relationship. A kinship term is the linguistic expression of a social identity. Since one term has no meaning without implying the use of its reciprocal in any social action, then the set of reciprocal terms is the label denoting the basic unit of the sociological structure. This we can call a status. Since we are here dealing only with kinship, we are more correctly talking about kinship statuses. Whereas in the linguistic analysis of kinship terms we hold constant a fictional propositus or EGO who has no linguistic identity but that of EGO, in the sociological structure there is no EGO, there is only a relation comprising two interdependent or reciprocal parts (kinship identities). The basic sociological structure of a kinship system, or of any status system for that matter, is a dyadic or reciprocal relation (cf. Adams, 1960:39; Foster, 1961:1174).

The kinship terminology of the Tsimihety can in fact be "reduced" to six terms, each expressing status rather than identity and incorporating the reciprocal terms. All kin who can identify themselves in the status grandparents: grandchild are described by the term *ampiafy;* those of the status parent: child by the term *ampianaka,* those of the status uncle/aunt: nephew/niece by the term *misidy,* brothers are *ampiralahy* and sisters *ampiravavy;* brothers and sisters are *ampianadahy.* These status terms are used not only to denote sociological positions with reference to genealogical space, but to describe the stereotype of behavior pattern associated with these statuses; thus the relationship *ampiafy* not only designates grandparents and grandchildren, it describes the respectful ease and familiarity of behavior expected and regarded as "normal" in such a status. These status terms may also be used as metaphors to describe behavior between two people not in the specific status position, but who behave toward each other as if they were. And the metaphor can be applied beyond the realm of human behavior to that of cattle, for example. In the same way, the specific identity terms can be used metaphorically when some aspect of a relationship bears a resemblance to the relationship that includes particular identities. My own identity toward inhabitants of one of the villages I studied provides a good example of the metaphorical use of kinship and status terms. When I first arrived I was referred to and addressed as *vahiny vazaha* (foreign white man). Eventually through my "adoption" by a particular old man who became my *dadilahy* I was addressed and referred to by various terms consonant with my *ampiafy* status to this particular old man. No one was under the slightest delusion that I was really a kinsman, but I behaved like one, and was identified like one.

Each and every Tsimihety recognizes a number of kin to whom he is genealogically and socially close. All such kin to whom an individual is close are categorized as *fianakaviana*. In theory this includes all kin who are the primary referents of the various kin terms. In practice more genealogically distant kin may be included if the sentiment between them is close, or if they live near each other and interact frequently and amicably. At certain important times of an individual's life, particularly at rituals marking events of the life cycle, an individual's *fianakaviana* come together and each component kin status performs as institutionalized role. Such events bring geographically distant kin together with co-resident kin, both cognates and agnates. However, even in their physical absence an individual's close kin remain classified as *fianakaviana* together with kin living near by. All *fianakaviana,* whether living apart or together, are obliged to visit each other regularly and to extend hospitality.

The closest *fianakaviana* of any male usually reside together, since post-marital residence is patrilocal. Conversely the closest *fianakaviana* of a female, while they live together, yet live apart from her. The co-resident *fianakaviana* include agnatically related males and females, the latter usually being unmarried, plus a man's mother, his paternal grandmother and/or his daughter. It does not include those co-resident females an individual classifies as *mpihavana* or affines, that is to say, his brother's wife, his father's brother's wife, or his son's wife. *Fianakaviana* then is an aggregative kinship category of bilateral dimensions.

The total residential group, which includes the *fianakaviana* and the spouses, is explicitly recognized. It is denoted by the term *ankohonana* (and less frequently *fehitry*) and it operates as a social unit. Formerly it was a commensal group, but common participation in a meal is less regular nowadays. As a commensal group it was termed *jao* which is also the term given to the meal. The *jao* is still typical, however, when the group works together at harvest time and at the time of field preparation. As a reciprocal co-operative labor group it is identified as *asa reky,* and it may include non-members of the *ankohonana,* depending on the ties of friendship between villagers. Finally, the Tsimihety distinguish the household, *tokontrano,* as a unit of social relationship. This term in effect describes the unit of husband and wife and additionally their children. Thus the term for marriage as a social act is *manazo tokon trano* (to take a wife/husband) as opposed to the ritual of marriage (*fanambady*).

The *fianakaviana* is an ego-based kindred of undifferentiated kin. It is not a grouping but a category or a general status denoting kin who have specific duties, obligations, and responsibilities toward one another. These are ritually expressed during the life cycle of the focal individual, particularly at his naming ceremony, circumcision, wedding, and burial. By virtue of Tsimihety post-marital residence patterns and exogamic stipulations in other social contexts, the category *fianakaviana* is differentiated, but not in terms of agnatic versus cognatic kin (as Freeman would suggest, 1961:204). The differentiation is in terms of those *fianakaviana* who live away (which includes such agnates as father's sister, cognates such as mother's brother and mother's parents) and those who live together (which includes an agnatic majority but also a cognate—a man's mother.)

The social group of *ankohonana* contains a majority of members who are agnatically related to each other, but this is an incidental not a purposive feature of its structure as is also the fact that many of its members are *fianakaviana* to each other. In the performance of the social tasks with which it is concerned, all members of the *ankohonana* have a status which is defined by their co-residence and by relative seniority, and not by kinship or descent.

It is to the descent aspect of kinship that we now turn.

III. TSIMIHETY DESCENT

Descent is a selective emphasis on specific kinship relations and as such is part and parcel of a kinship system. The selective emphases, or features of descent, have been noted by Fortes (1959: 206–7): "Descent can be defined as a genealogical connection recognized between a person and any of his ancestors or ancestresses. It is established by tracing a pedigree. . . . A descent rule states which of the two elementary forms of filiation and what serial combination of forms of filiation shall be utilized in establishing pedigrees for social purposes." The essentials of descent are the serial combination of particular genealogical links, and the continuity of these (cf. Scheffler, n.d.). Tsimihety appear to observe a rule of descent in the organization of social relations for certain purposes. The rule emphasizes the genealogical link between a father and his children, and this emphasis is continued through genealogical time, i.e. over generations with ultimate reference to the ancestors. The type of descent rule, or construct (Scheffler, op. cit.) is patrilineal, but since a female may transfer her patrilineal descent status to her children with degrees of priority varying with circumstances, Tsimihety provide an illustration of a departure from the ideal "model" of patrilineal descent structure.

The descent rule applies to the definition of status of individual Tsimihety with respect to tombs, ancestors, and land. It is a universal (Tsimihety) cultural imperative, or cultural given, that every Tsimihety should be buried in a tomb with his ancestors. He must be buried by his descendants. Every Tsimihety must have access to the ancestors, which is achieved through ritual and the establishment of an identity toward specific ancestors. Every Tsimihety must have land on which to live and cultivate. The rule of descent is used to define the status of Tsimihety individuals toward tombs, ancestors, and land, thereby ensuring recognition of rights, duties, and obligations. My emphasis is on the individual: descent is a rule that defines individual status rather than group status. In fact, whether descent gives rise to a descent group among the Tsimihety is highly debatable, and this is the question to which I shall return at the end of this paper.

A man expects to be buried in the tomb of his father by his son. A man (or woman) has the right to be buried in the paternal tomb. A three-generational continuum of patrifiliation is here implied. This fulfills the minimum condition for a rule of descent to be established (Fortes, 1959:207). Further implications are that a son, or at least a child, is essential to a person for the continuance of his social status after death. Unless a man has a son, he cannot become an ancestor. The birth of a son is not only a meaningful event in the day-to-day social life of a man, it is a confirmation of his ongoing status through a continuum that passes from life through death to ancestorship. Such knowledge on the part of an individual that he will become an ancestor by having descendants is possibly the crucial feature of Tsimihety cosmology.

The achievement of the status of father, then grandfather, is part of a status continuum leading to ancestor which defines and refines the social status of an individual among his fellows. If this is so, as I believe, then a critical moment to all Tsimihety is the birth of a new individual. Of fundamental sociological importance to Tsimihety, and to anthropology, is the sociology of birth and its association with the rule of descent which, as we have seen, is the rule behind a fundamental status system in Tsimihety life.

At birth a (Tsimihety) child is nothing—neither Tsimihety, nor kinsman, nor human being. Its only identity is male or female, and an "event" marked by an arbitrary name such as place of birth if this was unusual, or an object present at the birth (a child born in my presence was termed *Soivazaha:* white man bird). Mother and child remain closeted in the hut for at least a week. They are both in a ritually dangerous state (*trambona*) and fires are kept burning to ward off danger from spirits, etc. If the child dies during the time when it and the mother are *trambona* (until it cuts its first tooth) it is buried without ceremony somewhere in the bush. When the first tooth is cut it is given the first name, and thereby recognized as human. The name is more than just a signification of human status, it is a recognition of social status, not only of the child but of the parents and of the particular kin of the parents identified as *foko*. The actual name is decided on by consultation with the diviner (*ombiasa*).[6] The father of the child consults the *ombiasa,* and the name is discussed with the kin who are *fianakaviana*. The name is bestowed on the child before the assembled elders (*rayamandreny*) of the father's village, but also present are the mother's brother (*zama*) and, optionally, the mother's parents (and others of the mother's kin are invited to the feast). At the same time as the name of the child is announced, the father, mother, mother's brother, and (optionally) the four grandparents take the name of the child coupled with their kinship identity. This practice of teknonymy would therefore appear to confirm the status of husband/wife=parent; grandparent's/grandchild =ancestor's descendant; father/child=*fokondray;* mother/mother's brother/child-nephew=*fokondreny*. The name conferred on the child is not used until the child reaches adulthood. Instead it is called

[6] The term *mpisikidy* is often used in the literature to describe the *ombiasa* in his capacity as diviner. However the term *mpisikidy* is rarely used by Tsimihety, although the *ombiasa* uses the *sikidy* as a method of divination.

by a nickname that is often extremely unpleasant to make the child unattractive to the evil powers to which it is still susceptible. However, if the child falls ill, or has some misfortune, its real name will be changed. All things being equal, from this point on a man will have someone to bury him and a man's parents will become ancestors. A number of rights, duties, and privileges among a number of individuals have been publicly affirmed and clarified. From the child's point of view his right to inherit land, a place in his father's tomb, the protection of his kin, his secondary rights to be buried in his mother's tomb (rights guarded for her by her brother), to inherit his mother's land, etc., all are now public (i.e. social). He incurs a number of obligations to obey the authority of his senior kin, to observe taboos, to give of his labor, respect, hospitality, and obedience.

Though there is no confusion on the part of Tsimihety as to the role of the male and the female in conception, the determination of the status of a male and female toward a child is by no means automatic. Since the definition of status is sociological and not biological we should look to see how this is defined in Tsimihety. If it is a cultural axiom that a man must have descendants in order to continue his "life" on through death to ancestorship, how is such status achieved?[7]

Premarital sexual relations are very free, subject only to incest prohibitions which extend from forbidding incest with kin related to the sixth degree to kin related to the third degree.[8] Young

[7] It seems to me confusing to speak of ascribed status (Linton, 1936:115; Goodenough, 1965:5). Properly speaking only the qualifications for a particular status are inseparably part of the individual. The status he comes to hold, by virtue of apt qualification among a population, is the result of recognition of those qualifications by that population. This is shown up most clearly in the negative case where, for example, a man qualified to be *mpijoro* by virtue of his social seniority, may not function as such because he is senile. Or, as I have implied here, a man's descent status is by no means automatic. The achievement of descent status is, in the first instance at least, the result of the actions of others than the status holder it is achieved for him by his father and mother.

[8] The precise specification of the limits of exogamic prohibition is inherited from a man's father who shares it in common with all *fokondray*. The prohibition is expressed in terms of bilateral kinship and not by reference to patrilineal descent. Thus the Antivohilava forbid Antivohilava to marry each other within a range of three degrees and to marry any kin of the mother within the same limits. Antavaribe prohibit marriage with each other and with anyone an individual member recognizes as kin (*havana*). There is, however, some evidence of emphasis of prohibition on the father's side. A number of informants said

men therefore travel some distance to get their sexual experience. Most villages have a young men's house (*kotravahy lelahy*) where they may stay, and a young women's house (*kotravahy vaiavy*) in which young women entertain the young men. A young man usually gives the girl a gift after he has slept with her. Men after marriage are relatively free to have sexual relations with women other than their wives, but if a woman has extramarital sex relations the man has grounds for divorce and punishment.

During the course of his wanderings a young man often meets a girl he would like to live with. If he does not, his parents make inquiries, usually through their distant kin (*havana lavidavitra*), for a suitable wife. If the two young people approve of each other, plans for the wedding can go ahead. The majority of contemporary Tsimihety marriages are of a type termed *fanambadiana moletry*. This means a marriage at which a bride-price is handed over. The *moletry* includes cattle (from two to six head) and money (from CFA 100 to CFA 5,000). The word *moletry* was said to be of recent origin (cf. Bulletin, 1964:535), but the handing over of money and/or cattle appears to be long established, at least in Androna. The amount of the *moletry* is negotiated by the parents of the prospective spouses whose positions and confidence are usually bolstered by the presence of close kin (*fianakaviana*).

In terms of its structural role, the *moletry* is comparable to the bride-price institution described for peoples of East Africa (cf. Gluckman, 1950:189). In Tsimihety thinking and practice the *moletry* is correlated with the children expected to follow on a marriage. However, the *moletry* is not paid by a group, but by a man's father and sometimes by the groom himself. It is not the membership of a group that is paid for, but rather the status of father, and all that entails. The *moletry* is refundable in full if the marriage breaks up within a year, unless a child has been born, in which case the woman may retain a portion of the *moletry* (it belongs to the woman and not to any of her kin. It may be held in trust for her by her brother). After a year the *moletry* is not refundable if the marriage breaks up and

---

that marriage with the mother's kin within the prohibited degrees could occur and would not be too serious a breach of the rule. By performing the requisite sacrificial expiation (*mandoza*) the kinship of the spouses could be negated, and the ancestors reconciled. Where exogamic prohibitions inherited from both parents differ the narrowest prohibitions are strictly observed no matter which side, and if a breach of the widest prohibition occurs it is usually expiated by *mandoza*.

the woman has borne the man children. If she has borne him no children he may negotiate for the partial return of the *moletry*. A number of cases have occurred where the woman waits for a year and then leaves her husband, or provokes him into sending her home. She leaves a wealthier woman than when she came to him. To counter this a number of individuals have preferred to delay payment of the *moletry*, either in whole or in part, until after a child had been born to the union. It seems reasonable to conclude that at least part of the payment made by a man at marriage is for the right to call himself the father of the children of his wife. This interpretation is shown up more clearly in the more crucial example, which occurs frequently in Tsimihety, of the determination of fatherhood of a child born to a woman who has not been married.

A woman is not shamed by becoming pregnant outside of marriage, though this is not a preferred condition. When an unmarried woman becomes pregnant she has the option of telling the man she would like to recognize as the father before her pregnancy is obvious. Tsimihety girls are not oversexed or uncontrollably promiscuous and they usually form attachments and have sexual relations with one man or perhaps two and so usually know who is the father. The point is that she is not particularly concerned as to the biological father, but that she has a preference for a particular man she would like to become the father. The two are usually the same man. If, on the other hand, she has no preference she may wait until she is obviously pregnant and hope that one of her partners will claim fatherhood. If a man wishes to establish his fatherhood of a woman's child before she is delivered he announces his intention to her *fianakaviana*, brings her to his own village, and supports her until and through her delivery.[9] He similarly publicly informs the elders of his village of his fatherhood and he makes a payment to the woman (*valy tarana*) of either money or cattle or both. The child remains with the mother, going back with her to her own village until it reaches the age of about one to three years, unless the father is already married, in which case it will join the father's household before it is a year old. A man may theoretically claim a child at any time by making the necessary payment and announcement. However, I did not come across any case where a child was claimed over the age of seven years. If the child is a man's first he may take the name of the

[9] A married woman's first child, on the other hand, is usually born in the house of her mother.

child, but the mother does not do so, unless she marries the father. If a child is not claimed by its "father" it remains with its mother and its name is taken by the mother and the mother's brother. It is thereby granted full rights or primary status to burial in the mother's father's tomb and to all that this entails. It is fully protected by the ancestors of the mother and it has the right to inherit the property of the mother. If the mother does not marry, her rights to cultivate land are activated and her child will inherit these. If a woman does marry, her husband has the option of becoming the father of the child. If he does not then the child is brought up by the mother's brother and/or mother's parents and is granted full status rights to their land, tomb, and ancestors.

The status of *fokondray* is the right of an individual to be buried in his father's tomb, to inherit the land that has been cultivated by his father and to build a house in his father's village—if he so desires. He may mark the ears of his cattle with a design inherited from his father (*sofinomby*). He also has the right to the protection both supernatural and practical of his father. He is obliged to observe the taboos (*fady*) of his father, to obey his father, to bury his father, to look after his bones and to propitiate him. He holds this status with others who have access by the same rule of descent to common resources (tomb, ancestors, land) and in contrast to those who cannot establish their status by specific application of the rule of descent.

The status of *fokondreny* is identical with that of *fokondray* in kind, but not in degree. It is inherited through an individual's affiliation with his mother and thence through her descent status with her father and father's father. In the event that an individual's primary status of *fokondray* is not activated he may assume primary status through *fokondreny*. (Such situations arise frequently through adoption, the giving away of children—usually to those who are childless and who would therefore not become ancestors, and fatherless children.) *Fokondreny* can never become *fokondray*—but a man's children inherit his status of *fokondreny* as *fokondray*.

An individual who lives in the same village as his father's father and as his ancestors is described as living *ambenilahy*. All those living in the paternal village to whom the same specific application of the rule of descent is made have the same residential status as well as the same descent status. Others who share the same descent status but who do not live together are not *ambenilahy*. Actual genealogical continuity between co-resident *ambenilahy* is not necessary in either theory or practice. The *ambenilahy* is not a lineage in other words, though in many instances its genealogical structure resembles one. Such a co-resident aggregate with common descent ties tends to live in a clearly demarcated section (*fizarana*) of a particular village, if it does not comprise the entire population of that village. The sections are marked by a wider pathway between the houses, or they are arranged around the sides of the central dancing plaza. Those who are *ambenilahy,* and who live in the villages within the territory (*faritany*) to which they have collective rights of access inherited from the ancestors, are responsible for upkeep of the tomb, for propitiating the ancestors, and for guarding the tomb, and the rights of non-resident *foko* individuals in land and access to the tomb. In this capacity they occupy the collective status of *mpiambinjana* (guardians). When, for example, *fokondray* living far away come to bury an individual, or to attend a funeral or a wedding, the *mpiambinjana* must cater for them and provide them with what they need. Specific obligations are met on the basis of specific kinship statuses (such as actual boarding and lodging, etc.). In the event of a *fokondray* coming from afar and claiming the right to cultivate land in the *faritany* and to offer sacrifices to the ancestors it is up to the *mpiambinjana* to recognize the claim and establish the rights.

Persons who reside in the village of their mothers are described as *ambenivavy*. As such they enjoy only a secondary status in the village —they have less influence in the *fokon'olona* (council) and they may return to their father's village for rituals to be offered on their behalf. It happens not infrequently that a man sends his son to cultivate land that his wife has inherited. Even more frequent are the cases where a man sends one or more of his sons to his mother's village (their grandmother) to continue to cultivate land that she inherited, especially if it is good land. Any individual whose kin are related to him through his mother, but who are related among themselves by patrilineal descent, have the collective status of *ambenivavy* if they live together.

Another way in which a man can find himself in a position whereby it is difficult for him to activate his primary status of *fokondray* is if he goes to live with his wife in her village. Such a man and such a pattern of residence is termed *jaloko*. The land that he cultivates to support himself and his family is given to him by his wife's father with the approval of the *rayamandreny* or elders. In return he renders services to his father-in-law. If the *jaloko* continues to reside here (such unions are usually runaway love matches) it is likely that he will be represented to the ancestors by the *mpijoro* of his wife's *fokondray* and that he may eventually be buried in the tomb of his wife's father by his children, who will inherit land and their *foko* status through their mother (*fokondreny*). In these instances, which occur rarely, but with sufficient regularity for them to be verbalized as an institutional variant of marriage and descent by Tsimihety, "complementary affiliation" can be achieved through marriage as well as through kinship with the parent whose descent status is not primary. Such a status is termed *fokombady*.

Though residing patrilocally a man, after marriage, observes the taboos of his wife's father and of her *fokondray* (*fadindrazana*, taboos of the ancestors), just as she observes her husband's *fadindrazana*.

There are two specific statuses associated with the aggregation of Tsimihety into an assembly for a political or a ritual purpose. The senior male of the senior generation of the aggregate assembled at any given time is termed the *soja*. When the *rayamandreny* or elders of the village meet to discuss anything (*fokon'olona*) the "chairman" of the meeting is the *soja*, and the meeting is held in his house.[10] The order of speaking follows the rule of generation, and women take no direct path in such meetings (they gather in a neighboring house and often shout their suggestions). The head of a household (*tokontrano*) is termed *soja*, so also is the head or senior member of the *ankohonana, asa reky, fokondray,* or any aggregate.

In the offerings to the ancestors a ritual requirement is the pouring of a libation and the saying of a "prayer" which includes recitation of a genealogy.[11] Major rituals also require the striking of the sacrificial animal with a special cane (*koboay*). The officiant is the senior person (male or female) of the senior generation of the particular aggregate assembled. In such a capacity he or she is the *mpijoro* (offerer, sacrificer). In a small sacrifice (*joro*) the head of a household may perform the ritual, in which status he becomes *mpijoro*. But at major rituals, particularly those associated with death and with the rewrapping of the ancestral bones (*famadihana*), only that

[10] Nowadays meetings of a political or administrative nature in a village are most often called by the *chef de village*, an official of the government (elected by the village) and they are held in his house.

[11] In theory the *mpijoro* should recite the genealogy which accounts for the relationship of all those present. In fact he recites his own pedigree and includes everyone else by giving the name of the tomb—which contains all the ancestors.

person of one's *fokondray* nearest to the ancestors can effectively perform the ritual and is likely to know the ritual and the prayers.

Most of the *joro* performed are at the behest of individuals or on behalf of individuals, though *fokondray* participate and attend the accompanying feast. The *mpijoro* on these occasions does not act on behalf of the entire aggregate, but on behalf of the individual offering the sacrifice. This is also true at the *famadihana* when a number of *fokondray* rewrap their ancestors at the same time, but not as a united collectivity. On the occasion of the dedication of a new tomb, or when an existing tomb must be repaired, or modified (natural shelters are not always suitable *in statu naturae*) then the entire *fokondray* can be said to act as a collectivity, and the *mpijoro* to officiate on their behalf. The sponsors of rituals are individuals who furnish the victuals for the accompanying and mandatory feast. A number of individuals may combine in sacrificing to the ancestors and share the expenses of the feast, and primary kin (a man and his sons, or a set of brothers) often combine. Whenever a major sacrifice is offered, the *fokondreny* of the individual giving the feast must be invited, and the mother's brother (*zama*) plays an important, symbolic role, guarding the displayed head of the sacrificial animal. He is also permitted to demand anything in the way of food and drink from his nephew.[12]

An individual's status with respect to land is determined in a general way by a rule of descent. *Fokondray* ancestors when they came from the east eventually settled in a region and defined their boundaries with respect to their neighbors. They were, in many instances, granted the land by the Sakalava *mpanjaka*. Such an area of land, on which the ancestral tombs are located, is called *tanindrazana* (land of the ancestors). All those of the status of *fokondray,* defined with respect to collective ancestors who first settled the region, are entitled to cultivate rice fields within the boundaries and to pasture their cattle. Those of specific *foko* status who have collective rights to a given area of land are termed the *zafintany* (grandchildren of the land) of that area. It is perfectly possible, and it often happens, for there to be more than one *foko* who are *zafintany* in a given region, and it is equally possible and as frequent for one *foko* to be *zafintany* in more than one area. Nor do all those of one *foko* live

[12] The major rituals are carried out in the dry months (July to September). I was unable to attend a legitimate *famadihana* or body wrapping and certain other rituals. Further field-work is, however, envisaged.

where they are *zafintany*—they may be living on land belonging to another *foko* for a number of reasons (the land may be better, they may prefer scenery, there may be more land available, etc.). However, any individual who lives on land where he is not *zafintany* should seek permission to cultivate the land from those who are *zafintany*. Ideally this permission must be renewed annually. However, once a particular piece of land has been cleared and cultivated the rights to its use belong to the individual, and they are inherited from the individual. Permission to continue cultivating land once cleared is rarely withheld. Within the *zafintany*, rights to inherit particular parcels of cleared land pass through individuals. Land that has been left to return to bush after cultivation returns in theory to the general pool of the *tamindrazana* and becomes available to *zafintany*. In practice the timing as to when land becomes available to any one of *zafintany* status is very imprecise and is consequently a major focus of land disputes.

Those who are *zafintany* in the context of village affairs are regarded as *tompontanana*, seniors of the village. They carry most weight and influence in the *fokon'olona*, the village council or assembly, not only because they are often in the majority, but because of their seniority, and their ritual control of the land. It is the *soja* of the *tompontanana* who becomes *sojabe* or head of the village and, in the case of longsettled *vahiny* (strangers) who have become courtesy kin (*havana fanajana*) the *mpijoro* of the *tompontanana-zafintany-fokondray* may offer prayers and perform ritual on their behalf.

Those who are living *ambenivavy* (in their mother's village) and who have exercised their right to claim their mother's inheritance of land to cultivate can assume primary status in their *fokondreny*. This varies with individual circumstances, but when a man comes to live in his mother's village and it is a long way from his father's village, he may request the *mpijoro* to sacrifice on his behalf and the whole of his life may be directed within the context of this village with those who are *fokondreny* to him. In which case he becomes of full status and may even choose to be buried in his mother's tomb. He always has a right to such a status, but it is secondary to his right to burial in his father's tomb, to use the land cultivated by his father, and to communicate with the supernatural through his father's ancestors.

In some *tanindrazana* there is a special ricefield (*tanimbary omby*) which is owned collectively. In some cases it may be cultivated only by the *soja* and in others it may be cultivated by anyone with permission of the *soja*. In both cases whoever cultivates the land must offer a sacrifice at the time of planting and at the time of harvest. With the sacrifice goes a feast to which all inhabitants of villages within the *tanindrazana* are invited. Corporately owned rights to land that were exclusive to a descent group occurred, but very infrequently, in Androna and were the result of a known and specific action on the part of an individual ancestor. The land was termed *tanimbary lova* and I came across three examples. The particular ancestor (in all cases a recent one) had made public his desire that the land he had cleared should not be fragmented and should be reserved solely for the use of his sons and their male descendants. It should never be divided. In the case I knew best the land was allotted to individual males each year according to their stated needs by the *fokon'olona* of the lineage in question. Jurisdiction over this land was exercised quite independently of the other *foko* members and excluded them. But in the event of the land being unused (which would occur only at the expiration of the lineage) it would presumably revert back to common land of the *tanindrazana*.

IV. DISCUSSION

The foregoing description provides the amplification called for by Fortes (1959:211) of Firth's suggestion that "there are systems 'in which the major emphasis is upon descent in the male line, but allowance is made, in circumstances so frequent . . . as to be reckoned as normal for entitlement through a female.' " Tsimihety conforms approximately to Fortes's first conjecture that "membership . . . is strictly tied to the 'male line'—and therefore vested in males exclusively—but daughters (sc. sisters) have some kind of secondary or dormant rights of membership which they never forfeit and are able to transmit by filiation to their offspring" (op. cit.). I would prefer to substitute "status" for membership since the latter implies the existence of autonomous groups. Also validated is the distinction made by Fortes between filiation and descent. It is quite clear that there is only one descent rule followed by Tsimihety—patrilineal. But by filiation an individual is secondarily attached through a female to her patrilineal ascendants. With respect to the Tsimihety at least the term "complementary affiliation" can be extended to include the affiliation of a man with his wife, as well as with his mother, since a man acquires potential status rights with respect to his wife's patrilineal ascendants and the property to which they have access. Given the possibility of certain contingencies arising with respect to fundamental resources to which legal access is determined by a rule of descent, the combination of descent and filiation permits the individual a number of alternatives to maintain his status in those contingencies—though the status may become modified. It is not that the individual has a choice, to say so confuses the coherence of the analysis (cf. Schneider, 1965:66), but rather that circumstances of demography (overcrowding), biology (e.g. sterility), sentiment (the power of the love of a man for a woman over the opposition of their parents) can result in the misplacement of the individual in the general conceptual pattern of which patrilineal descent is a part. While his social position may be detrimentally affected in such contingencies, his access to suprasocial resources is maintained. The legal priority of patrilineal descent through patrifiliation is constant in Tsimihety as the determinant of status with respect to ancestors, tombs, and land, and we might add of the status of the individual to the cosmology.

There is a further, more general question raised by the foregoing account. This is the problem of the conjunction of a spatial and social definition of a population as a unit, or who it is that anthropologists are talking about. This problem has been raised most recently by Naroll (1964) and Moerman (1965) who direct attention to the difficulties of comparison that this problem raises. Here I wish to point to the difficulties this raises with respect to the analysis and interpretation of data. Fortes, whom I shall cite as perhaps the most prominent among many who follow the same path, states in a number of places that, for example, "descent operates where the total body of rights and duties, capacities and claims, *through which a society achieves its ends* is distributed among segments or classes, which are *required* to remain relatively fixed over a stretch of time *in order that the social system shall be able to maintain itself*" (Fortes, 1959:208/my italics) or "Study of the unilineal descent group as a part of the total social system means in fact studying its functions in the widest framework of social structure, that of the political organization" (Fortes, 1953:29). This holistic position has a very respectable pedigree in anthropology, its foci being Radcliffe-Brown back to Durkheim. The two quotations contain within them the essential Durkheimian assumptions: a "society" is an abstract and empirical whole of logical and empirical priority; it is composed of logical and empirical units (segments, classes, strata, etc.); its ultimate cohesion is maintained through the political functions of its components which provide for the definition and exercise of authority and definition and maintenance of boundaries; and finally that this entirety, a society, has an existence *sui generis*.

It is quite clear from the reports of some ethnographers (e.g. Goody, 1964:3; Moerman, 1965; Southall, 1956:3, and the present writer) that the neat coincidence of social concepts, social groupings, social boundaries, and political autonomy resulting in an empirical "society" as well as a model one simply does not exist. There is, for example, an entire cultural area of which it can be said that there is no coincidence of social, political, and cultural boundaries which would permit an analysis based on Durkheimian assumptions. This area is the Caribbean where the social organization of populations operates independently of the political organization and social groups (cf. Wilson, 1961, in press).

To return to Tsimihety, the unilineal descent "groups" (*foko*) which we could have described as the major segments of Tsimihety society have no political function. There is no level at which Tsimihety society have no political function. There is no level at which Tsimihety see themselves as a totality except as practitioners of customs in a certain way. But they share most of these customs with the other peoples of Madagascar, and neither in theory nor in practice is there any way in which we can talk of the priority of groups which act autonomously to cohere and maintain themselves by recruitment, allocation, and direction. It is only the highly artificial, but political, organization of "villages," "quartiers," "districts," and "provinces" established by the Merina, modified by the French, and taken over by the Republic, that gives rise to any sort of unit activity among Tsimihety. But this is quite divorced from Tsimihety social organization and not surprisingly Tsimihety take virtually no interest in it (the reports of early French administrators are full of complaints about the independence and non-co-operativeness of Tsimihety). It is perfectly possible to deal with kinship and descent constructs of Tsimihety as examples of the descent and kinship constructs presented by anthropologists, and developed by them into models of a social system and thence a society. But such a model, while perfectly logical, would be quite false if it was to be considered relevant to a "society" called Tsimihety.

It is for this reason that I have insisted that Tsimihety descent and kinship constructs are better understood as providing the linguistic and sociological terms for definitions of status legitimacy. A status includes the public or social identity of people to each other with respect to specified contexts involving access to common resources and the rights, duties, responsibilities, and obligations of people to each other and to those resources (cf. Leach, 1962:131, "Our ultimate concern . . . about the nature of descent and filiation is with the transmission of assets from one generation to another"). The focus of descent is not on group formation, exclusiveness, and maintenance, but rather on the individual, abstracted perhaps as a "social person," who is a legitimate member of a population. That population may be defined as it defines itself (as a speech community, a co-residential community, bearers of a common name, or practitioners of common habits and customs) (cf. Moerman, 1965).

Therefore, strictly speaking, this paper describes the practices only of those Tsimihety living within the area termed Androna. Tsimihety living elsewhere may well have different practices and even in Androna the degree of variation in, for example, the observance of exogamic restrictions, the validity of actual genealogical reckoning as compared to the descent "rule," the determination of land inheritance, are considerable enough to have made me hesitate to offer a description of Tsimihety social structure. I hope, in a separate publication, to document these structural variations and explore their significance.

14. Marriage System

In the Gikuyu community marriage and its obligations occupy a position of great importance. One of the outstanding features in the Gikuyu system of marriage is the desire of every member of the tribe to build up his own family group, and by this means to extend and prolong his father's *mbari* (clan). This results in the strengthening of the tribe as a whole.

We may mention here that the Gikuyu system of courtship is based on mutual love and gratification of sexual instinct between two individuals. And, therefore, a family is constituted by a permanent union between one man and one woman or several women. Through the marriage ceremony a man acquires sole right to sexual intercourse with the woman or women whom he marries. On signing the matrimonial contract the marriage ceases to be merely a personal matter, for the contract binds not only the bride and bridegroom, but also their kinsfolk. It becomes a duty to produce children, and sexual intercourse between a man and his wife or wives is looked upon as an act of production and not merely as the gratification of a bodily desire. The Gikuyu tribal custom requires that a married couple should have at least four children, two male and two female. The first male is regarded as perpetuating the existence of the man's father, the second as perpetuating that of the woman's father. The first and second female children fulfill the same ritual duty to the souls of their grandmothers on both sides. The children are given names of the persons whose souls they represent.

The desire to have children is deep-rooted in the hearts of both man and woman, and on entering into matrimonial union they regard the procreation of children as their first and most sacred duty. A childless marriage in a Gikuyu community is practically a failure,

SOURCE: Jomo Kenyatta, "Marriage System," Chap. VIII, *Facing Mount Kenya* by Jomo Kenyatta. Secker and Warburg, London, 1938, pp. 163–85. Reprinted by permission of the author and publisher.

for children bring joy not only to their parents, but to the *mbari* (clan) as a whole. In Gikuyu society the rearing of a family brings with it a rise in social status. The social position of a married man and woman who have children is of greater importance and dignity than that of a bachelor or spinster. After the birth of the first child the married pair become the object of higher regard on the part of their fellows than they were before.

Marriage is one of the most powerful means of maintaining the cohesion of Gikuyu society and of enforcing that conformity to the kinship system and to tribal organization without which social life is impossible.

The most interesting feature in the Gikuyu marriage system is the way in which marriages are solemnized, for the validity of marriage and the social position of women in the community is determined by the fulfillment of communal duties regulated by the marriage custom. We will give here a full description of the Gikuyu marriage ceremonies as they are performed today.

There has been some confusion in the minds of many writers who have tried to explain the system of marriage and the position of women in the African community. Some, especially missionaries, have gone so far as to say that African women are regarded as mere chattels of the men. Well-informed anthropologists agree that this is erroneous and a misconception of the African's social custom. From the following account of the institution of marriage among the Gikuyu, the reader may judge further as to whether "purchase" is or is not a feature of the Gikuyu marriage system.

CHOICE OF MATES

In the Gikuyu community boys and girls are left free to choose their mates, without any interference on the part of the parents on either side. From earliest infancy there is close social intercourse between the sexes, which provides them with an opportunity of becoming acquainted with one another for a considerable time before courtship begins. Thus, hasty judgment in choosing one's husband or wife is almost out of the question.

FIRST STAGE

When a boy falls in love with a girl he cannot tell her directly that he loves her or display his devotion to her in public, as this would be regarded by the Gikuyu as impolite and uncultured. He therefore discusses the matter with one or two of his best friends in the age-group to which he belongs. They then all pay a visit to the girl's home. On their arrival at the girl's homestead they enter her mother's hut. The girl and her mother exchange greetings with them. The mother then offers them refreshment and immediately goes away. Now the boys and the girl are left alone. At this stage the conversation may start in the following manner: One of the boys addresses the girl: *"Mware wa Njuguna?"* (Daughter of Njuguna), "Wouldn't you like to ask us why we have come here tonight?"

The girl answers: "No, it is not necessary to ask you that. Gikuyu custom provides that anyone passing by can come and have a meal with us."

The boy: "That is right, *Mware wa Njuguna,* but we are looking for a homestead where we could be adopted and be given food and shelter not only when we are passing by, but as children of the homestead."

At this remark the girl at once knows their object, and she asks them to state definitely which one of them is looking for the adoption. The boy then points out his friend who is in love with the girl. If she accepts him as her future husband she tells them to go away and come back some other time. Sometimes two or three visits of this kind are made. When she gives her final answer, she says to them: "I am willing that the son of So-and-so should be adopted into our homestead, but the ceremonial side of it is a matter for my parents. You had better talk to them about it yourselves."

If she does not accept him, she says: "Our house is not big enough to adopt anyone at present," and they go away.

SECOND STAGE

If accepted, her lover goes home and reports the matter to his parents. They then prepare honey or sugar-cane beer, which they take to the girl's parents. It is carried in two calabashes, one big and the other small. This beer is known as *njohi ya njoorio,* i.e., the beer of asking the girl's hand. When the parents of the two parties meet, the first thing the girl's parents do is to provide the visitors with food before they go into the question of matrimony. After this they state the object of their visit, but most of the conversation regarding their future son- or daughter-in-law is carried on in proverbs. The girl is called and, after being introduced, she is asked if she has agreed to become engaged. As she cannot answer directly yes or no, a little ceremony is necessary. Therefore, she is asked gently to fetch a particular horn used for beer drinking; then to fill it with beer and hand it to her father who, after sipping a little and spitting it out, sprinkles some on his chest. He then hands it over to his wife who does the same. The horn is filled a second time and is handed to the boy's parents, who repeat the same procedure. In each case the girl takes a sip first as a sign of consent.

If the lover has been refused he reports to his parents who, if they would like their son to marry the girl, may visit the girl's parents. The same ceremony takes place, but if the girl disapproves of it she will not pour out the beer or take the first sip. The visiting parents then go away.

When the parents' initial ceremony is concluded and the girl is willing to be engaged, close friends are invited and the beer is shared among them. At the conclusion of this friendly gathering they all join in a prayer, *korathimithia,* uttering blessings for the future unity and progress of the two families.

THIRD STAGE

When the boy's parents return home they begin to collect sheep and goats, or cattle if they are rich, for the first installment of the dowry, *roracio;* these would be taken by the lover to the girl's homestead and led to the hut of the girl's mother. This visit is followed by another in which some beer is brought, and the girl is consulted as in the first visit. This beer is called *njohi ya gothugumitheria mbori,* i.e., the beer for blessing the *roracio* sheep and goats. This installment is followed by another in a few days, and so on until the number of animals amounts to about thirty or forty. Beer is not necessarily brought each time. Even if a man is rich it is considered ill luck to bring all the *roracio* at once. When, according to the custom of the clan, the amount required for sealing the engagement has been sent, a day is fixed for the actual engagement ceremony, called *ngurario,* i.e., pouring out the blood of unity. In this all the relatives are called to the girl's homestead, where a sumptuous feast is provided, which includes the slaughtering of one fat sheep (*ngoima ya ngurario*) which has been sent from the boy's homestead specially for this purpose.

The significance of this ceremony is in the first place to announce publicly that the girl is engaged; secondly, to provide the relatives on both sides with an opportunity of meeting and getting to know one another; and, thirdly, to decide on how much the *roracio* should be. The amount varies from one clan to another and from district to district, although the amount required by the Gikuyu law is thirty sheep and goats. Sometimes, however, it runs to between thirty and eighty sheep and goats, apart from numerous presents exchanged on both sides. When a cow is included in the *roracio* it is valued at ten sheep and goats, while an ox is valued at five sheep and goats.

The main feature of this ceremony consists in the killing of a fat sheep kept for this purpose. The sheep must be of a certain color—black, white, or brown—in keeping with the symbolism adhered to for ritual purposes by the particular clan concerned. The blood is sprinkled along the gateway and toward Mount Kenya (Kere-Nyaga); the contents of the stomach are also sprinkled in the same way, and also on the sheep and goats or cattle which have been brought in for the *roracio*. This signifies that they are now purified and protected from any evils, and that the boy's parents have presented them to the girl's parents as a sign of good faith. From this time on the interests of the two clans are closely linked.

FOURTH STAGE

After all the arrangements are made in regard to *roracio,* the maturity of the girl is discussed. The boy's parents say to the girl's parents: "Is your daughter grown-up?"—meaning: "Has she menstruated yet?" At the end of the discussion a final day is fixed on which to sign the marriage contract. On the day in question all representatives of the two clans and friends are invited. They bring with them plenty of food and drink for the feast. The ceremony, which is called *gothenja ngoima,* consists of slaughtering six fat sheep, and in case of a rich man, an ox and five sheep. In doing this the girl's consent must be obtained. She is asked to provide the knife for skinning the sheep and to take a leading part in slaughtering the first animal. The kidneys of the first sheep are roasted and served to the bride-to-be, who eats them, indicating in this way that the engagement still holds good and that the families can proceed with the formality of signing the marriage contract.

When this is done, the people assemble and take part in the feast. This is followed by a big dance and the singing of songs. The boy, with his age-group, comes in procession, carrying special presents for the girl's mother and for the members of her clan. Any property, such as an ax, basket or large leather strap, which the girl may have lost as a child, will be made up to her parents by these presents. At about sunset, after the casual visitors have gone, the women representatives of the clan are called into the yard where baskets are kept containing their presents. These presents are contributed by one of the elders, while the womenfolk cheer every recipient with great excitement. This is followed by a dance and song, called *getiro,* for women only, which marks the end of the *ngoima* ceremony.

If the boy's homestead is in the neighborhood, a short visit is paid by a group of women, taking with them presents for the boy's relatives, but if the homestead is far away the visit is left to a later date. From this time onward the girl is regarded as having been blessed and given away to the boy's clan by her parents in agreement with the whole clan. She can now go and weed gardens with the boy's mother and other relatives in company with her girl friends. The function of the *ngoima* ceremony is to furnish a public wedding celebration in which all marriage agreements are concluded and in which the girl is betrothed to her fiancé, not only by her parents, but by the representative body of the clan acting collectively. She can now be taken to the boy's home as his wife at any time, without any further ceremony being performed at her parents' homestead.

WEDDING DAY

When the boy has provided himself with a hut and made the necessary preparation for housekeeping, he approaches his parents, especially his mother, and asks them to arrange a special day suitable for bringing his wife home. The arrangement is made according to certain propitious days of the moon, in accordance with the clan's history and traditions. For instance, many clans may not hold any wedding between the old and new moon, since this period is regarded as a "dark period" (*mweri we nduma*). The period preferable for embarking on any important project is the interval between the new moon and the full moon.

A Gikuyu wedding is a thing that baffles many outsiders and terrifies many Europeans who may have an opportunity of witnessing the events. This wedding drama misleads foreign onlookers, who do not understand the Gikuyu custom, into thinking that the girls are forced to marry, and even that they are treated as chattels.

In response to the boy's request, the family meets in council; the day is fixed for the wedding and kept secret from the girl—thus adding a dramatic touch to the proceedings. On the wedding day the boy's female relatives set out to watch the girl's movements. She might be in a garden, weeding, or in a forest collecting firewood, etc. When they have obtained the necessary information as to where she is working they search for her. On finding her they return with her, carrying her shoulder high. This is a moment of real theatrical acting. The girl struggles and refuses to go with them, protesting loudly and even seeming to shed tears, while the women giggle joyously and cheer her with songs and dances. The cries and cheers can be heard for miles around, and the Gikuyu people will know that the son of So-and-so has taken the daughter of So-and-so in marriage—while foreigners may imagine that the girl has been forcibly seized. It is probable that any person who is not well acquainted with the Gikuyu customs may easily mistake the drama for reality.

In some cases, where the families are large, a counterfeit fight is staged between the women of both sides. This provides great entertainment for the women and is followed by a liberal feast at the bridegroom's homestead. The girl's cries, which are uttered theatrically in a singing manner, include such phrases as "I do not want to get married! I will kill myself if you take me away from my parents! Oh! How foolish I was to leave my home alone and put myself into the hands of merciless people! Where are my relatives? Cannot they come and release me and prevent my being taken to a man whom I do not love?" and so on. This goes on until the girl reaches the boy's homestead, where she is led into her new hut, while children greet her, singing praises for their new bride. On her way home the bride is cheered by passers-by, who utter blessings for the bride and bride-groom and for their future homestead.

After the bride is comfortably settled in her new hut, the whole party of women from both clans, who a short while ago were engaged in a mock fight, join together and start dancing, singing, and cheering hilariously. In the evening the bride is visited by her age-group of both sexes, who bring presents in way of food and ornaments. The bride entertains them with songs called *kerero*, i.e., weeping, in which girls only take part while the boys listen. The *kerero* songs are mostly connected with the collective activities of the girl's age-group, and the part played by the girl. It is considered as the age-group mourning for the loss of the services and companionship of one of their number who, by marriage, has passed to another age-group.

The mourning songs are continued for eight days, during which time the bride is frequently visited by her friends and age-group of both sexes.

During this period the bride may not go out publicly or do any work. She has a special back path which she may use when she leaves the hut during the day to sit under a tree for fresh air. Her girl friends keep her company, together with the children of the family. The *kerero* goes on the whole day and a part of the evening, except for a few intervals between the arrival and departure of the visitors. About ten o'clock in the evening the bride and bridegroom are left to themselves until the neighborhood of nine o'clock next morning, when the visitors begin to pour in.

The question of physical virginity is very important, and parents expect their daughters to go to their husbands as physical virgins. This must be reported to the parents of both sides. The boy has to show by certain signs that the girl was a virgin; the girl, too, has to do the same to show that the boy is physically fit to be a husband. In case of impotency on either side, the matter is put before the families' and the marriage is annulled at once.

On the eighth day, when the *kerero* ceases, a sheep is killed, the fat of which is fried, and the oil is used to anoint the bride in a cere-mony of adoption into the new clan. After she has been admitted as a full member of the husband's family, she is free to mingle with its members and take an active part in the general work of the home-stead. When the adoption ceremony is concluded, a day is fixed im-mediately for her to pay a visit to her own parents. Care is taken in appointing the day, for she must not travel or cook during her menstrual period. On this particular visit she carries a small calabash with beer in it for the use of her parents in blessing her. On her way she is led by a small girl, who goes before her holding one end of a stick, the other end of which is held by the bride, who follows as though she were blind. She is supposed to be unable to see, and may not speak with any stranger she may meet during her journey. She goes all the way with bent head, hiding her face shyly, especially when somebody passes by her. She returns back in the cvening (if the parents are in the neighborhood) with presents from her parents. Sometimes when parents are rich she is given two or three sheep or goats. Her father-in-law also gives her presents; these vary in some cases from five sheep and goats to ten or a cow and a piece of fertile land. These presents are regarded as an act of "warming" the bride's hut, and they end the marriage ceremonial.

THE GIKUYU SYSTEM OF POLYGAMY

The Gikuyu customary law of marriage provides that a man may have as many wives as he can support, and that the larger one's family the better it is for him and the tribe. The love of children is also an encouraging factor of desiring to have more than one wife. The custom also provides that all women must be under the protection of men; and that in order to avoid prostitution (no word exists for "prostitution" in the Gikuyu language) all women must be married in their teens, i.e., fifteen to twenty. Thus there is no term in the Gikuyu language for "unmarried" or "old maids."

Before the advent of the white man the institution of serfdom and wage workers were unknown to the Gikuyu people. The tribal customary law recognized the freedom and independence of every member of the tribe. At the same time all were bound up together socially, politically, economically, and religiously by a system of collective activities and mutual help, extending from the family group to the tribe. The Weltanschauung of Gikuyu people is: *"Kanya gatuune ne mwamokanero"* ("Give and take").

For economic and political reasons every family was expected to be able to protect its own interests and at the same time help to protect the common interests of the tribe from outside attack. To do this effectively and to command the respect of the tribe, it was necessary for every family to have a number of male children who could be called up for military services in time of crises and alien aggression. It was also necessary to have a number of female children who could also render assistance by cultivating the land and looking after the general welfare of the tribe while the men were fighting to defend their homesteads. Furthermore, the society cannot do without them, for they are the salt of the earth, they have the most sacred duty of creating and rearing future generations. Female children are therefore looked upon as the connecting link between one generation and another and one clan and another, through marriage, which binds the interests of clans close together and makes them share in common the responsibilities of family life. For this reason, say the Gikuyu: *"Keimba kea mothoni na mothoni igoaga hamwe"* (literally, "Corpses of relations-in-law fall together"), meaning "Together let us live and if need be together let us die."

There is a fundamental idea among the Gikuyu that the larger the family is the happier it will be. In Gikuyu the qualification for a status to hold a high office in the tribal organization is based on family and not on property, as is the case in European society. It is held that if a man can control and manage effectively the affairs of a large family, this is an excellent testimonial of his capacity to look after the interests of the tribe whom he will also treat with fatherly love and affection as though it were all part of his own family. Thus the saying: *"Weega uumaga na mocie"* ("A good leader begins in his own homestead").

After a man has had the first wife, *nyakiambi*, a year or so generally passes, and then his wife starts to question him about getting a second wife, especially if she is expecting a child or immediately after she has had one. "My husband, don't you think it is wise for you to get me a companion? (*moiru*). Look at our position now. I am sure you will realize how God has been good to us to give us a nice and healthy baby. For the first few days I must devote all my attention to nursing our baby. I am weak . . . I can't go to the river to bring water or to the field to bring some food, or to weed our gardens. You have no one to cook for you. When strangers come you have no one to entertain them. I have no doubt that you realize the seriousness of the matter. What do you think of the daughter of So-and-so? She is beautiful and industrious and people speak highly about her and her family. Do not fail me, my husband. Try and win her love. I have spoken to her and found that she is very interested in our homestead. In anything that I can do to help you I am at your service, my husband.

"Even if we have not enough sheep and goats for the dowry our relatives and friends will help you so that you can get her into our family. You are young and healthy and this is the best time for us to have healthy children and so enlarge our family group, and thereby perpetuate our family name after you and I have gone. My husband, please act quickly, as you know the Gikuyu saying: *'Mae megother-era matietagerera mondo onyotie'* ('The flowing water of the river does not wait for a thirsty man')."

The husband, following his wife's advice, starts to act. He approaches his parents, and after consultation with them, arrangements are made to visit the girl and her parents. If accepted, he proceeds to pay the dowry and other gifts connected with marriages. When all arrangements are completed, he builds a hut next to that of the first wife and then brings the second wife home.

If the family in question is prosperous, after some time another companion is sought, and so the number of wives increases from one to fifty, and sometimes more. There is no limit. Of course, this does not mean that every Gikuyu man has many wives. There are a large number of Gikuyu men who have only one wife, simply because their economic position will not allow them to have as many wives as they and society would like. Taking the Gikuyu population as a whole, it can be said that there is an average of two wives per head, owing to the number of women who attain the marriageable age. Women generally marry between the ages of fifteen and twenty, while the majority of men start marrying from the age of twenty-five. Thus in every generation there are more women of marriageable age than men, which helps to balance the system of polygamy.

THE MANAGEMENT OF A POLYGAMOUS HOUSEHOLD

In a polygamous homestead the husband has his own hut (*thingira*), in which friends and casual visitors are entertained. Each wife has her own hut where she keeps her personal belongings. The cooking also is done in it. While collective ownership is a fundamental principle of the family group, the hut is considered as the private property of the wife and it is entirely under her control. Each wife is provided with several lots of land located in different places within the boundary of the family's land (allotment). The women usually cultivate bananas, sugar cane, sweet potatoes, maize, millet, yams, several varieties of beans, and other crops on these holdings.

The working of the land is collective, men doing the clearing of the virgin soil, such as cutting big trees and hoeing, while women come behind them turning the soil to prepare it for planting. The planting is also divided between men and women; the men take the responsibility of planting bananas, sugar cane, yams, and sometimes sweet potatoes. The women plant millet, maize, various kinds of beans and potatoes; the last are planted by both sexes.

Each wife is held responsible for what she produces from the land, and can distribute it as she pleases, provided that she has reserved enough food for the use of herself and family until the next harvest. She can sell any surplus stock in the market and buy what she likes, or keep the proceeds for family purposes. Nowadays the majority of women obtain money for their hut taxes in this way. Sometimes, when the harvest is good and there is an abundant supply of products, some are handed over to the husband, who buys sheep, goats, or a cow for the betterment of the homestead.

While the division of personal property exists between the wives, the husband is the head of the family and the one who contributes his labor power to all equally; he belongs to all and all belong to him. This brings the division to one collective ownership under his guidance.

Having described the division and distribution of labor, it is necessary to mention something about the distribution of love. No doubt some people wonder how one man is able to love many women. This is a very vital question, especially among those whose religious beliefs have taught them that to love more than one woman is a crime, and furthermore a sin against heavenly gods. On the contrary, the Gikuyu are taught from childhood that to be a man is to be able to love and keep a homestead with as many wives as possible. With this in view, Gikuyu male children are brought up to cultivate the idea and technique of extending their love to several women and to look upon them as companions and as members of one big family. The girls, too, are taught how to share a husband's love and to look upon him as the father of one big family. The idea of sharing everything is strongly emphasized in the upbringing of children, so when they grow up they find it natural to share love and affection with others, for it is said that "To live with others is to share and to have mercy for one another," and: "It is witch doctors who live and eat alone."

In order to avoid jealousy (*oiru*) among the wives, Gikuyu custom provides that each wife must be visited by her husband on certain days of the moon, particularly the three days following menstruation. Each wife has this special privilege. The wives, knowing that this is the best time to have children, see to it that the husband does not neglect his duty of distributing his love equally among them. Such conjugal relation is the only way in which a polygamous homestead could be kept in harmony. The three days immediately after menstruation are considered as the most likely for a woman to conceive. For this reason the husband does not generally cohabit with her again until after the next menstruation. If by then she has conceived, the husband allows a period of three months to elapse before having intercourse again, in order not to cause an abortion. After this time the husband may cohabit with her, but only in a special way. That is, he must not have full penetration; he may use only about two inches of his penis. The limit is indicated by a process in the *irua* operation, when the operator gathers back the foreskin into a tassel, called *ngwati* (the "brush,") which is arranged to hang at the right distance below the head of the penis. Its use is to increase sexual excitement, but it can also serve as a catch to check penetration. Fuller penetration is believed to result in destroying the womb.

DUTY OF THE WIVES

The women are essentially the homemakers, as without them there is no home in the Gikuyu sense of social life. Each wife has a special duty assigned to her in the general affairs of the homestead. She is responsible for looking after her hut and her household utensils, granary, and her garden. But the duty of looking after the husband, such as cleaning his hut, supplying him with firewood, water, food, etc., is shared by all, in turn. For example, every morning one of them cleans the husband's hut (*thingira*) and lights the fire, while others sweep the yard and do other work connected with the cleanliness of the homestead. At the same time sheep and goats are fed, cows (if they have any) are milked. Calves and kids are tended. The husband is served with food according to what they have prepared. Each wife provides food for her children. When the morning work in the homestead is over, each wife is supposed to prepare a plan of activities for the day. Some go to the forest to collect firewood, others go to cultivate their gardens in the company of their friends, relatives, or individually. During the day time everyone is engaged in some sort of activity or another. No one stays at home except the small children who are unable to accompany the adult members of the family to the fields, or those grownups who are engaged in some homework, especially that of grinding or beating grain in mortars.

In the evening the wives return home carrying various things: firewood, water, bananas, sweet potatoes, yams, and other foodstuffs. Immediately they set about preparing food for the evening meal. The wife whose turn it is provides the firewood and lights the fire in her husband's hut; no cooking is done in that hut except when meat is roasted. Otherwise each wife cooks in her own hut. When the food is ready, each wife takes the husband's share to his hut, where he entertains his friends and casual visitors. When the meal is over and utensils cleaned, the wives may go and spend the rest of the evening in the company of their husband or remain in their huts. But whenever special visitors, particularly members of the husband's age-group call, the wives are expected to join the company in the husband's hut. The reason for this is to show the solidarity of the age-group. If the visitors come from far away and they are to spend the night in the homestead, the arrangements for their accommodation are made according to the rules and customs governing the social affairs among the age-group.

On these occasions the wives exercise their freedom, which amounts to something like polyandry. Each wife is free to choose anyone among the age-group and give him accommodation for the night. This is looked upon as purely social intercourse, and no feeling of jealousy or evil is attached to it on the part of the husband or wife. And, having all been brought up and educated in the idea of sharing, especially at the time when they indulged in *ngweko* (love-making), their hearts are saturated with ideas of collective enjoyment, without which there could not be strong unity among the members of the age-group. When this choice is freely exercised, it is an offense for a wife to invite a man secretly to her hut, even a member of the age-group. To do so would be regarded as committing adultery. In order to guard oneself against matrimonial injuries this custom is strictly adhered to. Any man who is caught breaking this rule is punished heavily by the *kiama,* and sometimes the husband takes the law into his own hands, and before the *kiama* punishes the offender he is given a good beating by the outraged husband. There is a saying in Gikuyu which says that "Before a man embarks upon such an adventure of visiting another man's wife, it is advisable for him to arm himself, for there is no mercy for one who entices another man's wife or steals his cow." (*Ng'ombe na aka itire ndogo.*) The wife, too, is punished. She is taken back to her parents who, in order to establish good relationship, have to pay a fine of one or two he-goats to the husband. The fine is followed by a feast of beer drinking between the two families. Sometimes if this offense is repeated, the wife is divorced and the husband is entitled to get back all his *roracio,* and custody of his offspring. The divorce is preferred especially in a case where there are no children, but in the case of partners who have children, conciliation is considered as the best procedure, for in this case the matter has already ceased to be between individuals and has moved into the clan through the children, for children are regarded as the pledges of love and unity. It is only when the matter becomes really bad that divorce action is taken. We will deal with the divorce question later under that heading.

Owing to the many taboos (*megiro*) attached to the cohabitation of a married woman, and the social stigma that follows an offense, the breaking of this law is very rare. This is due to the fact that both wife and husband have ample opportunity of meeting their friends in a more open and legalized way, approved by the moral code of the community.

It is worth our while to mention a few of these taboos, *megiro,* which control the relationship between a married woman and an outsider and even the husband. For example, it is *megiro* for a wife to have sexual intercourse outside the homestead; this is considered as bringing evil and bad luck to the homestead; no wife may have sexual intercourse while her husband is away on a journey, on war or other activities, for to do so is to cause misfortune to the husband. No sexual intercourse while food is being cooked, for this will make the food impure and the result to those who would eat such food would be uncleanliness. Children must be put to bed before this; sexual intercourse is not held to be right if the children are away in the fields, for it is considered as a ritual shutting out the children (*kohingereria ciana*). Sexual intercourse is practiced ritually and these and many other *megiro* are considered important, and in order to maintain the harmony and prosperity of a homestead and to guard themselves against matrimonial injuries in the community, these *megiro* (taboos) must be rigidly observed.

DIVORCE

Among the Gikuyu divorce is very rare, because of the fact that a wife is regarded as the foundation rock on which the homestead is built. Without her the homestead is broken, therefore it is only when all efforts to keep the husband and wife together have failed that an action for divorce can be taken.

According to the Gikuyu customary law, a husband may divorce his wife on the grounds of (1) barrenness; (2) refusal to render conjugal rights without reason; (3) practicing witchcraft; (4) being a habitual thief; (5) willful desertion; (6) continual gross misconduct. A wife has the same right to divorce her husband on these grounds, except (6) owing perhaps to the system of polygamy. Besides the above-mentioned grounds, she can divorce her husband for cruelty, ill-treatment, drunkenness, and impotence.

In the case of barrenness or impotence, both husband and wife go through a practical test to prove who is to blame. The husband would allow his wife to have sexual intercourse with one or more of his age-grade. If this fails to bring fruitful result, a medicine man of repute (*mondo mogo*) is consulted with the hope of finding a successful solution. At the same time ceremonial blessing from parents on both sides is considered essential to fertilize the womb. Sometimes the wife succeeds in having a child in this way, and is saved from the embarrassing situation of being given a nickname of *thaata* (barren). But when all efforts fail, the case is considered as one above the power of man, and is attributed to the will of Ngai, the Great God. If there is no other disagreement between the husband and wife, the two can live together and perhaps have an adopted son or daughter, providing that the man is not in a position to marry another wife.

In case of impotence the man is given the same trial as the woman. If he can afford it, it is necessary to marry another wife, and in case he succeeds in having children by her, then it is said that the failure to have children by his first wife is due to the fact that their blood does not agree. But if a man knows that he is naturally impotent, and wishes to keep his homestead in harmony, he allows his wife or wives to have sexual companions or friends to fulfill the duty of procreation. The children of such a union are regarded exactly in the same way as if the real husband had been physically fit to function sexually.

When a wife is ill-treated by her husband she has the right to return to her father for protection. If the ill-treatment is proved, the father may keep his daughter in his homestead until such time as the husband pays a fine and promises not to ill-treat his wife again. If a wife has borne a child, the husband cannot claim his property which he had given as *roracio,* but in case of divorce the child is always left with the father. If the woman marries again her former husband has the right to claim at least half of his sheep and goats or cattle. But if she remains in her father's homestead and perhaps has friends, no property can be claimed. On the other hand, if she happens to have a child during that time, the former husband can claim that child as his, for as long as *roracio* is not returned, the union is not completely dissolved.

When there are no children in a matrimonial union the separation or divorce is much simpler than otherwise. In the Gikuyu system of marriage the presence of children is a sure sign of keeping the two coupled together in harmony.

15. Women in a Pastoral Society

UPBRINGING

Sex differentiation appears very early in the ways in which babies are looked after. While a girl is washed in warm water during the first four months, this treatment lasts only for three months for a boy; and certain amulets worn by babies differ according to sex, those worn by boys being for virility, and by girls for fertility. The mother wants her newborn child to come up to the racial standards of ideal physical beauty, and that demands special care while the body is still supple. The daily beauty treatment consists of pressing the nose of the baby between thumb and index finger so as to lengthen its line from the forehead downwards and make it thinner. The limbs are also gently stretched, and the head is squeezed between the palms in both fronto-occipital and parietal directions so as to obtain the rounded, globular skull that is the ideal striven after. Among the pet names, often quite absurd, which grandparents sometimes give their grandchildren are found expressions such as "big head" or "colocynth head." In spite of this beauty treatment designed to attain an anthropological characteristic which may have been lost through crossbreeding, the Bororo remain on the whole dolicephalic, and it is rare to find anyone who can boast of a small round skull.

During the first years of its life very little attempt is made to discipline the baby, and its early upbringing allows it a great deal of freedom. The child is nursed by its mother or mother-substitute whenever it wants, and neither weaning nor the birth of another child results in a psychological trauma. The mother avoids giving

SOURCE: Marguerite Dupire, "Women in a Pastoral Society" in *Women of Tropical Africa,* ed. by Denise Paulme, Routledge & Kegan Paul, Ltd., 1963, pp. 53–59. Reprinted by permission of the author and publisher. Originally published by the University of California Press; reprinted by permission of the regents of University of California.

the child any emotional shock or causing any jealous reactions by abruptly rejecting it. If, on the birth of a second child, the older one, who now has to be weaned, shows any signs of resistance to the weaning process, she will offer it her second breast while she is nursing the newborn child. Tiny children are without exception always treated with gentleness, affection, and patience, and both men and women, young or old, will immediately leave any task, however absorbing, to look after a baby that is crying.

The first lessons in social behavior are taught by the method of reciprocity, "an eye for an eye." A child who persists in hitting his brother is given a gentle slap on the arm; but if he gives signs, by indulging in whims and tantrums, of becoming difficult or spoiled, he will calmly be excluded from society by dumping him like a parcel outside the circle of women and children. It is taken for granted that the mother and all the other women of the camp will together give a child this early training based on patience and reciprocity.

At a very early age a little girl begins playing games which are a direct imitation of the work done by women. She joins in some games with her brothers—mostly games entailing some form of physical exercise, such as leapfrog, chasing each other over the sand, making miniature wells in the *gulbi* during the winter season —but she leaves them to "play at herds" while she models small pots or carries around on her back a doll made from a narrow-necked gourd or simply consisting of a stool, until soon the doll will be exchanged for her own small brother. As soon as she can stand up straight, she is put in the middle of a circle of women dancers, and the old women clap their hands and admire her for being so grown-up if her chubby little body manages to keep in time with the rhythm while she maintains a precarious balance. By three or four she is already quite a coquette, admires herself in a pool or turns round to watch her shadow when her hair is done in the style worn by the older girls; and she becomes skillful, like her mother, at polishing up her metal bracelets by rubbing them with sand. At two or three, the lobes of her ears are pierced, six holes in the right ear and seven in the left. The rings which are placed in them are scarcely more than a centimeter in diameter and allow for her becoming progressively accustomed to wearing ever heavier rings, which will not, however, replace the previous one until the holes have become large enough.

The stages in the upbringing of a little girl, unlike that of a boy, continue smoothly without a break. While a boy receives a profound emotional shock at about the age of six,[1] a girl has no such experience until she is married at fourteen or fifteen. By slow degrees her play activities become the tasks it will be her duty to perform. At six or seven she begins fetching water from the well, on foot or perched on a donkey; or, stick in hand, she helps to keep the beasts in order that are brought there to be watered. Under the guidance and supervision of her mother, she pounds grain, weaves winnowing fans and mats, decorates and mends calabashes, sews, until these activities gradually become the tasks that have to be done. And just as she becomes aware, at a very tender age, of her responsibilities as an elder sister by carrying a small brother on her back, looking after him, and defending him, so she also learns to look after the house in her mother's absence.

When children are four or five years old, a beginning is made to teach them the essential rules of the socio-moral code, the *mbo-Dangaku*. Thus a little girl learns, among other things, that sexual play between brothers and sisters is forbidden, that she must never look her fiancé (for she is already betrothed) in the face or go to visit him, or even mention the name of her future parents-in-law, and that respect must be shown to all old people. Her elders show her, by force of example, in which circumstances she is expected to display modesty of behavior and in which others she is free to behave as she likes.

Nor is her mental education neglected. It is given to her by her mother, who answers all her questions, gives her practical training in the use of customary equipment, and teaches her how to count by means of notches cut on a bed pole.

During these short childhood years spent in the paternal camp, the little girl learns to fill the two essential roles which her family expect of her: that of daughter and that of sister. Her relationship with her father is much less spontaneous and less affectionate than that with her mother. She actually sees very little of him, but she knows that she owes him absolute obedience. It is he, together with her mother, who has chosen a husband for her, often at the time of her birth, and she is not allowed to have any opinion in the matter. However, in practice, the father is not any more tyrannical toward her than he is toward his sons, and as often as not one is

[1] Male circumcision.

struck by his weakness and his difficulty in making his children obey him. Either at the naming ceremony, or just before his daughter goes to live with her husband, the father will present her with at least one heifer from his herd. Later he will avoid close physical contact with her, and once she is married, he cannot enter her house without a feeling of shame. But this attitude of restraint will be compensated for by the interest, affection, and generosity he will display to his grandchildren, which are indirectly intended for her.

The relationship between mother and daughter does not undergo these changes during the course of the years. The mother always remains her daughter's counselor, especially during the first years of her marriage and at the time of her first confinement. A daughter may want to let her mother have one of her own daughters as a household help, either as soon as the child is born, if it is the first girl to be born, or later when the mother is getting too old to manage all the household tasks by herself. However, once the children are married, a mother relies more on her sons than on her daughters, and this is certainly one of the reasons why a woman desires so much to have sons.

The relationship between brothers and sisters is determined and influenced by two main factors: kinship (as siblings or half-siblings) and seniority. There is much more affection, and a greater obligation to give mutual help, between full brothers and sisters than between mere consanguines. The fact of being born of the same mother, of having been brought up by her in the same hut, and of having shared in the affection of the same maternal kin reinforces considerably the relations resulting from mere consanguinity. These shades of difference in emotional attachment between brothers are important, and it is almost always brothers sharing the same father and mother who stick together and help each other in later life. In the same way, the bond between brothers and sisters who are all children of the same mother overrides any conflict of interests which may arise from sharing agnatic rights of inheritance. A woman would be ashamed to claim, in accordance with Muslim law, her share of the paternal inheritance if this had been assigned to a full brother, but if it were only a half-brother in question, her scruples would disappear, and in some cases she might pursue her own interests even if this meant disturbing the harmony of the consanguineous family.

Seniority, on the other hand, is an important hierarchical factor which affects all the members of one single generation alike, including cousins and parallel cousins, who have perhaps all been brought up together in the camp of their paternal grandfather if the pattern of common residence of the extended family has been followed, which was formerly the norm but is less frequent nowadays. All refer to each other as senior and junior, these terms deriving, in the case of parallel cousins, from the order of birth of their respective fathers. The eldest brother will eventually have to fill the role of father toward his brothers and sisters—a role which becomes important as far as the sisters are concerned in the event of their returning to the paternal camp after being divorced or widowed, as is customary if they have no married children to go to. The same attitude of restraint as obtained between father and married daughter will then be repeated between eldest brother and younger sister. It is similarly forbidden for the eldest brother to enter the hut of this younger sister, who may be classed together with the wives of his younger brothers; according to the institution of the junior levirate, these wives are prohibited from becoming secondary wives of the eldest brother. Thus between eldest brother and younger married sister affectionate relations are qualified firstly by the role of representative of authority played by the eldest brother, and secondly by the attitude of avoidance which he must adopt. Brothers and sisters being co-inheritors of the same paternal inheritance and also sexually taboo to each other, it can easily be understood that relations between them, however fond they may be of each other, can never be as free from constraint as those which exist between parallel cousins and, to an even greater extent, between cross cousins. Jokes are out of place between brothers and sisters once they are past childhood days, particularly jokes made by the older ones, who must adopt a more formal attitude toward their juniors.

The period preceding puberty is undoubtedly one of the happiest times in the life of a woman, in spite of the many household tasks that devolve upon a young girl. She is no more than nine or ten years old when she begins to take part in dances, where she and her companions meet young men and married men. Although she only plays a minor role in the men's dances, she is nevertheless the source of inspiration for songs which combine praises for the beauty of the women and of the cows belonging to the lineage segment. Her charms may be perpetuated in some monotonous little song, or she will achieve celebrity under some charming sobriquet (*moosaiDo,* "she who smiles," *liccel,* "little branch") given to her by her male companions. She may be dumpy, chubby, and awkward, but she knows of other ways of attracting men and becoming their special "little frog" (*paaBel*). She has every freedom, since no value is attached to virginity, and it is understood that girls will have had plenty of experience before marrying. There may be times when a girl finds herself alone with an older boy and is too inexperienced to defend herself against his importunities, but no one will be worried if she is heard weeping in the night. The adults will simply say: "The children were playing yesterday evening."

Girls become wiser as they grow older, and when it comes to the time for holding the most important dances of all (*yake* and *gereol*), it is they who do the choosing as they advance in couples toward the line of boys to select the one each has picked out for his particular gracefulness and beauty. The men will take the initiative again when everyday life is resumed, but meanwhile, during these celebrations, the *sukaaBe* (bachelors, and married men up to the age of thirty-five to forty) under their group leader the *samri* on the one hand, and on the other, the *surbaaBe* (young girls and childless married women) led by the *lame,* are performing a collective rite which is a duty that is expected of them. But when, late in the evening, the dancing is over and both groups have departed to their huts to take their rest, couples will form and, shouldering a rolled-up mat, will disappear into the cool, damp night of the winter season.

A young girl learns to assert herself, and will refuse an invitation which has the rowdy backing of the whole male group—for at this early stage affairs are a matter of group experience, into which jealousy does not enter at all, couples forming and unforming themselves without any restrictions. These "games" may be accompanied by feelings that are expressed in the discreet language of song, or by the exchange of small presents, the most common being a ring given by the girl to her lover, which he fixes to the ear of his favorite heifer. When the dancing has ended and the dancers have dispersed, rings such as these, or little scraps of material, can be found hung upon the scrub in the bush, now silent and deserted—mute witnesses that lovers have passed that way. Having complete sexual freedom at this period of her life, under the one condition that certain partners must be avoided, a young girl feels no shame in expressing her feelings and is full of initiative and audacity. This liberty contrasts strangely with the extreme modesty that has been inculcated into her since early childhood concerning anything to do with her marriage. The very mention of marriage makes her run away or hang her head in shame, and she absents herself as soon as her fiancé is mentioned, being forbidden to speak his name. She is very little acquainted with the life companion destined for her by her family, although she is not in the least embarrassed to talk about her lovers either to her girl friends or in public, and will say to anyone who cares to listen: "I like X, and I shall go to his camp because I want to live with him." These premarital relationships do not usually last very long, because the girl knows that she is destined to marry her fiancé. She knows that she cannot attain a status equivalent to that of *koowaaDo* except by going through the traditional form of marriage. It is only after marriage that a young woman may attempt to free herself from a union which has not been one of her own choosing.

16. Initiation Rituals of the Bushong[1]

Among the different Kuba groups, three forms of initiation rites are
practiced: the eastern Kuba (Ngende, Ngongo, and the Shoowa) follow a common form, the Kete of the Luebo region have their own,
and the Bushong of the south have yet another form.[2]

I was initiated according to the Bushong rites at the village of
Mapey in the south from October 23 to November 9, 1953. Initiation
rites at the capital have fallen into disuse and, apart from the capital,
may only be performed in villages which pay a special tribute to
the king and are known as "royal villages." The people of Mapey
allowed me to be initiated because the king himself vouched for me,
and because they hoped that I would refute the allegations of immorality brought by the missionaries.

The main advantage of undergoing initiation myself was that men
are solemnly bound to reveal the truth about their ceremonies to
other initiates. I was able to witness the important element of hoax
underlying the whole institution. The conventional accounts given
to women and non-initiates deliberately exaggerate the cruelty of
the ordeal and the heroism of the initiates. Even so-called confidential
statements about initiation may be wholly false. In a northern village
I received a detailed account of their initiation rites before they
discovered that I myself had been initiated in the south. The chief
then called his village council and in their presence confessed that
the secret of their initiation was that they had none. "We tell the
women these stories to impress them and to seem as courageous as
the men of the south."

SOURCE: J. Vansina, "Initiation Rituals of Bushong," *Africa,* Vol. 25, No.
2, April 1955. Reprinted by permission of the author and publisher, pp. 138–52.
[1] The author carried out fieldwork among the Ba-Kuba tribes as a research
worker of the Insitut pour la Recherche Scientifique en Afrique Centrale
(IRSAC).
[2] The Bushong are the central tribe of the Kuba peoples inhabiting Mweka
territory, Kasai District, Belgian Congo.

RITES

PREPARATORY STAGE

Before the ceremonies start, everybody talks about them. The men who are already initiated, the *biloomsh*, tell stories about the spirits of the dead who will haunt the village at night. After dark no woman or child may go out and strange noises are heard: the wailing of the dead and the growl of the "leopard." At nightfall a dignitary goes around the village singing, "Stay in your houses, the leopard is coming, the dead are coming, initiation is coming." In the day a naked man (*minyiing*) goes through the village covered with raffia fibers frightening the women and children. He whistles the same rhythm, dancing and whirling around. He speaks in a squeaky voice and strikes the children with a brush of bamboo twigs. The boys who are going to be initiated run after him and sing his songs which their fathers have taught them. They affect to despise the younger children.

In the evening the initiates dance. Drum rhythms, songs, and dance patterns are of a peculiar kind expressing courage, ferocity, and contempt for women. The elders gather outside the village to discuss the final arrangements. The leader of the novices, who should always be a son of the king, is allowed to attend these discussions. Fortunately I, as the holder of a noble title, was counted as such and attended their last meeting. The village head, the heads of the right and left sections of the village, their policemen, and the instructors of initiation were assembled to consider the participation of certain boys. The fathers concerned presented the case of their sons, some urging that they should be accepted, some refusing to let them enter. The veto of the father could not be overridden.

Terrifying stories circulated about the ordeal ahead. It was rumored that difficult taboos would have to be observed, for instance, the boys would be forbidden to have sexual relations, to smoke, to sleep on a bed, to talk about matters other than initiation, to have a fire, to enter a house, to touch each other, to start disputes, to walk in the village, to eat vegetables, even to talk to women, to laugh, to talk loudly, or to talk in a low voice. For any breach there would be a standard penalty of nine goats (about £26). For reporting the death of boys in initiation the punishment was death. Great hardships would have to be endured. Boys would sleep in treetops, they would be smeared with excrement, would suffer from the cold, be made to eat live rats, to journey through foreign lands, and, most fearful of all, they would have to go through the initiation tunnel (*mbyeen*) where horrible things would happen to all of them and some would be killed by the leopard. There would also be a brighter side: they would eat meat, drink palm wine, and go hunting. The women were made to believe that none of the boys would survive the ordeal in the tunnel.

IN THE SHELTER

After four days of preparation a shelter, covered on all sides by raffia fibers and medicine leaves, was erected on the central village square. The mask *Minyiing* was seen entering and leaving it. In the morning all the boys were assembled before the elders on the village square, the praise of initiation was recited, every boy paid a small fee and received a raffia rope around his neck. This was the beginning of the initiation (*nkaan*). The boys were now novices (*babyeen*). *Nkaan* means "binding" and *babyeen* "people of the tunnel." The rope around the neck symbolizes obedience. That morning the rope was laid on about fifty boys and in the days following many more asked to enter. Many of these were already initiated but wanted to do it again for the honor of initiation in the company of a high dignitary.[3]

Next day the novices entered the shelter, backwards. Inside they found the floor covered with raffia fibers on which they could sleep. This was the first secret of initiation. The uninitiated believed that novices sleep on the bare ground. During the following days the boys were busy making raffia fibers into loincloths. New songs were taught by the instructors and riddles were learned by heart.

Some of these riddles are "weak words"; they are seemingly intended as a kind of game but they have to be learned by heart as well as the "strong words."

Of the fifty riddles collected, about forty are more significant, of which the following are examples:

"We are together. The day a man dies we want to fly. Why? Because we were not present the day he was born." (Stresses the secret sphere of womanly activities.)

[3] I bore the third title in the land, that of *Mundy* (the researcher).

"How many people are there in our village? Two, man and woman." (Stresses the importance of sex.)

"The first collective gift with which we are washing a corpse? Tears."

"Which hoes did Woot forge first? The feet of men." (See p. 318 below.)

"A man without parents-in-law, without sisters—how does he hide? He hides (copulates) with his mother." (An allusion to problems of family and incest.)

The following was told me personally by the village chiefs as being a very strong and important one: "We have a difficult task. Neither father nor mother taught us to perform it. What is it? To sleep with a woman."

These are some instances of the traditional wisdom which is imparted to the novices. The initiates will go on all their lives learning new riddles.

The songs collected are the songs of the novices and those of *Minyiing*. Formerly the novices' songs were sung by them every morning while they were in the forest. Many of them are songs of sexual license; some refer to the roles of the instructors or to the dances. Special dances were also studied. The instructors told more terrifying stories about initiation. They explained that the greater the hardship the stronger the initiation. The boys were encouraged to dance on the village square every night. Drums, xylophones, and horns beat the special rhythms of the initiation dances. Songs stressed the sexual aspect of initiation.

Novices now discovered that most of the alleged taboos could be transgressed, but in secret; only if they were discovered by non-initiates did they have to pay a fine. A favorite joke was to say to an instructor, "We may not smoke. Have a cigarette." Certain taboos only were to be strictly observed: not to approach or talk to women, not to make a fire in the shelter or even to light a lamp, not to quarrel, not to speak loudly, and not to laugh. The boys had to speak in high shrill voices: "You are concubines of the king." A special language was learned, some of it consisted merely of whistling phrases of which only the tones were given, but some words had to be learned. The secret vocabulary was very small. All the boys were supposed to sleep in the shelter. A number of them did not do so because they were in mourning, and they were made to pay a fine of a white chicken.

Once in the shelter the boys were allowed to wear the mask *Minyiing* and to go into the village terrifying women and children. They also used another mask *Katum a lesh.*

In the last days of this phase of initiation we had to stay in the shelter day and night, eighty-four people in a room of 2½ by 3½ meters. There were many breaches of taboos: laughing, quarreling, talking, and I was made to record the fincs to be paid after initiation. The instructors nominated a "village chief" of the novices, a chief of the right side and one of the left, their assistants and policemen, and sectional clan heads of the new village the boys would live in during their camp in the forest. A leader of the whole group was designated, the youngest of the boys. He had nothing to do with village organization but would lead the other boys through the initiation tunnel. The boys were drilled in their respective roles: the village chief to speak slowly, to remain calm, and not to take part in work; the policemen to abuse, the chiefs of right and left to express public opinion and reconcile disputants.

Every evening an old man went singing through the village to make sure that all the people had regained their huts. Then, under the protection of their whistles, novices came out, went to smoke cigarettes or to visit their wives. After a time they heard the friction drum and re-entered their shelter.

Before entering the shelter the boys had been hunting and shot an antelope. This was a sign that the forest spirits were well disposed and that initiation could take place. After the hunt, the boys had to be confined so that the elders could dig the initiation tunnel and erect the wall of *nkaan.* They also dug a pit at the far end of the village which was supposed to be filled by the feces of all the villagers. Afterwards the novices were to be dipped in it. After three days of confinement, the coming out should have taken place. As it was All Soul's Day, the elders took advantage of an excuse for a day's rest and it was postponed until the following morning.

COMING OUT OF THE SHELTER

In the middle of the night the shelter was taken away from over the heads of the sleeping boys by the elders. Nothing remained of it in the village square. The boys squatted together. At about five o'clock in the morning all the elders gathered at the far (west) end of the village and the initiates made a mock charge at the boys. A few blew horns; others shouted and waved bamboo brooms. They made a few turns around the novices and finally attacked them and made them run toward the feces pit at the west end of the village. One by one the novices were dipped in it amid roars of laughter from the elders. But the pit was empty. Nevertheless, the boys who had come out of it had to run as fast as they could toward the spring. At the other side of the village, the women watched the novices running frantically in the mists and morning half-light. They could not see if they had been dipped in the feces or not. The boys washed at the spring and then went back to the village. On their way they were halted suddenly by an instructor who told them that two dead bodies were lying on the path. When each had paid three francs they were shown the corpses, which they were told were those of a sorcerer and of a lazy man. This ceremony may never be mentioned outside initiation. On their return to the village all taboos were relaxed. Everybody went home and had a good meal. Then the heads of the novices were shaved by their mothers, wives, or sisters, they were anointed with red camwood and clad in their best finery.

THE INITIATION TUNNEL

The drums called, and the novices gathered on the village square to dance the *kuyu* dance. At the west end of the village all the initiates, armed with sticks, were waiting for them. Pursued by the initiates the boys ran across the village to the east end, where the initiation wall had been erected. They all passed through the fibers of the wall (a wooden framework covered with raffia fibers) and found themselves before a masked man, *Nnup*. He wore a skirt of leopard skins and held a ritual knife in his hand. Now the instructors lined up the boys in order of rank. The youngest came first, then the different chiefs, the commoners grouped according to their clans, and the policemen closed the file. All the novices stripped themselves of their clothing and an instructor took the youngest on his back. He then dived with him between the legs of the *Nnup* mask who symbolically cut them off from the world. Between the legs of the mask, but hidden by his skirt, was the entrance to a tunnel. Underground one could hear the fearful growl of the leopard (friction drums). One by one all the boys disappeared underground. The watching women wailed and cried, the girls really believing that the boys were killed. In the meantime the novices crept on all fours through the tunnel.

Two men crouching in niches on either side of the tunnel pounced on them, and made them pay for the right to see the friction drum. Then they came upon a smith who was hammering in another niche. After paying a fee, they fell into a ditch full of water, from which they emerged at the other end of the tunnel. They came out between the legs of another masked person, *Kalyengl,* the mother of *nkaan.* The boys reborn (by emerging through her legs) let themselves fall on the ground and started to cry like newborn infants. Some old men washed them and carried them off to a nearby clearing in the forest. There they found the raffia garments which they had plaited in the shelter. Every dignitary had the insignia of his office counterfeited in raffia. While they were dressing an instructor told them that, alas, the head policeman, the last to cross the ditch, had died in the tunnel. They told me that in former times they killed him, but I am skeptical about this. After a few minutes the boy came along together with *Nnup* and *Kalyengl.* Now a line was formed. *Nnup* preceded the novices, who followed in the order in which they had entered the tunnel, *Kalyengl* brought up the rear. They carried long roots (*ngoonc*) in their hands, and proceeded by a dancing march through the village, from west to east. They were said to be ghost children, changelings of the former boys. The women believed that they would travel for at least a hundred miles among enemy tribes toward the *mashyaang* trees. They all brought food to their changelings to sustain them on their journey. At the end of the village *Nnup* and *Kalyengl* started dancing together and were driven out of the village by the people. Then the novices started their journey. They could not be followed, for the instructors covered the march with their friction drums. Not until nightfall did they reach a forest clearing where a few shelters had been set up. They slept there on the ground, with only their raffia cloths to protect them from the cold. But they were allowed to light a small fire.

LIFE IN THE FOREST CAMP

The following morning the instructors brought some more roofs so that the boys of each clan could build a shelter for themselves. Bedsteads were made, roofs patched up, and the officials among the boys started their duties. Some novices were sent to fetch water, others collected firewood. Corporal punishment for recalcitrants was banned, but the following sanctions were applied: a boy who had not

gone through the tunnel had to "commit adultery with the earth."
Stretched naked on the ground, he had to ejaculate into a little pit,
while the others mocked him. Other punishments consisted of tying
big ants' nests around the neck of the culprit; making him carry a
log with outstretched arms; pinching his nose with a wooden clip;
attaching a noose around his neck, the other end of which was tied
to the top of a small tree. The day passed in learning more riddles
and songs. During the afternoon the village elders came to the camp
and explained the rules of initiation. Knives were allowed, food
would be brought at night (stolen by the fathers from the kitchens
of their wives), the boys could draw palm wine but no woman might
see them. Should they encounter a woman they would carry her off
to the camp and all the novices would copulate with her (adultery of
nkaan). Formerly she was then put to death. Now they keep her in
the camp for some weeks.

At nightfall all the fathers came carrying food. The scene recalled
parents visiting their boys at school. They talked too loudly and had
to be reminded by the camp policemen that only whispering was allowed. That day too the raffia noose which had been worn since the
opening of the rites was discarded.

The following day new skirts of raffia fibers were made and new
riddles taught. An instructor took me aside to explain the mysteries
of initiation. The other boys can only learn this after their initiation,
if ever. They have to pay for it, and many of them are not interested,
so that they remain ignorant of the symbolism and myths of the
nkaan. What they were taught was that they had to endure many
hardships, to die as children and to be reborn as men.

The following night the boys set off at midnight, through the bush,
toward a village some ten miles away and from there along the main
road toward their own village. At eight in the morning they entered
the village and started dancing and singing on the village square.
When they were tired they might rest, hiding behind the initiation
wall, and when they felt hungry they went out of the village, hitting
the ground with their *ngoonc* roots in a certain rhythm. Their mothers then carried food out to the bush. The boys hid themselves until
their mothers had gone. When they had eaten they hid again, so that
their mothers could collect the dishes. It was forbidden for them to
enter the village except for dancing. In the evening they were conducted back to their camp in the bush by a very short path. They

discovered to their amazement that their camp was quite near to the village.

This phase lasted a few days. Morning and evening the boys drew palm wine and paid initiation fees by the calabash. Those already initiated went behind the initiation wall for the palm wine. In return the boys received instruction. The symbols displayed upon the initiation wall were explained. In former times the period of dancing could last for as long as six months, and the boys also went hunting and cleared fields in the forest.

CEREMONIES CLOSING INITIATION

One morning the boys were summoned to the initiation wall. They were told to hunt the chicken. One of them blew a whistle imitating the squeaking of a chicken. He started running around the village, pursued by the others, trying to catch "the white chicken." When they had run the whole morning through the bush they gathered behind the wall and announced that the chicken had been captured. Everybody went off to eat. That day all were supposed to eat chicken.

The following night the boys left their camp and went off to the territory of another village. In the past they went to make salt in some faraway marshes. (Nowadays they buy it in an African shopping center a good distance away.) They then came back in a file dancing *kuyu,* with their salt packed in leaves, and each wearing a special belt—"the badge of initiation." On the way back they stopped at a crossroads to plant a tree of commemoration (*kinkaan*). The tree was given the name by which that particular initiation would be known. Not far from the village the returning novices were met by the initiates, accompanied by two masks, one a snake and one *Cimbuun,* representing an antelope. *Cimbuun,* covered with raffia from which two antelope horns protruded, tried unsuccessfully to dance the *kuyu* dance. The snake wore a cap with a long tail decorated with red and black ribbons. He tried to approach the boys and to prick them with his deadly tail. The initiates fought him off, throwing magic leaves at him. Playing this mock battle, they entered the village, the women waiting, thronging one side of a square in the middle of the village. The initiates occupied another side, still throwing their magical leaves, the snake occupied the third, and the novices the fourth side. Now the youngest (the leader) of the boys danced forward, his salt in his hand. His mother came up, dancing, to receive the salt. The snake tried to prevent them, but the initiates threw their leaves and the mother finally received her salt. Thereupon the boy ran off toward his house. One by one all the boys danced the "salt dance," offering salt to their mothers, sisters, or wives.

That day all taboos were raised. The boys walked through the village, fed with their families, danced when they felt inclined, but they still might not enter the houses. At nightfall they were summoned to the village square and started dancing. The initiates drew hunting nets around them, forming an enclosure which they were not allowed to leave. They could either dance the whole night or sleep on the bare ground. The night we were in the net, a tornado came over between one and three o'clock in the morning, so we were allowed to shelter in an abandoned house.

The following morning the whole village gathered around the nets. The head policeman of the novices was called upon, and had to bite off the head of a live rat. One by one all the boys came out and the policemen killed more rats in the same fashion. The animals cut into pieces were given to the novices who had to eat them. Then all the boys ran off behind the initiation wall. The initiates grouped themselves on the village side of the wall and threw a burning brand over it. At the other side the boys received it in silence. Then a second brand, extinguished, was thrown over, and now shouting and rejoicing broke out. The initiation was over. The camp in the bush was burned the same day. The boys were now men, initiates. For a few weeks they would have to wear dark clothing as a final reminder of initiation.

THE BASIC MYTH

The inventor of *nkaan* was Woot, the first ancestor; all Bushong know that he committed incest with his sister, and afterward fled upstream. As he was the dispenser of fertility, the Bushong followed him to ask for his magic protection. This is the usual story of Bushong migrations, but the secret *nkaan* version is the following:

One day Woot, drunk with palm wine (that is the reason for asking palm wine as a fee before initiation matters can be discussed), lay naked on the ground. His sons mocked him, but his daughter found his loincloth and, walking backwards without looking at him, arranged it over his loins. When he awoke he rewarded his daughter by promising that her children would be heirs (the origin of matrilineal succession) and punished his sons by sending them to initiation. The whole initiation is a reenactment of the punishment Woot inflicted upon his sons. When recounting this, the initiators did not use the narrative tense. They told the story in this fashion: "You are Woot's son. You have offended your father. You must be punished; your father sends you to initiation."

Woot was not only the first father, he was the first king, and this is also reflected in the ceremonies. For them Woot is not dead. He disappeared upstream, but somehow he is present at initiation, which derives its power and sacredness from him. He also keeps the jealous sorcerers away from the novices.

Some of the myth had been forgotten by the village elders, but five years before they had told the following to one of my informants, and elders of other villages confirmed these scraps of information: Creation was initiated by Woot who had nine sons: *Woot icim,* the digger, who dug the river beds; *Woot aluun,* who made the hills from the earth displaced by *Woot icim; Woot iket* (or *itek*) who filled the river beds with water; *Woot aangdy maany mashepy,* who created forests and plains; *Woot a kash ikim,* who made the leaves; *Woot mameny makin,* who created rocks; *Woot a shodik,* who made all pointed things—needles, spines, boats, ears. His name seems to indicate that he bears some relation to *Shodik i maash* who personified the morass from whence, according to another myth, all people came. *Woot a pia* sharpens the iron things invented by *Woot a Mboom anon. Woot a shodik* and *Woot a pia* had a dispute; blood flowed because *Woot a shodik* wounded *Woot a pia* with a sharp iron sword. From this came death and all evil on the earth. There are several cycles of myths explaining the origins of the world, and no one of them is universally accepted. All the children of Woot were, however, the fruit of his incest with his sister. The taboo on knives among the novices is clear in view of the fact that the boys are Woot's sons sent to initiation. This, however, is not stressed by the informants.

Further details about Woot are not given during initiation ceremonies, but they are generally known and shed light on some details of the rites.

SOCIOLOGICAL INTERPRETATION

The preparatory rites can be divided into two parts: the preparation for the period spent in the shelter and the shelter period. The time spent in preparation varies from initiation to initiation. The first part does not generally exceed a week, but the time spent in the shelter is about a third of the time devoted to the *nkaan,* which can be up to a year. The preparation is a preliminary teaching period. The boys are told terrifying stories to impress upon them the importance of the rites they will undergo and the initiates dance every evening to extol the prestige acquired by initiation. The boys are convinced that manhood cannot be obtained without initiation. At night the wailing of the spirits serves the same purpose. The roar of the leopard has more significance. The leopard, the most dreaded animal of the forest; is at the same time the symbol of kingly power and the *paam,* the stern authority which is attached to it and gives it prestige. In the capital magical trees are erected to protect the village from the nightly visits of leopards, and everywhere this is the most dreaded occurrence. A story, believed by all, tells how the present king, before his accession, amused himself by taking the disguise of a leopard to scare villagers. Once he was caught by a very powerful sorcerer and starved for a week. After this lesson he never did it again.

The period spent in the shelter opens with the imposition of the raffia rope. Now the boys are bound by the raffia fiber, the symbol of initiation. Raffia is the most important material of Bushong culture. Palm wine, all clothing, and many building materials are made from it. The grubs who live on the rotten palm stem are a prized delicacy. All the implements of *nkaan:* the rope, the walls of the shelter and the initiation wall, the initiation clothing, the costumes of the masks and all the small implements of initiation are made with raffia.

The shelter itself is a symbol of Woot's genitals, for the boys enter it backwards in remembrance of the daughter who covered Woot's nakedness. The boys themselves while inside it are women, "the concubines of the king," so the shelter is the representation of the kingly harem too. Probably the idea of the king, Woot's successor, is merged with that of Woot, but sociologically this is important because village initiation is only a reflection of the initiation at the capi-

tal and the expression of total allegiance to a divine king, dispenser of
all fertility. This is also expressed by the boys being described as
wives of the king. Many of the king's concubines are only there for
political reasons, and sometimes men may reside near the harem as
"wives" of the king. Lastly the shelter period brings with it an exaggerated idea of the dangers of initiation. The magical leaves inserted
in the walls of the hut remind the boys of their danger from sorcerers
and witches. Only Woot's power can save them.

While they are inside the shelter the boys suffer considerable
strain. They may not laugh or talk, for they are in a period of mourning. They are "as if dead." That is why they may not light a fire. They
mourn the world of childhood they have left, and start an adult life
of hardship, without parental protection.

The various taboos are intended to regulate their behavior toward
women. They may no longer be familiar with women or younger
children. They are already out of their sphere. They are cut off from
the village since they may no longer enter their houses. They may not
eat vegetables, symbol of womanhood, but have to eat meat, the
food of men. But they may still talk to their female relatives and walk
through the village. The *nkaan* is not yet complete. The taboo on
smoking, the sleeping on the bare ground, and the like, of which it is
said that they should be transgressed secretly, are only intended to
reinforce the prestige of initiation in the eyes of women. The boys
learn to deceive womenfolk also by playing *Minyiing* and *Katum a
lesh* and by imitating the wailing of the spirits. These two masks,
which chase little children and mock the women, seem to be personifications of the status of the novices.

During the last days of the preparation for the main ceremonies,
when the wall and the tunnel are built, the atmosphere in the shelter
reaches a climax. As no one is allowed out (even for food) they remain hungry, awaiting what is to come, for three days. The different
taboos on not touching, slapping, or quarreling are intended to keep
order. It seems that they were effective in the past, but in our initiation, owing to European influence, they were not. The boy reckoned
that fines could not be enforced since the case was outside the jurisdiction of a district court. This initiation still emphasized another object of *nkaan:* the absolute control of the elders and dignitaries over
youths and commoners. On this principle the whole political structure
of the Bushong rests.

The coming out of the shelter and the entering the bush take place during the same day. The boys are driven to the pit of feces. They learn again that women must be deceived for the sake of male prestige, but up to the last moment they have to obey their elders without knowing what is coming. And symbolically they are dipped in a thing of *nyec* (filth) and persons associated with *nyec* are segregated from society. They acquire a status analogous to that of a sorcerer or the king, who live their whole lives surrounded by things of *nyec*. This segregation rite stresses the loss of shame (the main norm of Bushong behavior) and also the unqiueness and abnormality of the new status acquired.

The boys then run to the spring to clean themselves. The spring (and this can be inferred from the finding of the bodies of the sorcerer and the lazy man) is the primeval vagina, the ocean from which the Bushong, and indeed all people, came. It is also the source of life for a village. It means a return to the ultimate starting-point of everything. It emphasizes, I think, the notion of "not yet being created." At the same time the return to the village and the finding of the corpses represents the migration of the Bushong from the ocean, upstream in their quest of Woot. When the Bushong were pursuing Woot, he killed a sorcerer on his way, to scare them. The Bushong found two corpses, that of the sorcerer and that of a lazy man who had fallen asleep, and who also had lost Woot. The finding of the corpses suggests the wickedness of sorcery and the stupidity of laziness. A legend tells how seven men lost immortality because they slept at a crucial moment. The whole rite certainly conveys a feeling of terror to the novices. It is felt by them as a prefiguration of their own death in the tunnel. They believe that only some of them will survive the tunnel.

Then follows a complete relaxation; all taboos, except the one on loosing the rope, are suspended for a few hours, I think in order not to overstrain the boys and to give them time to shave, anoint themselves and don their best dancing clothes. This again is a reminder of the death they are to suffer. Corpses are always exposed for a few days after death in their best finery and anointed with red camwood. The boys are exposed before going to be buried in the tunnel. Shaving the heads recalls the shaving of the relatives of a man who has died from a "bad illness" (leprosy or other *nyec*).

After that the boys dance until they are chased by the initiates to the initiation wall. The dance is the breaking point of the preparatory period, the last moment of joy. The run to the wall, starting from the far end of the village, makes it clear that the novices are expelled from village life. When the corpse of a nobleman is brought from the tions. This rite exemplifies the principle of seniority in Bushong society.

The boys go through the wall. This means complete segregation from village life. When the corpse of a nobleman is brought from the capital to the burial place, it is lifted through a similar wall at the edge of the capital. "Now, his ghost cannot come back; he is cut off from us, we have nothing more to do with him," the people told me.

From now on the taboos will be strict. In the past, women who saw them after they had entered the tunnel were raped and killed, not so much to keep the secret of the novices' hiding place as to stress the complete contrast of two separate worlds, the bush and the village, and the dangers incurred by persons without a status. The wall itself is an abstract of all initiation symbols.

Nnup, the masked person wearing the leopard skin and other insignia of royalty and bearing the knife which kills, is the king, and he is Woot. The boys are naked partly because they have lost their sense of shame ("naked people are like beasts"), partly, I think, to convey the impression that a very important moment of their lives is reached. ("Everybody is naked when born, and when copulating.") The ditch is the leopard who swallows the children. The raffia fibers hanging before the entrance of the hole are his eyelashes, the earth which covers the tunnel is his skin, and the sides of the entrance are his jaws. Inside, the friction drum represents his roar. But (and this remains unexplained) the entrance itself is called the "head louse." The leopard again is Woot and also the king. If Woot kills the children, he re-creates the men. To grasp the full meaning of the tunnel it must be remembered that Woot is believed to be really there. The smith in the tunnel again is Woot. He is hammering out new men ("The hoes which Woot first forged were the feet of men"). The water again is the primeval vagina of the ever fecund first woman. It is the ocean, the starting point of Bushong migrations, it is the source, the life bringer of the village. The smith and the water represent the act of procreation. The mask *Kalyengl* gives birth. The crying and the washing of the boys symbolize childbirth.

Now the boys are forest spirit children. They belong to a new world, the world of the bush. The fibers from which they have made their skirts are not those of the cultivated palm tree but of a wild palm growing by the forest springs. The boys march with the two masks through the village dancing and slapping the ground with *ngoonc,* the root. *Ngoonc* also means a weaving rod. It is forbidden to strike anyone with such a rod because it was bewitched by Shaam a Bulongoong, a former king, and a culture hero of the Bushong. Instructors told us that the *ngoonc* was intended to strike women approaching the novices. The dance symbolizes the accomplished segregation from village life.

Nnup is Woot, *Kalyengl* is the primeval woman and sister of Woot, since she procreates with him in the tunnel. Their dance at the end of the village signifies incest; this is why they are driven out by the villagers: incest is rejected by culture. This interpretation is not far-fetched, as we shall see that one of the symbols of the initiation wall is concerned with incest, the primeval childbearing, and the sorrow which negation of incest implies. We note here that the Bushong call their mothers and sisters "the wives which God gave us," thus recognizing the problem of incest: that the most desirable women have to be given to other men.

The song of the march to the camp in the bush claims the complete sexual freedom to which society is opposed.

In the bush the boys learn building techniques and draw palm wine and go hunting—eminently masculine activities. They play the life of a hunting party, providing their own water and food, which in the bush is a male activity, though it is a female one in the village. Furthermore they learn about the social organization of a village: the rights and duties of the different chiefs, assistants, policemen, and each clan section has its own hut and its own head to settle minor disputes. All the difficulties of life are presented to them in a microcosm and they learn what adulthood means. At the same time insults with a strong sexual character (such as "Rotten is the vagina of your mother") are exchanged with the greatest freedom. Normally during this time the instructors teach what should be known about women: how their organs are made, how children are born, the correct way to copulate, and the behavior of husband to wife. This period of teaching lasts only three days. The women are made to believe that the boys are far away, but their mothers know that they are near because their husbands steal food nightly. They continue to cook as if the boys were at home. Only the younger children and unmarried girls are ignorant of the "secret."

The boys then come back to the village to dance. They receive their food outside the village, they sing their songs on the bush side of the wall, and they enter the village only in groups to dance. In the meantime the bush teaching goes on. The dancing seems to be intended to remind the villagers to do their part in observing taboos laid on them (not to go out at night: not to commit adultery with the boys' relatives). The songs stress the prestige acquired through initiation and the separation of the spheres of bush and village. This period used to last for up to six months.

The following ceremonies end the *nkaan*. The chasing of the chicken has a complex significance. The chicken is the symbol of the village (contrasted with the partridge). The feather of the chicken is a royal emblem worn during the coronation ceremonies of the king. It is then a substitute for the eagle, king of the birds. (The chicken is the biggest of birds.) Women do not eat chicken, and children may eat it only when "they know everything of life."

So the chase and capture of the white chicken represent the pursuit and possession of the knowledge of adult men. Eating the chicken is the first act of newly acquired male adult status. My instructors told me that the chase was also the pursuit of the heat of the sun. For when the cock crows, the sun rises. This could be another symbol of reintegration with village life. The forest, it is said, is cold, the village is warm. The sun too is a royal symbol, or, rather, it is the symbol of the Bushong whose first name was "people of the sun" (*bapil*). The village itself stands for organized social life.

The making of salt formerly took a month or two. It meant living in very hard conditions in rudimentary shelters in insect-infested marshes.

The planting of the *kiin* tree is a rite of commemoration. But medicine trees are also called *kiin* and the fact that the trees must be planted at crossroads is significant, for many charms are put at crossroads. The name of the tree (in this case: *ncwankaan*, "the initiation of the white man") is the name of the particular initiation class.

The dance of the snake and its expulsion by the elders of the village can be seen as the denial of the principle of segregation and the reconciliation of the different generations. The giving of salt to the women is the main integration rite. Salt is the symbol of cooking, which is the expression of the womanly responsibility in marriage. Marriage ceremonies stress the co-operation between husband and wife, and emphasize the understanding which must exist between them regarding food. The husband may not criticize his wife's food and she may not refuse him food. This is as important in marriage as sexual gratification. Giving the salt is thus the symbol of the traditional marital order on which the whole social structure is ultimately based. Its acceptance means a reintegration into the village world.

The final rites of enclosure in a hunting net, the eating of rats, and the throwing of firebrands are secondary. At the capital a hunting net is hung on the place of the *mbok ilaam* council to remind people of the following proverb: "To be caught in the king's net is bad, but the Bushong (councils) may save you; to be caught in the net of the Bushong is worse. Who will save you?" Hunting is a male activity and initiation cannot take place if the forest spirits have not shown their good will by sending an animal into the hunting nets. When the *nkaan* is over the new initiates go to the king and present him with the quarry of a hunt which took place the day after the closing ceremonies. The hunt is the essential "bush" activity. Thus the rite may be interpreted as an expression of the fact that the novices are not yet wholly integrated but are still children of the bush, and as a reminder of the force of law. No trespasser can escape customary justice, and this justice is needed to regulate conduct in a society.

The eating of rats is a last ordeal intended to impress the women. The rat is a thing of *nyec* too. The village elders told me that the novices ate a thing of *nyec* to show that they were so pure that a filthy act could not "spoil" them. Women are essentially unclean because of their menstruation and childbearing, and because during copulation they receive male sperm. Thus this rite opposes the male and the female spheres of life. The rat is a characteristic taboo of the king and of the whole nation. When a king is crowned live rats are given him in a basket by Pygmies. I could not obtain more information about this aspect of the rite.

The throwing of the sticks is a declaration of peace; the flaming brand being war, the extinguished one meaning peace. Formerly when a village in revolt wanted peace they sent their chiefs of right and left with an extinguished log to the court. The bringing of the quarry to the king (together with the initiation fees) stresses again that the *nkaan* is a matter wherein the king himself, descendant of Woot, is the real leader.

THE INITIATION WALL

The wall is composed of a framework of poles, all of different kinds of wood, on which palm ribs with their fibers loosely hanging are fastened. The wall is a long construction with three triangular peaks called "hills." The central peak is higher than the two others and reaches a height of about twenty-two feet. On the hills several masks are fastened and some representations of animals or little scenes.

The poles are "the trees of initiation." They represent the different village dignitaries and they bear their names (in the secret *nkaan* language). Woot invented all these titles, that is why they support the three hills. On top of the central hill a mask, *yool* (the policeman), is displayed. Its secret name is Woot. The two other hilltops are occupied by the masks of *Mboom* and *Cimon* (a Kete name, of which the Bushong name is *Mwash a Mbooy*). These are the effigies of the two sons Woot sent to the first initiation. They also represent the chiefs of right and left. At the capital the masks (of initiation) *Mboom* and *Mwash a Mbooy* represent the commoner and the king (kingly power) and the Bushong (power of the councils). Thus the whole structure displays the main principles of Bushong political and local (village) organization.

At the right (as seen from the village) of the first hill a tree is placed in which wooden figures of two francolins, a male and a female, are displayed. The male is trapped in a snare while the female is fluttering around him. They represent the novices trapped in initiation and the girls who cannot approach them. The francolin, the "chicken of the bush," reminds the novices that they belong to the sphere of the bush. As the chicken calls the sun, the francolins call the moon. The praise song of the francolin shows its symbolic importance. It runs almost like the praise song of the origin of the world and the primeval cataclysm. It shows a correlation with rain ("The francolin of the rain of the water god"). Rain is an emblem of water, and thus of fertility. Furthermore the cry of the francolin is like the little dancing drum which is called after him. All this is present to the mind of the novices when their instructors show them the birds. On the right of the central hill a Janus-like mask, *Kaloongaloong,* symbolizes the separation of village and bush. His two faces watch the observance of initiation rules in both village and bush. On the left side of the central hill a guinea fowl, also a "chicken of the bush," is the special emblem of the novices. The guinea fowl feather is the emblem of the chiefs of right and left in the village. Below the guinea fowl a palm tree, with palm nuts, supports the following scene: a parrot munches at the nuts while a monkey, trying to steal them, has been trapped in a snare. A man is climbing the tree to cut the nuts. His name is "the courage of the cutter" for he is going to defy the parrot. The parrot feather is the emblem of war, anger, and chiefly power. It is a dangerous bird with a terrible beak. The cutting of the nuts is, they told me, a symbol of all the arts and crafts Woot taught to the Bushong. Formerly they used to carve little figurines of a smith, a wood carver, and a weaver to show which crafts Woot gave them. As the palm kernels and the palm tree show, nearly everything in their material culture is connected with the palm tree, and it was Woot who taught the Bushong to use it. On the right side of the left hill a phallic mask *Mboong a kwong* is fastened. It represents a seated man displaying an enormous penis. They told me that it was the child of Woot, and represented the novices. Thus the sexual aspect of initiation and its relation to Woot is given.

At the foot of the central hill inside a little enclosed garden is a carving representing a woman in childbirth. All her sexual organs are overemphasized. On her face lines have been drawn to show that she is weeping. According to different explanations she is the primeval woman, mother of Woot and all living people, or the principle of perpetual creation. The enclosure is the symbol of the ban on incest. The plants inside it are charms to prevent her from copulating (some say with the Woot mask, others with the phallic mask). She weeps because she cannot copulate with anybody without committing incest. Her name, *Ngat a poong,* "wife of the eagle," suggests incest as well. The eagle is a royal emblem and especially the sign of Woot. This suggests the sister with whom Woot committed incest. Another reason for her tears is her fear on account of the courageous palm-nut cutter; or she weeps because of the pains of childbirth. All these are the formulation of values essential to the Bushong. The design of her face is identical with the initiation mask known at the capital as *Ngady a mwaash,* "the wife of *Mwash a mbooy*," the royal mask. The three masks of the royal *nkaan, Mwash a Mbooy, Ngady a mwaash,* and *Mboom* are thus present on the wall. At the capital the initiation dance represents a competition for the woman by the two male masks. The woman, wife of the king, has a lover, the Bushong. This is a transposition of the fact that every one of the 400 wives of the king has a lover, and the scene reflects also the giving of a woman to the king by every Bushong clan.

The mask of Woot has yet another significance. Woot is the leopard of initiation whose roar is the friction drum. He is the mother of *nkaan* too because he gives birth in the ditch (which is the leopard) to the novices. Between the wall and the ditch a further correlation shows that *Nnup* and *Woot* are one, and *Ngat a poong* and *Kalyengl* seem also to be one. *Kalyengl* is probably *Mweel,* Woot's sister.

Next to *Ngat a poong* a wooden crocodile recalls how the first king gave proof of his right to succeed Woot by using a crocodile as a canoe. It reaffirms the spiritual power bequeathed by Woot to the kings.

The whole *nkaan* gives the novices a world view: Woot, creator, origin of fertility, with his successor, the divine king, has abundance of life. He is the justification and the explanation of the environment; he created everything, all techniques, the social order based upon the prohibition of incest, the matrilineal clans, the local and central political structure. He still lives and his activities continue. The myth validates the structure of the whole society.

Another kind of symbolism is revealed in the three "hills" which represent the mountains Woot made when he fled upstream in order that the Bushong should not follow him. The same hills are represented in the tunnel by the different levels of the floor. The novices are the Bushong following Woot to regain the lost source of fertility.

CONCLUSION

The sociological significance of initiation can be given in a few lines. It is a typical *rite de passage* bringing the boys out of the sphere of women and children into that of men.[4] It is a school of technical and sociological training; it gives a cosmological view and trains the boys in symbolic thinking. As a result of this adults have organized the numerous symbols of their society into a loose system, each making his own meaning through different combinations of the same symbols. Even the initiation rites themselves differ slightly from village to village and from time to time, according to the changing views of the instructors. Initiation rites are thus a dynamic process adapted to the culture changes which occur incessantly. *Nkaan* also stresses the role of the king and of the loyalty which is

---

[4] M. Gluckman, "The Role of the Sexes in Wiko Circumcision Ceremonies," *Social Structure,* Oxford, Clarendon Press, 1949, notes the same opposition between women and children on the one hand and initiated men on the other.

due to him; it teaches discipline, emphasizes seniority, gives a feeling of superiority over villages which do not practice it, exalts male prestige, promotes village solidarity which is often lacking in other villages. The initiation sets generally coincide with the age sets in those villages (but not in the capital). Lastly it regulates sexual conduct.

When comparing village initiation with the *nkaan* at the capital we notice that the main ceremonies (the tunnel, the feces pit, the initiation wall) were similar at the capital. Here initiation was held once only during the lifetime of a king at his accession to the throne. A son of the king was the leader of the boys; the king himself played a part in it. Apart from the three masks already mentioned, other masks, "the slave of the king," "the ram," "the buffalo," were used, and the symbolism seems to have been even richer. Two dances of *nkaan* are still in use at the capital but they are debased into carnival ceremonies, although ritual songs are still hummed when the dancers are dressing. All the boys of the Bushong villages which were not "royal" attended the initiation at the capital. Although initiation is of Kete origin the symbolism is wholly transformed and expresses purely Bushong situations and values.

BIBLIOGRAPHICAL NOTE

The initiation rituals of many central Africans have been described. A bibliography concerning the Lunda peoples is given in M. McCulloch, *The Southern Lunda and Related Peoples, Ethnographic Survey of Africa, West Central Africa, Part I,* 1951, pp. 85–86, 101–9. M. Plancquaert, *Les Sociétés secrètes chez les Bayaka,* Bibliothèque Congo, Louvain, 1930, and D. Van Gool, 'Puberteitsriten bij de Bayaka', *Anthropos,* xlviii, 1953, pp. 853–88, describe the rituals among the Yaka. L. Bittremieux, *La Société secrète des Bakhimba au Mayombe,* IRCB, Bruxelles, 1936, and J. Van Wing, *De geheime sekte van t' Kimpasi,* Kongobibliotheek, Bruxelles, 1920, treat of the rituals among the lower Congo peoples, G. Wauters, *L'Ésotérie des Noirs dévoilée,* Bruxelles, 1949, gives important mythological data of the Songye tribes. See also Torday, *Les Bushongo,* 1910, pp. 81 ff., for an account of Bushong initiation rites.

ELLIOTT P. SKINNER

17. Intergenerational conflict among the Mossi: father and son

Intergenerational conflict is almost universal in human societies; that between father and son is often the most dramatic. Freud sees this conflict as the primeval rivalry between father and son over sexual access to the mother, and uses this basic postulate to delineate the nature of man and his relation to society. The Oedipus complex is a valid explanation for certain conflicts within the family which are ultimately responsible for an individual's maladjustment to his society. But it is questionable whether one is justified in extrapolating from individual psychology to the study of human society and cultural systems. The relations between generations and those between fathers and sons are also social relations and thus conditioned by the social structure and the cultural system within which they take place. Therefore, any serious attempt to understand these relationships must be viewed against the background of particular socio-cultural systems. Only when we know this background can we investigate and understand the individual reaction of father to son. I will attempt to analyze a pattern of conflict between father and son among the Mossi as a function of their socio-cultural system. I will show not only how the social structure of Mossi society builds and maintains these relationships, but how they support rather than impair the socio-cultural continuity of the system.

Before looking at intergenerational conflict among the Mossi as characterized by father-son relations, it will perhaps be well, in order to facilitate an understanding of the problem, to present a brief outline of the structure of Mossi society. The one and one-half million Mossi live in the Voltaic Republic which is just north of Ghana. They have traditionally been governed by rulers called Moro Nabas

SOURCE: Elliott P. Skinner, "Intergenerational conflict among the Mossi: father and son," *Journal of Conflict Resolution*, Vol. 5, No. 1, March 1961, pp. 55–60. © by University of Michigan. Reprinted by permission of the author and publisher.

who once held feudal-like control over the provinces, districts and villages which comprised their kingdoms. A rather complex hierarchial administrative apparatus extended the power of the rulers into the smallest village, and funneled taxes and tribute back to them. Most of the taxes were paid in grain and livestock, the basic local commodities. Other economic activities in the society were cotton manufacture and caravan trading between the forest and desert zones of West Africa.

The Mossi are divided into stratified royal, noble, and commoner patrilineages. Characteristic of this segmentary lineage system is a process by which royal sublineages descend serially until they merge with the mass of commoner lineages. Before the French conquered the Mossi in 1896, there were large classes of serfs and slaves of non-Mossi origin, but these persons have now been grouped into lineages and have become Mossi. The basic Mossi settlement pattern consists of virilocal, polygynous households grouped into villages. Marriages are arranged between unrelated persons through the agency of lineage members who establish "friendly" relationships. The two friends may ask their lineage heads for women to exchange as wives, or the "friend" who has received more gifts from his opposite number may give over a wife. Since it is mainly the older men who have women and goods at their disposal and can make friends, they are the ones who receive wives. As a result, young men usually lack wives and must content themselves with occasional lovers until they inherit wives from lineage members, or in lieu of this obtain women from chiefs and later on return the daughters of these women to the chiefs.

The Mossi are strongly patrilineal, and despite the advantages that may accrue to the fathers of girls in the marriage exchange, men desire male children to carry on the lineage. Men are accorded complete control over all of their children, and questions of paternity cannot weaken the patrilineal system because the Mossi emphasize sociological rather than biological parenthood. Any child born to a man's wife is unquestionably his whether he is at home or has been away for years. This patrilineal principle is further strengthened by the ritual prohibition against a woman giving birth to her child in any but her husband's village. If this happens accidentally, the husband's patrilineage must be propitiated lest harm befall either the child or its mother. Even when the Mossi mother takes the child to be reared in her own patrilineal village during the lactation period, she is not allowed to take it away in the usual manner. She must sneak away with it so that neither her husband nor his lineage brothers will see her.

A woman normally remains away with the child for about two to three years and only returns after the child can take care of himself. If she becomes pregnant shortly after she comes home, she again returns to her parents taking the baby and the young child with her. Ultimately the woman comes home, but if her first child is a boy she is enjoined by custom to leave it with her patrilineage so that she will be able to rear her younger child. The Mossi believe that it is "dangerous for two young brothers to urinate in the same hole" and fathers send their first son to live with the boy's maternal relatives until he is grown. The important point here is that a father has little contact with the one son who is most likely to be his heir and successor. Nevertheless, it is this first son, and not any of the younger ones, with whom a man is most often in conflict.

A first son does not return to his father's compound until he is past puberty, but does visit him from time to time. These visits are quite formal and from very early time the first son is taught to be circumspect with his father. He learns to efface himself before his father and not to seek attention from him even though he sees younger siblings playing with him. When the boy does return home he is made to live with other young men of the extended family either within the compound or in special young men's quarters outside the compound.

Sons normally work for their fathers most of the day and are only permitted to work for themselves in the late afternoon. Their corporate labor is used for the maintenance of the compound and to meet its standard obligations. The heads of households also use some of these resources to maintain the nexus of gift exchanges which are calculated to bring wives to the lineage. A Mossi boy may never question the use to which his labor is put by his father. His father may send him to help a friend build a hut, dig a well, or even cultivate a field. Mossi fathers believe that since they are responsible for the birth of their sons, they have the right to command all of their sons' goods and services. Implicit here, but not often stated, is the understanding that the sons, in turn, will inherit the father's goods.

The wives who normally devolve to a man either through inheritance or through marriage partners during the development cycle of the extended family are the source of actual or potential conflict between sons and fathers. Young men are required to treat their fathers' wives with the greatest formality, but this strict relationship is constantly undermined by the realization by both the boys and the women that some day they may be married to each other. The problem is further complicated by the fact that women and their future husbands live in the same household and are constantly seeing each other. To avoid unnecessary encounters between them, the Mossi practice a form of avoidance. Mossi fathers do not like their grown sons to visit the inside of the compound for trivial reasons. Furthermore, they do not like to meet their sons in the doorways of the compound. If a son is entering or leaving the compound he usually says something in a loud voice so that a person approaching him will know of his presence; the Mossi father does the same thing.

Mossi fathers of limited means, and even wealthy ones, are loath to procure wives for their sons. They declare that their sons do not want the responsibilities that go with having wives. Today, when many young men migrate to Ghana for work, the old men say that if boys wanted wives they would stay and aid their fathers to obtain them rather than go away to earn money for such trifles as bicycles. Moreover, the fathers point to the pattern of young men's sexual liaisons with married women as evidence of their opinion. The fact is that the Mossi father sees the possession of a wife by his son as representing the economic advantages which the son will gain when he dies. The antagonism between father and son is further heightened by the father's realization that the son's very advancement in the community is dependent on his father's death. Seen in this way, the father's death is imbued with a greater emotional impact than would normally be accounted for. Thus, fathers resist conferring the status of husband on their sons because this would mean that they themselves would have to adopt the status of elder, a status which, while conferring honor upon a man, also suggests his coming demise.

Mossi fathers are so sensitive about being eventually replaced by their sons that they often resent the boys' growth and development. The first son is the target of this fear and hostility because he is the one who will benefit most from his father's death. However, if the first son happens to die, then the son who is next in line becomes the subject of his father's uneasiness. Mossi men have been known to upbraid their sons for growing beards, the significance of which is seen in the fact that men do grow beards as a sign of mourning on the death of their father. Mossi fathers are also very anxious as to whether the "heads" of their eldest sons are "stronger" than their own. If a boy shows by his actions that he is not afraid of his father, then he is said to have a bigger head than his father and is in danger of being killed by sorcery instigated by his progenitor. As a rule, Mossi fathers tend to avoid any situation in which their eldest sons may be compared with them. For example, a man and his grown son do not walk together for fear of the embarrassment which would be created if a stranger, not recognizing the age differential between them, greeted the son before he greeted the father. Once when I asked a chief why his eldest son sat far away from him while his younger sons sat near by, he said, "Since he is going to inherit everything I own when I die, why should he come close to me now?" Some fathers even give their eldest sons separate compounds to see less of them. Mangin, writing about the Mossi some fifty years ago, said, ". . . the eldest son seldom remains in his father's household, especially if the father is wealthy or a naba [chief]; he is much too afraid that his son may do away with him, the sooner to come into his inheritance."

Mossi social structure induces opposition between father and son. Yet owing to the emphasis which they place on patrilineality, the Mossi value sons who can carry on the lineage. A man without sons is considered to have been a failure, and fathers are expected to take an interest in their sons. This is especially true with regard to the first son since he is most often the one who succeeds his father. Thus, while a Mossi father cannot show affection for his eldest son, he is always aware of what this son is doing and very often summons him at night to give him advice and counsel as to how he should behave. According to custom, the Moro Naba of Wagadougou places his son in a district about fifty miles from the capital and almost never sees him in public. Nevertheless, it is common knowledge that they often meet at night and that the father scarcely ever refuses a request from his son. So concerned are Moro Nabas over their sons that when the first son of Moro Naba Wobogo (1890–96) took ill and died, he had all the guardians of the boy executed.

The relationship between a chief and his son shows quite clearly the other side of the traditional opposition between a Mossi and his first son. Owing to a lack of primogeniture within the Mossi political system, any person within the ruling sublineage or even within the lineage is theoretically eligible to rule. A chief who has not angered his political superiors may be relatively certain that his son will succeed him, and fears that the boy will welcome his death. At the same time, the chief is also aware that during the interregnum caused by his death some other relative may inherit the chieftainship. He must therefore spend a great deal of his time establishing the right connections so that he may be relatively sure that his son will succeed him. It is very important for a chief that this should happen. If, by chance, his son should not succeed him, then for all practical purposes his line would lose its nobility and might even be reduced to commoner status. This would mean, among other things, that he himself would lose his position as an ancestor of the ruling chief, that his name would be dropped from the genealogy of the new line of chiefs, and that he would lose the veneration which normally would have come to him if his descendants had succeeded him. The Mossi say that aside from the possible conflict which prevents a chief's son from sitting with his father, there is another element, the fear that if both of them stayed together, they might be harmed by the same natural or supernatural agency. Thus, in a sense, this separation functions to ensure the continuity between father and son, a continuity which is treasured in this patrilineal society.

Although it is considered a sign of filial perfidy for a son to yearn for the death of his father—and no one would openly voice such a desire—the Mossi say that some young men "just wait for their fathers to die." The death of a father, whether wished for or not, does give a man wives and property, and does release him from a few ritual restrictions. The most important of these pertains to various aspects of funeral celebrations, a not unimportant thing since the funeral is the most important ceremony in Mossi society. If his father is still alive, a man may not beat the drums at a funeral, and he may not visit the compound of the dead person with the other celebrants at an important stage of the ceremony. More important, however, is the prohibition against a man taking a bow and arrow and dancing. It is during this dance that young men show their skill by dancing within a ring of people, pantomiming the activities of warriors, stalking, ambushing and killing their enemies. No young man would willingly desire the death of his father so that he could take part in these activities, but his prestige does rise when he can show his skill and finesse at this sport.

However, even after death the antagonism between father and son is not laid to rest. The son continues to reassure his father after death that he, at least, has not taken advantage of him, and attempts to disavow the conflict between them in order to gain his legacy. During the burial ceremony the father's body is carried through a hole made in the wall of the compound. It is then placed on the ground parallel to the wall but a few feet away from it. The first son is then carried through the same hole and made to stand between the wall and the body. Then he attempts twice to step over the body before going over it the third time. This is to show the people that he has been faithful to his father during his lifetime and has not slept with any of his father's wives. A man who had violated this norm would not go through this ritual for fear that his father's shade would kill him. Needless to say, a man who shows his guilt by refusing to perform this act is disinherited by the minimal lineage.

Until the end of the funeral celebration some months or even a year later, the eldest son or other relatives of the dead man are barred from using his property or appropriating it. If the dead man had been a chief, the command of his territory is even turned over to ritual or administrative personnel for the duration of the interregnum, and is not allowed to remain in the hands of his son or heir. It is only during and after the funeral ceremony that a man may fulfill the ritual obligations that will give him the right to utilize his father's property. The most important of these rites is that granting a man the use of his father's granary. This privilege is expressly denied the eldest son in his father's lifetime, while it is granted to the younger brother. During the burial ceremony the undertaker trusses up a living sheep and places it on the granary so that the dead person could take both meat and cereal with him to the land of the ancestors. The sheep is later removed and eaten, but no one is allowed to use the grain for any purpose. During the funeral ceremony the eldest son and the dead man's brother go to the granary where the eldest son is ritually shown his father's grain by his father's brother. Next the father's brother takes three calabash measures of grain from the top of the granary and mixes them with three measures which the eldest son takes from the bottom of the granary. The grain is then given to the eldest daughter of the dead man to be cooked for the evening meal. According to one informant, "this rite is designed to show the people that the eldest son has followed his father's prescription in everything, and those things which were forbidden to him before he can now perform with impunity."

It is not quite true, however, that the son can now do all the things formerly prohibited to him. He must still indicate that he has not usurped his father's property and so must ritually leave his father access to it. For example, if a son decides to take over his father's compound instead of building a new one, he has to close the gate his father used and open one for himself. Similarly, if he takes his father's wives he must close up the doors in their huts which his father used when he went to visit them and open new doors. If he does not do these things, he will be censured by the ancestors who will be angry when they discover that on coming to the compound they are visiting not the father but the son. As one man said, "One must close up the things of the dead and open things for the living." What is true about the doors which the ancestors use when they come to visit the living is also true about the sacrifices which must be made to the ancestors. If the heir inherits the head wife of his father whose task it was to prepare the repast for the ancestors, then she, now as his wife, may continue to do so. But if the heir's mother was the first wife and does not marry one of her husband's relatives, she is still considered the wife of the dead man and is forbidden to prepare the sacrifices. Should she try to do so she would be offering sacrifices to her husband since he would now be one of the ancestors, something a wife is forbidden to do. Any man who violates this rule is said to "have allowed his head" to set him against his father and runs the risks of ritual punishment by the ancestors.

DISCUSSION

The potential conflict between father and son in Mossi society stems from the structure of that society, especially its system of inheritance. In this strongly patrilineal structure, fathers have complete control over their sons and over all goods and services devolving to the family. Sons do not display their resentment of this control, nor do they ordinarily challenge paternal authority, but the possibility of their doing so, particularly in the case of oldest sons (who eventually replace their fathers), is recognized by members of the society. Institutionalized patterns of avoidance and separation between first son and father, while indicative of potential conflict, operate to prevent the hostility between them from disrupting their relationship. To interpret the avoidance between father and son and the ritual following the father's death as signs of a breach in their relationship would be fallacious, for the first averts situations which might arouse open conflict between them, and the second emphasizes paternal dominance. In this sense what appears to be disruptive is positively functional for the maintenance of traditional father-son relations. Thus the institutionalized recognition of potential conflict between father and son tends to preserve the existing norms of patrilineality in Mossi society.

JOHN H. HAMER

18. Sidamo Generational Class Cycles: A Political Gerontocracy[1]

INTRODUCTION

This paper considers age organization as a political means of dealing with problems arising out of the dispersion of men and wealth in varying ecological zones among the Sidamo of south-west Ethiopia.

The Sidamo inhabit an area shaped like a trapezoid beginning 169 miles below Addis Ababa, extending on a north-south axis from Lake Awasa to Lake Abaya, and on the east-west axis from the upper branches of the Loghita River to the Billate River. Their cultural boundaries are with the Arusi on the north, Walamo on the west, southward with the Gugi and Darassa, and the Jamjam (Northern Gugi) on the east. On the basis of village census data and registration of the majority of Sidamo household heads for the 1965 parliamentary elections, I would estimate the population to be between 100,000 and 200,000 persons.

Subsistence is based on a mixed economy of horticulture and herding well suited to a terrain varying from extensive dry grasslands at the 4,500-foot elevation to well-watered mountainous plateaus of over 9,000 feet. Cultivation of the basic subsistence crops of Ensete edulus, Zea maize, and a cash crop of coffee is important at altitudes above 5,000 feet and extending upward to around the 9,000-foot level. Climate can be characterized as moderate, with alternating dry (November–March) and rainy (April, June–October) cycles. Rain at the middle and high altitudes is sufficient to provide for a highly productive plant life while at the same time the

SOURCE: John H. Hamer, "Sidamo Generational Class Cycles: A Political Gerontocracy," *Africa*, Vol. 40, No. 1, January 1970, pp. 50–70. Reprinted by permission of the author and publisher.

[1] The field research on which this study is based was carried out in 1964–65 under the sponsorship of the Ford Foundation, Great Lakes Colleges Association, and Ohio Wesleyan University. I am most grateful to William Shack who was helpful in suggesting revisions for the first draft of this paper.

elevation is sufficient to protect people from the more drastic effects of malaria.

History

According to their mythology the original home of the Sidamo was in the north, with later migration to the south in search of more fertile land. The termination of this southern movement was the Dawa River in Borana country. Genealogical chronology suggests that early in the sixteenth century *Bushē* and *Maldea* the putative ancestors of most contemporary Sidamo set out from the Dawa River seeking more and better land. After years of desperate struggle they succeded in subjugating the original inhabitants in the present region of occupation between Lakes Abaya and Awasa. Whether *Bushē* and *Maldea* were brothers is not clear from the genealogical record. Shortly after the conquest of the land, however, their descendants quarreled with the result that *Maldea's* descendants either went north toward Arusi country or south of the Gidabo River, while the *Yamaričo,* as *Bushē's* descendants came to be called, settled at a point midway between the Gidabo River and Lake Awasa. For the next 150 years *Maldea's* descendants fought either with the Jamjam and Gugi to the south or with the *Yamaričo* on the north before they were able to consolidate their control over the territory now referred to as *Āletā.*

Whether the ancestors of the present Sidamo originally spoke a form of Gallenia may never be ascertained, but most people have at least some knowledge of this tongue. Regardless of origins, Sidamina is classified as a part of the Eastern Cushitic language stock and is usually associated with a group including Hadya, Kambatta, Alaba, Darasa, and Bambala (Tucker and Bryan, 1956:123–24). To avoid confusion arising out of ambiguous use of the term "Sidamo" as referring to either a tribe or a linguistic group embracing all of the aforementioned societies, the term will be used within the context of this paper to mean only tribe.

Community and Kinship

The Sidamo village (*kača*) is a collection of huts scattered across the hills and interconnected by a number of narrow winding footpaths. Villages are grouped around plateaus which along with forest land are treated as common property for purposes of grazing and the gathering of firewood. A *kača* averages between fifteen and thirty nuclear and occasionally extended family households, usually consisting of a man, his wife, and unmarried children. Though polygyny is a highly valued ideal only a minority of the household heads in our sample (13 per cent) had more than one wife. For those men with widely separated gardens there is a decided advantage in having a household on each plot. The occupants protect the land as well as look after the stock, and make sure the garden receives the animal dung so necessary for the successful cultivation of ensete.

The social nucleus of a Sidamo *kača* is a patrilineally related group of males three generations in depth. In each of the two villages of most intensive field research 60 per cent of the male household heads were found to be of the same lineage, connecting with a common ancestor in the fifth ascending generation from ego. The remainder were strangers from other clans whose ancestors through marriage or on the basis of individual request had been given land, and whose descendants are treated except for marriage and participation in clan rituals as members of the local descent group.

In addition to the generational class system the Sidamo are organized into a number of partrilineal clans. The field work on which this paper is based was carried out among a concentration of twelve of these descent groups, each of which is designated by the term *gurri,* known collectively as the *Āletā* people. Members of seven out of the twelve clans claim ultimate descent from *Maldea,* one originated from a neighboring Gugi descent group and four are of questionable origin. Between the *Āletā* and the southern boundary of the *Sidamo* is the *Hadičo* clan, while to the north and north-east are the *Yamaričo.* This designation in translation means those with purity of descent, and takes in the *Shabādino, Yānāssi, Wigā, Mālgā, Holō, Gārbičō,* and *Hābigōnā* clans, all descendants of *Bushē.* Interspersed among them are the *Hāvelā, Saolā,* and *Kēvennā* which though independent of the *Āletā* cluster claim descent from *Maldea.* The accepted and disputed ties are shown in the genealogical chart. All clans are further subdivided into subclans called *bosēllo.* With the exception of the *Āletā* people each clan has a chief called a *Morte* who has ritual and mediatory functions. Due to historical circumstances and the initial smallness in size of the latter descent groups there has always been a single *Morte* for all thirteen clans. Regardless of their inception all clans are corporate groups in the sense of Radcliffe-Brown's definition (1950:41); their members control property, are represented by an assembly of elders, and their male members assemble periodically for the performance of ritual sacrifice.[2]

The most basic political unit is found at the village level in the form of an assembly of adult males (*songo*), which meets frequently to settle disputes and make decisions regarding the allocation of unused land. In jural matters presentation and discussion of evidence is often made by young men who have not yet been promoted to elderhood, but are recognized as unusually competent speakers. Final decisions are made only by the elders with right of appeal to the neighborhood group (*olāuw*), clan, and sub-clan levels of the *songo*. The cases brought before these latter groups consist primarily of appeals in kinship and land dispute matters as well as inter-village conflicts and homicides.

The sanctioning authority of these gerontocratic assemblies is both secular and sacred. Secular penalties include the imposition of fines and social isolation, while the most severe sacred sanction involves the curse of the sky god (*Magāno*) which will not only serve to punish the wrongdoer, but in addition bring down disaster on his descendants. Nevertheless, the ultimate aim in any Sidamo dispute is the restoration of good will and harmony within the community.

ECONOMY

The planting cycle begins with preparation of the ground late in the dry season (February–March) to be followed by the planting of ensete seedlings and maize in April. A household head, his sons, and brothers are usually the only labor force involved in planting, while women are fully responsible for the harvesting of ensete (*wēsē*) in the dry season between late November and February. Though the Sidamo plant at least twenty-five varieties of ensete they do not follow the elaborate transplanting cycle of the Gurage (Shack, 1966:57–66). Only occasionally do they shift plants when the soil quality is poor or growth is stunted by the shade from those of greater maturity.

---

[2] The Sidamo make a distinction between performing a sacrifice which they denote by use of the term *kakāllo* from ritually feeding clan ancestors, a procedure which they refer to as *worāmo*. The latter may be translated literally as "to give a bull."

Herding is left to small children supervised by adolescent males. On the other hand, large-scale labor activities for house-building, clearing paths, damming streams or clearing ponds for the village water supply come from the *olāuw*. An *olāuw* comprises the total population of a number of contiguous villages. In addition to the aforementioned political functions of its elders this organization provides the labor for ritual activities such as burial and mourning rites.

A variable closely related to the productivity of labor is land, which in the past was sufficient for the needs of a man's male heirs as well as strangers who settled in the community. At marriage a father gives each of his sons a share of land and cattle, always making sure that the eldest receives slightly more than his younger siblings. Nevertheless, the youngest son, if he serves the father faithfully in the latter's declining years, will receive the remainder of the father's property. This may lead to his acquiring a larger patrimony than his oldest brother. As a consequence there is a basis for rivalry between brothers which it is clear from legend existed in the distant past, but has been exacerbated in the present by population increase and land scarcity.

Sidamo men aspire to positions of wealth, which helps to explain much of the past and present rivalry between brothers. For it is the amount of patrimony provided by one's father which forms the initial capital a young man needs to acquire ultimate wealth. The principal criteria for distinguishing the rich from the poor include: the extensiveness of one's garden; quantity and quality of clothing; spaciousness of dwelling; size of herd; a reputation for harvesting and selling much coffee; and resources for entertaining numerous guests. Only through control over large amounts of land and stock, however, is it possible to acquire these latter symbols. The pursuit of wealth leads men to seek to expand their initial patrimony of land and cattle by obtaining gardens and pasture in clan areas other than their own. This is why there is so high a proportion of "strangers" in many villages. For example, the census of one village in the area of field research indicated that 48 per cent of the household heads were strangers. If, however, a man is to have a large herd of cattle he must strengthen and maintain his kinship ties with people in the lowlands. So different are the middle and high altitudes from the lowlands that they attract people with different value interests. Those who live permanently in the lowlands are willing to put up with the heat and malaria for the sake of a continuous diet of milk and butter in contrast to persons who prefer the ensete and vegetable diet of the cool, damp, and relatively healthy highlands. When a man is young the practice is to spend much of the rainy season with his herds in the lowlands, returning to the plateau to harvest his coffee and prepare the land for planting. As his sons mature the seasonal care of the stock in the lowlands is delegated to them. Practically all highland dwellers have some agnatic or affinal kinsmen who live permanently in the lowlands and may be entrusted with the herd during the absence of the owner or his sons. These people return periodically to the highlands to participate in various rituals and to have their sons initiated into the generational class system. It is the generational class system which provides support for the political bonds between the two ecological zones by linking diverse descent groups through the process of generational complementarity.

GENERATIONAL CLASS CYCLES: THE *LUA*

The major purpose of this study is to describe and discuss the structure and political functions of temporal social classes for men, which are individually and collectively referred to as the *Lua*. It may be noted from the outset that there is no analogous structure for women and as a result their status is defined largely in terms of their family origins and that of their husbands.

Chronological age is not important in the *Lua*, rather it is the ordering of two sociologically defined categories of "old men" and "young men" which provides its *raison d'être*. A distinction is made in the ascription of political, judicial, military, and ritual roles on the basis of a sequence of socially defined generational classes, but only in a limited sense is it accurate to conceptualize the *Lua* as an age-grade system. In one cycle there are five named class intervals of seven years each and at any given time there will be three different cycles holding membership in successive class intervals. For ego there are four generations of real and classificatory agnates present at the start of a cycle, but these, along with non-kin members of the class intervals, are replaced in the succeeding 2⅖ cycles[3] as each new generation become members of the preceding class interval. The intervals as reckoned in terms of ascending generations are thought

[3] This will involve ninety-eight years, assuming ego is born shortly before or after his father's initiation.

of as proceeding in a clockwise sequence, while for those in descending generations the direction is counter-clockwise. The five classes as shown in Diagram I are arranged in circular order. Though *Fullāssa* is generally considered the oldest followed by *Wawāssa, Darāra, Morgīssa,* and *Hirbōra,* because sons always enter the class following counter-clockwise from that of their fathers there tends to be a circular interdependency between the *Lua* generations and cycles.

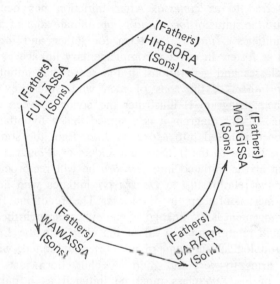

DIAGRAM I. Counter-clockwise order of *Lua* membership: Fathers to sons

Myths concerning the origin of the *Lua* abound and both the *Yamaričo* and *Āletā* peoples claim to be the originators, but there is in reality no way of knowing the etiological origins of the *Lua* names. The best that can be said is that they are associated with significant events of chance occurring at the time of initiation of a particular class. For example, *Morgīssa* is said to be derived from the word *Mīlla,* meaning to dry, and is associated with the induction of this class during a time of drought; *Fullāsa* comes from the word *fullsō,* a type of cattle disease said to have decimated herds at the end of one of the seven-year-class intervals; *Darāra* is from *darāro* meaning flower; and *Wawāssa* is a derivative of *wāki,* a word for a type of fever which is said to have once been of epidemic proportions, causing the death of many. In any event, whether a class starts during a time of troubles or at a particularly auspicious moment in history it is clear that the expectations and hopes are that it will bring peace, harmony, and good fortune to all of the people.

All males may be thought of as passing through three grades, depending on life span and time of birth *vis-à-vis* their father's initiation. These grades include that of pre-initiate, initiated members who have acquired the name of their *Lua,* and circumcised elders referred to as *čimessa.* After initiation has occurred men also acquire the status of *loco-ānna* to pre-initiate sons of an alternate class of initiates. *Ānna* is the term for father and *loco* may be translated as foster. In effect a complementary linkage is established between classes and generations in the sense that initiates become the foster fathers of the sons of men who were previously their foster fathers. Diagram II illustrates the bonds between classes and generations. In this diagram it is assumed that a hypothetical father has just been initiated into *Morgīssa Lua.* Ego, the son, will temporarily be linked to the initiates and elders of *Wawāssa* as a foster son. When ego is initiated into *Hirbōra* he will reciprocally assume the *loca-ānna* relationship to *Darāra* pre-initiates who are the sons of his former stepfathers in *Wawāssa.* The functional significance of this arrangement is the linkage of ego either through the father/son or *loco-ānna* relationships to all of the classes in the *Lua.*

The chronological age span of initiates is unlimited, varying from babes in arms to very old men. A child born just before the beginning of his *Lua* class must be initiated as a babe in arms unless he has older male siblings, in which case the latter will be initiated and ego will wait until these rites are performed in his "foster father's" *Lua* twenty-one years later. After that, however, he is considered a member of the same *Lua* as that of his siblings and will be promoted with them to elderhood at the end of the first class interval beginning a new thirty-five-year cycle. For example, if ego's *Lua* is *Hirbōra* and he is an infant with older siblings at the beginning of the class cycle he will be inducted with the *Wawāssa.*

In regard to upper age limits it is theoretically possible to conceive of a situation in which initiation age increases directly with changing generations. If a male who enters his class interval at birth begets a son at twenty-one years of age, the latter will be seven years at the time of his induction rites. Assuming the same conditions as

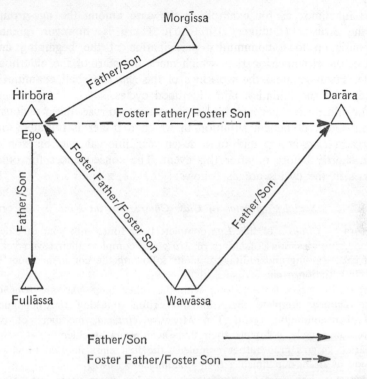

DIAGRAM II. Generational and class linkage

to age of male progenitor in each succeeding generation, the structural requirement that ego must enter the class immediately following his father's necessitates adding seven years to the initiation age of each succeeding generation. An approximation of this hypothetical situation helps to account for the chronologically old men who, along with the youth, form part of every class interval in the initiation cycle.

Unlike the Gada system of the Galla, marriage and the establishment of a family are unrelated to one's status in the class intervals. Also different from the East African age class systems is the practice of men remaining in the class interval of initiation for life, rather than being promoted through a series of grades with differing rights and obligations. All clan or, in the case of *Āletā,* tribal members who are eligible are inducted together and their positions as well as those of their officers have universal rather than primarily local functions, as for example is the case among the age-groups of the Arusha (Gulliver, 1963:26). There is, however, greater emphasis on local community participation at the beginning and end of the circumcision rites which mark the start of the elderhood cycle. To understand the workings of the *Lua* we shall examine in detail both the initiation and elderhood cycles.

For illustrative purposes it is convenient to use the previously mentioned hypothetical situation in which a father is initiated into *Morgīssa Lua* at the end of a seven-year interval and his son is born shortly before or after this event. The consequences for other classes in the cycles are as follows:

Social Correlates of Class Changes in the Lua

Hirbōra   *Čimessa* of this *Lua* complete their fourteenth year of elderhood. Initiates, sons of elders of *Morgīssa,* complete their seven years of cattle-raiding and military exploits following the commencement of their initiation cycle.

Morgīssa   Ego's father along with the other men who are sons of the *Darāra* complete their initiation ritual marking the beginning of their initiation cycle. The *Morgīssa čimessa,* members of the preceding cycle, complete their first seven years as elders.

Darāra   Ego's grandfather completes the first class interval of elderhood as his group finishes their circumcision rites.

Wawāssa   Ego's great grandfather's class has seven years left before completing its second cycle and being retired from the *Lua*. The sons of the *Fullāssa* have now finished their initiation cycle and are ready to begin the elderhood cycle. At the completion of the first interval of this cycle they will replace ego's great grandfather's class as *Wawāssa čimessa*. Ego becomes a "foster-son" of these men and will be under their tutelage until his initiation into *Hirbōra* twenty-eight years hence.

Fullāssa   The fathers of ego's "foster-fathers" begin the twenty-first year of their elderhood, with two more intervals remaining before retirement from the *Lua*.

The sequence will continue with sons of the preceding entering succeeding *Lua* classes of their fathers and being junior to the elders of a previous cycle in their respective classes.

In this way ego will be replaced by the sons of men in the next class of his cycle as initiates thirty-five years after his own initiation, and twenty-eight years later as elders, upon the retirement of his class. Though the Sidamo conceptualize class and generational differences, they do not have a term for cycle. This may be due to the way they view classes as continuous without beginning or end. The term "cycle" has been introduced by the author as an analytical convenience. Nevertheless, the *Lua* is probably not an institution of great historical depth. Based on a listing of all the class leaders, of which there have been twenty since its establishment among the *Āletā*, it can be estimated that the system is not much more than 140 years old. Consequently, not enough time has elapsed for the development of the cycle concept, but should the *Lua* continue, it is possible that a term will develop for ease in classifying the temporal sequences.

Classes are linked on an inter-generational basis starting with a temporary tie to the oldest existing class of one's great-grandfather, three cycles removed, and continued through a fictive "foster-son" relationship with the men two cycles ahead who replace the latter as elders. The superordinate role of the older over the younger generation is dramatically illustrated by the fact that ego cannot be initiated until his father's class, one cycle ahead, has entered elderhood through the completion of symbolic circumcision rites. To understand the political content of the ascribed authority role of one generation over another, as well as the opportunities for achieved leadership within generational classes, it is necessary to examine the events of the initiation and elderhood cycles.

INITIATION CYCLE

Preparations for initiation commence with the search for a *Gadane* and *Jet-lāwa* after the induction of the preceding *Lua*. These are the formal titles of the leader and his assistant provided for every new class.

In *Āletā* eight of the most distinguished *čimessa* will be called upon to designate the selectors of leaders from among the *Lua* to be initiated at their retirement. These eight elders may come only from the five clans whose ancestors participated in the defeat of the *Yamaričo* and were involved in the establishment of the first *Āletā Lua*. From their respective clans they will choose eight of the oldest and most qualified speakers among the pre-initiates who in turn will select the leaders for the next *Lua*. Selection is restricted to the five senior clans reckoning descent from *Maldea*.

As a reward for their leadership in the historic defeat of the *Yamaričo,* Gugi, and Jamjam, every other *Gadane* must come from *Hitala gurri.* When it is not the turn of the *Hitala* to provide a *Gadane,* the *Jet-lāwa* must be taken from this clan. The search is further narrowed to senior sub-clans in the above descent groups, and among the *Hitala* selection may be made only from the *Shāba,* senior clan section.

Since the sixteen elders must reach a consensus on the nominees to these leadership positions there are two culturally ambiguous means for testing the climate of opinion. One of the selectors may have a dream in which he has a vision of the new candidate and uses this as a means of appraising the attitudes of the others. Indirection is an important part of Sidamo communication and men are often afraid to express opinions directly for fear of placing themselves in jeopardy should others take offense. A dream, however, being associated with the spirit world, is dissociated from the personality of the dreamer and hence constitutes a topic which can be freely discussed, and should all the selectors concur in its legitimacy the choice can be made without further ado.

A second approach is to consult several *količa* for their opinion on the appropriate candidate. These men are specialists who have the ability to contact the supernatural world through possession by a personal spirit. The selectors contact these specialists from widely separate geographical areas and approach them with offerings of honey and butter. They place these in front of the *količa* who responds: "You came in order that I may select a new *Gadane* for (named) *Lua.* You will find this man in (named) *Gurri,* (named) *bosēllo,* and of (named) family." He then proceeds to describe the color and other physical characteristics of the candidate as they have been revealed to him through his spirit. When there is agreement among four or five specialists, the selectors are then able to narrow the field of prospects in terms of those who meet the relatively ambiguous criteria. It is at this point that character (*anāli*) is taken into consideration and includes such traits as unusual circumspection and wisdom in dealing with others, congeniality with all segments of the community, and a reputation for being a living embodiment of Sidamo ideals. It is also important that the man be physically whole since this attribute is associated with one who is spiritually complete. Since there is often disagreement among the selectors, given the high requirements for the position, and because there is a need to observe the behavior of the prospective candidates to determine the extent to which they measure up to the character criteria, the selection is usually not made until shortly before the initiation ritual is to begin.

Once chosen the *Gadane* and his assistant are recognized as permanent leaders of the new *Lua*. The class leader having been formally designated must perform three major roles: that of officiant at ritual sacrifice for members of the *Lua*[4]; as peace-maker in the settlement of disputes; and as organizer of the initiation rituals. Though he is the official head of his *Lua* and in the opinion of some informants commands more loyalty than men feel for their descent groups, he is in no way a military leader. His role as a man of peace is such that when the men of his class raid cattle from other tribes he goes part of the way and blesses their work, but never participates in the ensuing combat. Should the *Gadane* be unable to carry out any of these tasks he delegates them to his assistants, the *Jet-lāwa*.

The *Gadane* is responsible for organizing ritual sacrifice to promote the long life of the *Lua* and to protect it from disease and pestilence. A member may dream of his leader ameliorating the situation by sacrificing a cow of prescribed color and in a designated location. The *Gadane* will then be contacted and the *Lua* assembled to carry out the instructions of the dream. In addition to his role of officiant in therapeutic rituals he may be sought out by individuals for the bestowal of his blessing on such desirable events as the birth of a male child, recovery from a severe illness, or escape from poverty. This is referred to as taking *tano* to the *Gadane,* for in the event of success the person receiving the blessing agrees to present the *Gadane* with a bull or an ox.

The peacemaking functions of the *Gadane* and *Jet-lāwa* apply not just to the members of a single generational class, but may be utilized by all Sidamo. This is so much a part of their role that they must become living symbols of harmony by avoiding acrimonious debate with others and any participation in the military activity so highly esteemed by men. A *Gadane* or *Jet-lāwa* with a reputation for adeptness in settling disputes is in constant demand

---

[4] Until completion of the circumcision rites he would only be permitted to call the members of the *Lua* together for a ritual sacrifice, but the animal would actually be dispatched by an elder. Only *čimessa* are permitted to slaughter cattle.

by people in all parts of the country, and at any organizational level of the *songo* men will defer to his views or those of his assistant in the decision-making process. These officials may even intervene in inter- and intra-clan warfare by ceremonially throwing dried *siĉo* grass in the air as a sign that the conflict must cease.

INDUCTION CEREMONY

Formal induction of initiates involves a two-month ceremonial period in which they are from time to time either concentrated in one central camp or scattered about the countryside visiting the men of their father's and "foster-father's" *Lua*. The rites are centralized within the clan or tribe rather than held on a local community level. Among the *Āletā* clans *Goida* is the name of the plateau where the camp is located. This centralization of location along with the requirement that the initiation period cannot begin until all disputes involving the payment of bloodwealth for murder have been settled are means of dramatizing the cohesiveness of *Lua* social ties. Activities commence when the *Morte* calls the pre-initiates together to receive his formal blessing to be followed by the sacrifice of three bulls, one on the hill of *Golāma* overlooking the plateau where the *Āletā* won an important victory over the Gugi, another at *Birā* the original home of the *Āletā* clans, and a final one in the camp at *Goida*.

With the exception of infants all those about to be inducted enter the camp at *Goida* where they deposit handfuls of the *siĉo* grass at the base of a tree which is henceforth to be associated with their *Lua*. Should this tree die before completion of the initiation rites it will be feared that this is an evil omen, and the *ĉimessa* of that *Lua*, members of the initiates' father's cycle, will perform a sacrifice and pick another tree. One of the first acts of those soon to be initiated is the carving of two sticks, one from the wood of the *kitmalĉo* tree and another from the *gawaĉo* tree. Both these objects are called *lolōko* and one of them must be placed in the homestead of the initiate while the other is carried with him on visits to his fathers and "foster-fathers" during the two-month period. The surface is carved with designs of flowers and notched rings which are said to represent the circular scales of snakes. It is perhaps significant that the same type of circular design is carved on a man's funerary pole at his mourning ceremony.

Though informants could not suggest a reason other than custom for these stylized symbols, it seems likely that there is a tie-up with mythology concerning the origins of death. Snakes are said to have been given immortality by *Magāno* the sky god because of their obedience, while man lost his chance for eternal life through failure to show sufficient obedience and respect for this creator deity. Since only the owner and members of his *Lua* may touch a *lolōko* both sticks must be burned at the first *Feči* feast following initiation.[5]

Older men have already begun to assume the dignity of elders, and as a consequence they receive deferential treatment by being permitted to remain in camp with the leaders throughout the two-month period. The *Gadane* divides the younger men into groups of approximately 150 under the leadership of a *moriča* (foreman), who knows all the members of the "father's" and "foster-father's" *Lua* classes in the district to which they have been assigned. The young men are to be ritually fed by their "fathers" and "foster-fathers" and in their approach to the assigned areas they make known their presence in the following song: "We are the sons of (father's *Lua*)—we are the sons of ('foster-father's' *Lua*), and we come to our fathers to be fed." They will also honor the new leader of their class in song: "We are the people of *Gadane* (name)."

Each member of the father's class must contribute a bull to the group, which will be sent back to the camp to feed the *Gadane* and the older pre-initiates. This gift entails reciprocity on the part of the sons, in the form of a sacrificial bull at the death of their respective fathers. In addition, each father must feed the group of young men once during their visit to the area and through this act he may gain prestige by voluntarily slaughtering a cow as well as providing the conventional food of ensete (*wāssā*), milk, and coffee. The "foster-sons" of the senior division of the class about to be initiated also participate in the feasting. By this act fathers are not only demonstrating support for their own sons, but are affirming a tie with men of an alternate class in their own cycle who will not begin their elderhood rites for another seven years. Further, they are showing respect for the existing elders of this alternate class who replaced their grandfathers in the previous cycle and who have

[5] *Feči* is the feast marking the beginning of a new year in the Sidamo solar calendar. It involves feasting, dancing, and ritual washing of the face at dawn on the first day of the new year.

constituted the senior "foster-fathers" of their own sons. These men in turn signify completion of their role as "foster-fathers" by also feasting the groups of pre-initiates, but they are not expected to provide more than a modest feast, and there is no requirement that they donate cattle for the guests.

Initiation into a Sidamo generational class does not involve lengthy instruction in clan and tribal lore such as is often associated with this event in other societies. Even knowledge about the history of the *Lua* and the names of past *Gadana* and heroes is known only to elders; young men insist that they do not want to know these things as it implies old age and approaching death. Between intervals of ritual feasting the pre-initiates return to camp where they are instructed by their fathers in military skills such as fighting with the spear and shield as well as how to raid cattle from the enemy. The one other competency transmitted by the elders during this period is the proper method and rules for animal sacrifice.

The climax of the two-month ritual is the gathering at *Goida* of all groups that have been going about the countryside, the children and infants eligible for initiation, and the initiates of the previous *Lua* for a two-day period of feasting and sacrifices. On the first day the members of the preceding class mark the end of their first seven years by sacrificing a bull, while on the second day the new *Lua* initiates perform a similar rite to mark the beginning of their cycle and then are led out of the camp by the preceding class. At the edge of the camp the two groups fight a mock battle, boasting, hurling insults, and threatening with spears and swords as symbolic of the rivalry between the two successive *Lua,* with their fathers intervening to make sure the skirmishing does not get out of hand. The new class claims that it will raid the enemy more frequently and bring back more cattle in the ensuing seven years than did the previous one. Intervention of the fathers is usually effective in preventing the posturing and insults from getting out of hand, for not only must sons respect the authority of initiated fathers, but the fathers of the preceding *Lua* are the senior members of the new initiate's own class.

Following formal induction the initiates receive further instruction from their fathers in military tactics, and horseback riding in the lowlands around Lake Abaya. Then, before returning to their homes, they shed the goatskin wrist bands which have served as a sign of their status during the preceding two months. Full *Lua* membership has now been acquired and in *Āletā* the next obligation is to build a house for their *Gadane* and the *Morte,* as well as to labor for these two dignitaries in digging up a large garden plot. The final act in *Āletā,* though it is not the custom in the rest of Sidamo, is the presentation of tribute (*gumatta*) to the *Morte,* including pots of milk, butter, and money which must be presented by each new *Lua* member according to his ability to give. This is one of the earliest opportunities for a new initiate to enhance his prestige by demonstrating unusual generosity.

During the first seven-year interval the traditional procedure for members of the new *Lua* was to carry out numerous cattle raids in which they might demonstrate skill in taking large numbers of cattle under dangerous conditions. Though the animals were divided equally among the men, the extent to which they could boast about their exploits to the succeeding *Lua* was dependent on the total captured during this time. It was possible for a man to win a reputation for bravery through a daring act, such as stealing into a cattle pen and removing all the animals before the owner was aware of his presence. This form of skill was considered more important than killing Arusi, Gugi, or Jamjam owners, though a man could attain fame and acquire the right to special honors at his funerary rites by killing an enemy under circumstances requiring unusual courage. Through poetic boasting, one of the principal Sidamo art forms, the stories of such exceptional *Lua* exploits have been kept alive for generations and at mourning ceremonies and on the occasion of circumcision feasts men still vie with one another in reciting the deeds of heroes from their own and previous generational classes.

Other than for purposes of raiding cattle, participation in *Lua* sacrifice, attendance at mourning ceremonies, choosing selectors for the officers of their son's class, and mediating the mock combat when the latter leave the initiation camp, large numbers of the new generational class will not come together again. Until they begin the elderhood cycle their role *vis-à-vis* senior members of their own and other classes will involve service and deference. Under the supervision of the elders the most recently inducted classes provide manual labor in the local districts (*olāuw*) for house building, clearance of streams, trail maintenance, grave digging, and the erection of funerary fences. The deference which the younger must show toward older men is symbolized by the practice of following

Lua seniority in the order in which men receive food at public
gatherings, the sequence they follow in expressing condolence to a
deceased's relatives at a mourning ceremony, and in the presentation
of the traditional non-fermented horn of honey during the circumcision feast.[6] Members of the initiation cycle are further distinguished from elders by the way in which they wear the cotton
garment called *gūmffa*. Elders may wear the *gūmffa* as trousers,
but the young men are privileged to use it only as a loincloth.

Despite the obvious subordination of initiates to elders, there are
several ways in which the former may distinguish themselves and
not only gain prestige in their ascribed status but prepare the way
for leadership roles in the elderhood cycle. Raiding cattle, for
example, provides an opportunity for acquiring a reputation as a
man of courage and decisiveness under pressure and as previously
indicated the attainment of wealth through hard work, efficient use
of time, and intelligent dealing with other men in negotiations for
land and cattle is highly valued. Another method for becoming
potentially influential lies in consistency of attendance and participation in the *songo*. Before taking advantage of their prerogative to
make the decisions of the assembly the *čimessa* permit young
initiated men who demonstrate ability in debate to question witnesses,
discuss policy, and even suggest courses of action.

ELDERHOOD CYCLE

Junior will replace senior class members from the previous cycle
twenty-eight years after the former have been initiated and thirty-
five years following the attainment of elderhood by the latter. The
circumcision rites marking this promotion are of three parts; a
preparatory period for the accumulation of resources, the building
of a seclusion hut, the actual operation followed by several months
of retirement, and an emergence feast.

For the successful performance of these rites, the most lengthy
and expensive in the Sidamo ritual calendar, it is necessary for a
man to have support from as many as possible of his agnatic,
affinal, and uterine kin in accumulating sufficient resources to

---

[6] If men in attendance at mourning ceremonies are of the same clan, relative
chronological age will determine the order in which they approach the bereaved
kinsmen, but when they are of different clans, as is often the case, then the
principle of generational class seniority is followed.

support himself and his family during this period of enforced idleness. There is no restriction as to when the ritual may be held during the seven-year interval, but since men are least involved with gardening activities toward the end of the rainy season in the latter part of October or early November, it is usually scheduled at this time. The operation is performed individually or in groups of three or four *Lua* members from the same district (*olāuw*) on one of the two days in the monthly Sidamo solar calendar set aside for such activities. All the young men in the *olāuw* are expected to assist in building the seclusion hut (*barčīma desse*), while the women help in preparing large quantities of ensete flour mixed with butter (*būtla*) to be served at the circumcision feast. Also, if the man has killed one of the traditional enemy or individually taken cattle in a raid, large quantities of a non-fermented honey drink must be prepared.

The operation takes place at sunrise and is performed by a specialist (*Orgāsse*) whom informants indicated should always be an ethnic stranger, since one Sidamo should never spill the blood of another. The cutting is done with a special knife called *magalāli* which is made by the ironworking *tuntičā* caste and used only on this occasion. During the latter part of the rains, the *Orgāsse* is busy every day traveling about the countryside to perform these rites for which he is rewarded with money, ensete, and butter. His payment and feeding are the responsibility of the eldest sister of the newly circumcised man.

Circumcision is referred to as *barčīma,* the term for the four-legged stool on which the candidate sits supported by his youthful attendant and one or two men from the village. At the ceremony performed in the candidate's garden all men of the *olāuw,* his agnates, except those of his father's generation, and uterine relatives with the exception of the mother's generation, are expected to be present. This exclusion of kinsmen in the first ascending generation from ego is based on the fear that should they hear the rhythmical chanting following a successful operation their death will shortly ensue. As a preliminary to entering the garden, which is a privilege accorded only to males, an elder reckoned to be the oldest among those assembled sacrifices a lamb (*cutōte gōto*) and rubs some of the blood on his own and the foreheads of the candidate and his young attendant to "warm their blood." Then the men enter the garden where the operation is carried out in a small lean-to of ensete leaves.[7]

Once the man is seated on his stool the *Orgāsse* without saying a word cuts away the foreskin and departs. As in most such ordeals it is important for the subject not to cry out or in any way depart from a stoic countenance, as it is felt that such a sign of weakness could bring disgrace upon the whole *olāuw*. Several minutes of tension follow while those outside the enclosure await the signal that the blood has begun to coagulate and the man has succeeded in urinating; until this happens the operation is not considered a success and the man's life is in danger. Once the signal is given, however, the men burst into a joyous chant which they continue for several minutes. Next a second lamb (*horāffo*) is sacrificed, cut up, singed over the fire, and served to the men assembled in the garden. When this meat has been consumed and the newly circumcised candidate is thought strong enough to walk, they escort him to the seclusion hut where the old men proceed to bless the man, saying: "May this circumcision be good for you." All the people then crowd into the hut where they are served ensete and butter.

There can be little doubt that the prolonged period of seclusion in which the candidate elder remains not only within the hut but in a place of honor behind a bamboo screen is a symbolic process of rebirth. Indeed, during the first few days while the wound is healing the man is supposed to be so enfeebled that he is not even permitted to speak to his wife, or wives, and children. This period of helplessness is brought to an end with the ceremonial hunt for the *wāngi* bird whose colorful feathers are used to decorate the *lemočo* (bamboo) stick. Men and boys of the village search

[7] Among the *Yamaričo* a special ceremony is held before going into the garden for the operation which enables the candidate to acquire *anga*. *Anga* refers to genealogical purity and the ceremony symbolizes the continuity of the man's line of descent from *Bushē*. The *Ạletā* clans do not observe *anga* because of their descent diversity. This *Yamaričo* ritual is performed by a *čimessa* from the village who approaches the candidate, orders him to kneel, makes a slight incision in the back of the latter's neck and then says: "Vomit all that you have eaten from your birth until today, which is not what you are supposed to eat." Then the man pretends to regurgitate the food after which the *čimessa* slaughters a sheep and sprinkles the blood on his head. Instructions are issued about certain food taboos which henceforward must be obeyed, including the avoidance of such animals as pig and wild goat. Also, from that time on, the candidate must eat only meat slaughtered by a *čimessa*.

the hills and valleys until the bird is found and brought down by the sticks of the pursuers, after which all return in a triumphal procession to the circumcision hut. The *wāngi* is skinned, the feathers attached to the end of the *lemočo* stick, and before sunrise of the following morning the candidate's attendant (*jāla*) takes it to the bank of the river and buries it in the mud. The man then resumes his normal authority status *vis-ā-vis* his family, and the circumcision wound is considered healed. Other symptoms of rebirth are the completely sedentary activities of the seclusion period such that all of one's time is taken up with eating, sleeping, playing the game *sādaga,* and visiting with relatives and friends.[8] A final indication is the almost nurturing role of the *jāla,* a young boy selected from the village to run errands, wait upon, and prepare the food of the candidate.

Prestige is enhanced by the length of a man's stay in the *barčīma desse* beyond the normal two-month period, for it is a sign of his own wealth as well as the esteem of his kinsmen which is shown by the lavishness of their food gifts. Each of his siblings is expected to bring him a bull, butter, ensete, and milk; paternal-maternal cross and parallel cousins, though they may make joint contributions, are also expected to make similar presentations. Agnatic and uterine relatives of the first ascending generation, however, continue their avoidance and do not bring anything, those of the second ascending generation may make voluntary contributions, and a man's married children will be expected to bring bulls and other presents. All one's wife's brothers and her father, if he has not been promoted to elderhood, are obligated to show their support by bringing gifts similar to those provided by siblings and cousins. This gift exchange, which is symbolic of generational solidarity, is reciprocal, to the extent that ego is required to give the same to his male kin at their circumcision rites. The role of a man's sons is also important during the seclusion period for they are expected to care for his garden and cattle as well as to be always in attendance at the circumcision hut. His reputation for wealth and generosity may be enhanced by the manner in which he entertains visitors during their

[8] *Sādaga* is a version of a game played widely in Africa involving a board with two parallel lines of cup-shaped indentations, into which pebbles are dropped sequentially by the players. The object is to take the pebbles of the other player by ending the sequence of moves around the board with one's last pebble just opposite the cup in which the other player had dropped most of his. Players proceed turn by turn until one manages to capture most of the pebbles of the others.

presentation visits and, as a consequence, it is an important cost of the seclusion process, sometimes leading a man into debt that cannot be repaid for years. For example, one informant estimated the cost of such hospitality at more than $150.00. Eth., another at $300.00 Eth., which though high is considered acceptable for this important event.[9]

At the emergence from the *barčīma desse,* which may take place only on one of the two days reserved for circumcision rites in the solar calendar, the candidate leaves his hut before dawn and is escorted by the male members of the *olāuw* to the nearest river where he bathes and puts on new clothing, wearing for the first time new *gūmffa* in the fashion of the elders. An early hour for bathing is considered imperative since the river is pure at this time, not having been contaminated by people washing clothing or fetching water. There follows a triumphal procession back to the village with the new elder walking under an umbrella at the head, the other members singing the chant used at the time of the circumcision operation. Later in the morning a great feast is attended by members of the *olāuw* and the man's kinsmen minus his father, mother, and agnates of their generation. The oldest men are fed first in the place of honor behind the bamboo screen which divides the hut, after which they participate in previously mentioned poetic boasting, concerning great military exploits of past generational classes. In the afternoon the small children of the *olāuw* gather to be fed ensete and butter, while young unmarried men and women congregate toward sundown to sing and dance well into the night.

The elderhood cycle, which has now begun and will last until retirement thirty-five years later, entitles the recently promoted to respect from younger generations, exempts him from the communal labor involved in house building and road building, gives him full authority in settling disputes and making public policy. There are also certain symbolic indicators of the new status such as the right to slaughter sacrificial animals and the assignment of seats of honor at burial and mourning ceremonies. Informants indicated, however, that circumcision is more than a symbolic means of transferring privileges to a mature adult, rather it serves as a reminder to the individual that his character (*anāli*) is expected to change. This is especially notice-

---

[9] In a survey of the estimated income and expenditures of forty household heads in three villages, the mean annual income for 1964–65 was found to be approximately $248.00 Eth.

able in regard to the assumption of decision-making power, for a *či-messa* is distinguished from a young initiate in his circumspect, patient, and soft-spoken manner in dealing with others. A young man is excused for exhibiting uncontrollable anger and impetuosity, but an elder will be rebuked by others for such behavior. The *songo* provides the real test of these self-disciplinary attributes, for as previously indicated the ultimate exclusion or cursing sanctions are only invoked after a long and arduous probing of the evidence and alternatives involved in a specific case. Then instead of arbitrarily punishing recalcitrant disputants or imposing decisions on opposing factions in the community, the elders in a quiet but forceful manner seek to convince by logical argument. Sometimes the dialogue continues for hours or even days before their decision is accepted voluntarily by disputants, but only if persuasion fails should sanctions of force be used.

So important are the attributes of this gerontocracy in maintaining peace and harmony that they have been personified in the position of *Woma,* the ideal *čimessa.* In fact, informants with historical knowledge were unanimous in their opinion that the *Woma* position existed before the *Lua* or the *Gadane* and *Morte* roles had been established. A *Woma* is more than a competent mediator or ritual functionary such as a *Gadane* or *Morte,* for he combines in addition to their abilities the wisdom associated with very old age. Though there is variation from one clan to another in the selection and functions of these dignitaries certain general principles apply to all, such as the requirement that candidates must have survived two cycles of the *Lua,* and while they need not come from the senior sub-clan or, in the case of the *Āletā,* from the oldest clan in the tribe, they must be selected by members of that descent group. A *Woma* must always be available for consultation, so that the elders from the countryside may meet daily at his homestead to enjoy the satisfaction of associating with such a prestigious person as well as to form a perpetual *songo* for resolving disputes.

CHANGE

Since the conquest of the Sidamo by Emperor Menelik's armies in 1893 the *Lua* has continued despite a time lag in class intervals, owing to the interference and hostility of some Ethiopian government officials. Though individual governors have supported the rituals even to the point of giving a bull as a sign of friendship for the Sidamo people, most officials have reacted negatively because of the ethnic solidarity implications of the system and the fact that fighting often occurs with other tribes. Informants agreed, however, that the only significant change in addition to the delay in promotions has been the practice of purchasing cattle to be placed in wooded areas in Arusi, Jamjam, or Gugi country. Today, instead of actually raiding cows during the seven years following initiation the new *Lua* members simply go to the forest, kill a bull, cut off its tail, then, just as was done in the past, present these animals and the tail to their *Gadane*. Nevertheless, this relatively peaceful symbolic capture sometimes leads to conflict with the aforementioned groups.

There are signs that the reciprocal bonds of authority and service between generations are beginning to break down, for old men often complain that the young no longer have respect for them. Much of the strain may be attributable to the developing cash economy and the increasing opportunities for the young to acquire formal education away from the tutelage of the elders. The marketing of coffee is providing them with a previously unattainable degree of economic independence and their new literacy, though sometimes resented, is increasingly important to the old men who have little understanding of modern financial transactions (Hamer, 1967:84–85). Nevertheless, there is a consensus among all generations that the *Lua* continues to be significant in the lives of men because it is still considered "shameful" not to have a *Lua* name, elderhood continues to be an admired status, and the generational classes provide support for the mediating role of the *Gadane* who in the opinion of many informants is called upon more frequently than in the past to settle disputes. Even the Ethiopian courts will often request the latter to verify points of traditional Sidamo law and to assist in settling cases out of court.

The Ethiopian court system is providing an indirect influence for change to the extent that it is beginning to impinge upon the jurisdiction of the *songo*. With greater pressure to put more land under coffee production, boundary disputes have been increasing in recent years, and as a consequence men have begun to use the traditional or new judiciary depending on which seems to be most advantageous at the time. What constitutes an advantage is dependent on the estimate of probability for a favorable decision by the elders or whether the other party to the dispute can be frightened into concessions merely by threat of court action. In the long run this tends to undermine the authority of the old men and the whole gerontocratic system. The elders bemoan what they refer to as the "vengeful" spirit of youth which leads them to prefer the often disruptive force of police sanctions to the conciliatory, unity preserving, approach of the *songo*.

DISCUSSION AND COMPARISON

The existence of the *Lua* as a gerontocratic system of social control can be at least partially explained by examining the connection between several structural and ecological variables. One thing that makes the structure workable for men of all ages is that inequality between is balanced by equality within generations, while at the same time there exists an expectation of ultimately gaining command over the succeeding generation. Secondly, the asymmetrical relationship between generations permits the superordinate elders to allocate and protect wealth in land and cattle of subordinate pre-initiates and those who have already been inducted into the pre-elderhood stages of the class system. Within any generation the patrilineal descent system, which initially favors the eldest son in his acquisition of a larger patrimony and greater authority over his younger male siblings, is balanced by the initiation of all of the latter into the same *Lua* class with the former. Once inducted all have an opportunity to achieve positions of influence within the class by demonstrating superior military prowess, forensic skill, and ability to accumulate wealth. Encouragement of young men by their fathers in these areas of endeavor, combined with the initially ascribed advantage of the eldest son, leads to rivalry among siblings. This competition encourages the kinds of individual attainments which constitute criteria for informal leadership by the time a class is ready for promotion to elderhood. Thus, it is the elders who encourage noteworthy performance among the younger generation and then protect the gains of the latter by settling any conflicts that may arise as a consequence of the competition. In return young men must show respect for the elders and provide those services associated with youth, such as manual labor and military service.

There are a number of rituals serving to institutionalize the generational relationship, including the dramatic introduction through circumcision rites to the decision-making prerogatives of the elder, personification of the connection between wisdom and old age in the role of the *Woma,* and stress on continuity of obligation to deceased generations of elders effectively reinforced by periodic mourning ceremonies. The importance of social cohesiveness within generations regardless of divisions created by membership in different descent groups is emphasized through the role of the *Gadane* who serves both as a mediator and ritual point of focus for all class members.

Given the relatively dispersed small-scale Sidamo population that existed until recent times, the variety of ecological settings has been conducive to widely dispersed horticultural and pastoral subsistence activities. The variation in soil, climate, and rainfall conditions at different altitudes has made it possible not only to grow a number of plant supplements to the staple ensete, which generally provides sustenance when all other food sources fail, but ample pasturage has also been available in one area or another according to the season. Successful exploitation of these resources has been dependent on those aspects of the social and idea systems which encourage movement within and between different ecological zones. We have seen that the clan and residence pattern of the Sidamo is sufficiently flexible to render strangers fictive kinsmen; also the occasional extension of sibling terms to both paternal and maternal cousins who dwell in different localities is suggestive of a potential closeness through genealogical ties that would ease settlement and acceptance in clan territories other than those of birth. Furthermore, though males have primary rights as well as obligations to defend property within the boundaries of their own clan, there is nothing to prevent individuals from settling in the villages of their wives, if doing so will help to increase their wealth. In fact, the stronger the ties between cousins and affines, the greater the opportunity for a man not only to increase his own property, but to provide connections for his sons to help themselves in the following generation. Symbolic indication of the potential importance of these relationships is to be seen in the visitation and gift giving of cousins and affines during the period of seclusion preceding promotion to elderhood. Reinforcement of this bond comes at a time when a man has completed the initiation cycle and will have demonstrated to what extent he has succeeded in attaining fame and influence through oratory, bravery, and the pursuit of wealth. His sons are now ready to begin their initiation cycle, and if they are to become wealthy, they will need resources other than their patrimonies, which may be obtained through the aid of these kinsmen of their father's generation from widely separate locales.

Fathers can assist sons in acquiring wealth as a consequence of the quantity and quality of kinship alliances, but it is the generational class system that will protect the latter wherever they acquire property. The "old men" make decisions based on a knowledge of the traditional Sidamo way of life, circumspection, and adherence to truth. All of these are principles taking precedence over parochial clan loyalties. Because of the more inclusive rights and obligations resulting from these principles a stranger can ask for and receive land where he has no genealogical or even kinship ties and be entitled to participate in decision-making processes involving property, depending on his ascribed status in the generational class system.

Age organization seems to be most highly developed among mobile, diffuse, pastoral nomads. Spencer (1965:299–302) has suggested that in East Africa, Melanesia, and Australia it is a form of structure leading to a dichotomy between old and young men, giving the former authority to control the allocation of women through marriage which is the principal source of wealth and power in these societies. In this paper we have shown how in a predominantly horticultural society, where land is the major source of wealth, generational differences are utilized in support of a gerontocratic political system with the function of allocating and protecting property.

D. R. PRICE-WILLIAMS

19. A Case Study of Ideas Concerning Disease Among the Tiv[1]

Ideas and behavior relating to health and disease among the Tiv of Benue Province, Central Nigeria, have been reported in the literature at different times. Most of these studies have focused on the general principles involved as universal features of the Tiv people. The present study is concerned only with the ideas and social background of disease in one particular locality, namely an area within a certain "clan" called Mbara.

Tiv Division is divided administratively into large areas called septs, composed of a number of clans, which in turn subdivide into kindreds and sub-kindreds.[2] Each clan has a head called *Tyo-or;* the kindred head is called *Ortaregh* (collectively *Mbatarev*). The particular compound in which the present research was conducted was that of the *Tyo-or* of Mbara. It is important to note that in the year to which the following data refer (1959), fairly sophisticated notions about health and disease ran side by side with indigenous ideas. The former, however, were restricted to those young adults and children who had been influenced by missionaries and by the administrative education. Six miles from the *Tyo-or*'s compound lay a missionary dispensary and four miles away another one run by the Administration. Nevertheless the ideas and practices to be described were fairly widespread throughout the area, and it was not uncommon to find that those who visited the dispensaries, or who had even an outline knowledge of European medicine, also engaged in these purely indigenous practices.

SOURCE: D. R. Price-Williams, "A Case Study of Ideas Concerning Disease Among the Tiv," *Africa,* Vol. 32, No. 2, April 1962, pp. 123–31. Reprinted by permission of the author and publisher.

[1] My thanks are due to the authorities at the S.U.M. Hospital at Mkar, particularly to Dr. Grey, for permission to gather material on the incidence of disease in the area. The writing was greatly aided by the comments of Dr. Paul Bohannan on an earlier draft, and by my collegues of the Anthropological Department of the London School of Economics.

[2] The terms "clan," "kindred," "clan-head" are not used in the anthropological sense, but designate the administrative units.

GENERAL OUTLINE OF RESPONSE TO ILLNESS

The general feature of illness among the Tiv is that it is interpreted in a framework of witchcraft and malevolent forces. The sequence of events is that if a man becomes sick he assumes that he is either being assailed through witchcraft or that he has offended what are known as *akombo*. This is the key term in the unraveling of Tiv reaction to illness. It has more than one meaning. Basically it refers to non-human forces. As East has defined it in his annotation of Akiga's story: "The *akombo* are supernatural agencies. If a man is continually unlucky, or is attacked by illness which does not yield to normal treatment, he assumes that he has committed an offence against one of them."[3] At the same time as implying supernatural agencies, the term actually designates (with the appropriate name) the symptoms of a disease. Thus *akombo* X conveys certain symptoms and *akombo* Y other, different, symptoms. The term also refers to some emblem—a piece of pot, a gourd, an arrow with colored marks on it, and so on—which Tiv use as protections against the same supernatural agencies. Disease is a manifestation of only one kind of *akombo*. Abraham[4] designates eight classes: illness, birth, hunting, rendering arrows efficacious, fertility of crops, good luck, obtaining wives, and certain others which are kept for special reasons in a bin. This classification is, as Abraham himself remarked, not a watertight one, and suffers from the inevitable drawback of making systematic divisions where none such exist. Nevertheless it is true that Tiv employ classifications of *akombo,* although this may vary from one district to another. This particular point will be amplified in more detail later.

If a man does believe that he is ill for such a reason, then he will have recourse to a diviner (*or-u-ishor*), who will indicate to him the nature of his illness, that is, will categorize the particular *akombo* that is believed to be concerned, and will also indicate to the patient which particular kin are involved in this illness. The patient will then return to his compound, call together the relevant kin, and have a discussion with them. The next stage is to consult a man who is

---

[3] Rupert East (trans. and ed.), *Akiga's Story: The Tiv Tribe as seen by one of its Members.* O.U.P., 1939.

[4] R. C. Abraham, *The Tiv People,* 2nd ed. Crown Agents, 1940.

known in the area as being capable of performing the healing ceremony (simply called, in Tiv, *kwaghsoron,* literally "a setting right of the matter") related to the *akombo* involved. The patient will go through this ceremony in front of kinsfolk, take the medicine, and the sequence is finished. If he does not get better, then the whole sequence may have to be repeated.

THE *AKOMBO* SYSTEM

An unraveling of what may be called the *akombo* system is basic to the understanding of Tiv reaction to illness. For this purpose different aspects of it will be treated in turn.

1. PRACTITIONERS AND PATIENTS

If a man is ill he will go to a diviner himself, but a married woman will be taken by her husband or an unmarried woman by her father. The diviner himself may be an agnate of the patient or guardian, but this is not necessarily so. A man who has achieved some fame in the art will be consulted, irrespective of kin relationships. The performer of the *kwaghsoron* calls for special comment. In principle any man who has himself gone through all the necessary stages concerning any particular *akombo,* as described below, is then entitled to perform its corresponding ceremony—to "repair it," as Tiv say—for others. In practice anybody can set himself up as such a practitioner and rationalize the position. There is no particular status term for a person who repairs *akombo.* Tiv merely call the man by his individual name, or if pressed for a description say *or-u-akombo* (a man of *akombo*). That it is convenient to use the term here does not indicate that this is a Tiv usage. The only distinction that Tiv make, by common recognition, is that certain men know more about matters of *akombo* than others. This means that whereas there are a number of people who are able to perform the *kwaghsoron* of only one or two of the main *akombo,* few are able to perform all or a great number of them. In the Mbara clan there were only three such men, whereas there were a large number of those who were masters of a single *akombo.* An analysis of the kinship ties of such practitioners in the *Tyo-or*'s kindred showed that it was the brothers of the latter who were solely concerned. The following list shows the individual names of the brothers of the clan head with the names of the *akombo* they were said to be able to repair. (In addition another brother, Daga, was a diviner.)

Mode (the *Tyo-or*)	*Igbe*
Moji (died some years previously and followed by eldest son, see below)	Known as the main *or-u-akombo* in the kindred, and possibly the clan.
Foo	*Igbe*
Anakaa	Various minor *akombo,* and regularly assisted the present leading *or-u-akombo.*
Gatti	Various minor *akombo*
Agida (died during the research)	*Iwa*
Igor	*Iwa*

The eldest son of the deceased Moji, by the name of Ankungul, had taken over his father's role as the man who knew most about *akombo* in the kindred, and was thus the busiest and most prolific *or-u-akombo* in the kindred.

It was once put to the investigator by a *Tyo-or* of a neighboring clan that there should be only one leading *or-u-akombo* for an entire clan. When it was pointed out that in Mbara there were at least three, his reply was that this was a bad thing and made for conflict. While this is certainly true, it is suspected that Mbara was not alone in this. Indeed the lack of any formal procedure in matters concerning *akombo* and the questioning of knowledgeable people in other clans suggests that this was indeed the case. But the available evidence tells us that it is the concern of agnates.

2. CLASSIFICATION AND SYMPTOMS

By placing the focus on illness, in the sense in which this term is understood in the West, one is inevitably changing the emphasis from the way in which Tiv themselves regard *akombo.* For, in common with a great many other people, Tiv do not regard "illness" or "disease" as a completely separate category distinct from misfortunes to compound and farm, from relationship between kin, and from more complicated matters relating to the control of land. But it would be completely erroneous to say that Tiv are not able, in a cognitive sense, to recognize disease. As Bohannan has said: "The concept of a disease is not foreign to the Tiv: mumps, smallpox, . . . yaws and gonorrhoea are all common and each has a name."[5] What is meant is that disease is seldom viewed in isolation. As has already been noted, there are various other *akombo* than those of illness. However, within the class of *akombo* relating to illness, Tiv employ certain classifications which may vary from district to district. In the clan in which this study was done two main classifications which corresponded fairly well were given to the writer. The first was represented in a kinship manner: that is, *akombo* was a man who had sons, and these sons had further sons.[6] Each son and some of the sons' sons had signs (*kwav*) which indicated to those who could read them which *akombo* it was. The list given below represents *akombo*'s "sons" with their appropriate symptoms or signs as they were reported verbatim. The descriptions had a large measure of consistency for the area inasmuch as there was agreement on the symptoms for each *akombo* mentioned.

Swende   A cough. Spoils a woman's pregnancy. If it seizes (*kor*) a man, he cannot have children.

Twer   A person is unable to walk properly—he walks like a snake. The body gets very heavy. A person begins to shake.

Igbe   A person cannot stop defecating. Vomiting and headache. If a woman is pregnant the blood flows away too much.

Dam   Cough, headache, eye trouble. A person gets thinner and thinner. The mouth gets drier and drier. A person is unable to speak properly.

Imande   A person sweats all over the body. A big red spot may appear on the body. The mouth gets very big, the eyes become red. The toes look as if they have been burned.

Iwa   Pain around the waist. The penis doesn't work properly. Pain in the stomach. Eye trouble. A man's farm is unsuccessful. A thunderstorm will strike a man's hut or farm.

Kwambe   Boils or swellings all over the body.

Megh   If you run and break your leg. In hunting you cannot shoot properly. If you go to market and you are not able to sell anything. If you get married, you will not be able to bring your wife into the compound.

[5] Laura and Paul Bohannan, *The Tiv of Central Nigeria*. International African Institute, 1953.

[6] The classification was put forward only as an analogy. It must not be considered that Tiv really thought *akombo* to be a person.

Ahina   Bad cough. Spoils pregnancy. Has a connection with the
  birth of twins.

All these main *akombo*[7] or sons of *akombo* have smaller ones included in them which can be repaired separately, and which can
represent a stage of the larger *akombo*. For example, *kwambe* has
eight "sons" which represent not only stages but often a further
"sign." One of them for instance, *kwambeityo* by name, has the
particular sign or symptom of "blood coming through the teeth; a
wound which does not stop bleeding." Yet this is a wound which is
related to boils or swellings.

The second classification was put in terms of a large road deviating
into paths, and these into smaller paths. This classification corresponded fairly well with the previous one, even if some of the
nomenclature was different. The nine main *akombo* described previously were almost exactly the same. The notable difference from
the first classification was that there was a sharp division made between what was called *akombo ier,* which was the general name
given to matters of childbearing, and *akombo gbande* which referred
to sickness proper. This division appears to agree with Abraham's
original classification and makes explicit the distinction which Tiv
appeared to draw in their actual behavior relating to *akombo,*
though they were not always able to verbalize it. There were, in the
area studied, a great number of *akombo* concerned with faulty
childbirth, difficulties arising in childbirth, cases of barrenness in
women and sterility in men. To an outside observer it was difficult to
see why, for example, barrenness in women was sometimes brought
under the heading of *ier* and at other times of *gbande*. Elucidation on
this point was not always very successful, since Tiv are not necessarily
emphatic on abstract schemes of classification, but it transpired that
the categorizing decision turns on an action which the woman was
considered to have performed. For example, looking into a grave
where a corpse lies—something which Tiv women ought not to do—
is supposed to produce barrenness, and in this case the relevant
akombo is *gbande* and not *ier*. Actually the inference is the other way
round: the woman is barren, therefore she must have looked into a

---

[7] There are literally scores of *akombo*. The list given above represents merely
the main ones in the area about whose symptoms there was agreement. A study
of the literature and of neighboring areas at the time of this research shows that
akombo with similar names might have different symptons and *vice versa*. As
with much else in Tiv there is little orthodoxy about this matter.

grave. But the main point is that barrenness could be regarded in two different ways.

3. KINSHIP AND LOCALITY

A *kwaghsoron* is very seldom a private affair; a patient will call together his kin for them to witness that he has undergone the ceremony and for them to partake in the eating of the sacrificial goat or chicken—an important element. One role of the diviner is to indicate which particular kin are involved. There are two important relevant kinship terms: *ityo,* a patrilineage, and *igba,* used in the complementary sense for a man's mother's *ityo.* Sometimes this is called *igba ngo,* since there are three other terms relating to *igba: igba ter,* a man's father's mother's *ityo; igba ter u tamen,* a man's father's father's mother's *ityo;* and a man's mother's mother's *ityo,* which is called *igba ngo u tamen.*[8] When an individual visits a diviner, the latter may tell him either to call his *ityo* together, in which case a man will call together his brothers, or he will be told to call his *igba,* in which case the mother's brothers will be consulted. This is the simplest case, but the combination of generations and compound make for various possibilities. These are as follows:

(*a*) *ityo only.* An individual's brothers are summoned, and the *kwaghsoron* is performed in his father's compound, that is, his own compound.

(*b*) *igba only.* This is exemplified in the case when a man's wife is ill or barren. She is taken back to her father's compound and the husband's mother's brothers are summoned. There is also the case, which comes under this heading, when a man's wife is barren or ill, the *kwaghsoron* is held in his own compound, and the husband's mother also participates in the ceremony. In this instance (shown in the photographs of *akombo kwambe*) a brother of the wife is present, and also the witness to their marriage. All four of the *igbas* listed can be involved in *akombo* situations, the locality of the *kwaghsoron* turning on which particular one is involved.

(*c*) *ityo and igba together.* This occurs in the *ityumben* ceremonies, which are concerned with the birth of children and stages in infancy and childhood. Both the child's father's brothers and the child's mother's brothers are witnesses. The relevant *kwaghsoron* is

[8] See Laura and Paul Bohannan, op. cit., pp. 23–25, and Laura Bohannan, "Political aspects of Tiv social organization" (p. 38), in John Middleton and David Tait (eds.), *Tribes without Rulers.* Routledge & Kegan Paul, 1958.

sometimes held at the place where the mother and father were married.

4. THE CONTINUITY OF AKOMBO

As indicated above, ceremonies for each "big" *akombo* are composed of stages which could be performed separately. For example, *igbe* has the following stages: (i) *igbechire,* (ii) *igbekwan,* and (iii) *chicheven.* These can be taken one at a time until the final stage is reached, which is *igbe* proper. A person for whom all these stages have been performed is regarded as having mastered this particular *akombo.* This seemed to be the rule for all the *akombo.* But whether a stage of the final ceremony is performed on a particular occasion depends to a large extent upon the severity of the state of affairs. A small stage of *igbe* could be "repaired" (in which case there need be no sacrifice of animals, nor even kin present) if a man, as it was put, "just became entangled with *igbe* in some way." This could mean that he had merely improperly entered a hut at the doorway of which had hung the piece of black pot which symbolized *igbe.* At the other extreme a serious show of the symptoms that were said to characterize *igbe* would result in gathering of kin and the killing of chickens and goats. Nevertheless, a person is able to complete *igbe* by degrees. The continuity of *akombo* in this manner goes beyond one man's lifetime. It has been seen that *akombo* are connected with a lineage segment; at this point it needs to be added that the stages can be spread across the generations. One explanation often given for a person having a particular set of symptoms is that his father had not "completed" the relevant *kwaghsoron.* Thus it was explained that if *akombo iwa,* for example, seizes you, then it is because your father had not completed his *akombo.* If the father is alive then he must attend the *kwaghsoron* and participate in it. If he is dead then his son is in some way regarded as having completed it for him. The relevant unit of analysis is therefore not so much the individual as the lineage segment.

There is another aspect of the continuity of *akombo:* namely, the notion that they are regarded as a progression to the good things of life. Reference here is to what has been called in the literature *akombo biamegh* and *po'or. Biamegh* is a grand ceremony that will involve not only one's kin, or only the clan, but the entire Tiv land. When *biamegh* is celebrated (very rarely, for the expense is great), *akombo* specialists from all over the land will come to the place where it is being held, and the proceedings are likely to last for several days. *Po'or* is the name given to a bin in which, according to the old lore, human heads were kept. Again there are big rites connected with it. Both *biamegh* and *po'or* are what the Tiv call *akombo-a-tamen* ("great" *akombo*), which directly involve social groups and not individuals, and are concerned with such matters as possession of land, not with illness. The ramifications involved are complicated, and the writer is not equipped to go into them.[9] The point to be made here is that there is a positive notion of continuity with the other *akombo*. *Biamegh* and *po'or* are looked upon as extensions which cannot be entered until all the other *akombo* are completed by an individual or by his father in the way that has been described. With these two "great" *akombo* we are moving away from pure "disease" to questions of social control. In fact one *akombo* specialist, in contradistinction to other *akombo* specialists and to the literature, did not consider *biamegh* and *po'or* to be *akombo* at all. *Akombo,* he said, meant "sickness," but *biamegh* had to do with good clothes and enjoyment, property and so on— good things generally. The merging of concepts of disease with others concerning acquisition of property, status, and control is a complexity that would take much further research to unravel. Some general line of progression, however, is quite clear.

5. PAYMENT

All *kwaghsoron* ceremonies involve payments. These are made by the patient to the *or-u-akombo* in cash, and also in buying the sacrificial animals. Very often a man's brothers, especially the senior brother, will help him if payment is too heavy to be borne alone. These ceremonies can be costly. A chicken costs about 3*s.:* a goat, 30*s.:* a sheep, 40*s.* In addition, if the chicken were not considered to be big enough, payment in cash would be added "to make the chicken bigger." In some of the large *akombo* proceedings, a payment of some £4–5 may be made, on top of the initial payment for animals. It has been explained that the ceremonial for a large *akombo* can be done in stages and there are different payments for each stage. The stages, of course, require a smaller payment than for

[9] But see Laura and Paul Bohannan, op. cit., pp. 88–90, and East, op. cit., pp. 196–205.

the whole, but in many cases (the writer calculated) it would have been cheaper for a person to have completed the whole *akombo* at one ceremony. Here is an example of the payments relating to the stages of an *ityumben* ceremony.

(1) *ikombo:* a rat only required; (2) *atumba inhundu:* a fowl, plus 1*s;* (3) *angov:* a chicken, plus 6*d.;* (4) *ikungul:* 2 chickens (cock and hen) plus 4*s.;* (5) *icigh* (two kinds but the payment is the same): 1 fowl, 1 male goat, plus £3.

In this case the stages relate to different ages of the infant and child, but the following payments, relating to the *akombo* called *twer,* do not necessarily refer to definite ages in the adult but merely to parts of the whole which have to be done to complete it, each of which, of course, might be done at different periods of a man's life. The stages are given without names:

(1) Beer, 1 chicken; (2) 2*s.;* (3) 15*s.;* (4) 3*s.;* (5) 3*s.;* (6) 1 goat (two sub-stages here, 1 goat for each); (7) 1 goat; (8) (*a*) 1 goat; (*b*) 1 cock; (9) 1 frog and 1 cock; (10) *twer* proper, also called *gbandetwer.* A very big *akombo* involving a great many chickens and more than one goat. Informants were unable to give a definite price in cash; they merely said that it was "big."

The actual payment of money is handed over to the *or-u-akombo* at specific stages during the ceremony. Sometimes several small *akombo* (i.e. the stages themselves) are performed at one time: the payment for each is then made after each has finished. An extra 1*s.* is also paid for the actual medicine.

A further aspect of payment concerns the distribution of food. The sacrificial animals are cooked, cut up, and distributed at the ceremony. Pieces are then given to the kin present, the best going to the senior members. A distinguished guest, such as the investigator, was usually given the best piece. The food was often eaten there and then, but if any of the kin are visitors, e.g. a wife's brothers, the food is taken away, wrapped in large leaves, and eaten back at their own compounds. The display of food indicates to absent kin that the *akombo* has indeed been set right.

IDEAS OF CAUSATION

Linked to the notions of *akombo* and disease is the idea of action by witches. A person becomes ill, can die or be harmed in some other way, through the actions of people, collectively called the *mbatsav,* who operate their machinations secretly. The term comes from the central concept *tsav,* which refers basically to witchcraft substance, and is said to grow on a person's heart during his lifetime. Bohannan has also characterized *tsav* as meaning power, talent, ability.[10] *Tsav* is essentially a neutral power: it can be turned to good ends as well as to bad. In fact the *mbatsav,* as earlier ethnographers have shown, have the dual role of custodians of the land and its spoilers. With regard to disease the *mbatsav* can either make a person ill directly, or invoke an *akombo* force.[11] (This, incidentally, gives three postulated causes of disease, as an individual can, as already described, bring an *akombo* force on himself without the *mbatsav* necessarily being involved.) Actually the grades of severity of a disease suggest its causation. That is to say, if a *kwaghsoron* with its associated medicines fails to aid a person, then witchcraft is postulated and a moot is held to find the person or persons responsible. This continues right up to death; indeed there is very rarely a "natural" death, it must have been the result of *mbatsav.*[12] The identity of the latter is sought among kin. As Akiga has put it: "The Tiv do not bewitch people indiscriminately. You only bewitch a near relative, on your mother's or father's side, who has done you some wrong."[13] An examination of those who were thought to be *mbatsav* in the compound and neighboring area under research indicated that it was the agnates who were considered. It was further recognized that there might be degrees of bad *tsav,* inasmuch as there was wholehearted affirmation as to some particular people being *mbatsav,* but doubt as to others. This differentiation did not, as far as could be discovered, correlate with any status rela-

[10] Laura and Paul Bohannan, op. cit., pp. 84–85.

[11] For case histories of this see especially Nos. 3, 4, and 6 of Paul Bohannan, "Homicide among the Tiv of Central Nigeria," in Paul Bohannan (ed.), *African Homicide and Suicide.* Princeton University Press, 1960.

[12] W. A. Malherbe, in an unpublished manuscript kept at Mkar Hospital and lent to me by kind permission of the S.U.M. authorities, recognizes four classes of death, of which only one is death by witchcraft or *akombo,* while the remainder could be categorized as death due to accident or natural causes, for example starvation. While this may be correct as far as it goes, this kind of classification does not indicate that Tiv acknowledge two causes, of death or illness, which Bohannan (in a personal communication) has called a volitional and an instrumental cause. Sometimes a man dies as a direct result of witchcraft, for example, by poison. Sometimes a man dies through the medium of a "natural" illness, but brought on through witchcraft.

[13] East, op. cit., p. 246.

tions among kin. Again, sometimes the term is applied, irrespective of kinship relations, to people who tend to live alone or who are strange in some way, particularly if they are antisocial.

Ideas of causation are closely tied in with the fundamental Tiv axiom, stressed by the early ethnographers such as Abraham and Downes,[14] and reiterated by Bohannan, that good life, good health, and good luck proceed in an unbroken straight line if not disturbed by evil influences, such as the *mbatsav*. As explained under the heading of continuity of *akombo,* such disturbances can be referred to previous generations. . . . The matter of continuity, and responsibility of kin for their children, leads to the question of preventive practices. In view of the Tiv axion already quoted it may seem contradictory to speak of practices which are preventive. For if this axiom is held why perform them, since everything is already going smoothly? Yet preventive ceremonies do exist, especially for ensuring the birth of children. One explanation is that although the concept of prevention would certainly not be foreign to a Tiv, the semantic difference that is made in English between it and "cure" is not so sharp to him. In this connection one incident throws light on the distinction, or rather lack of it. When one *or-u-akombo* was demonstrating, purely for the writer's benefit, the manner in which he dealt with *akombo igbe,* three women joined in to go through the procedures and take the medicine. This clearly was not for display but because they wished to have the medicine. These women had not the symptoms for *igbe,* so the *kwaghsoron* was not performing any function of "cure." Their answer to the question why they had joined in was that in this way they would get stronger. In this manner "prevention" might be looked upon as a booster to an already established order, as in fact a prophylactic.

[14] R. M. Downes, *The Tiv Tribe.* Government Printer, Kaduna, 1933.

J. H. M. BEATTIE

20. Nyoro Mortuary Rites[1]

Like other people, Banyoro fear death. In rural Bunyoro, as in most other simple peasant communities where western medical aid, though becoming increasingly available, is still exiguous, illness and death are a part of everybody's experience. People contract sudden illnesses and die, and the rate of infant and child mortality, especially, is high; there are few families which have not lost one or more children. Nyoro peasants do not believe that death comes by chance; it is almost always attributed to sorcerers, ghosts, or other malevolent non-human agents. Yet although these various forces may cause a man to die, the death[2] that they bring upon him is thought of as being a power in its own right. As in other cultures, death is figuratively represented as a real being, almost as a person. There are many sayings which represent it in this way, and, also, explicit or implicit references to the personalized notion of death enter into many Nyoro personal names.[3]

When a person dies, old people—usually old women of the household, or neighbors—close the eyes and mouth of the corpse, shave the hair and beard, trim the finger nails, and clean and wash the

SOURCE: J. H. M. Beattie, "Nyoro Mortuary Rites," *Uganda Journal*, Vol. 25, No. 1, March 1961, pp. 171–83. Reprinted by permission of the author and publisher.

[1] My fieldwork in Bunyoro was carried out during 1951–53, and for a part of 1955, chiefly under the auspices of the Treasury Committee for Studentships in Foreign Languages and Cultures, London. The following notes derive mostly from two informants, the late Mr. Perezi Mpuru, whose untimely death in 1953 deprived Bunyoro of a native ethnographer of great potential ability, and Mr. Lameki Kikubebe.

[2] *Orufu.*

[3] Thus, for example, it is commonly said that "Death is unknowable" (*orufu turumanyirwe*), that is, it is unpredictable, and also that "Death is ignorant; it takes the young and leaves the old" (*orufu turumanya: rwita omuto, ruleka omukuru*). For some account of the part played by the concept of death in personal nomenclature, cf. J. H. M. Beattie "Nyoro Personal Names," *Uganda J.*, 21 (1957), pp. 101–2.

body. The limbs are straightened out in line with the body; it is said that if they are stiff they can be straightened by pouring water on them. The body remains in the house for a day or two with its face uncovered, so that relatives and neighbors may come and see it for the last time. During this period the women of the household weep and cry out loudly; men are not supposed to weep noisily.

When the deceased was the head of the household[4] a rite[5] used to be performed before the body was wrapped up, which symbolized the close attachment between the dead man and his dependents, an attachment now broken by death. Some grains of millet (the traditional staple of Bunyoro), mixed with simsim and fried cow-peas,[6] were placed in the dead man's right hand. This mixture, often eaten on ceremonial and other occasions, is called *ensigosigo*. Each of the dead man's children approached, took in his lips a small quantity of the mixture from the corpse's hand, and ate it. This signified the end of his fatherly care for them; in many contexts in Bunyoro close attachment between two people (parent and child, grandparent and grandchild, lovers, and others) is expressed by one taking from his own dish a small morsel of food, molding it in his fingers, and putting it in the other's mouth.[7]

When neighbors and relatives have seen the body, it is tightly wrapped up in grave clothes in preparation for burial; formerly bark cloth (now very expensive) was used, but nowadays blankets and sheets are more usual. If the deceased was a man, the body is wrapped by men; if a woman, by women. Formerly a rich man might be wrapped in five or six large bark cloths. The cloths now used should be newly purchased from the shops, and they should be contributed by the friends of the deceased and, especially, by his sons-in-law. Only if he lacked both friends and sons-in-law would money from his estate be used.

If the deceased was a household head, certain rites had to be performed by one of his sister's sons,[8] real or classificatory, as soon as possible after his death. All of these tasks symbolize the destruction of the household of which the deceased was the head and with which he was ritually identified. The sister's son has to wrench out

[4] *Nyineka.*
[5] Called *enteterwa.*
[6] *Enkole nyamugobe.*
[7] I am told that for hygienic reasons the ceremony of *enteterwa* is no longer performed.
[8] *Baihwa.*

the central pole of the house (this would only be possible in the old-fashioned beehive type of house, where there are several poles to support the roof), and he throws this in the middle of the courtyard. Also taken out is the dead man's eating basket,[9] his bowl, and the cooking stones from the hearth; like the household head, the fire which forms the center of the home is extinguished. There will be no fire or cooking in the house until the first three or four days[10] of mourning have passed. A banana plant from the household's banana grove, with fruit on it, is also added to the heap. Then the sister's son should go to the well with the household water pots; he brings back some water in it, and he then breaks it in the middle of the courtyard, among the other things. These various things are broken or just scattered in the courtyard, though the sister's son has the right to take utensils or other articles that are of some use if he wants to. Traditionally, that house would not be lived in again, but a new one would be built nearby, the traditional Nyoro house being a compact, beehive-like structure which can be built in a day.

Other acts that the sister's son is expected to perform are likewise symbolic. He should catch and kill the cock which was master of the dead man's poultry; it would not do for the cock to crow, and thus act like the head of a household, when its master was dead. Even a male goat may be killed, and it is said that in former days when Banyoro had cattle the chief bull of the herd might be slaughtered. Such an animal would not be slaughtered until four days after the household head's death, but its testicles would be ligatured at once, to prevent it from engaging in any sexual activity during the time of first mourning. The meat of a fowl or animal so killed belongs to the sister's son, but it would be shared with others of the household. This killing of male animals, so that when the head of the household no longer rules no other creature in it shall do so either, is called *mugabuzi*. If there is no sister's son to carry out these tasks, some other person, not a member of the family, is selected to perform them.

The grave is dug soon after death, the next morning if the death took place at night. The dead man may have selected the site himself, perhaps in his banana grove; in any case it will be very near his home. The grave should not be dug by the deceased man's relatives, but by his friends and neighbors: only men may dig it. The per-

[9] *Ndiro.*
[10] Three for a woman, four for a man: see post.

son who begins the digging is called the gravemaker (*kihanga mbya*). One man digs at a time. These people come to dig because of their regard for the dead person, and also because they know that when they die or lose a relative others will help them: it may be difficult to find gravediggers for an unpopular man, and this can be very awkward for his family. Banyoro express this obligation tersely in the phrase "a dead person isn't meat."[11] The point is not unsubtle, and shows the delicacy with which Banyoro think of neighborly relations; it is that one need feel no compunction in going to a burial, as one might in going at ordinary times to a house where meat was, for in the latter case the householder might have wished to keep it for himself or his cronies, or perhaps to dry and preserve it, in which case a visit would be an embarrassment to him.

The grave is long enough to accommodate the corpse at full length, and also for the two men who will stand in the grave to receive it. It is usually about seven feet long, about five to seven feet deep, and about four feet across. In traditional burial there is a narrower, coffin-like cavity along the bottom, about eighteen inches deep, in which the body is laid.[12] When the digging is finished one of the diggers descends with a number of strong sticks about three to four feet long; these will be laid transversely across the lower cavity to prevent earth from falling or pressing on the body.

Burial should take place in the morning or afternoon, not in the middle of the day, as it would be bad if the sun shone directly into the grave. When all is ready, the body is brought by some older men, who make sure that it has been properly wrapped. If the dead person was a man, the last cloth is secured at the front of the house, in the doorway; if a woman, in the inside room. At this time women are expected to moderate their weeping. The body is borne out through the gateway of the compound and taken to the grave. Everyone follows (except that a pregnant woman should not attend a burial; it might cause her to miscarry), and the group gathers round the grave. There is no weeping there. Two men get into the grave to receive the body, which may be let down with ropes.

The body of a man is laid on its right side; that of a woman, on its left; these are the proper positions for men and women to adopt when sleeping. The head is placed toward the east. Then the sticks

[11] *Omufu taba nyama.*
[12] Nowadays this lower cavity is not made when a coffin is used (sometimes it is not made even when there is no coffin).

are laid, close together, across the bottom trench where the body now lies, a mat is laid on the sticks, and old clothes or bark cloths on top of that. This prevents soil from falling on the body. The children of the deceased then sprinkle the first earth on the grave; they may scoop it up with their hands, but first they would, traditionally, brush a little in with their elbows, three times for a woman, four for a man. Males use their left elbows, females their right. The significance of this custom is that the survivors' hands are no longer of use to them, since they cannot now carry out their proper function of serving the deceased. Others may do likewise. This is an important act in showing good will toward the deceased and solidarity with his descendants; a person may curse[13] another by saying to him "even if I die, you shall not sprinkle earth on me,"[14] and such a curse is a very serious one. Care is taken to replace the red earth from the bottom of the grave first, leaving the darker earth from nearer the surface till the end, so as not to frighten people and make them unhappy by leaving the telltale red clay on the surface. If the deceased was a small infant, the mother may squeeze a few drops of breast milk into the grave before it is filled up. When the grave is half full of earth, the stick which was used to measure the corpse before the grave was dug is thrown in and buried; it is said that if this were not done, the measuring stick might be taken and used by sorcerers. When all the earth has been put back it is trampled down.

Until the burial is finished, no one should leave the grave; the gravediggers should not be left there by themselves. Nor, indeed, should anybody else. Anyone so left behind might say "they have left us so that death may come and kill us."[15] Also, the grave should not be left unattended before the burial; if it is it may demand another person to be buried in it. Should a grave be dug prematurely and the supposedly dying person recover, a large banana stem[16] is brought and buried in the grave instead.

The hoe used to dig the grave, which should be the one the dead person used, was formerly left on the grave, together with the basket which was used for removing the earth. These should not be used again by the bereaved family but the hoe at least might be picked up and used by others: nowadays it may be sold, and the proceeds

[13] *Kyena.*
[14] *Nobundifa otalinsensaho eitaka.*
[15] *Batulekeire orufu ruleke rutuite.*
[16] *Mugogo.*

spent on beer for the gravediggers. Other small personal effects of the deceased, such as his bowl or his drinking gourd, might also be left on the grave.

After the grave has been filled in, the gravediggers are given water to wash themselves with; it is believed that if they were to walk through their fields with earth from the grave still adhering to their feet and legs, their food crops would rot. They also cut a small bit of their hair, back and front, and throw this on the grave. After they have drunk their beer the grave is left, but after a few days (four in the case of a man, three in the case of a woman) lumps of smelted iron[17] may be heaped on the grave, or sometimes just large stones. These are put there simply to mark the grave so that people will know that it is there and will not dig or build there. To do so might bring back the death, especially if a house should be built over a grave, when all the people of the house might sicken or die. Ghosts and evil spirits are thought to haunt burial places, and they might make a person dream, perhaps demanding something very difficult to provide, like the sacrifice of a baby, if evil is to be averted.[18]

During the day of the burial nobody in the village does any agricultural work. For anyone to do so would suggest that he was a heartless person (and therefore very likely a sorcerer); also, it is said that crops planted or tended on such a day would not yield as they should.

Older informants say that formerly if a person died very ill-disposed toward someone in the family, the mouth and anus of the corpse might be stopped up with clay; it was supposed that this would prevent the ghost[19] from escaping and causing injury to the people against whom it had a grudge.

After the grave is filled in the party returns to the house, and the women's keening breaks out afresh. Everybody speaks of the goodness of the deceased, especially to his mother. The women cry out in various set phrases, of which the following are examples:

"He is dead, my strong buffalo, my beautiful one: he has gone; he shall not be forgotten."[20]

---

[17] *Butale.*
[18] Even today it is not uncommon for a family to move away altogether from a place where one or two of its members have died: "this place is bad for us; it haunts us" (*kururuma*), they may say.
[19] *Muzimu.*
[20] *Afuire, mbogo yange, omurungi wange; atalyeba.*

"He has gone for ever, that good man; he has gone: he shall not be forgotten."[21]

"Death has stolen him from me."[22]

And a wife, especially a favorite one, would often cry:

"Where shall I go? Alas, where shall I go? Now I am a beggar, like a dog, in this house."[23]

The men, who do not weep aloud, may tell the women not to mourn too loudly. But they pay no attention; women's tears, Banyoro say, are always nearer than men's.

On the evening of the day of the burial of a household head, the opener of the grave[24] officiates in a curious rite, in which he takes a handful of a juicy plant[25] and squeezes it with soot in his hand, so that the juice runs down his arm to his elbow. The children of the dead man, of both sexes, have to drink this juice from the elbow of the opener of the grave, as it runs down. This medicine protects them from certain kinds of illness ritually associated with the death. The shoot of a young tree growing from the root of a mature one is sometimes exposed when the grave is being dug, and this also may be used as a medicine for the children of the dead person: the symbolism here seems plain.

On the day of the burial of a household head, a log of firewood may be placed in the center of the courtyard, and the children of the dead man seated on it in turn. The opener of the grave taps each of them on the side of the head with a large food basket,[26] and a small amount of hair from the part of the head thus tapped is cut and thrown away.

After the burial there is a period of full mourning, which lasts for four days for a man, three for a woman.[27] This period is called *ekiragura,* the time of darkness, or the "black" mourning. During this

---

[21] *Ahezere omurungi agenzere omurungi; atalyeba.*

[22] *Rumunyagire orufu.*

[23] *Ndagyaha nyowe male ngende nakaha; munaku wabu mbwa nyowe.*

[24] *Kihanga mbya.*

[25] Called *mugosora.*

[26] *Kibali.*

[27] This constantly reiterated association of the number four with the male sex and three with the female occurs in many cultural contexts in Bunyoro. Its occurrence at death reflects a usage at birth; when a child is born the mother remains inside the house, by the fire place, for four days if the child is a boy, three if it is a girl, without going outside. The association through opposition of birth and death is expressed in the saying "the happiness of birth is equal to the grief of burial" (*okusemererwa kw'okuzarwa kwingana n'okuganya kw'okuzika*).

time no cooking is done. To begin with, the grown-up mourners should fast, though neighbors would bring food for young children; after a day or two increasing quantities of food (but not meat) already cooked, and also beer, are brought by neighbors. Gifts of money, often quite substantial, are also made to the bereaved family, and nowadays European commodities, such as sugar, tea and bread, may be brought. The mourners do not eat from proper vessels; they use leaves, and pieces of broken pots. The deceased's children tie dry banana stem fibers around their waist as a sign of mourning, and nobody in the household washes, shaves, changes his garments, or sleeps on a bed. They cut dry banana leaves[28] and sleep on these, usually spread around a fire made up in the courtyard. This is called *okugaragara,* and may be done by children, mother, clansfolk and wives of a dead household head (though nowadays mostly by men and boys); but married daughters or sisters' children who belong to other households need not do it. During these three or four days of deep mourning, friends and relatives may spend a good deal of time with the bereaved family, perhaps even spending the nights with them, so as to distract them, with conversation about other things, from thinking too much about the dead person and his ghost, which may, by this time, already be abroad.

At the end of these four (or three) days, the mourners go into the high grass a little way from the house, and wash with a decoction of a plant called *mubuza,*[29] shave one another's heads, pare their nails, and anoint themselves with oil. This shaving is called the "black" shaving.[30] They also change into clean clothes, perhaps leaving the old ones there. Some of the hair and nail clippings are

[28] *Isansa.*

[29] The symbolism here seems to depend on a pun; the idea is "to lose, get rid of, the death" (*okubuza orufu*).

[30] *Ekiragura.* Nowadays, when many men have adopted a European-style haircut, it is often enough if a small lock of hair is cut from the front and back of the head. At a funeral in 1953, one of my informants attended the hair-cutting ceremony four days after the burial of a neighbor's infant boy. He merely had two small locks of hair cut in this way. The child's father wished to do likewise, and asked my informant to cut them for him. But the mother of the dead child intervened and insisted that he (the father) should have the whole of his head shaved in the traditional manner. If he did not, she said, she would "do something to myself"—a threat of suicide. The father, a Christian, reluctantly agreed, saying "All right, I will follow the heathen custom *y'ekikafuiri,* but what good will it do? If I am shaved will it bring my child back to life?" In Bunyoro, as elsewhere, old is giving place to new, but not without interpersonal friction and strain in a very wide range of social situations.

collected and thrown on the grave, as also are the dry banana leaves
on which the mourners have slept. After this they return to the
house, led by the man who (if the deceased was the household
head) will take charge of the installation of the heir. This man, who
may be a brother or a close friend of the dead man, is called
mukuza, which means guardian or sponsor; he carries the spear of
the dead household head. On the way back to the house the party
passes through a small, flimsy hut, with a front and a back entrance, which has been erected for this purpose. This symbolizes the
"leaving behind" of the death.

On that day the heir is formally installed, and there is a feast. The
feast is called "the emerging from death."[31] A goat or fowl from the
dead man's estate may be slaughtered for it, and neighbors and
friends also bring contributions of cooked millet and other food, as
well as beer. In particular, the deceased man's sons-in-law,[32] as
also his sisters' husbands, should bring a pot of beer each. If they
do not do this it is said that their wives may not be allowed to
return home with them; the sponsor announces the name of each
one who brings beer. Before the feast begins the heir is formally
installed. He is probably the son of the dead man, and may be
quite a young boy. A special kind of grass[33] is spread in front of the
dead man's house, and the heir sits on the right side, the widow or
widows on the left. Other herbs have also been spread in the
courtyard; sweet-smelling lemon grass,[34] a species of yam,[35] and
a small herb with a pretty white blossom, perhaps a celosia.[36] The
heir is dressed in a bark cloth. Another old man, probably another
of the dead man's close friends, then takes a spear, and, raising it
as though he were about to strike the heir with it in the face, he
approaches him and says:

> "Now you are the heir to your father's stool[37]; be a man; the
> founder dies but a protector (of his line) remains. You should

[31] *Kuturuka orufu.*
[32] *Bako.*
[33] *Ehunda,* or *ebihira bakazi.*
[34] *Etete.*
[35] *Rwihura.*
[36] *Rweza.*
[37] *Kitebe.* This word, which literally means "stool" or "chair," symbolizes the
whole of the father's familial authority. It is often loosely used, as a collective
noun, to denote the local group of agnates subject to that authority.

always welcome your father's old friends.[38] Protect the daughters of the household and treat them fairly. Anything that you find too difficult you should discuss with us old men. Be strong in your father's place; if you refuse to welcome us, your father's friends who used to eat and drink with him, we shall never give you any help. Be a hero like him, and take care of all your clanspeople."[39]

The heir may also be addressed as Rwolekeire (from the verb *kwoleka,* "to show," and the prefix *ru,* referring to death): the meaning is that death is being shown another, future, victim.

After this the sponsor brings the boy into the house, where the dead man's stool has been placed on a bark cloth in its accustomed place, facing and to the right of the doorway, in the place called *rusika rwa nyineka* (the household head's partition, or room). He is seated on the stool. Then his father's spear, perhaps one or two of the tools he mostly used (such as an adze or an ax), and two sticks of a shrub[40] are handed to him. Coffee berries which have been cooked and dried, customarily handed round on polite formal occasions, are brought in, also *ensigosigo* (grains of finger millet and simsim). The sponsor picks up a pinch of this and sprinkles it on the ground, praying "may there be life, wealth, and childbearing; men die, they leave others behind."[41] And the heir also sprinkles some of it before and behind him, and so do the other people present, some of them repeating the same prayer. But the heir does not speak; he has to remain completely silent throughout the ceremony. After this everybody is given coffee berries to chew, and a round basket is put in the middle of the floor for people to put small gifts[42]

[38] *Abanywa b'emikago,* literally partners in the blood pact (*omukago*). This institution, formerly widely practiced and still highly regarded, is now dying out, but the terms are still used to refer to any particularly close and intimate friendship.

[39] The full text of this speech in Bunyoro is as follows: *Mpaho waba mugwetwa wekitebe kyaso, bamusaija, 'hafa katoma hasigara kalinzi,' noiriza abanywebemikago, nolinda abana bahara otalibatwara emikono enyuma, ekirakulemaga oyehanuzege abakuru nabanywani baso, bamanzi ha kitebe kyaso, obwolyanga kutuiriza itwe banywani baso abalyaga nawe nokunywa, titulikufaho nakamu, so yali musaija alya nabantu, naiwe bamanzi nkaso, nolinda bona aboruganda.*

[40] Called *rusinga.*

[41] *Obwomezi, okutunga, okuzara; abantu bafa basiga abandi.*

[42] *Ebirabuko.*

in for the heir, usually ten- or fifty-cent pieces, sometimes shillings. At this time, also, anybody who has a claim against the estate of the dead man introduces himself and explains about the debt he is claiming. Any claim not made now cannot be considered afterwards, except for very good reason, and only if the dead man's wives confirm it. After all this is finished, the heir leaves the stool and retires to remove his bark cloth. Then he begins to dispense food and beer to all the guests. The beer is drunk outside; it is not brought into the house. When everybody has eaten and drunk and the beer is finished, all the guests go home.

After this there is a further period, said formerly to have been two months but now more usually two weeks, during which the condition of ritual danger[43] consequent on the death persists, and certain ritual restrictions have to be observed. This period is called the white mourning,[44] in contradistinction to the "black" mourning, which was, it will be remembered, the period of three or four days immediately after the death. During the time of white mourning the young men of the household may not sleep with women, even with their wives, and they may not even place their hands on the shoulders of any woman (an act which symbolizes sexual intercourse). The women of the household in particular, especially the wives of a deceased household head, are subject to a corresponding prohibition, but children who have left the household and married elsewhere are not. This period is also called the time of "taking care of the *kigoye*."[45] The *kigoye* is a short length of plaited rope of a special grass,[46] the ritual significance of which is referred to below. "Taking care of the *kigoye*" during the period of white mourning implies essentially a ritual obligation on the part of the widow or widows of a dead household head to abstain from sexual intercourse with anyone during this time. At the end of the white mourning everyone in the family should shave their heads again; this is called the "white" shaving, to distinguish it from the earlier shaving, which was the "black" shaving.[47]

[43] *Mahano.*
[44] *Ekyera.*
[45] *Kulinda kigoye.*
[46] Called *esojo.*
[47] *Kumwa ekiragura.* The association of black with impurity, evil and danger, and of white with goodness and purity occurs also in many other Nyoro cultural contexts.

At the end of the period of taking care of the *kigoye* there used to take place a rite called "finishing the *kigoye*,"[48] which has now, I think, fallen out of use. The children of the dead man, with their mother (the deceased's widow) seek out the home of a distant mother's brother[49] in order to "leave the death" there. That is, they seek the home of some distant member of the child's mother's clan (in other words, of the clan from which the dead man obtained a wife); there need be no actual, or even presumed, genealogical relationship. But it must be a house where the bereaved family is not known; if they are known and news of the death has reached there, they will be refused entry, for they are bringing death to the house. If, by good luck, they find the house empty and the door open, they go in and, taking up some ashes from the hearth, they suck them and spit them out again. They also pick some grass from the roof or floor of the house, bite it, and twist it into a short, plaited cord. This they throw in the hearth, or elsewhere in the house. Then they drink some water from the household water pot, and go home. If they find people in the house, but are not recognized, they beg for a drink of water as though they were passing strangers, and surreptitiously pluck the piece of grass, twist it, and leave it there. If they are recognized all is lost, for if their intention is discovered the distant "mother's brother" will be very angry, and may even accuse them in the chief's court. Or, worse still, he might use sorcery against them, or even return the *kigoye* to their home, which would lead to further deaths there.

The next day the widow and her children visit the home of their "real" or nearest mother's brother (i.e. the widow's brother's or, if he is still alive, father's home). He receives them formally, seated on a bark cloth, and asks them: "Did you not spoil the *kigoye?*"[50] "No," they reply. The widow would then, in former times, have been required to perform a further rite before she could enter her father's, or her brother's (her father's heir's) house. A plaited rope of grass (the *kigoye*) is laid across the threshold and she is required to step over this. She may also be required to pass through the long stem of a banana leaf,[51] split longitudinally, which is held up for her to step through. Before she does so she swears as follows:

[48] *Kumara kigoye.*
[49] *Nyinarumi.*
[50] *Ekigoye mutakasise?*
[51] *Kizingonyi.*

"If I have done wrong with regard to the *kigoye* by sleeping with any man, may my *mahano* (magical potency) rise up and kill me this very moment."[52]

If she swears this oath and undergoes this ritual falsely, it is believed that not only will she die, but also she will bring death to her natal family and all her agnates. If it were already known that she had broken the rule of sexual abstinence, she would not be permitted to undergo the ritual or enter her father's house: when she visited there she would have to stay outside, and food would be brought to her in the courtyard. This prohibition lasts as long as the father or his heir lives.

If all is well and the rite is successfully performed, the father or his heir formally seats his daughter and grandchildren on his lap, a rite which in Bunyoro signifies a very close and intimate attachment.[53] The widow may also be decorated with garlands of yam and (?) celosia,[54] and sprinkled with water from a gourd[55] as a sign of welcome and blessing. The guests are then given coffee berries and *ensigosigo,* and they pray in terms similar to those used at their inheritance ceremony: "May there be increase, riches and child-bearing"[56] and "People die, but they leave others behind."[57] All who are present, including children, take pinches of the *ensigosigo* and sprinkle it behind and before. Then they are given food and beer, but they do not stay overnight.

On their way home, young men in the party should find a girl or woman—a stranger, with whom they will have no further contact—and place their hands on her shoulders. And the women should do likewise with some strange male. This gesture, symbolizing sexual intercourse, is the way of "finishing off the death."[58] It is essential

[52] *Obundaba nasobeze ekigoye nabyama nomusaija, hati bunu nfe ntalya nakenfuka.*

[53] This is called *kubukara.* It occurs, also, for example, at marriage, when the bride is seated on the laps of her parents before she leaves her home on her wedding night, and, with her husband, on those of her parents-in-law when she reaches their house.

[54] *Rweza* and *rwihura.*

[55] *Ndembezi.*

[56] *Okwomera, itungo, okuzara.*

[57] *Abantu bafa, basiga abandi.*

[58] *Okumara orufu.* The idea that a state of ritual danger (*mahano*) may be finished by a ritual act of intercourse occurs in other contexts also. For example, an initiate in the Nyoro spirit (*mbandwa*) possession cult may be required to

that the "victim" in each case should not know what is being done, for if he or she reciprocates, the "death" is returned to the person who is trying to get rid of it. For this reason a small boy or girl is often chosen. It is thought to be a bad thing for the unsuspecting recipient, who may become ill and even die as a result. If the person to whom it is done knows or suspects what is happening, she (or he) may resist. In one case of which I was told an unsuspecting foreigner, a Lugbara, whom the niece of a dead person met in a shop when returning home, was, literally, pressed to sit down by means of this ritual "laying on of hands." In another, a young girl, who knew what was being done, suggested fiercely but ineffectually against a similar assault by a young man. Real sexual congress is, of course, no less effective, but again the victim must be unsuspecting; if a woman suspects that she is being "used" in this way, she may return the death to her ravisher by seizing his sexual organs.

If any member of the deceased person's family "spoils" the *kigoye* by sleeping with someone during the period when this is prohibited, he may thus bring death into the mother's brother's house. A sister's child who does this is guilty of a grave ritual offense against his mother's brother, and he is not allowed to enter the latter's house again.

After these ceremonies have been carried out, the mourning is finished, and members of the bereaved family return to normal status.

Except where it has been otherwise indicated, these ceremonies are also carried out when a woman of the household dies. The girl who is to be her heir is chosen, seated on a bark cloth inside the house, and formally advised of her new duties and responsibilities by older women, friends or co-wives of her mother, who are present. These duties mainly relate to the necessity to be welcoming to guests, to cook well for them and so on.

Different funerary ceremonies are prescribed for the King (*Mukama*), and for twins of whom either or both die in infancy. I leave these for discussion in other contexts, adding here only a note on the method of disposing of the bodies of suicides. Suicide is not uncommon in Bunyoro, especially among women. It is almost invariably carried out by hanging from a tree. The proper mode of burial is to dig a grave directly under the tree so that when the rope

---

copulate with one of the initiators, in order to finish off the *mahano* brought about by the secret and sometimes fearful proceedings of initiation, which include, *inter alia,* ceremonial enactments of death and rebirth.

or cloth is cut the corpse falls directly into it. The tree has to be uprooted and completely burned; if this is not done it is believed that it may exercise an evil influence,[59] and other people will be drawn to hang themselves on it.

Incomplete and partial though the foregoing account is, it does suggest one or two points of comparative interest. Most of the symbolism involved is, of course, familiar from other cultures; the stress on the period of ritual and physical uncleanness, for example, the requirement of sexual abstinence, shaving as a rite of transition, and so on. But there are three features, in particular, which, although they may not be peculiar to Bunyoro, are especially expressive of Nyoro ideas and social values. The first is the stress on the importance of the household head, the second is the significant role played by the sister's son, and the third is the underlying antagonism between a man and his affines which is ritually expressed in the curious usage of "finishing the *kigoye*." I conclude with a few words on each of these three themes.

In Bunyoro the head of the family is a most important person. He is the owner[60] of everything the household contains, even the property of his adult sons; he is said to "rule" the household[61] as the king rules the whole country, and everybody in it is expected to be respectful and obedient to him. In a sense he *is* the household, so when he dies it also ceases to exist. This is the reason for its symbolic dismemberment and destruction by the sister's son. It is consistent with this situation that the installation of the new heir is, as we have seen it to be, a very formal matter. For the son who inherits is not simply taking over the property of the dead man; he is assuming his status, and may almost be said to "become" his father. In fact his father's son-in-law (who stand in a relationship of marked inferiority to their father-in-law's lineage) should henceforward address him and behave toward him as a father-in-law.[62] These important aspects of the household head's status are well brought out in the mortuary and inheritance rituals which have been described.

The relationships between sister's son and mother's brother is in Bunyoro an ambivalent one. The sister's son is a "child" of his mother's clan and lineage, and yet at the same time he is a stranger

[59] *Kururuma.*
[60] *Mukama.*
[61] *Eka.*
[62] *Isezara.*

in it. He is a "man from outside"[63]; the child of the "outsider" to whom his mother's group have given a daughter or a sister. This ambivalence expresses itself in Bunyoro, as it does elsewhere, in a number of ritual prescriptions and prohibitions, and it is significant that if there is any breach of these it is the mother's brother not the sister's son who suffers. In this way the sister's son has power over and is said to "rule" his mother's brother. These considerations make the sister's son the appropriate person to carry out the ritual destruction and scattering of effects which symbolize the end of the household head, and of the household which was identified with him. For these acts of violation are *mahano;* they are fearful and dangerous things to do, constituting, as they do, an assault on the principle of patriarchal authority, and no member of the deceased's family could possibly perform them. But the sister's son, who is not a member of the family but an "outsider," can do them with impunity. And he is rewarded with the meat (traditionally the head) of any animal or animals killed in the *mugabuzi* ceremony. It may also be suggested (on evidence from elsewhere; I have not put the hypothesis to Banyoro) that the sister's son is, for the group of his mother's brothers, an appropriate symbol of fertility, since he is living proof of their lineage's capacity to bear children. It is natural, then, that on the occasion of death, which, as we saw, for Bunyoro quite explicitly implies reference also to the idea of birth, death's opposite and complement, the sister's son should play an important role.

I now turn to the third theme and here I suspect that the rite of "finishing the *kigoye*," is also to be understood in the context of inter-group affinal relations. The death which has destroyed the household head has, somehow, to be got rid of by taking it into the clan from which his wife and the mother of his children came, for it cannot be retained in the agnatic group of the dead man. The notion that death, like some other kinds of spiritual powers, is a real entity which may be disposed of by taking it somewhere else but which can never be wholly destroyed, is consistent with other Nyoro ideas about these matters. Some of the spirits which are employed by sorcerers, for example, cannot be destroyed, but may be induced to leave their victims, and can then be disposed of by being left in the bush or elsewhere, where they continue to exist, and may seize other people. But why should the death of the household head be got rid of by depositing it in the house of a distant clansman of his

[63] *Muntu w'aheru.*

widow? I can only suggest, very tentatively, that the answer lies in the relationship of concealed and potential antagonism which, as Banyoro themselves acknowledge, underlies the formal relationship of good will which subsists between a man and the group of his wife's agnates. Whether, at the same time, the very fact that the household head's affines have "given life" to him and to his agnates by providing him with a woman to bear him children, makes it appropriate (because of the identity-in-opposition of birth and death) to return the death to them, I have not the evidence to decide.[64] Such a view would certainly be consistent with the ideology of Nyoro descent grouping, for just as the agnatic group endures—or should endure— so, ideally, does the household head. In a sense the heir *becomes* his father, and so for the paternal lineage there is no death. Hence, perhaps the need for its symbolic removal, and for its disposal among distant affines, members of the group which is most symbolic of mortality, and which, in Bunyoro, is regarded as both enemy and friend.[65]

[64] I owe this suggestion to Dr. Godfrey Lienhardt.

[65] For an account of the ambivalence of affinal relationships in Bunyoro see J. M. H. Beattie "Nyoro Marriage and Affinity," *Africa,* 28, No. 1, January 1958.

PART IV

African Political Institutions

Introduction

A wide variety of political systems exists in African societies. In the smaller scale societies, especially those on the "hunting and gathering" levels, most of the mechanisms for maintaining social control are still embedded in what may be called "social" institutions: the family, extended kin groupings, age-grades, and other socially important institutions such as the Title societies and Secret societies. At the other end of the continuum the complex African societies possess clearly recognized "political" institutions such as kings, administrators, and courts.

One major problem is encountered in studying African political systems. Most of the societies in which they are found are described as "tribes" (which, if anything at all, are "sociological or linguistic groupings") with the result that more emphasis has been placed on "kinship" as a mechanism for social and political control in African societies than is warranted. One notes with some dismay the numerous instances within this text where the anthropologist, conscious that he is conforming to an inadequate convention, eschews the terms district, chiefdom, or kingdom and describes the unit under consideration as a "tribe." African political organizations therefore are not always clearly understood, and the reality of African political life is often distorted.

The nature of social control in small-scale societies is well described by Colson in her article on the Plateau Tonga. In this society, people normally invoke cross-cutting ties and utilize matrilineal as well as patrilineal kinsmen and affines to help solve problems with their neighbors. When, as it sometimes happens, the normal recourse to kinsmen, shared values, and threats of physical harm do not resolve grievances, supernatural sanctions are believed to punish the wrongdoers.

Colson's suggestion that cross-cutting ties with the obligations to settle problems equitably are also used to resolve conflict in societies with highly developed corporate lineages cannot be too heavily underscored. Indeed one suspects that these mechanisms, and not the theoretical models of lineage segment mobilization, are what such people as the Nuer or Tallensi use for solving their problems. After all, regardless of whether lineages are "corporate" or not, their members must solve most of their problems within multilineal villages. What this implies is that the notion of the segmentary lineage system forming the framework for the political systems of such societies as Nuer and Tallensi are open to serious question. One's suspicion is aroused when, as the frontispiece of the study of the supposedly chiefless and lineaged-organized Tallensi, Meyer Fortes has a picture of the "Chief of Tongo." Similarly, one is alarmed to find in a book entitled *Tribes Without Rulers* that most of the societies treated therein have rulers. Obviously something is wrong: The ideology that the important problem-solving entities are the lineages, and not the localized groups with their councils and leaders, has led many anthropologists astray.

The more complex political systems in Africa are found in societies which not only have multilineal villages, but are usually ethnically heterogeneous as well. Most of these societies have myths that their political organizations came into existence as a result of either the peaceful or military domination of local communities by migrating strangers. Indeed, these myths became the basis for the erstwhile beliefs, cited by Wrigley above, that not only political organization but most important elements of African culture were introduced by "invading pastoral Hamites."

The Tutsi of Rwanda, whose complex system of domination of the Hutu is described by Lemarchand, are frequently cited as a case where Hamitic pastoralists conquered and dominated "Negroid" agriculturalists. Of course, the situation is more complex. First of all, many of the Hutu were already organized into small kingdoms when the invading Tutsi arrived. Where the Tutsi conquered some of these kingdoms, they took over many of the Hutu political symbols, such as the royal drum, and elaborated a type of polity not too different from "feudalism" but with specific African traits. Where the Tutsi did not "conquer" the local Hutu, they lived in symbiosis with them until the Europeans arrived, and turned over power to them. Tutsi domination of certain Hutu kingdoms is quite similar to the process by which the migratory Fulani established their control over many societies in Guinea, Mali, and Northern Nigeria. However, where they were unable to establish this dominance, they remained simple herdsmen with socio-political organizations much simpler than those found among the agricultural populations whom they conquered.

The Zande political organization is fairly typical of the large-scale political systems found in Africa. It also might be typical of African policies since, according to Evans-Pritchard, "It is particularly in Africa that relatively large-scale political societies can be studied." The Zande not only have the typical ideology of a conquest state, but the ruling group possesses numerous military and non-military techniques for establishing its domination over ethnically diverse populations. Like many comparable African states, the Zande state had classes of rulers and nobility, administrative apparatuses, judicial mechanisms, economic and fiscal policies, and a military organization. Moreover, the political institutional complex elaborated at the court of the king was duplicated at provincial and district levels. Thus the Zande possessed a political culture, and as they expanded their rule, they imposed this culture on conquered populations. The many similarities between the Zande state and so many African states in West, Central, East, and southern Africa also suggest that this political culture may be Africa-wide in distribution.

African legal systems have been of special interest to many scholars and have been well described. Drawing data from the many Tswana districts ("tribes") Schapera suggests that the role of the courts is not simply to administer justice in the abstract, but also to educate the people about their society's norms. This being the case, legal precedents, even when recalled by a remembrancer, are relatively unimportant, since almost by definition every case is a different one. Again, since to the Tswana the sociological factors in law are very important, justice is most often viewed as served by differential punishment for the similar offenses. Thus the Tswana tend to adhere to general principles of law in a manner not too different from the Barotse's principle of the "reasonable man," in which behavior is judged not in abstract terms but according to what the court deems reasonable at the time, at the place, and by the persons involved.

If the Tswana courts are fairly typical of traditional African legal systems, then the military organization of the Zulu represented the elaboration of the widespread age-grade, age-set systems as a fighting machine. The age-sets were organized into regiments, given distinct names, had their own battle cries, and had their own distinctive uniforms. Moreover, under Shaka's leadership, the Zulu army changed its military tactics and developed a more aggressive ideology. But like many African armies, the Zulu enlisted the power of the supernatural in their quest for victory. The shedding of the blood of an enemy was not taken lightly by the Zulu warriors, however, and before they were able to rejoin the society and be honored for their heroic deeds, they had to undergo other ritual acts in order to become clean. Cowards in warfare brought shame upon their relatives and were sometimes executed.

21. Social Control and Vengeance in Plateau Tonga Society[1]

I am here concerned with social control as it exists in Tonga society, where there are no obvious political institutions concerned in the maintenance of order. As in any society, control rests eventually on the sanction of force, here applied through a resort to vengeance on the part of an organized group if it feels that this is the only way to enforce its rights.

I am concerned with this problem because various people who have read the sketch of Tonga social organization which I have already published[2] have complained that they cannot see how controls can function in what seems at first glance to be an essentially unorganized society without clear-cut lines of allegiance to affiliate people to definite local groups. We understand the implications of the organized state with its delegation of authority to instituted leaders. Since the publication of Evans-Pritchard's studies of the Nuer, it has been possible to understand how stateless societies organized on lineage principles operate. But there are other forms of stateless societies, where the lineage system does not appear, and where no large group organized on kinship principles can be mobilized to enforce the rights of its members. Nor do local units relate themselves

SOURCE: E. Colson, "Social Control and Vengeance in Plateau Tonga Society," *Africa*, Vol. 23, No. 3, July 1953, pp. 199–211. Reprinted by permission of the author and publisher.

[1] Based on material collected among the Plateau Tonga of Northern Rhodesia during two field tours, September 1946–September 1947, and July 1948–July 1950, when I was employed as an officer of the Rhodes-Livingstone Institute. This paper was written while I was a Simon Research Fellow at the University of Manchester, and was read before the Royal Anthropological Institute on 27 November 1951.

[2] See my article in E. Colson and M. Gluckman (eds.), *Seven Tribes of British Central Africa*, London: Oxford University Press, 1951. In this and other earlier articles, I wrote of the feud as operating in Tonga Society. A talk on the feud among the Bedawin by Dr. E. Peters led me to reconsider my own material. I then realized that I had been using the term to cover isolated acts of vengeance, and that the Tonga did not, and could not, have the true feud.

to each other through any genealogical hierarchy, or any system of perpetual relationships phrased in kinship terms. The Tonga form such a society. Since the terms of affiliation and alliance which operate within it are unfamiliar to us, it is difficult first for the field worker himself to see them in their true perspective and then, when he has obtained an understanding of the principles involved, to find a method of making them clear to others.

Europeans have found it difficult to understand Tonga organization from the beginning of their contact with these people. Either they have attempted to find political authorities in the form of chiefs, or they have dismissed it as an unorganized anarchy. One who was in the area at the beginning of this century, when British administrators were just beginning to exert their influence, reported:

> One of the chief characteristics of the Batonga race is its disintegration. They have never been known to act in combination as one race, and the inhabitants of one village, and even of one family, will rarely co-operate to attain some common end. Not even for purposes of defence, nor to resist or avenge a wrong committed against one of their number, will the Batonga unite; and in my early experience on the Zambesi I have heard of the most atrocious murders being occasionally committed with absolute impunity, owing to the disintegrated state of society and absence of any central authority either in the district or at the kraals.
>
> To illustrate this I quote the instance of a man named Sia-masia, who had quarrelled with another Batonga, by name Sinasenkwi, from a neighbouring kraal. One morning Sia-masia observed the spoor of two lions close to his hut, and, upon reflection, concluded that Sinasenkwi had sent them by means of black magic. He thereupon repaired to Sinasenkwi's village, and there, in broad daylight, in the presence of all the villagers and of Sinasenkwi's relatives, stabbed not only the suspected wizard but also his wife and one of his children.
>
> When I inquired of Sinasenkwi's neighbours, why they had not interfered, they replied that the quarrel was one between Sia-masia and Sinasenkwi, and was no business of theirs.
>
> In another case, the headman of a village having been stabbed in the back, while entering a hut at a beer-drinking

festival, his people were appeased by a present of some goats from the murderers, and the matter was allowed to drop.[3]

Despite this observer's emphasis on disintegration and anarchy, the Tonga had their own methods of settling disputes and preventing general disorder, and even he comments that murders were occasional rather than frequent and that compensation was sometimes paid.

To understand how social control operates among the Tonga, it is first necessary to review the basic elements of their organization; we can then trace the interplay of these elements in an actual incident, and see how different systems of relationship act as checks on any general mobilization of one group against another, while at the same time influence is brought to bear upon the contestants to bring about a peaceful settlement of the dispute.

The Tonga, who occupy the plateau in the southern province of Zambia, live in small villages which are usually associated in little neighborhood groups, called *masi* (districts) or *tusi* (little districts). Villages are sometimes compact settlements with a definite pattern; more commonly they are collections of scattered homesteads under the more or less nebulous leadership of a headman. Today, on the average, they number about a hundred inhabitants, and probably in the past they were even smaller. A neighborhood or district may contain as many as seven or eight villages, but this seems to be the upper limit to which a neighborhood can grow. Each neighborhood may be separated from others of its ilk by bush or waste, or villages and fields may be continuous without any obvious boundary to separate one from another. The neighborhood does not form a kinship unit, nor are the villages related to one another through any institutionalized system of kinship ties, fictional or real. The Tonga have always moved about freely, in search of new land, better village sites, or more congenial neighbors. The man who first comes with his followers to settle in a previously unoccupied area is usually termed the "owner of the land" (*ulanyika*), and his heir may continue to receive respect for his primacy. But his control of the area is

[3] Notes by Mr. Val Gielgud, incorporated in H. Marshall Hole, "Notes on the Batonga and Batshukulumbwi Tribes," *Proceedings of the Rhodesia Scientific Association*, v, Part II, pp. 62–67, 1905. Mr. Gielgud apparently refers to the Valley Tonga, but similar conditions prevailed among the people of the Plateau.

equivocal at best. Other villages which follow him into the area do not recognize that he has rights in the land which override their own, nor do they necessarily look to him to settle their disputes, to perform ritual on their behalf, or to represent them before the world. No headman, moreover, holds his position by virtue of his leadership of an organized body of kinsmen. The male members of his village will be related to him in a number of different ways: some will be his sons; others will be his matrilineal kinsmen; some may be related to him through his father. Others may be affines, the husbands of his daughters or his sisters, or of women related to him in other ways. Others will be the relatives of these men who have followed them, and not the headman, into the village, and they may have no direct tie of kinship with the headman. Still others may simply claim the tie of common clan affiliation with the headman or with some other member of the village. Finally there may be strangers who have come to settle in the village though they can trace no tie of kinship or clanship with any previous member to ease the strain of adjustment to the local life.[4] Each village then lacks the integration brought about by the centralization of unilineal kinship ties, and each neighborhood is a complex of people, related to each other in a heterogeneous fashion. A man's place in his local community is affected by his kinship relationships to others in the community, but is not based upon these. His duties and rights in the community rise from the fact of his residence alone. Once he has moved into an area, has built his huts, and cultivated a field, he is a full member of the local group. He can look to other members of the group for assistance in ordinary daily activities. He is identified with the local community by outsiders. If he moves away, he loses this identification and joins with those of the new neighborhood where he settles.

Local organization is dependent upon the general recognition that to till one's fields and tend one's herds it is necessary to live at peace with one's neighbors, and this recognition of common interests finds expression in rites in which it is incumbent upon all members of the community to participate, under penalty of mystical sanctions which may affect, not only the offender, but the community as a whole, or any member within it. And the mystical sanction had its practical expression in mob action against someone who was thought to be endangering the others in the community. Therefore members of the community were expected to join together in the ritual for obtaining

---

[4] See my article, "Residence and Village Stability Among the Plateau Tonga," *Human Problems in British Central Africa,* No. 12, 1952, pp. 48–50.

rain, for the eating of the new grain, for the festival of the harvest. They also joined together for a rite of purification if a slaying polluted the soil of the district with blood, or if a stranger died within the boundaries of the district. If any member of the community dies all are expected to take part in the mourning.

But the local group does not assume responsibility for the actions of its members in other spheres. This is left to groups organized on kinship principles. The exogamous matrilineal clans, twelve in number, are dispersed groups without leaders or a corporate life to impress upon their members the obligations of clanship. Clanship does not imply common responsibility, though it mitigates hostility between fellow clansmen. Effective organization is dependent upon much smaller groups composed of those who consider themselves to be descended by matrilineal links from a common ancestress, who recognize their common obligations and rights and who join in common action. This is the group which is held responsible for the actions of its members, and which in turn acts to uphold their rights and to avenge their injuries. This is the group which should undertake the work of vengeance if just claims are not satisfied. The group as a whole, and not any particular individual within it, is expected to provide bridewealth for its members, and it shares in the bridewealth received for its women members. The group as a whole has the right to inherit the estate of its members and, if the deceased is a married man, is responsible for the provision of a substitute to marry the widows and father the orphaned children. The group as a whole is responsible for the payment of compensation for the offense of one of its members and formerly, if it failed, the injured parties might retaliate against any one of them and not against the offender alone.

But the matrilineal kinsmen who form the group tend to be dispersed into different neighborhoods, for though the Tonga are matrilineal, a man usually takes his wife to live in the locality where he has settled. And he is free to choose where he will go. His children may decide to settle with him, they may go to join maternal relatives, they may go off to live with others to whom they can trace some claim through kinship, or they may settle among strangers. And so, within a few generations, members of the group are dispersed across the countryside. But though they may live apart, they continue to act together and to form a group with common interests, so long as they remain in close enough contact to visit, to confer, and to share in one another's affairs. Membership is thus not directly governed by genealogical ties, and the exact degree of kinship is largely irrelevant in determining particular obligations to one another. A man belongs to a particular matrilineal group because he acts in common with its members, and he justifies his participation by the assumption of common kinship though he and others may not know the genealogical links between them. If he moves too far away to join with his kinsmen, or if he repudiates his obligations, he ceases to belong. Kin groups are thus continually reduced in size by the shedding of those who through distance or the existence of quarrels find themselves no longer able to participate in group affairs. The continued existence of the effective kinship group is dependent upon general good relations throughout the area within which kinsmen are scattered, or their intercourse is blocked and the group is shattered.

The matrilineal group is held together by common interests in property and by expectations of mutual assistance if the need arises. It is also buttressed by the mystique of kinship, which posits supernatural sanctions to bind them to each other. There is the sanction of the ancestral cult, for the matrilineal ancestors may vent their displeasure on any member or on all. There is also the sanction of *malweza,* which in some contexts simply means a "bad omen," and in others a supernatural retribution for an act or an occurrence which is thought to endanger the group. *Malweza* may strike any member of the offender's group, and not necessarily the offender himself. Incest, suicide or attempted suicide, physical violence offered by a man to his sister or by any person to someone of an older generation—these and many others are acts of *malweza.* After such an act, illness or misfortune suffered by any member of the group is likely to be attributed to retribution for *malweza.* The retribution can be averted only by a ritual peacemaking which restores the integrity of the group. It may be necessary only for the offender and the one against whom he has offended to make their peace in a ritual manner. Serious cases require the participation of every member of the group, while wider public opinion must be faced through the jeers of the clan joking relatives who are called upon to officiate in the rite.[5]

Joint responsibility of the group is thus extended into the super-

[5] See my article, "Clans and the Joking Relationship Among the Plateau Tonga," to appear in a forthcoming volume of the *University of California Publications in Anthroplogy.*

natural sphere, and incidents which would require compensation and a public settlement if people of different groups were involved, are here a matter for ritual actions which restore the unity of the group. If a man slays his kinsman, there can be neither compensation nor vengeance. To exact either would require the division of the group, and the end of its common kinship. The taking of a kinsman's property gives rise to grumbling, and in some cases to hints that the taker must be a witch since he thus openly shows his disregard of a living man's personality. But it is not theft. Adultery with a kinsman's wife is incest and therefore *malweza* if the two men are brothers. In other cases, the aggrieved husband may avenge his wrongs by driving off a beast or two from the offender's kraal, and the offender would bridle his resentment and accept his punishment. If a man's expectations of assistance in bridewealth were not met, he could convert his quarrel with his kinsmen into a quarrel between them and some other group by eloping with a girl whose relatives would demand compensation from those identified with him. But there is no open forum in which the wrongs done by one kinsman to another can be proclaimed to the world, which in any event has no interest or obligation to see that justice is done, for where only kinsmen are involved, no outsider may enter.

Thus kinsmen, though dispersed, act as a unit as the local group or neighborhood does not, and the crosscutting of local and kinship ties give flexibility to the organization of society. However, the Tonga have further elaborated this crosscutting of ties to bring about the relationship and interaction in set situations of each matrilineal group with others of like nature. This is done through the stressing of the role of the father. A man belongs to the matrilineal group of his mother, but he is a child of his father's matrilineal group and is identified with it also. And through the common interest which the two groups have in him, they are brought into association. Each group is expected to provide a portion of the bridewealth for the men, and they divide the bridewealth of the women. Both groups help to pay compensation if their child offends. If their child is killed, each group has a motive for extracting compensation, for each receives a share. Each group shares in the inheritance, and each has its role in the funeral ceremonies. The identification of a person with his father's group also receives ritual acknowledgment. A man may bring *malweza* upon his father's group as well as his own, for if he strikes his father, or any member of his father's group of an older generation, it is *malweza*. In return, he is dependent upon his father's group for his ritual well-being. Indeed he is more dependent upon them than upon his own matrilineal group, for he may approach his matrilineal ancestors directly. He is debarred from direct approach to the spirits of his father's line. Yet they may affect him, and indeed are considered to have a more powerful control over his life than have the spirits of his own line, and their anger is more dangerous to him and his than the anger of his matrilineal spirits. The Tonga say that if the ancestors of the paternal line are angered by neglect or by some offense against them, they will cause the death of the offender, and his maternal ancestors are powerless to protect him. If the maternal ancestors, however, are angered and wish to kill him, they must justify their action before his paternal ancestors, who will otherwise counter with: "This is our child. You have no right to kill him." But important as these ancestors of the paternal line are for good or evil, no man can approach them directly, for he is not a full member of their line. He must call upon some member of his father's group to make the offerings to them. Thus each matrilineal group depends upon the ritual offices of a number of other matrilineal groups for the well-being of its members.

This dependence is developed into a complex relationship, involving a large number of groups, for marriage rules force members of a group to seek alliances with the maximum number of other groups. Cross-cousin marriage is an approved form, but nevertheless the feeling is general that two closely related men should not marry women who are closely related. Nor do the Tonga approve of marriages which suggest that two groups are exchanging wives. It is impossible therefore for marriages, and the birth of children, to affiliate one group with only one or two others. Instead there is a dispersal of ties, and each person becomes a focal point upon which two groups achieve an integration of interests. A marriage is not an alliance between two people; it is a political relationship as well as a personal one, for each party to the marriage is identified with two groups, and all four are thus brought into association. These groups are: the husband's matrilineal group, and the group of his father, the wife's matrilineal group, and the group of her father. The husband's two groups share in the payment of bridewealth; the wife's two groups share in the receipt of the bridewealth. All four share in the rituals that institute the marriage and mark its various stages; they are concerned in the sickness or the death of either spouse. And even after the death of the two whose union constituted the original tie between them, two of the groups continue to be affiliated in their common concern for the offspring of the marriage. At the same time, each of the four groups is bound by exactly similar ties to many other matrilineal groups. Bad relations between two groups thus force all the others with which they are in association to have an interest in the development of the quarrel.

Since members of matrilineal groups are dispersed through a number of neighborhoods and marriages soon interrelate all those living in one neighborhood, neighborhood solidarity can be disrupted even though the original incident which provokes a quarrel between groups has occurred between people living in some other locality.

Still another set of ties exists which bind the people living in different localities to each other. These are brought about through the widespread lending of cattle, so that men herd cattle for friends and kinsmen living in various neighborhoods, while their own cattle in turn are handed over to other men for herding.[6] I shall not elaborate this system of relationships here, however, since in the case described below herding ties were not stressed.

With this background, we can begin to understand the stresses which occur within the social system when a major crisis breaks the peace. Today, with the presence of the British administration, the Northern Rhodesian police, the government-instituted chiefs with their courts and messengers, there is effective force to prevent the mobilization of units in vindictive action, but underneath this superstructure one can still see the interplay of the old forms of social control based on the interaction of kinship and local groups. These still work to reach a settlement over and above that which can be obtained through the courts. They are interested, not in the punishment of the offender, but in the re-establishment of good relations between the groups involved.

This will come out clearly in the particular case which I have chosen to present in illustration. It arose in 1948. It involved people of a number of different matrilineal groups, although those primarily concerned belonged to two groups, one of the Lion clan, the other of the Eland clan. Henceforth I shall refer to these groups as the Lions and the Elands, though it should be remembered that members of

[6] See my paper, "Cattle-keeping among the Plateau Tonga of Mazabuka District," in *Human Problems in British Central Africa*, No. 11, 1951.

these clans belonging to other matrilineal groups were not involved even when they were living in the same community. The incident also involved people of a number of different local groups, though again two adjacent neighborhoods were primarily concerned—Lupondo and Nampeyo. The incident itself was simple and direct; the issues were clear-cut, and the implications were accepted by all. *A,* a man of the Eland clan, living in the village of Gideon,[7] struck a man, *B,* belonging to the Lion clan, who also lived in Lupondo in the village of Moses. This was at a beer drink. After lingering for a few days in a coma, *B* died as a result of the blow. The police were summoned. The body was examined by the government doctor. *A* was arrested and committed for trial. Eventually he was convicted of manslaughter and sentenced to a year's imprisonment which he duly served. But this is only a fraction of the case as the Tonga saw it. From the beginning it was not a matter of *A* and *B* alone. *A*'s trial and punishment were not a settlement of the issues involved, and neither group was primarily concerned in this aspect of the matter.

B was a young man, settled in his wife's village. A large number of his matrilineal kinsmen live in the neighboring village of Joseph, whose headman is a Lion looked upon as the leader of their group. *B*'s father belonged to the Pigeon clan, and lived some twenty miles or more to the east in the district of Lupondo. None of *B*'s patrilineal kinsmen were living in the immediate vicinity of Lupondo, and the numerous Pigeons of other matrilineal groups did not concern themselves in the affair. *B*'s matrilineal kinsmen assumed complete responsibility, and summoned his father to come and join in mourning for their dead and in the decisions concerning what should be done.

A, a member of the Eland clan, lived in the village of Gideon, a Leopard headman who had married his mother's sister. His own father is Moses, a Hyena clansman, and headman of the victim's village. The majority of *A*'s close kinsmen live in the district of Nampeyo, which lies next-door to Lupondo. His mother and her sister married into Lupondo. After his mother's death *A* was reared by her sister at Gideon's village. His only sibling was living thirty miles away to the west, in the area where he had married, and though he was summoned to help in the settlement he took little part in the general discussion of the case. *A*'s mother's sister and her

[7] Names are fictitious, and following a convention of the Rhodes-Livingstone Institute are chosen from the Old Testament.

children all live in Lupondo. One is married to a Lion man of the same matrilineal group as his victim. Another who is married to a man of a different group lives in a village which contains many Lion people. Both had their children living with them. In their father's village, Eland and Lion people live side by side, and the Leopard people, of whom their father is one, are intermarried with both. In addition, there are other Eland people of this matrilineal group living in Lupondo villages.

At Nampeyo, where the majority of Eland people of this matrilineal group are living, the people have close ties with the people of Lupondo. One man, *D,* who belongs to the Eland group because his mother was a slave and he therefore took his father's affiliation, is married to a woman of the Lion group, a sister's daughter of the murdered man. Other Lion people are living in Nampeyo. Many of the Eland men are married to women from Lupondo, and their children have a stake in both communities. So numerous are the ties between the two groups that the people of Nampeyo almost automatically assume the obligation to attend funerals in Lupondo, though ordinarily you are only obliged to attend funerals in the neighborhood, and funerals outside the neighborhood if you are in some way related to the dead through an actual kinship or some affinal tie.

The leader of *A*'s matrilineal group is *C,* whose domination of the group is assured by a number of factors. He is a *musangu,* i.e. someone who under possession speaks for the spirits which control the rain and affairs of local import; he is a diviner with a reputation beyond his own area; he is a headman of a fairly populous village; he is an official in the Native Authority; he has a fair herd of cattle and, with his salary from the Native Authority treasury, he has sufficient wealth so that he is the logical person for his kinsmen to turn to in their difficulties. He is therefore considered to be their representative though many of them live outside his village, or his neighborhood, or his chieftaincy. As soon as he heard the news of the assault and the expected death of the victim, he went immediately to Moses's village to see the man and to announce that he and his people were very sorry for what had happened, that it was one man who had injured theirs, and that they as a group did not back his action. The relatives of the victim listened grimly while the injured man groaned occasionally in the background. But they showed no overt hostility toward *C*. Their attitude was that they would wait for the death before they showed their hand.

Then *C* returned to his village complaining bitterly about *A* who had always brought trouble to them and had now crowned his evil-doing with murder. *C* said that he and other elders among the Elands had long since marked *A* down as a troublemaker. They had sent him into the army with the hope that he would be killed in action. He came back unharmed. When *A* was seriously ill in 1946, local gossip had it that the elders of his group were attempting to kill him with sorcery to rid themselves of the trouble he caused them. Now their worst fears were realized. *C* said, "I'm sorry. I always said that his life was bad. He always liked to fight, and he fought with anybody including women and children. So it is up to us to pay." Again, he said, "When your child marries, you take the calabash and announce to the spirits that she has gone to be married to such and such a man. Sometimes there where she is married, she bears a mad child. But it is our relative. So what can we do? We cannot say that we will not pay this case." The other men who had gathered all agreed, "Of course we are going to pay, but we shan't know how much we shall have to pay until the settlement." Therefore, despite their general disgust with the murderer, they made no attempt to deny their responsibility as a group. *C*'s brothers were too old to be active in the matter, and *C* therefore turned to their sons, who lived with their fathers, and informed them that they must help their fathers to pay the case. The sons agreed, "Yes, we know that this must be paid. There is nothing to do but pay."

Meantime, *C* was sending a constant string of messengers to Lupondo to inquire after the injured man; and in return he was receiving messages from his kinsmen living in Lupondo who were demanding, "You must come and see the man whom *A* has killed. Why don't you come? Do you think that you will refuse to help us in this matter?" Then a messenger came back with the report that the man was dead, and that the Lion people had refused to greet him or the other Elands. Direct relationships between the two groups were now broken off. Because the body had been taken for examination, there could be no immediate mourning for the death, and the Elands did not know just how to proceed to indicate their repudiation of any attempt to deny their responsibility. Then Gideon of Lupondo, vitally concerned because he has both an

Eland and a Lion wife, and among his children are both Elands and Lions, called *C* to try to come to some arrangement which would ease the local tension. *C* suggested that they call in the father of the victim, who was closely associated with the matter, but nevertheless not the one primarily concerned. The people of Gideon's village objected that they did not dare go to find him since the Lion people were no longer greeting the Eland people, and it was dangerous to go among them. Finally, however, they summoned the father to discuss the matter. Meantime *C* was informed that the killing was of local importance as well as a matter of the kin group; for the people of Lupondo had maize in the pots to make beer for the harvest festival and they felt that they could not make their beer until the Elands had provided a beast to kill to cleanse the neighborhood of the blood spilt within it. In this case, however, the Elands were able to counter with the argument that anything they did to cleanse the district would be useless since they knew that in the last six years three people had been killed in Lupondo and no steps had been taken to cleanse the district of their blood.

While they waited for the return of the body to Lupondo so that the mourning could be held, there was a general uneasiness in the two communities. As the people sat about their fires they talked of the fear that would have afflicted them long ago before the Europeans came and forbade armed vengeance. *C* said, "Long ago, in a case like this, right after *A* had killed *B,* the people of *B* would be ready to attack us. First they would go to Gideon's village, because some of us live there, and they would try to kill some of them there and they would take all the women and children in that village to their village and shave their hair and give them new names. This would mean that now they were slaves. And after that *B*'s people would come here, following the relatives of *A*. They would be coming with many spears, and we would have to be ready because we would know that if they came it would be only to fight. If they wanted to discuss the matter and settle the case without a fight, they could not come here and we could not go there. But they would send an affine, and we would send an affine. When the two men met, they would explain what each side wanted. But we could not go there ourselves, because they would not wait to find out what we were coming for and would start to fight right away. Neither could we send our affine directly to them, nor could they send their affine directly to us. The two must meet somewhere and talk the matter out." When I pointed out that Gideon was not involved in the matter since he is a Leopard man, the answer was, "Yes, but there are Eland people in his village, and the Lion people would try to get them. Then Gideon would start to fight them because he would want his children back. And they would come to us and demand that we help them pay to recover their children."

While this was going on, the men said, there would have been a general disruption of community life. If a death had occurred, they would not have dared to go to the mourning if they knew that the Lion people were to be there, because they would be afraid that when the mourners danced with their spears before the house of the dead they would turn their spears on the Eland people. Nor would other groups welcome them at any gathering, for fear that fresh fighting would break out. Even today, they said, while they might attend the same funerals they would sit far apart, for fear that when the people began to drink beer they would fight. Also long ago, they said, the Eland women married to Lion men and living in a community with other Lion people would be afraid to remain in their homes, and on first news of the disaster would be running away with their children to try and seek protection. "They are afraid because their people have killed a Lion man." Nor could they return until a settlement was reached, because when people started to drink beer the Lions would say, "You have your child here, but you Elands killed one of us." And they would start fighting with the Elands who lived with them. Only after compensation had been paid would the women be able to retaliate with the answer, "Why do you talk like this? We have paid you." Nowadays, because of the fear of the Europeans, women are able to stay with their husbands, and the Eland women living at Lupondo stayed in their villages, although they felt they still ran the risk of sorcery or poisoning if the people were very angry.

Nevertheless, though Eland women continued to remain with their husbands in Lupondo while they waited for the mourning to start, they sent constant messages: "The Lion people are despising us. They refuse to greet us. They remind us all the time that we and our children are Eland, and we have killed their man. What are you going to do?"

And while the women were sending pleas to their relatives to settle the case in a hurry, their husbands were counseling their own kinsmen to accept a settlement: "The Elands have killed our man, but if they agree to settle, we must settle. Look, our children are Eland. Our wives are Eland. Will it bring that man back to life for us to lose our wives and children? If you despise them for what one man has done, how can they live among us?"

So far as they could, members of the two groups tried to avoid each other, but this meant that some of them could not perform their obligations. *D*'s wife was a Lion, and she went at once to her relatives to mourn with them. Her husband, an Eland, was required by the obligations of marriage to accompany her and take part in the mourning. It is his duty, along with all the other men who have married women of the line, to cook the food for the mourners and to perform the other necessary work about the place of mourning. He went, and got his brother, also an Eland, to accompany him. Then came word that mourning had started, and more and more people from Nampeyo who had kinship obligations to the Lion people went to the mourning. But the Lions sent no formal announcement that they were mourning. They were leaving the next step to the Elands.

C gathered members of his group and with them went to the mourning, where they were joined by Gideon and by the father of the murderer. First they went through the formal mourning dance, and then came to sit slightly apart from the silent group of Lion people. Between them sat a small group of men with ties in both camps. Then the Eland people and their children who had already come to mourn came out and joined *C* and his group, with considerable signs of relief. One old man, an Eland who had been living in Lupondo every since his kinsmen had ordered him out of Nampeyo many years before, said that he had not been greeted by the Lion people since the whole trouble started. After a slight pause, the Eland group exchanged greetings with the group between them and the Lions. They called forward the head of the Lion people, and the men greeted each other courteously. The head of the Lion people brought the father of the victim, and again greetings were exchanged. *C* and others of his party spoke again and again of their sorrow, that this was indeed a serious matter which they thoroughly condemned, that it was only one man who had done wrong and not all of them. The father commented, "Yes, that's all right. You are sorry. But I am the one who has lost a son." After a general talk on the evils of this particular case and the increase of violence at beer drinks, the leader of the Lions returned to his own group. *C* instructed his go-between Gideon who, as an affine of both the Lion and Eland people and the father of children belonging to both groups, was an ideal negotiator. Gideon relayed the matter to an affine of the Lion group, who in turn carried the words back to the waiting Lion men. Then the Lion affine withdrew, and the leader of the Lions joined the end of the neutral group. Gideon spoke to him and then to *C* and then he too withdrew, and *C* went to speak directly to the leader of the Lions. Relationships had now been restored between the two groups. *C* told them, "We have heard that you are mourning. We have come to mourn with you, and to find out what you want from us." The Lion people replied that they were not prepared to say what compensation they would accept until the court case had been settled. Then they would call upon the Elands to pay what was just.

Relationships having been re-established, the Lion and Eland men greeted each other, and food was brought to the visitors who ate. It was again possible for Eland and Lion people to meet and partake in the same rituals and in the same gatherings without danger of immediate hostilities. Each group had had good reason to desire this result, and each had been under considerable pressure from outsiders to settle the case. But it was only a truce, and a final settlement must wait upon the payment of compensation. Once the pressure of uneasiness and of general public anxiety was relaxed, however, the Elands were slow in paying. Normal relationships had been restored. They were no longer receiving frantic messages from their people living among the Lions that life was impossible until a settlement was reached. They began to find reasons why they should not give up their cattle. They argued that they too had lost a man, for was he not in prison? They suggested that the government law and its penalties had superseded the customary law of vengeance or compensation. They argued that they were poor in cattle and could not find the necessary animals to pay. They knew that the government would not permit the Lions to raid them. They also knew that general public opinion was interested only in the settlement of the differences, and not directly in the matter of compensation.

But public opinion still held them to be at fault, and found its mouthpiece through the invocation of mystical sanctions. *D* had a child by his Lion wife. It fell ill and the diviner announced that the illness was due to the spirit of the dead man which was angered because compensation had not been paid. His spirit could not attack the Eland people directly, for they do not belong to his line, but it could attack them through their child born of a Lion woman. When the child died, the Eland were told that this was due to their recalcitrance about payment. In similar cases, when sickness or death afflicts a person who has a tie with both groups, public opinion through the voice of the diviner will continue to remind the Elands that their responsibility is not at an end. Indeed, it can point the moral still more strongly, for any member of the Lion group who dies, or any child of this group, whether or not there is a tie with the Elands, may also be announced as having died from the same cause, and those who are bereft of a child will hold that the Elands are responsible.

The forces that operate to enforce public control in Tonga society no longer have free play because the presence of the European administration prevents recourse to the final sanction of force through the institution of vengeance. Nevertheless, it is still possible to see in this case how public control is brought to bear upon the groups which in theory are free to settle their differences as they will. In a society of this type, it is impossible to have the development of the feud and the institutionalization of repeated acts of vengeance, for each act of vengeance, like each original incident, mobilizes different groups whose interests are concerned in the particular case and that alone. It would also lead to a general community disruption, affecting those who must live in the midst of the turmoil and yet are not directly concerned with it. Permanent bad relations then are only possible when the groups involved do not have kinsmen living together in the same local groups, and where they are not tied by the network of kinship and affinal relationships to the same matrilineal groups. Then it becomes possible for vengeance to operate without the drag of local obligations and the crosscutting of kinship ties. But at this distance there is little likelihood of their members clashing. Where clashes are likely, local bonds and kinship ties intervene to force a settlement.

Tonga society, despite its lack of political organization and political unity, is a well-integrated entity, knit together by the spread of kinship ties from locality to locality, and the intertwining of kinship

ties within any one locality. It obtains its integration and its power
to control its members and the different groups in which they are
aligned by the integration of each individual into a number of
different systems of relationships which overlap. When a man seeks
to act in terms of his obligation to one set of relationships, he is
faced by the counterclaims upon him of other groups with which
he must also interact. This entanglement of claims leads to attempts
to seek an equitable settlement in the interests of the public peace
which alone enables the groups to perform their obligations one to
another and a Tonga to live as a full member of his society.

It seems possible that the crosscutting of ties also operates in the
same fashion in societies organized on the lineage principle, and
that a further analysis of the data would show that these societies
obtain their stability not because their local groups are unilineally
organized, but because of the presence within each local group of
people with a diverse set of ties linking them to those in other areas.

This has certainly been of primary importance among the Tallensi,
for whom Fortes reports:

> In spatial relations every maximal lineage belongs to one
> set of adjacent lineages in the *Bɔyar* cult and to a different
> set of adjacent lineages in the Earth cult. It has, therefore, two
> intersecting fields of politico-ritual relations so adjusted that
> its loyalties to the other component lineages of one field are
> counter-balanced by its loyalties to the component lineages of
> the other field. Both sets of politico-ritual loyalties are correlated
> with the same sort of social interests, symbolized in a single
> system of religious concepts and values. Their organization in
> two complementary configurations around polar symbols checks
> the dangers of disruptive conflicts that might spring from them.
> Thus the ties of clanship are regrouped around another axis
> of social integration. Every maximal lineage is a bridge between
> a *Bɔyar* congregation and a *Tɛŋ* congregation. In most cases,
> in fact, the component lineages of a particular *Tɛŋ* congregation
> all belong to, and in that context represent, different *Bɔyar*
> congregations, and vice versa. This is the fundamental mechan-
> ism of the remarkable politico-ritual equilibrium found among
> the Tallensi.[8]

[8] Pp. 107–8, in M. Fortes, *The Dynamics of Clanship,* London: Oxford University Press, 1945.

The Tonga and the Tallensi are very differently organized, but the same principle of crosscutting ties appears in both societies. I suspect that it is a general principle incorporated into most societies as a mechanism for ensuring the maintenance of order.

22. Power and Stratification in Rwanda: A Reconsideration[1]

Since the publication of M. Fortes and E. E. Evans-Pritchard's *African Political System,* anthropologists have drawn attention to a large variety of African societies that lack one or the other of the structural characteristics subsumed by the authors under their two major headings.[2] In an issue of *Anthropologica* devoted to the analysis of power in complex societies Professor Ronald Cohen notes that the dichotomy employed by Fortes and Evans-Pritchard leaves out "a very large group of societies of different varieties, a great deal more various in fact than would be assumed from the original group A category of Fortes and Evans-Pritchard, which they use to cover all societies that have 'centralized authority, administrative machinery and judicial institutions.' "[3] Rwanda, as he goes on to observe, is certainly a case in point.

. . . Besides having a centralized system of authority organized along hierarchical lines, traditional Rwanda was also characterized by the existence of inferior-superior relationships between two discrete ethnic groups, a fact which has long been recognized as one of the most critical factors in the socio-political organization of this particular society. Beyond this, however, there seems to be little agreement among scholars concerning the overall effects of ethnic

SOURCE: René Lemarchand, "Power and Stratification in Rwanda: A Reconsideration," *Cahiers d'Études Africaines,* Vol. 6, No. 4, 1966, pp. 592–610. Reprinted by permission of the author and publisher.

[1] I wish to record my indebtedness to the Social Science Research Council for their assistance while doing preliminary research for this paper, and to the Graduate Council of the University of Florida for their support while writing it.

[2] For a critique of Fortes and Evans-Pritchard's distinction between "state" and "stateless" societies, see in particular Paula Brown, "Patterns of Authority in West Africa," *Africa,* Vol. 21, October 1951, pp. 261–78, and Phyllis Kaberry, "Primitive States," *British Journal of Sociology,* Vol. VIII, September 1957, pp. 224–34. Cf. M. Fortes and E. E. Evans-Pritchard, *African Political Systems,* London, 1940, pp. 5–11.

[3] "Power in Complex Societies in Africa," *Anthropologica,* Vol. IV, No. 1, 1962, p. 6.

stratification on the distribution of power among and within Rwanda's constituent ethnic groups. No doubt, this lack of consensus reflects in part differences of opinion as to what concepts and methodological assumptions are most relevant to an analysis of stratificatory phenomena. Another and more fundamental reason is that most of the studies dealing with this area lack the time dimension necessary to an understanding of societal changes. The picture that emerges from the literature is little more than a snapshot view of Rwanda society at any given period of history.[4] In turn, the omission of dynamic elements from their total historical context has led certain scholars to vastly oversimplify, and therefore to misinterpret, political realities. That this bias can also lead to serious contradictions can be gathered from a closer eaxmination of the theories advanced by students of Rwanda society.

It is of course impossible within the scope of this paper to consider each theory in detail. The image of Rwanda conveyed by anthropologists emerges perhaps more clearly from the answers they give to the questions often raised by social scientists about problems of social stratification: What kinds of correlations can one discern between ethnic cleavages and the allocation of political roles? What is the nature of the boundary between the sphere of social and economic activities and that of political relations? How does one affect the other? Can one generalize about such questions without paying due attention to historical discontinuities and regional variations?

TWO CONTRASTING VIEWS

Among students of Rwanda society who have recently exercized themselves over these queries, Professor Jacques Maquet was the first to suggest a coherent set of hypotheses about the power structure of Rwanda and its relation to society as a whole. In *The Premise of Inequality in Ruanda,* Maquet presents the results of his investigation in the form of eight theorems which contain the gist of a functional theory of Rwanda society. As the title of his book suggests, Maquet's thesis is that the traditional ordering of relationships between the dominant Tutsi oligarchy and the Hutu

[4] A notable exception is Jan Vansina, *L'évolution du Royaume Rwanda des origines à 1900,* Bruxelles, A.R.S.O.M., t. XXVI, fasc. 2, 1962.

was based on a "premise of inequality" which permeated and regulated every phase of social and political life:

> Superiority and inferiority were foci of the Ruanda social structure to such an extent that as soon as they entered as a component in the content of a social intercourse, other components were regarded as less important and were colored by the hierarchical situation of the two actors.[5]

In practice this meant that all positions of wealth and influence were monopolized by the Tutsi elites, who stood toward their Hutu subjects very much like the medieval lords toward their vassals.

Inferior-superior relationships were institutionalized in a clientage system (*buhake*) which provided for reciprocal rights and obligations between the overlord (*shebuja*) and his client (*umugarugu*). The *buhake,* according to Maquet, formed the keystone of Rwanda society. His main argument is that the functions it performed on behalf of the clients tended to mitigate the built-in inequalities of the feudal system. Because of the protection which the clients could expect from their lords, and also because of the complementarity of economic activities involved in it, the *buhake* made for some measure of social cohesion while at the same time preserving the existing caste structure.

> By that agreement almost any Hutu was linked to a Tutsi and partook in the social power of the upper caste by identifying himself with a protector who was a member of the dominant group . . . Through the clientage institution Rwanda constituted a unified economic system which distributed agricultural and pastoral products among the totality of the population. The personal bond with a privileged caste member, and access to possession, however precarious, of cattle, seems to have been essential from the point of view of national solidarity.[6]

While the author admits of other factors which helped maintain social cohesion, his interpretation of the *buhake* as an institution

[5] Jacques J. Maquet, *The Premise of Inequality in Ruanda,* London, 1961, p. 165.
[6] Ibid., p. 150.

involving reciprocal gratifications is clearly central to his analysis. Ultimately, since economic and political power tended to gravitate into the same hands, the clientage system also tended to set the pattern of political relations.

A particularly significant aspect of the political structure was the substitutability of roles implicit in the "feudal" organization of society. The functions devolved upon hill chiefs, cattle chiefs, land chiefs, etc., were closely linked with the status hierarchy attendant upon the clientage system, so that the average officeholder would frequently combine a variety of roles. As a patron he could always use his "feudal" privileges to reinforce his authority as chief, or vice versa; as a client of a higher chief, however, he was also made aware of his obligations toward both his superiors and his subordinates. It was this network of interlocking roles which gave Rwanda society a measure of cohesion and stability. Equally instrumental in maintaining a caste structure were the various agencies of socialization embedded in the political system. The inculcation of what were regarded as typically Tutsi qualities—courage (*ubutware*), manliness (*mugabo*), self-mastery (*itonde*)—was the principal function attributed to the military establishment. As Maquet points out, the armies of Rwanda were among the most powerful instruments of social control available to the upper caste. It is true of course that in some areas the military chiefs were expected to perform essentially military and administrative functions, and the military skills acquired by the young Tutsi while serving their tour of duty were undoubtedly an important asset in the hands of the Tutsi to maintain their dominant position. But even more important in the long run was the role played by the army in legitimizing a *de facto* situation of inequality.[7]

Admittedly, it is difficult to do full justice to Maquet's interpretation in such a brief compass; but if one were to summarize in a nutshell the substance of his argument, one might put it in the following propositions: The "premise of inequality" was a major operative ideal in the political culture of Rwanda. Translated into concrete terms, this meant that "people born in different castes are unequal in endowment, physical as well as psychological, and have fundamentally different rights"—as well as different obliga-

[7] Ibid., p. 117. The socializing function of the army is further described by Alexis Kagame in *L'histoire des bovins dans l'Ancien Rwanda*, Bruxelles, A.R.S.O.M., t. XXV, fasc. 4, 1961.

tions.[8] Implicit in this definition is the idea that inequality was accepted by its members as a "natural" condition.

Maquet's interpretation has been forcefully challenged by Professor Codere, in an article which appeared in a recent issue of *Anthropologica*. Rejecting at the outset the notion that Rwanda society was "a functioning whole continuing in time through its mutually reinforcing structures and institutions and its vast network of reciprocities which benefit and obligate everyone of its members," Codere takes the view that power alone enabled the Tutsi to exercise continuous domination over the Hutu masses. "Based on the case of Rwanda the position arrived at in this study is that power can be held and exercised by a minority against the interests and without the consent of the governed."[9] Since power is defined by the author as "the ability of one individual to inflict harm and deprivation to one another," one must assume that the Tutsi minority kept the Hutu in bondage solely through the application or threat of coercitive measures. Unfortunately, Professor Codere does not tell the reader how the Tutsi minority, representing less than ten per cent of the total population, managed to gain and retain power over the years.

The most interesting part of Codere's analysis is that which concerns the effect of the Tutsi power struggle upon Hutu-Tutsi relations. Her reasoning runs as follows: Because of the "unremitting ferocity" which characterized personal relation *within* the dominant caste, the average Tutsi lived in a state of permanent anxiety "lest he be demoted from whatever position of power he held and suffer deprivation of property, status, or even life itself."[10] In order to maximize their security within their own caste the Tutsi were naturally inclined to use their power in the most ruthless fashion, which in turn served to deter the Hutu from attempting to gain ascendency in the political system. In other words, the use of naked power was the favorite "device" employed by the Tutsi to maintain their domination over the Hutu. Conversely,

> had the Tutsi been merely a comfortable and secure aristocracy, they might have developed slack and easy-going ways, but the

[8] Ibid., p. 165.

[9] Helen Codere, "Power in Rwanda," *Anthropologica*, Vol. IV, No. 1, 1962, p. 51.

[10] Jacques J. Maquet, *The Premise of Inequality in Ruanda,* London, 1961, p. 84.

brutal and relentless struggle for power among them kept them harsh and undistracted in their use of power, and thereby maximized the power they held as a group.[11]

The conclusion that logically follows is that the imposition of *pax belgica,* by mitigating the effects of the power struggle within the ruling group, prepared the ground for a Hutu revolt.

Inferentially, Codere casually dismisses Maquet's interpretation as a "Panglossian state of affairs." Rather than seeing Rwanda as a "network of reciprocities" she sees it as a polity where relations among individuals are strangely reminiscent of Hobbes' conception of the state of nature, i.e., a society where the "more powerful oppressed the less powerful or the powerless, [where] power was used to the hilt by those who possessed it, and [where] fear and insecurity perpetuated the system."[12] In a brief section on *The Revolution in Rwanda,* the author asserts that the Hutu-led revolution was a *Rwandese* revolution, in the sense that it was "neither inspired, created nor engineered by outside forces, Belgian, African, or any other."[13] The overthrow of the Tutsi feudal system was the logical *dénouement* of a conflict of aspirations that was inherent in the socio-political structure of Rwanda, and had little if anything to do with the Belgian presence.

The area of disagreement between the two foregoing views is about as wide as that which separates the devotees of "functional" analysis from the proponents of a "power" theory of politics. As noted earlier, these differences of interpretation tend to reflect differences in the techniques of investigation employed by the authors. For instance, one cannot fail to note that Maquet's interview schedules were communicated only to respondents of Tutsi origins, and most probably to residents of the central region of Rwanda. While there is no reason to question the sincerity of these informants, in all probability the evidence that could have been gathered from a sampling of Hutu respondents from the northern region would have brought some important qualifications to Maquet's findings. Far more objectionable is Codere's method of investigation, based on interviews with 356 Rwandese drawn from each of the main ethnic groups. What is objectionable here is not so

[11] Ibid., p. 84.
[12] Ibid., p. 82.
[13] Ibid., p. 63.

much the format of the interviews, and even less the sampling technique, as the circumstances under which they were conducted. To be sure, the application of interviews techniques to a crisis situation of the kind that existed in Rwanda in 1959–60 can yield some instructive insights into people's reactions to contemporary events. By definition, however, a crisis implies that the prevailing state of affairs is a highly abnormal one. As Codere herself admits, "a period of great tension and turbulence in a society has rarely been the setting for anthropological field work, and it was necessary to find or modify field techniques that would avoid or lessen the difficulties and profit by any advantages such a period presented." Despite her avowed reservations concerning the feasibility of anthropological field work under such circumstances, Codere's account of Rwanda society remains heavily colored by the emotions and racial antagonisms triggered off by the upheaval of November 1959. Her image of Rwanda is essentially that of a society torn by civil strife and bitter hatred. As such it provides a vivid and accurate description of the revolutionary circumstances which preceded the establishment of republican rule; but it only bears a remote reaction to the socio-political realities of traditional Rwanda.

Yet, looking at Rwanda in a broad historical perspective, one reaches the conclusion that neither one of these interpretations automatically excludes the other. Each theory emphasizes a particular aspect of Rwanda society, circumscribed both spatially and chronologically. Maquet's "functional" theory applies mainly to the central region of Rwanda (the seat of the "nuclear" kingdom) and reflects perhaps most accurately the state of affairs that prevailed around 1900; Codere's interpretation, on the other hand, applies to the peripheral areas of northern and western Rwanda in the period following the German occupation of the country, but has only limited relevance to an understanding of the social and political structure of central Rwanda prior to 1900. In order to separate the elements of truth contained in each theory from mere abstraction, one must look at some of the historical changes that have taken place in Rwanda over the last few centuries.

HISTORICAL PERSPECTIVES

As in the case of many other interlacustrine societies, the kingdom of Rwanda developed its present territorial base partly through conquest and partly through peaceful assimilation. The pattern of expansion seems to have been the same throughout the interlacustrine area. Under the leadership of a royal clan, successive waves of Hamitic pastoralists spread their domination over the indigenous Bantu societies, whose customs and traditions they progressively assimilated into their culture. In Rwanda this process began in the early sixteenth century, under the reign of Mwami Kigeli Mukobanya, and lasted until the inception of the colonial era. With the annexation of northern Rwanda in 1911 the boundaries of modern Rwanda were finally stabilized to their present configuration.

According to De Lacger, the history of Tutsi expansion falls into four separate phases.[14] The initial step involved the formation of a small nuclear kingdom in the region of Buganza and Bwanacambwe, under the reign of Ruganza Bwimbu in the fifteenth century. A second phase, beginning in the sixteenth century, brought about the incorporation of neighboring areas into what is today the central region of Rwanda (Nduga-Marangara). With the accession of Ruganzu Ndoli to power, in the seventeenth century, a series of invasions were launched against formerly independent Hutu communities which resulted in the creation of a "unitary" state. Finally, in the first half of the nineteenth century a group of independent Tutsi states—the most powerful of which was the kingdom of Gisaka in the east—were forcefully incorporated into the national boundaries of Rwanda.

Thus, while part of this territorial aggrandizement occurred at the expense of Tutsi states, much of it was directed against autonomous Bantu societies. The important thing to stress here is that the conquest of some of these Hutu states seems to have taken place much later than was assumed by De Lacger. Indeed, recent historical research shows that the absorption of the Hutu populations of the northern and eastern "marches" began in the middle of the eighteenth century and continued until the early part of the twen-

---

[14] L. de Lacger, *Ruanda*, Kabgaye, 1959, p. 113.

tieth century. Tutsi control over the northern region (corresponding roughly to the former *territoires* of Ruhengeri and Biumba) was not firmly established until the 1920's, and the Tutsi drive to the north did not commence until the late nineteenth century, under Mwami Rwabugiri. It was the same Rwabugiri who brought the eastern region (Bugoyi, Bwishaza, Kingogo) into the fold of the Rwanda monarchy. This does not mean that these areas had no previous contacts with Tutsi pastoralists (as we shall see, the annexation of Hutu lands was often preceded by a generous infiltration of Tutsi elements); but it does suggest that the formal annexation of the peripheral Hutu areas is a fairly recent phenomenon when one considers the total span of Rwanda's historical evolution.

In order to grasp the implications of this basic historical fact, something must be said of the different patterns of assimilation brought in the wake of Tutsi expansion. Where the conquered populations were already organized under a dominant Tutsi lineage (as in the case of the Mubari, Bugesera, and Nduga areas), ethnic affinities provided a major integrative bond, and hence made for rapid assimilation. The case of Gisaka is the only notable exception: according to d'Arianoff, no less than seven expeditions were launched against the Tutsi kings of Gisaka between 1835 and 1852 before they were finally brought to heel by Rwogera's warriors.[15] But in those areas that were occupied by autonomous Hutu communities, the conquering tribes were confronted with an entirely different situation. Some of these communities were organized in small autonomous "kingdoms" under the leadership of a "divine" king called *umuhinza* or *umwami*. Their political structure was similar in many respects to that of neighboring Tutsi states, and part of their rituals as well as some of their political symbols—the royal drum, for example—were subsequently adopted by the royal clans of Rwanda. Despite such similarities, the absorption of these Hutu communities into Rwanda society was undoubtedly a long and difficult task.

The consolidation of Rwandese national unity reflects a distinctive pattern of assimilation. The initial phase of Tutsi penetration was characterized by a gradual infiltration of Tutsi pastoralists among the indigenous population. Although the *buhake* had not yet been introduced into these areas, relations between Hutu and Tutsi were essentially of a commercial nature, involving the exchange of cattle

[15] A. d'Arianoff, *Histoire des Bagesera, souverains du Gisaka.* Bruxelles, I.R.C.B. t. XXIV, fasc. 3, 1952, pp. 86ff.

for agricultural products. This period of peaceful coexistence was usually brought to an end by a series of brutal encounters resulting in the pacification of the conquered territories and the establishment of military rule. After the invasions came the implantation of an embryonic administrative machinery. In some areas (as in the Kinyaga) army chiefs were appointed governors; elsewhere the Mwami would distribute the spoils of victory among the members of his family and his courtesans. Finally, a conscious attempt was made to achieve some measure of administrative and political unification: The Mwami would divide the provinces into districts, and the districts into *chefferies* and *sous-chefferies;* representatives of the Mwami were appointed in each subdivision; "royal" capitals were set up in each district and regular army contingents were dispatched to the outlying areas to maintain peace and order. It was only at this point that attempts at assimilation stood a reasonable chance of achieving their purpose.

In some areas Tutsi penetration was discouraged at the outset by the inaccessible or uninviting nature of the terrain, or because of the unfriendly dispositions of the indigenous tribes. In such cases the general pattern of amalgamation described above was usually telescoped into one or two phases, and did not last more than a few decades—sometimes even less than a decade. This is what happened in the Bushiri, Kingogo, Rwankeri and Ndorwa regions. In each of these areas the duration and intensity of contact between Hutu and Tutsi was minimal, and it was not until the early 1920's that a unified administrative structure was finally established.

These discontinuities in the timing of Tutsi expansion account to a large extent for the variant modes of political organization encountered by the European colonizers when they first entered the country. Where the penetration of Tutsi influences was most recent, the local elites continued to be drawn from the old Hutu ruling dynasties, and the traditional political roles assigned to them remained basically unchanged. In fact, so deep was the attachment of these societies to their traditional forms of government that many of them revolted against the innovations that were subsequently forced upon them by their Tutsi overlords with the assistance of the German colonizers.[16] In central Rwanda, on the other hand, where the long coalescence of Hutu and Tutsi had already produced a

[16] For further information see *Historique et Chronologie du Ruanda* (anonymous, n.d., n.p.).

stable society, the establishment of indirect rule merely served to confirm the pre-existing dominance of the Tutsi elites.

PATTERNS OF POWER

With these general observations in mind we must now turn to an examination of the different types of power relationships that have evolved in traditional Rwanda. For the sake of analysis, however, a distinction must be made at the outset between the central and the northern regions.

1. THE CENTRAL REGION

The stretch of territory corresponding roughly to the former *territoires* of Kigali and Nyanza constitutes the "core area" of traditional Rwanda. Historically, this is where Hutu and Tutsi have the longest record of continuous contact; politically, this is where Rwandese institutions first developed and achieved the highest degree of political stability.

It was in this region that, from a "pyramidal" kingdom based on autonomous descent groups, Rwanda eventually gave birth to a highly centralized polity in which all major offices came under the direct control of the Mwami. Although one knows very little of the actual circumstances which brought about this fundamental shift in the allocation of power, the processes by which it was accomplished can be reasonably inferred from the record of other interlacustrine societies. As in Buganda, where the authority of the *bataka* (or clan heads) was gradually curtailed in favor of chiefs appointed by the Kabaka (the so-called *saza* chiefs), the Rwanda kings consolidated their power by suppressing the autonomy of local hereditary lords and by replacing them with loyal retainers—almost all of them of Tutsi extraction. One finds in Max Weber's discussion of patrimonialism in medieval Europe an obvious parallel with what happened in Rwanda:

> The community was transformed into a stratum of aids to the rulers and depended upon him for maintenance through the usufruct of land, office fees, income in kind, salaries, and hence through prebends. The staff derived its legitimate power in

greatly varying stages of appropriation, infeudation, conferment, and appointment. As a rule this meant that princely prerogatives became patrimonial in nature.[17]

Similarly in traditional Rwanda chiefly positions became "patrimonial" in the Weberian sense of the term, inasmuch as they were the prebends distributed by the king to retain the loyalty of his "men."

The analogy of Rwanda with medieval Europe must be accepted with certain qualifications, however. As Gravel's study shows, Rwanda's political system had more in common with Japanese than European feudalism.[18] As in medieval Japan, the complex of rights and privileges attached to the ownership of land and cattle formed the basis of Rwanda society, and the Japanese word *shiki,* used to refer to such rights and privileges, including "the right of the patron, who, standing at the apex, ensures by his high position the immunity of state whether from tax or aggression,"[19] finds an exact counterpart in the kinyarwanda term *amarembo.* And just as in Kamakura, Japan, public appointments were treated as *shiki* pertaining to private estates, Rwanda's chieftaincies came to be regarded as *amarembo.* In short the benefices derived from clientship tended to form a tangle of mutual rights and obligations which ran through the entire political structure from the Mwami down to the most humble Hutu client.

Against this background one can better understand why clientship served as the linchpin which held the political system of Rwanda together, and why, once it was abolished, the entire structure collapsed, ushering in a bitter struggle for supremacy between Hutu and Tutsi. Since the exchange of goods and services served to express or extend political authority, a change in the economic system was

[17] H. H. Gerth and C. W. Mills, eds., *From Max Weber: Essays in Sociology,* New York, 1946.

[18] Pierre Gravel, *The Play for Power: Description of a Community in Eastern Rwanda* (Unpublished Ph.D. Dissertation, 1962). For a general discussion of the applicability of the concept of feudalism to African contexts, see Jack Goody, "Feudalism in Africa," *Journal of African History,* Vol. IV, No. 1, 1963, pp. 1–18; and J. H. M. Beattie, "Bunyoro: An African Feudality?", ibid., Vol. V, No. 1, 1964, pp. 24–36.

[19] G. B. Sansom, *Japan: A Short Cultural History,* New York, 1931, p. 274. For further information on the *shiki* system, see Ed. O. Reischauer, "Japanese Feudalism," in *Feudalism in History,* Rushton Coulborn, ed., Princeton, 1965, pp. 28–30.

bound to affect political relations. Moreover, in view of the close links between the allocation of political roles and the caste system, the abolition of the *buhake* was bound to destroy at the same time the structural roots of stratification.

In traditional Rwanda ethnic stratification was intimately connected with the value system and the pattern of political roles associated with it. Maquet's discussion of the clientage system vividly shows how the ownership of cattle, as the main symbol of wealth and authority, not only served to validate lord-client relationships, but also helped reinforce the power of the Mwami. As the supreme ruler of the kingdom, the Mwami was also the ultimate owner of cattle, which he would allocate to his chiefs as carefully as the latter would to their clients. Thus, by a skillful handling of *amarembo,* in the form of cattle and grazing lands, the kings of Rwanda managed to set up an amazingly effective system of administration. The standard system of administration at the district level consisted in a trinity of powers, represented by the army chiefs, the land chiefs and the cattle chiefs, all of them appointed by the Mwami. Below this intermediary layer, power was delegated to the hill chiefs who were themselves appointed by the army chiefs. The hill chiefs would in turn appoint a group of petty functionaries, called *ibilongozi,* to act as intermediaries between themselves and the local populations. As a rule the *ibilongozi* were the hill chief's favorite clients, just as the chiefs were somebody else's clients. The net result of this extraordinary fragmentation of power was to reinforce the omnipotence of the Mwami. Indeed, it is not a matter of pure coincidence that the most serious challenges to royal authority never came from the local notables but from the Mwami's own entourage.

Another important consequence of this diffusion of power at the local level is that it provided the Hutu with certain guarantees against arbitrary exactions. As Maquet points out,

> in a plural system there are several immediate superiors of approximately equal rank who are not interdependent. Consequently it is possible to have the support of one chief (or his complicity even) when resisting another . . . This is what happened in Rwanda.[20]

[20] Jacques J. Maquet, op. cit., p. 154.

On the basis of this generalization one could argue that the Hutu could always hope to secure a "fair treatment" for themselves by simply playing off one chief against the other—the *shebuja* against the hill chief, or the hill chief against the army chief. Although this is precisely what happened in many instances, the cohesion of the system as a whole did not depend exclusively on the opportunities arising from the interplay of rank and privilege among the Tutsi. Just as important, in terms of inter-caste cohesion, was the internalization of a set of values which tended to reflect and perpetuate a situation of inequality. As L. Mair observed,

> the status which the Rwanda scheme of values accorded to the Hutu was such that a Hutu who had no protector was at the mercy of any Tutsi . . . In the general insecurity of the pastoral states no person of small substance was safe without a protector, and this applied particularly to the Hutu who seem to have had no rights at all except as clients of a Tutsi who would assert his own rights in protecting them.[21]

If the need for protection accounts for the tendency of the Hutu peasants to "commend" themselves to a lord, one must also stress the general inclination of both Hutu and Tutsi to identify social justice with power. In the value system of Rwanda might and right are but two faces of the same coin. As Gravel succinctly puts it,

> if a patron is politically powerful, the client is always certain of being right in disputes. Just as there is no word to distinguish a lie from an error, there is none that distinguishes right from wrong. If one is powerful, one is right; if one is weak, one is wrong. There is no morality involved.[22]

Yet, to say that power is valued as an end in itself—partly because it is the base value through which other economic and social advantages can be obtained—does not imply that it will automatically be used arbitrarily, or against the interests of the lower caste. To go back to the point made by L. Mair, given the conditions of insecurity that prevailed in the traditional environment of Rwanda, it

---

[21] Lucy Mair, *Primitive Government*, Baltimore, 1962, p. 168.
[22] Gravel, op. cit., p. 215.

was clearly in the interests of the Hutu to seek the protection of a lord. In this connection, Codere's argument that "protection in such a sense deserves the quote marks it is usually given in describing U.S. gangsterism in the '20's"[23] does not withstand rational examination. Not only is it contradicted by the fact that in some places many Hutu continued to owe allegiance to their lords long after the introduction of political reforms, which would suggest a deep cultural commitment to status differences as a natural and proper form of social organization, but it also overlooks the restraining influences exerted through the various compensatory mechanisms described by Maquet. Another point which needs to be stressed is that once a Hutu had "infeudated" himself to a lord, if, for some reason or another, the arrangement proved unsatisfactory, he could always disengage himself from this relationship and turn to someone else for protection.

Finally, Codere's assumption that the power structure of Rwanda was everywhere under the control of Tutsi oligarchies, and hence made the Hutu everywhere "powerless," "oppressed," and "terrorized" is seriously opened to question. For one thing, one must remember that the structure of power at the hill level was in some ways quite different from what it was at the district or provincial level. As shown by Gravel's study of the "play for power" in Remera (Gisaka), political competition at the local level centered around three major institutions, namely the lineage, the chieftainship and the nuclear feudal cluster, the latter being the "smallest sociopolitical group of the hierarchy" and consisting of the "patron surrounded by all his clients, Tutsi and Hutu, bound to him in fealty."[24] More often than not the chieftain was also the head of the nuclear feudal cluster, and the combination of these two roles evidently weakened the autonomy of the lineage. Yet, the evidence shows that in some cases the strength of the local Hutu lineages was such that the Tutsi found it expedient to absorb these meddlesome "upstarts" into their own caste. In a fascinating discussion of the power struggle which took place in Remera, Gravel notes that "the Hutu lineages which have been *in situ* longest have acquired some sort of priority of rights on the hill. Their members are respected and the heads of the lineages have much influence on their neighbors, and have an important voice in local administration . . . The powerful lineages

[23] Codere, op. cit., p. 83.
[24] Gravel, op. cit., p. 221.

keep the power of the chieftain in check. If, however, they become powerful enough to threaten the chieftainship they are absorbed into the upper caste. Their Hutu origins are 'forgotten.' "[25] Besides showing the existence of opportunities for upward mobility across caste lines, Gravel's findings suggest that the "play for power" was neither confined to the Tutsi caste, nor bound to result in further Tutsi "oppression."

Another obvious qualification is that the higher echelons of the political hierarchy were not always monopolized by members of the Tutsi caste. In many instances the authority of the old Hutu dynasties continued to be recognized more or less explicitly by the kings of Rwanda. This is the situation that was to be found in the northern region of Rwanda at the inception of German colonial rule.

2. The Northern Region

A major feature of the Bantu societies of the northern region was the diversity of their formal political organization. Small-scale centralized political kingdoms seem to have developed side by side with societies organized on the basis of autonomous lineage groups. In general, however, the heads of the ruling patrilineages (*umuhinza*) were the real wielders of power, and the only limitation to their authority resided in the relative strength of other lineage groups. Although nothing resembling a livestock lease contract existed among these Hutu societies, in some areas a land lease contract developed between the lineages who originally owned the land (the so-called *abakonde*) and those who opened it up to cultivation (the *abagererwa*). Thus, the *abagererwa* who offered a tribute in kind to the landlord in exchange for usufructuary rights over his land stood in relation somewhat similar to that of the *umugaragu* toward the *shebuja*. It is indicative of the strength of indigenous Hutu traditions that this particular system of land tenure (*ubukonde*)—despite its obviously "feudal" character—should still be practiced in republican Rwanda.

The patterns of relationships that have evolved between the local Hutu dynasties and the neighboring Tutsi underwent many variations, depending on the region and period that one may wish to consider. However, taking as our frame of reference the different stages of assimilation that we already described, three major types of situa-

[25] Ibid., p. 229.

tions can be selected for analysis. One is the situation of peaceful coexistence that characterized the initial phase of Tutsi penetration. During this period, which in some places lasted well after the arrival of the Germans, the *abahinza* retained most of their powers and privileges. Some of them paid formal allegiance to the Mwami of Rwanda, and gave him the tribute that such allegiance implied; but except for such symbolic gestures, the political life of the Hutu communities went undisturbed. In the Mutara region, for example, one report notes that

> the political association of the two races was not achieved like in Rwanda [*sic*]. The Bahutu were under the command of their clan heads, who gathered the tribute destined to the Mwami. The Batutsi led the nomadic pastoral life which is still theirs. The family and the clan remained the basis of social and political organization.[26]

A rather different type of relation developed between the two groups when the Mwami of Rwanda took the initiative in curtailing or abolishing the authority of the Hutu chiefs. Although every effort was made to replace the local *bahinza* by Tutsi chiefs appointed by the Mwami, these early attempts at inaugurating a "direct" system of administration were met with considerable resistance on the part of the indigenous tribes. In Bushiru, for example, the appointment of a certain Biganda by Mwami Musinga caused a major revolt among the Bashiru. Biganda's successor, chief Mutambuka, does not seem to have been held in much greater esteem by his "constituents"; realizing how precarious his position was, he left his post only a few days after he was appointed to office.[27] In Mulera a similar fate befell chief Mucocori who, after being declared *persona non grata* by the indigenous tribes, decided to abandon all political ambitions. On the other hand, the few bands of Tutsi who lived in Mulera never seriously challenged the power of the local *bahinza*:

> The situation of this group of Batutsi, says one report, isolated in the midst of rugged and belligerent agriculturalists, induced them to adopt a great deal of prudence, moderation and

[26] *Historique et Chronologie du Ruanda,* op. cit., p. 181.
[27] Ibid., p. 128.

diplomacy . . . These Batutsi remained for a long time free of all political ties.[28]

It was not until the Germans took over the administration of the country that something approaching a Tutsi "protectorate" began to take shape. In contrast with the state of affairs prevailing in Burundi, the purpose of German punitive expeditions was to strengthen the authority of the Tutsi elites over the indigenous populations of the north, and to suppress whatever forms of resistance this policy was likely to engender.[29] Under the Belgian mandate this policy came to be regarded as a precondition to the establishment of a uniform and viable system of indirect administration.

During this last phase most of the *bahinza* were removed from office and their authority transferred to Tutsi chiefs appointed by the Belgian administration. Moreover, the role of chief was redefined in a way that rendered his "overrule" far more burdensome to his wards than he himself had anticipated. Indeed, if one were to look for evidence of coercion in the application of indirect rule, it is most likely to be found in northern Rwanda. To explain this situation, at least two specific factors should be mentioned. One is that the authority of the chiefs had no other base of legitimacy than the power of the Belgian colonizers. Only through coercion could these traditionally aloof Bantu populations be brought to comply with the demands made by the chiefs on behalf of the administration. The frequent penalties incurred by the chiefs suspected of "demagoguery" suggest that sheer compulsion was the only alternative to what otherwise would be regarded as a sign of voluntary negligence.[30] What made the chiefs' position especially uneasy is that they were invested with a range of functions that had no counterpart in traditional society: As agents of the administration they had to see to it that taxes were regularly paid, that crops were properly taken care of, that antierosive contour terracing was duly maintained, etc. To

[28] Ibid., p. 123.

[29] See Roger Louis, *Ruanda-Urundi 1884–1919,* Oxford, 1963, pp. 128ff.

[30] For example, a territorial administrator could write in a letter to the Resident of Ruanda, dated March 17, 1944: *"Il est grand temps qu'un sous-chef énergique vienne rétablir la situation et que les indigènes de cette sous-chefferie soient repris sérieusement en main, le sous-chef Ruhakana ayant versé dans une sorte de démagogie consistant à ne rien demander à ses contribuables de peur de les mécontenter."* I am grateful to the *sous-préfet* of Ruhengeri for permission to consult his files.

be sure, *corvée* labor of this kind was universally resented by the Hutu peasants. In the north, however, where natural resources were particularly scarce, these *prestations* were one of the most potent sources of hostility against the chiefs.

From this brief incursion into the history of the northern region one can draw little evidence in support of Maquet's interpretation. Although some sort of status hierarchy existed among the different Hutu lineages, until the European penetration nothing like a caste system seems to have taken root in this area. Where roving bands of Tutsi were encountered, their relations with the Hutu were marked by a keen awareness of, and respect for, the indigenous institutions of their "hosts." Even when sporadic attempts were made to gain formal control over the dominant Hutu patrilineages, as happened in Mulera under Rwabugiri's reign, the lower echelons of the power structure remained in Hutu hands.

CONCLUSION

The main conclusion to be drawn from the foregoing discussion is that traditional Rwanda did not form a single social aggregate, but rather an amalgam of two distinctive societies interacting with each other in different ways and at different levels. Relations among them did not exclude the use of violence, but violence *per se* does not suffice to explain the structure of action in each society. As it has been argued,

> the use of force is efficient only for a limited purpose. Force is a sanction, but never the essence of a society. A society based solely on force is a contradiction in terms that raises the classical question: *Quis custodies ipsos custodes?*[31]

Traditional Rwanda can best be thought of as a mixture of two distinctive types of situations—a situation of optimum functional integration, characterized by a caste structure; and a situation of "ethnic coexistence." History shows that neither one of these situations remained static. Absorption of the Hutu communities into the

[31] D. F. Aberle, A. K. Cohen, A. K. Davis, M. J. Levy, Jr., F. X. Sutton, "The Functional Prerequisites of a Society," *Ethics,* Vol. 60, October 1949, p. 104.

caste structure of the Tutsi invaders was an almost continuous process, involving a partial loss of cultural identity for the absorbed group, and its reintegration into a new system of social action. The process is described by Weber as follows:

> The caste structure transforms the horizontal and uncon-
> nected coexistences of ethnically segregated groups into a verti-
> cal social system of super- and subordination. Correctly formu-
> lated: A comprehensive societalization integrates the ethnically
> divided communities into specific political and communal ac-
> tion . . . Ethnic coexistences condition on a mutual repulsion
> and disdain but allow each ethnic community to consider its
> own honor as the highest one; the caste structure brings about a
> social subordination and an acknowledgement of "more honor"
> in favor of the privileged caste and status groups. This is due to
> the fact that in the caste structure ethnic distinctions as such
> have become "functional" distinctions within the political soci-
> etalization (warriors, priests, artisans that are politically impor-
> tant for war and for building, and so on).[32]

Weber's distinction between "caste structure" and "ethnic coexist-
ence" provides us with a key to an understanding of the evolving patterns of relations between Hutu and Tutsi. We have seen how, through various historical stages, two discrete ethnic communities were amalgamated into a single cultural matrix. What must be em-
phasized is that the caste structure of central Rwanda was rooted in a shared and "culturally elaborated image" of Rwanda society.[33] This image was projected into people's consciousness through several agencies of socialization (i.e. the lineage, the army, the nuclear feudal cluster, etc.) as well as through a considerable corpus of oral traditions and literary genres. Indeed, if one were to explain why this caste structure preserved its stern rigidity longer than any other interlacustrine society, one would probably have to mention first its traditional communication structure, as there seems to be a direct correlation between the differentiation of social and political roles,

[32] *From Max Weber: Essays in Sociology,* op. cit., p. 189.
[33] See Lloyd Fallers, "Equality, modernity and democracy in the new states," in *Old Societies and New States,* Clifford Geertz, ed., Glencoe, 1963, pp. 162ff. For a further discussion of the cultural referents of stratification, see S. N. Eisenstadt, *The Political Systems of Empires,* Glencoe, 1963, pp. 82ff., and pp. 224ff.

both at the central and the provincial levels, and the particular
types of literary expression associated with them. It is at this level
that one can perhaps best analyze the relationships between the
cultural and the structural roots of stratification. By way of an
illustration, one could argue that what made ethnic distinctions
"functional" in the Weberian sense, was not only the introduction
of specific institutions like the clientage system, but also the entire
body of symbols, ideas, and beliefs about the usefulness and legitimacy of such institutions. A situation of "ethnic coexistence," on
the other hand, implies the absence of functional integration and
the persistence of vertical cleavages among groups. Hence the feelings
of "mutual repulsion and disdain" which seemed to characterize
Hutu-Tutsi relations at the time of the European penetration.

This distinction is not only of mere academic interest; it is fundamental to an understanding of contemporary issues. Although space
limitations do not permit a full discussion of the origins of the
Rwanda revolution, one can at least draw attention to the dual
nature of the motives that inspired revolutionary action. The revolution that took place in central Rwanda was a *social* revolution, in
the sense that it developed its own dialectic from the social inequalities inherent in the caste structure. The crucial point here is
that such a revolution could not have taken place unless the old
particularistic, ascriptive order had already been undermined by the
spread of universalistic, egalitarian, achievement-oriented values. In
the north, however, this type of conflicting value-orientation was not
the most important motive force behind the revolution. In seeking
to evict the Tutsi oligarchy from its position of power, the northern
tribes did not seek to challenge the legitimacy of the old social order.
Their main objective, on the contrary, was to revert to the *political*
status quo in existence before the arrival of the Tutsi conquerors,
so as to regain their political autonomy as well as their cultural
identity. Thus, it is one of the ironies of Rwanda's history that in
destroying the old monarchic regime the republican revolution also
created the conditions for a partial revival, or a perpetuation, of
feudal institutions.

E. E. EVANS-PRITCHARD

23. The Zande State

I devote this lecture to a discussion of Zande political institutions. Classical anthropological theory was very largely constructed from research among peoples without developed political institutions and for a long time the political organization of primitive peoples was not given the attention it deserves. It is particularly in Africa that relatively large-scale political societies can be studied, and much advance has already been made in this department of social anthropology. The Azande are a specimen, and my intention is to give you a summary of what general conclusions have been reached about the nature of their political institutions and, in doing so, to draw attention to the complexity of the material presented by societies of the kind and also the need, in treating it, to take into consideration what historical data are available. For some societies such data are lacking or, in so far as they exist, show there has been little change in the period they cover, but the political state of affairs among the Azande which the first European travellers to their country observed had in some important respects only recently come about and was in the succeeding years to undergo further changes. In the course of this review I can scarcely avoid frequent references to my own research, conducted between 1927 and 1930, mostly in the old kingdom of Gbudwe in the Sudan. In the published accounts to which reference is given full acknowledgment has been made of the observations of others.

A description of Zande political institutions has to be to some extent a reconstruction, for though I found that, in general, social life had not, so far as could be ascertained, changed much following the setting-up of European administration, this was not so for political

SOURCE: E. E. Evans-Pritchard, "The Zande State," The Huxley Memorial Lecture delivered in London on June 27, 1963, and printed in *The Journal of the Royal Anthropological Institute*, Vol. 93, Part I (1963), pp. 134–54. Reprinted by permission of the author and publisher.

institutions. The power of the ruling princes had been weakened and the privileges and services which went with it had correspondingly diminished. Courts were maintained but the military companies which once had their barracks there were no more to be seen. Tribute in kind and in labor was on a smaller scale and so consequently was court hospitality. Princely oracles were still consulted but their verdicts carried no weight in the eyes of European officers who alone could determine penalties. Princes ruled their provinces as before but the paramount ruler, the king, to whom they had formerly paid allegiance, had been replaced by the District Commissioner. However, if much had gone, much remained, sufficient to enable one to observe directly the traditional system, even if in partial decay, for in the area in which I did my research administration had been slight till a few years before. Then, my informants were mostly persons who had grown up in, and had vivid recollections of, the old order and had been in close touch with courts of king and princes before the European era; and habits of thought can survive when the institutions in which they were formed are no longer active as before. Oral traditions about their past history were also useful, all the more so in that the Azande take their points of historical reference, as we do, in the succession of their rulers. Further material for reconstruction of the political system and in support of historical traditions is provided by the invaluable records taken down at the beginning of this century by de Calonne-Beaufaict (1921), Hutereau (1909; 1922), and Czekanowski (1924), and later by Mgr. Lagae (1926), Vanden Plas (1921), Major Larken (1926; 1927) and others. These evidences take us back some sixty years. We are further fortunate that during the second half of the last century Zandeland was visited by a number of European travellers, three of whom, Piaggia, Junker and Casati, resided for a long time among the Azande and have left us, as has Schweinfurth also, lengthy descriptions of their way of life (Antinori 1868; Schweinfurth 1873; Junker 1890; 1891; 1892; Casati 1891; Piaggia 1941). The early accounts have, it is true, to be used with critical caution. Their reliability is sometimes doubtful, as I have tried to show in my paper on "Zande Cannibalism" (Evans-Pritchard 1960a). But they give important and undoubtedly in the main accurate information about the political circumstances obtaining at the time they were written and they confirm in all important matters the traditions recorded by much later observers. These records take us back to a century ago, but in so far as they contain oral traditions current in the time of their authors they extend our knowledge of Zande history yet further back into the eighteenth and the first half of the nineteenth centuries.

Arab caravans began to trade in and through Zandeland for ivory and slaves from round about 1860 and in some areas immediately caused disturbances. By 1870 Egyptian government forces had appeared on the scene and greatly added to the confusion, and on the overthrow of that government in the Sudan by the Dervishes these made their contribution to the cruelty and chaos of the times. In the extreme south a fourth lot of Arabs, traders and slavers from Zanzibar and the east coast of Africa, added their share to the confusion. The Zande kingdoms were better able than less organized peoples of the region to resist the pressure of the intruders and to avoid the exploitation and enslavement to which some of their neighbors were subjected, but their history was much complicated by Arab activities, and dynastic rivalries and wars became entangled with forces and events which had a different origin and development. At the end of the century the Europeans arrived, French and Belgians from the west and lastly British from the north. Ostensibly they were fighting the Dervishes, but each Great Power was also endeavoring to extend its African domains at the expense of the others, and the Azande inevitably became involved in the situation. Their lands were eventually conquered and divided between three colonial empires. Gbudwe's kingdom was the last to keep its independence. It lost it in 1905.

Long before Arabs and Europeans came to add to the confusion a confused and disturbed state of affairs already existed. Zande history is one of wars and dynastic feuds. A considerable body of the Ambomu people, under the leadership of their Vongara royal house, moved, probably about the middle of the eighteenth century, from their homeland in the valleys of the Mbomu and Shinko rivers, in what is now the Central African Republic, in a south-easterly direction into what was till recently the Belgian Congo and then eastwards, southwards, and also northwards into the Sudan. In the course of these movements they conquered vast territories, driving before them or bringing into subjection a number of foreign peoples whose descendants were in varying degrees assimilated to their Mbomu conquerors, the resultant amalgam forming the Zande people as we know them today. To these almost ceaseless wars against foreign peoples were added wars between the Vongara kings and princes over the spoils.

I shall speak briefly of some of the consequences of this expansion but before doing so I would emphasize that, owing to the diversity of historical experience in different sections of Zandeland, it would be a formidable task to attempt to write a history of the Azande as a whole. They have been variously estimated to number as few as 750,000 and as many as two or three million, or even more. They occupy a territory which on a very rough estimate indeed is probably between 60,000 to 100,000 square miles. It ranges from savannah forest in the north to dense tropical rain-forest in the south. To write the history of this people it is therefore necessary first to write a series of local histories. The people of each area only know their own history and not that of the peoples of other areas, and they have their own time scale based on the succession of their kings, and there is no system of dating to help us collate events in one kingdom with those in another. This task has to some extent been under-taken, notably by de Calonne; and I have added my contribution in a short history of the kingdom of Gbudwe (Evans-Pritchard 1956a) and in a series of vernacular texts relating to historical events and political institutions (Evans-Pritchard of 1955–57). Nevertheless, in spite of ecological and historical diversity political institutions appear to have been everywhere fundamentally the same.

One consequence of these wars, movements, and migration seems to have been the growth of power of the Avongara. Azande themselves say that the authority of their leaders was strengthened by war and by the increase in the number of their followers each new conquest brought them. Another consequence has been ethnic intermingling of great complexity. I have listed over twenty foreign peoples (one cannot be more precise in the absence of adequate information) who have contributed to the Zande amalgam and there are in it many individuals representing yet other foreign stocks (Evans-Pritchard 1958a). It is not easy to determine ethnic origins with certainty but it is probable that, except in the area ruled by the dynasty of Yakpati, persons of foreign descent easily outnumber the Ambomu, and even in that area, to which the largest proportion of the Ambomu are said to have migrated, a census of between 33,000 and 34,000 of its inhabitants showed that the Ambomu are only twenty-nine per cent of the persons listed. Some foreign peoples still form communities, under Vongara hegemony, speaking their own languages as well as Zande: Sudanic, Bantu, and Nilotic. In the Sudan alone, in addition to Zande, there are still spoken in Zande country seven or eight different languages, and there were more before the Azande were pressed southwards by the Arabs; and in my day there were still old people who spoke yet other tongues, tongues once spoken by whole peoples now dispersed and in the final stage of total cultural assimilation. These foreign elements may be found at all stages ranging from political absorption but cultural autonomy to total assimilation, both political and cultural.

We may note some results of this process. Where the mass of the population was foreign, as tended to be the case the nearer the periphery of expansion, the ruling house seems to have been more autocratic and aloof, exacting a subordination the Ambomu would not have endured. Another result was the growth of a colonial policy. It was the policy of the Avongara not only to leave a submitted people in their territory but also to entrust authority over them to their own chiefs, demanding only acknowledgment of their paramountcy and tribute in labor and produce. Then prominent commoners of Mbomu or assimilated stocks were encouraged to settle in the conquered territory, thus making for further dispersal of their clans and for intermingling of clans in general. These colonists with their kinsmen and others who gathered around them formed nuclei from which were disseminated their speech, manners and customs, and political institutions till in course of time, except where they formed large and in one way or another geographically isolated communities, the foreigners became indistinguishable from the Ambomu themselves and thought of themselves together with the Ambomu as Azande. At some point or other a scion of the royal house would set up his court in their midst and encourage them to participate through it more fully in political affairs, thereby accelerating the process of assimilation, which was made easier by the fact that there was no marked difference in the standard of life to which both conquerors and subjects were accustomed. In the Sudan at any rate there were no attempts on the part of the conquered peoples at rebellion, and their lot was by no means harsh. Soon they were taking part in new conquests in Zande armies. Had it not been for the barriers presented by the Arabs and then the Europeans the processes of conquest, colonization, and absorption might have continued till ecological zones were reached which would have compelled the Azande to abandon their traditional way of life, for they had a political organization superior to that of most of their neighbors. We may also note that the ethnic admixture produced a not easily definable class differentiation between Ambomu and persons of foreign descent, the Auro, which manifested itself in differences of values, habits and speech. A man of Mbomu descent considered himself to be superior in such matters, and particularly on account of his frequent visits to princes' courts. However, there was so much movement from place to place, so much social mobility, and so much intermarriage that the class differentiation became less marked with each generation.

It follows from what has already been said that one of the results of the Vongara-Mbomu expansion, and evidence of it, is the wide scattering of the Mbomu clans and, in many cases, of the clans of the subjugated peoples also. It may not be entirely true, as Azande like to think, that in ancient times the Mbomu clans lived as more or less separate communities, each in its own territory and under its own elders, and that it was not until the Avongara became their rulers that the clans became everywhere mixed up, but it is significant that they entertain the idea, holding that the dispersal of the clans and the consequent atrophy of their hereditary leadership facilitated the rise to political pre-eminence of the Avongara. Certainly the clans are today widely dispersed. Members of the main Mbomu clans are found everywhere in that part of Zandeland which is in the Sudan, and some of those of the assimilated peoples also; and such information as is available for the Zande kingdoms that lie outside the Sudan shows that they are distributed throughout the whole area of Zande occupation (Evans-Pritchard 1959).

It is not merely that a large number of different clans are represented in each kingdom and each province of a kingdom but the same is the case on the neighborhood level. In one typical local community of 263 adult males (thirty per cent being Ambomu) sixty-three clans were represented; in another of fifty-four adult males (seventeen per cent being Ambomu) twenty-six clans were represented; and in a third of ninety-nine adult males (thirteen per cent being Ambomu) thirty-seven clans were represented. Zande local communities are therefore today in no sense clan groups. A fair number of such a community may be connected by kin or affinal ties of one sort or another, but as a group it is a political and administrative unit owing common allegiance to a king or provincial governor through his resident deputy. This is what gives the community its unity and distinctness and in that sense only can we call it a local group at all (Evans-Pritchard 1960b). I should add that it is claimed by Azande that the Ambomu are most strongly represented in provinces once ruled over directly by kings in person, because they like to retain their traditional relationship with monarchy as descendants of the first followers of the Vongara royal house. Whether it can be demonstrated that this is really the case by analysis of the census figures has yet to be determined.

It is possible that this far and wide dispersal of the clans may to some extent account for the large number of clans. Azande say that clans were broken up and then their fragments broken up again and that some of these bits and pieces, individuals as well as groups, lost touch with other members of their clan and started new descent groups or attached themselves to Mbomu clans or large foreign clans, so that it is no longer certain who belongs to the parent stem and who does not. It was found that in the census there was 188 clans represented by at least twenty-five recorded adult male members. There were many more with a smaller representation. They have not yet been counted, but if we take that fact into consideration and also that not all Sudanese Zandeland was covered by the inquiry and further that we have evidence that in other parts of Zandeland, where the constituent ethnic elements are different from those in the Sudanese kingdoms, there are clans not found in the Sudan, we may conclude that there must be several hundred Zande clans. The foreign origin of many of them is evident in their names, which Azande sometimes attempt to explain by a story which might account for the meaning they appear to have when the syllables of which they are composed are assimilated to Zande sounds (Evans-Pritchard 1956b).

The number of clans and their scattered distribution present some confused and complex historical problems which are made none the easier when we find that persons of the same clan may give different totems. Azande explain this by the habit, to which I have referred, of individuals and groups attaching themselves to some well-known clan. Some clans are thus spoken about as *kpamiakpamia,* conglomerate, clans. Whatever the explanation may be, it is a fact that even members of the same clan in the same local community may give different totems. I have listed for the Sudanese Azande 127 totems: fifty-seven mammals, twenty-two birds, thirty-four reptiles, one crustacean, and thirteen insects (Evans-Pritchard

1956c). Now, out of a sample in which forty-two of the best known clans were represented in only one case did all members of the clan give the same totem. Examples of people who claimed membership of the same clan giving different totems are the Agiti and the Abakpuro. Out of 289 Agiti 225 gave the *rungbu* snake (snakes are the commonest Zande totems, especially of the Mbomu clans), forty the thunder-beast (Azande regard thunder as a creature), twenty-one the leopard, two the *rungbura* snake, and one the tree snake. Out of sixty-two Abakpuro six gave the *rungbu* snake, one the thunder-beast, five the leopard, forty-eight a wild cat, and two the genet. This is another indication of the unimportant role played by clanship in the highly organized political society of the Azande (Evans-Pritchard 1961).

As we might expect, the counterpart to this ethnic amalgam is a composite culture, and Azande so regard their culture. The original Mbomu economy must have undergone great changes in the course of the last century or two. Some of the main Zande crops—manioc, sweet potatoes, maize, groundnuts, the tobacco plant—are all of American origin and could not therefore have reached Zandeland before the sixteenth century and probably not till the seventeenth, eighteenth, or even nineteenth century, and inevitably they would have been borrowed from some other African people as their spread preceded European penetration. The evidence points also to the Ambomu having borrowed the culture of the banana, and even their staple crop of today, eleusine; also the Ficus from the inner bark of which they manufacture their loin-cloths; also their main pulses. All this, and other evidence, suggests that before the Ambomu began their migrations they were primarily hunters with agriculture as a subsidiary interest, whereas today the Azande are predominantly agricultural. This consideration, a mobile economy, makes it easier to understand their migrations. It also has political significance, for the political development which undoubtedly occurred in the course of territorial expansion, the increase in power and administrative organization of the Avongara and the assimilation of foreign peoples, may well be connected with the greater stability dependence on cultivated crops would have brought about (Evans-Pritchard 1960c).

In other respects also Zande culture is a thing of shreds and patches. I hope soon to publish papers showing that some of their arts and crafts and a large sector of their material culture, and also some of their important institutions, were taken over by the Ambomu from foreign peoples they assimilated or neighbored.

What gave coherence and stability to this heterogeneous amalgam of ethnic and cultural elements was the superior political organization of the Avongara-Ambomu which enabled them to impose their language and institutions on the subjugated peoples. It is this organization I shall now examine. Traditionally Azande lived in isolated homesteads spread over the countryside with several hundred yards, and sometimes greater distances, of bush between them. Early travelers through their country noted that eventually they came to a break in this distribution of homesteads and for several miles none were to be seen, and they discovered that this indicated that they were crossing from the domains of one king to those of another. These kingdoms appear to have all been of the same pattern.

In the course of Zande expansion the conquests came to be ruled by several dynasties, though the different royal houses were all closely related members of the same family or clan, the Avongara. I leave out of account here the fact that the Azande in the extreme west of their territory are, together with the related Nzakara people to the west of them, ruled by a clan of quite different ethnic origin, the Bandiya. M. de Dampierre has recently made a study of this region and has put me right on this matter, in which I had been led astray by following earlier authorities. I also leave out of account a small section of Azande, the Adio or Makaraka, who live to the extreme north-east of Zandeland and are not ruled by the Avongara but come under the authority of their own elders. The Vongara dynasties are all descended from King Ngura, the ruler of the Ambomu people some seven or eight generations ago, whose sons and grandsons founded them in the territories they carved out for themselves. I do not think we need doubt Zande statements about this.

What is open to question is the manner in which the Avongara became leaders of the Ambomu. It has been suggested that they were an intrusive foreign (non-Mbomu) stock, but there is no evidence for this view. The belief that they have a secret language of their own receives no support from such facts as are known and is also contrary to logic. It may have arisen from the habit cultivated by small sons of princes of speaking Zande backwards, in reversed syllables (Evans-Pritchard 1954). The Azande have their own story to account for the origin of their ruling house (Evans-Pritchard 1957a), and, in spite of some improbable events related in it, I think it provides the most likely explanation: that a certain man called Basenginonga, or by some other name, achieved pre-eminence among a divided people by his wise judgments and hospitality. His descendants then increased their authority and power, Azande say, in the course of migrations and wars. That many individuals have gained a following and founded dynasties is a plain fact of history, and examples could be quoted from Africa: Chaka, Sebotoane, Moshesh, and others. Cases closer to the Avongara are the ruling houses of the already mentioned Bandiya and the Mangbetu, both ruling over a cluster of peoples with similar political institutions to those of the Azande, whom they neighbor. But only in the latter case does the evidence seem conclusive that the establishment of the ruling dynasty was due to the initiative of one man (who was possibly a Vongara). The line of descent from Basenginonga to Ngura is uncertain, but there is every reason to accept the lines of descent from Ngura to the present day as substantially correct.

The descendants of Ngura established six dynasties and their genealogies have been carefully recorded by a number of observers, and de Calonne has mapped out the territories ruled by them. Scions of each dynasty established themselves as rulers of independent kingdoms, the number of which varied from time to time with the fortunes of war; and it cannot even be said with precision how many there were at any given time, both on account of lack of adequate information and also because, for a reason which will soon be apparent, the definition of what constitutes a kingdom has to be in relative terms. However, if we define it as an area whose inhabitants acknowledge one man to be their sovereign and he acknowledges the overlordship of no other man, then round about 1880 there were probably some fifteen kingdoms. They varied in size but all stretched for several days journey on foot. Gbudwe's kingdom was, at a very rough approximation, 10,000 square miles. We have to guess at the size of their populations, but there are indications that they were not likely to have been less than 50,000 and were probably nearer 100,000 in some of the larger kingdoms, such as Gbudwe's.

However, though a kingdom had clearly demarcated boundaries, designated by rivers, and can be so defined, in discussing the ruler-subject relationship Azande place the emphasis on personal allegiance rather than on tenure. It is true that in a sense the king owned the land and could order a subject off it, and in that sense anyone who lived on land over which he held dominion was *ipso facto* his subject. But no one was tied to any particular piece of land or district. The country was thinly populated, perhaps ten to the square mile, or even fewer, and people settled very much where they pleased, frequently moving their homes from one place to another. Landed property had little importance in a political context. There was no suggestion of tribute and services being paid as rent. Furthermore, if a Zande was dissatisfied with his lot in one kingdom he could move to another. He might have to use discretion in doing so, but it was done; and he then transferred his allegiance to the ruler in whose territory he went to live. That the relationship was thought of in terms of personal allegiance rather than of tenure, of leadership rather than of possession, is illustrated by the fact that the people of a kingdom were designated by reference to a person rather than to a territory. The people of one kingdom were *avuru* Wando, the subjects or followers of Wando, the people of another were *avuru* Malingindo, the subjects or followers of Malingindo, and so on. This designation of the political community might be compared to that obtaining in Europe before the idea of possession gained precedence, but whereas in Europe it was defined in relation to the people—King of the Franks, Duke of the Normans, King of the English—among the Azande it was in relation to their ruler. In speaking about a kingdom Azande do not have so much in mind its boundaries as the relation of a community of subjects to a person; and it was more followers than land that the kings wished to gain in their struggles for power, the territory seized being incidental to the acquisition of new subjects. Also, as we shall see, a kingdom had no territorial longevity. On the death of the sovereign it broke up into separate kingdoms ruled over by his elder sons, and the inhabitants of each then became the subjects of independent rulers, whereas before these rulers had acknowledged the paramountcy of their father. Consequently one cannot speak of a Zande kingdom in the sense that one can speak of, for example, the kingdom of Bunyoro, where there has been a succession of monarchs whose authority can be clearly defined in territorial terms, as can the succession of dynasties in England. Perhaps we may see in the Zande mode of designation for, and their conception of, their political communities a heritage from their past, from the time of their great migrations, when whole populations moved, . . . and the tie between the leaders of these migratory bands and their followers was a personal one and could not adequately be thought of in terms of any particular tract of country. The mode of speech suggests also that the Vongara royal house have not always had the exalted position the first European visitors to their courts found them to possess but rather that they reached it in the course of these movements and attendant wars, which is what the Azande themselves say and other evidences point to: that "war begat the king." It is only in a historical, or looking back, sense that Azande stress the territorial aspect of a kingdom, when they refer to what used to be a king's domains, e.g. *kumbo Ezo,* what was the kingdom of (or the heritage of) Ezo.

Before I describe the organizational structure of a Zande kingdom it is necessary to decide on the terms we are to use, especially in translating the Zande *gbia*. This word can be used for the superior person in any relationship involving authority on one side and subordination on the other, which for the Azande means all social relationships, though its first meaning is any member of the Vongara clan, the nobility. We have, however, to distinguish between grades of status in the nobility. A king was ruler of a kingdom in the sense already defined. I speak of "princes" in a political sense only, to denote those members of the aristocracy who ruled a province of a kingdom as representatives of its monarch, by whom they were appointed and to whom they were responsible. I speak of "nobles" in reference to all members of the aristocratic clan, giving the word a social rather than a political sense, for although all kings and princes were also in this sense nobles, most members of the clan have in recent times held no, or very minor, political office, though they have always had, and still have, a superior social position with which went certain privileges. When a king appointed a commoner to rule a province I speak of him as a "commoner governor" when it is necessary to make a distinction between governors who were commoners and those who were nobles, the princes. Azande often use the word "Azande" in the sense of commoners in contrast to nobles, but I shall use the term in the broader cultural sense which denotes the whole people: the Vongara aristocracy, the descendants of their original Mbomu followers, and the descendants of the conquered peoples, the Auro.

A king divided his realm into provinces, between river boundaries, keeping a large central one for himself and establishing in each of the others his representatives to rule in his name. His central position enabled him to be within reasonable distance from the courts of his governors, but the reason generally advanced is that he was protected against surprise attack from another kingdom, which would first have to pass through one or more of the frontier provinces, giving time for the whole kingdom to be alerted. Broad paths led from the royal court to the provincial courts and it was the duty of the governors to see that when the grasses were high they were leveled to the ground on both sides of them. Junker has a drawing of a man engaged in this operation. In the early part of a king's reign the governors would tend to be commoners for as a rule kings did not trust their kinsmen, but when his sons grew up—some might be only striplings at the time—he gave them the most important provinces. Each governor exercised in his province the same authority over his subjects as the king did in his, and it was only in degree that his functions differed from theirs; and their courts were constructed on the same model of, and run on the same lines as, the royal court. Nevertheless, a king could deprive a governor of his office at will and he did not hesitate to do so if he suspected his loyalty or for cowardice or maladministration, and he could transfer him from one province to another to suit his convenience. In the kingdom of Gbudwe, of the administrative structure of which I have made a detailed analysis (Evans-Pritchard 1960d), there appear to have been *circa* 1900, including his own, twenty-six provinces, mostly ruled by his sons. The number of provinces in a kingdom varied from time to time and provincial boundaries were changed if the king thought fit to alter them. They varied also in size and to some extent in their degree of autonomy. That ruled over by Gbudwe's second son Mange to the east of the Sueh river was so large and populous and also so far removed from his father's court that he was almost an independent monarch and, though he formally recognized his father's authority, he kept well away from him.

The administrative arrangements in each province were on the same pattern as that of the kingdom as a whole. Each was a kingdom in miniature. The prince in his province was like the king in his realm. He placed his court in a central position, thus protecting it from raids and making it easily accessible to his agents. These agents or deputies correspond to the governors of provinces in the kingdom, though they lacked their power and authority. They had charge of the various districts into which a province was divided for administrative purposes and the governor ruled through them. They were responsible to him for good order, payment of tribute in kind and labor, settlement of disputes which were not of such a character as required handling by the governor himself, military service, etc. Just as paths ran from the king's court to the courts of his provincial governors so paths, though narrower ones, ran from the provincial court to the homesteads of the governor's deputies in each province.

The question of succession to these provinces or fiefs—I use the word without prejudice: they little resembled the feudal fiefs of Europe—scarcely arose. If a prince died the king put another in his place, and though he might choose a younger uterine brother of the dead man he could nominate whom he pleased. He sent one of his men-at-court with the new princely ruler to present him to his subjects and they formally accepted him after some of them had made speeches admonishing him to govern wisely. They had no choice in the matter. A prince could, if he so wished, allow a younger brother or older son to exercise authority over part of his territory while remaining responsible to him—a sort of "parage." The king would raise no objection. As far as he was concerned the fief was undivided and he dealt only with the prince in charge of it. A prince could not alienate his fief. When the king died the fief, if its ruler was a noble, not if he was a commoner, became *de facto* an independent realm and the prince its king, if he survived the internecine strife which then took place.

It must be emphasized that though the royal authority was recognized everywhere in the kingdom, and the provincial governors, nobles and commoners alike, were careful to pay the king tribute, to visit him every month or so (Mange was an exception), and to avoid giving him any cause for dissatisfaction, nevertheless, the king retained direct control over only a portion of the realm and had to delegate to others power in the rest of it. Effective power over the subject consequently passed into the hands of his governors and particularly of his elder sons; and they in their turn had to delegate some of it to their deputies, though to a far lesser degree. Given the size of a Zande kingdom and the simplicity of communications there would seem to have been a limit to the extent of an area, and of its population, over which a man could exercise direct personal control.

The system of provinces could be described as a complex segmentary structure in which there was a certain degree of opposition between province and province. This was expressed in terms of the jealousy and enmity with which princes viewed each other, especially those ruling adjacent provinces, and this occasionally led to fights, though they were unlikely to be more than casual affrays, for the king took the line that all alike were his subjects and would punish the offender. There was an element of local particularism which tended to persist in spite of change of governors, for the same people continued to have a common tie to whomsoever at any time held office. It was expressed in and through the local ruler. The people of the province of Gbudwe's son Rikita were not only *avuru* Gbudwe, subjects of Gbudwe. They were also *avuru* Rikita, subjects of Rikita, as distinct from the subjects of other princes, and it was Rikita, and not his father, with whom they had personal contact and to whom they fulfilled such duties as subject owes to ruler. The rivalry, however, was between prince and prince and not between prince and king, who was too powerful to be overthrown by any one of his sons, for he had a powerful force at his immediate command and could rely for support on his other governors, too jealous of each other to combine against him. Consequently, though it is true, as was the case in Europe in feudal times, that the subject was bound to his immediate lord by ties stronger, because more personal, than those which attached him more remotely to the king, he was not put in a position of having to chose between two allegiances.

In every Zande kingdom about which we have sufficient information to judge, the process was the same and repetitive. A king planted out his sons in provinces. Even during his lifetime the elder sons, the earliest planted out and with the largest provinces, were almost independent monarchs ruling autonomous states in their own right. On the king's death these elder sons achieved complete autonomy and set out to enlarge their patrimony at the expense of neighboring peoples and of their weaker brothers. When they thus gained kingdoms of their own they in their turn planted out their sons and so the process was repeated generation after generation. There can be no doubt about the facts. They have been recorded in detail by several hands, most notably by de Calonne.

The evidence inclines one to believe that in the period of rapid expansion, up to some four or five generations ago, in the main the elder princes who found themselves in possession of large tracts of the patrimony on their father's death enlarged their domains at the expense of foreign peoples instead of wasting their energy in fighting each other for dominance. As the momentum of expansion slowed down and its limits were reached in most directions, so that the territories of the various branches of the royal house became stabilized, the domains of a prince could be enlarged only by conquest of those of his brothers or other kinsmen. Civil war and the elimination of all but a few was the only alternative to fractionization into ever smaller fragments.

I turn now to ask what were the relations between rulers and ruled, between king, or his representative, and subject, and how both viewed them. The main royal functions as seen from both sides are in part pointed to in the myth of the origin of the Vongara clan: judicial, military, and economic or fiscal; and we may add to them administrative. As each of the governors had the same functions in his province as the king had in his it must be understood that when I say that the king did this or that, this is shorthand for the king or his governors, unless specified otherwise.

All cases of any importance, crimes and torts involving punishment or compensation on any scale, had to be settled at the king's court, usually by the king in person, who gave judgments and imposed penalties in accord with custom and precedent. He came out from his private quarters every two or three days to sit in judgment with his men-at-court sitting in a semi-circle in front of him. As most Zande cases concern witchcraft and adultery in which evidence was either lacking or circumstantial the facts had to be determined by putting questions to the poison oracle (Evans-Pritchard 1937), and while anyone could consult his own oracle about his affairs, only the king's oracle or that of a person acting on his instructions or with his consent had validity in law. The king therefore had the judicial machinery entirely in his hands, and the first of his duties was to see that it was properly used, that fair and, in Zande eyes, reasonable judgments were given. As the sole source of justice the king benefited from court fees and gifts made to him by successful litigants.

Besides being supreme judge the king was also commander-in-chief of the forces of his realm. There were companies of warriors, some of senior men and some of bachelors, each under its own officers, and the bachelor companies had barracks round the court. Some of their members would generally be in residence there. These regulars, if we may so call them, were volunteers; and a prince had no difficulty in recruiting young men for, among other incentives, there was the expectation that he would aid them in obtaining wives, which was often a problem for men in a society where so many of the women were taken to spouse by the nobles and wealthier and older commoners. When a prince carried out a raid across the border into another kingdom or there was war between kingdom and kingdom the whole manpower of the province or kingdom could be mobilized and incorporated for the duration of the fighting into this skeletal organization. The men of the raided province were under obligation to proceed at once to the point of attack and their resistance was consequently not in company formation. Border raids, called *basapu,* organized by marcher governors were, on one or other sector of the frontiers, annual events. If one province was attacked adjacent provinces came to its aid, but in the case of raids there was no mobilization of the whole kingdom. Affrays of this kind only lasted a few hours. These raids seem to have had little purpose beyond the boosting of a prince's renown and a demonstration of loyalty to him. Their sociological function, however, may be said to be the maintenance of a political system in which kingdom was in balanced opposition to kingdom by keeping the border in a state of turmoil, or the threat of it, making the physical boundary a clear political one and emphasizing on both sides allegiance to the king and his representatives (Evans-Pritchard 1957b). Large-scale wars or campaigns, between kingdom and kingdom or against Arabs and Europeans, called *sungusungu vura,* which might last for several days or even several weeks, were less frequent. Gbudwe in the course of a reign of about thirty-six years is recorded to have fought nine of these campaigns. When there was fighting on this scale the king sent messengers to his provincial governors ordering them to mobilize their forces; and should the kingdom be in jeopardy and the operation a defensive one, to proceed immediately with their companies to the scene of operations. Only the king could order general mobilization of the whole kingdom, and it was he who seems generally to have directed, with the aid of his poison oracle, the strategy and tactics of the campaign, though each contingent was directly under the orders of the governor of the province from which it came, and each had to solve its own commissariat problems (Evans-Pritchard 1957c). The military organization of the kingdom was thus also in the hands of the king and his representatives; and it may here be noted that the people of a kingdom saw themselves as a distinct unity, a political community, in relation to their king particularly in war, for participation in such wars was a demonstration that the men on either side were followers of one king and not of another, and this was the only activity in which the whole of a kingdom took part together. Its corporate military action was the clearest criterion by which a Zande kingdom might be defined.

In a broad sense the king considered himself responsible for public order, the upkeep of communications, and intelligence for the whole kingdom. He did not interfere with the internal administration of his governors unless their rivalries led to affrays or a governor proved to be incompetent, but he stood no nonsense from them and he expected them to keep in touch with him by messenger if anything untoward happened or there was intelligence of an attack on the kingdom and to report in person every month or two on the affairs of their provinces. He placed special emphasis on the duty of the marcher governors to keep watch on the frontier, to obtain advance information through their spies and oracles of an impending attack, and in the case of one to go to the assistance of the threatened province at once. The king also, through his deputies in his own central province, which was by far the largest, had the same administrative functions as each of the governors had in theirs.

The maintenance of a court of justice, of a military organization, and of administration meant that there were always a fair number of persons at court; the king's sons and kinsmen, visiting governors, deputies paying their respects, members of the bachelor companies in barracks, litigants awaiting court procedure, pages, suppliants for gifts, and others, and these people had to be fed during their residence at court, often of several days continuous duration or more, even, at the courts of governors who might not at the time have the wherewithal to assist suppliants, of weeks. Otherwise they could not, and certainly would not, have remained there. An abundance of food was therefore required, and the king had no means of acquiring it other than by the labor and gifts of his subjects. The considerable quantities of food sent out to his guests from day to day were obtained in three ways. The military companies were used for labor in the royal cultivations. The companies and the wives of the senior ones in his own province cleared the bush for the main royal crops, weeded them, and harvested them; and they were aided in the most arduous of these tasks, the clearing, by detachments sent by each of the commoner governors of provinces of the realm. Gardens so worked by public labor must be distinguished from the king's private gardens, cultivated by his wives and their female servants with some assistance from his personal pages, for, in theory at any rate and probably in practice in the main, the crops cultivated by his subjects were used for public entertainment and not for consumption by his own household. It is likely that when occasion required each was used to supplement the other. The second source of food was tribute of the subjects of his own province. This could be regarded as a tax, but, although some pressure may have been brought to bear on persons to contribute who did not regularly attend court, it was regarded by Azande as more in the nature of a whip-round from time to time to supply their ruler with the means of providing for their own consumption at court. The deputies in each district collected from the people of it whatever was seasonable in the gardens or bush and sent it to court, and people also presented part of the game they killed. Again, such tribute was not intended for the king or his wives but for public hospitality. If a subject wished to contribute some particularly relished food, such as game or beer, to the king's personal table he made him a personal and private gift. A third source of food—and this the paramount alone enjoyed, was the annual tribute sent to him by his provincial governors. Every year caravans brought a portion of the tribute paid to these governors by their subjects to the paramount's court. The labor of preparing all this food for eating was the king's responsibility. It fell to his wives and their female servants, of whom he had therefore to have a large number—a matter I discuss later.

Besides revenue in food the king was given by his immediate subjects and by his governors various products of art and craft: baskets, hats, mats, barkcloth, stools, bowls, pots, etc. These were for the use of his household. In the case of King Gbudwe's kingdom, products common in some parts of the realm were scarce or not to be found in his own province and were therefore doubly welcome. From the same sources he was presented with spears and other metal artifacts, and he obtained quantities of these valuable objects in fines and court fees, from the spoils of war, and in other ways. Some he used for marrying wives, but he had to distribute many, perhaps most, of them to his warriors and to suppliants who came to beg his aid, not only from his own province but from those of his governors also. Prisoners of war, girls and boys, were sent to the king, and these, or some of them, he also gave away. He also gave away to his courtiers and to those who had served in his military companies women for wives; and these appear to have been, besides captives of war, women paid in fines or seized from the homes of men who had incurred royal displeasure. I cannot say how many, or how often, women were princes' rewards to their subjects, but I fancy that they were few and seldom, although the giving of them was spoken about by Azande and their princes alike as the supreme example of princely munificence in the past.

Now, in a subsistence economy without money or markets there is nothing much a ruler can do with surplus food or such objects as hats or barkcloth except to give them away, and although spears could be exchanged for wives they must have been mainly given to subjects, for it was impossible for a king or prince to refuse a suppliant, though he might keep him waiting a long time before giving them. We might say that what has been described is a form of gift exchange, but this, though true up to a point, would leave out of consideration some important features. The subject gives to the ruler and the ruler gives back, but the psychology is different in the two transactions. The subject is performing a duty and the king graciously receives his tribute. He confers a favor in accepting a gift and also in dispensing largesse; in both he places the subject in an inferior position. Also, although it was an exchange it was an uneven one. Most of those who gave received nothing in return because they did not frequent the courts. The food and other gifts the king gave away went to those who served at court: his bodyguard, his kinsmen, his pages, his deputies, his governors and their retinues, and other retainers. The people as a whole were maintaining the court. Then, the king and princes were left with a surplus. We have to bear in mind further that by distribution of food and other gifts the rulers were able to maintain a political organization through which they accumulated wealth in fines, fees, gifts to win favor, etc. They were the wealthiest members of the society, and this was to be seen in their dress (though simple, better than that of commoners), in their well-fed appearance, and in particular in the abstinence from manual labor and in the number of their wives, which exceeded, and sometimes far exceeded what even the most prosperous commoners could attain to; and in an economy of this kind women are the real wealth—their labor and child-bearing, their productive and reproductive functions. The more wives a man had the greater the hospitality he could offer, thereby attaching to himself followers who provided him with yet more labor and other services; and the more the children begotten by him. Further, apart from the economic advantage of many wives the rulers were also exploiting their subjects through their labor and tribute alike. It could be said that all these services went to support the state, from the maintenance of which all benefited. This is also true up to a point, beyond which it would have to be said that the state did not benefit all equally, that the upper rank in the state, the Avongara benefited much more considerably than the commoners. Nevertheless, I think it would be a mistake to view the matter in purely economic terms. Royalty did not want wealth so much as personal prestige; or, perhaps one should rather say that princes liked riches because they liked to win renown by giving them away. It was that which counted most, and in the thought of the people the economic advantages were subsidiary to the power they served to sustain.

I must at this point make it clear that the Zande kinship was a purely secular office, lacking religious or magical attributes or functions as such; kings were powerful enough to have no need of them. The ruler-subject relationship was a matter-of-fact one in which mutuality of service was recognized and given on both sides. The way the Azande saw it was that the king was father-ruler to his people and they his children-subjects. In paying him tribute they showed him respect, and he on his part gave hospitality to such guests as cared to visit him. In discussing their rulers commoners often tell one that they themselves are a quarrelsome and unruly people and that if it were not for their noble masters there would be no order, for they would not obey one of themselves; and I think they are right. They recognize that there must be a final authority whose decisions are not to be disputed, and that is why they obey their rulers; and they accepted in the past that in the last resort the king must exercise force if his decisions were questioned or his orders not carried out or if someone acted contrary to law, custom, and good manners. The king had the force at his hand in his military companies, his retainers, his deputies, and in general the men-at-court. He instructed them to execute, or mutilate a man and seize his wives and destroy his home, and it was not disputed that he had a right to do so. However, there was a curb on despotism. If a prince tried to exact too much from his subjects, went after their wives, or was cruel there were sanctions they could apply. They could cease to visit him at court, isolating him, and if they found that they were no longer able to feel secure in person and property they moved their homes to another province and transferred their allegiance to its governor. An unpopular prince would also find that when it came to civil war on the death of his father he would not receive the support of his subjects. Then there was a further, and perhaps more important, curb than fear of losing subjects or their support. Zande kingdoms were in Montesquieu's category of those of which the principle was honor. Kings and princes felt obliged to behave according to the traditional pattern of their status, to be courteous to their subjects and not to go beyond what custom prescribed for them, to do nothing shameful. All in all we may say that though the royal power might appear to have been unlimited, as in theory it was, in practice it was limited by the fact that a ruler had to exercise it through others, and these others could only exercise it if they retained the confidence of those over whom they represented royal authority. It was remarked by early travelers that there was a big gap between appearance and reality, the king in the last resort being unable to get his followers to do what they were determined not to do.

The secret of success of the Zande administrative organization seems to me to have been the deputing of authority. A king or prince ruled through his representatives at all levels: governors, deputies, leaders of military companies. Without them he was helpless. He seldom left his home, where he spent most of his time with his wives and small children. He was not only a remote but also a lonely figure, and he would have had no idea of what was going on, far less have been able to control it, if it had not been for the loyalty of those he appointed to office; and these men passed the king's authority downward to others so that a large number of persons enhanced their self-importance by sharing in it. The king's authority in the end depended on its distribution right down the scale. In short, the enjoyment of royal authority was largely its enjoyment by those through whom it was exercised, and they could sometimes circumvent it or use it in their own interests and for their own prestige. Much was done in the king's name that he had not ordered and might never hear about. People were even executed in his name but not at his behest. What we are saying is that underlying the apparent despotism of the sovereign was a bureaucracy that served the royal power for its own sake, for the privilege of sharing in it, for the love of power, even though delegated power. This they achieved by personal relations with the ruler, which most people did not have, by frequent attendance at court; and I now say a few words about court arrangements (Evans-Pritchard 1957d).

A king lived in the center of his realm, like a queen bee in a hive. His court consisted of three parts: an outer court, an inner court, and the private quarters or harem. In the outer court cases were heard, wars were declared, and administration was conducted by the king in person or in his absence by one of his sons who might be present; and food was sent out daily for those in attendance, the members of companies, deputies, and all those whose ambitions made them regular visitors to court; for ordinary persons, unless they had some special business there, tended to keep away from court, taking the view that though it might offer rewards—office, gifts, being-in-the-know—it also had its hazards: accusations of witchcraft, sorcery, and adultery with the king's wives, and the danger of being bewitched by jealous rivals for royal favors. Most people, especially the foreign elements, preferred to stay at home and mind their own business. They took such troubles as they might have to the king's deputy in their district. Between the outer court and the private quarters was a small inner court called "the place of secrets," at the side of which the king's pages had their huts. Here food was served to nobles, who ate by themselves, and to senior office-holders. A page summoned them from the outer court when the bowls and pots of food had been carried from the private quarters to this inner court. There also the king could discuss affairs privately with his more important retainers away from the general public. A path ran from this court to the royal harem which, as the king had many wives, might cover an extensive area, for each wife had her own homestead and garden; and in the vicinity were also the main crop cultivations. The wives had to grow and prepare food for themselves and their children and also to prepare food for the king's subjects in the two courts. The king appointed one of them his cook, and she alone prepared his meals. At the court of a king or of a wealthy prince the wives were organized into companies on the model of the military companies, each with its mistress, whom we may dub a queen. The royal public cultivations were worked by the subjects, and their tribute was paid to the name of one or other of the queens and she distributed the produce of the cultivations, and the food paid in tribute, to her followers to prepare for consumption in the courts. The queens were given servants, usually young girls, by their master, as were also sometimes other wives, and these servants performed the more onerous household tasks. Sooner or later the king would have relations with them—it is said secretly for fear of comment from his wives—and if they bore him children they were given their own homes and henceforward ranked as wives.

One of the most important features of the Zande royal house lack-

ing in the monarchies with which we are familiar in most of our historical reading was the large families they begat by their numerous
wives. Some kings had dozens of wives. In practice a ruler could
demand the hand of any unmarried girl, though he paid bridewealth
for her and, apart from that consideration, men were glad to have
their daughters among the royal wives as there was some prestige in
this and favors might come from it. A king did not, however, treat his
in-laws with the deference a commoner was expected to show his.
The king-to-subject relationship was not affected by the son-in-law
to father-in-law one. Since a king had marital relations with all his
many wives we can readily see how it came about that the royal clan
is now probably the largest in Zandeland. In the census taken in the
Sudanese part of it it was the largest, numbering 1,382 adult, or near
adult, males. If it is represented on this scale in other parts there
might be over 10,000 Avongara of both sexes and of all ages. Considering that they all trace their descent back to King Ngura, who
lived some seven or eight generations back, this is an astonishing
figure; but it is not an improbable one; and it is comparable with
figures from other societies known to me, for example the increase
in membership of the royal houses of the Shilluk and Anuak peoples,
and also of the Sanusi family in Cyrenaica where polygamy is limited
by Koranic law. This increase among the Azande has led to the
formation of an aristocratic caste or class, not just a differentiation between rulers and subjects but the emergence of a privileged grade of
people who, even though the great majority of them hold no office,
have by birth a superior status. They avoid, in so far as they can,
manual labor, but most of them can no longer avoid it altogether,
and the situation becomes more difficult for them in each new generation. As they increase in number they lose in prestige and wealth and
are forced, except for the few, to live more and more as commoners
do. So today we have to distinguish between princes and an aristocratic class, noble by birth but lacking political authority. I speak of
what was happening in Zandeland when I was there over thirty years
ago. In the past the situation was different. The Avongara must have
been fewer the further back we go. Also such evidence as we have
suggests that they lived less lavishly when they were less powerful.
Then, in the past the Azande were still enlarging their territories
and royal sons could be provided with provinces to rule so that they
were spread more thinly and ruler and noble were synonymous. We
must bear in mind too that large numbers of them must have been

eliminated in wars and by assassination, a point to which I shall soon turn.

Sons of princes had a shorter and less intimate home life than sons of commoners. They lived with their mothers till shortly before puberty. They were then told by the king or their elder brothers to leave the harem and build huts for themselves near the outer court, and from that time they never entered the harem again. They only saw their father when he entered the outer court, and it was only occasionally that they saw their mothers, when by arrangement they met them at the edge of the royal homestead. If their father spoilt them when they were little they from now on had to endure what a commoner's son did not suffer. They were often hungry, and their older brothers made them fag for them and gave them a hiding if they did not carry out their duties promptly and properly. This education undoubtedly inculcated self-reliance and shaped their characters in other respects. Most Europeans who have known Zande kings and princes in the days before their power was broken have paid tribute to them. Cunning and ruthless the Vongara rulers may have been, and had to be if they were to survive, just as the Italian princes in Machiavelli's time had to be, but what European travelers admired in them was their natural dignity of bearing, unostentatious pride, courteous manners, cordiality, composure, reserve, intelligence, prudence, and so forth (Evans-Pritchard 1957e). Pride and reserve, even shyness and in some cases nervous aloofness, polished manners, simplicity of adornment, shrewdness of judgment, and a high degree of intelligence, poise, and an air of authority were characteristic of most of the princes I met, and even of the nobility who lacked office. One could pick them out among commoners at a glance.

The elder sons were planted out by their father, sometimes while still in their teens, to rule provinces of the realm, at first under the guidance of a trusted courtier if they were very young; and sooner or later all sons received fiefs unless their father thought them incompetent. The relations of these princes with their father were of mutual reserve. Court etiquette inhibited any intimacy between them, imposing a screen of shyness. The fathers seem always to have suspected their grown-up sons of trying to seduce their wives, suspicion resting on oracular disclosures rather than on factual evidence, and though they seldom rebelled against their fathers—some cases have been recorded—the fathers feared disloyalty and also assassination by sorcery at their hands. I return to the relation between brothers after a few words about royal daughters.

There can be no doubt that the Avongara, especially those in high positions, though they sometimes gave their daughters in marriage to commoners, on the whole disliked the idea of their subjects possessing their daughters; and such marriages were not solicited by the husbands and seem to have been generally unsatisfactory and unstable. Husbands had little control over wives of royal blood, and the princesses, having been brought up in idleness, were not prepared to lead the hard and busy life of a commoner's housewife. Nor were the husbands at all comfortable in the knowledge that the nobles regularly had incestuous relations with all but the full sister, so that a man who came to visit his half-sister or cousin might commit with her the adultery for which his residence as a guest gave him opportunity. Moreover, the son of a commoner father and a noble mother had a somewhat ambiguous status in society and was liable to be thought by commoners and nobles alike to be putting on airs. Consequently, though this is very difficult to determine, girls of noble birth seem in the past, and even when I was living among the Azande, to have been given in marriage to kinsmen, sometimes to cement a friendship, or more commonly to have been kept as mistresses by their fathers and brothers, for nobles did not hesitate to have congress with their own daughters and with their sisters on the spear-side. Other princesses became more or less courtesans, like the Shilluk princesses, wandering from man to man, commoners and nobles alike, who took their fancy, and probably ending up in some prince's harem, though it would be difficult to say in what capacity, whether as kinswoman or paramour or both. They would then have been given servants to labor for them and could live a life of ease, and, so Azande say, they were much given to Lesbian practices. As women in Zande society have a subordinate position it would have been thought highly improper for them to have had a political status which required the exercise of authority over men.

I return to the royal sons. The rules of succession to royal office must be sought in historical actualities rather than in any principle, for there does not appear to have been any theory of primogeniture or any other order of succession. Indeed, we may say that there was, properly speaking, no succession at all. It stands to reason that the elder sons were in a better position to gain their father's personal heritage at his death than his younger sons, for they were already firmly rooted as rulers of principalities which were almost autonomous states. When they were able in the past to expand at the expense of foreign peoples there was little incentive to try to annex one another's domains, but there could be bitter competition to acquire the personal royal domain with the prestige and large population that went with it. The issue was fought out, the competitors being supported by the people of their provinces; and I was told that the victory was likely to go to the prince who had the confidence of his late father's immediate subjects, their backing being the deciding factor. Thus Gbudwe, who had no province or not one of any importance at his father's death nevertheless obtained control over his personal demesne because he was the choice of its warriors. It will be appreciated that this was a powerful sanction for a prince to act correctly in his dealings with commoners. Provincial governors had only personal loyalty to rely on. Their people were not attached to them by traditional allegiance to a particular line of descent associated with the locality, nor as representatives of a local clan predominant in the area, nor through a maternal link with the principality, nor in other ways found in some African polities; which was also another reason why princes had no inducement to oppose the king.

Dynastic rivalries have, at any rate in later periods of Zande history, frequently led to wars and assassinations to which Arabs and Europeans added their quota. The facts are beyond dispute. Zande history is very largely a chronicle of patricides, fratricides, and the slaughter of sons and cousins on a Visigothic scale (Evans-Pritchard 1958b). The slaughter was appalling. Very few of the kings died a natural death, and those who, in our way of thinking, did so are thought by Azande, who regard all deaths as brought about by human action, to have perished by curses or sorcery on the part of their kinsmen. In these struggles for power only the most cunning and ruthless survived. We can say of them what Ganshof says of the quarrels between the sons and grandsons of Clovis in the sixth century, that they "resembled nothing so much as the fighting of wild beasts" (Ganshof 1952). These rivalries, largely between brothers, arose from the fact that when a king died no one son inherited his domains. Each became the monarch of his erstwhile province. The weaker found it expedient to pay homage to the stronger, and the stronger made war on each other to get possession of the late king's personal demesne; and when that issue was settled they made war on each other because, as I have noted earlier, it was through war that subjects demonstrated their loyalty to a ruler, though Azande put the matter rather differently, saying that kings made war from pride and for honor and renown. The situation was much the same as for the Frankish kingship, and for the same reason, that a kingdom was divided among the king's sons during his lifetime and at his death. Foreknowledge of the invariable struggle for dominance and survival which ensued at the death of their father could scarcely have failed to have colored the attitude of Zande princes to one another, and we need not therefore be surprised that rivalry, suspicion, and hatred were common among royal sons. It will readily be understood also that in these circumstances a prince would be foolhardy indeed to rebel against his father, for none was powerful enough to assert himself single-handed against the monarch, while their rivalries among themselves would have prevented an effective combination to overthrow the royal authority.

I have tried to sketch a broad picture of the Zande political system in so far as it can be reconstructed, and especially of the place of the kingship in it; and I have emphasized a few points which seem to me to be significant for an understanding of this particular people's political institutions and for African states in general. I have given few details. They are contained in the books and papers listed in the bibliographical references. I do not suppose that further research today could reveal directly much beyond what has been recorded with regard to the matters I have discussed. They are what Azande call *kuru pai,* old things or things of the past. I wonder if there is a single Zande alive who can remember having seen King Gbudwe. Further research can, however, show us what changes the institutions have undergone during more than half a century of alien rule and so shed some retrospective light upon them.

24. The Sources of Law in Tswana Courts: Legislation and Precedent

The Tswana peoples referred to in this paper inhabit the Bechuanaland Protectorate, where they number altogether about 27,000. In pre-European times they derived their subsistence mainly from animal husbandry and the cultivation of crops, each household producing its own food. Today they are still essentially small-scale subsistence farmers. But to satisfy the new wants developed by contact with Western civilization over the past century, many persons also pursue new occupations, including above all temporary wage-labor for Europeans. In some areas more than half the able-bodied men are away every year working in the Union of South Africa. Their absence, often prolonged, has led to conspicuous changes in traditional customs and beliefs, and, as will be seen from some of the examples given below, has also given rise to new grounds for litigation.

Politically the Tswana are divided into "tribes," each occupying its own territory and managing its own affairs, subject only to the overriding control exercised by the European Administration of the Protectorate. Each tribe has its own chief, who even under European rule still has important executive, judicial, and legislative, functions. In performing his duties he is helped by several grades of council, one of which, the "tribal assembly," embraces all the adult men. Within each tribe the major administrative unit is the "ward," a body of people living in their own village or part of a village under the leadership and authority of a "headman," whose office, like the chief's, is normally hereditary from father to son. The headman, in addition to his other duties, judges cases between members of his ward or involving them as defendants or accused. His verdicts can be taken on appeal to the senior tribal court, of which the chief is

SOURCE: I. Schapera, "The Sources of Law in Tswana Tribal Courts: Legislation and Precedent," *Journal of African Law*, Vol. 1, No. 3, 1957, pp. 150–62. Reprinted by permission of the author and publisher.

the judge, and beyond that appeal can be made to the court of the local district officer.[1]

In a study published in 1943,[2] I showed that among the Tswana chiefs have from time immemorial had the power to change the law, either by abolishing or amending an existing usage or by establishing a new rule of conduct. Within relatively recent times legislation of this kind has become fairly common, owing mainly to the new conditions created by the impact of Western civilization. The European Government of the Protectorate not only recognized most of the laws decreed by the chiefs, but preferred to encourage them instead of imposing its own; and the Native Administration Proclamation (No. 74 of 1934, replaced by No. 32 of 1943) explicitly authorized Native Authorities to make rules, subject to the approval of the High Commissioner, on matters relating to "the preservation of law and order and the provision of local services."

Although seldom recorded in writing, which itself is of course an innovation in Tswana life, such laws are usually well known to the people. Sometimes, after having been decided upon by the chief in consultation with his confidential advisers, they are merely announced to a tribal assembly; but as a rule they are first referred to such an assembly for discussion and approval before being put into force. In any event they receive wide publicity at the time of promulgation. With rare exceptions, moreover, they present no special complications in wording or content. The great majority, indeed, are little more than straightforward prohibitions or injunctions. Thus, to cite some examples from the written list of laws compiled by the Ngwaketse chief Seêpapitsô in 1913: "No one may undergo *bogwêra* or *bojale*" [the traditional initiation ceremonies for boys and girls respectively]; "Wagons may not enter or leave a village on Sundays"; "No one may drink *kgadi*" [a highly intoxicating kind of mead]; "The heirs to an estate should share the property (of their deceased father) with their mother and sisters"; "If a man sends away, i.e. divorces, his wife (without proper cause), he must give her all the household goods." Similarly, it is now tribal law everywhere that cattle and Kafir corn may not be sold to traders,

[1] Cf. Schapera, *A Handbook of Tswana Law and Custom*, new ed. 1955, and "The Development of customary law in the Bechuanaland Protectorate" (pp. 102–16 in the symposium, *The Future of Customary Law in Africa*, Afrika-Instituut, Leiden, 1956).

[2] *Tribal Legislation among the Tswana* (London School of Economics Monographs on Social Anthropology, No. 9).

nor may big game be hunted, without special permission from the chief, and that registered taxpayers must each pay a stipulated sum annually to the local tribal treasury.

Decrees such as these today form part of the law enforced in the courts of every tribe. But, as in the pre-colonial period, the great bulk of the work done by the courts still consists in applying what is commonly though not altogether accurately described as "native law and custom," i.e., rules not specially promulgated but established by popular practice and long usage. Since Bechuanaland became a British Protectorate in 1885, the jurisdiction of tribal courts has been curtailed in various ways, notably by the exclusion of cases in which a person is charged with an offense punishable by death or imprisonment for life, divorce proceedings between people married according to Protectorate civil law, and cases "arising under the law relating to insolvency, or involving matters or relationships between the parties to which native law and custom are inapplicable." But the chiefs' courts, in particular, continue to deal with a very wide range of disputes and offenses. These include, for example, questions of marriage and divorce, status and custody of children, rights and duties of parents and guardians, membership of tribe or ward; ownership and inheritance of property; contracts relating to sale and purchase, permissive use, donation, or service; wrongs such as defamation, insult, assault, seduction, adultery, damage to property, theft, sorcery, and rape; and penal offenses such as disobedience of political authorities, contempt of court, and violation of prohibitions imposed by the chiefs.

My object in this paper is to show how the courts determine the law in cases that are not governed by decree, and to indicate what effect their judgments may have upon its development.

Until fairly recently written records were seldom kept of cases dealt with by the courts. The only conspicuous exception was among the Ngwaketse, where Chief Seêpapitsô (1910–16) recorded all the cases tried in his court, a practice revived by his son Bathoen II on becoming chief in 1928. The Native Tribunals Proclamation (No. 75 of 1934) made it obligatory, *inter alia,* for all officially recognized tribal courts to keep proper records. Special books were provided for the purpose by the Administration, and after some initial difficulties and delays the practice became established everywhere. During field trips to Bechuanaland at various times in the period 1938–43, in the course of which I visited all the main tribes, I went systematically through the record books of the chiefs' and certain other courts, making a short abstract of every case entered, and, where it seemed of special interest, taking a verbatim copy. Altogether I dealt in this way with about 1,950 cases from nine different tribes (Kgatla, Ngwato, Tawana, Ngwaketse, Kwena, Tlôkwa, Malete, Khurutshe, and Seleka-Rolong), the records consulted for each tribe ranging over a period of from one and a half years to five, according to the date of my visit and the time at my disposal.

The following discussion is based almost entirely upon this case material. My reason for the limitation is that the case records are presumably still available for consultation in the tribal archives, whereas the many other cases that I myself had previously witnessed (my field work in Bechuanaland began in 1929, and I visited the Territory almost annually thereafter), or of which I had been told in the course of studying law and other aspects of tribal life, are obviously not accessible to the same kind of check. I would only add that among the Kgatla, who at the time of my field work were keeping their records in English, all the cases dealt with here were recorded in the vernacular. The entries varied greatly from one tribe to another in clarity and wealth of detail; sometimes little more than the nature of the case and the essential features of the judgment were recorded, occasionally very briefly and in a manner difficult to understand, but sometimes (notably among Ngwato, Kgatla, and Ngwaketse) all the evidence was adequately summarized and the judgments were set out very fully.

So far as the Tswana themselves are concerned, the records, at least at the time when I was in the field, seem to have had little influence upon the trend of legal development. They were inspected from time to time by the local District Officer, whose main concern was to see that the courts were functioning correctly and not exceeding their powers, and they were also produced at his court in the event of an appeal. But there was nothing in the nature of published law reports by which the decisions of the judges were systematically made available to people other than those present in court when they were delivered, nor, so far as I am aware, did members of the public ever show any interest in reading the records themselves. In brief, the records had not yet (and so far as I know have not yet) begun to be used as the basis for a system of written case law.

In this connection one feature of the Tswana judicial system needs to be stressed. People involved in a dispute or accused of an offense always appear and speak for themselves, i.e., they plead in person. They may and indeed should be supported by their near relatives and neighbors; but in the traditional system there were no professional lawyers to advise them on points of law or to help them conduct their cases, and the Native Courts Proclamation (No. 33 of 1943) explicitly states that "no advocate or legal practitioner may appear or act for any party before a Native Court" (section 22). Even the judges are not required or expected to have special competence in the law. As already mentioned, the headman of every ward is *ex officio* also judge in any dispute between members of his own ward or in charges brought against them by outsiders; but should he himself be away or for any other reason unable to try a case, the man next to him in seniority, i.e. his brother or some other close agnate, replaces him for the time being. Thus it is by no means uncommon for a youth who has barely attained his majority to act as a judge. For example, Molefi became chief of the Kgatla at the age of nineteen (1929), Bathoen II became chief of the Ngwaketse at the age of twenty (1928), and Tshekedi became acting chief of the Ngwato at the age of twenty-one (1926); and each of them began at once to preside over and give judgments in the highest court in his tribe.

In reaching his decision on questions involving customary law, the judge formerly had no written records to which to refer; even nowadays, from what I saw at the trials that I attended, he does not bother to consult the records of his own or other courts, or my own *Handbook of Tswana Law and Custom* (1st ed., 1938). He continues, as in the old days, to rely upon his personal knowledge of the law and upon the guidance of others present in court. All cases are heard in public, and any tribesman is free to attend and take part in the proceedings. But in every court there are usually one or more men who, because of constant attendance and long experience in such matters, have become well informed about details of law and procedure. Such men, sometimes referred to as *bagakolodi* (remembrancers) or *banna ba lekgotla* (men of the court), not only play an important part in the questioning of litigants and witnesses; in the second stage of each trial, when the matter is thrown open for public discussion, they also review the evidence, state the law as they know it, and if possible cite precedents. In this way they help the judge to arrive at a verdict. He is not bound to accept their advice, but unless he himself has had a good deal of experience it is seldom that he will decide otherwise than as they suggest.

(a) This brings me to the first point that I wish to make here. As I have already indicated, the decrees of the chiefs are usually straightforward and well publicized, and it is therefore taken for granted that any man concerned will be well aware of them. But the extent to which people are familiar with their traditional laws and customs must obviously vary greatly according to their age and experience. Hence we find that often enough a judge, in the course of his verdict, will state what the law is on the matter at issue. This statement not merely indicates the grounds for his decision, but, I suggest, *also serves the important function of instructing the people present in the legal norms of their society.* A few simple examples may be cited.

Among the TAWANA, a man who had forcibly attached another's household goods to secure payment of a debt was fined two head of cattle, because, said the judge, "the law is that a person should not seize from another, but must bring him to the chief" (*Sement* v. *Makgala Kopo, 86/1938*).[3]

Among the KHURUTSHE, a man killed an ox that was eating corn in his garden. He was ordered to give the animal's owner a heifer as compensation: "according to our law", said the judge, "you are not entitled to seize payment for yourself, you have behaved like a thief" (*Kombane Chepete* v. *Maboiwa Mpambi, 9.5.1941*).

Among the KWENA, a man who had removed the rafters from his step-mother's hut and used them for himself was ordered to replace them and look after the woman properly, "because according to our law and custom she is your mother" (*Mmano Kebohula* v. *Kenalekgosi Kebohula, 33/1936*); a man who had assaulted another in the latter's compound was fined an ox, "because it is against native law and custom to go and fight a person at his home" (*Thebeng* v. *Gaorekwe, 3/1936*);

[3] In most instances, cases in the record books are numbered consecutively for each calendar year; thus, 86/1938 is Case No. 86 of 1938. Where this has not been done, I give the full date of the hearing. Unless otherwise stated, the record book cited is that of the chief's court.

a man who after publicly divorcing his wife went one night to her parents' home and induced her to come away with him was fined "for doing what is contrary to Native law and custom" (*Botshabelo* v. *Letlamma,* 10/1937); and several others were also fined "for violating Native law and custom" by not reporting to the chief that they had foreign tribesmen living with them (*Chief* v. *Moalatshwang,* 14/1936; *Chief* v. *Moitoi,* 15/1936; *Chief* v. *Basiang,* 4/1937).

Among the MALETE, a woman soon after becoming a widow wished to return to her parental home, and claimed from her late husband's younger brother the cattle given to her by her father when she got married. The judge found that the cattle were certainly hers, but ruled that, "according to Tswana law and custom", she could not take them and go back to her own people: she must remain with her husband's people, and his brother must look after her and the animals (*Maria Leketo* v. *Molefe Leketo,* 27/1938).

Among the NGWAKETSE, a man who pushed his father away during a quarrel was sentenced to a thrashing, "because it is Ngwaketse law that a child should not raise his hand against his father, or become incensed when he is scolded, that is a great offence" (*Motlohelwa Moitoi* v. *Medupe Motlohelwa,* 18/1939); another man who violently assaulted his step-mother and in other ways ill-treated her was both thrashed and sent to gaol, "because custom forbids a child, no matter how old, ever to quarrel with his parents, let alone assault them" (*Kgosidikae* v. *Keitumetse,* 22/1940). Among the KHURUTSHE, a man who slapped his senior in the face was told, "It is against Native law and custom for a junior to strike his senior", and was reprimanded and warned not to repeat the offence (*Modie* v. *George,* 30.8.1939); and among the KGATLA, a man was punished in an assault case, "because it is an offence to swear at a person older than yourself" (*Leshome Mabeko* v. *Moremi Moatshe,* Mathubudukwane ward court, 4/1938).

Among the NGWAKETSE, again, a woman refused to pay a man for looking after her cattle, because she had entrusted them not to him but to another woman whose herdsman he was. The judge ruled, however, that "according to our law and custom" one woman does not give another cattle to herd; he therefore ordered her to pay the plaintiff as requested (*Segole*

v. *Mrs. Bent,* 39/1930). So, too, when a man who had moved away from his father claimed that the latter was wrongfully detaining some of his cattle, he was told that "according to custom" a son is not entitled to his cattle if he separates from his father without the latter's consent (*Joseph R. Sebonego* v. *Ratsie Sebonego,* 4/1936).

In another NGWAKETSE case, a man who claimed compensation from another whose donkey stallion had injured his mare was told that, "according to custom", a man cannot be held responsible if his bull injures a cow in copulation (*Dibeela* v. *Tlhobolo,* 15/1912).

(b) The records show further that the court's judgment may be influenced by the knowledge that the persons concerned are presumed to have of the law. Thus:

> Among the KWENA, a man who hit another on the head with a stick was fined an ox, "because as an elderly man he should have been aware that he was doing wrong" (*Gasebatho* v. *Philip,* 21/1936);
>
> among the KGATLA, a man who had refused on demand to give up cattle that he was looking after for someone else was not only ordered to do so, but was also fined, "because he is an old man and ought to know the law" (*Kgamanyane S. Pilane* v. *Ntwai Moeng,* 22/1938);
>
> in a matrimonial dispute among the NGWATO, the husband's conduct was found specially reprehensible, "because he is an old man, from whom younger people should learn how to behave" (*Dikeledi* v. *Makgoeng,* 153/1938);
>
> and in another NGWATO case a village headman who had abducted another's wife was fined more heavily than usual because in his position he was expected to set a good example to others (*Monyanda* v. *Radipitse,* 151/1938).

(c) On the other hand, ignorance of the law may at times lead to more leniency than might otherwise have prevailed.

> Among the TAWANA, when a visiting alien fought with a local tribesman at the latter's home (and to assault a man in his own home is a serious offence), the judgment was: "The

accused is a foreigner who does not know Tswana custom, and although he admits his fault he should not be punished in the usual way; had he been a Tswana he would have been thrashed; as it is, he must pay an ox to the victim" (*Motlhanke Morapedi* v. *Jeremiah Tjoko,* 12/1937).

(d) In some instances the judge goes even further, and deliberately uses his decision as a means of instructing people in the correct modes of behavior.

Thus, among the NGWAKETSE, incoming mail is normally distributed at the chief's office, people gathering there on post-days and claiming their letters when the clerk reads out their name. On one occasion a woman claimed, opened, and read, three letters addressed not to her but to someone else of the same surname. The latter sued her for theft. The chief ordered all the other women waiting outside his office to come and listen to the case. The woman concerned admitted that she had not acted in error, since she could see from the envelopes that the letters were in fact not intended for her. The chief ordered her to pay two head of cattle to the plaintiff, and continued: "I specially asked all you other women to come here, so that you should remember the punishment for opening letters not addressed to you" (*Bokgola S. Sepato* v. *Mpaesele B. Sepato,* 9/1934).

It will be noted, incidentally, that here we have an instance of the customary law being applied to meet a new kind of situation arising from the spread of Western usages to the Tswana.

Among the NGWATO, a man took action against some of his servants who had run away from him. In giving judgment, the local headman said: "In this matter Tswana law and European law are the same: a servant wishing to leave his master must give proper notice, and not simply run away". He therefore ordered the servants to return to their master, and added that if they still wished to leave him they could do so after giving proper notice (*Ramatudung* v. *Makgafole and others,* Madinare district court, 44/1940).

(e) The preceding cases have all been cited merely because they illustrate the role of the courts in making known the law, or indicate in what circumstances knowledge of the law is expected. They presented no special difficulties or unusual features, and I chose them for mention primarily because the record shows that the judge specifically stated what the law was on the matter at issue.

In other cases the record indicates also that the judgment was based upon what may be called the "expert opinion" of the "remembrancers."

Among the TAWANA, a divorced woman claimed from her former husband certain livestock which she said she had earned for herself, and which he refused to hand over. The record continues: "Letsholo says that according to custom a woman on divorce is entitled to take any cattle which she brought with her or which she earned while living with her husband, but she is not entitled to take anything he himself may have given her". On the strength of this, she was awarded the animals she claimed (*MmaMokgama* v. *RraMokgama*, 209/1939).

Among the NGWAKETSE, similarly, a husband was ordered to hand over to his divorced wife a sheep that she had been given as part of the *bogadi* (marriage payment) received for her sister, but which he claimed because he had contributed towards the cost of the wedding feast. "Rabodietso explained the custom: an animal obtained for *bogadi* belongs directly to the person getting it; people who contribute towards the feast may be given meat from a slaughtered ox, but not a living animal" (*Olebile Mafshiakgomo* v. *Tlametlo Moranyane*, 10/1937).

Among the KGATLA, when a man claimed his elder brother's children, who were living with their mother at her parental home, "the advisers" said that according to custom he must first pay something towards the cost of their maintenance (*Johannes Lesejane* v. *Motlhabatau Raletsane*, 28/1938).

In the same tribe, the chief had decided to use two huts in an abandoned compound as quarters for teachers employed by the tribal administration. The compound originally belonged to a widow, who had moved to another village some time before. Her husband's nephew (brother's son) now claimed that he had inherited it, though he was not living there, and he demanded £35 compensation for its loss. Five men at the court, including ex-chief Isang, gave evidence showing that the chief was entitled to such action, and citing past instances of its having been taken. The court held that the chief had the right to take "ruins" for tribal purposes, and the claim was therefore dismissed (*Sebele Motsisi* v. *Chief Mmusi,* 27/1938).

Among the MALETE, a man whose wife had deserted him claimed the return of his *bogadi.* "Sekgere stated: if a man divorces his wife, he recovers both *bogadi* and *serufo* (betrothal pledge); if there is a child, he recovers *bogadi* but not *serufo;* if there is no child, he gets back all his cattle". The judgment was: "According to Tswana custom, if a man divorces his wife, the *bogadi* goes back to him" (*Robert Mpelane* v. *Ntanyane Motsumi,* 21/1941).

(f) Expert opinion is usually taken in cases of what may be termed "foreign custom." Some Tswana tribes, notably Ngwato and Tawana, contain fairly large groups of people differing from the ruling section in law and custom. If a dispute involving only such people comes to the chief's court, he sometimes settles the matter according to their own usages, which he ascertains from senior members of their community.

Such cases have occurred, for example, among the TAWANA, where an inheritance dispute between two Herero, and a claim for recovery of debt against the heirs of another Herero, were both decided, as the judgments say, "according to Herero custom" (*Kasondoro* v. *Tjinjokamoaha,* 95/1938; *Makgala Kopo* v. *Sons of Daniel,* 18/1937). Among the NGWATO, similarly, in a matrimonial dispute between two Kalaka, the question of whether they were in fact married was settled in terms of what some senior Kalaka present described as the norms of their own people (*Samuel* v. *Onalenna,* 534/1940).

But when a dispute involves people of different cultures, the law of the ruling section is applied instead.

Thus, among the NGWAKETSE, a Xhosa father sued a youth who had seduced his daughter. He maintained, correctly, that in Xhosa law he was entitled to damages, even if the girl did not become pregnant. The chief ruled against him, because, reads the judgment, "The Ngwaketse have a law against rape, and a law about impregnation, but there is no law against cohabitation alone" (*Nosekate Marman* v. *Botlhoko Leburu,* 60/1932).

If circumstances warrant it, moreover, foreign custom may be overruled even in a dispute between members of the same ethnic community.

Among the NGWAKETSE, a Mmanaana-Kgatla died in 1934, leaving a wife and children. His younger brother refused to act as seed-raiser, saying that he wanted his own wife and not an older woman. Deceased's father, Bagwasi, thereupon himself began to cohabit with the widow, by whom he begot two children, who were held to be the dead man's legal offspring. In 1937 Bagwasi's wife complained to the local headman, saying that she was ashamed of what her husband was doing, and that he was also neglecting her. The headman replied that Bagwasi was acting in conformity with Mmanaana-Kgatla custom. The wife then carried her protest to the chief. The Mmanaana-Kgatla present at the hearing contended that Bagwasi was doing nothing wrong, and cited eight similar instances known to them. The chief and other Ngwaketse said, however, that such a form of cohabitation, between a man and his daughter-in-law, was disgraceful and contrary to their own usages. Bagwasi was therefore ordered to stop living with his son's widow. He ignored the order, for which offence he was tried by the chief in the following year and fined three head of cattle (*Mmalontshwane Bagwasi* v. *Bagwasi Tlhabiwa,* 20/ 1938).

Here, it will be noted, the chief applied a principle somewhat like that by which European Administrations often refuse to recognize as legally valid certain native usages, because they are "repugnant to natural justice and humanity." In a somewhat similar case among the Ngwato, the judgment not only refused to recognize a "foreign custom," but extended the ruling more widely to cover Tswana practice as well:

The eldest son by the first wife of a Kalaka named Makwati had died some time previously. Six years afterwards, Makwati took a woman to be the "wife" of his son and to bear children in "his name". The other sons (half-brothers of the deceased) refused to cohabit with the woman as seed-raisers, whereupon Makwati himself did so. After his death, the status of the woman and her children was questioned by the other heirs, since, if she was accepted as the wife of the first son, her children would rank as Makwati's main heirs. Some of the Kalaka present at the hearing said that they did not know the custom of "ghost marriage", but that the woman could be regarded as a substitute for the dead man's mother, in which case her children would still rank as the main heirs, their mother belonging to the great hut. The chief, in giving judgment, described both "ghost marriage" and the sororate as pernicious customs, and said that in these modern days people should beget or bear children for themselves, not for others. And, because he refused to regard such customs as still having legal validity, he ruled that the woman should be regarded as Makwati's own junior wife, her children being inferior in status to all the others borne by women married previously (*Toitoi* v. *Osenyeng,* 132/1938).

(g) As shown by the case just cited, the courts do not merely apply the existing law, but *if considered advisable may even abolish or modify certain rights that formed part of the old legal system.* Owing to education, economic progress, and the spread of "civilization" generally, many changes have unobtrusively developed in Tswana tribal life. Some traditional practices have by now been so widely discarded, even though not specifically prohibited by legislation, that if they give rise to legal proceedings the chief in his judicial capacity will sometimes refuse to regard them as still valid.

Thus, among the NGWAKETSE, a matrimonial dispute was heard at the chief's court in 1939. The newly-married bride was only fourteen years of age. Without inquiring further into the merits of the case, the chief on ascertaining this held that the girl's father had acted shamefully in marrying her off when she was so young, and ordered restoration of the *bogadi* and annulment of the marriage (*Kefilwe Malau* v. *Sane Mumereki,* 16/1939). This verdict constituted a distinct departure from

Ngwaketse usage, which gave full recognition to infant betroth-
als.

It has also been held in some tribes, that a man who remains
working abroad for several years continuously, thereby neglecting
his wife, has no case against her or her lover if she is unfaithful
to him during his absence (*Tshiako* v. *Kepalilwe,* NGWAKETSE,
1/1938; *Otleseng* v. *Lonaka,* TAWANA, 10/1936).

(h) Conversely, a chief has sometimes ruled against the recognition of innovations, and in effect has thus refused to establish
new legal norms or, perhaps more correctly, has perpetuated
traditional ones.

Among the KWENA, a man named Sephuthabakwa was in 1938
fined by the chief's court for having demanded and received
cattle from men to whom he had given part of his arable land,
and he was also ordered to restore the animals to their former
owners. It was explicitly stated in the judgment that he had
behaved very badly: land belongs to the chief and tribe, and
cannot be sold (*Kokole* v. *Sephuthabakwa,* 3/1938).

Among the NGWATO, it appeared in a case of seduction that
the youth charged with the offence was willing to marry the girl.
Both she and her parents were also agreeable, but his own
parents were not. The people at court thought that in the
circumstances the marriage should be allowed. The chief dis-
agreed; he said that if it were permitted, the effect would be
that in future youths could depend on getting their own way
by seducing girls whom their parents would not let them
marry, and the result would be an increase of immorality.
He therefore prohibited the marriage, and ordered the boy's
father to pay compensation to the girl's, the cattle to be
taken from those already set aside for the boy (*Sepako* v.
Tsholofelo, 72/1938).

Among the TAWANA, again, it was found in the course of a
matrimonial dispute that the couple concerned were not really
married, but that the man had merely been living with the
woman at her parental home. In giving judgment the chief
said: "From today attention must be paid to men living away
from their own people; it is because of them that women are
becoming concubines. Should any man again be found living

with a woman whom he has not sought in the usual way from her parents, and the case comes to court, both he and the people of their wards will be dealt with severely" (*Lemmonnyo* v. *his wife,* 103/1938).

Three months later a case did come to court. The chief reminded the people of his previous warning "that he should never again find a man living with a woman to whom he is not married, since this is not Tswana law and custom"; he fined the man four head of cattle, the men of his ward one ox each "for not complaining about him to the chief", and the men of the woman's ward one ox each "for not driving her lover away". He concluded his verdict with the words: "It is the law of the chief that no man may go to live at the home of a concubine, and that no man may live with a woman unless he has taken her to be his wife" (*Chief* v. *Kgwabi,* 144/1938).

Although apparently an innovation, the "law of the chief" in this case merely reaffirmed a traditional norm, and the decree thus falls within the category that I have been discussing, because its object was to prohibit new practices that he regarded with disapproval.

(i) But the courts have by no means always opposed innovations. Indeed, much of their work at the present time consists in dealing with situations that did not occur in the old tribal life. These include, for example, commercial transactions or labor contracts involving payment in money, such as loans on interest, the hire of wagons, guns, and sewing machines, the employment of herd boys for monthly cash wages, and the employment of specialists to build or thatch huts, dig wells, or break in untamed horses; partnerships (as in running a business, sharing the use of a well, or transporting goods for traders); personal injury or damage to property through collisions (with bicycles, wagons, etc.); and sometimes even forgery. In all such instances the courts have usually had little difficulty in adapting the principles of the customary law to the matter at issue, though sometimes, as already mentioned, a chief might decide to control the new practice by decree.

Occasionally, however, cases come to court where there is clearly a conflict between old and new, and the chief has to decide which to adopt.

Among the Ngwaketse, a man complained that the woman for whom he had given *bogadi* refused to come and live with him. The woman replied that as a Christian she wished to be married in church. To this the man would not agree, since it meant subjecting himself to the provisions of the Protectorate civil law. The woman's mother supported her, but her father's younger brother, who was her guardian (her father being dead), sided with the man. The chief told her that she must choose: her guardian had threatened to disown her if she did not follow his wishes by marrying the man according to "Native law and custom", whereas if she did not marry in church she would be expelled from the congregation. She asked the chief to decide on her behalf. He said that he agreed with the guardian. This judgment evoked a protest from a leading Christian tribesman present in court, who said that it was discriminating against the church; but the chief refused to enter into the matter, saying that if the Christians wished they could get together and raise it on another occasion (*Gaotilwe Mmolai* v. *Samma Baratedi,* 21/1915).

In the case just cited, the chief preferred traditional usage to an innovation, but in another case, also tried by him, he followed a different course.

A man had died leaving a widow and one son. His younger brother cohabited with the woman under the levirate, begetting four sons; he then married her by civil rites, after which they had three more sons. The question at issue was the status of these children. The only son by the first husband claimed that according to the seed-raising custom they were all his father's children. The second husband claimed however that those born after the civil marriage belonged to him. The chief decided that the children born before that marriage were by tribal custom undoubtedly the dead man's, but he decided also that those born afterwards should belong to the second husband. He thus established the principle that in tribal law a widow might be legally married by her husband's younger brother and bear children to him and not to her first husband (*Motsopye* v. *Setlang,* 8/1914).

In another case, much earlier in date than any of those so far cited, a chief was unsuccessful in his attempt to alter the law in his judicial capacity.

Among the KWENA, as among most other Tswana tribes, it is the traditional rule that a man who abducts another's wife should forfeit all his property to the injured husband. In 1902 a man named Kgotodue abducted the wife of one Lesokwane. Chief Sebele I, who tried the case, ordered Kgotodue to pay Lesokwane ten head of cattle as compensation, but added that he could take the woman to wife. Thereupon, says the official report of the District Officer, "the majority of the headmen objected to this, on the ground that it would be creating a bad precedent, which might lead wealthy men into breaking up others' homes, as it would be practically allowing a man to buy another's wife for 10 head of cattle." Sebele was accordingly forced by the pressure of public opinion, and the advice of the Government, to alter his judgment, and ordered Kgotodue to have nothing more to do with the woman, lest he be deprived of all his property (*Government Archives,* Mafeking, J. 359).

(j) The main conclusions suggested by what has been said above may be summarized as follows:

(1) In non-literate communities of the kind until recently found among the Tswana, the role of courts is not simply to administer justice but also to educate people in the legal norms of their society. This does not imply that education is not also a function of courts in societies such as our own; often indeed it is only through newspaper reports of cases that people become aware of the law on certain matters.

(2) But where writing is (or was until recently) completely unknown, and where legal textbooks and other written aids to study are consequently non-existent, the principal if not the only way in which anybody can become really familiar with legal norms and practices is by constant attendance at court cases over a fairly long period. Hence we find that among the Tswana there are certain men whose age and experience tend to give them special authority in judicial matters, even though they themselves do not necessarily hold official positions of any kind. It is because of them, because of the help that they give in the discussion of cases, that the

lack of special legal competence in a judge is not so great a handicap as one might expect.

(3) Since, in every individual case, the judge's decision is shaped at least partly by the opinions of the people present, it is unlikely that judicial precedents can be as significant as is sometimes asserted of similar systems. Whether or not a precedent exists depends in fact merely upon whether someone present has seen or heard of a similar case before.

(4) In the circumstances, and considering the inevitable limitations of personal experience, the tendency will be for judgments to be based more upon recognized general principles than upon specific decisions of the past.

(5) This in turn means that the law is not rigid but flexible, and can be readily adapted to meet new situations or, if need be, to reject customary norms that are now considered obsolete.

(6) What effect the introduction of written records in Tswana courts will have upon the development of Tswana law is still uncertain. I should imagine, however, that unless and until professional lawyers become part of the legal system the courts will continue, as in the past, to rely upon personal experience and opinion, and not feel bound to adhere in all instances to previous decisions.

25. The Military Organization of the Zulus

Zulu history and the character of the Zulu people have been to a very great extent molded and determined by their military system which, during the nineteenth century, influenced almost every phase of Zulu life. Indeed the whole nation was organized into what might be called a great military camp with war the only thought of the people.

The Zulus owed their military power to Shaka, who not only changed the old methods of fighting merely for present superiority to those of crushing his enemies out of existence altogether, but also completely reorganized the army. One of his first reforms was to do away with the custom of hurling an assegai, mostly without effect, at a distant foe, and to substitute one short assegai with its consequent fighting at close quarters. To give his warriors a demonstration of the superiority of the new method, he arranged a sham fight with reeds, the one side hurling their reeds, the others charging upon their opponents with a single stabbing reed. The immediate and complete victory of the latter demonstrated beyond doubt the advantage of the new method of attack.[1]

When Shaka came to the Zulu throne, he found the usual *Nguni* organization of the men into age-sets or circumcision guilds, each of which consisted of about fifty men of the same age. The oldest of these Zulu age-sets had been circumcised, not so the younger ones, for the custom had by Shaka's time already fallen into disuse, though the classifying of groups according to age had continued for state purposes. Shaka thought these groups too small to subserve his military purposes, so he reorganized his father's people as he had seen Dingiswayo do in Mthethwaland. The eldest he drafted together

SOURCE: E. J. Krige, "The Military Organization of the Zulus," in *Social System of the Zulus,* Longmans, Green & Co., Ltd., 1936, pp. 261–79. Reprinted by permission of the author and publisher.

[1] Bryant, *Dictionary.*

to form an *ibutho* or regiment, which he called *amaWombe* (they were the last of the Zulus that were circumcised); the next group he named *uDubinhlangu,* and the younger men were called *umGamule.*[2] These names were probably specially created by Shaka, for it is unlikely that he would have used any of the original names for the different age-sets that went to make up each one of these regiments. As the Zulu power grew, and conquered tribes came to be incorporated into the nation, the strength and size of the army increased, for the only exceptions to the universal enrollment were the unfit and diviners.[3] There have been various computations of the strength of Shaka's army, from Farewell's of 14,000 to Fynn's of 50,000. Bryant, however, believes it could never have been more than 20,000.[4]

REGIMENTS AND THEIR DRESS

A Zulu regiment was usually from about 800 to 1,000 strong, and between its members there were to be found bonds of great solidarity. They were men of the same age, many of whom had since early boyhood associated with each other, for the *amaviyo,* or companies within the regiment, were no other than the old *intanga* of the district, and between them and the other regiments there was a spirit of great rivalry and keen competition. The different regiments were constantly competing, not only in military exploits, but also in dancing at the royal kraal, so that when on any occasion they all had to be present together, they camped, each regiment by itself, some distance apart, to prevent quarrels. In spite of these precautions, however, faction fights were common.

Each regiment had its own regimental songs and war cry, besides the national war cry. The regimental war cry was uttered as the regiment set off to engage the enemy, but during the actual fighting, the national one was always used.[5] The regiments were further distinguished from one another by their different regimental dress,

[2] Bryant, *Olden Times in Zululand and Natal,* pp. 642–43.
[3] By the time of umPande, too many people were getting out of being soldiers by becoming diviners, so umPande collected them together to form a regiment of their own and made them stay together in one kraal (Stuart, *History of the Zulu Rebellion,* p. 72).
[4] Bryant, ibid., p. 647.
[5] R. C. Samuelson, *Long, Long Ago,* p. 263.

chiefly noticeable in their headdress, though it sometimes happened that the principal distinguishing feature of a regiment was the color of its shield. No two regiments had the same kind of shield, although in many cases a single regiment might have two or more types of shields.[6] There were regiments with black and white shields, white shields with black patches, and so on, so that when the regiments were dancing or going through other military evolutions, this uniformity must have been very striking. Far more impressive than their shields, however, must have been their regimental dress, which in many instances was extremely rich and beautiful. The picked regiments wore monkey and genet tails, while the young regiments and others wore the oridinary *umutsha;* but each regiment had its own peculiar headdress. Indeed, the dress of the *Indabakawombe,* umPande's favorite regiment, was so rich that we have descriptions of it in more than one source.[7] The head was decked with a pad of otter skin passing over the forehead and secured at the back, while the rest of the headdress was formed of ostrich feathers and the long tail plume of the Stanley crane. There were lappets over the ears and behind the head, made of leopard skin, ornamented with tufts of the scarlet breast feathers of the weaver bird. From the neck, arms, and knees, tails of cattle streamed, and from the waist was worn the graceful and costly *insimba* (war kilt), made of four hundred rolls of civet skin sewn to imitate tails of monkeys, a thick garment which adapted itself to every movement.[8] The headdress of the Isangu regiment consisted of "a grotesque fillet of white ox-hide with lappets of the same of a red color. On the back of the head was a shaved ball of eagle or bustard feathers, and two bunches of the long tail of the kaffir-finch formed graceful ornaments as they floated in the air."[9]

Every Zulu warrior was armed with a shield, one or more throwing assegais, and one stabbing one,[10] and to return without the latter meant death. No sandals were worn, because Shaka did away with them, believing that his soldiers would act more promptly without footwear.[11] The warriors supplied their own uniforms and

[6] Stuart, ibid., p. 74.

[7] For a complete list of Zulu regiments from Shaka's time to the present day, see Appendix VIII in *Social System of the Zulus.*

[8] Angas, *The Kaffirs Illustrated* (Plate XXX), and Delegorgue, *Voyage dans l'Afrique Australe,* Vol. II, p. 223.

[9] Ibid.

[10] Stuart, *History of the Zulu Rebellion,* pp. 67–68.

[11] Delegorgue, ibid., p. 218.

assegais, though their shields were made from the hides of the king's cattle. These they fashioned themselves, except when they "begged" shields at the king's kraal.

There were special decorations for warriors who had distinguished themselves in war. Beads and other ornaments or assegais were given by the king's favor to such men,[12] and the principal *induna* of each military kraal, who had considerable authority to give punishment or reward, always had a supply of brass armlets and collars for the decoration of those who deserved distinction.[13] A man who had killed another in battle was entitled to wear a necklace of horns with charred blocks of willow intervening,[14] while another necklace, worn as a sign of bravery, consisted of a number of pieces of a certain kind of root strung on sinew, or bits of wood, each one representing an enemy slain.[15] To those who had been outstandingly brave in battle the king gave presents of cattle, which they could take home, and the cattle taken in war were nearly always liberally distributed.

There were, broadly speaking, two main classes of warriors. The "white" warriors, who were married and wore the headring, were distinguished by predominating white or rather light shields, as well as by the shining appearance the polished headring gave to the shaven head. The "black" warriors were the young unmarried men, who had a predominating amount of black in their shields.[16] In Shaka's time, however, marriage was only allowed to very few of the warriors, so that the "white" warriors of his day were unmarried veterans. The married men in Shaka's reign were regarded as "inferior"; they formed regiments carrying red shields[17] and lived at home. The "white" warriors were the pick of the soldiers.

THE IKHANDA OR MILITARY KRAAL

Though, in general, each regiment had its own military kraal, this was not always the case, and often on formation it was sent to share an *ikhanda* with some very much older regiment. As men in

[12] Shooter, *The Kaffirs of Natal,* p. 238.
[13] Gardiner, *A Journey to the Zoolu Country,* p. 94.
[14] Stuart, *History of the Zulu Rebellion,* p. 75.
[15] R. C. Samuelson, *Long, Long Ago.*
[16] Stuart, ibid., p. 70.
[17] Isaacs, *Travels in Eastern Africa,* Vol. II, p. 346.

the older regiments ever more and more fell out on the field, bodies of young men were periodically drafted in to maintain the regimental strength and thus, for example, with the *izimPohlo* were subsequently embodied the *uGibabanye, imFolozi, uFojisa, inDabankulu* and others. Gradually, however, the old regiments did disappear.

Every military kraal was built on the same lines as the royal kraal, which was always a military kraal. The circle of huts was divided up into sections, the most important of which was the *isigodlo* which occupied the top end. Here lived a number of the king's women and girls under some female relative of the king who kept them in order. She presided over the kraal, and was particularly charged with the distribution of provisions.[18] The girls at an *ikhanda* were chiefly occupied in cultivating fields, the produce of which was used by the *ikhanda,* more particularly by the *isigodlo* itself.

At the head of each *ikhanda* was an *induna* who had considerable power. He saw that all the men in his military district rendered a reasonable amount of service each year at the *ikhanda*—from two to three months at least, and though the power of mobilizing for war was the prerogative of the king, every *induna* of a military kraal had the right in occurrences of a sudden and local kind, such as a raid or insurrection, to call out the men under his command.[19] Under Shaka the *induna* had power of life and death, but Dingane restricted this power to three of his chief *indunas* only, viz., uMdlela, Dambuza and Wohlo, the *induna* of Congella.[20] The resident *induna* was allowed to have with him his wives, but for the rest, with the exception of the *isigodlo,* no women were allowed to live in an *ikhanda,* and infants were rigidly proscribed.[21] Ranking below the *induna* were an officer second in command and two wing officers. Then came the captains of the *amaviyo* (companies), who sometimes had from one to three junior officers.[22]

Warriors did not eat *amasi* at the *ikhanda,* but lived on "hard" foods, or so-called strengthening foods, such as meat, beer and cooked

[18] Gardiner, *A Journey to the Zoolu Country,* p. 146.
[19] Stuart, *History of the Zulu Rebellion,* pp. 71–72.
[20] Gardiner, ibid., p. 94.
[21] Ibid. This held only in Shaka's time. Dingane relaxed the rule somewhat, and allowed children first at Congella, because he had been brought up there as a child, and later at a few other kraals (ibid., pp. 124 and 143).
[22] *War Office Précis,* p. 112.

mealies,[23] which were supplied from their own homes, or which they fossicked themselves when and where they could.[24] Very often beer for the soldiers was made from grain grown in the king's fields at the *ikhanda,* and the king also supplied them with "an ox or two now and then."[25] Shaka and Dingane are said to have supplied the whole food of the soldiers in the military kraals, but this in reality could have applied only to the royal kraal.[26] Here the warriors were provided with beer in the morning and beef in the evening,[27] and this food was partaken of in public. The morning beer was set before the assembled crowd within the inner fence and the bowls were emptied on the spot, being passed from one to the other.[28] For the evening meal every section (*iViyo*) collected separately within the enclosure. The meat was brought out on mats about two feet square and one was placed on the ground before each section. "They gathered thickly round this circle, often two or three deep, and the carver (officer of the section) then, with an assegaihead upon a short stick, apportioned rations to every second or third man who, in turn, divided it with his collateral neighbours by the joint effort of their teeth, the recipient being always privileged to the first bite."[29]

LIFE AT THE IKHANDA

In time of peace, the soldiers at the *ikhanda* were occupied in constructing or repairing kraals, cattle enclosures, fences; or they hoed, sowed, weeded, and harvested the royal crops. Small groups

[23] Delegorgue, *Voyage dans l'Afrique Australe,* Vol. I, p. 421.

[24] Bryant, *Olden Times in Zululand and Natal,* pp. 78, 79. Ferguson says the beer of the soldiers was made from a tax in grain levied on the civil villages in the midst of which the *ikhanda* lay, but this conveys a wrong impression, for the grain was more probably voluntarily supplied from the homes of the warriors for their maintenance.

[25] Shooter, *The Kaffirs of Natal,* p. 238.

[26] Gardiner in *A Journey to the Zoolu Country,* p. 54, makes this statement apply to all military kraals, but if this had been correct it would hardly have been necessary for soldiers to "beg" shields at the royal kraal; while, if the grain for beer had been supplied by the chief or levied as a "tax" on the people, a fairly elaborate organization would have been necessary to administer this properly.

[27] Ibid.

[28] Ibid., p. 55.

[29] Ibid., p. 56.

were constantly engaged in smaller matters—carrying grain to or from a distance, or carrying messages to men of rank in all parts of the country—and occasionally great hunts were organized.[30] There was no organized drill, but instead there were dances which served a similar purpose, though they were indulged in by the soldiers rather for amusement than with any idea of exercise. In these dances, in which on occasion women and even cattle took part,[31] the movements were frequently similar to those of soldiers in battle, while sometimes they were neither more nor less than sham fights. Describing the life at the barracks, Bryant says: "While ease and freedom were abundant, stern discipline continuously reigned, but it was wholly a moral force, the young men being thrown entirely on their honour, without standing regulations and without supervision. . . . They were there for the sole purpose of fulfilling the king's behests. They acted as the state army, the state police, the state labour gang. They fought the clan's battles, made raids when state funds were low. They slew convicted and even suspected malefactors and confiscated their property in the king's name; they built and repaired the king's kraal, cultivated his fields and manufactured his war shields, for all of which they received no rations, no wages, not one word of thanks."[32]

PREPARING FOR WAR

The time for campaigning among the Zulus was generally in winter after the crops had been harvested, and often it was decided at the Feast of the First-fruits to have war almost immediately. Before war was decided upon, the king usually summoned his councilors, most of whom were also leaders of regiments, without whose advice and concurrence it would have been unwise for even the despotic Zulu king to act. True, the king could summon a different lot of councilors if he could not get the first lot to agree with him,[33] but to get the concurrence of his councilors was essential. To mobilize the army, the king sent a message to the *induna* in charge at

[30] Stuart, *The Zulu Rebellion,* p. 76.
[31] Ibid.
[32] Bryant, *Olden Times in Zululand and Natal,* p. 78.
[33] Isaacs tells us that Shaka was generally at variance with half his *indunas,* and prevented their meeting by having their regiments some distance apart (*Travels in Eastern Africa,* Vol. II, p. 347).

the different military kraals, ordering all warriors to proceed to the Great Place. This order was instantly executed, the greatest pains being taken to lose no time for fear the king might order the seizure of their stock for dilatoriness. So swift were the movements of the Zulu army that within twenty-four hours those regiments stationed within fifteen miles of the royal kraal had already assembled at the meeting place, and within a period of from two to five days the whole army was collected at the Great Place. The regiments camped apart to avoid regimental fights and cattle were slaughtered by the king to feed them.

In spite of the rapidity required of all warriors in their execution of the king's command to mobilize, no warrior would go to war unless he had first visited his home to pray to his ancestral spirits for their protection. When about to leave home, two or three men would enter the cattle kraal, and at the upper end call upon the ancestors. An old woman sometimes took her stand outside the gate with a broom in her hand, and with this she would silently flick the calf of each warrior to ward off dangers.[34] It was also customary for warriors, when summoned to war, to put on their war dress and enter the cattle kraal with great solemnity, there to leap about as if fighting, in order to "get up steam" (*ukuvusa umhlonga*).[35] There were many charms against the weapons of the enemy, and warriors would be careful to arm themselves with some of these to prevent harm befalling them in the war. A newly married man would be the first to secure himself from these dangers, because it was believed that he would be more quickly stabbed by the enemy than the others.[36] A well-known charm against the enemy was the skin of a hedgehog, which was cut into small circular pieces (as big as a five-shilling piece) with the hair on, and sewn to a leather thong which was laid around the head, so that the piece of hedgehog skin was on the forehead.[37] A warrior might also carry a certain kind of iris that had powers of dulling away sharpness, or dulling the enemy's power.[38] When going to battle, the Zulus often chewed *umabophe,* a

[34] Stuart, *The Zulu Rebellion,* p. 87.
[35] Colenso, *Dictionary* (Hlonga).
[36] Callaway, *Religious System of the Amazulu,* p. 443.
[37] R. C. Samuelson, *Long, Long Ago,* p. 371.
[38] Bryant, *Dictionary.* It is said that a man going to war will deliberately enter the hut of his newborn child, which is otherwise strictly taboo. This, by making him unattractive and "not clear," will bring him good luck, for he will not be easily seen by the enemy (Fuze, *Abantu Abamnyama,* p. 53).

climbing plant with red roots, and spat it out in the direction of the enemy. This had the power of causing the enemy to make mistakes.[39] No one going to war would eat *umDumbi* (a kind of wild potato), because it would make him afraid in the fight, ready to flee for nothing. This is so because the leaves of *umDumbi* plants are easily shaken by the wind and this property is transferred to the warrior.[40] There were, in addition, also various taboos to be observed by warriors at all times. Warriors never ate the marrow of any animal, nor would they eat fish or birds, lest they should lose their courage and their cattle.[41]

While the army was being mobilized, secret messengers would be dispatched by the king to get belongings of the enemy chief, by means of which he would be able to gain ascendancy over the enemy; and the king and his doctors were kept very busy with their churnings and other medicinal preparations, without which no Zulu king would dream of going to war.

STRENGTHENING THE ARMY

The Zulu army never went to war without being specially strengthened by the doctors of the king, a process which took a few days, and which was begun as soon as all the warriors had arrived at the royal kraal. Here, as in the First-fruit Ceremonies, the army was strengthened and given courage by eating the medicated flesh of a bull killed in a special way, and the regiment chosen to bring this bull to earth unarmed was usually the favorite regiment of the king, because this was regarded as a very great honor. Before any of these ceremonies were begun, a day was spent in preparations. The chosen regiment devoted its time to collecting firewood for the beasts that were later to be killed and eaten, while cadets were directed to gather the green branches of the *umthole,* a kind of mimosa, to be burned as a charm with the roasting flesh of the bull.

The following day, in the early morning, the regiments went to the spot appointed for the troops to *hlanza* or vomit. Here there was a hole six or seven feet deep, in which the warriors were to vomit, and beside which stood three or four great pots or baskets

[39] Tyler, *Forty Years Among the Zulus,* p. 110.
[40] *The Collector,* No. 927.
[41] Isaacs, *Travels in Eastern Africa,* Vol. II, p. 303.

of decoctions on special articles "not unlike small life-belts made of straw, bound round with plaited fibre."[42] At this spot, and in charge of all proceedings, were the war doctors of the king. Each warrior had to take a mouthful or two of the decoctions, which acted as emetics, and then vomit into the hole. The doctors would not allow more than about four at a time at the hole, and they beat with sticks those who were not reacting properly and who had thus probably only pretended to take the medicine. Most of the men, knowing what was to come, had fasted the previous night. The whole process was gone through to "bring together the hearts of the people," and it was usually well past midday (about 3 P.M.) when all the regiments had been through it. The hole was then carefully filled up by the doctors to prevent hostile tribes obtaining any part of the substances used.

The first regiment to go through the *hlanza*-ing was the one chosen to deal with the bull selected by the king, and as soon as they were finished, they went to drive the bull into the cattle enclosure where they tackled it. It was first kept running around for two or three hours to tire it and then, at about midday, was rushed and brought to earth. The men then held on to it as best they could, while a number of them proceeded to twist its neck. As soon as it was dead the doctors came up and chased away the warriors before beginning to cut up the bull, lest one of them should cut off a portion and take it to the king's enemies.

The beast was then skinned and the flesh cut up into long strips (*imbengo*) and roasted on a huge fire made of the wood gathered the previous day. After having been roasted, the strips were smeared with black powders of pungent, bitter drugs, the names and identity of which were kept a deadly secret.[43] Sometimes sinews, extracted from behind the knee of the hind leg of a beast while still alive, were cut up and boiled with the medicines, to give the soldiers strength in the knee and ability to stand strongly against their enemies.[44] But the most potent of all these medicines was human flesh, and in the Zulu War (1879) a white man, O. E. Neal was killed by the Zulus, who used parts of his body for doctoring the *impi*.[45]

At about three or four o'clock in the afternoon, when all was ready,

[42] Stuart, *History of the Zulu Rebellion*, pp. 78–83.
[43] Stuart, *History of the Zulu Rebellion*, pp. 78–83.
[44] R. C. Samuelson, *Long, Long Ago*, p. 308.
[45] Stuart, ibid., p. 378.

the regiments came up to eat the *imbengo*. They formed an *umkhumbi* or half-moon, several men deep, and the doctors and their assistants then began to fling the strips of medicated, half-cooked flesh into the air above the heads of the different sections, to do which satisfactorily they had to pass through the *umkhumbi* at specially prepared openings. The warriors, holding weapons and shields in the left hand, caught the meat with the other, and there was a general scramble for each piece. On catching a strip, a warrior bit off a lump and pitched the rest back into the air to be violently contended for again. Once a strip fell to the ground, however, it lost its virtue. Only the juice of the meat was meant to be swallowed, the rest being spat out onto the ground, but often the men were so hungry by this time that many of them would gulp down the flesh as well. One bull was enough for the whole army, and more were never killed.[46]

Only boys under puberty were allowed to eat the remains of this bull, but it was often hard to find the boys when wanted, because all those who were commandeered were obliged to sleep at the place where the bull had been killed and roasted till next morning. To all such boys it was strictly taboo to pass water from the moment of coming up till permission was given them to depart. The entrails of the bull were secretly buried in the king's cattle enclosure, which was cut off from the main inner circle of the kraal, and the hole was guarded all night by a watchman. Every atom of the bull that was left over, including bones and hide, was burned to cinders, which the doctors collected and threw into some deep pool.[47]

After the army had been strengthened by the eating of the *imbengo,* cattle were apportioned to the various regiments, and these were killed and eaten in the evening, which was spent in singing the great national chants, recounting war experiences and generally working up the enthusiasm of the warriors for the forthcoming campaign. Sacrifices were offered to the spirits of the king's ancestors, and the departed spirits were invoked by officers of high rank, "men of sufficient status to remonstrate with the king on great occasions."[48]

[46] Holden mentions that sometimes there was further doctoring of the warriors. Incisions were made on the warriors and into these medicines were put (*Past and Future of the Kaffir Races,* p. 344).

[47] Stuart, *History of the Zulu Rebellion,* p. 83.

[48] Ibid., p. 82.

The ancient graves of former kings were also visited during this period and the spirits invoked at each, and asked for their blessings and help in the war.[49] Thus the Zulus made quite sure that all the forces of the universe that they could control were in their favor: their own ancestors were on their side; the king's vessel predicted success; their king had not only in his possession the means, in the form of possessions of the enemy, of overcoming their foes by magic, but had been strengthened as representative of his people; while the warriors themselves had been instilled with the necessary courage and ferocity to achieve victory. They were now to keep away from the weakening influence of women, and the girls and the women who brought food for their fathers and husbands had simply to set it down and return home at once.

Before the departure of the warriors, it was customary for the king to address them, to reassure them as to the result of his "churnings" and to excite them.[50] A few regiments would be summoned into the enclosure, there to challenge one another, and the king would say, "I've summoned you to hear how you mean to behave to the enemy." Thereupon one man would jump up and say, "I shall do so-and-so, I can do better than you," challenging some other warrior, *giya*-ing all the time.[51] The challenged man would then come out defiantly and answer the challenge, though occasionally someone would refrain from taking up the challenge. Such a man was treated as a coward and made to suffer great indignities. Sometimes the warrior would lay a wager on the matter, but this was merely to make the whole thing more exciting, for the wager was never paid. After the war the same regiments were called before the king to discuss the campaign, and it was seen who had won the wager.[52]

[49] This was done during the 1879 Zulu War when black oxen were so driven (Stuart, *uKulumetule,* p. 224).

[50] Shooter, *The Kaffirs of Natal,* p. 341.

[51] When a warrior *giya*'s the spectators shout out his praises, and in a military life like that of the Zulus, where praises had to be won by brave deeds in battle, these praises led to great emulation. They were an encouragement, not only to the man who had won them, but to others who had not yet distinguished themselves. In view of all this publicity, the position of a coward, who would have no one to praise him if he dared to *giya,* must have been invidious.

[52] Stuart, *History of the Zulu Rebellion,* p. 82.

SPRINKLING THE ARMY

When circumstances were such that the warriors had to proceed forthwith against the enemy, the ceremony of sprinkling them with medicine was gone through, though it appears that generally this was left until enemy country had been reached, or a battle was imminent. If such sprinkling was done at home, the procedure was more elaborate than when it took place just before a battle. The warriors formed a semicircle in the enclosure and then the doctor came out of a hut, his face smeared with black powder, and carrying a smoking firebrand in his hand. He flourished this at the men, first in front and then behind; then, throwing away the brand, he sprinkled them with a branch in each hand. Next he sent the men to the stream, while his boy followed them with a basket of medicine which he put into deep running water, so that the water flowed in the basket and out of it. The soldiers drank of the water below, some even from the basket itself; then they moved downstream and each one vomited into the water. The warriors now washed their bodies and moved back in company formation to the cattle kraal, chanting as they went. Thus cleansed inside and out, they dipped their fingers in war medicines prepared on potsherds.[53] This sprinkling of the regiment was done differently by different doctors, but the essential features always were cleansing internally by emetics and externally by washing in a stream; dipping the fingers into a dish of medicine, *ncinda*-ing (sucking off) it and then spitting it out, uttering imprecations against the enemy; being smoked with drugs; and being sprinkled front and rear by the doctor, while standing in a circle around him. In one case that we have on record, the doctor held something glittering in his hand, moving it about quickly so that the soldiers caught only imperfect glimpses of it. In another, the doctor used an assegai thrown by the enemy, which had failed to reach its mark. He bent the blade of this assegai, tying in the bend a small, round vessel of charms, and this he stuck into the ground by sharpening the wooden haft. Then each company approached, while the doctor shouted, "Here is a marvel, here is the one that missed its mark, etc." On filing past, each man shook the vessel with his fingers, saying,

[53] Ibid., p. 347, quoting Mbambo's case (N.H.C., December 1907).

"I shut." The effect of this was to cause all the enemy's assegais to miss their mark.[54]

ON THE MARCH

Often the destination of the army was concealed till the moment of starting and then confided only to one general; even in his speech to the army, the king would hint at a different direction from the actual one.[55] Sometimes, just as the warriors were setting out, women would pull off their dresses by opening them in front, and run naked before the soldiers to bring misfortune on the enemy.[56] The army marched in extended regimental columns with scouts in advance, on the flanks and in the rear, and when far from the enemy the warriors usually rolled up their shields and carried them on the back.[57] The young soldiers carried their own karosses, mats, etc., but carriers were attached to every army to carry the belongings of the principal men.[58] These carriers (*udibi*) marched two or three miles on the right or left flank of the main body, driving before them a herd of cattle, some of which were to provide food during the march, but most of which were to assist in finding and driving home the enemy's cattle.[59] Accompanying these carriers were also girls carrying beer, corn and other food for their male relatives; when this was exhausted they returned home. The provision bearers and herds seldom kept up with the army for more than the first few days, after which each warrior carried his own equipment. While still in Zululand, the soldiers were allowed to help themselves to food at the various kraals they passed, but they always took care to break the cooking vessels they had used.[60]

The Zulus could march with remarkable swiftness, being able to go forty miles in one night and forthwith give battle. If the army came to a stream in flood which was out of their depth but did not exceed fifteen yards in breadth, they plunged into it in a dense mass, holding on to one another, those behind forcing the others forward,

[54] Stuart, *History of the Zulu Rebellion,* p. 84.
[55] Shooter, *The Kaffirs of Natal,* p. 341.
[56] *The Collector,* No. 926.
[57] Stuart, ibid., p. 86.
[58] Fynn, in Bird's *Annals of Natal,* p. 87.
[59] Shooter, ibid., p. 402.
[60] Shooter, *The Kaffirs of Natal,* p. 347.

and in this way they succeeded in crossing with the loss of only a few.[61] Passwords and countersigns were made use of, especially when traveling at night, and when the army camped at night temporary shelters (*amadlangala*) were erected.

On reaching hostile territory, or when in broken country, the army marched in closer formation and divided into two. An advance guard of about ten companies moved from ten to twelve miles ahead to give the enemy the impression that they were the main body, and it was held to be a serious breach in tactics for the army to fail to divide like this.[62] Spies were sent in twos and threes to locate the enemy, and as soon as the advance guard found it had been perceived by the enemy, runners were dispatched to warn the main body.

When an engagement was imminent, the men were again sprinkled by the army doctors with *intelezi,* and the following is an example of such a sprinkling that took place in the Zulu War. A small fire, made with green leaves and a fatty substance that caused great smoke, was kindled; through this the men passed in twos. They trod lightly in the fire itself, the man on the left with his right foot, and the man on the right with his left. As they passed by, the doctor next sprinkled them with medicine from an earthen pot, using for the purpose two black brushes, one in either hand. Then they came to a second doctor, who lifted to the mouth of each a ladle containing some other medicine from a pot at his side, instructing them at the same time not to swallow this. When the whole *impi* had been dealt with in this way, they were told they were now invulnerable against bullets. Then they were led to the top of the nearest hill where they *chints'a*'d (squirted) the liquid toward their foes with terrible imprecations.[63]

ATTACK

Either before or just after this sprinkling, the men were drawn up in a semicircle and instructed by the officer in supreme command as to the routes to be taken, what regiments were to form the right horn, and what the left. Then the warriors, once more reminded

[61] Stuart, *History of the Zulu Rebellion,* pp. 199–202.
[62] *War Office Précis,* p. 212.
[63] Ibid.

of their challenge and exhorted through praise of departed kings, dashed forward to the attack.[64] The Zulus attacked in the form of an *umkhumbi,* or semicircle, usually making a feint with one horn, while the other, concealed in the bush and grass, swept around to

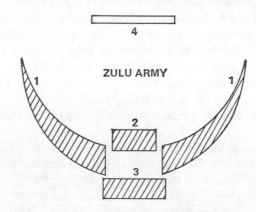

surround the enemy. The "chest," consisting of the greatest number of men, and also the most experienced (for the "black" regiments always formed the horns), now advanced and tried to crush the enemy.[65] Behind them was a large force which came to their aid when the army was in difficulty, or joined in the pursuit of the enemy. They were usually seated with their backs to the enemy,[66] while the commanding officer and staff took up their position on high ground to watch and issue directions, which were delivered by runners.[67]

TREATMENT OF THE WOUNDED AND THOSE WHO HAD KILLED AN ENEMY

The army doctors not only prepared the soldiers for battle, but also treated the wounded. When Isaacs was wounded on the expedition against Phakathwayo, in which he accompanied Shaka's army, a young heifer was killed and some of the entrails were parboiled with gall and excrement and roots. He was then made to take three sips of

[64] Stuart, *History of the Zulu Rebellion,* p. 86.
[65] Ludlow, *Zululand and Cetewayo,* p. 47.
[66] *War Office Précis,* p. 114.
[67] Ibid.

the medicine, sprinkle some over his body and then spit on a stick, point it thrice at the enemy, and throw it toward them, saying, *"Hhezie."* After this the doctor gave him an emetic to eject the medicine he had swallowed. When Isaacs at first refused to drink the decoction, he was told unless he did so he could not take milk, as the cows would die, and if he approached the king without having used the charms, the latter would become ill.[68]

On slaying an enemy, it is usual to stab the bowels of the victim lest the unreleased spirit of the victim turns the slayer into a lunatic.[69] The first thing to be done by a man who has slain an enemy is to take off his *ibeshu*, or loin covering, and put on that of the man he has killed. This he must wear until he can resume his own by having cleansed himself. He will now carry the assegai that has been responsible for the death of the enemy, with the blade pointing downward, and not, as is usual, horizontally in his hand.[70] A man who has killed another, whether in battle or otherwise, may neither mix freely in society nor partake of *amasi* until he has undergone a process of fortification (*Qunga*). He contracts potentially, though not actually, a certain disease (*iZembe*) appearing as dysentery, kidney diseases, and others, culminating in insanity, which he will contract properly unless he undergoes this *Qunga* process.[71] Hence those warriors in the army who have killed others eat and live entirely apart from the main body for many days, during which they are doctored with certain herbs and finally washed all over with drugs. They are treated with great respect, the best portions of meat being served to them. A man who has killed an adversary must carry in his hair a sprig of wild asparagus, and he may not take up his residence again in his own kraal till he has had sexual intercourse with some female or another not of his own tribe (or in case of necessity, any boy). This female, though not experiencing inconvenience herself, will transmit the *iZembe* disease, which the man has potentially contracted by killing an enemy, to the first male with whom she has intercourse. Till the warrior has found such a female he must, even at home, continue to live out on the veld. Upon entering his kraal he must *ncinda* a large variety of medicines or fighting charms called *iZembe elimnyana* (black *iZembe* medicine) before partaking of

[68] Shooter, *The Kaffirs of Natal,* p. 344.
[69] Stuart, *History of the Zulu Rebellion,* p. 88. Ludlow says it is done lest, when his bowels swell, theirs do too.
[70] Bryant, *Dictionary.* See under iNxeleha and iZembe, also Qunga.
[71] Ibid.

any food. These he *ncinda*'s with milk mixed with other charms, called *iZembe elimhlophe* (white *iZembe*). This done, he is clean, and may freely enter society and partake of *amasi,* but until he dies he must never again eat curds made from milk of a cow whose calf has not yet shown the horns; and every year he must refrain from eating the first fruits of the season, or beer made from the new corn, until he has fortified himself in all cases by certain medicinal charms.[72]

OBSERVANCES OF THE WOMEN IN WARTIME

While the men are away at war, the women must be very careful in their behavior at home, lest anything they do brings danger upon those who are absent. Quarreling is refrained from and all must be quiet. Ordinary ornaments are not worn, but, instead, wives and mothers mark their faces by rubbing them with specially prepared black paste of ashes, earth, and other similar ingredients. These marks are of various designs, some taking the form of a circle (of diameter about one and a half inches) over each eye meeting at the top of the nose, and a circle on each cheek. A necklace of two or three berries may be threaded to a cord, as also a rabbit tail, and worn to ward off evil. "The black marks on the face, and the wearing of berries, represent the formal suppression of ordinary personal feelings or the deliberate assumption of a callous disposition."[73] The tops of the skirts (*isidwaba*) of the women are reversed, the nap being turned outward, and to safeguard the home, a sprig of wild asparagus is often stuck in the thatch over the doorway of a hut.[74]

To scare away death from their husbands, women go about beating together large stones or rattling small ones between both hands (*Gqunga*),[75] while special precautions are taken to sweep the huts vacated by the men, and to make a fire in each one to encourage their return and prevent their remaining away forever. Their sleeping mat is shaken and rolled up, an ear of millet put in it, and it is stood upright at the end of the hut, a departure from the normal horizontal position of rolled-up sleeping mats. Sometimes the wooden headrest

---

[72] Bryant, *Dictionary* (Qunga).
[73] Stuart, *History of the Zulu Rebellion,* p. 88.
[74] Bryant, ibid.
[75] Ibid.

and other articles used by the warrior are suspended along the mat.[76] As long as this mat casts a shadow on the wall the husband is safe. To make quite sure of this a woman may take the mat and stand it upright in the sun: if it casts a large shadow, he is alive; if the shadow is short, he is dead. Sometimes bitter apple berries (*solanum*) are rolled slowly along that side of the hut in which the warrior slept, being aimed to go out by the door and carry out with it all possibility of harm.[77]

RETURN HOME

After an expedition the troops were permitted to return to their homes for a short period to recover from fatigue.[78] On their way home they sang their old tribal war song, and as soon as the women heard it, they came with faces smeared with light-colored clay, shrieking, "*Ki, Ki, Ki, . . . kuhle kwethu*" (joy in our homes), at the top of their voices, as a welcome. The warriors now threw away the loincloths worn during the war and cleaned up their spears, fitting them all with new handles. At home a black male beast was killed, the horns were cut, possible to be used as necklaces by those who had killed an enemy, though this is not stated, and strips of the skin were cut to be worn on the wrist.[79]

Within a short time, however, the warriors all gathered once more at the royal kraal to give an account of the details of the war operations. Those regiments who had challenged one another prior to setting out, now met again in another discussion, and from these discussions it was discovered who had been cowards and who had distinguished themselves. The latter were honored with a *nom de guerre,* and a hero would receive as many as ten head of cattle from the king. The cowards in Shaka's days received the fiat of their master and

[76] Arbousset, *Exploratory Tour in South Africa.*

[77] Stuart, *History of the Zulu Rebellion,* p. 88. Stuart mentions that certain customs are observed by mothers-in-law, too, to safeguard their daughters' husbands, but unfortunately does not mention what they are. He also states that when a husband is killed, "various other customs are conformed to by the woman," but gives no further information of their nature.

[78] Isaacs, *Travels in Eastern Africa,* Vol. II, p. 346. It would seem from Stuart's account in *uTulasizwe,* pp. 66–67, that the regiments first go to the royal kraal where they give the king an account of the war, and then repair to their homes.

[79] Stuart, *uTulasizwe,* p. 67.

were impaled.[80] Later on, in the days of umPande and Cetshwayo, cowards were no longer killed but nevertheless had to suffer many indignities, one of which was to have their meat dipped in cold water. Girls have been known actually to uncover themselves in the presence of a fiancé who had shown cowardice in order to shame him, after which the engagement was, of course, broken.[81] In these ways did the Zulu nation show its approval of the Spartan qualities engendered by the military system under which it lived.

[80] Isaacs, *Travels in Eastern Africa,* Vol. II, p. 346.
[81] Stuart, *History of the Zulu Rebellion,* p. 89.

PART V

African Aesthetics and Recreation

Introduction

African aesthetics and recreational activities have not received due attention. Some forms of African plastic art have been collected and have been the subject of scholarly monographs, but African music, oral literature, dance forms, and plays are only now being studied and reported upon in any detail. This neglect of African art and aesthetics is revealing when it is noted that most of the first ethnographers in Africa, especially the Germans, paid a great deal of attention to these aspects of African culture. The British scholars, who replaced the Germans as the foremost students of African civilization, were more interested in the social and political organizations of the Africans then being colonized than in either their art or religion. Only with the arrival of American and French scholars was the interest in the aesthetic and recreational aspects of African cultures revived. Today, a growing number of African scholars are writing on their art, and other Africans are modifying it to meet the needs of the contemporary world.

The most important characteristic of African aesthetics and recreational activities is their multi-functionality. It is possible, after diligent search, to find examples of "art for art's sake" and the same for recreation in African societies, but on the whole, art and recreational activities are almost always related to other aspects of life. This point is clearly recognized by the Fante who told Christensen, "there is no proverb without a situation." Although the Fante possess and use a rich stock of verbal art, Christensen found it difficult to collect many proverbs in the abstract. Instead, he learned to appreciate the subtlety and aptness of many Fante proverbs, maxims, and aphorisms by hearing them within the context of court cases, as social commentary on behavior, and in other live situations. Used by the Fante in such ways, these verbal art forms reveal the society's behavioral norms and ideals as much as they give free rein to their narrator's skill, ingenuity, and knowledge of the ways of his people.

Denise Paulme's treatment of the folk tales from West Africa not only supports the generalization that art forms are usually related to other aspects of culture in African societies, but her analysis appears to indicate that they reveal the general concerns of these societies. The tales she collected among the Bété are often funny and one can understand why they are used "for laughing" by these people. Nevertheless, Paulme was able to show how these tales mirror the "deeper" social structure of the Bété and reveal many of their more conscious values. Perhaps the most fascinating aspect of Paulme's article is the comparison of Bété tales with those of the Dogon, and the demonstration that the changes in the characters or behavior of the protagonists are also congruent with differences between these two societies. Her "transformational" and "structural" analysis of these folk tales are quite impressive. Moreover, her ability to compare these widespread African myths with similar ones in the Middle East and Europe has important implication for diffusionist studies.

While African folk tales are fairly well known, there is less known about the existence of African poetical forms. Poetry in Africa, as in Europe, owes a great deal to the Arabs and Arabic aesthetic elements in Swahili poetry are quite easily demonstrable. Knappert shows how the Swahili poets modified the classical Arabic metric forms, and insists that like good Muslims they remain fatalistic about the transitoriness of this world, emphasizing instead the promises of Paradise. But one wonders whether the poets' equal concern with love and indeed with life is not as African as it is Arab. Moreover, there is the evidence that the Swahili poets are very concerned with local affairs in contrast to those of the Orient, and that later Christian poets find in Swahili as ready a vehicle for expressing Christianity as did their ancestors for dealing with Islamic beliefs. Julius Nyerere's attempt to diffuse Shakespeare's plays to many people in Tanzania by means of Swahili demonstrates once again the versatility and adaptability of East African poetic forms.

Praise-singing, really a form of prose poetry, is found in many parts of Africa, but is especially well developed in the Western Sudan. Here the praise-singer (often called the *griot*) is not only a flatterer who "fills the heart" of his auditor, but functions as historian and musician at many ceremonies and rituals. Smith describes how the Hausa *maroka* or praise-singer eulogizes nobility, and performs at: religious ceremonies, wedding celebrations, meetings of age-grade organizations, work parties, the homes of wealthy individuals, and the salons of courtesans. Nevertheless, *roko* or praise-singing is more than an artistic or economic institution since its "non-economic and non-contractual features are used to regulate the social system." Certain *maroka* have the right and duty to make demands on and to interact with specific persons, thus demonstrating the latter's rank, privilege, or state of life.

African music, whether in the form of praise-singing or instrumental, is more varied and complicated than is usually realized. Besides the human voice, the instruments used run the gamut from idiophones such as the very common rattles to chorophones, popularly known as stringed instruments. In addition to these, as Nketia shows, there is hand clapping and foot stamping, much of which is often closely interwoven with instrumental music to produce sounds aesthetically pleasing to different African societies. Nketia states that the African creative performer has a body of technical *usages* to guide him, and permit him to exploit the full possibilities of his instruments.

African music normally emphasizes dynamic rhythm and usually organizes melody within the rhythmic framework. But perhaps the most important characteristic of African music is what Nketia calls, "the interaction between musical structure and social use." For him, music is always "an event" whether involved with praising kings, or linked to children's games, ceremonies of life cycles, or various types of festivals. And given the changing nature of African societies, African music tends to be very flexible permitting creation, re-creation, borrowing and adaptation.

Until now, not too much attention had been paid to autochthonous African theater which normally implied masquerades. This is indeed a pity since the masquerade is one of the most complex art forms in African societies. It involves music, poetry, dancing, praise and exhortation, singing, ritual, social, political and religious commentary, and of course, the plastic art. Masked figures and dancers, whether representing the ancestors or other supernatural or comic personages, always add drama to aspects of social life be they court cases, ceremonies such as initiation, weddings and funerals, and such other activities as planting or marketing.

The Ekine society found among the Kalabari is so multi-functional that Horton consigned it to a *borderland,* that of religion and art. He tells us that the ends of the society are as "artistic" as they are "religious," but so important are its social and political functions that at one time people were led to believe that the Ekine society governed the Kalabari people. Among its fascinating aspects is its means of determining status in Kalabari society. Indeed status in the Ekine society is governed by technical skill involved with the masquerade and not by socio-economic or political factors outside of it. Like many institutions of this type, the Ekine masquerades often engage in social commentary, but the personification of supernatural entities in the plays renders the ridicule of the foibles of men more acceptable and enhances the art of the performers. These plays also contribute to the socialization of both young and old into the norms of Kalabari society, but the Ekine does not attempt to "keep women in their place." Indeed, the occasion of the plays permits men to engage in a form of potlatch where they compete with each other to see who can provide the most luxurious clothes in which the women of their Houses attend the plays—a gesture as important for showing status as in providing costumes and masques for the actual performances. Thus, the role of the Ekine society among the Kalabari, like the role of Proverbs among the Fante, poetry among the Swahili, praise-singing among the Hausa, and African music, shows an intimate association of both art and life in African societies.

26. The Role of Proverbs in Fante Culture

A knowledge of what has been traditionally termed "folklore," and more recently "verbal art,"[1] has long been considered essential for any well-rounded ethnography. Among many non-literate peoples this art form sanctions and validates other aspects of culture such as religious, economic, social, and political institutions. This paper will discuss the role of one of its elements, the proverb, in a West African culture.

The materials presented here were obtained during field research among the Fante of the central coastal area of Ghana, formerly the Gold Coast.[2] The Fante are one of the several ethnically related groups known collectively as the Akan, which total approximately two million people inhabiting the greater part of the southern half of Ghana and contiguous areas in the Ivory Coast. The Akan exhibit a high degree of cultural homogeneity and for the most part speak mutually intelligible dialects. Much of what is stated here concerning Fante proverbs and culture also pertains to the Akan as a whole.[3]

The proverbs considered here were collected in three main ways.

SOURCE: James Boyd Christensen, "The Role of Proverbs in Fante Culture," *Africa*, Vol. 28, No. 3, July 1958, pp. 232–43. Reprinted by permission of the author and publisher.

[1] William R. Bascom, "Verbal Art," *Journal of American Folklore*, lxviii (1955), pp. 245–52.

[2] Grateful acknowledgment is made to the Fulbright Program, Social Science Research Council, and the Wenner-Gren Foundation for making the field research and subsequent work on the field materials possible.

[3] Many of the Fante proverbs collected by the writer have already been published in R. S. Rattray's *Ashanti Proverbs* (Oxford, 1916), although the translation differs somewhat. Rattray's work in turn is a translation of 830 of the 3,600 Akan proverbs appearing in the work by J. G. Christaller, *Twi Mmebusem Mpensa-Ahansia Mmoaano* (Basel, 1879), which is a collection compiled by Christaller and his associates and published in Akan. This shows the universality among the Akan of a large number of proverbs, although many are localized and regional variation does occur. Unfortunately, these rather rare works of Rattray and Christaller were not available to the writer while in the field, so the extent to which the Fante had proverbs in common with the other Akan could not be more accurately ascertained.

Some were obtained from informants during conversation where they were offered in validation of traditional procedures. Others were taken down during "contests," where two elders were competing to see who could quote the most proverbs. Elders were also requested to recount and explain proverbs. The last procedure, even with informants who were known to be masters of this art form, was not particularly rewarding. An informant who would invariably emphasize a point by use of a proverb would often prove a rather sterile source when asked for proverbs *per se,* without a problem or a situation to suggest one. One elder explained this difficulty by quoting what he maintained was a traditional saying, "there is no proverb without the situation." Their ability to remember proverbs seemed to be greater during conversation or in a contest than when discussing them as such. A very competent interpreter was used for the translations, and an attempt has been made to keep these as literal as possible while still making the saying appear meaningful in English.

Certain aspects of Fante culture have been singled out to indicate the various uses of the proverb. Proverbs have long been used in anthropological literature to illustrate or stress a feature of belief or behavior. The practice is evident in the writings of students of the Akan such as Rattray, Fortes, and Busia, to name but a few. However, the intent here is to accentuate the role of the proverb in a society rather than to emphasize the ethnographic fact.

Space will not permit more than a brief outline of the relevant ethnographic data, and while a lengthy list of pertinent proverbs could be included under each topic of discussion, the number has been limited to what is believed to be adequate for purposes of illustration.

Some of the aspects of culture discussed here have a larger number of proverbs listed in the discussion than others. This is not to be taken as a reflection of the interests of the Fante, or that they are more overtly concerned with the area of experience which has the greatest number of proverbs listed. For example, religion has been specified as the cultural focus of West Africa,[4] which certainly holds true for the Fante. Every aspect of culture is inextricably linked with the ancestral spirits, nature deities, or some form of animism. While a long list of proverbs relating to religion could be supplied, it has been given rather summary treatment here.[5]

[4] See M. J. Herskovits, *Man and His Works* (New York, 1948), pp. 542–61.
[5] An article dealing with the religious concepts of the Fante and relevant proverbs is scheduled for publication elsewhere.

West African proverbs, like those from elsewhere, may be grouped in two general categories: the truism or "proverbial apothegm," which has limited application because of its literal or definite assertion; and the "metaphorical proverb," which because of the metaphorical use of a simple event or statement has wide applicability. While truisms may lack the imagery or artistry of the metaphorical variety, they play the same role, and any differentiation is made on the basis of form rather than function. To the Fante, the word for proverb, *epe,* is also used for any traditional saying or statement, and even for riddles. Since our concern here is primarily with function, some truisms are included.

It is perhaps needless to indicate that proverbs reflect the ideal or norm of behavior rather than the actual. Moreover, the technique of presentation utilized does not imply that a given proverb is limited in its use to the area of experience under which it is listed. As elsewhere, some proverbs have wide applicability, and could be quoted with equal validity in reference to the beliefs and behavior patterns of the Fante in several aspects of culture.

JUDICIAL PROCEEDINGS

One facet of Fante culture in which proverbs play a prominent role is judicial procedure, where they are repeated as a traditional part of the hearings and are cited by the litigants. From before control by the Europeans down to the present, the Fante have had a rather complex system of courts and hearings. Presiding at any dispute or trial may be a group of elders, a chief and elders, or a panel of chiefs, depending on the nature of the case. A dispute, after submission to a group of elders for arbitration, may be further referred to higher authority, such as a sub-chief or the paramount chief of a state. The latter, known as the *omanhen,*[6] was the ultimate authority prior to the *Pax Britannica.*

The plaintiff and defendant generally present their own case to

[6] While there is only one paramount chief or *omanhen* (from *oman,* "state" and *ohen,* "chief") in each Fante state, there are numerous chiefs of varying degrees of importance. The term "chief" is used here to refer to an individual who occupies the sacred or ancestral "stool" of his clan. However, all clans do not have a chief and a sacred stool, as some are headed by a senior elder or *abusua panyin.* See J. B. Christensen, *Double Descent Among the Fanti* (New Haven, 1954) for material on the clan and other aspects of Fante culture discussed here.

the court, call witnesses and cross-examine those who give testimony for the opposition. During a hearing, proverbs are quoted by the litigants in much the same manner as precedents are cited during hearings in England or the United States. In this sense, proverbs may be regarded as the verbalization of social norms or "laws" which govern interpersonal relations. To illustrate, a man suing for collection of a loan, in addition to giving his interpretation of the issues, may intersperse his testimony with such statements as "One does not fan (the fire) that another may bite (eat)" or "One cannot gather and another use." The litigant who is the most eloquent and can muster several proverbs to support his case has a decided advantage, other factors being equal.

Many proverbs may be regarded as legal maxims since they are utilized most frequently in disputes. For example, a request for the postponement of a case may be supported by the statement, "It takes time to make a dress for the hunchback." Another proverb often quoted to indicate prior ownership in a land dispute is, "The bathroom was wet before the rain fell."[7] When requesting elders to quote and explain proverbs they tended to give those proverbs having bearing on property disputes. Moreover, when asked to discuss the meaning, or cite an example of a situation in which a given proverb would be applicable, the answer was frequently couched in terms of a dispute or court case, indicating that to the Fante there is a close association between proverbs and litigation.

Important in litigation and in all matters involving a chief is the *kyeame* or "spokesman." Every chief has his spokesman who serves him in several capacities. Tradition requires that a chief should never address the public directly, nor be spoken to except through the *kyeame*. The latter should be well-versed in customary law, and have a broad knowledge of proverbs to illustrate and emphasize his statements, this latter attribute being one of the criteria by which the competence of a spokesman is evaluated. It is of paramount importance that this spokesman be competent in public speaking, for while he may not change the meaning of the chief's words, he is permitted, if not expected, to manipulate, embellish, and revise the phraseology and choice of words. Stammering, or at least affecting it, was considered appropriate or even desirable behavior for a chief.

---

[7] "Bathroom" here refers to a four-sided screen, shoulder high, made of bamboo or occasionally sheet metal. The Fante, who are meticulous about at least one bath per day, carry a tin gourd of water into this enclosure to bathe when a river or the sea is not convenient.

The importance of the spokesman in the Fante political and judicial system is illustrated by the maxim, "There are no bad chiefs, only bad messengers." Because of his proximity to the chief, he can be an extremely influential person. In criminal cases the *kyeame* served in the role of prosecutor and in civil cases he acted as arbitrator, drawing the pertinent facts from the litigants and witnesses. He was charged with maintaining the decorum of the court, and when tempers rose he could restore order by use of a proverb. He would announce, "Some must inform the sea to stop being rough so that the coconut branches may stop rustling."

Findings of the court are also announced by the spokesman, again utilizing proverbs. In litigation over a loan, he may sum up the findings with, "One does not buy a cock that it may crow in someone else's town." It is also traditional at the close of a hearing to address the guilty party or unsuccessful litigant by the apothegm, "If you had taken a cudgel and killed your friend, then you would have killed him without profit."

There has long been a tradition that one of the emoluments of public office, such as the position of chief, was the "gifts" offered to show respect and to secure attention. Several proverbs reflect the sad plight of the poor, such as "The wealthy man is senior," or "A good name cannot be eaten, it is money that counts." That the less affluent citizen may encounter difficulty in court because of this pattern of giftgiving is recognized by the Fante, who quote a maxim with little imagery but considerable acumen, "A poor man cannot win a court case," or, in the same vein, "The poor man's plea receives hurried treatment."

THE CLAN

The key to the social structure of the Fante is the matrilineal clan or *abusua*. All members of the clan are believed to be related through descent from a common ancestress, though this relationship is often more mythical than real. The members of any one clan within a community or chiefdom are divided into many matrilineages, i.e. the uterine descendants of a female three to five generations back. While it may not be possible to name a common antecedent or prove a biological bond between all of the various matrilineages of a clan, all members of the *abusua* consider themselves related, and marriage within the clan would be regarded as incest. It is in the matrilineage and, in some contexts, the clan as a whole that the individual Fante traditionally found a high degree of security. From the lineage he secures land to cultivate, inherits property or office (from a uterine brother or maternal uncle), obtains aid in case of debt or virtually any form of difficulty. The lineage also co-operates in the worship and propitiation of the ancestors, and kinsmen are responsible for the elaborate burial and funeral so important to the Fante.

Collective responsibility and co-operation are outstanding attributes of clan and lineage membership, and numerous proverbs attest this expected pattern of behavior. Some of these are as follows:

"If the lizard is a blacksmith the monitor does not lack a cutlass."

"The lizard and the crocodile have the same stomach—if one eats, the other should also get a morsel." (The lizard, monitor, and crocodile are regarded as being of the same clan.)

"The poor kinsman does not lack a resting place."

"If you are getting your hair cut by your mother's child you do not look into a looking glass." (Kinsmen are to be trusted.)

"Because the tortoise has no clan he has already made his casket."

"The right arm washed the left arm, and the left also washes the right."

"A bird roosts with its own clan."

"The good paw paw tree has a plucking stick near it." (The wealthy man will have less fortunate kinsmen around him.)

Several proverbs illustrate the rules of conduct governing inheritance and intraclan and lineage relationships. Though women sometimes wield considerable influence, the affairs of the lineage are dominated by the men, for, as a simple apothegm states, "It is a house where there is no male that the female speaks." In regard to inheritance of position and property customary law indicates the logical heir to be the eldest surviving uterine brother, or, lacking this, the eldest sister's eldest son, and thence on to other uterine kin according to their seniority and matrilineal proximity to the deceased and primogeniture. Whether the position involved is that of a chief, or merely the head of a matrilineage, the preferred heir is a male within the matrilineage. To illustrate this the Fante quote "A maggot has its own route," or, similarly, "Anything that wiggles has its own path."

Though seniority in the matrilineage is a guiding principle, as illustrated by the maxim "The elder brother is the master," it is not compulsory that the elders appoint an heir on this basis, as other factors may intervene. The heir inherits property and wealth to administer for the benefit of all of the clan. Thus the decision of the elders may be to pass over the next in line and appoint a younger sibling or maternal nephew who is regarded as more reliable and competent, or whom they feel has earned the right on the basis of aid and service to the deceased. As the Fante put it, "What is in the hands of him who will go tomorrow is taken and given to him who goes today," or, "The red bracelet is fitted for the leopard and yet it is the duiker's mother who is dead."

That one person inherits the role of administrator of lineage affairs is indicated by the proverb, "Of all the fingers there is a special one that is used to eat the bean." That a sudden display of affluence on the part of a young man may result from inheritance of wealth rather than his own initiative is shown by the proverb, "If it does not take long for a tree to grow, then it sprang from a stree stump." That a man must assume the obligations and debts of his antecedent as well as any material wealth is an established principle in customary law. This is illustrated by such proverbs as "All mushrooms grow in the same place, but some are eaten and others are not," or, "The same snare that catches the deer sometimes catches a snake," and, more to the point, "A good man also sins." While a man has the privilege of indicating his preferred heir before his death, it is believed unwise to show a high degree of favoritism to a specific sister's son. A man may become completely dependent on his relatives in his old age, perhaps one he has slighted, for as it is aptly stated, "One does not know which thigh the day will find one sleeping on."

While one may count on the assistance of one's kinsmen in time of need, waiting around for a mother's brother to die is considered foolish, and complete dependence or "sponging" is not permitted, as is indicated by the maxim, "If you depend on someone else for breakfast, you go without food." Moreover, litigation between kinsmen helps no one, for as a proverb states it, "If you pick the pieces of meat from your teeth, and eat them, that does not mean you have eaten meat," which has a connotation similar to our own statement of "Robbing Peter to pay Paul."

THE ELDERS

A feature of Fante political and social structure is the prestige and authority accorded the elders (*mpayinfo*) and the deference and respect shown the aged. Even though the Fante have an elaborate system of chieftainship there is also a strong element of gerontocracy, particularly on the level of lineage affairs. Every chief, from the paramount to the sub-chiefs, has his circle of clan elders to serve as his councilors. Consultation of the lineage or clan elders was required in major and minor transactions, whether it involved land tenure, marriage, divorce, or minor problems such as who occupies which room in a house. For example, since marriage is a contract between two kin groups, all bridewealth and gifts must pass through the hands of elders. A gift by a young man directly to his betrothed could not be counted in a settlement in the event of a divorce. The proverb most often quoted to the writer, and applied to innumerable situations, was "One does not pluck the feathers from a fowl before presenting it to an elder." In short, one would not ask an elder to identify a fowl after its feathers had been removed, or one should never present one's senior with a *fait accompli,* but seek him out first.

The following proverbs are some of the many that indicate the importance placed on the role of the elder:

"The word of the elder is more powerful than the *suman.*"
(A *suman* is an amulet or charm having supernatural power.)

"A child who can wash his hands clean may eat with the elders."

"The child bows to the elders."

"The head that is first is senior."

"We follow the words of the mouth of an elder, not his thoughts."

"If your grandmother tells you something, do not tell her that you are going to find out from your mother, for who brought forth your mother?"

"Five articles cannot be compared with nine."

"An elder does not break wind in public, but in the latrine."

"One who is cutting the path does not know it is crooked." (Thus one should seek or take advice.)

THE CHIEF AND THE STATE

The Fante are divided into eighteen small states, the present populations of which range from 2,000 to 35,000. Before British control each of these was autonomous. At the head of each *oman* or state was an *omanken,* chosen from the "royal family" which was the particular clan having the privilege of providing the ruler. While the *omanhen* and sub-chiefs were accorded considerable authority under customary law, they were by no means autocrats. A system of checks and balances was present in the indigenous political structure that ensured the commoner a voice in his government, in fact, there was a strong element of democracy present in the system.[8] The *oman* or state (the term also applied to the citizens as well as the territory) could accept or reject a candidate for the position of paramount chief. As long as the chief used discretion and did not antagonize too many of his followers, he was permitted to remain in office. However, should a majority of the people, or a sufficient number of influential citizens, decide the *omanhen* had deviated to a degree that warranted his removal from office, he could be forced to abdicate or be removed from his position.

The field worker among the Fante soon becomes familiar with the dual nature of the political system, for a paramount chief will rarely grant a concession of any importance without consulting the representatives of the people. Often matters of state are decided during an open meeting of all people who care to attend, and anyone may voice an opinion.

Consequently, what would appear to be an incongruity occurs between some of the proverbs relating to this aspect of Fante culture. Many stress the supremacy and primacy of the *omanhen,* but, conversely, others point out that the ultimate power lies with the state. This is not a contradiction, but rather indicates that as long as the paramount chief has the support of the people he has the authority accorded him by tradition, but the prerogative to appoint and remove

[8] For a discussion of the political system of the Akan see K. A. Busia, *Position of the Chief in the Modern Political System of Ashanti* (London, 1951) and J. B. Christensen, "African Political Systems: Indirect Rule and Democratic Processes," *Phylon,* First Quarter (1954).

chiefs rests with the people. In many of the proverbs the elephant is used synonymously with the *omanhen:*

"One cannot make the same tracks as an elephant."

"A snare is destroyed when an elephant places his foot on it." (Plots against the chief are easily quashed.)

"A cow can only be tethered to a strong tree." (The chief can check even the strongest.)

"One does not state what he thinks in front of a chief, but behind his back."

"After the elephant there is no other animal."

"When you follow the elephant you will not be ensnared in difficulties."

"The chief has ears like those of an elephant."

"When the chief's breast has plenty of milk it is for all the world to suck."

The role of the people is indicated in the following:

"When the chief has good advisers, he reigns peacefully."

"If Otsibo says he can do something, then he does it with his followers."

"Though the elephant is huge, his domain is looked after by the duiker." (In proverbs the *oman* is often depicted as the duiker.)

"Though the coconut tree is smooth, the palm-nut tree is the king." (The palm-nut tree is likened to the people because of its many products.)

Proverbs also exist for sanctioning the removal of a chief who fails in his duties, such as, "If you see a stick that will pierce your eye, break it off." Proverbs also recognize that public opinion may be fickle or that attitudes may change. That the chief who once received the adulation of his followers may later be the target of their anger is illustrated by "The throat that gulps down good soup is the very throat that receives the bullet in time of difficulty."

CHILD REARING

"A wise child is talked to in proverbs" is another Fante maxim that is widely observed, for the proverb is commonly used to admonish the child who misbehaves as well as to praise the obedient one. Many of the proverbs dealing with the respect due to elders, obligations to kinsmen, or the proper attitude toward chiefs are used to indoctrinate children in regard to the acceptable standard of social behavior. The following are proverbs that are oriented primarily toward the rearing of children:

"The monkey jumps to where it can swing." (The child should not "Bite off more than he can chew," or "Look before you leap.")

"The male cat is not one man's pet." (Told to a child who complains that too many adults are sending him on errands or requesting his services.)

"If you follow a bad dog you come across a dead rat."

"The child should not mock the short man."

"Short palm tree, stop complaining, for the tall palm started as you."

"The child who provokes his mother and father eats food without salt."

"If the foreleg is larger than the thigh then there is an illness." (A child should not consider himself superior to his parents.)

"When a child behaves as an adult, he sees what an adult sees." (He is punished as an adult.)

Proverbs also outline the correct procedure for parents in regard to child rearing, like "Spare the rod and spoil the child" in our own culture. Examples are:

"If one is unable to eat one's palm nuts they become full of worms." (If a parent cannot control his children, they become spoiled.)

"The hen's feet do not kill her chicks."

"When a child cries, he is not imprisoned." (Actually, he is not "bound to a log," the pre-contact technique of restraining prisoners.)

"One does not send a child on an errand, then look to see whether or not he is pleased."

"Human beings who are found useless are not classified as beasts." (Children are not to be treated as animals.)

"One has not been an elder before but one has been a child." (Adult behavior should not be expected of children.)

"It is the child who is sent for water that breaks the pot." (Children learn by doing.)

"If you, an elder, say, and do not do, you will not be feared by the young."

While it is considered permissible and appropriate for an adult to correct any child he sees misbehaving, spanking or whipping should be undertaken only by the parents or a close relative. The duty of spanking usually falls to the father, Fante mothers being somewhat indulgent. Generally speaking, the women do not favor any form of corporal punishment for children, and the father threatening such action is likely to be told by his wife that "The stick that is used to hit the sheep is not used to hit the fowl" (adult punishment is not administered to a child). That spanking is the prerogative of the parents is illustrated by the proverb, "Unless a boy's parents are present, you cannot wash his yaws." The Fante also cited the latter proverb to indicate certain limitations placed on the avunculate. Unlike some of the other Akan, where a man has complete control over his sister's children, the Fante father retains authority over his children until their marriage, when they pass to the control of their clan elders.

ENTERTAINMENT

Recitation of proverbs served as a form of entertainment when quoted in contests. Two contestants would alternately cite a proverb and a panel of judges would rule on duplication and authenticity. If one contestant delayed too long before submitting an appropriate citation and his opponent could offer a new proverb, the latter was declared the winner. Such contests were carried on at casual gatherings in the evening or at ceremonies and celebrations.

There is also an association between proverbs and the gold weights of the Akan. Before the introduction of modern coinage the currency of the Akan was gold dust, and the weights used for assessing amounts, exchange, and payment were cast in bronze by the *cire perdue* technique, and made in either a geometric pattern or anthropomorphic or zoomorphic forms. Today the manufacture of gold weights is almost a lost art, though many of these pieces are still obtainable.

Proverbs or a ceremony often suggested the design or form of a weight, although these are invariably human or animal in form. Some weights suggest only a specific, well-known proverb, but others, such as a tortoise or crocodile, may suggest to different individuals any proverb that contains that particular animal.[9] For example, a very common "proverb weight" is a pair of crossed crocodiles having two

[9] See R. S. Rattray, *Ashanti* (Oxford, 1923), ch. xxv. Rattray's discussion of the nature and function of the Ashanti weights is applicable to the role of this form of plastic art among the Fante.

heads and tails but a single stomach. This particular weight elicited different proverbs from informants, although they all had do do with the collective responsibility of the lineage. These included the first two proverbs quoted under the discussion of the clan and lineage above.

Proverbs may also be depicted on the flags of the *asafo* or military companies. The *asafo,* whose primary function in former times was defense of the state, still retain their political and ceremonial roles, and they are most often seen parading at ceremonies for chiefs or at the funerals of deceased members of the company. The occasion often arises for an *asafo* company to visit a village or state other than the one where a majority of their members reside,[10] and at such times they may display an ensign with a proverb pictured on it. The use of flags by the military undoubtedly post-dated European contact, but the practice described here in regard to flags can hardly be classed as "fakelore" rather than folklore, as it has been common for two or three hundred years and is probably a transposition of proverb weights to a new medium. These "proverbial ensigns" depicted either a heroic deed of the company displaying it or could have a derogatory significance. The latter form would often refer to some past incident when another *asafo* company or town had suffered defeat or had not behaved honorably. For example, a cat, a mouse, and a bag pictured on the flag would refer to the maxim "There is a reason why the cat becomes passive when the mouse goes into his bag for food," signifying that the spectators did not retaliate to some insult in an exemplary manner in the past. Since some Fante states were formed by migrants from another established *oman,* they could be reminded of their junior status by a picture of a bird and its young, symbolizing the proverb, "If the parent does not go in search of food, the young ones go without." Such effrontery as this had been known to precipitate intra-tribal wars in the past.

Proverbs and riddles could be played by the drummer of the *asafo* company, and this would usually occur when the drummer of the local company engaged the drummer of a visiting company in a contest. These are not the famous "talking drums" (*ntumpan,* Fante, *ntumpane,* Ashanti) of the Akan, which consist of a "male" and "female" drum of different tone, and are normally the sacred drums of the state. The technique involved in communication by the talking

---

[10] See Christensen, *Double Descent,* ch. vi, for a detailed discussion of the *asafo.*

drums has been described in detail by Rattray, and the same principles generally apply to the *asafo* drum.[11] But unlike the *ntumpan,* the drum used for proverbs by the *asafo* consists of a single drum, played with one stick and the open hand.

The repertoire of proverbs and riddles of the *asafo* drummer is limited to those that carry the additional label of "drumming proverbs." These are sayings that have become well known or standardized by the drummers through decades or centuries of repetition and is familiar to those of the audience who understand the drum language. While it is theoretically possible to reproduce any proverb on the drum, the limitations of the talking drum are such that other than standard communications or common drumming proverbs would be virtually incomprehensible to the listener.

BEHAVIOR AND VALUES

Among the Fante correct procedure in interpersonal relations is stressed and the large number of proverbs which outline this pattern of accepted behavior reflects this emphasis on "doing the proper thing."[12] Many behavioral norms and values found in Euro-American culture are also found among the Fante. In the following series of comments on personality and human behavior it may be noted that many are similar in meaning to European proverbs and would be used by the Fante in a comparable situation:

"If a rat goes to a funeral, he stays with a burrowing animal." (Similar to "Birds of a feather flock together.")

"The fox and the fowl do not live together."

[11] Rattray, *Ashanti,* ch. xxii. Most often the *asafo* drum is used to accompany the dance or to sound standard military messages. However, speech could be indicated. This was done by representing tone, emphasis (loudness or softness), pauses and accents which combine to make a form of linguistic music. The instrument is not a pressure drum, and as near as the untrained ear of the writer could ascertain, a change of tone was achieved on the single drum by using the open hand, which produced a tone different from that made by use of the drumstick, or by hand pressure on the drumhead while striking it. Inquiry of the drummers as to how they approximated speech was not particularly fruitful, as they maintained they just played the way they had been taught. What the drummer played could best be described as a musical phrase, familiar to the audience.

[12] It is recognized that to have a section of the paper dealing with behavior and values is somewhat unrealistic, as virtually all of the proverbs in the article are related to behavior and the value system.

"The crab does not give birth to a bird."

"A sheep does not give birth to a goat."

"No one needs to teach the leopard's child how to spring." (This and the two previous proverbs are used to imply "Like father, like son.")

"The blacksmith hammers where it needs it."

"The lizard does not eat pepper for the frog to sweat." (A man must be responsible for his own actions.)

"There is no hatred if it does not get to the ear."

"If water is not near you, you go near it."

"The hunter is he who has game on the hearth."

"The reason two deer walk together is that one has to take the mote from the other's eye." (Similar to "Two heads are better than one.")

"An empty barrel makes the most sound." (Barrels have been known on the coast for over two centuries, as goods from Europe often arrived in such containers.)

"What is good fortune for one is misfortune for another."

"If the mouth slips, it is more slippery than the foot."

"If you visit Kweku, Kweku will visit you." (Similar in meaning to "As ye sow, so shall ye reap.")

"If you get your bundle ready, you will be helped to carry it."

"If you are not one of those who go to sea, you say the sea is calm."

"A hopeful palm tree does not produce wine." (Like "Do not count your chickens before they are hatched.")

"The bird that sits in the tree too long gets hit with a stone." (This is the antithesis of "The rolling stone gathers no moss.")

"It is regular walking that stops the path from growing weeds."

"If you only talk about weeding out a thorny bush, no thorns get in your skin."

"If you play push with the porcupine you do not become free from sores." ("Push" is a children's game. The proverb is similar in meaning to "People who play with fire get burned.")

"Things gained easily, disappear easily."

"One bird in the hand is worth ten in the sky."

Disapproval of adultery or promiscuity is evident in such statements as "A woman at childbirth is not covered with a cloth," or, "It is not possible to remove a woman's loin cloth without her knowing it." Attitudes toward the female may at times be other than complimentary as indicated by the following proverbs:

"A wife is like a blanket, for even though it scratches you, you are cold without it."

"Even if a wife is unfaithful you do not have to sleep alone."

"Do not tell your wife anything that cannot be said in public."

What often appears to the European as indolence or lack of desire to come to grips with a problem on the part of the African may be answered by a proverb such as "You do not carry the sticks that are used to brace the vines the day you plant the yam." This was the Fante way of resisting pressure or implying that important decisions require a great deal of contemplation and discussion. In a similar vein, the belief that problems should be met when they arise and that one should not seek out trouble is indicated by, "The cloth for the swollen testicle is sewn when the testicle gets swollen."

To summarize, the foregoing discussion, in addition to illustrating the pronounced tendency of the West African to moralize and speak indirectly by the use of a proverb, shows the many facets of Fante life where the proverb plays a role. The Fante, when discussing custom and tradition, constantly emphasize, or to their mind prove, a statement by quoting an appropriate maxim. Thus working with proverbs may prove an aid to the ethnographer in ascertaining the ideal norms of behavior, and in some areas of experience proverbs may be taken as the verbalization of customary law.

27. Oral Literature and Social Behavior in Black Africa

In 1958 we gathered some thirty folk tales from among the Bété, a Krou Krou (Kru) population who live in the Gagnoa and Daloa areas of southwest Ivory Coast. In 1956 the Bété officially numbered 184,000.

All these tales belong to the type *nine gbaleade* or stories "for laughing." The *nine* are for light entertainment during the moonlit nights when no one wants to go to sleep too soon. One would never hear them during daytime. They are simple stories grouped into songs, *Wumunu nine;* riddles, *gosa nine;* and proverbs, *nine sisakpasi.* The *nine gbaleade* we will deal with here are humorous stories told for pleasure, because the *gbaleawi* are those with whom one can joke without restraint—the younger brothers and sisters of a wife, for instance. This is in contrast to the *wota,* the elder *wota,* whom the husband respects and also avoids as often as possible.

None of these tales appears to be specific to the Bété: not only is the principal character, the Spider "zakole," obviously borrowed from the Agni and Baoulé folklore, but almost every intrigue is really a variation on an already well-known theme. Because of this fact, two approaches were possible: ignore those tales that added nothing to the study of a society of which they were not indigenous; contrariwise, retain them, and deal only with what differentiates them from other versions. In the changes that were judged necessary to make the stories acceptable to a new audience, could one not see reflected the concerns that belong only to that society? Would one not better understand how this society approaches problems that are equally found elsewhere?

[1] Translated by Marguerite Chesbrough and Elliott P. Skinner from Denise Paulme, "Littérature Orale et Comportements Sociaux en Afrique Noire," *L'Homme,* Tome I, No. 1, Janvier–Avril 1961, Paris, pp. 37–49. Reprinted by permission of Denise Paulme and the editors of *L'Homme.*

Here are the ideas suggested by the Bété version of three stories whose versions have already been noted among the Dogon in the Sudan. All three stories are about kinsmen and in-laws, marriage and the relations between the husband and his wife, his parents and his in-laws.

The first very short Bété tale is in riddle form, and in a way is reminiscent of the topics an eighteenth-century Parisian hostess would relate in order to test the subtlety of her guests.

BÉTÉ TALE—THE THREE DROWNED WOMEN

A man, his sister, wife and mother-in-law are crossing a river in a canoe. The canoe capsizes. Neither of the three women can swim. Whom do you think the man will rescue?

The narrator adds, as a commentary: "If you rescue your sister and let your wife drown, you will have to pay a new bride price (to acquire a new wife). If you rescue your wife and abandon your sister, your relatives will assail you with reproaches. But if you choose to rescue your mother-in-law, you are an idiot."

DOGON TALE (without title)

A man was working in his field with the help of his sister and his wife. There had been a heavy downpour and they had to cross a roaring river to return to the village. The two women lost their footing in the river and while the man was rescuing his sister, his wife drowned. The following year the sister went to live with her husband and left her brother alone in his house. One day he was working alone in his field, close to that of his brother-in-law, when some passers-by, seeing him alone, offered to sell him a captive girl they had with them. The widower had no money, so he called his sister and asked the strangers if they would agree to an exchange of girls. The deal was made and leaving the new wife with the widower, they took the sister with them. His unfortunate brother-in-law did not protest when he discovered what had happened, because he felt that the widower indeed needed a wife to take care of his household—and besides, the brother did not exceed his rights in selling his sister. Alas, all this would have been avoided had the man rescued his wife rather than his sister. The narrator ends his tale thus: "A husband should put his wife before his sister. This is the lesson of the story."[2]

[2] D. Paulme, *Organisation sociale des Dogon,* Paris 1940, pp. 479–80.

This tale indicates that the Dogon have no difficulty dealing with a problem to which the Bété, by their own admission, have not been able to find a satisfactory solution. The factors in the problem are the same in both societies: both of them are governed by patrilinear rules of filiation and by patrilocal residence. In both societies it is necessary to pay a bride-price to the relatives of a girl in order to obtain a wife. However, the resemblances end here, since the Dogon and the Bété react differently to the same institution. If we can believe our informants, in former days the Dogon wife did not go to live with her husband until the birth of their third child. At that time she had to resign herself to living far from her own family. Nowadays, the time that a woman spends away from her husband is even shorter, but even so, the new household does not come into being until there is a sign of pregnancy. Among the Bété it is quite different. Not only must the first child be born under his father's roof, but married life traditionally started with an abduction. Whether forewarned or not, the "bride" was taken from her parents' home and sequestered for three days. Whatever her feelings are, the appearance of violence must be maintained. Afterwards, the young Bété wife shows a greater concern about her brother's household than about her own because she feels that she has been responsible for setting it up. Was it not the bride-price given by the husband of the elder sister that was used to obtain a wife for the younger brother? This explains, if not justifies, the frequent intrusions of a married sister into her brother's married life. Let her sister-in-law show a "lack of respect" only once, and a woman will set all the older married female members of the lineage upon her. Like furies they invade the village and take the guilty one prisoner; even her husband cannot leave his house without agreeing to pay a fine chosen at the whim of the sisters. The poor wife, in order to obtain money for the fine, has to go to call upon her own relatives. The danger is that once away from her husband, she often prefers to stay with another man rather than take the trouble to collect the ransom. It is easy to imagine a Bété husband's difficulties in keeping a wife who can never forget that in her own village she herself has all the privileges of a sister. Thus, the issue posed by the storyteller in the Bété tale (between a sister and a wife which one to choose?) is of immediate interest to his audience.

How can one explain such strained relations, are they purposely made difficult? One answer may be that it pleases the quarrelsome and vocal Bété to make use of the slightest pretext for offense. In earlier days, wife abductions were met by a punitive expedition against the village of the seducer, a welcome diversion for men habituated to hunting, during monotonous periods when no big feast, no big gathering, gave life to the society. However, fighting never lasted very long. It stopped after the first encounter, the warriors preferring the effect of surprise to a staged campaign, and a compromise instead of the defeat of an opponent upon whom they depended, after all, in everyday life. They preferred just a little fire, not a huge conflagration that could destroy the whole village. In other words, the Bété seem to find difficulty coping with the fact that social life calls for half measures that often leave no one really satisfied. They are perpetually dissatisfied. They agree that marriage is indispensable for the survival of the lineage, but find this very irritating at the same time. In submitting his wife to perpetual exile, the husband is condemned to endure at least the whims of his sisters and the sullen silence of his wife. Nevertheless, all the men really desire polygamy which, in former times, was the prerogative of the outstanding warrior. Among the burdens of marriage, one should not forget the demands of the parents-in-law.

Even though the Dogon tale reported above does not refer directly to the mother-in-law, the commentary of the Bété narrator leaves no doubt about the sentiment of the son-in-law toward this important in-law, "wota wono," (literally: woman, "wono," in-law, "wota"). These sentiments are more crudely expressed in the tale of the "Spider and his Mother-in-law." If in the preceding *nine* the son-in-law ignores her, it is deliberate; here he fully intends to drown "the one who eats everything."

BÉTÉ TALE—THE SPIDER AND HIS MOTHER-IN-LAW

The Spider, his wife, his child and his mother-in-law were in a forest camp when a famine arrived. The Spider left to look for food but his search was in vain. He is very distraught: "Man searches," he says to himself, "and all he finds are stones." One of the stones hears him and replies: "Take me, I will nourish you.—How?—Put me in the bottom of a pot, put water on top of me and put the pot on the fire." The Spider obeys and a miracle happens! The pot is full of rice, and everyone eats to his heart's content. But the insatiable mother-in-law scrapes the bottom of the pot to get the rice grains which are stuck to it, and in her gluttony she also gets the stone and swallows it. The son-in-law asks himself: "Where is my stone?" "I ate it," confesses the mother-in-law. "You will have to give it back to me; you will have to take a purge." The mother-in-law takes a purge and produces the stone. The Spider puts the stone back into the pot, fills the pot with water and puts it on the fire. But the charm is broken, and this time the pot does not fill with rice. "Tomorrow," says the Spider to his mother-in-law, "we will return to the stones and ask them for something to eat." They both set out on their way.

On the road they meet a man named Médé who asks them: "Where are you going?" and offers the son-in-law some palm wine. He also says to him: "Take this path and you will find a palm tree which I have cut down and tapped." The Spider does not waste any time, puts down his bundle in which his mother-in-law is hidden, and leaves to look for the palm wine. The mother-in-law, taking advantage of her son-in-law's absence, asks Médé to free her, and tells him what they are looking for. Médé, curious about the secret of the stones, takes the mother-in-law's place and hides in the bundles. (The mother-in-law disappears.) The Spider comes back after drinking the palm wine, shoulders his bundle and continues on his way, without noticing the change of persons hiding in it. As he comes to the river, he says to his mother-in-law: "Today your life is over." The terrified Médé shouts: "It is me, Médé, that you are carrying, and not your mother-in-law!" But the Spider refused to listen to the frantic Médé and throws his bundle into the water; Médé dies in vain."[3]

The Bété really like this story. Up to this moment I have not been able to determine whether they really felt sympathy for the son-in-law (the Spider appears in all the *nine gbaleade* as a scoundrel always ready to pull a fast one on his partners) or if they are more amused at a plan doomed to failure: Does the son-in-law really believe that he can get rid of his mother-in-law just by throwing her into the water?

In still unpublished Dogon tales I found to my surprise the same theme but with characters and motives entirely different. Of

[3] This was the only time I heard the name Médé mentioned; it does not belong to the Bété. Perhaps it is borrowed from the Gouro, where "Médé" means snake?

interest is that the mother-in-law is completely absent in the Dogon version of this tale which belongs to the class of tales called *So Taniye*.[4]

DOGON TALE—THE CUCKOLDED HOGON

One day, the Hogon finds his wife committing adultery. He orders the guilty rival put into a waterskin and that it be thrown into the water to drown him. A robust servant is chosen for this job; he puts the waterskin on his back and makes for the river. En route he has to relieve himself and asks a Peul who is minding his flock nearby to keep an eye on the waterskin. In his absence the prisoner inside the skin starts complaining: "I have eaten so much honey, I have a bellyache." The Peul is intrigued, opens the skin and asks to have a taste of the honey. The prisoner escapes through the opening of the skin and puts the Peul in it. When the servant returns, he puts the skin on his shoulder and proceeds to drown the Peul without paying the slightest attention to the latter's outcries and pleadings.

Meanwhile, the Hogon's rival takes the Peul's cattle now left without a keeper. Six days later, he returns to his village with the flock of cattle. When questioned, he explains that he found the cattle at the bottom of the pool in which he had been thrown. When these rumors reached the Hogon, he asked that he too be thrown into the pool. This was done, and the Hogon never came back. People say that since then, young men are never drowned for committing adultery.

The plot of the two stories is approximately this: being deeply offended, a man wants to take revenge. He takes his opponent captive, and the latter seems to be hopelessly lost; however, at the last moment, the prisoner uses some trick to get free and a third person who has nothing to do with the quarrel will have to pay for it.

[4] *So Taniye:* "astonishing word," cf. G. Calame-Griaule, "Esotérisme et fabulation au Soudan," *Bull. IFAN,* t. XVI, series B Nos. 3–4, July–October 1954, pp. 307–21. The *Taniye* tends to be an explanatory tale: "The reason why . . ." "Once upon a time . . ."

	Offended	Offender	Nature of Offense	Victim + Conclusion
BÉTÉ	Spider (son-in-law)	Mother-in-law	"ate everything"	Médé dies in vain.
DOGON	Hogon (husband)	Lover	sexual	The Peul becomes a victim of his gluttony; the Hogon of his greed.

It is interesting to note that greediness is a motif in both versions. However, while the Hogon as well as the Peul die from their greediness, the old Bété lady who even eats the stone remains unharmed. The portrayal is marvelous and very deft. On the other hand, the Dogon narrator draws only a bare outline of the lover who really stays in the background. In contrast, he gives much more detail of the two other characters, the husband and the final victim. The latter is a Peul, that is to say, a man from a different walk of life, a born enemy of the peasant. The Peul's cattle constantly trample down the peasant's meager crops, and therefore a Dogon will not miss an opportunity to ridicule the Peul. The Peul's character is better drawn than that of the Médé in the Bété version, whose intervention remains inexplicable and he ends up drowned "for nothing." Indeed, there could hardly be any hostility on the part of the Bété toward the Peul who are unknown in Bété country. Up to today, the Bété occupy a border forest area whose inhabitants live primarily by hunting and from simple agricultural techniques which are still quite close to "gathering."

Thus, from an economic standpoint, the differences between the two tales reflect the different anxieties of their respective audiences. The enemy "who eats everything" is in one, the mother-in-law; in the other, the wandering nomad and his cattle.

The Hogon in the Dogon version is the counterpart of the Bété's Spider. Elder and revered chief of the community, where he lives somewhat apart, the Hogon appears in the story only in the guise of a deceived husband. Nevertheless, his wrath over his wife's behavior, and the brutal punishment he orders for his rival, precludes any sympathy for him. The end of the tale is in tune with its beginning: the man who abuses his power is also covetous. He cannot resist the perspective of new riches and will perish, a victim of his greed. The reference to a sacred chief in the context of this vernacular story is interesting. According to traditional Dogon belief, the Hogon does not die. His corpse is hidden from the public's eye and is said to change into a great snake. This is why the audience smiles at the disrespectful hint in the story that the Hogon could die from drowning.

With some qualification, the moral of the Dogon tale could be said to indicate the necessity for the old to limit their authority over the young, and for the dead over the living. The world of the dead—to which the Hogon already belongs, since in former days his elevation to office was sanctified by a funeral ritual—should not interfere in the affairs of the living. Therefore, for having infringed this rule, and demanded an excessive punishment for an offense which did not hurt him personally, the representative of the ancestors will be twice ridiculed. Having made this point, the narrator takes the opportunity to ridicule the hated Peul and to make allusion to the cattle coming out of the water, the great myth of the origin of all cattle in the Western Sudan.

But this is not all. The story, or rather its theme, has a wider distribution in Black Africa than any of the Bété and Dogon. Already in 1905, Ch. Monteil had published two versions of it, one from the Khasonké and the other from the Soninké country.[5] Neither of these tales puts the intrigue within the contest of married life which, it must be admitted, is only hinted at in the Dogon version. In them, the role of the offender (the Bété mother-in-law, and the Dogon lover) is given, in an even vaguer manner, to the "Child of Evil," called in Soninké "Marandenboné," a kind of trickster whose actions are always contrary to what is expected of him. In the Khasonké tale, the victim is a blacksmith who loses his patience over the mischief of the "Child of Evil." Exasperated, the blacksmith puts his tormentor into a goatskin which had been used for honeyed meal. But the Child of Evil succeeds in escaping with the help of the blacksmith's two small daughters, who take his place. They would end up not drowned, but burned:

> ". . . the blacksmith, after putting fire to a pile of wood, got
> the goatskin, and hearing two sweet small voices coming from

5 Ch. Monteil, *Contes soudanais,* Paris, 1905.

its interior resembling those of his two little girls, cried out: 'Yes, yes, you son of a devil, you can split yourself up if you like, you will burn just the same!' He threw the bundle onto the fire. After a moment the goatskin exploded, and the poor blacksmith saw his two dear little girls burning to death."[6]

We thus find the mother-in-law transformed and appearing in the guise of an obnoxious being—an identification to which the Bété would not object. But while the Khasonké blacksmith is cruelly punished for having wanted to get rid of an exasperating tormentor, the Bété son-in-law who wanted to discard his mother-in-law is not punished at all, only ridiculed as a deceiver deceived.

Why is this offended Khasonké a blacksmith? That he should be the Hogon in the Dogon version is already surprising enough. And why do the Soninké give the blacksmith's role to a "sorceress" who also throws her own children into the fire? This gesture alone makes us wish that the one who committed it be punished. As there is no reason or commentary given on such gesture, we feel better disposed toward the "Child of Evil" whose strange behavior is justified by nothing and does not call for our criticism.

The answer to this lies elsewhere. In his foreword to Monteil's anthology, H. Basset mentions the similarities between the Sudanese "Child of Evil" and the tale of *Mqidech* or *Haddidouan* known throughout North Africa. Its numerous versions describe the struggle of the weak but clever child (Petit Poucet, in the French literature) against an ogress whom he finally overcomes:

> ". . . the ogress glares at the hero whose shrewdness defies all her traps and all her double-dealing, to her great humiliation, until the day when he lets himself be caught. He works for the ogress, and is finally sentenced to die to serve as meal to the ogress's anthropophagous friends. But at the very last moment he succeeds in substituting the ogress's daughter in his own place, forces her to eat her daughter, kills all the children of his hosts and returns home."[7]

[6] Ch. Monteil, op. cit., pp. 158–65.
[7] H. Basset, *Essai sur la littérature des Berbères*, Algiers, 1920, pp. 134–35. On Haddidouan see notably: S. Biarnay, "L'Historie d'Haddidouan," *Étude sur les dialectes berbères du Rif*, Paris, 1917, pp. 312–18; E. Destaing, *Étude sur le dialecte berbère des Beni Snous*, t. II. Paris, 1911, pp. 75–84.

What makes the Sudanese versions obscure and unsatisfactory becomes clear. The parallels would seem to be as follows:

	Offender	*Offended*	*Final Victim*
North Africa	Haddidouan (Petit Poucet)	Ogress	Ogress's daughter
Soninké	Child of Evil	Sorceress	Sorceress's daughters
Khasonké	Child of Evil	Blacksmith	Blacksmith's daughters
Dogon	Lover	Hogon (=husband)	Peul + Hogon
Bété	Mother-in-law	Spider (=son-in-law)	Médé

In the process of transformation, the tale loses its first meaning
and takes on a completely new one; the initial role of the characters
is so modified that in the end their relations appear reversed. The
"Petit Poucet" whose courage together with his physical weakness
command our sympathy, and for whom we tremble wishing for his
final triumph, becomes, by transformation, the loathesome mother-
in-law who consumes all the resources of a son-in-law unable to
get rid of her. The metamorphosis of the ogress in the Berber tale
(it would be as such an ogress that we could see the mother-in-law)
is no less curious. While mutating from a woman to a man, the
character also gets rid of its terrifying aspects. With the ogress as
character, the initial theme of overcoming brutal force with shrewdness gets lost. The result is a noticeable uncertainty in the Soninké
and Khasonké versions where their meaning is no longer clear.
Indeed, the audience does not know with whom to side. That
there was once an ogress in this tale is seen from traces left in the
Sudanese versions. The transition from the Soninké sorceress to the
Khasonké blacksmith is quite understandable. In traditional African
societies the blacksmith is a disconcerting and sinister figure. Even
though he has his place in the social order, he remains obscure
and lives a marginal life. He is also a bit of a magician and of
course there is the implication that he is a sorcerer. To fight against
one as well as the other, must one not first know their secrets?

There are also intriguing similarities between the blacksmith and the Hogon. The Hogon too is a double-faced figure: beneficial, but in some ways detrimental, since one attribute seldom goes without the other. To understand the tale one must note that the Hogon is in fact a living dead. Hogon and blacksmith, both are bogeymen, and one cannot be sure that they did not at one time or another participate in a communion of human flesh.

In the hands of the Dogon, this somewhat moribund tale takes on new life. The figure of the "Child of Evil," having lost its *raison d'être,* is forgotten, and even the Hogon appears only as the cuckolded husband. More importantly, the Dogon version transforms the thrust of the tale into a problem of double antagonism: first the antagonism born out of the trials of life, where the cultivator has to endure the incursions and robberies of the nomadic Peul. This antagonism is satisfied with the Peul perishing, a victim of his gluttony. Then there is the deeper antagonism between the living and the dead, illustrated by the role of the Hogon. The dead need the living, therefore they too, just as the Peul, must moderate their exigencies. They must be reminded that they cannot always have it their own way. Thus the conclusion of the tale: "From this time on, young men are never drowned for committing adultery."

Finally, the Bété, who see all problems of life only in the context of family relationships, could not see the struggle in question in any terms but as between son-in-law and mother-in-law, a seemingly hopeless combat no less unequal than that between David and Goliath. Nevertheless one knows from the beginning what the outcome of the combat will be. There is a world of difference between the original ogress and the starving son-in-law. One inspires awe and the other sympathy, or at least compassion. However, the Bété narrator takes care, from the very beginning of the tale, to hint that the son-in-law, whose tribulations he will narrate, is in fact the Spider, that is to say, a trickster known for his insincerity. It is all right to feel sorry for the Spider, but his victims may also rejoice at his final downfall.

Our last tale is a very widespread one. Its Bété version was brought to my attention under the title "Seri, his wife and his dog."

BÉTÉ TALE—SERI, HIS WIFE AND HIS DOG

One day, Seri and his dog went to the forest to tap some palm wine. Seri finds a palm tree and starts climbing when all of a sudden his knife slips out of his hand and falls to the ground. Seri curses, and says to himself: "What shall I do now? If I climb down I shall be too tired and shall not have the strength to climb up again. Why is my dog not a man? I could then tell him to bring me the knife." The dog hears this and replies to Seri: "I shall climb up and bring you the knife. I shall also give you a gift. But if you do not be careful with it, you will die." Seri replies: "I shall certainly be careful." So the dog brings him the knife. Seri taps the palm tree and both he and his dog climb down.

As they touch the ground again, the dog pours a few drops of a potion into Seri's eyes and nose. Immediately Seri can understand what all the animals are saying. They then return to the village.

That evening Seri's one-eyed wife was husking rice. A hen with her chicks approaches the mortar, and the hen says to her chickens: "Children, go to the side where the woman cannot see, and there will be lots for you to eat. As for me, I am going to peck on the other side, to attract her attention." Seri, who hears this, bursts out laughing. His wife asks: "Why do you laugh?" Seri replies, "If I tell you I shall die." His wife gets mad. "I know why you are laughing but you would not admit. it. It is because my mother is dead." Seri protests but his wife refuses to listen to him.

That night the woman wept. The mice came and ate the rice she had put aside. While she was chasing the mice one of them says to his companion: "Her mother died but her grief does not keep her from keeping an eye on her rice." Seri on hearing this bursts out laughing again.

The following morning, the wife feeling offended went back to her parents. Seri goes after her and begs her to come back with him but she refuses. The situation is explained to the wife's parents who ask Seri: "Why did you laugh?" "It is a secret," replies Seri, "and if I tell I shall die." The wife's parents remain inflexible: "If you do not give a clear answer, you cannot take your wife back." Thus constrained, Seri tells why he laughed and dies since he violated his promise.

From that time on, if a man refuses to obey, one does not insist.

Now, here is the Dogon version:

DOGON TALE—WOE TO THE ONE
WHO CANNOT KEEP HIS TONGUE[8]

One day, a dog and a young girl went to the collective fields. The girl prepared a meal and gave half of it to the dog. To show his appreciation, the dog taught the girl the language of the animals. "But," he said, "it is a secret and you must tell no one." That evening they returned to the village. The girl went to sit with a one-eyed woman who was pounding millet. A rooster and a hen were scratching for food on both sides of her. The woman only saw the hen and chased it. The rooster said to the hen: "Come to the other side where she will not see you." The young girl on hearing this starts to laugh. The one-eyed woman, thinking the girl was laughing at her, grew angry and struck her. The girl started to cry and the dog came running to defend his friend. "It is not about you that she laughed," he tells the woman, "it is of what the rooster said to the chicken." Having said this, the dog fell dead.

The scene and the action of the two tales do not even conform to the same format. While the Bété husband is double-crossed by his mother-in-law in the first tale, here he succumbs a victim of his wife's stubbornness. The Dogon version only speaks of the dog who died defending his friend—a tale whose level is not above that of anecdote. Nevertheless, the way in which the tale develops, the details of the one-eyed woman, and the conversation between the hen and her chicks obviously come from the same source.

The Dogon narrator does not offer any commentary with his tale. When we heard it, we did not think to ask him for one. His protagonists are simply "a young girl," *ya,* and "a woman," *yana.* Today, knowing what we have since learned, we would certainly have asked him for an interpretation. The patrilineal principle and virilocal residence rules of the Dogon mean that a woman living in any community will by necessity either be a daughter, *ya,* or a wife, *yana.* The young girl lives with her father and with the other married or unmarried men of her lineage until she goes to live with her husband, at whose house she becomes a wife, *yana* (to be exact, *yana* means mother; from *na* which means mother). There, at least at the beginning, and because she comes from elsewhere, she will be considered

[8] D. Paulme et D. Lifszyc, "Les animaux dans le folklore dogon," *Revue de folklore français et de folklore colonist,* VII, 1936, p. 289.

a stranger. It is thus possible, without falsifying the sense, to transpose our text in reading "nonmarried sister," every time we see "daughter," *ya.* In other words, the conflict which is the subject of the tale is not between just any woman and any girl, but between a wife and her sister-in-law. It might be recalled that in the first Dogon tale cited here, we are taught why a husband, when faced with the choice between his sister and his wife, will spare his wife to sacrifice his sister. Thus the problem of choice could arise at any time, and with it the problem of the relationship between two women. Our tale offers an unhappy example of these relations: *ya,* the young girl, lives at her father's among her patrilineal relatives. When the day is over, she sits down in the courtyard and lets her married sister-in-law prepare the meal. Moreover, according to custom, as long as she remains among her own relatives and until she herself goes to join her husband, all the household tasks are left to the wife and her brother.[9] It is easy to see how the latter would resent being ordered about by a *ya* who according to tradition has the right to ask her to light the fire and to grind the grain. Already exasperated by the girl's idleness, she will not have much sympathy for a laugh which she could take as being spiteful. Of course there is also the superiority of the wife over the younger unmarried girl, who, despite appearances, must learn to respect her. Thus if our interpretation is correct, the moral of the story would be also to teach tolerance and mutual appreciation. One last point: the girl here, the *ya,* does not yet have the status of a married woman. This brings again to mind the similar behavior of the Bété sister. If this woman can order about the wife of her brother, it is, in the eyes of the Bété, only because the dowry paid for her in the first place made the marriage of her brother possible—a reference to something that happened in the past. This theory does not apply in the Dogon story where the sister in question is a younger girl, thus a junior sister. Why must a married woman, a mother, *yana,* obey the orders of a mere young girl? It appears to us that perhaps an answer could be found in the Dogon practice of the levirate. The behavior toward the younger sister of the husband seems in effect, based on that which is observed toward the younger brother of the husband who is the presumed inheritor of the older brother's widow. This is a possible future but not certain event that could influence the relationship of the two women.[10]

[9] D. Paulme, *Organisation sociale* . . . , p. 384.
[10] D. Paulme, op. cit., p. 385.

Let us, however, refrain from attaching too much importance to
the concept of past and future, which, after all, belongs to categories
of western thinking. Relationships between relatives and in-laws in
African societies belong to the eternal present. Each one plays a
role in his behavior toward another: father or mother, son or
daughter, son-in-law or sister-in-law, the age or sex of the actors is
irrelevant. Their position on the social checkerboard is far more
important than their physical appearance. That a young girl avails
herself of privileges and simulates the behavior of a husband sur-
prises no one—only a European would be puzzled.

Let us now leave the Bété and the Dogon and look at these tales
in other contexts.

The two so dissimilar versions of the same tale are not the only
ones found in Africa, south of the Sahara. Previous scholars have
noted them in the following places: in the Ivory Coast itself; in the
neighboring Ghana; in southern Dahomey; in Nigeria; much farther
south among the Mbaka of Angola; and very far eastward among
the Zandé of the Upper Ouellé, which is at the border of the eastern
Sudan.[11] Some versions might also have escaped us.

All the tales have the same outline with only the Dogon text deviating substantially. In that version a hunter in the forest is taught
the language of the animals—by his dog. Among the Baoulé of the
Ivory Coast, the pursuit of game led him to the burrow which gives
access to the world of the genies; in Ghana to the lair of animals;
and among the Ekoi of Nigeria, to the kingdom of the dead. The
theme of the hunt has been omitted only in the Popo's version which
tells only of how "a husband," by feigning death, outwits a vulture
and discovers the secret. The rest is the same: (1) the man overhears
a conversation between animals in the barnyard and bursts out laughing; the faulty eyesight is attributed to the mother of the wife in the
versions of the Ashanti, Popo and Ekoi; and in the Angola text,
the mother-in-law appears "in rags"; (2) the wife is offended by her
husband's merriment which she believes is at the expense of her

[11] Version baoulé, H. Himmelheber, *Aura Poku,* Eisenach, 1951, pp.
112–15; version akan (Ghana), W. H. Barker et Cecilia Sinclair, *West African
Folk-Tales,* London, 1917, pp. 105–13; version ashanti, R. S. Rattray, *Akan and
Ashanti Folk-Tales,* Oxford, 1930, pp. 243 sq.; version popo (sud Dahomey),
R. Trautmann, *La littérature populaire à la Côte des esclaves,* Paris, 1927;
version ekoi (Nigeria), P. A. Talbot, *In the Shadow of the Bush,* London, 1912,
pp. 99–101; version mbaka (Angola), Héli Châtelain, *Folk-Tales of Angola,*
Memoirs of the American-Folk-Lore Society, 1894, pp. 218 sq.; version zandé,
Lagae (Père C. R.), *La Langue des Azande,* Gand, 1921, t. I, pp. 243–45.

mother and refuses to stay with her husband; (3) in the face of his in-laws' insistence ("you cannot take our daughter back if you do not tell us your secret") the husband tells, and dies. In the Zandé version, the offended person is the father-in-law who had asked that his son-in-law come to braid his hair. The son-in-law overhears a hilarious dialogue between ants, laughs, and the end is the same. The son-in-law, told that he cannot take his wife back with him if he does not reveal his secret, talks and dies.

While this tale is largely African in distribution, it is one of the best-known ones in folklore and is classified by Aarne and Thompson under type 670. *The Thousand and One Nights* contains one of its more famous versions where the hero is not a hunter but a wealthy tradesman. The tale does not reveal how he came to his secret, perhaps he brought it back from one of his trips which were as adventurous as those of Sinbad. The point of interest to us is that the tale in *The Thousand and One Nights* has a happy ending, an ending radically different from any of those in the African versions—except one. Here the wife is also offended by her husband's bursts of laughter and his not being able to reveal his secret except under penalty of death. The poor man is at the point of giving in when he overhears a conversation between the dog of the house and the rooster, where the latter says:

> "How absurd! Our master has only one woman and cannot bring her to heel while I have fifty who all do exactly as I wish. Let him recover his senses, he will soon find the right way to get out of this dilemma." "Well, what do you think he should do?" asks the dog. "He should go to his wife's room," replied the cock, "lock himself in with her, then take a stick and give her a thousand blows. I guarantee you that she will behave after that and that she will no longer pester him to tell what he cannot reveal."

The husband follows the rooster's advice and all goes well:

> ". . . He opened the door, all the relatives came in and rejoiced to see the wife cured of her stubbornness. They complimented the husband on the excellent remedy he had used to make her come to reason."[12]

[12] *Les Mille et Une Nuits,* trad. Galland, Paris, Garnier, t. I., p. 20.

We mentioned earlier that there was only one African version that ends with the husband's victory. It is the Ashanti text: Just as he was about to reveal the secret, the husband hears the rooster order his hen to shut up. The husband changes his mind, and divorces his wife. The tale ends thus: "This was the first case of divorce among us and we owe that to the rooster."

In summing it up, the diverse African versions of the tale could be analyzed about as follows:

	Hero	Secret has been revealed to him by:	His laughter offends:	Conclusion:
DOGON	young girl	dog	the wife	the dog dies
BÉTÉ (most common African version)	hunter (=husband)	dog	wife or mother-in-law (one-eyed woman)	the husband tells and dies
ZANDÉ	hunter (=husband)	dog	the father-in-law	the son-in-law tells and dies
THOUSAND AND ONE NIGHTS	Tradesman (=husband)	?	the wife	the husband punishes his wife
ASHANTI	hunter (=husband)	python	mother-in-law (one-eyed)	the husband divorces his wife

This comparison reveals the following points:

1. Most of the versions of the tale in Black Africa end badly for the husband (who learns the secret during a hunting trip). He succumbs to the obstinacy of his wife backed up by the in-laws to whom the son-in-law has to be perpetually obliged.

2. In *The Thousand and One Nights* version, the husband (a wealthy merchant) triumphs through the use of brute force. The in-laws, having tried without success to change his wife's mind, approve the husband's decision to be master in his house.

3. The Ashanti version contains details which while omitted in the

Oriental texts are present in all African versions. The mother-in-law here has an important role. Let us look at the conversation between the hen and her chicks.

> . . . Returning to the village, Kwasi Gyaba finds his mother-in-law who has come to visit her daughter. The mother-in-law was blind in her right eye and was pounding grain. Two hens who were there start a conversation. "How is it that you can peck in peace while I am constantly chased away?" "Did you not notice that she is blind in the right eye?" "Come to this side, she will not see you." Kwasi Gyaba on hearing this breaks out in uncontrollable laughter. The mother-in-law thinks he is laughing at her . . .

The Ashanti version is also the only one where the husband escapes death and saves his honor while, it must be admitted, ruining his marriage: "This was the first case of divorce." The very special characteristics of Ashanti marriage must here be mentioned: half of the people live in a matrilineal household and only one third of the married women live with their husbands.[13] If a man is living with his mother or with his sister, he could certainly do without a wife to keep his household. This is obviously not the case in the other African societies. Generally speaking, and certainly for the sake of a good tale, the African husband who is foolish enough to offend his wife and his in-laws will have nowhere to turn. His end will be miserable.

[13] M. Fortes, "Kinship and Marriage Among the Ashanti," p. 262, in A. Radcliffe-Brown and D. Forde, *African Systems of Kinship and Marriage,* Oxford, 1950.

28. Some Aspects of Swahili Poetry

Poetry is the common heritage of all the people of the Swahili Coast. Its centers are found all along the shores of the Indian Ocean: between Barawa in the North (now part of Somalia but still in the nineteenth century a center of Swahili poetry) and Lindi in the South. Known centers of today are Lamu, Mombasa, Pemba, Zanzibar, Bagamoyo, Tanga, Dar es Salaam, Kilwa, and Mikindani. Though the dialects of these towns are different, there is a free exchange of poems in manuscripts between one town and another.

Today one finds poems written in Roman script or even typed, but the old tradition, which is still kept up by many poets, is to write in Arabic characters with at the end the date and the words "Written with God's help by the poor, destitute, and ignorant writer Fulani bin Fulani." The old type of poets wrote poetry for the love of God; their poverty was in line with their artistic principles.

All the Swahili educated in their old traditions can read and write Arabic script. The form of Swahili-Arabic writing now in use in Mombasa is based on the Urdu variety of Arabic script and is so well adapted to the language that it is now actually better than Roman script as it represents dental consonants, aspirates and velarized sounds. To overcome the extra cost of printing in Arabic, the latest publications are photographic reproductions of original manuscripts; this shows that traditional poetry is still very popular.

The date of birth of Swahili poetry is not known, but I would put it very tentatively around 1500. It is possible that Swahili was written before that date but there was probably no extensive literature in Swahili before the sixteenth century. As for the place of birth, the evidence seems to point in the direction of Pate, as all the manuscripts of the first half of the eighteenth century, the oldest known period,

SOURCE: Jan Knappert, "Some Aspects of Swahili Poetry," *Tanzania Notes and Records*, No. 66, December 1966, pp. 163–70. Reprinted by permission of the author and publisher.

are in the Pate dialect. These poems (Hamziya, Herekali, and Inkishafi) are written each in a different meter and show such a high degree of artistic perfection that it is certain they stand at the end of a long period of development. The three poems that remain indicate that there must have been a rich literature at that time.

The oldest known poet who used the Swahili language is the legendary King Liongo who ruled the lower Tana area, according to Hichens, at the end of the twelfth century. This does not seem to be corroborated by any archaeological evidence; Kirkman placed him in the last part of the sixteenth century (*Man and Monument in East Africa,* p. 82). That would just about fit the linguistic peculiarities of the poems attributed to him.

The most prominent poet of the classical period was no doubt Muyaka bin Haji al-Ghassaniy, who lived 1753–1837, according to notes of the late Sir Mbarak Ali Hinawy. Muyaka's "Diwani" was collected by the Rev. W. E. Taylor in the eighteen nineties and was later published by Hichens with an introduction by Sir Mbarak. Muyaka excelled in the *shairi* meter, which became so popular that *ushairi* now means poetry in general. The *shairi* meter is built up of stanzas of four lines each, every line containing sixteen syllables. In all Swahili poems every line must have the same number of syllables; one cannot, as in European languages, insert lines of different length in one poem. The place of the stresses in the line seems to be free, and the poet uses the stress in order to create a special rhythm in his poems.

The following is a quatrain from Muyaka in the *shairi* meter:

> *Naliwazato moyoni, humumo moyoni mwangu:*
> *mambo pia duniani, Mtenzi ni Yeye Mungu.*
> *Zizungukapo zamani, yazingapo malimwengu*
> *Mava yatakuwa vyungu, vyungu vitakuwa mava.*

> I was thinking deeply in my heart, here in this heart of mine:
> about all the things of this world, the one Actor is God.
> As the time rolls by, so the things of this world revolve:
> Dust will become pots, pots will become dust.

In Swahili, the heart is the seat of reason and common sense, not the center of feelings and emotions as in English. The theme of the transience of this world is a popular one with Swahili poets of all ages; it is bound up with the Islamic tradition. We find the same atmosphere of resignation in all other parts of the Islamic world.

The Swahili poets write entirely in an oriental style, and both the themes and the meter are of oriental origin. Swahili culture as a whole is not African but oriental. The Swahili have always lived as it were with their backs turned toward Africa, looking eastward across the ocean toward Arabia, Persia, and India, from where they received their standards of religion, culture, and literature. Where the Africans enjoy life on this earth and celebrate it in songs and dances without another world worth longing for, the Swahili on the other hand look away from this transitory world toward a better life in Paradise; and whoever leads a life of dignity and restraint in this world can be certain of a good place in the eternal world after this one.

In both worlds God is the only Actor: people are as it were like puppets in His hand. God causes the Universe with all its planets to revolve, and all the visible things it contains will change their appearance as time rolls by. Every attempt to escape from this gigantic system of divine laws is doomed to fail: we can never hide from the sight of an all seeing God. On this, Muyaka wrote:

> *Aliyekimbia wole, mwendo wa myaka sitini,*
> *akenda umungojele, ukele mitilizini,*
> *ukamba ndoo tukale, mwandani, wangu mwandani!*
> *akiuuza U nani? ukamba Simi weleo?*

> He that fled from his Fate, a journey of sixty years,
> while he was going, it was waiting for him, sitting in the gutter:
> it said: Come and let us eat, my dear friend!
> When he asked: Who are You? It said: Am I not your Fate?

Rhyme in Swahili is effected by making the last syllable of two lines identical, as if we were in English, for example, able to rhyme mango with bingo. In the *shairi,* there is rhyme not only at the end of a line but also in the middle before the caesura. The end rhyme of the first three lines is found again in the middle of the fourth line, on the caesura. A very rich but very difficult pattern!

Modern poets still use the same forms of verse line and stanza to write their lyrical and philosophical poetry. Most poets require several stanzas in one poem to express their thoughts properly, but some of the best-known poets need only one stanza: the genuine quatrain. The famous Shabaan Robert wrote a book of quatrains, *Marudi Mema,* after he had translated Omar Khayyam's quatrains into

Swahili, with which I hope to deal in another article. Here is one quatrain from the *Marudi Mema:*

> *Nipe maneno launi*   *mepesi kwa kukariri,*
> *yenye wema na amani*   *na moyoni kufikiri,*
> *yenye wema na amani*   *kwa watu yasikasiri:*
> *yawe tamu ulimini*   *na moyoni kufikiri,*
> *yatie watu imani*   *njema ya kutadhibiri.*

Give me colourful words, easy to repeat,
good and peaceful for people and not lacking anything:
let them be sweet on the tongue and in the heart, to reflect upon,
may they give people faith, a good thing to recite.

We see how the poet has changed the original rhyme scheme so as to suit the form of a quatrain: all the middle syllables rhyme and so do the four end syllables.

Another well-known poet who died recently, Sh. Amri Abedi, did not follow Shabaan Robert in this. He retained the old design which was originally intended for verses with one final rhyme running throughout the whole poem:

> *Pendo ni tamu ajabu,*   *likutanapo na pendo*
> *hulevya kama sharabu,*   *likatawala vitendo,*
> *na maradhi likatibu,*   *kiwete hupata mwendo,*
> *usipende asopendo.*   *pendo ni huku na huku.*

Love is wonderfully sweet, if it meets love.
it inebriates like drinking, it rules our actions,
it cures diseases, the lame will be able to walk,
do not love someone who has no love; love is everywhere.

> *Ukitaka moyo wangu, ni tayari kukupao,*
> *nawe wako uwe kwangu, usiwe kwa mungineo;*
> *hapo takufanya wangu, niwe wako wa pekeo,*
> *mpumbavu apendao, pendo upande mmoja.*

If you want my heart, I am ready to give it to you,
and your heart should be with me, it should be with no one else;
now I will make you mine, let me be yours alone,
a fool loves with love from one side only.

More difficult than the meter of sixteen syllables is the one with fifteen syllables in the line, the so-called long *ukawafi.* It can have a rhyme in the fifth syllable of every line, at the first caesura. It is mostly used for religious poetry, some of the oldest and best poems in the Swahili language being written in it. Nowadays it is seldom practiced because it requires a great poetic skill. Ahmed Nassir Juma, of Mombasa, gave me one quatrain in which he managed to rhyme not only in the fifth, but also in the tenth syllable of every line, at the second caesura:

Mvita ifile, kisiwa chetu kitwa kitini
mezima myale, na kulla mtu yumo kizani
uwi na ndwele nyoyoni mwetu ndipo shinani
na mizi tele na utukutu uso thamani

Mombasa died, our island, its head is down,
the sparks are extinguished, and every man is in darkness,
evil and disease are in our hearts here at the roots,
there is an abundance of amulets and exorcism, which are of no
    value.

This lamentation probably refers to the fact that the prominent Swahili families in Mombasa see their wealth waning; some even have to sell their proud houses in the town and move to more modest country dwellings. The pious Swahili see this as a punishment from God, because they have been slack in the performance of their religious duties. So the evil is in their own hearts; there is the root (*shinani,* lit. "in the stem") of the disease. Instead of following the precepts of orthodox Islam, the people have indulged in such heathen practices as amulets and exorcism. The word *utukutu* refers to the ideophone *tukutu tukutu,* a realistic imitation of the sound of the drums in a nocturnal dance to exorcise the evil spirits. All this is anathema to the pious Muslim, who knows that all evil can be averted by zealous prayer and strict obedience to God's commandments.

A shorter line with similar structure is a peculiar type of song often used for a sort of light philosophy. Here is an example from Ahmed Basheikh Husein, a well-known poet from Mombasa who lived in the first half of this century. The first part of the line has only four syllables, the last part only three. The middle part retains five syllables, so that the total number of syllables in the line is twelve. Inner rhyme occurs normally only in the fourth syllable, i.e. at the first caesura:

> *Jitihadi   haiondowi   kudura*
> *hazifidi   nyingi za watu   busara*
> *halirudi   landikwalo   hata mara.*

Efforts do not avert fate;
the arts of men are to no avail;
the written (word) does not go back even once.

Kudura is here short for *kudura la Allah* "God's power," which cannot be turned away by human efforts, nor is man's wisdom of any use. God's word has been written on the *Loho,* the Writing Board in Heaven; that cannot be reversed, no human effort can wipe it off.

Here is another example of this rare form of song:

> *Hizi nyonda   walla hazina   imani*
> *hukuzinda   zikakutia   kizani*
> *asopenda   hana raha   duniani.*

This love, by God, it has no faith,
it tricks you and put you in the dark;
but he that does not love has no pleasant life.

Swahili poets often complain that love is unfaithful and therefore has no mercy (*rahama*).

A last example dates from the time of Al-Akida, when Mombasa was independent and refused to pay taxes to the Sultan of Zanzibar:

> *Sumaili Basha   anena hakiri*
> *Lingajaa kasha   poso na mahari*
> *Sumaili   Basha   hamuoi siri,*

Isumaili Pasha says that he does not give his consent, though his treasury
contains enough money for the proposal and for the bride price,
Isumaili Pasha does not give away (his daughter in marriage) secretly.

The song is a disguised allusion to the political situation of the day and therefore contains a number of *double-entendres.* Firstly, there is another word *hakiri* "poor, destitute," so that the first line might be translated: "Isumaili Pasha says that he is poor." In the second line, *poso* could also be identified with *posho* "provisions for the journey," whereas *mahari* "bride price" has another meaning: "skill, cunning." In the third line, the word *kuoa* can mean "to marry" or "to write." The hidden meaning (*maana batini* or *kujua ndani*) of the song is thus: "Isumaili Pasha says that he is poor, though his cupboard is full of provisions and he has cunning; Isumaili Pasha does not write a secret contract." What on the surface seems to be an innocent song about a marriage is in actual fact an outlet for political feelings.

In the last example the rhyming of the fourth syllable has been susperseded by the rhyme in the middle of the line, on the sixth syllable. The following specimen shows the common form of the song (*wimbo*):

> *Raha ya duniya   ni mambo matatu*
> *la kwanza afiya   la pili ni kitu*
> *la tatu bahtiya   kupendwa ni watu,*
> *Moyo si kiwanda   hauna nafasi*
> *siitii nyonda   haudhi nafusi*
> *huyuwi kupenda   kupendwa huyisi*
> *Nina langu kwanda   fungu la usemi*
> *K'iketi na nyonda   sitindi ulimi*
> *nayuwa kupenda   na kupendwa mimi.*

The pleasure of this world is three things:
the first is health, the second is possessions,
and the third is to be loved by people.
My heart is not an open space, it has no room;
I will not put (one-sided) love in it for I would only suffer from it
   myself,
You do not know how to love, nor do you know how to be loved.
First I make use of my talent (lit, "share"), the gift of speech;
when sitting with my love, I never stop my tongue,
I know how to love and how to be loved.

The singer is a young man of the world who has just won his sweetheart from a rival. He considers good health and wealth even more important than love. He is not going to suffer pains of love without any response from the beloved. When in the company of his sweetheart, he knows what to do: the gift of the gab makes girls fall in love. He is speaking scornfully to his beaten rival.

There are numerous *nyimbo* in this form, most of them dealing with the subject of love in a light manner:

> *Mahaba ni sumu   iuayo siri*
> *hayana mwalimu   wala dakitari*
> *hutia wazimu nao ufakiri.*
>
> *Mahaba ni sumu   ni sumu katili*
> *mahaba ni tamu   kwa kiwiliwili*
> *mahaba ni tamu   kwa watu wawili.*
>
> *Apendaye kweli   haonyeki dawa*
> *hawi na akili   hapati kutua*
> *usiku halali   usiku belua.*
>
> *Dawa ya mahaba   ni ukipendacho*
> *ndicho kitu tiba   kikupumbazacho*
> *fanya taratibu   ukipate hicho.*
>
> *Na dawa ni wewe   wangu muadhamu*
> *sina mwenginewe   na hilo fahamu*
> *mimi mbwako wewe   hata wa salamu.*

Love is a poison which kills secretly
there is no scholar and no doctor (who can cure it) makes one
  crazy and it causes poverty.

Love is a poison, a lethal poison;
love is sweet for the body,
love is sweet if there are two together.

He who really loves, no medicine can be indicated for him;
he has lost his senses, he is not able to rest,
at night he does not sleep, the night is a trial.

The medicine for love is that which you love,
that is your cure that will make you cheerful again;
act with prudence so that you may get it.

The cure is you, my beloved,
I have no other one, remember this;
I am yours until the end.

If one leaves off one more syllable from the song-line of 6+6 syllables, one can form a new type of meter, the short *ukawafi* of eleven syllables in the line. Here is an example in the dialect of Barawa (Kibarawa) now in Somalia:

> *Taka nikwambire nisikwambire*
> *kijungu cha pengo usipikire*
> *mke mwenye mwana usimuore*

> Whether you want me to tell you or not;
> do not cook in a pot with a sherd missing;
> do not marry a woman with a child.

This verse refers to the preference of men in East Africa for virgins; a woman who is divorced or a widow is compared to a pot with a piece broken off.

The best known example of the *Ukawafi* of eleven syllables is the famous poem Inkishafi, published by William Hichens (Sheldon Press, 1939, p. 88):

> *Kwalina mabwana na mawaziri*
> *wenda na makundi na asikari*
> *watamiwe nti za makaburi*
> *pingu za mauti ziwafundiye.*

> There were once lords and ministers of state;
> they went out with troops of soldiers.
> But the earth graves gaped for them,
> The shackles of death tied them down.

It is easy to hear how different the rhythm of this meter is from the one above, though they have the same number of syllables in the line. This last type with always four lines in the stanza is exclusively used for religious poetry. Next to the Inkishafi, the Durra Mandhuma (see Dammann, *Dichtungen in der Lamu Mundart,* Hamburg, 1940) is a very popular poem for pious Muslims. It is typical of classical Swahili poetry; in modern collections of Swahili verse I found only one example, in Sh. Amri Abedi's Diwani (p. 112) where he speaks to a corrupt official who led a lecherous life until he fell from power:

> *Dunia si njema imekutupa!*
> *Sana hako mtu wa kukukopa!*
> *Vya bure ukala ukanenepa!*
> *Sasa utakonda kuvijutia!*

> The world is not nice, it has rejected you!
> Now there is no one willing to lend you anything!

You ate and grew fat, in vain!
Now you will grow meagre and regret it!

The *long ukawafi* has fifteen syllables in the line; it is likewise almost exclusively classical and mainly in use for the *historia sancta,* the hagiography of the Islamic world, the history of the Prophet Mohammed and other saints of Islam. One of the long poems in this meter is a Maulidi (or Mauludi) published by G. Neuhaus (Berlin, 1935). A Maulidi is a poem in Arabic or Swahili which deals with the birth and life of the Prophet; it is traditionally recited on the day of the same name, when the birthday of Mohammed is celebrated. In stanza 71 an episode is dated from Mohammed's life: The young Prophet who had not yet been called by the Lord, arrives in Mecca from a long caravan journey to Syria. It is a hot day and all the travelers suffer from the heat. Hadija, the future wife of Mohammed, is sitting on the roof of her house and sees the caravan arriving:

> *Alimuonaye mefuata na malaika*
> *na hari ya yua kwa mabawa   humufunika*
> *kaonya na wendi walo wote   kifurahika*
> *na Maisarati akanena   aloyaona.*

> She saw him, how he was accompanied by angels,
> who shielded him from the heat of the sun with their wings.
> She showed her friends this and they all rejoiced.
> She told Maisara, her councillor, what she had seen.

Hadija, the sensible woman, understands that this is a sign from God, that He has shown her His angels protecting Mohammed in order to let her know that He wants her to marry Mohammed. Hadija then sends a messenger to invite Mohammed who is then only a humble camel boy. Of course her father is strongly opposed to the marriage, but, curiously enough with the help of heady wine, he is persuaded to consent, and so the two are married and live happily together until she dies.

By far the most important part of Swahili literature is the huge treasure of *utenzi* poetry. Most of this is still unpublished, and new titles are still being discovered. The *utenzi* meter of eight syllables in the line and four lines in the stanza is used for the major part for epic verse. Some of these epics are short, only a few hundred stanzas,

but some are long, such as the *Utenzi wa Rasi l'Ghuli* which has more
than 4,300 stanzas, or the Epic on the Life of Mohammed which
has more than 6,000 stanzas and is thus the longest epic in an
African language. I deal with the *utenzi* at greater length in my forthcoming "Traditional Swahili Poetry."

In modern times Christian poets have joined the ranks of their
Muslim colleagues and added a voice to the chorus that uses
Swahili for its language of expression. Though making use of all the
extensive linguistic potential of the Swahili language, they tread new
paths in the field of culture. Their leader is beyond doubt Mathias
Mnyampala, whose *Utenzi wa Enjili Takatifu,* a versified life of
Jesus in the *utenzi* meter, has already gained popularity in Tanzania. Here is his rendering of passage from the psalms in the
shairi meter:

> *Jalali wangu Mchunga,   nikidhi yako rehema,*
> *sinache natangatanga,   nitaburuku kwa wema,*
> *niweke kwenye kiunga,   cha malisho ya uzima,*
> *na majani ya rehema,   na vijito vyenye raha.*

> Majesty, my shepherd, bestow Thy grace upon me,
> do not let me wander about, let me be blessed with goodness,
> place me in the Garden of the food of bliss,
> and of the green leaves of Grace, and near the revulets of Peace.
>   (Psalm 23, 1).

Most of the hymns in the Christian hymnbooks are written in a free
rhythm. It appears however, that in a language in which the stress
accent is much less prominent than in English, one cannot rely on
stress to create rhythm. In a language like Swahili with open syllables
and a weaker stress accent, one has to rely on the syllable as the
basis for the rhythm. It is therefore advisable to keep the number
of syllables always equal. President Nyerere himself showed the way
when composing his translation of Julius Caesar: the whole drama is
written in the *shairi* meter, though often without a caesura. His
translation is certainly a pioneer's work: it is the first play in Swahili
verse, and the first piece of Swahili poetry written in blank verse.
Yet the Mwalimu realized that in the matter of rhythm and meter a
Swahili poet could not yet dispense with the old rigid forms. As
Goethe says: "The master shows himself when he is limited."

29. The Social Functions and Meaning of Hausa Praise-Singing

In this paper I illustrate an objective method for the determination of the meaning and values of social institutions, using data on the custom of praise-singing (*roko*) among the Hausa of Northern Nigeria. To direct attention to the method of analysis clearly, I shall present the field data and their examination separately. In concluding, I shall indicate certain problems which seem to arise from this paper.

THE HAUSA MAROKA

CONTEXT

The Hausa of Northern Nigeria live in a group of states most of which were formerly parts of the Fulani Empire of Sokoto, an empire that was established during and after the *jihad* of 1804–10. Under Sokoto, the principal kingdoms of the empire, such as Kano, Adamawa, Bauchi, or Zaria, occupied a position of vassalage, and many of these large states had smaller vassals themselves. There was a general autocratic pattern of state administration through titled fief holders, mainly of Fulani descent, who supervised rural communities, each with its own capital and chiefly line. The king lived in the capital city of his territory, which was usually a town of considerable size and of great importance strategically as well as economically. There he kept his court, at which the fief holders were required to attend regularly. Fief holders administered their scattered fiefs through staffs of titled intermediaries, known as *jakadu* (sing. *jakada*). The village chief of a rural area lived in the capital of his community, which was normally a walled market town situated on or near one of the main caravan routes, and surrounded by a few daughter-hamlets. Political

SOURCE: "The Social Functions and Meaning of Hausa Praise-Singing," *Africa*, Vol. 27, No. 1., 1957, pp. 26–43. Reprinted by permission of the author and publisher.

organization within the village reproduced patterns from the central state system. Thus, there was a hierarchy of offices linked with the administration of wards and hamlets of the local community; a pattern of competition for office among socially important men; succession to the chieftainship through an electoral process by members of the agnatic chiefly lines (*dangin sarauta*); and a set of occupational titles, such as chief of the blacksmiths, whose holders were entrusted with the collection of occupational taxes and the supervision of certain craft functions.

The Hausa and their Fulani rulers are Muhammadans and practice an economy based mainly on agriculture and trade, with a flourishing diversity of craft production for local needs and for exchange in neighboring markets. Kinship is markedly bilateral among the subordinate Hausa population, and strongly patrilineal among the ruling Fulani. Women practice a culture that differs widely from that of their menfolk, but has complementary relations with it. Women are legal and political minors, except for a few who hold titles and official positions, such as the Magajiya, head of the with the choice of giving away more than he can afford or taking a production for subsistence and for exchange, permits a wide variation in the form of this combination at an individual level. Occupations are ranked loosely in terms of prestige, and criteria of age, ancestry, office, wealth, and ethnic status are also involved in the status placement of males. Among women somewhat different factors are important, such as family connections, seniority within the husband's household, marital record, fertility, age, and the like.

Religion sanctions Fulani rule, since the conquest was phrased as a *jihad* or holy war, and Islamic knowledge is greatly esteemed. None the less, the pre-Fulani cult of spirit-possession (*bori*) still flourishes and has many devotees, especially among women, the prostitutes (*karuwai*) being its principal champions. It is of interest that *bori* is not universally regarded as being in conflict with Islam. The term prostitute (*karuwa*) covers all unmarried adults among the Hausa, but refers particularly to those mature women who prefer to remain unwed. Marriage is virilocal and polygynous, and divorce is both easy and frequent. Concubinage was formerly important, the women involved being normally slaves. A strong religious militancy characterized Hausa-Fulani culture during the nineteenth century and found its principal expression in state-organized slave-raiding.

PRAISE-SINGING IN HAUSA CULTURE

This brief outline of Hausa culture and society is necessary for an understanding of the form and practice of *roko* (eulogy, praise-singing). Hausa classify *roko* as a craft (*sana'a*) but, unlike most other crafts, such as dyeing, weaving, building, etc., its product is an incorporeal good incapable of further exchange, an article of immediate consumption. Unlike other service-specialisms, such as barber-doctoring (*wanzanci*), slaughtering (*yanka* or *mahanci*), commission agency (*dillanci*), or even drumming (*kida*), the product or the service performed—praise or blame, shouted or sung with all available force—is consumed by all within earshot, as well as by the person to whom it is addressed. In fact, without this wider audience and publicity, *roko* as a general practice cannot obtain. Moreover, unlike other Hausa craft products, *roki* does not usually depend on voluntary agreement between the craftsman and his customer. At certain levels *roko* is an explicit expression of status, and neither the producer nor the consumer can voluntarily avoid the performance. At other levels the producer may indeed inflict his attention on persons against their wish. These non-economic and non-contractual characteristics of *roko* indicate clearly that the practice constitutes a social institution with an indirect regulative function. Understanding of *roko* thus proceeds through a systematic relation of the practice to its several social contexts, and, in this process, contributes to the understanding of Hausa society.

Roko is practiced by *maroka* (m.s., *maroki;* f.s., *marokiya,* praise-singer, eulogist). *Maroka* may be of either sex but are usually male. With the sole exception of female eulogists who sing praises for kings only, female *maroka* confine their attentions to women, and males address theirs to men. As the institution of praise-singing is developed more elaborately in masculine Hausa culture, our discussion will be concerned principally with male practices, although women's *roko* will be described also.

Roko is often, but by no means always, carried on to the music of drums. Often the *maroki* is himself a drummer. Sometimes he is not, and there are many drummers in Hausaland who are not *maroka* but perform quite different services, such as sending drum messages for butchers on the eve of market to the nearby settlements about the type of stock to be killed on the following day. Other drummers are employed to stimulate competition and keep the rhythm of work at farming work-parties (*gayya*), while still others beat the royal drums (*tambari*) on ceremonial and religious occasions.

The drum is not the only musical instrument employed in *roko*. Double-gongs (*koge*) of a silver-tin alloy, long trumpets of silver or beaten brass (*kakaki*), wooden horns (*fare, pampani*), or reed instruments which sound like bagpipes (*algaita*) figure prominently in the praise-singing addressed to rulers and senior titleholders, such as District heads or vassal-chiefs. The use of these instruments is controlled by a body of rules. Thus, only kings may be praised to the accompaniment of *kakaki*, only certain vassals may be praised with *koge; fare* and *algaita* may not be used in singing the praises of any official below the rank of District head, or its equivalent.

In the *bori* (spirit-possession) cult, the spirits are called and entertained by singing their praises. This requires special musical instruments, such as the *garaya*, a type of guitar, and the *goge*, a type of violin, which are not otherwise employed. Drumming to accompany the praising of spirits is carried out on an upturned half-calabash, which stands in a bowl of water (*kidan ruwa*, the drumming of water) or in an empty vessel (*kidan amada*). These types of drumming are typically practiced at women's ceremonies. In the praise-singing which individual men carry out for one another, the *kalangu*, a double-membraned talking drum shaped like an hourglass and slung under the left arm, or the *ganga*, the large double-membraned Hausa drum, are normally the only drums employed.

The ways in which the praises of nobility, male and female commoners, and spirits are sung thus differ considerably. These differences are linked with other variations of form and function in the types of *roko* appropriate to the differing social contexts in which the spirits, the nobility, and commoners of either sex are addressed. Even so, this list of contexts is not complete. *Maroka* play an important part in the group activities of young people, at dance-meetings, at *ajo* (public collections on behalf of bridegrooms to assist with the marriage-payments), at weddings, and at the two main Muhammadan festivals (*Sallah*): Id-el-Fitr and Id-el-Kabir. The social contexts of otherwise similar events, such as marriages, vary also according to the type of community in which they are held. Hausa distinguish the state capital (*birni*) from the capital of a village area or local community (*gari*), and both from small outlying hamlets (*kauye,* pl. *kauyuka*), and rank these types of settlement in this order. But while Hausa who live at the capital of a state regard all other settlements of the kingdom as *kauyuka,* persons who live in village capitals reserve this depreciatory term for their daughter-hamlets. Urbanization is contrasted with "bush"-dwelling and is clearly accorded prestige, but the definition of a town sometimes varies according to the type of community to which the speaker belongs.

The complexity of Hausa society and culture is mirrored in the institution of *roko.* Such factors as age, ethnic origin, office, social class, wealth, descent, sex, occupation, and area of residence are all significant in defining the positions of persons in the various social contexts in which *roko* occurs, and the institution of praise-singing, which, as we have seen, has a primarily social function, reflects these conditions faithfully in its variant forms.

POLITICAL PRAISE-SINGING BY MAROKA TEAMS

Some *maroka* operate in teams. This normally occurs where there is a fairly complex musical accompaniment, for example, the two drums, *kalangu* and *ganga.* In such teams the *kalangu* is usually played by a small boy, who serves his apprenticeship in this way and is often a son or relative of the team leader. The more complex the musical equipment used in *roko,* the more stable the team. This is especially true of the *maroka* teams that high officials maintain, and which are attached to the official title (*sarauta*) rather than to its holder. Such groups, linked today to the office of district head, will normally contain, besides the drummers and eulogists, two or more pipers and an occasional hornblower. If the office is one of hereditary vassalship, there will also be one or more persons responsible for drumming on the *tambari* at set times and for keeping the fires burning before them. Such *maroka* groups have stable authority structures expressed in the allocation to its members of graded titles, such as Sarkin Makada (the head of the drummers), Galadiman Busa (the senior piper), etc. Normally the team assembles weekly at the District head's entrance hut (*zaure*) on Thursday nights, when the Muhammadan Sabbath starts, and celebrates his office, ancestry, and power in set terms. The district head is usually present, and may request that the praise-songs of titleholders who are his particular friends or patrons should also be sung. This weekly ceremony terminates after an hour or two when gifts of money to the *maroka* are thrown on the floor by the District head.

At Sallah, when the District head has to attend the king at his capital, the band of *maroka* accompanies him on horseback, and plays him into the city with bugle and drum. After the Sallah rite on the prayer-ground outside the city (*masallacin Idi*), the District head, together with his subordinate village chiefs and administrative staff, declares allegiance to the king by a cavalry charge with drawn swords outside the palace, while the *maroka* who take part in this gallop, drum, pipe, and blow their master's title-praise (*kirari*) on horseback. During the distribution of largesse which marks Sallah, the *maroka* are rewarded by their lord with meat, kola nuts, clothes, money, occasionally a horse, and titular promotions. Within the group, these and other rewards from the lord are divided by the senior *maroka* among the team in proportions corresponding to their titular ranking. Although the members of such official *maroka* teams may be unrelated officially, they tend in time to establish affinal links with one another, and may not leave the unit or its headquarters without the permission of their lord.

Often enough, these musical retainers also perform other services for their master, such as political agency (*fadanci*), thereby extending the range of interests linking them to their lord and also augmenting their incomes. Such agency involves relations of clientage between musician and master and receives the rewards appropriate to that social tie. It is common for musicians who are attached to a District headship to become attached to its holder by the relation of political clientage and agency. In form and function, this type of *maroka* team strongly reflects its political context.

It also reflects the pattern of territorial organization. *Maroka* teams attached to District headships are located at the district capital, generally the largest town in a district which may average seven or eight hundred square miles, as in Zaria. Within each district, the District head's band of musicians is unique, and though its individual members may sing the praises of particular village chiefs, as a band the team normally confines its attention to the District head and his most senior official assistant, the Alkali or District judge, except at the installation of village chiefs, or with the foreknowledge and consent of the District head.

At the capital of a kingdom, on the other hand, there will normally be several officials equivalent in rank to the territorial head of the city. Above all these stands the king, whose *maroka* establishment outshines that of the District head in size and complexity as much as kingship outranks the subordinate office. Excluding the king, the capital contains *hakimai* (officials of the first rank) such as the Chief Judge, the Judge of Divorce Pleas, the Town chief, the Treasurer, the Native heads of such Departments as Public Works, Prisons, Sanitation, Education, Medicine, Agriculture, Forestry, Veterinary and Police Services, together with the traditional titled Imams (Muhammadan priests). Each of these senior officials heads an administrative structure, the executive offices of which carry high prestige within the kingdom and are normally held by aristocrats. Apart from these noble officials, there will also normally be at the capital a considerable number of aristocrats who are without lucrative office at the moment, but whose opinion and support play an important part in the allocation of most offices of major importance, including the kingship. Thus, as a center of political and administrative activity, the capital contains a large number of departmental officials and other aristocrats and provides a sharp contrast with the district headquarters, which can provide no one to rival the District head in status or power.

Differences in the organization of *maroka* at the state and district capitals reflect the political differences of these two types of community. The *maroka* team of a district headquarters enjoys a unique and exclusive group relation with the office of District headship, while its members may have individual relations of political clientage with the District head. But, with the exception of the king, senior officials at the capital do not usually maintain separate *maroka* teams, and thus there is less scope both for the titular organization of these bands in the city, and for their maintenance as stable units through the control exercised by a particular official or lord. None the less the norms and forms of political praise-singing are much the same in the capital as at the district headquarters. For the praise of a senior official or high-ranking aristocrat to be sung appropriately requires a team of *maroka* containing at least two singers, two drummers, and normally a piper or hornblower. A smaller band with fewer instrumental types is something in the nature of a reflection on the status and prospects of the senior official it inappropriately addresses.

The political situation of the capital therefore requires and supports the informal organization of *maroka* in bands for the purpose of attending on these senior officials and aristocrats. Titles are consequently less in evidence among these bands than among their rural equivalents, and stability is less general also. As in the districts, these teams address high officials at set times and in set terms, praising the title, the virtues, and the lineage of the individual. Gifts are expected and received by these *maroka* in return for their services, and each band tends to scatter its visits on the eve of Sabbath or at Sallah among the senior officials, unless particularly favored by one or other of them with gifts.

Maroka bands playing to senior officials at the capital as independent and unattached teams are freer to address other persons both individually and as a band than are the country teams attached to particular titles. They are also often under economic constraints to extend their group operations, owing to the relatively unfavorable position of their members as town-dwellers with scanty resources of land from which to supplement cash incomes from their craft by subsistence farming, and also owing to the higher prices of foodstuffs in the town. Wealthy merchants are the obvious persons whose praises offer appropriate rewards, and a good deal of attention is paid to them individually. Since many of these merchants (*attajirai,* rich men) are *nouveaux riches* and of low origin, and since there are considerable numbers of strangers (*baki*) in their ranks at most capitals, they are badly placed to refuse demands from *maroka* for money, as they present easy targets for innuendo and invective if praise fails to reap its reward. Rich merchants therefore appeal to *maroka* in one way, while *maroka* appeal to them in another. Sometimes, however, mistakes occur and the visitor regarded as a man of wealth by the local *maroka,* or, alternatively, the local man erroneously reported as wealthy to the visiting *maroka* is faced with the choice of giving away more than he can afford or taking a severe verbal drubbing. Generally, however, and from motives of self-interest, *maroka* seek to avoid unremunerative exercises of their art.

The type of musical entourage which a king supports has no parallel within the state, but cannot be fully described here. The king's musicians and *maroka* form an organized group containing one or more titular series and effective authority hierarchies. The troupe is both more numerous and specialized in its musical functions, and more permanently attached to the title, than are the teams linked to District headships, which are similarly organized.

Many of the royal *maroka* proudly describe themselves as royal slaves, and point to the fact that their ancestors held titles as royal musicians under earlier kings. It seems that there is at least a core of such *maroka* hereditarily attached to the throne. The king's musical troupe is also peculiar in containing one *marokiya* (female praiser), who formerly had the title of *Boroka* in Zaria, but is nowadays known as *Zabiya* (the guinea hen) from the shrill ululating sound which it is her function to let out at odd moments, such as during the king's address to his assembled subjects after Sallah. Other specialized musical functions in the royal troupe include blowing on the long silver horns or shorter wooden ones, playing on the *taushe* (a small hemispherical drum), and singing the royal praises in Fulani, the last being the task of *maroka* recruited from among the Bombadawa Fulani. Royal *maroka* are in constant attendance at the palace, and announce the arrival of distinguished visitors such as the Resident, Divisional Officer, District Chiefs, and the like, by trumpet fanfares, drumming, and shouting. They also salute the king on the Sabbath eve and nightly during the annual fast of Ramadan, when the royal drums (*tambari*) are regularly played. The king's *maroka* address no one except their master, unless to herald visitors into his presence. They are allocated compounds, farm lands, and titles by the king, who may also give them horses and frequently provides them with clothes, money, or assistance at weddings, as well as with food. It is unusual for any but a very few of these royal musicians to act as political agents for the king, although they are all his clients and retainers. The combination of agency with the role of *maroka,* which occurs frequently at the level of District headship, is marginal at that of the throne and for obvious reasons. As befits their position, the royal *maroka* are unique within the state and only work as a team.

MAROKA TEAMS AND WEDDING CELEBRATIONS

Among the Hausa the celebration of weddings has always required the presence of *maroka*. Normally also, the *maroka* attending such feasts work as a group, with drumming and praise-singing if commoners (*talakawa*) are involved, and some bugling or pipe blowing for persons of wealth or noble status. The principal beneficiaries of the gifts made publicly at weddings are the *maroka* themselves. *Maroka* do not perform at the naming ceremonies which are held for week-old infants, when the newborn are formally in-corporated into the Muhammadan Hausa community. At these ceremonies, and also at the wakes that follow death, the *mallamai* (Koranic scholars and teachers) are the principal recipients of gifts. In some sense, therefore, it may be said that the strictly religious aspect predominates over the secular at naming and funeral cere-monies, while the opposite is true of weddings. Weddings, and es-pecially the weddings of persons of high status or wealth, are oc-casions at which the *maroka* come into their own.

One example will serve to illustrate the part that *maroka* play at a wedding. The groom in this case was a District head, his bride a maiden whose father was a senior official living in Zaria city. The groom had made marriage payments of £22. 10*s*. to the bride's family and had given her cloths costing £40. He also provided his other wives with cloths costing £6, and bought £14 worth of kola nuts to distribute among the guests at the feast. His subordinate vil-lage chiefs brought him gifts of money totaling about £40. His principal bond friend, another District head, gave the groom £2 as a token gift and gave £5 to the groom's *maroka*. Another District head who attended the ceremony also gave £5 to the groom's *maroka*, and a wealthy merchant from Zaria city gave them £20. The total cash gifts received by the groom were therefore £42, as against £30 which his *maroka* received from only three of the per-sons present. At the very least the *maroka*'s receipts must have ex-ceeded the gifts made to their master by £5 or £10. But this com-parison would probably not be accepted by the bridegroom or his liberal friends. They would regard the £30 which the *maroka* received from the lord's friends as gifts made to them *on his behalf*. Gifts to a lord's dependents are therefore declarations of solidarity with the lord. The *maroka* benefit directly from such patterns of gift-giving; but these patterns indirectly express personal attach-ments, and also, but still more indirectly, they express and affirm certain values and principles of Hausa society.

Among the Hausa, wedding ceremonials are elaborate and com-plex, and proceed simultaneously at the compounds of the bride and the groom. At each compound the sexes celebrate the wedding separately. The men hold their feast in the forecourt and the en-trance hut, while the women hold theirs inside the compound (*cikin gida*) which is the women's quarters. Male *maroka* address the male assembly at the forecourt, while female *maroka* perform inside. The two sets of feasts have quite different contents.

Women assembled in a compound to celebrate a marriage generally call the *bori* (spirits) to witness and bless the union, and to join in celebrating it. This is usually done at night, when the heavy work of preparing food for the feast is over. The ceremony normally begins with *kidan amada,* or *kidan kwaliya* (drumming on an empty upturned half-calabash), while the women present crowd into one of the huts. While the gathering is getting settled, and for some time after, this *kidan kwaliya* continues, and one or more of the female *maroka* present will sing the praises of individuals in the assembly, stressing their fertility, generosity, descent, family connections, seniority, and other desirable qualities. Indirect references are also made to female bond-friend and client relationships, which are expressive of status as that is conceived among females, and these references are designed to stimulate the person addressed to give freely. Senior women of the families involved in the marriage, or co-wives, especially those of the compound in which the gathering meets, are attractive targets for individual address by the *marokiya,* since these relationships imply personal rivalry, with the effect of increasing the desire not to be shamed as ungenerous in the competitive giveaways[1] that *maroka* stimulate. Gradually the *kidan kwaliya* changes to *kidan ruwa* (drumming on the calabash upturned in a basin of water) which is used to call the spirits at female gatherings. Calling the *bori* then begins, the *marokiya,* who is often a prostitute, taking the lead.

Like all Hausa, each of the spirits has at least one praise-song (*taki, kirari*); and the number and elegance of the praise-songs reflect the prominence of the person addressed, human or spirit. To call a particular spirit, one keeps on playing through its series of praise-songs until it possesses one of the persons present, usually one who is already dancing. In theory, the same spirit may prefer different songs on different occasions, momentary preference being expressed by its response. After its arrival the spirit controls the selection of tunes, until, as sometimes happens with unimportant spirits, the audience requires its departure. As with humans, so with spirits, it is most improper to play anyone's praise-song unrequested when addressing someone else. This is one of the means by which *maroka*

---

[1] Giving of gifts.

insinuate disrespect at a public gift-giving, and when applied to spirits it normally leads to their departure in a huff.

During the period of its attendance, the spirit, through the body of the person possessed, conducts itself in the manner expected of it by the Hausa. Thus the spirit Dan Galadima is a prince, son of the king of the spirits, Sarkin Aljannu, and he conducts himself as such. He requests a turban, is somewhat particular about the cloth produced, sees that it is folded in a mode appropriate to his royal status, and generally behaves in the manner associated with highly placed officials of royal rank. He settles himself in the center of the hut holding court, muttering to himself about political and administrative problems, and frequently ordering such articles as perfume, kola nuts, blouses, bangles, and money to be given to the musicians and the *marokiya* who play his praise-songs. If the order is directed generally at the assembly rather than at any single person, there is a brief flutter until it is carried out and the spirit is appeased. Orders to particular individuals have to be obeyed on the instant. The *maroka* benefit considerably. As the spirits mainly possess persons who have already been initiated (*girki*) within the cult, the uninitiated majority of the audience on whom the bulk of these spirit orders and requests falls, participate actively, if indirectly, in maintaining the cult by discharging these requests for transfers to the *maroka* directly. Here the structure of relations expressed in the donation is identical with that found to obtain among males at weddings.

At the entrance hut where the males foregather, there is usually a fair number of persons listening to the *maroka* as they drum and sing the praises of the *gida* (compound, family line) and particularly those of its male head. Descent, age, generosity, relations of solidarity with important persons, and other prestige-giving conditions are referred to time and again, and gifts received by the *maroka* on behalf of the principal addressed are followed by singing the donor's praises also. At the wedding of an important man, this drumming and praise-singing at the compound entrance begins in the forenoon and may conclude after dark. When less wealthy people in the country marry, less time is spent on praise-singing, and for the marriage of divorcees, the ceremonial normally starts after dark, when the bride moves to her new home, and rarely lasts more than three hours. There is no limit to the number of *maroka* or other persons who may attend a wedding, other than that set by wealth or interest. Though *maroka* bands are common in the capital and richer towns at marriages of important men, others who work singly may also attend, and these solo craftsmen are more common in the country parts when poor folk are the marriage principals. Since the bride moves to her husband's home on the Hausa wedding day or, in the case of divorcées, a week thereafter, the husband's compound is the focus of greater public celebration after the wedding than that of the bride; but the bridal procession is normally accompanied by *maroka* and drummers and enters with them into her new home.

OTHER SITUATIONS FAVORABLE TO MAROKA TEAMWORK

Nowadays in the towns weddings may be preceded by meetings known as *ajo,* a Yoruba custom recently introduced into Hausaland. *Ajo* is a formal public meeting which is called on behalf of a man about to be married for the purpose of contributing to his marriage payments and expenses. This custom has found favor among junior officials of the Native Administration, whose salaries and indebtedness make it seem attractive. Senior officials do not practice *ajo* and rarely attend them. *Ajo* is usually held at night and is presided over by the principal bond-friend (*babban aboki*) of the bridegroom, who sits at a table with certain other friends of the groom, all males, and writes down the amounts given and the names of the donors. Women attend by invitation—the younger wives of the males present, some female relatives of the marriage principals, and well-known *karuwai* (prostitutes). The *maroka* are engaged in bands, and there may be two bands present at an *ajo.* The *maroka* provide impersonal music, such as *Chaji,* a popular Hausa song, until the principal bond-friend opens the ceremony with a short speech. The *maroka* then launch into the praise-songs of the bridegroom, his family, and the like, which specify their descent, prominence, important connections, and fortune. The bridegroom is never present at an *ajo.* The praise-songs of the *maroka* stimulate donations which are handed to the chief *maroki* of the band, who counts the money, announces the amount and the donor's name, and interrupts his praising of the groom briefly to sing the praises of the donor. This continues in an orderly fashion, unless personal jealousies or rivalries of love or office among some of the males present produce a competitive situation, which the *maroki* must then exploit. After the meeting is over, the *maroka* employed for the *ajo* receive an agreed portion of the takings or a flat payment of about £3 or £4. An *ajo* normally lasts about two hours, is not attended by uninvited *maroka,* and does not involve donations of money by the women present. In fact, the presence of these women, most of whom are generally confined to their compounds under the practice of purdah marriage (*auren kulle*), would be pointless if it did not provide an audience and stimulate the generosity of males by rivalry. The women are normally seated on chairs in a group at some little distance from the men, and throughout the proceedings maintain an aloof and mildly disdainful expression.

Thus far we have been describing situations in which the sexes are normally separated and do not actively cooperate to provide the context of *roko.* This is functionally accurate as a description of *ajo,* since the females present are required to be noncommittal, but it is not true of the praise-singing that takes place at the salons of important or notable city prostitutes (*manya-manya karuwai*). These salons are held nightly and are presided over by the prostitute in whose compound they meet. The males attending, apart from *maroka* who often perform there in teams, are predominantly wealthy and aristocratic, if the prostitute is a lady of high prestige. Normally these guests are polygynists and already known to one another. If the prostitute has a high reputation her clientele is proportionately limited and tends to be stable. The salon exists as much for witty conversation, easy social intercourse, and display as for any other purpose. Such a situation requires and attracts *maroka.* Since generosity is obligatory on the guests, both to avoid innuendo and to declare appreciation of the mistress of the salon, praise-singing stimulates an indirect competition for the lady's good opinion among her noble clients, the more so since the leading *maroki* can artistically discredit one lover and recommend another, and may often enjoy the confidence of the lady herself. The prostitute's salon also presents another feature which *maroka* can exploit, in that it is formally contradictory to the principles of Islam, and often also to the rules of the king. The lady, as an open rebel against both these codes, occupies a far less ambiguous position in relation to them than do her noble clients, and she is under no obligation to reward the praise-singers. None the less, the prostitute's response, overt or other, as well as the fact that her compound provides the meeting place for the group, involves her participation in the *roko* at her salon. The traditional prototype of this situation is the girls' dances on market and feast days in country or town.

At these dances, the unmarried maidens (*buduruwai,* sing. *buduruwa*) dance solo parts to the drumming of *kalangu* and *ganga.* Those waiting their turn to dance accompany the drums with chants and songs. The girls are competitors in an indirect contest of dance skill and other attractive qualities, hence the dancing is solo. Young men cluster about the dance circle, watching the dancers and generally admiring the girls. The master of ceremonies, whether formerly a *maroki* or not, becomes a *maroki* in this situation if he is to function as master of ceremonies at all. This frequently happens against the will of the person concerned, who may be simply a drummer enjoying the spectacle of the girls dancing after the market is over. Invariably, however, competition sets in between the girls on the one hand for admirers, and between the youths on the other for the most attractive of the nubile girls. This type of situation transforms the drummer-in-chief into a *maroki,* however little he wishes to exploit it. The pattern here is for the admiring male to give the drummer money so that he will continue to drum while the girl of his choice dances, or alternatively so that he will interrupt his dance drumming for another to sing her praise and request her to dance, boldly mentioning the name of her admirer and the amount given. This, once started, initiates a keen competition among the young men to declare their attachment to a particular girl by outdoing one another in donations on her behalf, while others who admire other girls try to interrupt these declarations to secure the attention of the *maroka* for the maidens of their preference. For an hour or two the pace of gift-giving and the size of the gifts increase as the competition narrows down to some specific rivalry for a particular girl. Those girls and youths defeated earlier in the contest enjoy the spectacle presented by the final stages of the competition, when elimination of the rival becomes necessary to avoid the shame of defeat, and uncertainty as to the victor provides a dramatic suspense. A skilled *maroki* can both create this situation and exploit it superbly, but no novice can easily revoke its momentum once the development has started.

In similar circumstances, when adult males compete for the favors of admired prostitutes and divorcees, debts are hastily contracted to continue the competition, clothes are given away and whatever else comes to hand—housekeeping money, one's wife's clothes, small livestock, and so forth. This type of situation develops most drama when all the principals are adult and two men of equally high status

compete for the favors of a desirable prostitute at the brothel run by
the Magajiya of a rural town.[2] But whether the girl for whose sake the
successful competitor has made his expensive public declaration is a
maiden or a prostitute, the implications are largely the same. The
successful competitor has declared his desire for the female concerned and will later approach her for his reward. The girl also,
granted average good looks in the winner, is pleased at the attention
bestowed on her and at her momentary triumph over her age mates
and sex rivals. According to informants, she is normally grateful to
her admirer.

Thus the situation at girls' dances is essentially the same, for all
parties concerned, as the competition for a prostitute at a rural
brothel. Both these contexts differ formally from the situation inside
a courtesan's salon, principally in the fact that whereas the *maroki*
controls the public performance and is free to exploit it as he will,
the mistress of the salon controls the situation within her compound
and can silence the *maroki* if he becomes offensive or stimulates a
type of contest that she does not wish among her clients. Thus, as the
independence of the prostitute increases and finds expression in control of her own salon and a select clientele, the *maroki*'s control of
the situation provided by heterosexual participation in giveaways
declines.

Competitive giveaways in heterosexual groups cannot provide the
necessary conditions for the maintenance of stable *maroka* teams,
except in large settlements. They tend to occur sporadically, rather
than predictably, and regularity is essential for the maintenance of
groups of this sort. Though a regularly recurrent pattern at the
young people's dances, these giveaways do not often yield sufficient
reward to warrant group work by adult *maroka,* since the young
folk involved do not normally have much money. On the other hand
the giveaways at young people's dances are well adapted to the
needs of an individual *maroki,* working singly and with a keen eye
and tongue for the situation. Where competitive giveaways involve
adult males and prostitutes, skilled handling by the *maroki* is essential to extract all the drama and donations implicit in the situation.
Thus the *maroki* is as essential to the adult competitions as the
drummer (*makada*) is to the girls' dances. At these adult displays of
rivalry, the gifts made remain with the *maroki,* unless publicly stated

[2] See Mary F. Smith, *Baba of Karo,* Faber & Faber, London, 1954, pp. 224–
26, for an instance.

to be intended for the lady whose favor forms their object. Competition for the favors of maidens rarely involves public donations *to* them via *maroka,* but this sometimes happens as a final gesture when adults compete for the favor of prostitutes at brothels, the gifts involved being of a value that meets or exceeds the lady's expectations.

Among the Hausa, play associations of young people (*taron tsaran juna,* age grades) are divided on sex lines and contain parallel organizations of the boys and girls of a local community. Each division forms a separate authority structure, controlled through a series of titular statuses, such as Sarkin Samari (Chief of the youths), Mama (Chief of the girls), Galadima, Iya, and other titles drawn from the central state system. Competition for titles proceeds within each division by gifts, clientage, and other means current in Hausa political systems. Each title has a defined sphere of control, an appropriate etiquette, and relations with others of the series as well as with subordinate groups. Membership of the girls' associations lapses at their first marriages; but membership in the young men's associations sometimes continues for prominent persons beyond that stage. The head of the girls' group arranges and presides over certain of the girls' dances, can levy fines for non-attendance, refusal to obey orders and the like, and can command the attendance of girls on male titleholders. Seniority by age is linked with status seniority in each association. The two associations meet together once each year for a ceremony known as *kallankuwa,* during which they establish a straw township of their own on some fallow farm land outside the town walls. *Kallankuwa* lasts for three or four days and consists in a formal dramatization of the state political system on which these associations are modeled. It is principally at this time that titular promotions are made, the young people's "law-courts" hold session, and the allocation of subjects and fiefs to titleholders take place. The political pattern of this play form also requires sexual intercourse between members of the two associations, and to some extent the authority structure of each group permits this to occur despite the wishes of individual girls. Hence the opposition of some parents to these age grades, and their refusal to permit their children to enter such groups.

An essential role at *kallankuwa* and in the organization of the age grades generally was performed by the *maroka* of the community. They provided the young people with instruction in political organization and in the behavior appropriate to different levels of these group structures, and supplied the primary incentives to individual participation—praise or shame. By their presence they gave continuity to the groups, and by their praise-singing they transformed these groups from an empty shadow play into a living reality for the members. Their role in the pattern of sexual competition and dances has already been described. For *kallankuwa,* as for political praise-singing, *maroka* teams were necessary, and, since the festival was an annual one for which the young people of both sexes saved in order to compete effectively with one another, the *maroka* were assured of adequate rewards for their participation.

Kallankuwa concludes the list of situations favoring group performances by *maroka*. Such situations are of set pattern, fairly predictable, and have clearly defined conventions. In contrast, solo praise-singing normally creates its own situation, is limited to males, and has different conventions. Where the *maroki* is primarily a drummer, he may seek to exploit the occasion of a wedding by attending uninvited to sing and drum the praises of individuals who are present. But it is not usual for the pure *maroki,* the solo verbalist who does not drum, to invade a wedding party for this purpose. The presence of other *maroka* in teams is an adequate safeguard for the host, his friends, or his kin.

SOLO PRAISE-SINGING

The *maroki* who does not drum or perform with any assistance gives the purest expression to the nature and meaning of *roko* in Hausaland. Normally he is a rover, arriving unexpectedly in rural areas and augmenting his knowledge of the important individuals he intends to address by information obtained from local *maroka*. He selects the situation in which he will perform with care. It may be late at night when all are in their compounds, or early in the morning before the folk have left home, or some other situation, such as markets provide, which allows no escape to the man addressed, and leaves the *maroki* free to declaim without interruption. The market place, especially when empty, is a good platform in rural areas, since the houses of traders and prominent people are normally near at hand, and the space permits considerable range to the *maroki*'s addresses.

He begins by calling the name of the person he intends to praise several times, working into a rhythm and thence into the individual's praise-song. This continues for some time with increasingly frequent and direct demands for gifts. Normally the person addressed, if already out of sight, continues to remain so as long as possible and sends out his gift by a boy. The *maroki* now chants his thanks, *godiya, na gode, na gode,* then announces the amount of the gift. If it is clearly adequate by community standards, he concludes his address to the first individual with a brief repetition of his praise-song and a recommendation of the donor to Allah, and turns his attention to a second individual near by. If either of the persons addressed sends a gift that the *maroki* regards as inadequate, then this is announced, and the voice pattern changes from singing to a rhythmic declamation in an unnatural pitch. Innuendo marks the alteration initially, but later, to indicate impatience at tardiness in the arrival of an appropriate gift, this innuendo becomes sharper, harsher, and its delivery takes a staccato form. This is virtually an ultimatum and rarely fails to produce surrender from the individual addressed, who has probably had more than he can stand already. He now sends whatever gifts he regards as likely to satisfy and pacify the *maroki*—money, clothes, or something light, salable, and of value, such as a new hoe, which also indicates lack of cash. After one such demonstration of his powers, the *maroki* will normally be content with a brief praising of some local official such as the village chief or a ward head, and will depart with grateful acknowledgment of their gifts. He cannot afford to alienate the community by continuing a serial declamation of this sort. While the declamation proceeds, however, no one present makes any conspicuous movement against or away from the *maroki*. To do so is to invite his attention and to miss the drama involved. Traditionally, no one has the right or power to silence the *maroki* while he addresses an individual with praise-songs; but there is a category of legal offense (*zage,* defamation, abuse) that the *maroki* must avoid if the matter is not to go to court at some later date. During the past two years, however, laws forbidding or limiting this type of solo declamation directed at individuals have been promulgated in various Hausa kingdoms.

This type of solo declamation occurs mainly in rural areas, but is similar in many respects to the group performances of *roko* which are addressed to the *nouveaux riches* in the larger towns. The kinds of person to whom the individual *roko* is addressed are all relatively prosperous, such as butchers, commission agents,

other market factors, senior blacksmiths, dyers, large farmers, builders, and famous *maroka* themselves. Two important categories of
adult males are never addressed in this manner—the nobility,
official or other, and the religious leaders or scholars, *mallamai*,
including the priests or imams. Women are also excluded by their
sex from being direct objects of *roko* by solo *maroka*. Since their
official position invests even quite junior state employees of the
Native Authority with relatively high status and power, this group
too is normally excluded from the objects of individual praise-
singing, being regarded as part of the official nobility. But government employees such as Ibo, Yoruba, or Hausa of low family
are not regarded as exercising similar power or enjoying equivalent
status, and provide possible targets for this type of address. The
gifts which a *maroki* regards as adequate vary in relation to the
prosperity, prospects, and reputation of the commoner (*batalake*) to
whom he is giving his unrequested services.

The content of a solo declamation consists in statements of the
individual's ancestry, their notability, his prosperity and influence,
the number of his dependents, his fame, and its range. If he has
any well-known and important political connections, such as clientage with a senior official capable of protecting him, these are alluded
to indirectly. If the declamation becomes hostile, the same themes
recur, though with unfavorable emphases and connotations. Insinua-
tions about the ancestry of the person addressed are made at this
time and, for many commoners at whom this type of declamation is
directed, this may imply slavery. Unfavorable references to the
individual's meanness, fortune (*arziki*), treatment of his dependents,
occupation, reputation, and possible disloyalty to his community or
political patrons are also liable to be made. The ultimate insult—
imputation of ambiguous paternity—is never openly mentioned, but
overshadows the process of increasing pressure.

In the sense in which the term "moral" is normally used among
Europeans, the moral status of the individual concerned is utterly
irrelevant to the declamation, its content, and its significance. Sexual
deviance, including incest, perjury by swearing of false oaths on the
Koran, and other forms of behavior regarded as "immoral" in
Hausa culture, are never referred to in the declamations of *roko*,
even by implication. Such behavior is punishable either by law
(*shari'a*) or by the taunting songs that children sing around the
village. Politically significant misconduct, on the other hand, is
dealt with by the officials of the Native Administration (N.A.).

Yet other types of behavior are proscribed under the fear of semi-automatic magico-religious sanctions. But the punishment and praise which are the alternative weights in the balances wielded by solo *maroka* are awarded purely for behavior within the situation of *roko* itself, and with the tacit consent of the community.

ANALYSIS

We can analyze the data presented above in order to determine the function of *roko* in Hausa society or to decipher its meaning. These two types of analysis have different references and proceed in different directions. For that reason they are best carried out separately, although often they are confused.

Functional analysis has reference primarily to the social structure in regard to which social functions are determined; but semantic analysis—the determination of meanings—refers to the values or conceptual aspects of particular forms as more or less consistent ideational systems, the correspondence and relations of which to other parts of the social structure remain to be investigated. The determination of social functions proceeds by systematic examination of the part which an institution plays in the series of contexts in which it is found. The ultimate reference here is to the inclusive social context analyzed as a system of a particular type, a continuing structure. In this analysis the emphasis is uniformly on the relations of the institution with other parts of this system, that is, with the *external* relations of the particular form. But, to discover the meaning of the form in question, it is necessary to make a parallel study of the *internal* relations of its elements in all the situations in which it occurs. The consistency or inconsistency of these relations and their value reference can only be defined precisely by the comparative study of the form in all the contexts in which it occurs, in order to discover its systematic content. For the determination of values through a study of meanings, regulative institutions such as *roko* present inviting material.

Among the Hausa *roko* is an informal regulative institution through which praise or shame are distributed. As an informal regulative institution, it simultaneously imposes social control and reflects honor on the formal agencies of social control. Thus, in certain circumstances, notably at solo declamations, it enjoys considerable license, while in other contexts, such as the situations of political praise-singing, the conventions that govern its performance prohibit innuendo or disrespect.

In both political praise-singing and solo declamations addressed to individuals, only the person addressed may reward the *maroka*. On the other hand, at *bori* seances, *ajo* wedding celebrations, and public heterosexual competitions, gifts are normally received by the *maroka* on behalf of another person. These differences in the structure of gift-giving reflect other differences in the two sets of contexts. When an individual, lord or commoner, rewards *maroka* directly, it is in return for personal praise and is a declaration of status in that it constitutes performance of the role attaching to the status in question. An inadequate reward is a failure to perform the role attaching to the attributed status, and therefore provokes the *maroka*'s disrespect and the community's disapproval.

Donations which the *maroka* receive on behalf of another, whether human or spirit, are either declarations of solidarity with the person on whose behalf they have been made, as in the context of *ajo,* weddings, and séances, or are attempts to win a female's favor and at the same time to vindicate status within the community by displays of liberality. In the context of weddings and séances the gifts made to *maroka* on another's behalf also declare the value placed by the donor on the institution which provides the context of gift-giving. This declaration of cultural attachment finds no parallel in the donations made on behalf of women or girls at public give aways. In its place there is the purely individual declaration of desire, the objects of which are evaluated in terms of beauty, intelligence, and the like. Thus, in the one case, declarations of solidarity with other persons also involve declarations of attachment to institutions of Hausa culture, while in the heterosexual situation gifts made on behalf of women express attachment to more general qualities, such as beauty, youth and the like.

The function of *roko* as an informal regulative institution is thus to express certain social and cultural values, to enjoin their maintenance, and to declare certain types of relations which ideally hold between these values. The individual addressed, the type of address, and the context of the address, are all suitable or unsuitable for *roko* of different types to the extent that they represent the values to which the *roko* is ultimately addressed.

Exclusion of religious leaders and Koranic scholars from the category of persons at whom *roko* may be directed shows that the valuations which this institution expresses are independent of those of Islam. The set patterns of *roko* in which the nobility are addressed express high valuations of power, authority, office, lineage, prosperity, tradition, and influence; and the fact that innuendo and disrespect are prohibited in this context of *roko* indicates the direct functional relation of this institution to the structure of social control. It is therefore appropriate that the most elaborate developments of *roko* are associated with the highest levels of power and authority, and that periodic ceremonials reassert the relation between the nobility and the values of the social structure. In this respect it is utterly irrelevant whether the official addressed is a reprobate or a saint, a tyrant or an honest administrator; *roko* is directed toward structural values as such, and not at individual character.

But such a functional analysis of *roko* needs to be supplemented by semantic analysis if the institution is to be fully understood. The object of semantic analysis is to define the structural values which it is the function of *roko* to express. The determination of these values proceeds by examining the serial of contexts comparatively to discover whether their content and relations form a coherent referential system in themselves. Unless functional analysis is supplemented by such a study of meanings, it is impossible to demonstrate objectively what structural values it is the function of *roko* to express.

The female ceremonial of *bori* expresses most clearly the values basic to *roko*. It does this by personalizing these values, together with their relations and appropriate behavior, in spirit form. The spirits of *bori* represent and express such values as tradition, status, descent, authority, power, prosperity. They also enjoin the expression of solidarity with these values by requiring donations from the audience to the *maroka*. The values expressed in *bori* are basic to *roko* because they are basic to Hausa society, and because *roko* is the institutionalized mode of their expression. Like the gods of Greece, the Hausa *bori* are amoral representations, but there is no possibility of doubting their character as personifications of social values.

In the age-grade activities, such as *kallankuwa*, we are dealing with another projective expression which dramatizes certain social values, notably values of status and authority, together with intelligence in the learning and performance of roles. In the competitive giveaways of dance ring or brothel, cultural values of beauty and youth are expressed, together with the social values of status-maintenance. Notably, no "moral" values of chastity or fidelity are implied. At *ajo* and weddings the purely social values of solidarity and liberality are invoked, and gifts are made to *maroka* on behalf of another which not only declare solidarity with persons held to represent such values as lineage, maturity and so on, but also express approval of the basic institutions of Hausa marriage and kinship. It is significant that at weddings, where the secular element predominates over the religious, *maroka* are required, while they are excluded from the naming ceremonies and wakes, at which the religious elements predominate over the secular.

The meaning and basis of *roko* as a regulative institution are most clearly apparent in the solo declamations directed at individuals. The *maroka* who make such declamations are normally strangers to the community, but are for that reason perhaps the best available spokesmen for the values to which they give expression. This relatively informal type of *roko* has clear conventions that define its form and content. The declamation consists, briefly, in an application of public pressure to prominent members of the community to validate their status by appropriate role performances within the *roko* situation through the mechanism of gifts to the *maroka.* Praise and shame are the sanctions involved. Validation of status within the community, and hence affirmation of membership in that community—these are the values expressed. It is in this light that the gifts made to the *maroka* must be finally evaluated. The *maroki* regards them as evidence of generosity or meanness in the donor, but the community more correctly understands their symbolic character as expressions of identity with its system of values. Thus the individual who makes the *maroki* a gift in such a context is primarily concerned, not to maintain or increase his community prestige, but to declare his loyalty to the system of social values. As these values are unchanging, the content of *roko* is constant, except in so far as its different social contexts, such as political praise-singing, *bori,* weddings, and the like, emphasize one aspect of the system rather than another.

By means of the sanctions that *roko* wields over the *nouveaux riches,* their individualism is inhibited in social relationships, and the continuation of personal good fortune (*arziki*) is made contingent on their conformity to social norms and expectations. The gifts that these people make to *maroka* are thus statements of their adherence to these social norms, and the *maroki* receives the gift *on behalf of the society*. It is for this reason that convention prohibits interruption of the solo declamations directed at the individuals, despite their often painful character, and also that in these situations gifts on behalf of the individual addressed are inadmissible. This is so because the real meaning of this situation is that the individual addressed should declare his identity with the values necessary to the maintenance and functioning of Hausa society.

As agents of public opinion, the *maroka* are only concerned with problems of the correspondence and relations between abstract social values and individuals who occupy positions to which these values are attached in various situations. Hence the generality of the *maroki*'s address, and the fact that specific faults or virtues of the individual are irrelevant to his appraisal. The moral worth of the individual is immaterial when the social value of his total status is being assessed, or the correspondence between his behavior and that expected as the expression of status. Thus the poor man may not be addressed by the *maroki* at all; and the nobleman in office is not asked to rule justly, but simply to rule, and by his acts to manifest his status. Although the social values that *roko* reflects are as constant as Hausa society, their expression in terms of individual lives is thus inherently relativistic, and therefore the sanctions attaching to their realization will vary with individual circumstance.

Of course the *maroka* and the Hausa in general are little conscious of the meaning we have found in this institution. But this does not imply that our analysis is simply a subjective interpretation of their customs. If the method by which we arrive at our conclusions is scientifically valid and objective, the conclusions to which it leads cannot simply be regarded as "interpretation."

CONCLUSION

The method illustrated here is identical with that proposed by Radcliffe-Brown in his lecture on Taboo, and bears on identical problems. In Radcliffe-Brown's words, "What method, other than that of guessing, is there of arriving at the meaning? I suggest that we may start with a general working hypothesis that when, in a single society, the same symbol is used in different contexts or on different kinds of occasions there is some common element of meaning, and that by comparing the various uses of the symbol we may be able to discover what the common element is. This is precisely the method we adopt in studying an unrecorded spoken language in order to discover the meanings of words and morphemes."[3]

The problems which are raised by this method partly explain its relative infrequency in current anthropology. As Radcliffe-Brown pointed out in his discussion of Taboo, it is necessary to discriminate between the function, meaning, purpose, and value of social forms. Each of these categories of analysis refers to something distinct, and all are necessary to the complete understanding of the custom under study. Unfortunately, however, there is often such overlap in these categories that it has become normal to regard the function of an institution as "proof" of its meaning, and evidence of its value. In some analyses, moreover, function is confused with purpose, and unverifiable teleological propositions are advanced. If semantic analysis of social institutions is to be developed in anthropology, then the attribution of functions will have to proceed by methods that exclude the extrapolation of meaning and value and make the confusion of purpose and function impossible. This, I think, was Radcliffe-Brown's point.

Moreover there are problems of defining and classifying values and especially of determining their relations to the social structures within which they occur. There are basically only two alternative approaches to these questions: the inductive comparative approach that proceeds by the semantic analysis of a number of empirical social systems; and the deductive theoretical approach that draws on conceptual analysis current in philosophy and attempts to classify elements and systems of value in more or less familiar terms. Anthropology will gain from the simultaneous development of both these approaches, and indeed cannot escape this dual pursuit without unequivocal definition as either a natural or a moral science. Yet if the inductive approach to the study of value-systems may not lead directly to a satisfactory classification of the elements and systems it defines, the deductive approach promises to tell us little definitively about the relations of the values that it classifies to social structure and social process.

[3] A. R. Radcliffe-Brown, *Structure and Function in Primitive Society,* Cohen & West, London, 1952, p. 146; also pp. 142–48.

30. African Music

I

Important contributions to the study of African music have been made in recent years by a number of scholars working in different areas. Publications on African musical instruments in South Africa, Uganda, the Congo, Nigeria, and a few other places have appeared as well as studies of single instruments such as xylophones, flutes, and drums in restricted areas. The study of song texts has received some attention, and the analysis of rhythm, particularly as exemplified in drumming, is well on the way. A major contribution to the study of the latter has recently been made by Jones, who has provided extensive transcriptions of a number of rather complex forms of drumming found among the Ewe of southeastern Ghana (Jones, 1959).

In addition to these publications, one should mention also the extensive recordings of traditional and contemporary African music that are now available for study—such as the recordings of the African Music Transcription Library and the International Library of African Music, discs issued by Musée de l'Homme and a number of recording companies in America, Britain, and various African territories. Although a recording is by no means complete in itself as data, there is no doubt that it could be a valuable source of information in the hands of a person with some practical experience of African music and who knows how to listen to it and use it. These recordings and the publications now available, therefore, provide a small but growing body of data on African music to inspire one with the hope of adequate coverage in the not-too-distant future which will lead to a better grasp of both the principles

SOURCE: *AMSAC Newsletter,* Vol. III, Supplement No. 19, 1961, pp. 3–6 (January–February), 4–8 (March–April). Reprinted by permission of the author and publisher.

of this music and what the music itself means to those who make it.

In drawing attention to these, I do not of course imply that all of them are of equal merit or that their approach is uniformly satisfactory. But whatever may be said about them from other angles, there can be no doubt that they add considerably to our knowledge of African music by providing a body of useful and reliable data. Indeed it is only in the light of this body of data that we can begin to take an overview of African musical practice with a little more confidence than before. It is only because of these publications that we can now go beyond the apparent structural characteristics of this music discussed by Wallaschek (1893) on the evidence of travelers' accounts, by Ward (1927) on the basis of a very small sample, and by Hornbostel (1928) on the basis of limited studies of recordings and ethnographic data.

Attempts that have been made since these early studies to provide such an overview of African music are relatively small, although the works of scholars are seldom devoid of generalizations. The most recent of these are two articles by Merriam (1959a & b) which, though brief, summarize viewpoints and relevant information about African music in a more rounded way than anything that has come to my notice. Both of them deal with African music as a "style," or more precisely as a body of closely related styles that are uniformly different in certain particulars from other known musical styles. His approach is both critical and descriptive and "meaning" in African music is stated in terms of social function and familiar categories of music theory: rhythm, melody and form, scale and harmony, and a few other aspects of special interest.

This paper is contributed both as a supplement to those of Merriam and an extension of a previous paper on "Drums, Dance, and Song" which deals largely with the social implications of African music (Nketia, 1959a). Here we shall be concerned with artistic processes and the musical values in terms of which African musical style manifests itself. The observations are based not only on published data but also to a large extent on my personal experience as a carrier of one tradition of African music—the music of the Akan—and as a person who has attempted to use the resources of this music creatively, as well as on the results of my research in Ghana.

In a paper on such a vast subject, one can only speak in

general terms. It is hoped nevertheless that the observations presented here will provide a point of reference from which one can proceed to explore various problems of meaning in African music.

II

A fundamental question on which our understanding of music in any culture rests is the question of what constitutes music or what the concept of music involves. This is sometimes taken for granted, yet as musicologists have shown, different cultures provide different answers. Oriental cultures are said to have musical cosmologies "in which tempi, pitches, rhythms, and modes are linked to and express concepts, emotions, and moral qualities" (Meyer, 1956:2; Sachs, 1943:110). Western art music since the middle ages uses, according to Meyer, "musical symbolism depicting actions, character, and emotions" (1956:2), and psychological investigations have shown that these are things that many Euroamerican listeners look for in their music (Lee, 1932) even though composers are not unanimous in their insistence on expressive symbolism (cf. Copland, 1953:13–14).

As a starting point in our discussion of musical values in African music, we may similarly ask: what constitutes music in Africa, and what does the concept of music involve? There are at least two ways of approaching these questions. We may attempt to define the concept of music by reference to "how the African *thinks* about his music," to the "musical mind" of the African—an approach often stressed by Jones in his writings on African rhythm (see, e.g., Jones, 1959), or we may approach the problem by considering what the African *does* when he makes music, what resources he uses, how and when he uses them, and from these deduce—in the light of our knowledge and experience of this music in its cultural context—what can be stated to constitute music and what the concept of music involves. This paper takes the second line of approach. Beginning with the raw material of African music, it proceeds in an ascending order to the music in its cultural context, considering at every stage what constitutes this music and what the concept of music involves, particularly from the point of view of the creative performer.

Our first question then is, what is the nature of the sounds employed in African music? To the African, a musical sound does not consist only of what textbooks describe as "sounds with regular and periodic vibrations" (see, e.g., Culver, 1941:4–5), but any sound—whether regular or not; whether pure, compound in tone, or in the class of sounds referred to by Seashore as "the pitchless sound we call 'noise'" (1938:20)—any sound that can be produced by the human vocal apparatus or by some mechanical means. Thus the sound of a flute or rattle, the sound of an iron bell, the concussion of rocks, as in multiple rock gongs discovered by Fagg in Nigeria (Fagg, 1956), the clatter of sticks, the noise of seeds in the shell of a fruit, the sound of the stamping feet—all these provide potential sounds that may be utilized in music by the creative performer under specific circumstances. That is to say, the type of sounds that enter into the concept of music includes not only sounds with definite pitch but also those with indefinite pitch. It includes sounds that can be sustained, as well as those that cannot be sustained.

This concept of the musical sound has several repercussions—on the choice and design of sound-producing objects or instruments, on the texture of the music one may hear in Africa, on the processes and techniques by which musical sounds are generated into music, on the aesthetic evaluation of the music made out of them and on the organization or control of music-making in community life.

The broadness of the concept of the musical sound does not mean that all sounds that may be heard in an African society have the same value or that any sound is regarded as music or musical. On the contrary there is discrimination and evaluation. Different reactions are shown to what may be the same sound physically according to where and how it is used. There is a concept of "noise" as a psychological fact that would apply in the African sense as much to a broadcast of a Schoenbergian Concerto as to the sound of an automobile. This should not come as a surprise when we consider what Western critics have said about their own music, when we find that in 1853 a German critic described Wagner's *Tannhäuser* Overture as "shrill noise and broken crockery effects" (Miller, 1934:23).

If in Akan society someone scraped off mud on a bottle with the lid of a cigarette tin, he would produce noise as a by-product. If he performed this act of scraping in the performance of *ahyewa* music, the sound, though similar, would have a different meaning.

It would be purposeful in a musical sense. Further there would be a controlled method of scraping so as to produce an ordered sequence of the type characteristic of all other sound sequences and combinations regarded as music or manifestations of music. The musical sound is thus also a culturally defined concept. It is not only the sound in isolation that must be considered but also the sound in combination and in a given situation.

A further point that arises from the broadness of the concept of the musical sound in Africa concerns aesthetic evaluation. Musical sounds do not only have a functional value in structure and in situations: they also carry aesthetic ideals in the qualities that are selected or aimed at. This means that the whole gamut of possible sounds is not used without discrimination. Preference is shown for one quality of "pitchless" sound over another, for one type of material for making an instrument over another, for one type of design over another. There are "musical woods" suitable for constructing different instruments (see Tracey, 1949); there are techniques of sound production that sometimes take into consideration different qualities of tone, as for example in drumming (Nketia, 1958a). As Jones has shown, these qualities may form part of the formation of rhythm patterns (Jones, 1959).

Discrimination in sound qualities can be seen within single African cultures in the design and construction of instruments in the same family or species. For example, among the Akan there is a wide variety of drums differentiated both in their range of pitches and in their tone qualities, and these are employed in various musical combinations. Similarly aerophones (wind instruments) made out of the tusks of elephants are found side by side with instruments made out of bamboo or the bark of cane.

The Akan are by no means alone in this respect. Wherever particular musical instruments are used, there tends to be more than one variety. Accordingly when one takes Africa as a whole, one meets an enormous variety of musical instruments, each group or culture area specializing in a number of them. This is not often realized, although it is the one aspect of African music that has been well documented (e.g., Kirby, 1934; Maguet, 1958; Soderberg, 1956). It may be of interest, therefore, to give examples of these here in order that the range of sounds that enter into the definition of the concept of music may be evaluated.

All the four major classes of instruments set up by musicologists from studies of musical cultures are found in Africa: There are idiophones, membranophones, aerophones, and chordophones. In form many of them look simple, sometimes rough-and-ready, being made of very simple materials which nature supplies: wood, bush rope, horse hair, skins, ivory and animal horns, gut, gourds, clay or metal forged or cast by local craftsmen. However, as Kirby has pointed out, they should not be judged merely by how they look but by their music and the musical techniques which they call for. They may look "primitive only in form but not in function" (Kirby, 1932) for they reflect the same kind of acoustical principles that underlie the construction of similar instruments in the West.

Idiophones are undoubtedly the most common of these instruments. They are "instruments made of naturally sonorous materials not needing any additional tension as do strings or drums" (Sachs, 1940:455). There is a very wide variety of these (see, e.g., Wachsmann, 1954). They include stick beaters, clappers or percussion sticks, percussion beam: rattles of all description such as gourd rattles, wicker rattles, rattles made out of fruit shells, strung beads or cowries. There are also stamping tubes made out of bamboo or gourd tubes, metal beaters like iron bells, clangers and castanets, thumb or hand pianos and xylophones.

Membranophones (drums) form another important class of African musical instruments. It has been pointed out that there are some African peoples who do not use drums as well as others like the Watutsi among whom the drum is restricted to royalty (Merriam, 1953; 1957; 1959a; 1959b). In the light of our present knowledge, however, such groups appear to be in the minority.

As with idiophones a large variety of drums are found and are usually graded in pitch and tone quality. There are hourglass drums, kettledrums, open and closed bottle-shaped drums, cylindrical drums, goblet drums, pot drums, gourd drums, and frame drums. Each ethnic group uses one or more of these.

A number of drumming techniques are used so as to bring out the essential tone and rhythmic potentialities of each drum. There is a technique suitable for each drum, though some of them are played in more than one way according to where they are used. There is a stick technique which may be used; a hand and stick technique in which the hand may be used for muting or beating; a hand technique in which various parts of the hand or the fingers are used in a spread or cuplike formation according to the quality of tone desired, and a stick and armpit control technique used only for the hourglass drum.

The sounds of drums are interpreted in three different ways according to the type of drum and the mode of drumming employed. They may be interpreted as "signals"—call signals, warning signals, or as "speech" in which case words, phrases, and sentences would be attributed to them, or as music—that is, as sounds with definite implications of movement which may be articulated in the dance.

These uses of drum sounds sometimes overlap. There are some societies like the Akan, the Dagbani, and the Yoruba who sometimes use verse as the basis of musical rhythms. (See Nketia, 1958a, b, & c.)

In addition to drums a number of aerophones (wind instruments) are found. The use of the horns of large animals or the tusks of elephants as aerophones appears to occur in a number of places in Africa. The horns are specially treated, and sometimes decorated; they are commonly side-blown, and have a narrow range of tones.

In Akan society the sounds of horns have a linguistic and a musical use, and both usages may overlap in the same piece. That is to say, what is heard as music sometimes conveys a verbal message.

Trumpets made out of gourd or carved out of wood are also found in some parts of Africa.

Of wider distribution than the above are flutes and whistles. They may be carved out of solid wood or constructed out of bamboo, the bark of cane or reed and may be vertical or transverse. The pitch ranges vary. Some societies construct flutes of wide compass; others design them in sets of varying pitches which can be combined in different ensembles.

Lastly varieties of chorophones (stringed instruments) are found in various parts of Africa. There are lyres, plucked lutes and bowed lutes (such as the one-stringed fiddle of West Africa or the two-, three-, and four-stringed fiddles of the Congo), varieties of zithers (such as raft zithers, tube zithers, and musical bows) and harps. These instruments however are of comparatively narrower distribution than other instruments. They tend to be used as domestic instruments or instruments played for self-delectation. But there are some societies that use them for outdoor functions as well.

Of the sounds produced by the variety of musical instruments we have mentioned, those that are most easily made by anyone are percussive. The technical skills demanded by the others in execution tend to preclude them from the ordinary performer, while clapping the hands, stamping the feet, clicking the thumb and the forefinger provide ready extra-vocal sounds that may be used in any situation. Further, sound-producing instruments that can be readily improvised are the percussive type. One may resort to a packing case, a stool or chair or anything that comes handy in an improvisatory situation. Furthermore, there are a few activities that are in themselves sound-producing—grinding, pounding, threading, floor beating, paddling. It is worthy of note that some African socieites make these pleasant by providing songs that may be combined with the resultant sounds, thus turning the situations into musical events.

Studies of musical instruments also show a predilection to add buzzing idiophonic contrivances. Thus one sometimes meets drums with buzzing metal pendants. Such buzzers may be found attached to the neck of lutes. The resonators of xylophones are fitted with mirlitons which give the resultant sounds a nasal or buzzing quality. In some places the players themselves wear buzzers on their fingers. One also comes across resonators filled with pellets, or resonators to which chains are attached for the same purpose.

The dramatic character of a dance situation is in some societies heightened through the use of percussive devices worn by the dancers—such as ankle bells or a belt of cowry shells worn at the waist. There may be stamping. Sounds may be made by striking shields, for percussive sounds heighten the dance drama to which music performed by the musicians contributes.

In ritual situations, one comes across isolated use of percussion, particularly rattles and bells where special effects are desired; but in general, percussive sounds mingle with other sounds.

When we examine the type of instrumental combinations used by creative performers in Africa, again we find percussive sounds mingling with other sounds. The most common type of instrumental ensemble is the drum ensemble. Where other instruments are used, one finds a drum or drum ensemble being combined with them. Thus in some places a flute ensemble is accompanied by drums or idiophones.

Ensembles of xylophones are found and range from two to the large orchestral ensembles of the Chopi which may have as many as thirty instruments graded by pitch into five groups. Xylophones may also be combined with drums.

It is evident from these examples that while there is a large variety of sounds—the sounds of aerophones, chordophones, the sounds of idiophones of definite pitch such as xylophones, there is a general cultural focus on percussive sounds, which are used sometimes as primary sounds, sometimes as secondary sounds and sometimes as background sounds. This emphasis on percussion which shows itself even in performance techniques imparts to African music a textural quality that is at once complex in its composition and exciting in its appeal. An aspect of the art of African music consists in varying the complexity of this texture as well as its intensity through the preselection of instrumental devices and the structural mold into which the sounds are fitted. This variation, however, is largely confined to musical types rather than to individual items or to performance. That is to say, texture is an identifying characteristic of formal types. Hence the variety of instrumental sounds tends to be distributed in relation to the formal types that are recognized.

A corollary of this is that all the individual items that constitute a musical type share not only in a common textural form but also a common "emotional" or aesthetic character. Often the musical type as a whole is considered to be gay, lively, exciting, etc., and individuals show their preference for one type over another in this respect. In addition to this, individual items may carry additional implications through their internal structure or verbal content. Hence a gay and exciting musical type may include songs with joyful words or songs with sorrowful texts, reflective statements, and so on.

The selection of sound qualities does not stop with instruments. There are also aesthetic norms of vocal sound qualities that are pursued in varying degrees by members of each ethnic group who constitute in this respect a "community of taste."

Merriam has said that African singing is generally resonant and open in quality (Merriam, 1957; 1959a & b). However, one would find different degrees of openness as well as usages that emphasize somewhat tense vocal quality, such as one meets among the Frafra of Ghana. Similarly variant oral and nasal qualities or even of pulsation especially in Islamized areas will be found. Cultural norms also vary in the use of tessitura.

Differentiations in vocal timbres are sometimes found in the same culture and are used according to the requirements of particular forms of music. In Ashanti there is a peculiar voice quality used by court minstrels in singing about ancestor chiefs which is different from the quality of voice aimed at by the lute player and singer. Sometimes there is imitative singing or vocal characterization, for example in song interludes in folk tales. Wherever Ananse, the hero in Akan folk tales, sings, a pronounced nasality is used by the narrator.

An interesting example of imitative singing has been recorded by Rouget in Dahomey where vocal imitation of trumpets is used to commemorate a trumpet ruse used by King Abaka in one of his wars (Esoteric records, ES 259).

The phenomenon of voice-masking also occurs now and again in restricted contexts. The instances I know of in Ghana occur among children and are not considered regular ways of making music. An example, however, has been mentioned by Wachsmann as occurring in East Africa. At possession dances women hum a tune into the "kazoo," a simple membranophone (Wachsmann, 1957).

When one turns from single voices to two or more voices, again one finds variant usages both within single cultures and groups of cultures. There are African peoples like the Akan who tend to favor separate choruses for men and women. In mixed bands one would frequently find the singing performed largely by one group. Part singing is mainly in thirds and the incidence of octave parallels is small. On the other hand the Anglo (Ewe) of southeastern Ghana emphasize mixed choruses, and the incidence of octave parallels resulting from the pitch levels of men and women singing together is great. There are other African peoples among whom octave parallels separated by intermediate fourths or fifths constitute a regular scheme of chorus singing. (See Jones, 1959:216–22.)

The musical values implied in the foregoing are textural. The interval usages—the parallel structures—are a function of textural organization. There is, however, not enough data at present to show how textural patterns function formally and aesthetically in different African societies. In Akan society these patterns are to some extent part of the identifying characteristics of song types.

From the foregoing brief review of the sounds of African music, the following general observations may be stated or re-emphasized:

(1) African music makes use of a wide range of sounds of

definite and indefinite pitches, all of which are contextually distributed.

(2) The musical sound, however, is a culturally defined concept and aesthetic norms are applied in each culture in the selection of sounds.

(3) Taking Africa as a whole, there are broad aesthetic concepts of musical sounds which are traditionally applied and easily perceived in use.

(4) There is a general emphasis on percussion which adds to the complexity or intensity of musical textures. From the way such sounds are used and the responses they evoke in various situations, one may postulate the predominance of a dramatic concept of music. The silent moments of a ritual situation may be punctuated by momentary odd beats on a double bell. The exciting moments of a drama of possession may bring rattles into action. The animation of a dancing ring may be created and sustained by percussion. Dull as hand clapping or the beats of an iron bell may seem to those whose cultures treat percussion as "kitchen instruments," they have not only an organizational function in African music but also provide an added source of pleasure. For those accustomed to these in their music, their absence in the particular musical types with which they are identified would be felt as an impoverishment.

(5) The corollary of the above is that while aesthetic selection is made of sounds or of textures, it would seem that sound qualities or textural variations form part of structure and have no referential meaning. They form part of the identifying characteristics of musical types. Hence conscious exploitation by the individual performer of subtleties of variant tone qualities of which a selected instrument of a given timbre is capable does not appear to be a clearly defined artistic ideal in performance. Where they occur they are dictated by structural requirements or the situation, that is, by the drama of given moments rather than abstract symbolism.

III

We have considered the sounds of African music in isolation in order to draw attention to certain values that are implicit in their selection and range and in so doing provide part of the definition of music and what it involves from the African point of view. We shall now consider the structural processes in which these sounds are used and the implications they may have for our understanding of African music as a "style" or "idiom," and as an activity in social life.

Vocal and instrumental resources are used in building up pieces for performance by single individuals or groups. There are set songs, set pieces in all African societies which are used over and over again. That is to say, there is everywhere a repertoire which is used and enlarged by the addition of new pieces. Some of the items of a repertoire are abandoned or forgotten with the passage of time, but there is always a process of creation and re-creation in African music. Hence the creative performer is of particular importance in African societies. He is often not only a person with a command of repertoire but also someone who is able to make creative additions to repertoire or to individual pieces in the course of a performance.

From a structural point of view, therefore, music is always an event: it happens as the result of the activities of the creative performer and those with whom he collaborates. Hence the processes of creation and structuring are part of the concept of music. The creative performer must be guided by a knowledge of tradition, a knowledge of how to construct a phrase, how and where to add a second part, how to build up new material and place it against something that is already going on; how to increase the animation of the piece. A performer can always reproduce what he has learned, but always the best performers of African music are creative performers who can bring their own individual artistic contribution into what they are doing.

Basically the creative performer has a body of *usages* to guide him. He learns these through social experience in much the same way as craftsmen, storytellers, and others learn their skills. In vocal music he would be aware of the methods of "converting" texts or verse into music, of singing a verbal phrase instead of speaking it: that is to say, he would establish quite unconsciously a relationship between the rhythm and intonation of words.

Secondly he would be aware of phrasing, and his musical structuring would be guided by usages of pauses in speech which define breath groups, word groups within the phrase or the sentence.

His musical art will then consist in how he treats the verbal groups in relation to one another in terms of levels of pitch. It is here that the musical processes of melody construction are sharply differentiated from the intonation processes of speech. The internal tonal relationships of words in groups may be reproduced in the melody, but the junctional relationships between the groups may be different. There are various ways of modifying the internal relations, but the use of these will differentiate the artist from the ordinary run of performer.

The next set of considerations are purely musical ones. In respect of pitch variation, the performer would be guided by the interval usages of his tradition: that is, he would follow the usual patterns of melodic movement and how they operate in songs, moving in stepwise motion or in larger intervals according to the organic relationships demanded by the configurations he builds up within phrases and at the junction of phrases. An Akan singer, for example, would build up his phrases with intervals of seconds, thirds, and fourths according to certain procedures of melodic movement which need not be discussed here.

In addition to interval usages, the creative singer would of course be aware of starting points, phrase endings, and their relationship to phrase initials. He would be aware of the various ways in which songs or phrases end and how to arrive there.

All these can of course be stated in more objective terms. (See Merriam, 1959a & b.) What we know at present of the details of these processes in the music of various African peoples is too scanty to permit generalizations of a more specific character. That African peoples use diatonic scales—in pentatonic, hexatonic, and heptatonic forms—has been established, but we do not know enough about the internal relationships of the tones of melodies which make use of these. From the point of view of what the creative performer does, these internal relationships are far more important than theoretical abstractions of scales.

The next set of considerations concern the "flow" of the song. It must have a lilt, it must have a drive. These are imparted to it through the choice of tempo, through the absence or presence of a regulative pulse which the creative performer carries in his head and in terms of which he organizes the constituents of his phrases, through the choice of points at which to begin phrases in relation to this regulative pulse, where to pause, what orders of durational values to use, what phrase lengths to employ, and so on. Instructive examples of most of these aspects have been given by Jones (1959).

The regulative pulse is an important aspect of the African concept of rhythm. It is a subjective organizing element, which is sometimes externalized through movements of the body or some part of the limb, or sometimes through extra-musical noises which the performer makes quietly with his vocal apparatus at points in the music where the phrases start after the regulative pulse. It may also be externalized by implication in musical sounds which may accompany the song, such as hand clapping, beats of sticks, or an iron bell, etc. But this does not replace the subjective pulse: it sustains it; it helps the performer to keep his bearing or find it if he should lose it temporarily through concentration on some other feature of the piece. The individual performer who sings and claps or accompanies himself on some instrument follows a single regulative pulse. It is also a common point of reference for the musician and the dancer.

On the choice and use of song texts little need be said here. The importance of the texts of African songs as avenues of literary expression, social criticism, and commentary, etc., has been frequently emphasized and amply illustrated in writings on African music. (See Merriam, 1959a:51–53; Nketia, 1959:70.)

What has been said of the construction of songs can be repeated for other types of melodies, except that considerations of text may not be relevant. But this is not always so. The Akan flute solo is said to have a verbal basis, and there are even drum pieces that are similarly orientated.

Where an instrument is capable of a wide melodic compass, the creative performer will naturally produce phrases which are akin in shape to those of songs. In instruments of narrow compass—limited to two or three tones—the emphasis is invariably on using the tones as a frame for the formation of rhythm patterns.

In general the character of music performed by instrumental means tends to reflect very closely the capabilities and limitations of the instruments used. Obviously instruments without sustaining power cannot be assigned notes of long duration. The music that is suitable for them is one which minimizes their natural limitations by providing notes that can be played in fairly rapid succession. Hence the cultural emphasis on percussion results in music that is racy in character and precludes long-drawn-out notes except as marginal units.

Consider for example the music of African xylophones. All the transcriptions that have appeared show (a) fast tempo (b) succession of eighth and sixteenth notes in stepwise patterns, sometimes opposed to longer notes, and (c) repeated notes. This kind of structuring gives full scope to the capabilities of the instrument. (See Tracey, 1948, appendix.)

A look at drum scores again shows similar musical treatment. (See Jones, 1959, Vol. II.) The tempo is fast. Jones gives an average of seven seconds for eighth notes. Most scores show durational values of sixteenth, eighth, and quarter notes as the most predominant.

Plucked strings generate percussive sounds of decreasing intensity. Hence here also one finds the same kind of techniques being applied.

The general cultural emphasis on percussion and percussive effects tends to influence the structuring of the music of instruments with sustaining power. The incidence of long notes is greater in the music of bowed lutes and aerophones which I have heard, but the use of notes of short duration in rhythmic configurations is almost as important a feature of this music as it is in the music of strongly percussive instruments.

The relative importance of tone and rhythm in African music will be evident from the foregoing. Music proceeds by the introduction of new elements—a new tone, a fresh impulse, a new durational unit, or combinations of these. The rate at which changes take place, the extent and direction of such changes determine the character of a piece, a musical type, or even a style.

African music emphasizes rapid succession of durational values or changes in impulses and shows preference for this to rapid changes of tone. A piece of music with a narrow melodic range is felt to be dynamic and satisfying if it has a rhythmic drive. Hence in instruments of short compass tone mainly functions as a frame for organizing and modifying rhythm patterns, for heightening contrasts. In general a repeated tone would be of greater interest than one held for the same amount of time.

Because of the emphasis on dynamic rhythm, the organization of rhythm in African music is more complex than the organization of melody. Indeed, often rhythm provides the dynamic framework in which melody is organized. Various artistic considerations will be found operative. For example, where two or more lines of music are going on simultaneously, all the parts need not show the same degree of complexity. Indeed, they could be graded in complexity, and the rate at which each part introduces new patterns may be controlled. Some parts may be assigned invariable rhythm patterns while others change at varying rates from one pattern to another. Where complex parts are assigned to more than one part, generally they contrast and are made to move independently so as to bring out this contrast. In singing, voices may be combined simultaneously or in alternate sections. But when other sounds are added, these must run counter to the voice or voices in some particular way.

All these are structural processes which form part of the musical skills of creative performers. They function in individual pieces as well as in musical types. Ability in handling them enables the creative performer to create and re-create pieces in appropriate contexts.

In respect of structural processes, then, the following general observations may be noted:

(1) The resources of African music are used in different formal structures. There is a close relationship between type of sounds and design of pieces, e.g., in the music of percussive instruments.

(2) The structure of songs observes certain relationships between intonation and melodic processes. Deviations form part of the art of song construction.

(3) Melodic progression is governed by traditional interval usages in respect of sizes of intervals and their positional distribution.

(4) There is a general emphasis on *drive,* resulting in fast tempo as a norm, and emphasis on notes of short durational values.

(5) Rhythmic organization is more complex than tonal organization. Melody is organized within a rhythmic framework. The nature of this framework has been described variously as emphasizing "off-beat phrasing" "heterometer"—bars of irregular lengths or meters, etc.

(6) Rhythmic part structuring is conceived horizontally, often with different points of entry as well as different patterns. All the parts need not be complex. The use of a dominant unchanging pattern in one of the parts as a common point of reference is one of the important techniques of rhythmic part-structuring.

(7) Vocal parts—whether in parallel thirds, octaves, fourths, or fifths—may be sung simultaneously or structured differently according to how musical roles are distributed. When other sounds are added, it is generally expected that they should run counter to the voices.

(8) The above processes are used in individual songs and musical

types. Generally there is a repertoire, but the creative performer may add to it or re-create individual pieces to fit new situations or musical ideas that arise in the course of a performance.

IV

An important aspect of music in Africa is the interaction between musical structure and social use. Our examination of musical values would, therefore, be incomplete without a note on the contextual distribution of musical types or individual pieces.

The musical types that are maintained in African societies are used in well-defined situations in community life. They may be organized on the basis of occasions for which musical provision is considered necessary or desirable, such as formal occasions on which ceremonies are performed—festivals, ceremonies of the life cycle, occasions of worship. Musical provision may also be made for informal occasions —recreation, storytelling and some forms of manual labor.

Musical types or pieces may also be organized for performance on the basis of participants. These may be considered in terms of sex or age. There are specific songs for the young such as those incorporated into children's games—particularly counting or number games, language games, games involving dancing or movement. A few examples of these in Uganda have been given by Sempebwa (1948:20). There are also songs in children's stories and rites. A Dahomean child is taught a song that he sings on the loss of his first tooth (Herskovits, 1938:275) while the Ashanti of Ghana have a special song of insult for the habitual bed-wetter.

In most societies, the majority of musical types are intended for adults, though these may be subdivided by sex. There are maiden songs, dirges, grinding and other domestic songs sung by women as well as men's songs such as special communal labor songs, hunting songs, and warrior songs.

Sometimes kinship provides a basis of musical organization. There may be a class of songs used exclusively at kinship ceremonials such as one finds in Adangme society (Nketia, 1957a) or in the classification of funeral dirges of the Akan people of Ghana (Nketia, 1955).

In many African societies, music provides a basis of association. One comes across a number of musical associations or "popular bands" that specialize in one or more forms of recreational music and dancing. They perform when they feel like it and often provide entertainment for the whole community. Membership of such an association carries with it certain privileges, such as the right of full participation in music and extra-musical activities of the association, the right to have the band at the funeral of a relation or at one's own funeral.

The musical types in which popular bands of the associative type specialize tend to enjoy a short life and are then abandoned by enterprising people for a new type. In this way "popular" music is created and re-created all the time. New dances come in vogue and disappear all the time. This had been the tradition in Ghana.

The emergence of Highlife bands, jazz bands, and calypso bands in West Africa is in fact a continuation of this process of creating and re-creating new forms of popular entertainment and dancing, this process of forming restricted bands of musicians in given communities. A traditional popular band in Ashanti and other parts of Ghana can be hired for a funeral just as nowadays a Highlife band might be asked.

In addition to popular bands, one finds a number of other associations that are primarily nonmusical associations but which also have their distinctive forms of music. Among such associations are occupational associations like hunters' associations which are found in Ghana, and warrior organizations which form part of the traditional social or political structure. One finds also religious associations or cult groups with their forms of music.

The royal courts of Africa frequently also have special music provided for entertainment and for ceremonial functions.

That is briefly the pattern of musical organization one finds in Africa. Where there are no special musical associations, the village community itself may also function as a musical group and will be generally organized—through the distribution of musical roles and responsibilities which are assumed on occasions of performance. The creative performer may make music on his own. But it is usually as a member of a performing group that he contributes his special skills. Most African societies expect that there should not be a great gulf between leaders of music-making and other participants in a situation of performance. Nevertheless their talent, their skills, their special contribution are always recognized, appreciated, and sometimes rewarded.

A typical musical situation in community life would be one involving several individuals performing different musical roles. The structure of musical types is accordingly often keyed to the performing needs of the situation, and of the participants. Songs are arranged in the form of solo and chorus parts which allow for participation by everybody, while giving scope to creative performers for making their special contribution.

Pieces to be performed by a number of drummers have the outline of the parts laid out. But the master drummer is given the freedom to build up the sequences of the rhythmic themes provided in relation to other events in the situation, particularly the movements in the dancing ring.

One finds also consideration given in the organization of musical types to styles of dancing or dance routines as opposed to the serial actions performed by a dancer in the course of the same routine or a defined style. Thus in possession dancing among the Ga or Akan of Ghana, different drum pieces would be played, and each one would correspond to a particular style of dancing or a dance routine (Nketia, 1957b). As Tracey has shown (Tracey, 1948), the Ngodo dances of the Chopi are similarly organized in terms of a series of orchestral movements corresponding to various phases of the dance routine.

The picture one gets from a study of African music then is a series of interlocking relationships of sounds, structure, and situation, each carrying a number of values. These values together define the concept of music in African culture and what it involves. As well as being an art, African music is also a social fact, and people make music just as they fight and make love. But there is a cultural focus on it as a rallying point in community life and in the life of associations bound together by common beliefs and common values.

There are no cosmological connotations of music as far as we know. Neither is referential meaning based on *musical* symbolism a predominating factor in music-making. Yet African music carries a dispersal of meanings—aesthetic, emotional, dramatic, and social—which are conveyed at particular phases in the process of music-making.

African music is "controlled" music in the sense that there are norms of selection, structuring, and use which persist. Yet it is flexible in that it permits creation and re-creation, borrowing and adaptation (see Nketia, 1959). It encourages tradition and innovation. It is dynamic and adaptable to change. The contemporary scene in Africa today shows that in the processes of social change that are taking place, African music will not lag behind. Already new forms of music are being created in response to the demands of new institutions and new values.

31. The Kalabari Ekine Society: A Borderland of Religion and Art

One of the pillars of traditional Kalabari culture is the *Ekine* Men's Society, otherwise known as *Sekiapu*—"The Dancing People." But although many Kalabari talk of *Ekine* as "one of our highest things," it is an institution remarkably difficult to pin down and define.

On the face of it, *Ekine* serves many disparate ends. At a superficial glance, it appears as a religious institution, designed to solicit the help of the water spirits[1] through invocations and dramatic representations of them by masquerades. A second glance suggests that these masquerades are recreational as much as religious in their intent. Yet again, many of the masquerades seem to be important status-symbols. And finally, *Ekine* often appears as a significant organ of government. A day-to-day description of the society's activities in any one community would reveal these aspects as tightly woven or tangled together. In this paper, however, it will be our task not only to unravel them, but to attempt a distinction between those that are essential features of the institution, and those that are incidental.

ESSENTIAL VALUES OF *EKINE*

Perhaps our best point of entry to the complicated tangle of values realized in *Ekine* lies through the myths that recount the origins of the institution. For these supply not only a theory of how *Ekine* came into being, but also the Kalabari idea of what it was founded for.

The most elaborate of these myths tells how the dancing water

SOURCE: Robin Horton, "The Kalabari *Ekine* Society: A Borderland of Religion and Art," *Africa*, Vol. 33, No. 2, April 1963, pp. 94–114. Reprinted by permission of the author and publisher.

[1] For a sketch of Kalabari society and of the various categories of Kalabari gods, see my "Kalabari World-View: an Outline and Interpretation," *Africa*, July 1962.

spirits abducted *Ekineba,* a beautiful woman of a certain delta town, and took her to their home beneath the creeks. The mother of the water spirits was angry at what they had done, and commanded her children to take *Ekineba* back to the land of men. Before returning her, however, each water spirit showed her its special play; and when she returned to her home, she taught the people all the plays she had seen. The plays became very popular and were constantly performed. But the young men found it difficult to obey a certain rule which the water spirits had imposed on her—namely, that whenever her people put on one of her plays, she must always be the first to beat the drum. After they had disobeyed this rule three times, the water spirits lost patience and took *Ekineba* away for good. Since then, men have taken her as the patron goddess of the masquerade; and the *Ekine* Society which organizes its performance is named after her.

This myth and its variants give us a valuable lead.[2] In the first place, they stress that the various masquerade plays of *Ekine* are derived from the water spirits and in a sense represent them. Apart from anything else, then, the plays are seen as religious activities. Yet, at the same time, they are said to have caught on among men because they were enjoyable in themselves. And this suggests that Kalabari also see them as an art or recreation.

Let us first of all take a closer look at the religious aspect.

1. *Ekine* AS A RELIGIOUS CULT-GROUP

Every Kalabari community has its own *Ekine* society, independent of those of other communities. Each society stages a cycle of thirty

[2] The *Ekine* myths exemplify recurrent Kalabari patterns. Thus the most elaborate of them shows a new institution introduced by a goddess who is typical of the village heroes generally: a figure coming from outside the community, who lived with men and taught them, but who finally disappeared leaving no descendants when men failed to keep to the rules she had laid down. The theme of a woman introducing the plays and men taking them over also exemplifies a recurrent mythical pattern, in which men assume control of what women originate. The latter probably reflects a paradox of which Kalabari show themselves aware in a number of situations: that of a society whose most important assets—people—are brought into the world by women and are then taken over by men. This theme of the woman creator of the male institution seems widespread in West Africa. A striking example is recorded in B. Holas, *Les Masques Kono,* Paris, 1952. From the Kono assertion that women first discovered and danced masks, Holas infers that male-dominated Kono society was once matriarchal. An interpretation similar to the one I have just offered seems more in accord with known facts and probabilities.

to fifty masquerade plays—a cycle which in former times was probably completed in the drier part of every year. The commonest way of beginning the cycle is for *Ekine* members to go down in canoes to a spot far out in the creeks known as "Beach of the Water Spirits." Here they call in the spirits, telling them that their plays are about to begin and that they should come to attend them. The spirits are believed to return to the town with their invokers. This done, the *Ekine* members offer a dog to their patron goddess, with a prayer for the success of her plays. All is now ready for the masquerades to start.

Each masquerade play is associated with one or more water spirits; and the actual performance is preceded by invocations and offerings to these spirit "owners." During the play, which usually takes place on the following morning, the water spirits themselves are supposed to be "walking with" the dancers who represent them, and their close attendance often passes over into a state where people say that they have actually possessed their dancers. Possession, though quite an ordeal for the masquerader, is in fact encouraged, and is regarded as the seal of a successful performance.

When the last of the plays has been performed, a second set of rites winds up the cycle. The usual form of winding-up ceremony is called *owu aru sun*—"Stretching the Canoe of the Water People." Dancers representing every play perform together in a single morning, just before the ebb of the tide. At the ebb, all the maskers go down to a special beach known as the "Pouring-out Place of the Water Spirits," where they strip off their costumes and bathe. In so doing, they are believed to be dispatching the spirits back to their creeks.

In all this there is much that resembles the normal run of Kalabari rituals designed to solicit help from the gods. At a cursory glance, the preliminary invocations and offerings to masquerade spirits are not very different from those given to other spirits. And the masquerade itself looks like one more among the several forms of dramatic presentation that appear at the climax of typical Kalabari religious rites. On looking closer, however, we see some important differences of emphasis. Thus in the usual Kalabari ritual, both the invocations and offerings, and the dramatic presentations that follow them, are largely directed toward obtaining general benefits such as health, wealth, plentiful issue, and peace. In the masquerade rituals, on the other hand, this is not really so. True, the preliminary invocations often include requests for the usual benefits. But they are as much taken up with requests for the success of the masquerade perform- ance itself. Indeed, they contain a whole inventory of the things that make for a successful performance. They ask that the masker should be given nimble legs and light arms; that nothing should press heavily upon him; that his ears should be wide and clear to hear the drum; that it should seem as if he and the drummer had planned every step of the performance between them; that the drum should "enter the dancer's legs"; that the spirit of the masquerade should possess him. The place given to such requests is consistent with many other signs of concern for the masquerade as something valuable in itself. There is, for instance, the vigorous practice with which the dancers prepare for the actual performance—an element which is quite absent from other Kalabari rituals. And again, there are the offerings made to a variety of village gods before a major play, all with the sole aim of ensuring its success. Unlike other dramatic pres- entations, then, the masquerade is not a means of getting some- thing out of the gods: it is an end in itself.

The religious aspect of *Ekine* activities reveals further peculiarities when we come to ask what place the spirit "owners" of the mas- querades occupy in the total Kalabari world picture. For we find that these gods are hardly ever drawn from the ranks of the water spirits who control the community's surrounding creeks, and who therefore have to be taken into constant account in the struggle to keep alive. Rather, they are drawn from among the countless hosts of water spirits who are vaguely known to inhabit the creeks beyond the domains of the community. Such spirits, because they live beyond the normal range of communal activity, are hardly ever called upon to help cope with any of life's vicissitudes outside the context of the masquerade.[3]

Stranger still, some of the spirits involved are not only unim- portant in practical terms: they are actually dangerous. Thus the myths of masquerade spirits like *Egbelegbe* and *Agiri* tell how, be- fore these spirits were taken up by their present hosts, a succession of other communities had got rid of them after finding them danger- ous to their players and insatiable in their demand for human sacri- fices. Only the present hosts, so the myths go, were brave enough

[3] A solitary exception is *Ngbula,* whose characterization as the native doctor of the water people is consistent with the use of his costume to drive out evil spirits during a disease epidemic.

to ignore the dangers and persuasive enough to make these spirits accept animals rather than human beings as their food.

A final peculiarity appears in the fact that, although all the more important plays are associated with water spirits, there are some which are not. The well-known *Kirimani* play, for instance, represents mere animals who are in no way objects of a cult; and one or two other plays represent frankly fictitious figures.

In short, *Ekine* as a cult-group is principally devoted to marginal and even obnoxious gods whose only service to men lies in ensuring the success of the plays that represent them. The function of these gods, moreover, can be at least partially taken over by figures that are not gods at all. *Ekine* is certainly a religious institution; but it is an unusual one by Kalabari or any other standards. Its activities only make full sense when we remember the clue offered by the origin myths, which suggest that its ends are as much artistic as they are religious.

2. *Ekine* AS A SOCIETY OF ARTISTS

Since the masquerade performance itself seems to be the end to which most *Ekine* rituals are directed, it is time we looked at it in more detail.

(*a*) *Verbalized content of the masquerade.* The subject matter of the various plays, revealed in comments and accompanying songs, shows a considerable variety. Perhaps the commonest theme is that of the ferocious male warrior, laying about him with machete or spear, his violence set off by the plump, comely, slow-moving figure of his wife. This pair is portrayed by some of the most widely distributed masquerades such as *Agiri, Egbelegbe, Egbekoro,* and *Seki*. Then there is the dignified, opulent "house head" portrayed by masquerades like *Gbassa* and *Alagba*. Or the massive, stolid character portrayed by the maskers of *Otobo*—a water spirit who is thought of as part man, part hippopotamus, and who is addressed in song as "Beast who holds up even the flowing tide." By way of contrast, there is the cunning, amoral hypocrite portrayed by *Ikaki*—"Tortoise." Or the sexy, good-for-nothing aristocrat *Igbo,* of whom they sing: "His father sent him to market to buy yams; but instead he bought woman's vagina. O! *Igbo,* son of a chief! O! *Igbo,* son of a chief!" Or again, there is the native doctor *Ngbula,* grunting around with grim concentration in search of bad medicines and evil spirits:

suspicious like all of his profession that people are talking ill of him, and breaking off from time to time to make ferocious charges at his supposed detractors among the *Ekine* members. Female water spirits, too, sometimes take the central place in a masquerade. Notable among these is *Igoni;* a garrulous, self-pitying old widow who alternately bemoans her own and everyone else's troubles.

Another element of most masquerade performances is the *Egberi* or "Embellishment." This is a short tableau representing some episode in which the principal figure of the play becomes involved with other water spirits. Common themes of *Egberi* are domestic episodes, such as quarrels between husband and wife's brother over custody of wife and children, and quarrels between husband, wife, and lover. A common minor protagonist in these domestic scenes is *Kekobo*— "Testicle Man." *Kekobo* suffers from an enormous elephantiasis of the scrotum, usually conveyed by suspending a calabash between the dancer's legs. Elephantiasis is a complaint that is said to affect sorcerers and other wicked people; and *Kekobo* is an oft-recurring reminder of evil in the world, at once comic and slightly sinister. Other themes of *Egberi* include troubles in lineage or "house," which often feature sorcery duels between rival water men equipped with medicines in the form of leaf sprigs. Sometimes, too, we see the figure of a powerful city-state king, embroiled with a group of recalcitrant chiefs.

All in all, the themes of Kalabari masquerades cover a great diversity of social experience, ostensibly drawn from the world of the water spirits, but recognizably reflecting the life of Kalabari town and village. The masquerades take no particular stand on behalf of the accepted moral code. Nor, though Kalabari confess to enjoying some plays because "they bring hidden things to the town square" (this is a reaction to portrayals of such things as sexual intercourse and scrotal elephantiasis, which the spectators usually find highly comic), is the open portrayal of unmentionable things one of their major aims. It is simply that they are inspired by things as they are, and not by things as they ought to be. The whole of social experience is grist to their mill—both public happenings and things generally kept secret and concealed. Indeed, by adding together the contents of all the plays, one could build up a patchwork that covered most areas of Kalabari social life.

(*b*) *The drums and the dance.* Diverse as they are, however, the verbalized themes of the masquerade are never very elaborate. All that can be said about the characters portrayed in a particular play takes no more than a sentence or two. And the plots of the *Egberi* tableaux are sketchy in the extreme—especially if one compares them with the rich narrative which Kalabari weave about the water spirits in other contexts. There is, in fact, a good reason for this sketchiness and brevity. For the masquerade is not intended as the enactment of verbal narrative. Its dominant symbols are those of rhythmic gesture, dictated by the drum; and in so far as its verbal commentaries have a use, it is one of directing attention to the broad area in which the meaning of the dance gestures lies. Words here provide no more than a bare, crude outline of meaning, and it is left to the language of the dance to fill in the detail which makes the masquerade rich and satisfying to its audience.

If an *Ekine* member is asked how he recognizes a particular play, he does not start to talk about the character portrayed or about the plot of the *Egberi*. He starts by imitating the rhythm of its drums; and perhaps, if there are no women about, by dancing a few of its characteristic steps. By this, he is able to convey the distinctive features of the play: for every masquerade has its own characteristic set of drum-rhythms, beaten on a characteristic combination of drums.[4]

The first requisite of every masquerade dancer is that "he should hear the drum well." On the one hand, this means understanding the drum language and the instructions conveyed in it by the drummer.[5] On the other hand, it means an ability to translate the rhythm of the drums smoothly and faultlessly into the appropriate dance steps. In fact, since Kalabari can supply verbal meanings for many drum-rhythms, they make no hard-and-fast distinction between understanding drummed messages and translating rhythms into dance gestures; and they are apt to treat these two skills as indivisible. In several masquerades (*Alagba, Otobo,* and *Igbo* are examples), an explicit test of "hearing the drum" precedes the main body of the performance. For each dancer, the drummers beat the names of a score or so of the most important heroes and ancestors of the community; and as each name is called, the dancer must indi-

[4] In his article on Northern Ibo Masquerades (*JRAI,* Vol. xc, Pt. 1, 1960), J. S. Boston shows that in this culture-area, too, it is a distinctive set of rhythms which is definitive of a particular masquerade play.

[5] Spoken Kalabari is a three-tone language. Drummed Kalabari reduces the three tones to two by equating middle and low, then abstracts the resulting two-tone patterns from their context of verbal syllables.

cate correctly the direction of the owner's shrine. Every *Ekine* member must pass this test before entering the senior grade of the society. If he fails, he is expelled from the society altogether and can only rejoin after paying a fine of seven dogs to the patron goddess *Ekineba*. He may also be unmasked in front of the whole village—a disgrace which *Ekine* members maintain is enough to provoke suicide.

The value which *Ekine* sets on the dancer's attunement to the drum does much to explain why its members consider possession by the masquerade spirit to be the crowning achievement of the expert performer. In Kalabari thought, all symbols of the gods are instinct with their presence. Now the drum rhythms of each masquerade are symbols of its spirit "owner," and as such they too are vehicles of his presence. So, saying that the spirit "owner" has taken charge of the dancer's body is a natural way of describing the ideal state of attunement in which the drum rhythms seem to have taken over the man's movements from his conscious will and thought. That these are indeed two ways of describing the same experience is suggested by the reply of a gifted dancer whom I asked what it was like to become possessed during the dance. As he put it: "One plays until, as it were, the drum pushes one around."

There are, in fact, three major requisites of a good masquerade performance. First of all, an orchestra that can beat the drum rhythm not only correctly but in a way that "shakes a man's spirit." Secondly, a dancer good enough to translate the drum rhythms smoothly into the gestures of the dance. And thirdly, the correct performance of preliminary offerings and invocations. These last are crucial. For though a dancer must have talent before he can be possessed, it is only these preliminary rites that can induce the spirit "owner" to crown the performance by descending on him.

For Kalabari, then, the water spirits are not just beings represented by the masquerade. They themselves are part of the raw material which has to be coaxed into playing its part in the total work of art, just as any recalcitrant block of wood has to be coaxed by a sculptor. And now, I think, one can understand the cult of some of the masquerade spirits like *Agiri* and *Egbelegbe,* whose presence seemed so puzzling earlier on. For, dangerous and unbeneficial as they are, possession by them gives rise to some of the most spectacular of all performances. And in the risks which *Ekine* members take by putting on their plays, we can see the artist rising to the challenge of a highly difficult yet highly rewarding medium.

(*c*) *Costumes and headpieces.* The base of the masquerade costume is a skin-tight white tunic, covering the hands but leaving the feet free, into which the dancer is sewn. Strapped on over this is, first of all, a narrow cone made of palm midrib sections, which projects horizontally backward from the buttocks and forms the masker's tail. Then, in front, a large stomach pad is strapped on to form another protruding organ known as *Igoli*. These two projections give the masker the characteristic body shape of a water spirit. In many masquerades, too, a circlet of locust beans (*Igbiri*) is tied round each ankle: these circlets sound in time with the dancer's steps and supplement the rhythm of the drums.

The upper part of the costume is sewn on to the underside of the masquerade headpiece, and it drapes down over the dancer's torso when the headpiece is set in its place. So far as costume is concerned, there are certain cloths and accouterments that generally go with particular masquerades, but there is a good deal of variability. The more definitive part of the dancer's material equipment is the headpiece—*owu sibi*. Each play has one or more headpieces that are always distinctive. Some, like those of the *Gbassa* and *Alagba* plays, are made from cloth and tassels sewn on to large conical frames made of palm-midrib sections. More often, however, the headpiece includes a wooden, sculpted "mask." The headpiece is regarded as the seat of the masquerade's spirit "owner"; and to it are directed the various invocations and offerings which precede the play proper.

Where the headpiece includes a wooden mask, the latter is regarded as something distinct from the rest of the dancer's costume. It is said to be the "name" of the masquerade, while everything else is just "decoration." Some say that it is because of the mask's presence that the dancer becomes possessed by the play's spirit owner; and they maintain that possession is most likely in those plays whose dress includes it. This view of the sculpted mask, as something whose function is first and foremost to establish the presence of a spirit rather than to impress spectators, explains a good deal that is otherwise puzzling about its use. Thus its commonest position is atop the dancer's head, with its principal features facing the sky and visible to spectators only when the man bends. Sometimes this concealment is increased when the mask is set in a great horizontal ruff of cloth and tassels sewn on the frame. And in yet other cases, it is entirely enclosed in "decoration," and so totally invisible from any angle. Thus, in the *Egbekoro* masquerade, it is enclosed in a wrap of animal fur; and in one version of the *Otobo* masquerade, it is buried in an enormous stand of palm fronds.

This is not to say that the sculpted mask is never visible to the spectator. Thus in the *Ngbula* play, part of the character of the native doctor is his ugliness, which helps him in driving away evil spirits; and this ugliness is incorporated into the dance spectacle through the mask, which stands upright and visible on the dancer's head. Again, in the *Seki* and *Daraminaye* plays which represent water people believed to be half man, half crocodile, the long animal jaw of the mask is eminently visible; and by its striking extension of the human form it makes possible a new range of dance gestures.

But even where the sculpted mask does form part of the dance spectacle, it is never singled out for the sort of criticism and approval that greets the dance itself. To a lesser extent, this is true of both headpiece and costume generally. An exception, perhaps, is provided by those plays which portray opulent and chiefly figures: for in these a degree of flamboyance in cloths and ornaments is an appropriate mark of the sort of characters being represented, and this provides an excuse for all manner of conspicuous display on the part of the dancers. However, these flamboyantly dressed masquerades seem somehow contrary to the spirit of the institution; for I have heard *Ekine* members contrasting them almost scornfully, as "dressing-up masquerades," with "real, strong, playing masquerades" like *Ngbula, Seki,* and *Igbo*—all of which involve difficult and exhausting dance sequences and a minimum of showy costume. This brings us back to the point that the real core of the masquerade lies in the dance, and that by and large other elements are only considered important in so far as they contribute to it.

As a complex and sophisticated art, the masquerade is sustained by long training and careful organization. Almost as soon as they can walk male children are encouraged to imitate the masquerade performances of their elders, and their fathers or other male relatives often help them. At the age of fifteen or so, the boys pay a small sum to join *Kala Siri*—a junior replica of the *Ekine* society which operates in intervals between masquerade cycles proper.[6] *Kala Siri*

[6] From here until the end of this paper, I shall use a comprehensive "ethnographic present" to cover cultural patterns which are still fully extant in some communities, but which elsewhere live on only in the older man's

organizes replicas of many of the plays performed by *Ekine* itself; but it omits the plays of those strong and dangerous spirits who might retaliate violently for any mistakes made; and it does not court the presence of the masquerade spirits by preliminary offerings and invocations. *Kala Siri* is supervised by the "Drum Master" of *Ekine,* whose services are rewarded by gifts.

The members of *Ekine* proper keep a look-out for promising youngsters in the *Kala Siri* plays. Any *Ekine* member may sponsor such a youngster for entry into the society; and having paid a small sum in cash or trade gin, the latter becomes a member of its junior grade—*Iwo Sekiapu,* or "New Dancers." He stays in this grade until the end of the first cycle of plays in which he has successfully danced a masquerade involving the shrine-pointing test. Then he joins the senior grade—*Elem Sekiapu* or "Old Dancers." After this he may also pay some small sums of money to join a number of clubs within the senior grade, each of which holds the right to play a

---

memories of his youth. Since the present paper aims to give a picture of the position of *Ekine* in the traditional culture which will be valid for the majority of Kalabari communities, this usage seems preferable to a long and tiresome string of qualifications.

In fact, there are a number of modern changes, bearing upon different communities with variable force, which have brought varying degrees of disruption to *Ekine* activities. Thus there is a switch from a pattern of productive activity based on the village itself, to a pattern involving shifting residence in a variety of fishing camps often twenty mules or more from home; and where this switch has been most marked, people spend the greater part of the years away from the village. This makes the organization of frequent masquerades almost impossible; for each demands the presence of a goodly proportion of *Ekine* members, and it is extremely difficult to get such a quorum into the community at any one time. Another factor has been the avoidance of overt participation in traditional religious practices, which has become a powerful status symbol in certain communities. Where large numbers of mission-educated people have plowed back the fruits of their education into the traditional status system, power and influence have become associated with churchgoing, and hence with overt rejection of the old religion. This has had its most marked effect in the three offshoots of the New Calabar city-state. In these towns, many of the chiefs and other influential people are mission-educated and retired from jobs in commercial firms or government service. Although many of them privately subscribe to traditional religious beliefs and methods of dealing with misfortune, and many are enthusiastic spectators of the masquerade, few care to participate actively in *Ekine*. Fortunately, I was able to check the very full accounts given by older men in these New Calabar communities with firsthand observation in remoter villages like Soku, where these modern changes have not impinged with such force, and where the traditional patterns of *Ekine* activity appear to be largely intact.

particular masquerade and to teach it. The plays so vested in clubs are usually among those considered to be the most difficult and most demanding of specialist knowledge: thus they include *Igbo,* said to be the most taxing of all masquerades.

Each grade of *Ekine* has its head man—*Edi*—who is elected from among the senior-grade members of the society. Both senior and junior *Edi* offices are usually held by experienced dancers and their main duties are those of organizing plays. The other two standard offices in *Ekine* are those of *Ekine Alabo*—"Priest of *Ekine,*" and *Akwa Alabo*—"Drum Master." *Ekine Alabo* performs the invocations and offerings to the patron goddess *Ekine Ba,* and his office is generally assigned to an elderly member of the society with a long dancing career behind him. *Akwa Alabo* is the principal drummer of the society, and is the most talented drummer available in the community at the time of his predecessor's death.

It is notable that the criteria for entry to the various grades and offices of *Ekine* are all connected with skill in some aspect of the masquerade performance. They do not involve the considerations of wealth, pedigree, and political influence which govern advancement in Kalabari society at large. *Ekine* members themselves often stress this. Thus they say: "In *Ekine,* everyone is equal to everyone else. Whatever people say on the path outside, it is not our business who owns whom, or whose father is greater than whose. We are here for laughing, drinking, and for the play." There is, moreover, a feeling that these values have to be defended against the very different ones that prevail outside—a feeling which is crystallized in the society's attitude toward the dead. Thus every *Ekine* member is ritually expelled from the society when he dies, so that no dead person is ever a member. And any invocation of one's ancestors is strictly forbidden within the society's house. These rules are often explained as designed simply to prevent the dead from "worrying" the living *Ekine* members when anything annoyed them. But a deeper and more perceptive explanation was given by the senior *Edi* of the Buguma[7] *Ekine,* who said: "If people started pouring wine to the dead in the *Ekine* House, they would start to remember their forefathers; and from there, who-is-bigger-than-whom case would come out." Underpinning as they do the whole ideology of lineage and kinship, the dead encourage all that competition for status and influence which relies on lineage and kin support, and all

---

[7] The largest of the three offshoots of the New Calabar city-state.

the invidious comparison based on the length and eminence of a man's Kalabari pedigree. Hence, by excluding any relations with the dead from its activities, *Ekine* stresses that such competition and comparison must be kept outside its confines.

Masquerading itself, of course, is a potential source of invidious comparisons between *Ekine* members. But here again, the organization of the plays does everything possible to eliminate it. Thus no matter what the play or who the player, the society's rules compel all members to turn out for the wake which is held on the night before the actual performance, and to join in the songs praising its water spirit "owner." On the day of the performance, all except the oldest and most decrepit members of the society must turn out to escort the actual masqueraders; and by giving of their utmost in dancing, capering, chasing off spectators who encroach on the arena, and emitting the hoarse, spirit-shaking cheers peculiar to *Ekine,* they must help to "make the play strong." The good *Edi* is the one who continually brings it home to those under him that each play is the collective concern of the entire *Ekine*—both those masquerading and those not. He is the one who continually reminds people that the play's success or failure affects not only the reputation of the masker, but that of *Ekine* as a whole. His job, in short, is to ensure that every member of the society identifies himself with whoever is actually dancing any play.

Not only, then, are the rules of behavior laid down in *Ekine* designed to exclude most of the preoccupations which reign beyond its confines: they are also designed to ensure that, in their concern for the masquerade, *Ekine* members react to the play and not to the player.

This difference between the values that dominate *Ekine* and those that dominate the society at large means that those people who are important within the society will often be different from those who are important outside. In the city-state of New Calabar, the prototype of the great *Ekine* member is *Jiji,* a famous character of olden times of whom it is said that, when he got too old to dance on his own feet, he had himself carried around the dancing arena, fully clothed, on the back of a young man. *Jiji* is described as an aristocrat of long pedigree, but not as a chief or as a man of any political importance. He is depicted as carefree, always engaged in sexual adventures; living for laughs, drinks, and above all for the masquerade. Though his character has probably been exaggerated through the years, prominent *Ekine* members of today do not entirely belie his image.

It is quite usual to find that the principal offices of *Ekine* are held neither by the head of the town or village, nor by anyone else prominent in its government or its politics. Indeed, they are often held by people who are "cool," who "like to laugh and play," and who do not "look for cases"—by people, that is, who are in many ways the antithesis of the aggressive, thrusting politician. The same is often true of the core of dancing enthusiasts who give the society its real vitality.

But this does not mean that no one who is prominent in the village at large plays a significant part in *Ekine* activities. On the contrary: in Kalabari judgment, every grown man ought to be able to perform some masquerade of his choice with reasonable skill and enjoyment. And someone who is neither interested nor able is likely to be distrusted. In the olden days, indeed, he might well have been suspected of sorcery. There is a certain logic in this distrust; for a person who is unable to stand back from life and portray it in the masquerade may well be so totally committed to the struggle to be one up on his fellows as to pursue it by forbidden means—perhaps even by using lethal medicine. Hence every man who aspires to some standing in the community must cultivate his taste for the masquerade in order to make himself a completely acceptable person. (One hears here an echo of the English cultivation of a sense of humor, and the distrust of its absence. Is it just my imagination, or do the more ruthless circles of our society—like Big Business or academics—lay greater emphasis on this accomplishment than anyone else?)

3. RELIGION AS THE SERVANT OF ART

At this stage of the analysis, one might still ask the question: Why, if the masquerade is first and foremost an art, and a highly developed one at that, should it have remained so closely associated with religion?

Here, I think, one should pause to ask the further question: What exactly is involved in our reacting to some human performance as a work of art? Briefly, two main factors seem to be involved. First of all, we must be able to cut off our practical, workaday reaction to the subject matter of the performance, and exchange this reaction for an attitude of contemplation. To take the crude but effective example of a film about sex and violence, we must be able to suspend the workaday reactions of excitement or disgust that the subject matter would normally inspire in us, and look at it with an eye that is engaged yet somehow aloof. If we cannot achieve this, we are unable to approach the film as a work of art. And if nobody can, we may well say that the film is not art at all, but mere pornography.

A second vital condition is that in approaching the performance, we should be able to suspend our personal reactions toward the actor, and concentrate upon the part he plays. In so far as we respond to the actor as the individual we know in the world outside, we have not succeeded in treating his performance as art. Most Englishmen encounter this sort of failure as children, watching school plays in which they know all the actors intimately. On such occasions their personal reactions to the performers sometimes interfere so much that they are unable to appreciate the play.[8]

In modern Western theater and ballet, these vital requirements can usually be met without too much difficulty. In the first place the complexity of modern industrial society ensures that the theme of any play or ballet is often such that the majority of the audience have had no firsthand experience of any situation exactly similar. Hence the problem of cutting off workaday reactions to the theme of the performance is not acute. Secondly, the actors in modern theater or ballet are not personally known to the majority of their audience. Hence the problem of suspending all personal reactions to them does not arise.

In the type of small-scale, homogeneous society exemplified by a

[8] This line of approach is derived from ideas put forward in Edward Bullough's famous essay " 'Psychical Distance' as a Factor in Art and an Aesthetic Principle," *British Journal of Psychology*, 1912, Vol. v, No. 2), and from the application of these ideas to Greek religion made by Jane Harrison in her *Ancient Art and Ritual* (Oxford, 1948). This little book seems neglected by anthropologists, probably because it champions the discredited myth-from-ritual theory of religion. But the use which it makes of the concept of "Psychical Distance," chiefly to account for the origins of Greek dramatic art, is independent of this mistaken theory and so merits attention for its own sake. The ancient Greek situation as analyzed by Harrison seems analogous to the one we are dealing with here. Thus she sees Greek drama arising as an art in religious rites representing the ancient heroes: because these figures were losing their religious importance at the time, they could elicit contemplation rather than practical reaction. A point of contrast, of course, is that the Kalabari dancing water spirits are not part of a decaying religious system: on the contrary, they are part of a very live system, of which, however, they happen to be marginal members.

Kalabari town or village, the problem of meeting these requirements is much more serious. In the first place, the greater uniformity of social experience means that the audience will have had firsthand exposure to the subject matter of almost any dramatic performance. In their case, the subject matter is always near the bone. Secondly, the performers are always personally known to most of their audience, so the latter are confronted with all the difficulties that face the spectator of the school play.

Now it is in this situation that the religious context of the masquerade would seem to have been crucial to its growth and survival as an art. First of all, by developing the themes of the masquerade around the figures of water spirits, Kalabari have been able to disentangle them from particular human beings whom everyone knows. Thus the figure of the water sorcerer disentangles the act of sorcery from its association with particular people whom everybody has to deal with. And the quarrel between the water-spirit husband and his father-in-law disentangles the strains of marriage from their association with the quarrelsome in-laws who provide the community with some of its current social problems. In this way the water spirits lift the subject matter of the masquerade out of those contexts in which it evokes regular practical reactions. As gods, of course, one might expect them to evoke the practical reactions appropriate to beings whose help is crucial in the control of the everyday world. But precisely because they are gods who have very little practical importance, they do not evoke any such reactions. As for the animal figures which crop up from time to time among the water-spirit protagonists of the masquerade plays, their function seems much the same. Thus, on the one hand, they disentangle the themes of the plays from the human contexts in which they evoke practical reactions; and on the other hand, as creatures who occupy a rather marginal position in the field of human endeavor, they elicit no strong practical reactions on their own account. So it is that the water spirits, and to a lesser extent various animals, make it possible for the masquerade to satisfy the first of our two conditions.

Now, too, one can understand an otherwise curious inconsistency in the way Kalabari talk and think about their masquerades. Particular plays, as we have seen, are treated as portraying attributes of their water spirit "owners" or episodes in their lives. To take one example, the character of the grunting, suspicious native doctor portrayed in the *Ngbula* play is that of the water spirit *Ngbula* himself; and the ugliness of the sculpted mask which crowns the dancer's head is also the ugliness of *Ngbula* himself. Yet the origin myths of the masquerades, which you may recall from the beginning of this paper, imply something rather different. For by presenting the masquerades first and foremost as plays, originally performed by the water spirits and then taken over by men, they imply that the content no more portrays the characters of the original spirit players than it portrays those of the present-day human players. This inconsistency, I think, is a response to the inherent paradox of the masquerade performance itself. Thus the masquerade hangs its themes on the figures of gods who form part of Kalabari reality; but it is by making the claim to be representing this particular area of reality that it helps its audience to treat its content not as part of real life but as art or "play." By saying in one breath that the masquerades portray water spirits, and in another that they are merely plays once performed by water spirits, Kalabari leave the two terms of the paradox unreconciled. But if they were reconciled, the masquerade might lose its impact as an art.

As we have seen, the second of our two conditions poses an equally serious problem in the Kalabari community. And here again, the religious context of the masquerade seems crucial. Thus, because their actors are enveloped in water-spirit disguise, Kalabari are able to get round the problem posed by the audience's personal acquaintance with the performers: for the disguise makes it relatively easy to suspend one's reactions to the player and transfer them to the play.

It is now that many of the prohibitions which the *Ekine* society imposes on women begin to make sense. Anthropologists have often treated West African masquerades as a male device for dominating women. By making women think that they are spirits, so the story goes, the masqueraders are able to impose their will and inflict punishment on a hapless weaker sex. However far this may be true in other areas,[9] it is certainly far from the case here. First of all, it is apparent that women are not in any way victims of these performances. Far from it, indeed. For women are the principal spectators of the masquerade; and one of the implicit principles of the latter's performance is that spectators must never be injured or

---

[9] That it is not true among the Yoruba is suggested by Ulli Beier's article "Gelede Masks," *Odù*, No. 6, June 1958; and for the Northern Ibo the same thing is suggested by J. S. Boston, op. cit., p. 56.

seriously chased. It is those men who actively participate in the performance, either as maskers or as an attendant *corps de ballet,* who run the risk of injury during one of the more violent plays.

Nor is it true that the real nature of the masquerade is intentionally kept secret from women, in order that they should feel terror for objects they suppose to be spirits. Both men and women know the myths of origin of the masquerade plays, and no one tries to keep them a secret reserved for men. Women, moreover, are allowed to see the disembodied headpieces of masquerades when these have been painted or sewn, and are set up in their shrines on the eve of a performance; and on such occasions they even queue up with men to make small personal offerings of coins to the water spirits involved. Yet again, the masquerade costume does not entirely conceal the human player beneath, since it leaves the feet quite naked for any woman to see. And, when a novice fails the shrine-pointing test which we mentioned earlier, it is considered quite appropriate to demask him in front of all the women in the community.

Women, then, are not forbidden the knowledge that masquerade dancers are human. What they are forbidden is to see, hear of, or suggest any connection between a masquerade and a particular player. Thus they must not see men in the process of putting on their masquerade costumes. They must not greet any masquerade by the name of its performer; nor must any man so greet a masquerade in their presence. They must not talk of any man as the performer of a particular masquerade; nor must they hear such talk from men. They must not abuse an *Ekine* member with the words: "You animal"; for animals, too, are among the protagonists of the masquerade plays.

The common feature of these various prohibitions is that, by concealing the identity of the individual player, they damp down the tendency to react personally to him rather than aesthetically to the play. In this, they serve to uphold the vital part played by the masquerade costume. The inconsistency offered by the demasking of the incompetent novice is more apparent than real: for while it is appropriate that during a properly conducted masquerade all reactions should be diverted from player to play, it is equally appropriate that any gross failure should be held against the player and not against the play.

It is because they are ordained, not as victims of the masquerade, but as its eternal spectators, that women are singled out by these prohibitions. For men, all of whom are potentially involved in its performance or behind-the-scenes organization, such prohibitions would defeat their own ends. For men, it is the code of behavior enjoined within *Ekine* that concentrates their attention on the play rather than the player.

In summing up the relation of religion to art in the Kalabari masquerade, it is important to avoid giving the impression that the one has been deliberately pressed into the service of the other. What does seem true is that religion has provided a prop without which the masquerade could never have grown into the major art that it is.

VALUES REALIZED INCIDENTALLY THROUGH *EKINE*

Because the masquerade is not a restricted, specialist skill for whose performance the rest of the community pays, but an accomplishment which every normal man is expected to cultivate as part of his equipment for living, the values of *Ekine* can never be perfectly segregated from those that hold sway beyond its confines. On the contrary, as we shall see in what follows, the influence of these other values seeps insidiously into many aspects of *Ekine* activity.

1. THE MASQUERADE, THE INDIVIDUAL, AND THE LINEAGE

It is common for the enthusiastic *Ekine* member to specialize in the performance of a particular play, and to practice this play with especial fervor. The play chosen may be one already established in the village. More rarely, it may be one that the would-be performer has brought in from another community after making the customary payment to the latter's *Ekine* members. Just very occasionally, it seems, the play may be one which the individual introduces after some sort of visionary guidance from the water spirits.

Now although the conjunction of a particular masquerade with a particular dancer must not be formally acknowledged or revealed in front of women, the latter as well as their menfolk do come to possess a good deal of tacit knowledge about the specialist performers of various plays. In their approval of the performance, reaction to the player often creeps in alongside reaction to the play.

Approval is expressed by throwing coins to the masker which are collected by his escorts; and *Ekine* members admit that the women, who are most vigorous in this, often know whom they are throwing to. They say that such gifts are frequently tokens of willingness to start a love affair as well as of appreciation of the performance. The masquerade, then, plays an important part in male rivalry for women.

The performance of the masquerade in which he specializes may also provide an individual with the opportunity to indulge in the conspicuous display and expenditure of wealth which are an integral part of Kalabari status-rivalry. This applies especially where the play concerned is one of the "dressing-up" masquerades which demands a certain luxuriance of costume. In such a play there is much that a man can do to emphasize his own prosperity by the incorporation of costly old cloths and trinkets. These potlatch elements are most pronounced in the New Calabar city-state, where a house head who introduces a new masquerade may lay on an enormous wake-feast for his fellow *Ekine* members, provide the women of his house with costly clothes for their parade round the dancing arena to sing the praises of the water spirit "owner" of the play, and dress the costume itself with corals, silks, and gold braids.

Over and above these various ways in which the masquerade can be used to enhance individual status, there is something which is perhaps of even deeper significance. The organization of Kalabari society provides few alternative avenues for gaining status. A person becomes somebody of account by developing a generalized influence over others—first of all in limited contexts like that of his age-set and his lineage, then later in the community at large. Because this is the one major way of achieving status, judgments of a person's worth tend to be of an absolute and uncompromising type. Either he is "a man," or he is not. In this taxing situation, the particular masquerade which a person has chosen to adopt assumes a specially weighty significance. Skill in its performance is not just something which compensates to some extent for lack of political influence in the community—though it may do so. It is something much more. For the various masquerades played by any *Ekine* society are by and large incommensurable with one another: they are just different. Hence, by deciding to specialize in a particular masquerade, a man both makes a free choice and at the same time involves himself in an activity which is not fully comparable with the activities of others.

This element of non-comparability looms very large where, in other things, the individual's sense of worth is almost totally vulnerable to a relentless measure based on his influence or lack of it. In such circumstances, the adoption of a special masquerade becomes almost a guarantee of the individual's sense of secure identity.

Only in this context, I think, can one understand the great feeling with which men reminisce among themselves about the plays in which they have chosen to specialize. Only now, too, can one understand why, in many villages, one of the most important and deeply felt parts of a man's funeral rites is when *Ekine* members, at the request of his relatives, stage his special play.[10] So closely is the masquerade associated with the sense of individual identity that in the city-state of New Calabar, where large and elaborate ancestor memorials are made to represent dead house heads, it is the miniature replica of the headpiece of a man's special play that is used to differentiate his memorial figure from those of others. The human-body motif in all such figures is a completely standardized one which shows no attempt at portraiture; and the headpiece replica which surmounts it is the one portion which conveys the reference to an individual.

Where a man has purchased a play from another community, where he has produced something entirely new as a result of visionary inspiration, or where he has merely become the outstanding dancer of a mask in an established play, his heirs[11] acquire an exclusive right to provide the dancers for future performances—though of course only those who are *Ekine* members can make use of the right. This seems to be the reason for the great variation in dancing rights which one finds associated with the plays of any particular *Ekine* society. Thus, where a whole play has been purchased by an individual from elsewhere, rights to perform all its masks pass to the purchaser's heirs. On the other hand, where a man has been an outstanding dancer of one mask in a play consisting of several, rights in this particular mask become the property of his

[10] Since it is performed out of its turn in the masquerade cycle, the funeral play is not accompanied by the usual preliminary invocations and offerings.
[11] For the descent-system of Kalabari, see the outline at the beginning of my "Kalabari World-View," *Africa*, July 1962. Suffice it to remember here that where the deceased's wife or wives were married with small bridewealth, property rights pass matrilineally—first to his full brothers and thence to his full sisters' sons. Where there was a large-bridewealth marriage, property rights pass to the deceased's own male children.

heirs, while rights in the other masks of the play remain communal. Hence we find a continuum ranging from plays whose dancing rights are wholly vested in a particular lineage group, through plays with some rights restricted and some communal, to plays in which all the rights are communal.

In the performance of these restricted masquerades, there is an important element of reverence for the dead. Where there are permanent sculpted headpieces for them, these are kept in the ancestor shrines of the lineage groups who have a right to provide their dancers. And in the preliminary offerings and invocations which take place on the eve of a performance, prayers addressed to the ancestor first associated with the play mingle with those addressed to its water spirit "owner." These prayers ask the ancestor to help make the plays a success, and they remind him that "Your child is taking out your play today, so that your name shall not disappear." In other words, a man's special masquerade is not only a symbol of his individuality in this life: it is also a means toward his posthumous survival in the community that gave him birth. Since Kalabari think of the after life in terms of continuing relations between the dead and the living, this is something of importance to everyone.[12]

In so far as the performance of a restricted masquerade is an act of reverence for a dead man on the part of his descendants, it is also an assertion by them of the collective status which they derive from him. As such, it is apt to include the sort of potlatch elements which sometimes characterize the special plays of individuals. Here again, such elements are most marked in the trading state of New Calabar, especially when a house brings out the play introduced by its founder. The dresses of the house women parading to sing the praises of the water spirit "owner," the lavish food and drink distributed to *Ekine* members during the wake, and the finery of the maskers themselves —all these assert the prowess of the house in a powerfully conspicuous display of wealth and generosity.

In its association with the status of individual and lineage, we see the masquerade being used to realize values basically opposed to

[12] This aspect of the Kalabari masquerade shows interesting parallels with the Yoruba *Egungun* masquerade as described by P. Morton-Williams in "Yoruba Responses to the Fear of Death," *Africa,* January 1960. *Egungun,* however, is first and foremost symbolic of the dead, whereas the Kalabari masquerade is only incidentally so.

those which are implied by the formal doctrines, rules, and organization of *Ekine*. Thus, while all the rules of *Ekine* are directed toward ensuring that people react to the play and not to the player, the dancer himself, without actually violating any of these rules, is able to slip between them in various ways so as to use the masquerade for the enhancement of his individuality. The result is the curious paradox of the masquerade headpiece, which for *Ekine* is a means of effacing individual identity, but whose miniature replica on a memorial figure actually symbolizes such identity. Again, while the rules of *Ekine* exclude from its confines both the dead and the lineage ideology which they sanction, a lineage group which has an exclusive right to provide the dancers for a masquerade can slip between these rules in such a way as to make the play serve as both a remembrance of its founding ancestor and an assertion of its collective prowess. Here too the result is a spectacular paradox—that of ancestral libations, forbidden within the *Ekine* meetinghouse, but poured elsewhere to ensure the success of the very masquerades which *Ekine* exists to promote.

In the masquerade, then, the aesthetic values promoted by *Ekine* are constantly struggling with other values which dominate the social world beyond its confines. But this should not surprise us. For although at the core of *Ekine* membership there is often a group of dedicated artists who, in a conflict situation, would support the values of the society against those of the outside world, there is a larger proportion of ordinary people who would make the opposite choice.

2. *Ekine* AS AN ORGAN OF GOVERNMENT

According to Talbot, the first serious ethnographer of this area, "Among Kalabari and Okrikans, before the coming of the white men, the power of government was mostly vested in the Sakapu club, just as in the Ekpe society among the Efik of Calabar and the Ngbe of the Ekoi."[13] This picture of *Ekine* as an all-powerful secret society was perpetuated by Newns in his later administrative report on the area.[14] Newns depicted the authority of the New Calabar house heads as a recent development from a traditional pattern in which most significant communal authority was vested in *Ekine*.

[13] *Tribes of the Niger Delta*, London, 1932, p. 300. See also the author's *The Peoples of Southern Nigeria*, Vol. iii (Oxford, 1926), p. 765.
[14] Intelligence Report on the Kalabari Clan, Nigeria, 1942.

Kalabari informants, too, often answer vague general questions about *Ekine* by saying "It was our old-time government."

This picture of *Ekine* as the principal organ of government contrasts oddly with what we have described so far; and, in fact, it credits the institution with an undue political importance. How this appraisal of it arose is rather a mystery. Part of the explanation, perhaps, is that Talbot automatically assumed *Ekine* to have the same functions as the Cross River political associations which he knew so well. Another part may be that Newns was dealing with the New Calabar house heads at a time when they were causing the administration a lot of trouble: in his anxiety to find some more viable basis for local government, it is possible that he unwittingly magnified the political significance of non-chiefly institutions. Present-day Kalabari generalizations about *Ekine* and "government" may be in part due to the digestion of Talbot and Newns. In part, too, they may stem from the peculiar associations of the word "government" for some of the less educated informants—associations often centered upon violent, high-handed action by the police: for, as we shall see in a moment, there were certain restricted situations in which action of this type was frequently taken by *Ekine.*

Be all this as it may, when we turn from vague general statements about *Ekine* to direct observation and to recollections of older men about actions of the society in specific contexts, we get a rather different picture. First of all, any public delict or offense against village laws is a "town case" which is dealt with by the village assembly and never by *Ekine.* Examples of such offenses are murder, sorcery, or canoe theft. In any matter of communal policy making, whether it has to do with fending off attacks from a neighboring group or with deciding how and where to dig a village well, it is the village assembly and not *Ekine* that both deliberates and executes decisions. Where the village has a system of "Watchmen" to act as guardians of law and order, these are appointed in rotation by the assembly and not by *Ekine.*

Where, then, is the "governmental" significance of *Ekine?* Principally, this seems to be in the sphere of arbitrating private delicts—cases where one individual or group is considered to have wronged another without infringing village laws, such as those involving debt, defamation, or adultery. In such cases, the person who fancies himself wronged complains to *Ekine,* which then summons the accused and assembles for a hearing of both sides. Heavy fines are often imposed as penalties or compensations, and *Iwo Sekiapu* (the junior grade) is sent forcibly to distrain goods of equivalent value if the accused fails to pay. There is no appeal.

In New Calabar, accounts of nineteenth-century politics suggest that these formal judicial processes were, in the past, often made the cover for intrigues that gave the society an added dimension of political significance. According to such accounts, powerful figures within *Ekine* were wont to gang up on rivals, incite people to complain against them to the society, and then get them saddled with crippling fines. If they could not pay the fines, they were forced to part with their slaves in lieu, and so might be politically ruined.

Restricted though its governmental functions are to the sphere of private delict, *Ekine* is still undeniably important as part of Kalabari political organization. Yet in trying to define the institution in Kalabari terms, I think it would be a mistake to regard its political functions as more than incidental. For one thing, where we find an origin myth for some Kalabari communal institution, this generally states not only how the institution came to be founded by one of the heroes, but also what purposes it was founded for. But in the case of *Ekine,* the myth of its foundation by *Ekineba* makes no mention whatsoever of its judicial functions. Again, though *Ekineba* is the patron hero of the institution, she is never invoked or in any other way involved during its judicial operations. Finally, as we have already seen, status-differentiation within *Ekine* is in terms of skill and experience in the masquerade, and not of age, political influence, forensic skill, or any other criterion immediately relevant to its judicial aspect.

Perhaps one can sum up as follows. Kalabari villagers are wont to call on a great variety of individuals and groups as arbitrators of private delict. Choice in this is very flexible, and *Ekine* offers just one possibility among many. If it is especially favored in such cases, this is because it contains all the important adult males in the community, and even if such people do not participate in a particular case, their support of the institution lends weight to its proceedings and prevents them from being challenged. Thus, if a person who fancies himself wronged calls in *Ekine* to judge his case, the person whom he accuses cannot object as he can to other groups that might have been called in. If he refuses to turn up to the hearing, this just increases the presumption of his guilt. Again, *Ekine* has such influence behind it that no one will challenge its use of force to collect the fines it imposes. In addition to all this, the ideals of the institution forbid its members to bring into it the struggles for status and influence which rage in the village outside; so, as an arbitrating group, it has all the formal trappings of impartiality. And where the successful resolution of many disputes lies in persuading people that they can climb down from extreme positions without loss of face, such an appearance of impartiality may be crucial—whatever the reality behind it.

In short, the values, organization, and membership of *Ekine* make it incidentally suited to certain judicial functions. But these functions are not among the essential purposes of the institution. Despite earlier accounts presenting *Ekine* as a primarily political association, none of the evidence we have reviewed controverts the judgment that, for Kalabari, *Ekine* is essentially a society dedicated to the production of an art.

SUMMARY AND CONCLUSIONS

In this paper I have dealt with an institution that is associated with a bewildering variety of diverse and often conflicting values. In trying to explain its meaning for Kalabari, I have distinguished essential values and incidental values. The essential values are those which the myths of origin say that *Ekine* was founded to promote. They are the values to which the formal rules and prohibitions of the institution relate. And they are the values taken into account in assigning status within it. As we have seen, these essential values can only be called aesthetic.

By contrast, the incidental values are those which find no mention in the formal doctrines, rules, and status-criteria of the institution. At several points they are actually in conflict with the essential values. In a sense, attempts to realize them through *Ekine* are an "abuse" of the institution.

I stress this rather banal distinction between essential and incidental, uses and abuses, because social anthropologists often ignore it to the detriment of their ethnography. Often it is the incidental values and abuses of an institution that seem most relevant to that mysterious thing—a purely "social-structural" analysis. Where this is so, the tendency is to lay all the emphasis on the incidentals, play down the essentials, and end up with the picture of a society whose members are preoccupied with a constant, nightmarish struggle to be one up on the Joneses or to fit in with the Smiths, Browns, and Greens. Applied to *Ekine,* this sort of analysis would have concentrated almost entirely upon the judicial functions of the institution, and upon the masquerade as a means of individual and group status-assertion. The result would have been like an analysis of the art of Picasso which concluded that the main significance of his paintings was as means whereby millionaires could assert their financial capacity.

As an art, the Kalabari masquerade raises a number of points that seem relevant to the wider study of West African art generally. I should like to bring up two of these points before closing.

First of all, the masquerade belies the easy and oft-heard generalization that in traditional West African culture there was no such thing as art for art's sake. For although its performance is intimately associated with religious activity and belief, here it is the religion that serves the art, rather than vice versa. It is possible that some studies of West African culture have not found art practiced for its own sake, simply because they have not looked for it in the right direction.

This brings us to the second point. In describing the masquerade performance, I took pains to stress that its central element was the dance, and that the apparatus of costume and headpiece filled a subordinate place in the whole. I also stressed that the sculpted mask was first and foremost an instrument for securing the presence of a spirit, and not something produced as a work of art. This in fact is true of Kalabari sculpture generally. Now it would be dangerous to generalize on the basis of this one example. But taken together with reports on some other West African cultures such as that of the Ibo,[15] it does make one suspect that, at least in certain areas of West Africa, the dance overshadows sculpture, painting, architecture, and literature as the leading traditional art.

Now, so far, the study of West African art has been carried on almost entirely by Europeans. And I think it is probably fair to say that in pursuing it, we have been strongly influenced by our own ranking of the various arts. For us, painting, sculpture, and literature rank far ahead of the ballet. To call someone a connoisseur of painting or sculpture is for us high praise; but for the enthusiast of ballet,

---

[15] See the comment by K. C. Murray on pp. 95–100 of *The Artist in Tribal Society,* ed. M. W. Smith, London, 1961.

we have only the term "balletomane," which implies a warped sense of values. When we come to study West African art, there is a tendency to bring these attitudes along with us. We make a beeline for the sculpture and eulogize its aesthetic merits; but we consign the dance to the category of mere ritual, not to be taken seriously as art. Even when we find that people do not appear to treat their sculpture as an art at all, we often try to defend our preconceptions against the evidence of our senses by saying that this apparent lack of appreciation conceals a great depth of aesthetic feeling which for some strange reason is never expressed in words.

This preconceived ranking of the arts expresses itself not only in academic studies of West African culture, but also in practical policies. Take the example of Nigeria, the country to which Kalabari now belong. In the last two decades, Nigeria has been flooded with teachers of painting, sculpture, and literature, to the virtual exclusion of ballet instructors and choreographers. As a result, modern Nigerian art is dominated by painters, sculptors, and writers. For all their talent, however, they still largely lack a critical audience among their own countrymen. As a result, while they strive to develop an authentically African style, it is hard for them to work without one eye cocked on a largely European public. This leads to deep conflicts in their work, and has probably obscured their true potential.[16] Meanwhile the dance, for which there already exists a large and critical Nigerian audience, has been allowed to stagnate. In short, it is just that art whose further development might have yielded the biggest returns, that has been most neglected in modern Nigeria.

In this and other newly independent West African countries, the younger generation of artists and intellectuals is much preoccupied with the development of a modern culture that still has its roots in tradition. Such a development, it would seem, must involve not only coming to terms with tradition within each particular branch of the arts, but also examining the order of priority that is assigned to the various branches. For in Nigeria and other West African countries today, the current order of priority seems to owe more to European than to indigenous tradition.

[16] A good discussion of the modern Nigerian painters and sculptors is to be found in *Art in Nigeria 1960,* by U. Beier, Cambridge, 1960.

PART VI

African Beliefs and Religions

Introduction

Myth and religion tend to depict and to treat the major issues in African societies, and when not consciously used as charters or explanations for important institutions or aspects of life, they often indicate the norms or ideals of the people concerned. Creation myths are especially revealing since they seek to explain the origin of God, of the universe, of man, and attempt to account for the latter's joys, sorrows, and ultimate destiny. However, in so doing, they also reveal a people's views about the character of man and their values of good and evil. The very elaborate creation myth of the Mande-speaking peoples of Mali describes how God, *Mangala,* made the world in the form of seeds, within which were forces such as twin personages that gave rise to mankind, the natural world, and its attributes.

As in a number of African creation myths, there are primeval twins who from the beginning take an active part in creation so that one has the impression that man plays an important part "in making himself" and that the Creator can withdraw from the active affairs of men. Thus, much of man's subsequent fate is not so much the result of God's need for worship, or of his other concerns, but of man's own activities. The myth explains how man grew fruitful and multiplied and provides the basis for inclusion into the family of man all the different ethnic groups known to the Mande. So widespread are the variations of this Mande myth in West Africa that Dieterlen believes that it really served as a charter for the "international" lineages of the Keita (Mali) empire and "expresses a widespread tradition of the unity of African peoples."

There are some intriguing similarities between the creation myth of the Mande and the cosmology and cult organization of the Oyo Yoruba. In both myths man takes part in the creation of the earth. On the one hand, Pemba and Faro descend to the barren land, so characteristic of Mande country, and have to induce the primeval blacksmith to strike a rock and appeal to God for the life-giving water. On the other hand, Oduduwa, the ancestral Yoruba hero, descends in the ark with a bag of sand, and through the agency of a chicken creates the dry land out of the waters so characteristic of the Nigerian rain forests. But the similarity goes even further: every pool in Mande country becomes a center of cultivation made possible by the activity of Pemba's female twin and ultimately the original home of human lineages and their totems; in the Yoruba myth, the land created by Oduduwa becomes the domain of the Earth Goddess.

The cosmology of the Yoruba is quite detailed, and reflects the political structure of the Yoruba kingdoms, the importance of the royalty and of lineage groups. Morton-Williams believes that the Supreme God of the Yoruba is an *otiose* figure like their often secluded divine king, so that much religious attention is focused upon the Earth, whose fructifying powers are of greater moment to man. Indeed she has her own cult, whereas the Supreme God does not have one. Most of man's ritual needs are met by the lesser gods, and his morality is supervised by the lineage ancestors. Man, however, is not completely at the mercy of the supernatural. He often chooses the lesser gods whom he wishes to worship, and through the Ifa's diviners can obtain advice about the kind of behavior that displeases the ancestors, also the type of sacrifice a lesser deity will honor to ensure health, children, and the good life.

If myths and religious systems of the Mande and Yoruba reflect largely autochthonous African beliefs, the religion of the Coptic Christians in Egypt and Ethiopia represent intrusive beliefs that adapted to these African societies. Indeed, the long historical relationship between Egypt and Ethiopia and the Middle East, and the many similarities between the teachings of the Nazarene and ancient Egyptian beliefs made this adaptation possible. Nevertheless, there were some aspects of orthodox Christianity that, taken together with the political problems of the day, prevented the Old Egyptians from adopting it in its original form. Davis indicates that the Old Egyptians, like the contemporary Zulu, could not accept the alien view that there was coequality of Father and Son. And when political factors were added to these cultural differences, Egyptian Coptic Christianity diverged from Western Christianity and in turn imparted its rituals and beliefs to other Africans in Nubia and Ethiopia.

Nubian Christianity is relatively unknown since it disappeared in the sixteenth century as a result of Islamic Arab conquest. In contrast, the Coptic Christianity that diffused to Ethiopia has not only survived and given rise to amazing underground rock-hewn churches, but also has adapted to the major cultural patterns of Ethiopia. Sumner shows how the liturgy of the Ethiopian Coptic church has been Africanized. He calls attention to the repetitions, parallelisms, and the "joy" that is characteristic of Ethiopian prayers—traits that are obvious to anyone familiar with other African religions. He notes also a concern for unity and a sense of community that induce the priests to pray for the king, the nobles, the army, the neighbors at home and abroad, and also for those "fathers, brothers, and sisters" whose tardiness should normally be censured. Sumner is astounded that Mary is so revered by the Ethiopic Church, but this should not be surprising, given the widespread importance of the female (Earth) goddess in Africa, whether as the Egyptian *Isis,* the Mossi *Tenga,* the Ibo *Ale,* or the Yoruba *Onile,* addressed in prayers as *Iya,* Mother.

The struggle of Islam to retain its originality in Africa is widely documented by numerous scholars. Its arrival in Egypt in the seventh century with the Arab invaders was widely hailed by people tired of Byzantine rule. And except for stanch Coptic Christians, many Egyptians adopted Islam and largely abandoned their traditional religion. However, Islam had only differential success during its four historical phases in Africa. As Trimingham states, "The African idea of the harmony of society maintained itself, over and against any idea of Islamic exclusiveness. Consequently, Islamic elements of challenge to traditional life were largely neutralized."

In those areas of Africa where Islam gained adherents, the results were very much alike. According to Trimingham, this was due to the fact that Islam brought the same institutions that modified African life, and it was around these Islamic institutions that the African institutions that persisted or survived crystallized. Thus, Islam, like all of the religions and belief systems in Africa, came in time to reflect the nature of its society.

32. The Mande Creation Myth[1]

In the course of the investigations carried out by the Missions Griaule in French West Africa during several decades, our attention has been drawn to the fact that numerous populations in the French Sudan and Upper Volta claimed to be descended from a common stock located in Mande. Mande is the traditional center of the ancient Keita empire (called by the Arabs the Mali empire), which was founded in the thirteenth century by Soundiata Keita. The cultural center of this area today is Kangaba, which the inhabitants call Kaba. A list of the peoples in West Africa who claim to have come from Mande has been drawn up and published.[2]

From 1953 to 1955, detailed investigations were carried out for the first time in Bamako and Kangaba itself among the descendants of the Keita lineage living in both areas as well as among members of the Kouyaté lineage in Kangaba and of the Diabaté lineage in Kela, who are their bards.[3]

Every seven years a ceremony takes place at Kangaba,[4] when the local Keita and their relatives assemble in large numbers for the rebuilding of the *kamã blõ*, a sanctuary first erected in this place by Mansasama, a descendant of Soundiata. This sanctuary is believed to have been a copy of the one first built by the Keita in more an-

SOURCE: Germaine Dieterlen, "The Mande Creation Myth," *Africa*, Vol. 17, No. 2, April 1957, pp. 124–38. Reprinted by permission of the author and publisher.

[1] This article is based on the author's "Mythe et organisation sociale au Soudan français," *Journal de la Société des Africanistes*, xxv, 1955; it was delivered as the first of three public lectures in the University of London in June 1956.

[2] See D. Zahan, "Aperçus sur la pensée théogonique des Dogon," *Cahiers Internationaux de Sociologie*, iv, 1949, pp. 113–33; G. Dieterlen, *Essai sur la religion bambara*, 1951, p. xiii.

[3] We want to thank here all the informants who worked with us.

[4] This ceremony was last performed in 1954, when we were able to witness and study it closely.

cient times not far from Kri and close to Nyagassola. The mountainous region which extends from Kri eastward to beyond Sibi is considered by the Keita, who call it Kouroula, to be the birthplace of their lineage.

Before the rebuilding of the Kangaba sanctuary, a sacrifice is performed at the old shrine by Keita lineage members. During the Kangaba ceremony, which lasts five days, the Dyabaté from Kela village, who have the privilege of performing this special part of the ritual, enter the sanctuary before the new roof is placed in position and, for a whole night, they recite the creation myth, the story of the mythical generations, and, lastly, the genealogies of the Keita and of their related and allied lineages.

According to the myth and the genealogies, the peoples who originated from Mande are reckoned to be forty-four or forty-eight. These numbers are related to the first five mythical generations of ancestors which many peoples of the Western Sudan recognize. The number forty-four recurs in similar contexts among several populations that we have studied. The fifth generation generally includes forty-four descendants. The system of matrimonial alliances among these Sudanese peoples—for example, that of the Dogon—is related to this conception of distinct but related groups derived from these mythical ancestors.[5]

The bards (*griots*), who have special knowledge of genealogies, assert that, among these peoples, thirty lineages, scattered widely in Africa, derive from Mande and have a common origin. These lineages are: five Masaré, or true Keita lineages,[6] called *mammuru si ke duru,* who are descended from five Keita brothers, themselves descendants of Soundiata, the first chief; five Moslem lineages called *mori si ke duru:* Bérété, Touré, Haydara, Fofana, and Saganogo; four lineages of occupational castes, collectively known as *wara nani ñamakala,* which include the genealogists or bards, *dyelu;* the blacksmiths, *numu;* the leatherworkers, *garanke;* and the basketmakers, *fina* or *fine.*

There are sixteen other families of "noble captives," called *tõ ta dyõ tã ni woro,* "sixteen captives who have taken the war equipment,"

[5] See G. Dieterlen, "Parenté et Mariage chez les Dogon," *Africa,* xxvi, 2, 1956, pp. 107–48.
[6] The lineage name is Masaré and the *dyamu* is Keita (lit. "who has taken all things"); the *dyamu* was first given to Soundiata and his descendants cannot officially use it before they are twenty-two years old.

who are considered to be voluntarily allied to the Keita with whom they sometimes intermarry: Traoré, Koné, Kamara, Kuruma, Mogasuba, Dansuba, Dagnogo, Koulibali, Dyara, Danté, Dougonno, Sogoré, Diallo, Diakité, Sidibé, Sangaré.

These lineages are believed to be represented not only among the single linguistic group of Mandingo, Malinke, Bambara, Dyula or Khasonke, but also among most of the populations of Senegal, Sudan, Ivory Coast, Guinea, Togo, etc. The following list, which is not exhaustive, gives some idea of their extension:

Those said to be derived from the Keita include the Kissi, Dogon, Toma, Guerze, Lobi, Mande, Baule; those belonging to the Traoré and the Koné are: Koniagui, Bassari, Bobo *ble* and Bobo *fi;* Wolof are derived from the Traoré and the Keita, Minianka from the Koné, Baga from the Koné and the Kamara, Kabre and Sosso from the Kamara (or Doumbia), Kurumba of Upper Yatenga from the Kuruma.

All the Fulani who were questioned also asserted their original connection with the four large lineages: Diallo, Diakité, Sangaré, and Sidibé.[7]

Such facts explain why many peoples in the Western Sudan, when they come to the Upper Niger area, far from their own country, change their names and use that of one of the traditional Mande lineages.[8]

The geographical axis of the organization that has just been outlined is the upper part of the River Niger, from its source to Lake Debo. The main ritual centers which are located at both ends of this axis are Kri and Kri Koro[9] in Mande, Baka and Akka near Debo. But all along the stream, at special places called *faro tyn,* important rituals are performed. Some villages (such as Kaba, Koulikoro, Nyamina, Tamani, Sama, Segou, and Dyafarabé) represent places where

[7] See also G. Monteil, "Réflexions sur le probléme des Peuls," *Journal de la Société des Africanistes,* xx, 2, 1950.

[8] When he goes to Mande, a Dogon is called Keita and a Mossi is called Traoré.

[9] The Dogon organized in a restricted area a geographical representation of the myth. In the Sanga region, the course of the Gona is divided into sections and marked by rocks for a distance of four miles in imitation of the River Niger from Kaba to Akka. Caves in which the initiates undergo instruction have been made in a section called Ka, and rituals are performed all along the stream. The whole Dogon myth is to be published in *Le Renard Pàle,* volume 1, by M. Griaule and G. Dieterlen. For the Bambara, see G. Dieterlen, *Essai sur la religion Bambara,* 1951, chap. 1.

proto-historical or historical events occurred in connection with the history and extension of the lineages already mentioned.[10]

The religious, social, and political aspects of this organization are based on an important myth, known to the initiates, which is recited in full at certain ceremonies (see p. 634). In order to understand this organization, which may be called international, it is necessary to know the myth. We shall summarize it in the Mandingo version of Kangaba; but it is found, under similar forms, among many peoples, some of whom—Bozo, Bambara, Kurumba, Samogo, Dogon, as well as the blacksmiths and bards—have already been thoroughly studied.

God, *Mangala*,[11] first created the *balãzã* (*Acacia albida*) seed, which was, however, a failure. So he abandoned it in order to create twin varieties of eleusine seed, *fani berere* and *fani ba*[12]; thus, as the Keita say, he "made the egg of the world in two twin parts which were to procreate." God then created six more seeds and associated with this group of eight seeds the four elements and the "cardinal points" in order to mark out the organization of the world and its expansion. Thus there was: in the west (*klebi*): *fani berere* and *fani ba;* in the east (*koro*): *sañõ* and *keninge;* in the north (*kañaga*): *so* and *kende;* in the south (*worodugu*): *kaba* and *malo*. Finally the whole was enfolded in a hibiscus seed.

The seeds are thus conceived as twins of opposite sex in the "egg of God," which is also called "egg of the world" or "placenta of the world." They are often represented in drawings as an open flower with four petals which are also sometimes called the four "clavicles" of God.

In the same egg, according to the myth, there were in addition two pairs of twins, each consisting of one male and one female, archetypes of the future men. One of the males, Pemba, desiring to dominate the creation, emerged prematurely, before gestation was complete, tearing away a piece of his placenta as he did so. He came down through empty space; the piece of placenta became the

[10] During a first journey in the *Mannogo,* the laboratory-boat belonging to the National Centre for Scientific Research, these facts were verified on the spot. The place names on the Niger reveal the unity of the system: Tamani, Dyaka, Nyamina are words whose native etymology is closely linked with the events referred to later in this article.

[11] Bambara call the creator God *Ngala* (and sometimes Bemba).

[12] Bambara call these two varieties of Digitaria *fini wele-wele* and *fini ba.*

earth, but it was dry and barren and he could do nothing with it. Seeing this, he went back to heaven and tried to resume his place in the placenta and find his twin. In this he could not succeed, for God had changed the remaining part of his placenta into the sun. So Pemba then stole from one of God's clavicles the eight male seeds which he carried down in a calabash flask (*bara*).

He sowed these seeds in the piece of placenta which had become the earth. In this first field, which the Keita locate near Bounan (a village not far from Lake Debo), only the *fani berere*—one of the eleusine seeds—germinated in the blood of the placenta; the other seeds died for want of water. Because of Pemba's theft and his incestuous act (for Pemba had put the seed in his own placenta, that is, in his mother's womb) the earth became impure and the eleusine seed turned red as it is today.

The other male twin, Faro, assumed, while in heaven, the form of twin *mannogo* fishes, which are represented in the Niger River today by the *mannogo ble* and the *mannogo fi*.[13] The first represented his strength and his life, the second his body. In order to atone for Pemba's sin and purify the earth, Faro was sacrificed in heaven and his body was cut into sixty pieces which were scattered throughout space. They fell on the earth where they became trees, symbols of vegetal resurrection. God then brought Faro back to life in heaven and, giving him human shape, sent him down to earth on an ark made of his celestial placenta.

The ark came to rest on the mountain called Kouroula, in the area called *kele koroni* "ancient space," which lies between Kri and Kri Koro.[14] This area was then given the name of Mande which the inhabitants translate as "son of the person" (*ma*) or more explicitly "son of the *mannogo*," the "person" being Faro whose first bodily form was that of a silurian fish.[15] The place is also called "the mountain that encircles the world"; it is said that "Faro came out of this mountain, he took his life from the cloudy sky of Mande."[16]

Where the ark came to rest near Kri there was a cave called *kaba*

---

[13] The scientific names of these fishes are *Heterobranchus bidorsalis,* for the *mannogo ble,* which the Bambara call *polyo ble,* and *Clarias senegalensis* for the *mannogo fi*.

[14] See page 636.

[15] The same idea appears among some Sudanese peoples who believe that man has the shape of a fish in his mother's womb during the first months of gestation.

[16] *Faro bwora dyĕ lamin kuru si ya bwora kaba mande fe.*

koro, or more commonly *ka.* Near this cave appeared a hollow in the earth which became the first pool, *ko koro* or *ko ba.*[17] On the ark stood Faro, brought back to life, and also the eight original ancestors of men, created from Faro's placenta, that is to say four pairs of male and female twins called *mogo si segi.* The males of these twins were called: Kanisimbo ("from Ka's womb"), Kani yogo simbo ("from the same Ka's womb"), Simboumba Tangnagati ("the big remaining part of the womb which took command"), Nounou (from *nono,* milk). In the ark were also all the animals and plants that were going to multiply on earth.

The first human beings, like Faro himself, had a common vital force (*nyama*) and complementary spiritual forces *ni* and *dya,*[18] each of which had both a male and a female form. Also, in their clavicles were deposited the symbols of the eight seeds created by God. Emerging from the ark they watched, for the first time, the rising of the sun.

The bardic ancestor, Sourakata, then came down from heaven at Kri Koro holding in his hands the skull of the sacrificed Faro. This skull became the first drum. He played on it only once to ask, in vain, for rain. He then put the drum in a cave. The ancestral smith then came down to Kri, while Mousso Koroni Koundye, Pemba's female twin, came down "on the wind" at Bounan.

When he saw the prevailing drought the smith struck a rock with his hammer to ask for rain, and water poured down from heaven, filling the hollow *ko koro* with purifying and fertilizing water. Two fishes then came down: *mannogo ble* and *mannogo fi,* manifestations of Faro. *Mannogo fi* is the archetype of man who was to be Faro's "son"; *mannogo ble* represents Faro himself, and on earth and in the water was to be the intermediary between him and mankind. This is why, for the Mande, this fish has become the basic taboo of a great number of people including the Keita.

[17] Lit. "old pool" or "big pool," also called *nyame ko ba,* from Nyame, the present name of a nearby village.
[18] Such forces are double: the male *dya* of a man goes with the animal tabooed for his lineage while the female *dya* stays under water, under Faro's power; a similar combination stands for women, the *dya* sexes being reversed.

REVELATION OF THE WORD AND
BUILDING OF THE FIRST SANCTUARY

Simboumba Tangnagati, one of the male twins, who had entered the pool with the first fall of rain, was then given by Faro the first thirty words and the eight female seeds from God's clavicle. Now, coming out of the water, Simboumba said: *"nko* (I speak)."[19] In order to plant out the seeds he had received, Simboumba Tangnagati left the area of the pool and, that very day at sunset, built a sanctuary on a hill near Kri Koro. This building, called *lu daga blõ* (hall of the upper house), stood on the top of a hill; it was regarded as the "egg of the world" and was consecrated to the *mannogo ble.* It was made of black earth from the original pool, and its roof was made of a bamboo from the same place which represented Faro's hair. The roof had six edges symbolizing the *mannogo ble*'s beard, Faro's speech, and the spilling of water; inside the building Simboumba Tangnagati drew the sign of the *mannogo ble.*

From the door of the sanctuary Simboumba Tangnagati, who thenceforward was to be responsible for the seeds, the rain, and speech, gave men the first thirty words while the seeds were still in the sanctuary. He talked the whole night, ceasing only when he saw the sun and Sirius rising at the same time. This sun was what remained of Pemba's placenta, while Sirius, *sigi dolo,* was the image of Faro's placenta. During this night-long speech, the bard who was present carried a staff, symbol of Faro's resurrection, made of *ñogoñogo* wood[20] that had grown in the first pool.

The following night the *mannogo ble,* coming out of the Kri pool where he had been hidden among the rice, entered the sanctuary.[21] The next day Simboumba Tangnagati put the seeds on the *mannogo ble*'s head, at a place where there were signs. Then the rain started to pour down on the hill where the *blõ* was. The *mannogo ble* then left the sanctuary and went back to the Kri pool. Then the rain, bringing down earth from the hill, spread it out near the pool.

[19] Before sowing, the *gwa tigi* (head of the family) recalls this event. He starts the ceremony by saying: *"nko,* I speak."

[20] The *tana* of the Kela bards today is a similar staff and is made of the same wood.

[21] On the essential part played by the fish in the growing of crops see below, p. 651.

The first human ancestor, Kanisimbo, now sowed in this earth some of the seeds which Simboumba Tangnagati had put in the *blō*. This first field was called *kanisimbo foro*. It was rectangular like the ark and orientated in an east–west direction. Kanisimbo marked off its limits with the rope made of *ñogoñogo* fibers from which the ark had been suspended during its descent to earth. The field was eighty "cubits" long and sixty "cubits" wide. The "cubits" marked out the work and also represented the length of a man's forearm. Kanisimbo then gave the rope to Simboumba, who used it to tie down the roof of the sanctuary.

In the middle of the field Kanisimbo built a shrine made of three upright stones supporting a fourth. On the east he sowed the *fani berere,* on the west, the *fani ba,* on the north, the small millet *sañō,* on the south, rice, *malo,* and in the center, maize, *kaba.*[22] Finally hibiscus seeds, *da,* were sown all around the field.[23]

After the first storm that followed upon the building of the *blō,* two stars began to circle around Sirius (*sigi dolo*). They represented the two descents of the seeds: the one, called *ñō dolo,* symbolized Pemba's male seeds, the second, called *dyi dolo,* Faro's female seeds.[24]

THE BUILDING OF THE SECOND SANCTUARY

During this period Mousso Koroni Koundye, Pemba's female twin, left Kri and fled to Bounan. There she grew the impure *fani berere* seeds and she and Pemba ate them together. Faro went after her and made her return to Kri, whither she carried back part of the crop. Between Bounan and Kri, however, she dropped seeds all along her

[22] There are two original varieties of maize as there are of eleusine: *kaba sagada ule,* "the red corn which arrived first," and *kaba satabe,* "corn that arrived later on."

[23] It is said that this first field is still used and that the crops harvested there have to be kept in a special granary. The custodian of the *blō,* who is the patriarch in Kri Koro, is responsible for it, but sowing and harvesting are done by everybody. During the harvest meal made of *fani berere, fani ba* and *sañō* is poured into the pool before the custodian and the village patriarchs may eat the first crops.

[24] "*Sigi dolo* and Faro are alike," the Keita say, for Sirius is also called Faro *dolo.* If Sirius shines bright during the sowing, there will be "lots of rain and lots of millet." *Ñō dolo* and *dyi dolo* are also called by the Bambara *fani dolo* and *keninge dolo,* "sorghum star." The sorghum seed symbolizes, for them, all the seeds Pemba could not succeed in growing.

way, "sowing at night and cultivating by day."[25] The wild animals sent by Faro tried with varying success to stop her.

Back in Kri, Mousso Koroni, in her fear, hid the *fani berere* brought from Bounan for seven years. Then, on a moonless night (*kalo laba*), she sowed it "when the sun was in the south."[26] She kept trying "to catch the sun," which was made of the rest of her and Pemba's placenta. By sowing when the sun was in the south, at the time when it looked as if it were going to "fall," she thought "it would dry her field if Faro should attempt to flood it." But the moon when it rose revealed what she had done. The pool *kokoro* overflowed, poured down the hill, and flooded her field, and the *mannogo ble* swallowed the seeds. It sowed part of them on the same spot and turned the rest into fishes' roe.

Men then came down to reap the field which Mousso Koroni had sown and thus, by recovering the seeds, witnessed to Faro's victory. They first built a second Mande *blõ* which was an exact copy of the original one. In order to find the right place for it, Simboumba Tangnagati, the third ancestor, took his own seeds in a flask (*bara*)[27] and followed the path the water had made when it flowed out of the pool. The *mannogo ble* showed the way. The place where the water had stopped in Mousso Koroni's field lay between Kaba and Kela and this spot became Faro's first seat (*faro tyn*). The second *blõ* was built near it, at sunset, after rain had fallen. It was dedicated to the *mannogo fi*.

Inside this second sanctuary, also made of earth from the pool, Simboumba Tangnagati drew the sign of the *mannogo ble,* including all the marks he had on his head, and then the sign of the *mannogo fi.*[28] The bamboo roof had six edges representing the beard of the *mannogo fi.*

The two stars which circled around *sigi dolo*—*ñõ dolo* and *dyi dolo* —were symbolized by two balls of earth from the pool, dried and hung from the roof of the sanctuary; other signs represented Sirius, the sun, the moon, and the move from the first to the second

---

[25] The way the eleusine seeds are now sown is copied from the way Mousso Koroni scattered her seeds all along her way.

[26] I.e., the winter solstice.

[27] The seeds sown in the fields produced the calabash called *fle* or *file* which is used for offerings to the river.

[28] For the various signs used by the Keita, see "Signes des Keita," in M. Griaule and G. Dieterlen, *Signes graphiques soudanais,* 1951.

sanctuary; each word was associated with a star and also had its sign.

A well (*kolo*) was dug near the sanctuary for Faro and for the *mannogo* which is thought to enter it whenever the roof is being repaired. To draw water from the well and pour it on the sown fields is called "to take the *mannogo* and put it in the field." Around the second sanctuary a field of *fani berere* was made to replace the one made by Mousso Koroni. Afterward it was changed into a maize field, maize (*kaba*) being a basic seed for the Keita. While his brothers went back to the hill, Simboumba Tangnagati, the third ancestor, settled down at the foot of the hill and took command "because of the word."

The first village was laid out at the four cardinal points around the central field which contained the sanctuary and was called Kaba, thus recalling that its center was a maize field, *kaba*. Kaba is also the name of the place where Faro came down to earth in the Kouroula mountains and in other contexts means "cloudy sky."

FARO'S JOURNEY

Faro now traveled east in order to flood all the places where Mousso Koroni had dropped eleusine seeds and he finally reached Bounan and flooded Pemba's field. He was able to recover all the seeds that had been stolen, for he sent the *mannogo ble* everywhere to eat the seeds and it was followed by all the other fishes.[29]

Thus the River Niger, which has been formed from this series of floods, represents Faro's body; and it is said that "Faro lies face downward in the Niger." His head is Lake Debo, his right arm is the Bani, while his body is the Niger itself. The Bani and Niger are also called *bala,* which is male, and *bogolo,* which is female; the river from its source to Sama is Faro's single leg and Sama itself is his genitals. But on the opposite bank Faro, who was androgynous (or a twin), took the opposite sex; thus between Tamani and Sama, from being male on the right bank he became female on the left bank. All along the river a series of *faro tyn* marks the places where he halted: the place where he drowned Mousso Koroni's seeds that the *mannogo ble* had eaten; the place where he left his seeds in the

[29] The fish called *ngarakasa* preceding them.

shape of silurian fish for the future birth of men. For Faro is said to be unique and ubiquitous, and procreative.

So, above Koulikoro, Faro himself is responsible for the course of the river; below Koulikoro, one of his descendants is the guardian of each place marked out by the ten *faro tyn*. According to the Keita, as we shall see, the following places are connected with and participate in the myth and ritual of Faro: twenty-two main *faro tyn* between Kaba and Akka connected directly with Faro: these are supposed to represent the twenty-two parts of his body; twenty-two from Koulikoro to Mopti, which are connected with the second generation, i.e. Faro's children; twenty-two from Mopti to Akka connected with the third generation, i.e. Faro's grandchildren. The fourth generation is associated with pools, wells, and streams.

These four generations are also associated with the four ancestors who came down on the ark. The first generation settled in all the places where Mousso Koroni had sown her seeds; the second settled where the *mannogo* "dug in order to stop Mousso Koroni from sowing more seeds"; the third lived in the places where the maize (*kaba*) was sown to mark "the extension of Mande as far as Akka."

With each of these places on the river is connected a wild animal who is believed either to have prevented Mousso Koroni's sowing or to have protected the ritual field of Faro; later on those animals became the totemic taboos (*tne* or *tana*) of the various lineages of Mande.

Each of the *faro tyn* has a special name,[30] connected with the spreading of water and with Faro's expansion on earth: at Kaba, *senebo,* "coming out of cultivation," meaning the fields of *fani berere* taken back from Mousso Koroni in which the seeds from the Kouroula hills were sown; at Kourouba, *kandyi,* "Ka water," meaning the water and rain that Faro brought down onto the earth; at Dangassa, *senebo,* "coming out of cultivation," meaning the field of *fani ba,* that one of the two eleusine seeds which was kept pure and was never eaten by Pemba; this seed also came from the hills. Thus the cultivation of the two original eleusine seeds is separately represented by the first three *faro tyn*. Pemba was the first who sowed,

---

[30] We have not yet secured an exhaustive list of these places; the names of the villages where the twenty-two *faro tyn* located between Koulikoro and Mopti are to be found are: Koulikoro, Kamané, Nyamina, Mignon, Tamani, Sama, Segou, Koukou, M'Péba, Markala, Sansanding, Sama (the second), Senenkoun, Siranin koro, Macina, Tourara, Koumaré, Dyafarabé, Noukoun, Saouné, Ngoni, Mopti.

cultivated, and ate the *fani berere;* later, after Faro's arrival, men did the same with *fani ba.* The *kandyi faro tyn,* which is situated between the first and the third, is a sign of the coming of water and of Faro's activities, for "men now grow both sorts of eleusine thanks to Faro's water."

At Samayana, above Bamako, the *faro tyn* is called *sirakuru,* "the ark road." Here Faro changed his direction; in heaven he walked straight but on earth he walked in a sinuous way like a watercourse, and this purifies and regenerates the soil; at Bamako it is called *sutadunu,* "the corpse drum": the whirling water roars and its noise represents the rhythm of Faro's drum, *faro dundun,* which is played for weddings and funerals.[31] The roaring of the water refers to Faro's revelation to men of the second word which happened farther along the river; at Kayo[32] Faro dug a deep hole in the rocks, thus showing his strength; at Koulikoro the *faro tyn* is situated near a sharp rock which juts into the river. Faro placed his first child there to guard the way while he changed to the other bank and became a female; at Mignon, which means "patient," Faro rested after he had dug the hole. He made the river "broader like a wide road." Faro's vital force (*nyama*) is in Nyamina; at Tamani, "soul of the drum," he gave men the second word, which was the symbol of fecundity for it multiplies like births; at Sama, which means "the delegate," he sent a "delegate of the word."

At Dyafarabé, which means "to part the *dya,*" Faro's *dya* separated from his body and his *ni* to take its place in the River Dyaka. All human *dya* dwell there along with his. The *faro tyn* is called *gangare,* "horseman," and Faro may be seen on it in the form of a white horse. Faro at last reached Bounan[33] where he vanquished

[31] The *faro dundun* is made of *lange, dyala, dogora,* or *si* wood and is shaped like the smith's hammer. The smith invented it for the funeral of the first man to die. For the part played by the *faro dundun* in marriage rituals, see G. Dieterlen, "Les rites symboliques du mariage chez les Bambara," *Zaïre,* viii, 8, 1954.

[32] The word is a synonym for *kaba.*

[33] *Bunā tu la faro dona bunā.* According to some information which is not yet complete, the field is now drowned by the Ouallado Debo "in which one cannot grow seeds any more." The publishing of such information is postponed until further inquiries have been made. A *pembele* is said to have been found in Bounan together with a thing called "iron canoe," recalling Faro's ark. Bounan is said to be derived from the word *"buguna"* which means "to brood over."

Pemba and ordered the *mannogo ble* to eat the seeds from his field. Then, "spreading the river like a mat (*debe*)," which gave its name to Lake Debo, Faro and the *mannogo ble* stopped in Akka. Akka symbolizes "Faro's clavicles"[34]; the word comes from *hake* "limit" and also signifies the end of Faro's travels.

It is said also that "the place where Faro's ark stopped is situated between Akka and Baka," for the distance between these places represents the length of the ark that came "with the river" from Kaba.[35]

At the end of Lake Debo stand three hills, Gourao, Mamari, and Gambe; they represent, on the one hand, the three main seeds: *fani berere, fani ba,* and *kaba,* and, on the other hand, the three ancestors who stayed in Kaba and the Kri hills that symbolize them in Mande.

According to the Keita, the Bozo are the descendants of the first men who followed Faro along the river and occupied the banks. They are Faro's *dya*.[36] They are said to have been the first to grow and harvest the *fani ba* sown by Faro and the *mannogo ble* in the field taken back from Pemba.

REVELATION OF THE SECOND WORD

The second word, revealed by Faro to Simboumba Tangnagati, was handed down by him to mankind after Faro's victory and the extending of his power on earth. This revelation occurred at the place on the river which represents his genitals. Faro being essentially procreative, this place is linked with his seed and with the birth of mankind.

The four male ancestors who descended in the ark married by exchanging their twins two by two. In order to transmit the word, Simboumba Tangnagati decided to sacrifice in the sanctuary on the hill (*lu daga blō*) the first twins of mixed sex born of these marriages. He asked the bard to make an arm-drum (*tama*) with the

[34] *Akka faro kamankolouhiri.*

[35] We have not so far identified the place previously called Baka by the Keita of Mande. Further investigations are being pursued. Baka means "Ka's mother."

[36] *Bozo faro dya.* The name of the first Bozo is supposed to be Binakinaki, from which is derived the name Bounakinak, often given by the Keita to this people.

skin of the twins. The tree *gwele*,[37] from which he carved the drum, grew on the hill and symbolized Faro's only leg. Making a double drum of it meant dividing this single member into two legs like those of men, and also recalled Faro's journey on earth with the water. *Tama,* the name of the drum, comes from *ta* (to go away) and refers to this journey.[38] This is also why the bard, since the word was revealed, has, as the Mande say, to go on walking till he reaches Akka, "to follow Faro and testify to the distance he travelled." The two drum skins gave complementary male and female sounds, and the sacrifice was made to ask Faro for the birth of twins in every lineage.

To go from Kaba to Tamani, where the sacrifice was offered, men were led by the *mannogo ble* which entered the sanctuary with the rising water. Thus he showed the way to men, going before them. They went east, along the right bank of the river; by day they walked in the direction of the rising sun, by night, toward Sirius, which, at that time, rose in the east as soon as the sun had set. For the revelation of the word at Tamani, Simboumba Tangnagati carried the seeds from the sanctuary on the hill in order that he might "speak upon them." These seeds were to multiply, as words multiply, in the fertile area of Faro's genitalia. At each *faro tyn* which marked the activities of Faro and the part he played in providing seeds and procreation, twins were sacrificed in order that twin births might be frequent.

When they saw, as on the first occasion by the entrance to the shrine, Sirius rising along with the sun, the first men halted at the place of Faro's fecundity. Then, joined by Mousso Koroni Koundye, they crossed the river on steppingstones; the bard remained alone on the right bank. Simboumba Tangnagati played on wrought-iron bells (*simbo*), image of Faro's mouth, and said fifty words. These the bard Sourakata repeated on the opposite bank of the river, while he played the drum *tama* on both the male and female sides of the instrument.[39] The fifty words proclaimed the propagation of human beings throughout the earth and the common origin of all

---

[37] *Prosopis africana.*

[38] Popular etymology.

[39] It is also said that while he was playing "the bard walked along the river from Tamani, female, to Sama, male," i.e., a distance equal to the length of the ark. His journey also symbolizes the peregrinations of the bards today.

lineages from Mande; it is said of them: "black people belong to the millet race and they should all possess the same knowledge."[40]

The place where the bard stood gave its name to the village of Tamani. On the opposite bank the place where the men stood was called Do, "secret"; there is only a small bare hill there and nothing to recall the men's halt because it was to be kept secret from Mousso Koroni, who was still seeking to reach Sirius and the sun: "Mousso Koroni must never be able to find the spot."[41]

The men, followed by Mousso Koroni, then went back to Kri along the left bank; Nounou alone went on beyond Kri and along the same bank to Sama, where he crossed the river led by the *mannogo ble,* and stopped at the site of the present Ségou Koro.

Meanwhile the bard went his way along the right bank of the river, walking east to Akka, the *mannogo ble* going before him to show the way. At Akka the bard gave his drum *tama*[42] to the Bozo who were the first to arrive there.

Now the bard had left at Ka the head of Faro which he had been given in heaven after the sacrifice, but he had brought the drum to Akka. So Akka is the head of Faro risen from the dead. The two drum skins recall the two geographical areas, Kaba and Akka, and the narrow central part of the drum is the river itself and hence Faro's journey. The thirty ropes with which it is tied represent the first thirty words and also the thirty lineages. On his way back the bard came to Ka bringing the *simbo* which looks like "the head of Faro alive." It was put aside in the same cave, together with the skull that had become the first drum.

Sourakata's journey, symbol of the continuous traveling of genealogists today, and the revelation of the word of which they have, from that time, been the heralds, gave one of its present names to the river: namely *dyali ba,* "the great bard." The name refers both to Faro, owner of the word, and to the first bard who was Faro's "spokesman." While he was staying in Akka, the bard saw the ark and, on his return home, he carved a harp of *dogora* or *dura*

[40] *Mana fi ñõ si ye, an ka hakili to ñõño.*

[41] At Do there is said to be a deserted village located near the present Segala Bozo.

[42] The patriarch of Akka was to be in charge of the sanctuary, decorated with paintings in four colors, which contains the *tama,* on both sides of which annual offerings of eleusine are made. In Bounan an annual sacrifice is performed before the communal fishing, because it is said that "if the place is not purified Faro does not give any fish": more investigations on this subject should be carried out.

wood[43] and shaped it like an ark; the four strings of the harp symbolized the four cardinal points.

NOUNOU'S PART

Nounou, the fourth human ancestor, who was a hunter and a medicine man, was led by a *mannogo ble* across the river at Sama and followed it "in order to possess both banks and see if the bard's speech could be extended." He carried with him his three medicine shrines. Suddenly he came to a hill called *kulubana* which blocked the road and prevented him from occupying the whole region.[44] This was at a place now called Segou Koro where he settled down.

Mousso Koroni, still trying to find the seeds she had lost and to fight Faro, joined Nounou, "leaving traces wherever she went."[45] Following her treacherous advice, he tried to cross the hill and, to this end, caused the *mannogo ble* to be caught in order that he might sacrifice it and obtain his own *sañõ* field, with eight plots, on the hill at Segou Koro. Nounou died on account of this; for he had committed sacrilege by killing the *mannogo ble*. He was buried in his house in Segou Sorokimo.[46]

The antelope, *dage*, which Faro had sent to watch the shrines, carried Nounou's vital force in its horns and ran from Segou Koro to Mande, along with Nounou's souls which had come back to life. Using the shrines and the trees that grew in the field and had become the basic medicines,[47] Nounou changed himself into a snake and hid in the Ka cave on the Kouroula hills in Mande. The *dage* and the *mannogo* became taboo for his descendants, who were called Kouloubali (or Koulibali), a name which, according to popular etymology, recalls the name of the hill.[48]

Mousso Koroni, left alone, went wandering about, begging and

[43] As among the Dogon, the instrument is more properly made of four different woods, each one being a symbol, since vegetation is linked with resurrection.

[44] *Bana* marks Nounou's stop by the hill, *kulu*.

[45] Moving east toward the sun and *sigi dolo* which she hoped to reach.

[46] A yearly sacrifice is still performed on his grave at the time of sowing.

[47] These are the *balãzã*, the *ñogoñogo*, the *dyala*, and *so*, symbols of Faro's resurrection, as are all plants.

[48] At the present time, when a hunter kills a *dage* a ceremony is held at which the hunters dance to honor him.

"leaving traces in all the fields she tried to cultivate." Starving and miserable "she at last went east and was never seen again."

The three ancestors who stayed in Mande, when the time came for them to die, disappeared under the wooden shrine built in the initial field and also became snakes (*miñã*). Today in the Ka cave in Kri live four mythical snakes representing the four ancestors.[49]

From the descendants of the ancestors of the ark human beings multiplied. There were first the five mythical generations from whose supposed marriages a complex system of matrimonial alliances derives.[50] The fifth of these generations consisted of forty-four descendants, among whom twenty-two males symbolically represented the twenty-two *faro tyn;* they are said to be the several ancestors of all the lineages who regard themselves as "coming from Mande."

The myth thus briefly outlined is not only recited but is also expressed in the social life of the peoples living along the upper Niger. The themes and the ideas found in the myth appear in their social organization, their juridical systems, and their rituals. To illustrate this we give some examples from our field data on the Bozo, Somono, Fulani, and Bambara of this region. We shall then describe in detail two basic rituals of the Mandingo.

I. The Keita of Mande divided the fishing rights in the river into three areas related to the three sections of *faro tyn* mentioned above. The Somono of Kaba were the *dyi tigi*, "masters of the water," also called *batigi*, "masters of the river," from Kaba to Koulikoro. Those of Segou had the same rights from Koulikoro to Mopti. The Bozo were given the area from Mopti to Lake Debo. Each area is divided into small sections allotted to the various villages along the banks. Bozo and Somono paid a duty in fish annually to the Keita or their relatives, who are known as *dugukolo tigi*, "masters of the earth," along the banks. Rights and duties may have changed slightly in the course of time, though they are still very carefully observed in most of the places we investigated.

The prohibition of intermarriage, which is strictly observed by Somono and Bozo today, is ascribed to the belief that the an-

---

[49] According to information received but not yet checked, there are snakes modeled in clay in the cave where sacrifices are performed.

[50] This part of the myth is more developed among the Dogon but a discussion of it is outside the scope of this paper. It has been described in an article by the author published in *Africa* (see note 5, pg. 635 above).

cestors of the Bozo broke the interdict concerning the *mannogo ble* which, originally, could neither be caught nor eaten. The prohibition of marriage between Bozo and Dogon, although both are regarded as Keita, is similarly explained.

II. The great annual ceremony of the Fulani of Macina is performed in November at Dyafarabé on the occasion of the "crossing of the river" by the cattle. The animals, preceded by the herdsmen, swim across the Dyaka River. This is not merely because it is the usual route of the seasonal migrations; for those who take part in it, the ritual links the Fulani to the Bozo and effects a ritual purification of the cattle.[51] The animals must cross the Dyaka in order, as they say, "to get back one of their *dya* (souls) given to Faro" during their seasonal migration beyond the river.

III. Two public ceremonies in which masks are displayed, performed by many peoples living along the Niger (for instance Bambara, Bozo, and Marka), are related to the myths concerning eleusine seeds and fish. The first ceremony is performed at night, at the time of the eleusine harvest; the second takes place during the daytime, when the great annual fishing party is organized by the chiefs of the areas mentioned above.[52] The ceremonies vary slightly from one area to another, but they all include a more or less complete representation of the creation myth.

IV. In Kaba, each year, a ritual field of *fani berere* is sown and harvested at the first *faro tyn*. At the harvest a silurian fish is sacrificed and offered by the priest of the cult; this commemorates the sacrifice of Faro in heaven. The blood of the animal is poured into a new calabash which is left in the river after offerings of the first eleusine crop have also been placed in it. Like Faro, the silurian fish is believed to come back to life and to multiply through its own blood. Similar offerings of *fani ba* are made at the third *faro tyn* in Dangassa. In every village the harvesting of eleusine is accompanied by offerings of first fruits to the ancestors.

[51] Before the animals make the crossing, sacrifices are performed by Bozo who carry in canoes the animals too young to swim.

The most ancient Bozo lineage recognized in the Dyafarabé area is the Salamenta lineage from the village of Kara; Salamenta are Keita (according to information from Mr. Daget, Head of the Hydrobiology Laboratory of Dyafarabé, I.F.A.N.). Salamenta used to pay a tribute of fish to the Traoré from Dya who once ruled the area.

[52] Such ceremonies were observed in Pelengena, Bambougou, Tchongoni, Sansanding, and Dyafarabé (night ceremony) as well as in Banankoro and Bambougou (day ceremony) in 1953, '54, and '55.

The silurian fish and eleusine also play an important part in the ritual of rebuilding the sanctuary which takes place every seven years in Kaba (see p. 634). Each ceremony marks the end of the "long year" and the beginning of the new year. It commemorates the settlement of the Mande, the coming of the rain, the revelation of the word, and the expansion of the lineages. The Keita, the bards of Kela, and representatives of the sixteen allied lineages alone are permitted to perform this ritual. The public or semi-public ritual lasts five days and is preceded by secret rituals forbidden to the public.

The public ceremony begins with the marking out of a large open space, representing the original field of eleusine, around the sanctuary, and the erection of gates. The old roof is then taken off and a new one is built by young men, while girls of pure Keita origin repair the building and paint it red, white, and black.

Before the new roof is put on, the bards of Kela enter the sanctuary and, throughout the night, recite the creation myth, including Faro's travels and his victory over Pemba, and then the story of Mahomet. They recite the eighty mythical words and the mottoes of all the lineages "coming from Mande." Thus, even if all the lineages do not send representatives to the ceremony, the recital of their names and mottoes by the bards is regarded as ensuring their participation, and thereby their continued existence.

The following conclusions may be drawn from the wide extension among a great number of peoples in the Western Sudan of a myth which provides the justification for certain fixed relations among them and enables them to share the same rituals.

1. It is quite possible that the origins and interrelations of these peoples as asserted in the myth have no ethnic or historical reality, and the myth may well have been established for political reasons at a time when ruling groups from Mande gained control of large parts of West Africa. Nevertheless it serves to validate the relations and mutual obligations which exist among them today, and which are deeply felt and respected. The myth, therefore, expresses a widespread tradition of the unity of African peoples.

2. The investigations already carried out should be pursued and further developed along several lines:

    (*a*) further analysis of the notions of family and kinship in the wide sense among these peoples;

(*b*) analysis of the internal composition of the lineages who claim to "come from Mande" in order to determine the basic elements of their structure;

(*c*) historical study of the distribution and migrations, and of the conflicts which have occurred among the peoples who today are integrated;

(*d*) the collection and comparison of the traditional texts recited by the bards within the various groups, which include genealogies of each of the lineages derived from the Mande;

(*e*) a comparative analysis of the creation myth and its variants, of the symbols and their relation to the social organization, among groups where it has not so far been examined.

33. An Outline of the Cosmology and Cult Organization of the Oyo Yoruba[1]

I. A NEW MODEL OF THE YORUBA COSMOS

The structure of the Yoruba cosmos is broadly evident in their creation myth and can be discerned as presupposed behind many other myths, praise songs of the god, and other symbolic utterances. These formulations help us, too, to construct a more detailed model of this cosmos than is available in any single mythical form. A model worked out from these sources is preferable methodologically to one derived from interrogating informants to get at their personal ideas and formulations, because these myths and liturgical expressions are relatively permanent features of Yoruba culture and are the materials for informants' constructs. Furthermore, it is not on intellectual grounds that myths survive and one must therefore beware of jockeying informants into making untypical intellectual abstractions from them and then using these abstractions as one's main primary source material. However interesting in themselves their own attempts at a generalized statement of the cosmos may be, informants can better be used to clarify overcondensed or allusive passages in myths and to check one's own interpretations, and again, to supply evidence for the details of the analysis through, for instance, their assertions about the locations of the various gods, spirits, and the ancestors.

The Yoruba creation myth, which will be known to many readers from the writings of Frobenius and several more recent investiga-

SOURCE: Peter Morton-Williams, "An Outline of the Cosmology and Cult Organization of the Oyo Yoruba," *Africa*, Vol. 34, No. 3, July 1964, pp. 243–61. Reprinted by permission of the author and publisher.

[1] This paper has been developed from a shorter one read to the First International Congress of Africanists in Accra, December 1962, and is printed here with permission of the Joint Secretaries of the Congress. I am grateful to Professor Daryll Forde for encouraging me to expand the earlier paper and for finding room for it in *Africa*.

tors,[2] has its local variations; in the most widely current version, Oduduwa, founder of the kinship in Ifẹ[3] and ultimate begetter of all Yoruba kings, is the protagonist. God sends him from the sky in a canoe, which floats on the waters of the earth. Oduduwa has a bag of sand[4] which he opens and pours on the water, and then a five-toed chicken, sent down in the canoe with him, scratches and scatters the sand, which becomes the first dry land; then people are created and the town of Ifẹ is built, where Oduduwa rules, the first king. This is only one of several versions known in Ọyọ. In the palace at Ọyọ the myth is told with a different protagonist, Ọranyan, the first king of the Ọyọ Yoruba. He comes down from the sky carrying soil and two chickens, all tied up in a woman's kerchief. The chickens scatter the soil to the right and left of Ọranyan, who becomes the owner of all the land; and this, the myth ends, is how it comes about that the kings of Ọyọ, the *Alafin,* are called *ọba onilẹ,* kings who own the land.

In all forms of this myth the threefold structure of the cosmos is clear enough—a pre-existing, primeval sky and ocean and a subsequently created habitable world. Yoruba have names for these three: for the firmament (visibly sky, mystically heaven), *ile ọrun,* house of the sky, or *ọke ọrun,* hill of the sky; for the lowest level, *ilẹ,* which, it is important to observe, means Earth rather than water. The primeval waters must be thought of as both equivalent to the Earth in some sense and also as having covered the Earth before being displaced by the dry land. The middle zone, the habitable land, is called *ile aiye,* the house of the World.

This term *aiye,* world, has a wide meaning: it means the civilized, ordered world, organized into states and governed by kings, the place where people live amid their cultivated land; it includes the pattern or idea of life properly lived and the notion some European languages convey by "the times," as in "times aren't what they

[2] Frobenius, 1912; English translation, 1913, i, pp. 283f. The earliest reference to the creation myth seems to be R. Lander's (Lander, 1832, p. 180—journal for May 15, 1830).

[3] The orthography current among the Yoruba is used in this paper. The letters have the values of the *Africa* alphabet of the International African Institute, except that *e* is replaced by *ẹ*, *ɔ* by *ọ* and *ṣ* by *ẹ́*, that *p* is the double plosive *kp,* and that when *n* follows a vowel it serves only to indicate that the vowel is nasalized. Tones are not marked, but they may be found by reference to R. C. Abraham, *Dictionary of Modern Yoruba,* London, 1958.

[4] The Yoruba word *ẹrupe,* generally translated "sand," primarily denotes dry, powdery earth or soil, rather than the sand of the sea beach.

were." It has recently been reported by the Rev. Dr. E. B. Idowu that the Yoruba conceive of evil as being essentially located in the World, as a property of *aiye* in its mystical aspect.[5] Much more could be said about the meanings of the word *aiye,* but I shall limit myself here to saying what it does not mean: it does not seem to include the distant uncultivated bush or the forest, or even, on occasion, long-standing, wooded, fallows.

We must, therefore, imagine the cosmos as made up of Sky and Earth enfolding an island-like World. Beyond the limits of World, Sky and Earth may be thought of as touching, since it is believed that certain spirits pass freely between them. We are at once reminded of the dual relationship of the God of Heaven and the Goddess of Earth symbolized by the two halves of a whitened closed calabash among the south-western Yoruba, where they are called Qbatala and Oduduwa, or in Dahomey, where they are called Mawu and Lisa.[6] It should, however, be noticed that this image was not encountered in Oyo, or in Ifę either.

This model of the cosmos has, typically of Yoruba religious conceptions, some relativity of scale in its application. It allows us to think of the whole world of mankind as *aiye* lying between Earth and Sky; or to think of each Yoruba kingdom separately as *aiye,* its limits the edges of its cultivated land, which in turn are surrounded by unfarmed land merging into the domain *ilę.* We can do this figuratively, although in fact states are connected to one another (in the old order as well as today) by well-maintained paths and roads and the farms of one state may adjoin those of another. We are dealing with the idea of the state and of the cosmic order, not with geography. The three domains of Sky-Heaven,

---

[5] Dr. Idowu's is the only published discussion of the Yoruba conception of *aiye* that I know (Idowu, 1962, pp. 177–80). His discussion centers on the problem of the source of the evil that can conflict with and spoil the worldly destiny God gives each human being upon his leaving the Sky to be born and live in the World; and it is a convincing and valuable addition to our knowledge of Yoruba metaphysical ideas.

[6] Ellis, 1894, p. 41; Herskovits, 1938, ii, pp. 10–14; Mercier, 1954, pp. 218–20. Maupoil, 1943, shows an elaborate construction (fig. 1, p. 62), which represents the cosmology of his principal informant, the famous Gędęgbę, chief Ifa diviner to the last two kings of Dahomey. Gędęgbę, uterine nephew of King Gezo, was of Ęgbado Yoruba parentage, and met many Yoruba diviners in Abomey; but he passed all his life in Abomey and his ideas are the remarkable fruit of his own joining of Fon and Yoruba conceptions. Cf. p. 664, n. 17, below.

World, and Earth have their proper denizens. There are some regional variations in beliefs about who they are, the main line of contrast being between eastern Yoruba, including Ifẹ, and the western, dominated by Ọyọ. The rest of this description applies to the Ọyọ Yoruba.

The House of the Sky is the domain of the Supreme God, Ọlọrun Olodumare (Ọlọrun means "Sky-Owner"). He is male and rules the sky as a king. Next to him are his principal subjects, being called, collectively and specifically, *oriṣa*. These we may also call "gods." In some myths they appear as royal children of the Supreme God, and in others as his creations who stand to him rather as vassal kings stand to their suzerain, the Alafin of Ọyọ in this world. They, rather than Ọlọrun, control, or interfere with, relations between Sky and World, and what goes on in the World, although Ọlọrun is the ultimate source of their powers. In terms of the contrast between their and God's relation to the World and mankind, there is a rather close analogy with relations between the Alafin of Ọyọ, a secluded king rarely to be seen by his subjects but ultimately responsible for everything that happens in his realm, on the one hand, and his duty appointed agents, the state officials, who are his intermediaries with all the corporate groups in his realm and with his subjects individually, on the other.[7] The principal *oriṣa* are each the head of a hierarchy of lesser (usually more localized or specialized) *oriṣa,* much as both high officers of state and also vassal kings head hierarchies of lesser officials. A third kind of being in the sky are the *ara-ọrun,* sky-people, who are the spirit doubles of the living and souls awaiting rebirth. The term *ara ọrun* is sometimes used also to denote a set of spirits otherwise called *ẹgbẹ ọrun,* "the band of heaven (or sky)," who are from time to time incarnated in *abiku* children; the Yoruba belief is that a woman who gives birth to a succession of children who die in infancy is repeatedly bearing the same *abiku* spirit, the spirit returning to its companions when they call it back.[8] Yoruba, nevertheless, do not confuse these troublesome spirits with a person's *ara ọrun,* or *ọrun,* as it is more simply called.

---

[7] Idowu (1962, pp. 48f.) uses this analogy of God and king, too. Because so much writing on Yoruba religion has been derivative from earlier writings, and often without acknowledgement, it is worth saying that I obtained it quite independently, so that it must represent a widely held Yoruba view of God's role.

[8] Morton-Williams, 1960*a*, p. 35 and plate 1.

The Earth is the domain of the goddess Onilọ, Earth-Owner, who is sometimes simply called Ilẹ, i.e. Earth personified. She is conceptually the counterpart of the Sky God, since Earth and Sky are coeval; and she is asserted by those Yoruba who worship her to have existed before the other gods, the *orişa*. In her rites she is addressed as *Iya,* Mother. She receives the souls of the dead, who become Earth-dwelling spirits.

Associated with her, or perhaps better thought of as manifestations of her power, there are certain vengeful spirits who punish misdeeds on the part of members of her cult, the Ogboni.[9] She also has in her domain the ancestors and other dead, who can pass through to the sky whence they can be reincarnated through the power of Olorun and the *orişa.* Last, certain forest spirits and tree spirits, called collectively *ẹgbẹ ọgbẹ,* the company of the forest, are also in her domain.

Spiritual beings, whether of Earth or Sky, are collectively termed *irunmọlẹ.* Etymologically this word can only mean earth-spirits; but it seems to include all spirits in so far as they can be encountered on earth. It is not ordinarily used by Ọyọ or western Yoruba to refer to *orişa,* except when they are thought of as being possibly involved in uncanny phenomena which could have been caused by any kind of spirit. For instance, traveling from town to bush one becomes aware of the nearness of the Earth Goddess's domain and of the presence of *irunmọlẹ* when the branches of trees stir and the leaves rustle, although no wind blows, or a dry tree spontaneously catches fire.

Life in the third cosmic realm, *ile aiye,* the house of the World, is good only when good relationships are maintained with the gods and spirits of the other two. Spirits of every category have their peculiar and essential roles to play to enable mankind to live, prosper, and reproduce itself.

God himself gives each human being his fate, his distinctive character, before he is born, as W. R. Bascom has well described[10]; thereafter, the human creature is in the care of the *orişa* rather

---

[9] I have described some of these in a previous paper (Morton-Williams, 1960*b*, pp. 36f. and plates I and II). See also p. 672, n. 26, below, on the ambiguous location of the ancestors; some Yoruba tend to think of them as essentially inhabiting Earth, others as being with the *oriéa* in the Sky. The Ogboni burial liturgy says "we are bringing him [the dead] home to become an Earth-dwelling spirit."

[10] Bascom, 1960, p. 409, cf. Idowu, 1962, Ch. 13.

than of God, who has no cult in the world, though men appeal to him in extreme despair. He is also invoked at some stage in prayers and sacrifices to the *oriṣa* and in certain conventional utterances, most noticeably in pious remarks to the parents of new-born children.[11]

The *oriṣa* give to their worshipers the blessing of children, health, and, if their God-ordained fate permits it, wealth. They are vengeful if affronted through neglect or impiety. It is not, however, in relation to their devotees but in relation to the world as a whole and to the community that the various hierarchies of *oriṣa* have specific functions—control over lightning and the tornado, over activities such as hunting, smithing, war, and now driving, involving the use of iron; over smallpox, the fertility of farm and forest, and so on. Within a hierarchy certain *oriṣa* may have specialized roles serving its more general function. Besides being defined in terms of their role, *oriṣa* are also differentiated individually or as members of a hierarchy through prescribed or tabooed offerings, by other taboos observed by their worshipers, by the use of certain drums and distinctive dances in their rites, and by the human idiosyncrasies attributed to them, both such broad categorizing characteristics as being of a "hot" or "hard" or "cool" disposition and also, for some of them, individual traits (such as the arrogance and impatience of Ogun) described in their myths and praise songs. Among the multitude of *oriṣa* (201, 401, and 1600 are con-ventional numbers), nevertheless, only the principal members, some-times only the head, of each of the dozen or so hierarchies served in Qyǫ can be seen, through myth and the behavior of worshipers when "possessed" by one, as a clearly characterized personage. The lesser members of any hierarchy are said to associate with their principals, as their "followers," because they are of like dis-position. It is noteworthy that definite personalities or dispositions are believed to characterize members of their various cults too, and there seems to be good empirical support for this belief—

11 Examples: (i) To the mother of a newly-born child *Qlǫrum a wo o!,* "God will watch over it!" (ii) Conventional greeting: *O daaro o! Qlǫrum ji wa o!* "Good night! May God awaken us!" There is no need to suppose a direct Christian or Muslim intrusion into Yoruba culture here, whatever may be the ultimate source of Yoruba—or other West African—religious ideas. We should remember that not only Islam but Christian and Jewish influences penetrated the Sudan from the East many centuries before Qyǫ was founded.

worshipers' characteristics being either remarkably like those of the gods or else clearly complementary to them.[12]

The ancestors have powers for their lineage members and their wives, just as the *orişa* have for their adherents, of bestowing children, health, and prosperity, if properly served. Their displeasure is roused by moral shortcomings in a way that the anger of the *orişa* is not, since they are concerned with behavior between kin and in the community, and with the good reputation of their descendants, not, as the *orişa* are, with relationships to environmental and cosmic forces.[13]

There is a fierce spirit, Oro, whose place in the cosmos is hard to assign. He has the power to cleanse a town of that evil propensity of women, witchcraft. His voice is the bull-roarer or rhomb, and, as might be anticipated from the use of this ancient instrument, his cult is open only to men. The cult does not appear to have been as prominent in Oyọ as it was (and is) among the southern Yoruba; indeed, as will be argued later, the Oyọ may have adopted it as lately as the nineteenth century, after they had settled in their present town, a hundred miles south of Old Oyọ. In Oyọ the head of the cult recited a myth telling that his ancestors obtained the rites from God through a diviner to enable them to call upon Oro to prevent their

[12] This is not the place to discuss this thesis; but cf. Wescott and Morton-Williams, 1962, pp. 25–27.

[13] It is true that Şango in particular among the *orişa* is said to hate liars; but, as Joan Wescott has said to me in a private communication, it is the Şango possession priests who cannot tolerate deceit. I think the explanation may be along these lines: more readily than adepts of other cults, they are sent by ritual drumming, drugs, or other means into states of frenzy which are regarded as possession by the *orişa*. Fairly small shocks such as a sudden loud noise unconnected with ritual may result in "possession." The possession itself nearly always takes the form of raging displays of domineering power that commonly include rather bizarre and even gruesome actions. In their ordinary state of consciousness this ferocity is unconscious and therefore is projected and experienced as an attribute not only of the god Şango but also of the world, before which it seems the priest experiences himself as rather womanish—a contributing cause of the transvestitism of these priests. Indeed, because their conscious control is so precarious in the face of their own unconscious forces, they, more than most people, need reliable external relationships and cannot easily stand the shock of finding they have been lied to. Paranoia of this sort can easily enough misinterpret a casual lie as a vicious act of aggression, with shattering consequences. The eventual result, as I observed it in Oyọ and elsewhere, was an obsessive thirst for vengeance which was to be obtained through magical command of Şango's powers to punish. The peculiarities of Şango priests are further discussed in Wescott and Morton-Williams, 1962, pp. 25, 27, 28.

children dying. Myths of the cult's origin collected elsewhere are concerned to show why its secrets must be kept from women. In the few of its myths that have been published by others[14] Oro is described as a spirit of the land where the first human beings settled, or as a supernatural hunter "owning" the land and heard calling in the forest. No myths tell of him as inhabiting heaven and periodically visiting the world, as the *oriṣa* do. Some of my southern Yoruba informants associated him with the power of the collective male dead in the earth. It might be urged that he is a spirit of *aiye,* World, but on the other hand he is called from the forest, marginal to the domains World and Earth, and does not dwell in the town. On balance, I incline to assign Oro to the category Earth spirits, but this may be imposing system on Yoruba notions where there is none. It is clear enough that his cosmological status is of no interest to the Yoruba: what this spirit is concerned with is the solidarity of men and their relations with women in *aiye,* expressed in the symbolic language of witchcraft and rites to counter it.

Unlike the Supreme God, Ọlọrun Olodumare, the Earth Goddess Onilẹ has a cult, because she interacts directly with mankind. She is polluted by the shedding of human blood, except in sacrifice, and demands costly rites of purification and atonement. The *aiye* rests on her and she supports people during their time in the world; and she receives them when they die. Her cult, Ogboni, has an important function in the organization of the Yoruba state, and her goodwill is essential to the well-being of the king and his kingdom.

As we shall see, a person worships a narrowly limited number of spiritual beings—certain gods and his spirit double, and, we may note in passing, his own head, a spiritual component that controls his success in life, yet is partly independent of his will; but any of the spirits, whether or not he has ever worshiped or invoked them, may come into interaction with him, and he needs a means to ascertain their intentions. Again, at the level of the community, the kingdom, it is important to know what each spiritual power is doing. This can be achieved because God has sent into the world a pair of divine

---

[14] See Batty, 1890; Parkinson, 1906. Frobenius, 1926 (I have seen only the French translation, 1949, where see pp. 91–98) cites a myth in which Oro is invented as a magical procedure and then described as the voice and power of the dead "grandfather"—possibly a too literal translation of the Yoruba *babanla,* ancestors—literally "great fathers"). Bascom (1944, pt. iii) writes: "informants in Ifẹ said Oro came from heaven and is therefore an oriṣa" and also their ancestor; but he does not report any myth to this effect.

mediators. In some respects like *oriṣa,* they are analytically and in their main roles, as Yoruba themselves recognize, *sui generis.* These mediators are Ifa, the spirit of divination, and Eṣu, the divine Trickster. By a careful regard for the intentions of the *oriṣa* and other divinities, as revealed by Ifa, and by a careful respect for the norms of society, one can hope to avoid too much interference from Eṣu, whose intervention, always without one's being aware of it until too late, magnifies one's petty misdeeds and shortcomings into dire offenses against the gods, ancestors, or the king, so that, it has been reported, he is sometimes spoken of as the anger of the gods.[15] There is a considerable and growing literature on these two most interesting divinities.[16]

We can summarize the Yoruba cosmology, or the model of it we have abstracted, in the accompanying diagram, Fig. 33-1.

II. CONTRASTS WITH OTHER MODELS OF THE YORUBA RELIGIOUS SYSTEM

This scheme is so unlike the conventional statement of the Yoruba religious system that we must digress for a moment to say something about that conventional model. It places the various spiritual powers in a hierarchy: at the top, the High God, Ọlọrun, without a cult; next in order of rank, the *oriṣa,* usually including Ifa and Eṣu and sometimes arbitrarily graded into two orders of greater and lesser deities; then the ancestors; and last, minor ghosts, tree spirits, fairies, and so on. The Rev. Dr. E. G. Parrinder, one of the most widely read of more recent writers, reserves the last category for impersonal forces in charms and amulets, putting the petty spirits and fairies in the same class as the minor *oriṣa.* I will just say in passing that Yoruba charms and magical objects are made with the help of *oriṣa,*

[15] Wescott, 1962, p. 337; cf. Frobenius, 1913, i, pp. 230ff.

[16] Among the many published sources, the following may be consulted. For Ifa, Maupoil, 1943, is the outstanding account of Ifa divination and associated myths, beliefs, and rites. Primarily an account of the Dahomean system Fa, which itself derives from the Yoruba Ifa, it includes much Yoruba material; see also Bascom, 1941, 1942 (a useful critical supplement to Clarke); Clarke, 1939; Epega (1931); Frobenius, 1912 (1913), ch. 12 (Frobenius, 1926 [1949], ch. 9 is substantially the same account). For Eṣu see Frobenius, 1912 (1913); Idowu, 1962; Verger, 1957; Wescott, 1962; Wescott and Morton-Williams, 1962. See Herskovits, 1938, ii, for Fọn and Gun (Eastern Ewe) ideas and myths about Lẹgba, which merge indistinguishably with those about the corresponding Yoruba *Eṣu* (who is also called Ẹlẹgbara).

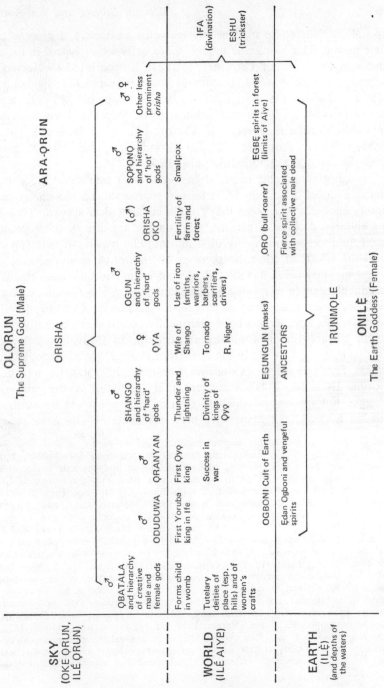

Figure 33-1. The Yoruba cosmology.

who allow them to be used as storage cells, as it were, for some of their power. This hierarchic model, more or less developed, is to be found in the work of Crowther (1852), Bowen (1857—Burton's original), Burton (1863), Baudin (1884), Ellis (1894), Frobenius (1912), Talbot (1926), Epega (1931), Bascom (1944), and Idowu (1962). Its fullest exposition is to be found in three doctoral theses on Yoruba religion: S. S. Farrow (Ph.D. [Edinburgh], publ. 1924), E. G. Parrinder (Ph.D. [London], publ. 1949), and J. O. Lucas (D.D. [Durham], publ. 1950).

Enough ethnographic material has now been published[17] to show that this model is inadequate. It fails to reproduce Yoruba categories closely enough and ignores the Yoruba cosmological system. That it has endured so long is curious. Christianity appears to have prejudiced the investigators, many of whom are clergymen, so that (apart from the effects of romantic theories of "primitive monotheism") a complementary being to the God of Heaven might have been readily imaginable only in terms of a Manichean Enemy, a notion quite alien to West Africa; while Eṣu was cast for the role of the Christian Devil. Possibly, too, later writers have uncritically accepted as generally true for all Yoruba Baudin's and Ellis's accounts of Ifọnyin and Awori Yoruba beliefs (gathered in the area from Porto Novo to Lagos) in a female Earth Goddess (Oduduwa) paired with Ọbatala and not Ọlọrun. Even so, Ellis's statement that "Odudua is the wife of Ọbatala, but she was coeval with Ọlọrun, and not made by him, as was her husband" ought to have been elucidated.[18] The inadequacy

[17] The work of P. Verger deserves especial mention here.

[18] The duality of the Dahomean Mawu-Lisa has been inescapable, but, although they are sometimes said to be fused in an androgynous being, missionaries have gone so far as to equate Mawu (the female member of the pair) with God the Father and Lisa with Jesus Christ! (See Baudin, 1884 (1885); Ellis, 1890; Labouret and Rivet, 1929; Mercier, 1954; and Verger, 1957, ch. 16). The Dahomean Lisa is obviously cognate with the Yoruba Orisala (The Great *Oriṣa*), an alternative name for Ọbatala (loan words from Yoruba drop the initial vowel in Fọn and *l* is regularly substituted for the Yoruba *r*). The Dahomey Mawu I believe to be cognate with the name of the consort of Ọbatala in Ifẹ, Yemoo (contracted from Iye Mowo—*iye*, requiring substantial analysis and demonstration, because in the western "mother," Ifẹ dialect, Mowo, or Moho, proper name). But a full discussion requiring substantial analysis and demonstration, because in the western Yoruba area bordering on Dahomey, Ọbatala is paired with Oduduwa, must be postponed. P. Verger (Verger, 1957, ch. 14, 15, 16, esp. pp. 449, 552), too, has concluded that the *vodun* Mawu is equivalent to the *oriéa* Yemo(w)o, in a notable review of the published evidence and his own field material. He also discusses inconclusively the question whether there existed

of the model, indeed, has been implicit since the earliest writers, because it has failed to find a place, cosmologically, for the Ogboni cult, although the vast importance of Ogboni, to the south-western Yoruba at least, was recorded by Baudin (1884), Ellis (1894), and Dennett (1910), and Frobenius even became initiated into the cult because he realized that in it lay the key to the secrets of all other cults. A cult so plainly unique in function could only be classed with *oriṣa* cults or with so-called ancestor cults on positive evidence that the spiritual beings worshiped were either *oriṣa* or ancestors. No such evidence has been discovered; instead, the functional distinctiveness of Ogboni has been minimized by most writers (though Biobaku's publications[19] on Ogboni in Abẹokuta have corrected this approach); and it has been assumed that all cults that have obvious political or executive powers in the state (or that can impose legitimate coercive sanctions over non-members) can be grouped together functionally (in fact, Ogboni, Oro, and Egungun, to name only the most widely distributed of these, operate their sanctions in quite different ways). It has then been further assumed that the objects of worship, though undisclosed because of the secrecy of the cults, are therefore similar and are somehow concerned with the ancestors—and this although Baudin (1884, Engl. transl., 1885, pp. 63f.) wrote: "The divinity of the Ogboni is Ilẹ (the earth), one of the names of Odudua the great goddess," which Ellis (1894) repeated; and Bascom (1944) plainly stated that the "symbol" of Ogboni was Earth.

My own model has, then, advantages over the one used by my predecessors and colleagues in their analyses. Its main outlines conform to Yoruba cosmological categories, as given stereotyped expression in myth. It matches Yoruba religious conceptions in assigning the different categories of spiritual beings each to its proper domain and not merely classifying by function and inferred relative importance. And by respecting these Yoruba cosmological ideas, it helps us to understand more thoroughly the correspondence between the religious system and the religious organization and to see how religion functions in culture and society.

---

in the hinterland of Western Dahomey or Togo, apart from Christian influence, a separate belief in a male sky god also called Mawu. Among the Krobo of SE. Ghana, the Sky God is called Mawu, the Earth Goddess Kloweki (Mate Kole, 1955, p. 134).

[19] See Biobaku, 1952 and 1956.

III. THE CULTS IN ǪYǪ

Each of the various hierarchies of *orişa* is worshiped through a cult with a priesthood organized into a hierarchy of ranked offices. There are likewise cult organizations for Egungun and Oro, and the rites for the Earth are performed by a strongly corporate cult association with a powerful hierarchy of priests. Lineage ancestors are worshiped with offerings made by the lineage head or senior priest in the lineage at their graves, and also through some of the rites of the Egungun masked cult. Ifa, the divination spirit, is served by a corporation of diviners and he provides the benefits and sanctions of an *orişa* for a diviner's near agnate, wives, and dependents. Eşu too has an organized cult but, consistently enough with his propensity for disorder and lack of regard for authority, his priests do not form a titled hierarchy.

To the distinctions in the proper domain of the various categories of Yoruba deities there correspond differences in the spheres of activity of their cults.

The *orişa* are believed to control external natural forces, including epidemic diseases. The cult associations could impose religious sanctions upon the community (and to a very limited extent are still occasionally permitted to do so); but they could do so only under special circumstances—either when the *orişa* had indicated that it was making demands, for instance through the outbreak of a smallpox epidemic (which indicates that Şọpọnọ[20] is dissatisfied), or the destruction of a part of the town by fire after lightning (indicating the same of Şango), or when the community was making demands upon the *orişa,* such as for rain (Şango) or for success in war (Ǫranyan and Ogun). On such occasions, the priests divined to ask the *orişa* what offerings were required and, later, to ask if the *orişa* was satisfied with the offerings made. Beyond these special occasions it was the duty of the cult association to ensure that the *orişa* was properly and adequately served at its annual festival, and its service might involve some constraint of the community; to ensure the next harvest, for example, no one was permitted to eat new yams before

---

[20] Şọpọnọ, who is responsible for smallpox, is an ordinary *orişa in Ǫyǫ;* its homologue, Sagbata, in Dahomey, is, according to Herskovits and others, an earth deity.

Orișa Oko's annual festival had been observed. Șango, as will be seen, is in a rather special position, as he is not only an *orișa* but also a royal ancestor—he came to furnish the most potent symbol of the power of Oyọ kingship, and he sanctioned certain of the Alafin's diplomatic acts or relations. Șango, however, had two cult associations, one in Oyọ town and the other in the nearby village of Koso, supposedly the site of his apotheosis, and the latter was directly organized from the palace—it was in fact the king's cult of Șango.

The Ogboni, the cult association for Earth, which had judicial and political functions, sanctioned bloodshed, for to shed human blood on the ground was a grave sin against Earth, Egungun and Oro sanctioned sorcery and witchcraft. All three, more generally, sanctioned competition or rivalry with the government within the kingdom. In contrast to the *orișa* cults, then, they wielded sanctions upholding important features of the social structure or rules directly related to these features, as will be shown in more detail later on. The ancestors were concerned with proper behavior in the household and lineage group and also sanctioned marital relations.

The cult of the divination spirit, Ifa, was the concern of a corporation of diviners and was held to provide information necessary for taking decisions within the general sphere of government (beliefs about the activities of spirits were an essential principle of explanation in making events intelligible), while the cult of Ifa's counterpart, Eșu, was considered vital for the general peace and order in the community, and in particular for quiet in the market, where there might be several thousand people.

Admission into a cult is sought from a variety of circumstances. It is expected that a Yoruba will attend and contribute toward the cost of rites for the *orișa* worshiped by both parents; but he does not necessarily become initiated into these cults or even observe their taboos (*eewọ*)—there must first be some evidence that an *orișa* requires his service. This may be a simple matter of asking a diviner which of the parents' gods the child should serve. It has been said earlier that children are the gift of *orișa;* and it is expected that the child will one day become a worshiper of the *orișa* through whose agency his parents conceived him. Ordinarily, this is one of the *orișa* worshiped by the parents, but not necessarily so, because a childless woman may be told that a neglected *orișa* is the one who has a child for her. If it is not already one of their *orișa,* then the parents undertake its worship for the child until he can be initiated into its cult.

Later in life, a person may find his way into a new cult through having been "possessed" by the god, or as a result of personality disorders, or by being called by the god in dreams, or through the agency of Ifa. But, while several gods may be worshiped, the cult of only one as a general rule commands most of a person's participation and enthusiasm, or excites much desire to learn its esoterica and perhaps undergo training for its priesthood.

The highest and, in most instances, all the titled priestly offices in a cult are vested in certain lineages; but it will be obvious that cult members are recruited from a large number of lineages, and it rarely happens that only one *orișa* is served within a lineage, though the lineage members may think of themselves as predominantly—or even exclusively—worshipers of a particular *orișa*.[21] Thus cult membership results in associations that cut across the lineage organization, with its associated compounds, and this alternative set of organized associations has been given governmental functions complementary to those based on locality. These functions, resting on their control of various religious sanctions, gave religious leaders political roles, and provided some of the cults with privileged revenues arising out of their administrative functions.

It may perhaps be recalled from my earlier paper, "The Yoruba Ogboni cult in Ọyọ,"[22] that the two main organized groups in the Ọyọ government are the king with his palace organization, confronted in structural opposition by a corporation of titled officials, the Ọyọ Mesi, the Council of State. A third corporation, the Ogboni cult of the Earth, had a mediating role between them, the Ọyọ Mesi having seats in the Ogboni lodge but no priestly offices in it, so that they could participate in its deliberations but not command them. The Ogboni cult met in its lodge in the palace forecourt and the king was represented there by a woman, who reported its transactions to him but could not take part in its decisions. The Ogboni was recruited from free Yoruba on a basis of age, presumed wisdom, and some prominence in secular or religious life. It worked closely with the corporation of diviners.

These three central organizations of government all had a hand in the control of the cults. First, it was the king's duty to ensure that all the gods were worshiped, and in the course of an annual cycle of

---

[21] On the numbers of *orișa* served within a small agnatic group, see Dennett, 1910, pp. 181f.
[22] Morton-Williams, 1960*b*.

festivals he received the homage and tribute of each group in turn. He had the last word in the appointment of successors to vacant priestly offices. His three main roles—judicial, religious, and military —were largely delegated to three eunuchs. The Qtun Efa (Eunuch of the Right) represented his religious person. Each cult group negotiated with the king and his high officials through its official intermediary, who was either a woman of the palace appointed *iya kekere*, "little mother," of the cult, or a titled slave, the *baba kekere*, its "little father."

Secondly, the main temples of the various *orişa* hierarchies were distributed throughout the various wards of the town; the principal temple of Şango, a deified Alafin, was in the royal ward, the others in wards governed by different members of the Qyǫ Mesi. Lesser temples of each cult were often set up in the compounds of titled priests, or the priests otherwise set aside a room as a shrine, and most worshipers set up a small shrine in their own compound. The titled priests, like compound heads, frequently communicated with the ward head and joined in periodical assemblies of ward elders; they were responsible to the ward elders and to that member of the Qyǫ Mesi who was ward head for the religious well-being of the ward. The Qyǫ Mesi also received customary gifts when priests celebrated the annual festival at their temple or shrine. Further, certain members of the Qyǫ Mesi were responsible for rites important for the whole kingdom. In the Qyǫ Mesi was reconstituted by Alafin Atiba, first king of New Qyǫ, in the middle of the nineteenth century, and as it endured until 1956 when it was again reconstituted, five of its seven members held this responsibility and it is said that four of these five had held it in Old Qyǫ; the fifth, the Aşipa of Qyǫ was first admitted to the Qyǫ Mesi by Atiba who built New Qyǫ on the site of the camp of an Old Qyǫ man holding the title of Aşipa, the chief title of the *egbe ode*, the association of hunters.

The head of the Qyǫ Mesi, the Başǫrun, divined once a year to find the state of the relationship between the Alafin and his spirit counterpart in heaven; a bad relationship could, it was said, be made to justify a demand for the king's suicide. The Alapini was head of the *egungun* cult, which had an important function in government, as we shall see later. The Agbakin headed the cult of Qranyan, first Alafin of Qyǫ, to whom human sacrifice had to be offered before any war as a condition of success. The Laguna was head of the cult of Orişa Oko, god of the fertility of farmland and of game in the bush.

The Aṣipa, in virtue of his role as chief of the hunters' association, was head of the cult of Ogun, god of the use of iron, and the ọdẹ were, under his command, the advance guards of the army and scouts in defensive war. The Ọyọ Mesi, then, had a twofold part in the control of cults. One was a rather general and limited control of cult activities going on in their wards (such as the Aṣipa's over the rites of Ọbatala, whose temple was in his ward). This control was nevertheless important because the cults were not only charged with the satisfactory worship of a god whose goodwill was essential to the kingdom; cult associations also commanded powerful religious sanctions, since they could obtain magical powers from the gods and use them against their enemies. The other kind of control the Ọyọ Mesi had was through the Baṣọrun's role in the service of the king's ọrun (spirit double) and the role of certain others as heads of cults that were both vital to the spiritual well-being of the kingdom of Ọyọ and also, as far as the cults of Ọranyan, Egungun, and to some extent Ogun were concerned, were cults that gave their leaders political power—Ọranyan and Ogun in external relations, Egungun within Ọyọ.

Furthermore, the Ogboni numbered among its members priests of many cults; it had a say in the timing and conduct of festivals through its right to be represented when Ifa was consulted on behalf of the town, and so an advisory as well as a directly administrative function in the control of religious affairs.

It would be hard to overestimate the importance of divination in this system, where statecraft had to take so heavily into account the intrusion of autonomous spirit powers. These powers, seen from the human point of view, were a factor that made rational decision impossible unless the diviners could reveal the intentions and desires of the various kinds of spirits. The Alafin had a hierarchy of Ifa diviners to serve the needs of state. The principal diviner, the Ọnalemọlẹ, lived not far from the palace in the royal sector of the town and, through the Osi Ẹfa (and not, interestingly, through the Ọtun Ẹfa, the eunuch for religion), he had access to the king at any time. The various Ọyọ Mesi chiefs, like anyone else who constantly had to take decisions, had each their consulting diviner; the Aṣipa, indeed, as head of the original village that had grown into New Ọyọ, had (and still has) his own high priest of Ifa with an appropriate following of titled diviners.

The Ọnalemọlẹ had a wide range of duties. He obtained Ifa's

judgment on the merit of the candidate for succession after the death of an Alafin, and, again, of any candidate for high political or religious office before the Alafin would give his assent to the appointment—Ifa might reject the candidate outright, or make a conditional judgment stipulating that various offerings or purifications must first be made. He had to find Ifa's diagnosis of the general spiritual relations of Ọyọ regularly, at sixteen-day intervals, and, besides this, of any strange, portentous event. Aided by his hierarchy of diviners, he interpreted the signs and formulae of the Ifa oracle, which were generalized pronouncements in mythical language, into statements of specific application to the here and now. It has been said, of divination in general, that the oracle replaces a dilemma with an enigma (Metman, 1963); it was the duty of the diviners at the king's court to resolve the enigma after they had produced it, the king needing information and not riddles.

Of all the *orişa* cults, the cult of Şango requires special mention, even in this summary paper. It was linked closely through beliefs about Şango as a deified Alafin and, through its organization, with the powers of the king of Ọyọ, who was himself, both as a descendant of Şango and also as king, the vessel for some of Şango's powers. The principal Şango temple was situated in the Alafin's ward in Ọyọ shrine in the ward of the Başọrun. The cult was organized on an empire-wide basis, with some central control. Succession to the highest ranks in the cult (a hereditary high-priesthood whose members were not expected to become possessed by the god) was vested in certain Ọyọ lineages, most of them in the royal wards of the town; and all possession priests, though resident in the various kingdoms of their birth, had to come to Ọyọ for the final stages of their initiatory training and to be equipped with the paraphernalia of priesthood.[23] Since possession priests were not only in a violent frenzy when possessed by the god, but were also believed to have the power to direct lightning, and since, further, they were authorized to collect what might be ruinously high purification fees after lightning had struck, the cult was a powerful corporation, and, outside Ọyọ itself, not fully under the jurisdiction of the local state. Again, the powers of Şango were, it seems, made use of by the Alafin in the administration of the more distant parts of the Ọyọ empire. The Alafin in the late eighteenth century appointed titled slaves as his agents (*aşoju ọba:* king's observers, is the Ọyọ term for them; they are also called

[23] Wescott and Morton-Williams, 1962, 23f.

ajęlę) to ensure the loyalty and fiscal honesty of certain vassal kings, especially along the trade route to the Atlantic ports. Dr. Biobaku has recorded the interesting Egba tradition that the *ajęlę* were all initiated priests of Ṣango,[24] as such they were believed to have magical powers, notably the power to direct lightning, and in possession were, like other priests of this deified king, accorded royal rank and in this state could confront and make demands upon vassal kings with impunity. In Ọyọ the Ọtun Efa (eunuch in charge of state religion) told me that while not all the *aṣoju ọba* were priests of Ṣango, those that were not always had Ṣango priests in their entourage.[25]

The Egungun cult, the masked association,[26] had a part in the government of Ọyọ. Masked associations were powerful in many Yoruba states as in so many West African societies. In Ọyọ the *egungun* was prominent, but not as powerful (in New Ọyọ, at least) as it was in the south-western Yoruba states. Egungun masks brought back the spirits of important ancestors and also brought the gods to town,[27] so they were considered dangerous and powerful and not merely awesome. The cult was directed by the Alapini, one of the Ọyọ Mesi, but the most powerful *egungun*, Jęnju, was owned by the

[24] Biobaku, 1957, p. 8.

[25] Clapperton, 1829, Engl. edn., p. 10, American edn., p. 36; Lander, R. L. and J., 1830, i, p. 67, describe the Alafin's representative in Ijanna (they call him "the king of Jennah") as wearing a red hat, which might be indicative that he was a Ṣango priest, as red cloth is emblematic in the dress of Ṣango priests. Some of the lineal descendants of the last of these representatives worship Ṣango to this day; but they, or others of his descendants, also worship Ogun, Eṣu, and Egungun, so it is hard to decide what can be safely inferred from this fact. These people say their ancestors brought them all from Old Ọyọ, and the names of persons believed to have been born through the agency of all these *orіṣa* occur in the genealogies over several generations.

[26] Morton-Williams, 1956; Beier, 1956. Bascom, 1944, has some material on the cult in Ifę, but his account shows that the cult there differs from its structure in the Ọyọ empire.

[27] Egungun were said in Ęgbado to come from the earth; but the Yoruba sometimes call them *araọrum*, "sky people" (a term used primarily of the spirit-double). I have heard this term for *egungun* in Ọyọ, and Idowu notes it, too, presumably as used in Ifę. Yet, as Verger writes (1957, p. 507): "Egun est évoqué, appelé, en frappant le sol trois fois avec une baguette (*iṣan*)." Since there are also *egungun* masks representing, and sometimes occupied by, *orіṣa,* who are certainly sky-beings, there is nothing to be gained, as far as this cult is concerned, by splitting hairs over the precise location of the ancestors. "Both" Earth and Sky beings comes nearer than "either/or" to Yoruba habits of mind.

Alafin, who kept the mask in the palace, assigned it to a slave or eunuch to wear, and employed him to execute witches and sorcerers.[28]

The Oro cult, a men's secret association, was not granted in Qyọ the political and police powers it had in the south-western Yoruba area, powers that were vividly described by the nineteenth-century visitors to Abẹokuta.[29] In southern and western Yoruba kingdoms, as well as punishing witches and sorcerers in the name of supernatural powers, the Oro and Egungun cults were also used to threaten or even to make away with those who, while lacking a titled office, were, by wealth or following, in a position to challenge the constituted authorities. In present-day Qyọ which, it will be recollected, was founded some time after the fall of Old Qyọ in the 1830's, the number of Oro initiates is small and its head is not one of the principal state officers, but is the head of a village community, Jabata, that came to settle within the walls of New Qyọ in the mid-nineteenth century, Jabata is said to be a community of Ṣa (Sha) Yoruba origin, a western Yoruba people now mainly in Dahomey. The Oro cult is conspicuously developed among the Ṣa, as it is among the Ẹgba and other southern Yoruba people, while it has seldom been reported among northern Yoruba. I conclude not only that adepts in the cult from Old Qyọ were not resettled in New Qyọ, but, further, the cult may not have existed in Old Qyọ. It seems that at least over the last century it was restricted to performing rites to neutralize witchcraft as a force at large and was not permitted to make attacks on particular reputed witches.[30]

We are now able to summarize the cult organization in the Qyọ kingdom diagrammatically (Figs. 33–2 and 33–3).

Two important points remain to be discussed. The first concerns the roles of men and women in government. In Qyọ representatives of four categories of men: the king and men of the royal lineage, free men, slaves, and palace eunuchs, all held positions of authority within the state, secular and military as well as religious. Women too in Qyọ could achieve state offices, but only through the cults. It has already been said that certain palace women (some the widows

[28] I was told, probably truly, that Alafin Ladugbolu (d. 1947), like some of his predecessors, had sometimes worn this mask himself.

[29] Bowen, 1857, Burton, 1863, Campbell, 1861, and Farrow, 1926 are among the more readily accessible descriptions.

[30] See Morton-Williams, 1956 and 1960a for a discussion of some of the functions of Oro.

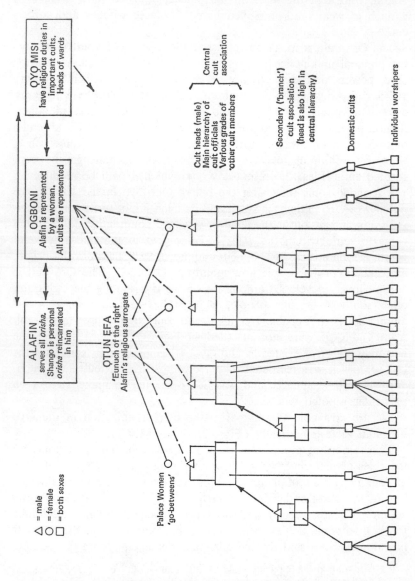

Figure 33–2. The pattern of religious organization in Ọyọ: Structure of cults.

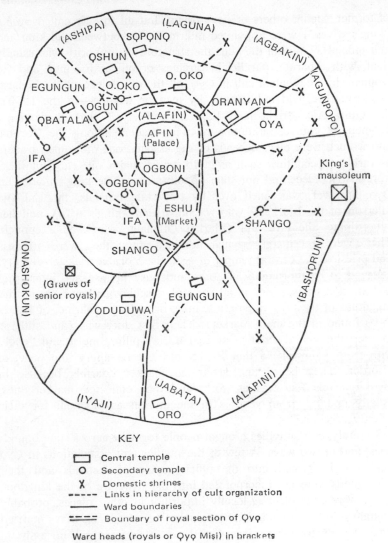

KEY

▭	Central temple
○	Secondary temple
X	Domestic shrines
----	Links in hierarchy of cult organization
——	Ward boundaries
≡≡≡	Boundary of royal section of Ǫyǫ

Ward heads (royals or Ǫyǫ Miṣi) in brackets

Figure 33–3. Pattern of distribution of temples and domestic shrines in Ǫyǫ (simplified).

NOTES:

1. All *orisa* have shrines in the palace, except Sango, who has his own royal village, Koso, on the outskirts of Ǫyǫ.
2. There is no central temple for Ifa. Certain Ifa rites are performed in a grove outside the town.

of former Alafin, others of slave origin, but all loosely called *ayaba,* "king's wives") were appointed intermediaries between the king and cult officials.[31] Within the cults the structure of authority was usually dual, with separate, parallel hierarchies of offices for men and for women (in the Ọbatala cult in Ọyọ, all the offices except the highest, Ajẹ, could be held indifferently by men or women—in the 1950's, the Ọtun Ajẹ, "right-hand [i.e. deputy] Ajẹ," was a woman). Women, of course, outnumber men as traders among the Yoruba, and women were elected heads of the associations of women traders in various specialties, such as cloth, yams, palm oil, etc. But these were lowly offices and not state appointments. The king's market in Ọyọ, however, was ruled over by two state officials, the Ẹni Ọja (Person of the Market), who was an *ayaba* (king's wife), and her subordinate, the Arẹ Ọja (Market Official), who was a eunuch. These were not merely secular administrators; they were priestess and priest of the central temple of Eṣu, the Yoruba trickster-divinity, believed to be thoroughly at home and busy in markets, interfering with market transactions in all sorts of mischievous ways (in all the kingdoms of the Ọyọ empire, a temple, or at least a shrine, of Eṣu is to be found in the main market). Their first duty was (and still is) to keep the sacred emblem of Eṣu a clay pillar, moist and "cool" with fresh palm-oil, so that Eṣu would not be angry and provoke disorder. They heard and arbitrated market quarrels because in these quarrels Eṣu was at work, and they collected market dues, usually in kind, from vendors in the market as payment for their priestly services.[32]

Secondly, cult activities brought people together across state boundaries, and in two ways. A few of the smaller cult associations in Ọyọ were not integrated into the official cycle of festivals and their priesthoods were not incorporated into the structure of the kingdom. These were cults of *oriṣa* locally important in other places, probably brought into Ọyọ by immigrants—including, of course, wives married from distant towns. Shrines for these *oriṣa* were set up only in the compounds of worshipers, not in public open spaces, and their festivals were domestic affairs during which cult members would celebrate in one another's compounds in turn. At present in Ọyọ (it is impossible to know what happened in the old days of imperial Ọyọ) the cult members also send delegates with gifts to the main

[31] Cf. Johnson, 1921, pp. 63ff.
[32] Cf. Johnson, 1921, p. 66.

center of worship of the *orişa*. For instance, the national goddess of Oşogbo, a large town and kingdom of Ijeşa origin on the river Oşun, is the *orişa* Oşun, deity of the river,[33] she is worshiped in a few compounds in Oyo and six or seven of her worshipers travel every year to Oşogbo, 70 miles away, for her annual festival there. Conversely, Oyo *émigrés* are sometimes represented at Oyo festivals.

In concluding, we may observe that at the present time the majority of the population of Oyo is Muslim, with a substantial Christian minority. Some people both serve *orişa* and are either Muslims or Christians, but the traditional religion is in rapid decline. Certainly it lacks the powers in the state that it formerly had, yet the cult organization has not altogether vanished and the Alafin still plays his role, though a dwindling one, in the traditional pattern of religious ceremonies, and the annual cycle of festivals, with a few gaps, continues in a modest way. The higher cult offices still carry obvious prestige and bring in small incomes, and the magical power of initiates is still feared. But recruits for even some of the highest priestly offices are often hard to find and much lore is dying with the old people who know it. The rivalries of modern party politics have penetrated the cult organization, bringing into the open old factions or mere jealousy and hardening them into permanent schisms.[34] This has done perhaps as much, during the last few years, as conversions to new religions and the exclusion of cult groups such as Ogboni from modern administration to hasten the end of the traditional pattern of religious life in Oyo.

[33] Verger, 1957, pp. 405–12, gives information about the cult of Oşun.
[34] Splits along political lines are not confined to the old cults. In several communities, including Oyo, the Muslims have divided into Action Group and N.C.N.C. congregations, each sometimes with its own mosque and imam.

34. Coptic Christianity

Christianity, which eventually became the religion of the original Egyptian race—the Copts—first entered the country through the missionary campaign of St. Mark. It is not certain, however, that Mark himself actually visited Egypt. The teaching of the "Man from Nazareth" displaced the ancient pagan religion, although it took several centuries to do this completely. The original Eyptians who adopted Christianity have since then been called Coptic Christians. The process was gradual and the period witnessed a change in language as well as religion. After the Greek conquest of Alexandria, the Greek word for Egypt—Aiguptos, which was the Greek form of the Old Egyptian *Haka Ptah* (house of the old God Ptah)—was first applied to the river Nile; then to the "land of the Nile."

Literally therefore, one meaning of the term Copt implies "nationality" rather than "religion." This is confirmed by the fact that Greek and other Christians who lived in Egypt did not at this time apply the term Copt to themselves. Later, in the middle of the seventh century when the Arabs took Egypt, the name Copt ceased to mean "inhabitant of Egypt" and acquired the sense of Christian descendants of the Old Egyptians, in contrast to the Muslim invaders. Later still the term acquired a new and final meaning, that of Egyptian *monophysite*, without regard to previous nationality.

Today any person who joins the Egyptian Church and accepts their monophysite doctrines at the same time assumes their name. On the other hand, while Old Egyptians who embrace Islam are called Arabs, the term Arab is now also applied to all Egyptians without reference to religion. Monophysite Christians may be correctly called Jacobite, after the monophysite patriarch, Jacob Bardaeus, consecrated in A.D. 535. Thus today Old Egyptian, Jacobite, monophysite,

SOURCE: A. J. Davis, "Coptic Christianity" *Tarikh,* Vol. 2, No. 1, 1967, pp. 43–51. Reprinted by permission of the author and publisher.

and Copt have the same meaning. Finally, the Arabs call the Copts *Qibti* or *Qibt* (plural) but when no reference to religion is implied Egyptians are called *Maisri*.

EVOLUTION OF LANGUAGE

The old population which took the name Copt, which is also derived from Haka Ptah, is that branch of the Egyptian race which speaks a language that is a mixture of Old Egyptian (the language that used the *hieroglyphic* script) and Greek. By hieroglyphic we mean a picture standing for a word. Originally these "pictures" were not traced by the pen on paper, but were carved with great effort by chisel and hammer on granite and marble. Sometimes the carvings were several inches deep. This peculiar writing came to be known to us through being carved on temple walls, on obelisks, on monuments, and on pillars and images.

Scholars have been able to demonstrate that this writing had passed through three separate stages. Originally it was a pure "picture" form of writing. But, because carving and chiseling was laborious, shortened forms came into being, and this "picture writing" came to be called hieratic. To begin with this was largely the script of the language of the priesthood and a few learned people. Later, the hieratic form evolved into the demotic (script of the people) alphabet, which the Phoenicians used. It was that alphabet, with modifications, that became the basis of European and Asian scripts.

As the living speech of Old Egyptians grew continually more different from the old form of the language, it again needed a new alphabet. Thus when the Greeks occupied Egypt the language of the victors gradually became that of the defeated, and a Greek alphabet emerged. This Greek alphabet, plus six letters for which the Greeks had no equivalent, were retained within the demotic system. Thus a new alphabet, with its associated Greco-Egyptian language—Coptic —was born. The new language assimilated new words and new ideas brought into Egypt by the foreign colonies and this led to a new epoch.

Thus between about 500 B.C. and A.D. 200 a complete transformation had occurred. While the abbreviated picture writing that the people used gradually gave way to the Greek alphabet, Coptic Christianity was gradually developing out of the ancient Egyptian religion, until by the fifth century we find its mature form. The influence of the Greek language is of great importance in this process since it is only in the expressions of that language that the various interpretations of the Trinity can be fully understood. Later in this article we will see in detail how the Coptic interpretation of the Trinity was different from that accepted by the Council of Chalcedon.

TRANSFORMATION OF RELIGION

The development of language was thus closely related to the development of religion in Egypt, and this was helped by the similarities between the "old" and the "new" religion. The years between the influence of Mark in Egypt and the persecutions of about A.D. 300 saw a great transformation in Egyptian thought and feeling. The efforts of those who followed the teaching of Jesus of Nazareth soon went far beyond the expectations, or even the hopes, of those who were close to him, and with this success over the Old Egyptian God, *Amon-Re* (Light of the World), there followed Egyptian disenchantment with their "sacred animals" and disillusionment with the old worship of rocks. There had already been a weakening of Old Egyptian thought about *Amon-Re* as a result of the difficulty of understanding hieroglyphics, and the consequently meaningless nature of much of the ritual surrounding worship of the God, and this earlier loss of confidence in sacred rocks and animals prepared the way for the new religion from Galilee.

The change was also encouraged because the Egyptians had beliefs that made it easier to accept the basic doctrines of the new religion. The idea held in pre-Christian Egypt that God is one and that the numberless names, idols, and images all pointed to aspects of the same principle found its way into the new religion. The Old Egyptian god whose substance exists externally, that is, in material form; a god who gives himself his own being; and a god who is eternal; all these were ideas in common with Christianity. Similarly the Old Egyptian idea of a divine judgment was not unlike the Christian belief in the Second Coming. The Egyptian idea of the eternal conflict and difference between good and evil supported the teaching in the new religion of a hell and heaven. The concept of the immortality of the soul was a truth that would be confirmed by St.

Mark himself. In the group of *Isis, Horus,* and *Osiris* these were similarities to the Christian doctrine of the Trinity.

There were also Old Egyptian "popular traditions" that helped the new religion. Thus Old Egyptian ideas that sins had to be atoned for and that sin was hereditary, as well as ideas about the fall from original purity, easily found themselves expressed in the new religion. Thus many factors favored the spread of the new Christian religion so that by the end of the third century it was the dominant faith.

ALEXANDRIA: SEAT OF COPTIC CHRISTIANITY

The city of Alexandria, founded by Alexander the Great, whose tomb it held, became the residence of Kings descended from his companion-in-arms, Ptolemy, the son of Lagus. The Library of Alexandria, a center of study and instruction, was organized on the model of the Greek teaching tradition. Because much of the Mediterranean trade passed through its sheltered port, Alexandria soon outgrew Carthage, developed into the largest city in the Mediterranean, and became the great center of Hellenistic and Jewish culture. The large collection of scrolls in its library led to the growth of a fine university that attracted many scholars. It soon became the center of all Greek intellectual life. It was the headquarters of the philosophers: the meeting place of thinkers and poets; and the residence of artists and mathematicians. The names of Samothrace, the collector of Homeric texts, Euclid, the mathematician, and Herophius, the anatomist who founded a medical school are associated with the history of Alexandria.

Through the harbor of Alexandria the traders of the world came to the treasures of Egypt. Greek merchants, adventurers, and officials gained a foothold everywhere in Upper and Lower Egypt; they mingled with the indigenous population and, in doing so, as we have seen, produced a mixed Egypto-Hellenic race, who formed the link between pure Hellenism and Old Egyptian thought.

Then, in 47 B.C., Julius Caesar occupied the city and destroyed its first library. In 30 B.C., after the suicide of Cleopatra, Alexandria fell into the hands of Octavius and Egypt became a Roman province. But by later centuries of Roman rule it had become once again a great center, this time a center of Christian learning rivaling the reputation of two other great centers, Rome and Constantinople. In the meantime, Christianity had become the religion of the "Old Egyptian" population. A famous historian—Eusebius—records that sometime after the Roman occupation, Egypt was evangelized by Simon Peter and John Mark. Although there is some doubt about this, the Egyptians hold that Mark was the first Patriarch or head of the Coptic Church, that he suffered martyrdom in Alexandria, but that the work he had begun remained and grew.

ORIGEN

The city of Alexandria was famed throughout the world, and so were the men who lived in the city during Christian times. One of the most remarkable was Origenes Adamantius, known to us as Origen of Alexandria. Origen brought a new dimension to Alexandria's reputation. His education, unlike that of his equally great predecessor, Clement of Alexandria, was first religious, then philosophical. He learned Hebrew, studied grammar, and mastered the principles of the important philosophy of his day, Neoplatonism. His literary output was immense and he wrote on such varying topics as the resurrection, prayers, and on exhortation and martyrdom. Origen attempted to combine the fundamental principles of Greek philosophy with the beliefs of Christianity in order to prove that the Christian view of the universe did not contradict Greek thought, which was highly respected in his day. He was the most formidable theologian in the Church before Augustine of Hippo.

In A.D. 230, Origen was ordained by the Bishops of Caesarea and Jerusalem, but Demetrius, his own Bishop of Alexandria, banished him from Alexandria. He went to Caesarea, where in 231 he founded a new school more famous even than the one in Alexandria. The reason for this banishment was that his orthodoxy was questioned.

Orthodox belief held that Christ was co-eternal and co-equal with the Father. Origen believed that Christ was created by the Father, and was therefore inferior to him. It was the idea behind this belief that was eventually, though in a rather different form, to be the main point of disagreement between Coptic Christianity and the rest of the church. Origen also felt that a Christian should draw from the Scriptures whatever could be found there or deduced. He was thus also condemned because it was felt that his doctrine would encourage private judgment and speculation.

DISPUTES AND QUARRELS

"Christians of those times had much stronger desire to dispute and quarrel than to discover truth" is the opinion of one historian. As Antioch, Constantinople, and Alexandria favored different systems, argument occurred. The whole period saw Christianity torn by disputes and rash decisions. New ideas and practices often originated more from argument than from religious conviction.

The first of the fierce discussions was about the "nature" of Christ. In its broadest sense the problem was the relationship of the Son to the Father. Whether that nature was human or divine or both was the essential question.

Generally, the Church had agreed that the divine nature of Christ was co-eternal with the Father, that the Son was of the same nature with God, the Father. Origen had taught that the Son was subordinate (inferior) to the Father. Widespread dispute followed. By the second decade of the fourth century it reached a high point through Arius, a presbyter in the Church of Alexandria, who felt, in general agreement with Origen, that Christ was neither eternal nor of the same substance as the Father, and was therefore inferior rather than equal. Origen was of course dead, but in 318, Bishop Alexander of Alexandria called a synod of nearly one hundred Egyptian Bishops at which Arius was condemned and deposed. This naturally caused great excitement in the Church among Arius' many followers. The controversy quickly spread beyond the boundaries of the city as the condemned man looked elsewhere for help. Bishop Alexander was then invited by Emperor Constantine to hold a council of all the Bishops of Christendom to discuss the matter. By virtue of his divine commission, Constantine felt some concern for the Church. To strengthen it and give it peace seemed to him necessary to complete the security and the unity of the Roman Empire. As a consequence he took an active part in the Council of Nicea where it was held that Jesus Christ was *fully man* and at the same time *fully God,* and Arius was condemned again. Rejection of Arius' doctrine remains to the present day a cardinal teaching in the Christian Church.

Disputes continued all the time. Nestorius, Patriarch of Constantinople, denied that Mary was the Mother of God, but rather insisted she was the Mother of Christ, Eutychius, also of Constantinople and chief opponent of Nestorius, even suggested that Christ had only one nature and that was divine, implying that his humanity was absorbed in divinity. In a local synod in Constantinople in A.D. 448, Eutychius was condemned and deposed. But Emperor Theodosius favored Eutychianism and called a Council at Ephesus in A.D. 449, where Eutychius was reinstated. The tide was to change once more, and upon the death of Theodosius (A.D. 450) his orthodox successors, Empress Pulcheria and Emperor Marcian, called the famous Council of Chalcedon to right the wrongs of Ephesus and to discuss Eutychianism. The ideas of Nestorius and Eutychius were rejected.

Chalcedon's chief work was its definition of the "nature" and the "person" of Christ. In opposition to the view of Eutychianism that Christ has one nature it declared that Christ combines two distinct natures, one divine and one human. Moreover, it declared, the two natures exist separately in one person—hence the phrase "Christ is two natures in one person." While this definition became the test of orthodoxy in the East and in the West, it was rejected by the "Old Egyptians."

THE COPTIC CHURCH AND NEW IMPERIAL MASTERS

The Coptic Church, as it is today, owes its distinctive character to the dispute about the natures of Christ which was defined in 451 at the Council of Chalcedon. The formula that the Council adopted is roughly as follows:

> The Son of God, the second person of the
> Trinity being fully God and eternal, of one
> substance and equal with the father . . . is of
> *two whole, perfect and distinct natures* . . .
> joined together in one person. . . .

In short the Chalcedonians held that "Christ is two—divine and human—one person." The formula was rejected by the Old Egyptian Christians and they substituted in its stead: "Christ is *one* nature in *one* person." For the Old Egyptians the number two could not precede the term "nature" because the latter was a synonym for "person." Two natures meant for them two persons. As a consequence the group that rejected the "two natures" formula and substituted the "one nature" idea regarded the Council of Chalcedon as wrong. The Egyptians who supported the Council were called Melchites—Royalists—because they agreed with the Emperor Marcian in his attempts to gain uniformity of doctrine. On the other hand, those who opposed it were the Copts, and these were described as monophysites; which is a combination of two Greek words *monos* (one) and *physis* (nature).

A BRIEF TRIUMPH

Egyptian Christianity was thus split into two, and various imperial conquerors of Egypt sought to use this division for their own ends.

After a brief period of Persian rule, the Emperor Heraclius of Byzantium drove them out in 626 and was welcomed by Melchite and Copt alike. But Heraclius did not tolerate "heretics" and, as a result, the Copts looked to their own Coptic-speaking Patriarch as the leader against imperial control, successfully resisting the attempts of the Melchites to impose orthodoxy. Some fifteen years later the invading armies of Amr ibn al'As, who was conquering in the name of Islam, captured Egypt from the Byzantines. The Copts rejoiced at the appearance of an invader, hoping with Muslim aid to throw off the Melchite hold. The Melchites were destroyed. Benjamine, a famous monophysite, who earlier had been expelled, returned to head the Church. He and his followers then took possession of every Church and monastery in Egypt.

THE TURN OF THE TIDE

By 700 however, the tide of events suddenly changed once more when the Amir of Egypt demanded the first tribute from Coptic monks. The relationship between the two communities continued to deteriorate as the Copts became a less and less important section of the population. They were avoided by Muslims and cut off from intellectual stimulus and growth, so much that, during the Crusades, the western Christian found co-operation with the Copts impossible. In addition, their churches were systematically destroyed, their images broken, and their icons burned. Moreover, taxes got heavier as oppression increased. Throughout the ages Coptic Christians recanted and accepted Islam. In 1345 it is recorded that 600 Copts accepted Islam in one day. By the seventeenth century, due to a governmental decree, Coptic ceased to be the language of every day and became a liturgical language only.

Thus the long association with Islam had a discouraging effect and provided a new cultural element in the community. While many kept the Coptic faith they adopted the language of their conquerors and continue to speak Arabic to the present day. In the twentieth century fate smiled again, and the closely knit community that had been loyal to its Muslim rulers held posts of honor, and by the law of the country obtained equal rights with other sections of the Egyptian population.

THE COPTIC CHURCH TODAY

"Wisdom hath builded her house, she hath hewn out her seven sacraments." Remaining faithful to this passage from Proverbs (IX:1) the Copts acknowledge seven sacraments, namely: Baptism, Confirmation, Matrimony, Eucharist, Penance, Orders, and Unction for the sick.

Male children are baptized on the fortieth and female on the eightieth day after birth. According to Coptic tradition these are the days of purification. When death is apparent, the child is baptized at once. The water used requires a special consecration, and the child is completely immersed. Confirmation, while it is a sacrament in itself, is linked with baptism. The individual has to wear a white garment. After a special prayer, the eyes and the forehead are anointed with holy *chrism* (oil with salve); then the nostrils and mouth, and ears and the hands on both sides, then the breast, knees, and the instep of the feet and the back of the arms are similarly anointed. Finally the individual is crowned. Thus the anointment, the white garment, and the crown are symbols of a confirmed Coptic Christian. The Eucharist is given to infants immediately after baptism. For adults it is generally given after a period of fasting and after having received absolution.

The priests take it every week. The bread used is baked into wafers on which a cross is stamped, and the wine is unfermented. Penance or confession takes place whenever it is desired. During the week before Easter, it is observed by all. It is also required by someone on the point of dying. Orders are the consecration of officers of the church. The sacrament of Matrimony is performed in the church or at the bridegroom's home. Anointment (Unction) for the sick is also performed in the church, but if the person is unable to be present he may be represented by a relative or friend.

When the majority of the people accepted Christianity at the beginning of the fourth century, the Bible was translated into the modified language of the "Old Egyptians." There are three main versions of the Coptic Bible: *Memphic, Thebaic,* and *Bashmuric.* The first is named after the city Memphis, the second after Thebes, and the third after a province in the Delta. These Coptic versions of the Bible are translated closely from the Greek. Thebaic and Memphic are the dialects of Upper and Lower Egypt. There is also an Arabic version of the Bible which is sometimes used in the churches. This of course is due to the influence of the Muslims.

The head of the entire Coptic Church is called Patriarch, and his seat is in the beautiful cathedral in Cairo. At first he resided in Alexandria, but the seat of the See was ultimately transferred to the growing new capital. Cairo, which ever since has been the residence of all Coptic Patriarchs. The Copts refer to him as Qodsak (Your Holiness). Patriarchs are traditionally appointed by lot from nine monks of the Convent of St. Antonius. Next to the Patriarch are the four metropolitans or archbishops; those of Alexandria, of Manufia, of Jerusalem, and until 1950—when an Ethiopian was chosen —of Ethiopia. In addition to these four there are twelve bishops representing the twelve apostles.

Under each bishop are the chief priests who rule the local churches. Among the higher ranks of the Coptic priests marriage is forbidden. In the lower ranks, if a priest's wife dies he cannot remarry. After the chief priests are the archdeacons and deacons. Their main functions are to read in the Church and assist the priest in his public service. Generally, their number is limited to seven to each church. Sometimes young people are chosen because "they are less defiled with sin." They are ordained by their archbishop, who cuts a lock of their hair. Then there are the subdeacons who look after the candles and the censers. They are followed by the lector, who reads the lesson before the people, and the doorkeeper. Finally there are the monks who inhabit desolate corners of Egypt. They live by alms.

In the Coptic Church the more pious usually take off their shoes. This practice, however, is no longer essential. All the lessons are read standing. The lamps represent the stars and are filled with olive oil, because at the deluge from among all the trees God saved the olive trees. Icons of Christ, the Virgin Mary, and the saints adorn the walls. No music except cymbals and triangles accompanies the songs of praise and there is no "beginning notice" (such as the ringing of bells, which is forbidden by the Muslims). Many of the churches do not have pulpits but a reader's desk instead. And finally Coptic Churches tend to be in out-of-the-way places—probably because of Islamic dominance. Many features thus reflect the isolation of Coptic Christianity from the rest of the Church, as well as the influence of Islam; this last is also seen in Coptic marriage and funeral practices.

The Coptic Church was the national religion of Egypt in fact only from the Council of Chalcedon to the Arabic invasion, and in theory it was not even this, because the Orthodox Church was recognized as the official church until the Arab conquest. Copts regard their history as virtually ending with the coming of the Arabs, and in many ways this is true. They were accepted by the Islamic state as *"dhimmis"* (client people) and their numbers have declined. Nevertheless they have always been prominent as civil servants in the Arab administration, and are today well represented in the Egyptian parliament.

35. The Ethiopic Liturgy: An Analysis

The Ethiopic Liturgy has been the object of a limited degree of scientific research. Samuel A. B. Mercer,[1] to mention one specialist, has attempted to establish the Liturgy of Ethiopia in its probable primitive form, in the Greek of the fifth century. But the Liturgy is more than an object of technical research; it is a witness to life. It is marked with a long history; in it the faith of praying generations has been crystallized. It may be considered as a fruit of the rich Ethiopian cultural soil, and hence may enlighten us on some of the characteristics of the aesthetic religious background of the people. A prolonged contact with the liturgical text, of which I made an English translation in 1958,[2] has rendered this text, as it were, transparent in all its beauty—a beauty that is nearly unknown to the outside world, except for a narrow circle of scholars. After a short historical introduction, I should like to present here my impressions as a translator.

Ethiopia became a Christian empire toward the middle of the fourth century. Its first apostle, St. Frumentius, received the episcopal consecration from the hands of St. Athanasius, patriarch of Alexandria. He transplanted into his country of adoption the ecclesiastical traditions of Alexandria, and within these the Divine Liturgy itself,

SOURCE: Claude Sumner, "The Ethiopic Liturgy: An Analysis" *Journal of Ethiopian Studies,* Vol. 1, No. 1, January 1963, pp. 40–46. Reprinted by permission of the author and publisher.

[1] S. A. B. Mercer, *The Ethiopic Liturgy* (Milwaukee: The Young Churchman, 1915), pp. 393–465: photographic reproduction of the text of the Anaphora of the Apostles according to MS. Mercer 3. See also F. E. Brightman, *Liturgies Eastern and Western* (1896), pp. 228–44; J. M. Harden, *The Anaphoras of the Ethiopic Liturgy* (London: Macmillan, 1928), pp. 31–50; Marcos Daoud, *The Liturgy of the Ethiopian Church* (Addis Ababa: Berhane Selam Printing Press, 1954), pp. 56–78.

[2] C. Sumner, *The Ethiopic Liturgy* (Addis Ababa: Artistic Printing Press, 1958). Translation of the Liturgy of the Apostles, in its non-solemn form, from a manuscript presented to the author in 1957 by Abba Petros Hailu.

that is, what is called in the Western Church the "Mass," or the complex of prayers and ceremonies, words and actions that constitute the Eucharistic Sacrifice.

On the high plateaus of old Abyssinia, which was soon to be cut off from the rest of Christendom by Islam, and was often isolated within its own territory because of a lack of means of communication, the primitive Liturgy, called Liturgy of St. Mark, developed by successive stages. First came the translation, made, so it seems, toward the end of the fifth century, most probably from a Greek original. The language used was that spoken at the court and in the kingdom of the North, Ge'ez or ancient Ethiopic,[3] a language belonging to the Western and Southern group of Semitic languages. Today a "dead language," Ge'ez is found only in liturgical and literary texts, where it plays a role comparable to that of classical Latin.[4] The other phases of development are marked by several additions, incorporated in the course of time. Thus, to the first Liturgy, probably entitled "Liturgy of St. Mark," there were added the Anaphoras[5] of the Apostles, and then all the other Anaphoras that slowly and progressively made their way into the Missal. There are in all fourteen or seventeen Anaphoras, according to different editions of missals.

Here is the outline of the solemn Liturgy as presented by Abba Petros Hailu. Besides the rite of the introductory preparation, it is divided into two parts: the Pro-Anaphora ("Ordinary of the Mass") and the Anaphora ("Canon of the Mass"). The first part, except for the Lections from the New Testament, is always the same for all the Anaphoras. It comprises the Mass of the Catechumens and contains the Offertory, the solemn "Absolution of the Son" (characteristic of this rite), the Litanies, the Censing, Lections of the

---

[3] Ancient Ethiopian or Ge'ez is designated by the term "Ethiopic," while "Ethiopian" is reserved for the following meanings: all that refers to Ethiopia in general or to the Semitic languages spoken today in the same country, as for instance, Amharic, the official language of the empire.

[4] C. Sumner, "Du guèze à l'amharique moderne," *Étude expérimentale de l'amharique moderne* (Montréal: Éditions Bellarmin, 1957), pp. xiv–xix.

[5] The Eucharistic service consists of two parts: the Pro-Anaphora, a term equivalent to "Ordinary of the Mass," invariable except for the Lections from the New Testament, and the Anaphora, equivalent to "Canon of the Mass." As it is the second part, the Anaphora, which varies according to the day on which the Liturgy is used, the expression "different Anaphoras" is common among the Orientals, as the expression "different Masses" is among the Latins.

Epistle and of the Gospel, and the Pre-Anaphora, itself composed of several prayers having the Creed as center. The second part, the Anaphora, varies according to the day on which the Liturgy is used. It opens with the Eucharistic Prayer, which comprises the Sanctus, the Consecration, the Anamnesis, the Epiklesis, the Fraction of the Host, and the Lord's Prayer. Then follow the Commemorations of the Living and of the Dead, the solemn Elevation, the Profession of Faith in the Eucharist, the Consignation, the Communion, the Thanksgiving, and the Final Blessing. The most frequently used Anaphora is that of the Apostles, from which all the excerpts reproduced in this article have been taken.

CONTEMPLATIVE CHARACTER

What first strikes one who is familar with the Latin Liturgy is the contemplative character of the Ethiopic Liturgy. The Latin Mass is "practical," in the original meaning of the Greek πρᾶξις (action); habitually a gesture accompanies prayer, or a prayer underlines the meaning of the gesture. But the Ethiopic Liturgy is more static, less spectacular; one could say that the prayers have a value for themselves. The priest, standing at the center of the altar with his arms extended, will recite or chant long prayers, without any bodily movement troubling the peace of his contemplation.

A second characteristic of the Latin Mass, on the other hand, is that it is classical in its structure; its prayers are sober and concise with very few allusions to the first person singular. But to the Eastern mind, all this seems rigid and thin. Nothing manifests more the difference between the Western and the Eastern mentality than the forms of greeting. In the Western way, a simple handshake is enough, or even a gesture in mid-air, as if one were chasing a fly away. But in Ethiopia, where the rhythm of life is more humane, greetings are a ritual. One raises his *šämma* or veil, bows deeply; and then the litany of protocol questions begins: about one's health, the wife, the children, the house. . . . At the foot of the altar, the same attitude is found again. The Kyrie Eleison, reduced to nine repetitions in the West, is here said forty-one times. The priest feels, as it were, the need of affirming his faith in the Eucharist in front of the faithful who accompany him with their repeated "Amen":

> *I believe, I believe, I believe and I confess until the last breath*
> *that this is the Body of our Lord and our God and our Saviour*
> *Jesus Christ . . . I believe, I believe, I believe and I confess*
> *that His Godhead was not separated from His humanity . . .*
> *I believe, I believe, I believe and I confess that this is the*
> *Body and the Blood of our Lord God and Saviour Jesus*
> *Christ . . .*[6]

Repetitions, parallelism, long and abundant prayers—to all these characteristics a personal note is added. The celebrant mentions his own name in the Divine Liturgy. Thus, at the end of the Prayer of St. Basil to the Father, the celebrant says:

> *Loosed and freed be all Thy servants and Thy handmaids, by*
> *the mouth of the Holy Spirit and by the mouth of me Thy*
> *sinful and guilty servant.*[7]

PREVALENCE OF SYMBOLISM

A third characteristic is the prevalence of symbolism. Whereas the symbols in the Latin Mass usually have a historical explanation, in the Ethiopic Liturgy the symbol is introduced for its own figurative meaning, without historical reference. It often evokes another symbol, which in its turn is widened and reflected back. When, at the beginning of the Holy Liturgy, the priest covers the chalice and the host with the veil, he says:

> *This which we have placed upon the blessed paten is like to the*
> *sepulchre in which Thou hast rested three days and three nights;*
> *so make our hands like the hands of Joseph and Nicodemus,*
> *who wrapped Thy body, acquiring thereby tranquility and peace*
> *for themselves, and honour for the Father, and the Son, and*
> *the Holy Ghost, both now and ever, world without end.*[8]

[6] Sumner, "Profession of Faith in the Eucharist," *The Ethiopic Liturgy,* pp. 58–59.

[7] Ibid., "Prayer of St. Basil to the Father," pp. 53–54.

[8] Ibid., "Prayer of the Veil," p. 20.

The greeting of the celebrant to the "Holy Church, dwelling of God"[9] refers to Mary, Mother of God. The symbol of the dwelling evokes another which the people develop in lines of splendid beauty about the golden censer.

> *The priest — Hail,*
> *The people — Holy Church, dwelling of God!*
> *The priest — Pray for us,*
> *The people — Virgin Mary, Mother of God.*
> *The priest — Thou art*
> *The people — the golden censer who didst bear the blessed*
> *coal of fire which was taken from the Holy Place and which*
> *remits all sins and destroys all offences; that fire is the word*
> *of God who became man of Thee and who offereth Himself*
> *to the Father as incense and pleasing offering.*[10]

THE NOTE OF JOY

These short notations having been made, mostly through comparison with the Latin Liturgy, let us proceed to the text itself. What are the elements or characteristics which are most striking? I could indicate in the first place the note of *joy* that is manifested with such spontaneity and insistence. While blessing the chalice into which he has poured the wine, the priest says:

> *Christ, our true God, and our Lord, who didst go to the marriage feast when they called Thee in Cana of Galilee, and didst bless it and didst change the water into wine, also in like manner do Thou change this wine into Thy Blood.*
> *Bless it and hallow it and cleanse it; let it become the joy and gladness, the life of our souls and bodies. At all times may the Father and the Son and the Holy Ghost be with us, other than Whom there is no God. Fill it with the wine of rejoicing and exultation, for things good, for life, for salvation and for the remission of sin, for understanding, for healing and for counsel of the Holy Ghost, both now and ever and world without end.*[11]

[9] Ibid., "Prayer to the Blessed Virgin," p. 21.
[10] Ibid.
[11] Ibid., "Blessing of the Chalice," pp. 13–14.

Joy expressed in the symbolism of the change of water into wine at Cana, of wine into the precious Blood in the Divine Liturgy; joy that finds its rhythm of exultation in the repetition that is taken over seven times, this selfsame joy, in the prayer after the Lord's Prayer called Embolism, will burst out into the cry which traditionally in Ethiopia expresses an intense emotion, yeigh, yeigh, yeigh:

> *The host of angels of the Redeemer of the world, "yeigh, yeigh, yeigh," stand before the Redeemer of the world. They stand around the Redeemer of the world, "yeigh, yeigh, yeigh," before the Body and the Blood of the Redeemer. Let us come, we also, near to the Redeemer of the world, "yeigh, yeigh, yeah;" by believing in Him, the Apostles followed in His footsteps.*[12]

SENSE OF COMMUNITY

A simple glance at the Missal suffices to reveal a deep sense of community. Indeed from the beginning to the end of the Liturgy, the Christian people alternate with the priest or the deacon. Whereas in the Latin Mass one has the impression that the dialogue ceases at the moment of the Offertory and is renewed only sporadically from then on, the community of the faithful constantly participates in the Ethiopic Liturgy. It is a moving spectacle during the Liturgy to hear men, women, and children singing together, sometimes with many variations, the responses which are transmitted from generation to generation. Even at the most solemn moment of consecration, silence is broken by the voice of the faithful who sing:

> *Amen, amen, amen. We believe and confess, we glorify Thee, our Lord and our God; we believe that this is verily Thy Body.*[13]

This sense of community has found its way even into the composition of certain prayers in which the social hierarchy of Ethiopia,

[12] Ibid., "Embolism," p. 52. Embolism is the expansion of the two last petitions of the Lord's Prayer when said by the celebrant of the Liturgy.
[13] Ibid., "Consecration," p. 46.

is clearly structured: the emperor, the court, the army, the judges and the nobles, all the people, without omitting the multitude of the neighbors, abroad and at home.

> *All the people and all Thy flock bless Thou* (the priest blesses the people). *The peace that is from heaven send Thou into our hearts, and the tranquility of our life give unto us, vouchsafe peace to our King N., to his court and his armies, and to his judges and to his nobles, and to the multitude of our neighbours abroad and at home; adorn them with all peace.*[14]

A supreme delicacy at the end of the Liturgy is a special mention for those who arrived late. The Liturgy may last some two hours and a half. . . .

> *We pray for those who came late to the Liturgy, and for our fathers, brothers and sisters . . .*[15]

CONCERN FOR UNITY

At a time when the ecumenical sense uplifts the Christian conscience, it is consoling to note to how great an extent the Ethiopic Liturgy has been marked by the concern for unity. Before the Gospel the priest blesses the four cardinal points; his thought rises from the Church dispersed throughout the world to the triumphant Church in whose unity the whole Church will one day be joined:

> *May the Lord on high bless us all, and sanctify us with all spiritual blessings, and make felicitous our entry into His Holy Church, joined as it is with His holy angels, who chant unto Him with fear and with trembling, and glorify Him at all times and all hours, both now and ever world without end.*[16]

There is a sense of community, a sense of the Church; yet one should not be led to believe that the Ethiopic Liturgy emphasizes so much the social aspect that the personal one is ignored. As in

[14] Ibid., "A Prayer for Peace," pp. 34–35.
[15] Ibid., "Purification," p. 67.
[16] Ibid., p. 30.

the Latin Mass, the prayer before communion has a personal character; but, apart from the fact that this prayer is said by the people, it has recourse to the awareness that the faithful have of their unworthiness, not only to the merits of Our Lord, but also to the "splendors of creation."

> *Oh my Lord Jesus Christ, I am not worthy that Thou shouldst enter under the roof of my unclean house, for I have provoked Thee to anger and offended Thee and have done evil in Thy sight and have stained my body and my soul, that Thou hast created in Thy own image and likeness, by transgressing Thy precepts, and in me there is no good deed, nay not one; but for the sake of Thy splendid creation, and because Thou didst become man for my salvation, for the sake of Thy precious cross and Thy lifegiving death and Thy resurrection on the third day, I pray Thee and entreat Thee, O my Lord, to purify me from all transgressions and curse and sin and impurity.*[17]

If it is true that personal devotion has its part in the Liturgy, the specifically theological values are underlined with a great density of expression and a tone that is more than once dramatic or poetical. The sacrificial aspect of the Liturgy, the role of the Holy Ghost, the mediation of Mary—the Ethiopic language expresses these truths with a vigor that recalls certain biblical phrases.

SACRIFICIAL ASPECT

While he drops a particle of the Sacred Host (Despotikon) into the chalice, the priest says:

> *Lord, our God, here is the Body of Thy Son, which is a sacrifice most pleasing to Thee; on this account forgive all my sins; because Thine Only-begotten Son died for me. And here is the Blood of Thy spotless Christ which was shed for me on Calvary. Behold, this precious Blood speaks, cries out in my behalf.*[18]

[17] Ibid., "Prayer before Communion," pp. 60–61.
[18] Ibid., pp. 59–60.

This prayer is like an echo of the words by which the people drew out the sacrificial sense immediately after the consecration of the two species:

> *We proclaim Thy death, O Lord, and Thy holy resurrection;*
> *we believe in Thy ascension and Thy second coming.*[19]

ROLE OF THE HOLY GHOST

The first thought of the priest, immediately after the initial sign of the cross, refers to the role of the Holy Ghost, Who, certainly through an allusion to the Annunciation as related in the first chapter of St. Luke, will overshadow this offering as formerly He came upon the Virgin Mary and overshadowed her—and in both cases the Word is given to mankind.

> *In the name of the Father, and of the Son, and of the Holy*
> *Ghost, Amen. How wondrous is this day and how marvellous*
> *this hour in which the Holy Ghost will come down from the*
> *high heaven and overshadow this offering and sanctify it.*[20]

The role of the Holy Ghost is particularly emphasized in the Epiklesis. D. Attwater, in *The Christian Churches of the East*,[21] defines the Epiklesis as "a prayer asking the Holy Ghost to come down upon the bread and wine and turn it into Christ's Body and Blood, and imploring the grace of the sacrament for the recipients."

> *We pray Thee, O Lord, and we implore Thee to call down*
> *Thy Holy Spirit upon this Bread and upon this Chalice, so*
> *that He change them into the Body and Blood of our Lord and*
> *Saviour Jesus Christ, world without end.*[22] *Uniting all those who*

[19] Ibid., "Consecration," p. 47.

[20] Ibid., "Introit," p. 11.

[21] D. Attwater, *The Christian Churches of the East* (Milwaukee: Bruce, 1948), I, 234.

[22] See Abba Petros Hailu, *Messa Etiopica detta "Degli Apostoli"* (Rome: Casa Editrice degli Lazariste, 1946), p. 47. The liturgical ending, "world without end," here refers to the permanence of the change, under the action of the Holy Ghost.

*are to receive His Body and His Blood grant that it may
be for their sanctification and that they may thereby receive
the fullness of the Holy Ghost and that, confirmed in the faith,
they may give Thee glory and praise through Thy Beloved
Son Jesus Christ.*[23]

MEDIATION OF MARY

The action of the Holy Ghost, the sacrificial aspect of the
Eucharist—these theological values have been set off in a prominent
position by the Ethiopic Liturgy. But there still remains a point
that is dear to the heart of every Christian Ethiopian—the devotion
to Mary. This country looks upon itself as a fief offered by Our
Lord to His Mother and accepted by her as tithe of the universe;
there are some thirty-three feasts in her honor; a rigorous fast
of fifteen days precedes the Assumption; baptismal names are often
borrowed from her: Son of Mary, Plant of Mary, Servant of Mary;
popular proverbs exalt her power: "If you praise Mary, you will
reign with her." Is it astonishing that in such a Marian country
her name finds a place in all the hymns and all the religious
offices?[24] The priest at the altar rejoices because he shares the
joy of the Mother of God, whose intercession, royalty, and universal mediation he sings:

*Rejoice, O thou of whom we ask salvation, O holy, full of
glory, ever virgin. Mother of God, Mother of Christ, offer up
our prayer on high to thy beloved Son, Jesus, that He forgive
our sins.*

*Rejoice, O thou who bearest for us the very light of right-
eousness, Christ our God; O holy Virgin, plead for us unto
God, that he show mercy unto our souls and forgive us our
sins.*

*Rejoice, O Virgin Mary, Holy Mother of God, verily an advocate
for the race of mankind; plead for us to Christ thy son, that
He make us worthy of the remission of our sins.*

Rejoice, O Virgin, who art truly Queen.

[23] Sumner, "Epiklesis," *The Ethiopic Liturgy*, pp. 48–49.
[24] See J. B. Coulbeaux, *Histoire politique et religieuse d'Abyssinie* (Paris:
Geuthner, 1929), pp. 73–74.

Rejoice, O pride of our race, who for us didst give birth to the Emmanuel; we beseech thee to remember us, thou who didst implore mercy for us in the presence of our Lord Jesus Christ, that He may forgive us our sins.[25]

In an age in which the world does not know whether it stands on the edge of an abyss or on the shores of a new land, a voice may reach us through centuries of Christian wisdom, a message of "light," which everyone may conceive in his heart, like Mary, the "Holy Church, the dwelling of God, the golden censer."

[25] Sumner, "Praises of the Blessed Virgin," *The Ethiopic Liturgy*, p. 26.

36. The Phases of Islamic Expansion and Islamic Culture Zones in Africa

I. THE SPREAD OF ISLAM

The spread of Islam in Africa is marked by four phases, which also represent methods and depths and correspond to types of contemporary Islam.

1. THE WINNING OF NORTH AFRICA (A.D. 638–1050)

The first stage was the conquest by the early Muslim Arabs of all the Mediterranean littoral from Egypt to Morocco; then there followed a period of pacification, quickly succeeded by a breakup of the short-lived political unity into many Muslim states. Islam slowly won over the Berbers, but their Arabization took place during the next stage, following a new break-in of Arab nomads.

2. THE SPREAD OF ISLAM INTO THE SUDAN BELT (1050–1750)

This period witnessed the slow and largely peaceful spread of Islam southwards across the Sahara and up the valley of the Nile into the Hamitic and Black Africa of the Sudan belt. Across the Red Sea and by way of East Africa sea routes it spread into the plains of the Eastern Horn, where it gained the 'Afar and Somali. Settlements were formed along the East African coast, where a new cultural group—the Swahili—was formed, but Islam had no effect upon the Bantu and other peoples of the region.

This phase began with the upsurge of the Berber Murabitun (from 1056) and the dispersion throughout North Africa of Arab nomads of the Bani Hilal (from 1045). These events principally

SOURCE: J. S. Trimingham, "The Phases of Islamic Expansion and Islamic Culture Zones in Africa," in *Islam in Tropical Africa*, ed. by I. M. Lewis. Reprinted by permission of author and publisher. London: Oxford University Press, 1966, pp. 127–43.

affected the desert and North Africa, for though the Murabits conquered the Negro state of Ghana on the edge of the southern desert, they were soon expelled. The Arab tribes did not spread Islam, but their conquest of the Berbers of Mauritania, south of Morocco, led to their Arabization. The Berbers of central Sahara, the Tuareg, were neither conquered nor Arabized.

The spread of Islam across the Sahara into the northern Sudan came through the work of Berber traders and clerics in the west and an influx of Arab tribes (A.D. 1300–1500) in the east, where the Christianity of the Nilotic Sudan disappeared.

The feature of this period is the adoption of Islam as a class religion—the imperial cult in the Sudan states like Mali and Kanem and as the cult of the trading and clerical classes. Just as various religious strata existed side by side in the mosaic of Sudanese religion, so when Islam came on the scene there was no feeling that it was incompatible with an African religious outlook, and, strange though it may seem, Islam was incorporated into the Sudanese religious scheme. Religious life was characterized by accommodation or, more correctly, by a dualism or a parallelism of the old and the new—the African idea of the harmony of society maintained itself over against any idea of Islamic exclusiveness. Consequently, Islam's elements of challenge to traditional life were largely neutralized.

The next period witnessed the triumph of Islam throughout the Sudan belt in a form that claimed its exclusiveness, while the modern period has seen the emergence among new converts of a secular Islam different from traditional African Islam.

3. The Era of Theocracies and of States where Islam is the State Religion (1750–1901)

The nineteenth century was characterized by the appearance of a new, intolerant, and militant Islam. Clerics made their appearance (the first in Futa Jalon in 1725) who waged the *jihad* or holy war and formed a number of theocratic states as they are usually called, though they should really be called divine nomocracies, since they all claimed to be ruled by divine law. These states appeared throughout the Sudan belt from Guinea (Futa Jalon, 1776) and Senegal (Futa Toro, 1776), through Masina (1818) and Sokoto (1802) to the Mahdia of the Nilotic Sudan (1881).

These states degenerated, and most of them were conquered or came under the rule of a new type of despot, for example, alhajj 'Umar (1854–64) in western Sudan and 'Abdallah al-Ta'aishi in Nilotic Sudan (1885–98).

The great change introduced by the nineteenth-century reformers lay in the stress placed on the uniqueness and exclusiveness of Islam and its incompatibility with worship within the old cults. These reformers brought an intensity into the former unchallenging Islam, so Africanized as to be at the point of losing its identity, which drove Islam into the center of life as a transforming factor, whereby the very equilibrium of society was changed. Although under their successors this exclusive reference waned, yet sufficient had been done to bring Islam forward as the supreme arbiter of life and dominant in spite of all the accommodation with pagan practices which was in fact allowed in life.

The conquests of the reformers resulted in a great expansion of nominal allegiance to Islam,[1] but their greatest contribution to the implanting of Islam came from the way they broke up social and tribal groups (prisoners, slave villages, forcible removals) and destroyed organized cults, leaving Islam as the sole cement for new or reconstituted organizations. This process was accelerated during the next phase, when all these territories came under European occupation.

4. THE COLONIAL PERIOD TO THE PRESENT DAY

The latter part of the last period coincided with the occupation of Africa by European powers with all its accompaniments: penetration of new forces, economic, ideological, and religious (Christianity). This period witnessed the continued expansion of Islam at an accelerated pace and over regions that had previously been closed to Islamic propaganda. It was only during this period (especially between 1890 and 1930) that Islam spread from the East African coast among the Bantu of the interior.

Although the nineteenth-century era of militant Islam was that of its greatest expansion in area, the subsequent period of Euro-

---

[1] Many groups in the north with different types of organization remained uninfluenced until the period of European occupation loosened bonds. These included the centralized Mossi states, which were never conquered, Bambara (village state structures), and primitive palaeonegritics of the southern Sudan belt. Even in the northern Sudan belt there are few exclusively Muslim zones.

pean rule, while it stopped forcible conversions, facilitated its expansion in other ways. Peaceful conditions after years of warfare and slave-raiding, combined with new facilities for communication, enabled traders and clerics to circulate everywhere and spread the ways of their religion. In addition, the Muslim conquests of the previous century, followed by the impact of Western civilization, weakened the religious-social structures of many pagan societies. Add to these, the migration of villagers to towns, plantations, and mines, the pressure of new ways of life, the weakening of respect for elders, traditional customs and social sanctions, all these opened the way for the penetration of a religious culture like that of Islam, which could provide a new center for communal life and help to maintain social stability.

In parts where Muslim states had been established (even though overthrown as in French territory) Islam's spread and the nature of its adoption followed the old fashion. But other parts have witnessed the secular diffusion of Islam and the creation of neo-Islamic communities where Islam's position is much like that of Christianity in Western countries. This is due to the fact that the diffusion of Western influences accompanied the diffusion of Islam.

These four historical stages correspond to four different degrees of types of Islam found in Africa:

(*a*) The Islam of the first phase of expansion among Hamites. Two culture zones (Egypt and the Maghrib) where Islam is integrated into every aspect of life.

(*b*) Traditional African Islam, where Islam is fitted into the indigenous system and embraces many grades of allegiance. Religious dualism and tolerance are characteristic; chiefs recognizing all the religious usages of their peoples.

(*c*) The basic Sudan pattern, where Islamic law is incorporated into the pattern of social life. Intolerance and at the same time parallelism.

(*d*) The secularized Islam of neo-Islamic communities, where Western penetration accompanied the adoption of Islam.

II. THE RESULTANT ISLAMIC CULTURE ZONES

Islam spread through the accidents of historical necessity. We do not find the same pattern exactly reproduced throughout the

Islamic world, for the formation of a new Muslim community like the Swahili or, and this is the more general and normal pattern of change, the transformation of an existing community through its adoption of Islam comes about through the interplay of the aggressive culture, as expressed by Muslims from particular culture areas, upon people who have been molded in very different ways.

In the meeting of Islamic and African cultures two currents of attraction and repulsion are set up; their interaction, the play of the various elements of the two cultures upon each other, eventually leads to a synthesis. One current is moving toward differentiation and the other toward homogeneity. From this interaction derives the actual state of Muslim peoples until the impact of Western secular culture.

Regional diversity derives from both internal and external factors of differentiation: (i) geographical and ethnic factors and the pre-Islamic religio-social substratum, and (ii) external influences, the nature, and differences in the historical penetration of Islam. Thus, East African Islam shows the strong influence of the Hadramaut, while West African Islam's characteristics link it with the Maghrib.

These factors operate to develop a culture along regional lines. On the other hand, Islam has acted toward unifying African culture. It is a strong cultural influence, and once it has been adopted by an African community it becomes eventually dominant. Certain Islamic institutions are universally adopted, and these elements not merely create a bond of understanding between peoples but develop common attitudes and patterns of behavior. A distinctive outlook on life is created and a new religio-social pattern is woven.

Although the regional differences are clear, the dynamic tension between Islam and African culture finds expression in a remarkable unity of African Islamic culture. In spite of the fact that Islam normally penetrated integrated communities (exceptions are artificially formed groups such as the Swahili communities and slave villages), thereby transforming them, the Islamic aspects of the resultant culture are much the same everywhere. This is due to the fact that Islam brings the same institutions that modified African life, and it was around the Islamic institutions that the retained or kindred African institutions coagulated. The culture areas may therefore be regarded as having a common Islamic heritage.

However, since the integration of African and Islamic cultures is not complete (for Islam was only able to preserve its uniqueness by parallelism), African Islam may often have to be understood and studied in a double aspect as the local African manifestation of world Islam, and as Islamic variants of African culture.

In discussing the spread and historical role of Islam in Africa, as well as differences in the form that Islamic institutions eventually took, we need to divide Africa into various zones or Islamic culture areas. Such zones have no absolute values, the agreements are more important than the variants, but they are a useful method of treatment. There are three main Islamic culture zones: Egyptian, Maghribi, and Negro, each differentiated by the degree to which it has absorbed and been molded by Islam and to the underlying cultural differences. The distinctions between the Negro African zones are due more to differences in the African cultural basis than to Islam. The culture zones are:

Egyptian: Basic Near Eastern Islamic culture, with Egyptian Nilotic culture showing itself in the village culture of the *fallahin.*

Maghrib: North African Mediterranean culture, though with Berber regional basis.

In the intermediary Saharan-Sahilian desert area the Moors and Tuareg belong to the Maghribi cycle and the Teda to the Central Sudan cycle.

Western Sudan: Negro Islam.

Central Sudan: Negro Islam.

Eastern or Nilotic Sudan: Hamitic-Negro.

North-eastern Hamitic (Eritrea, Ethiopia, and Somalia): The Islam of the nomads of the Eastern Horn.

Coastal East African: Swahili Islam.

Egypt and the Maghrib. The first two cultural regions, Egypt and the Maghrib, are those into which Islam spread from an early date and became so deeply implanted as to influence all subsequent history and every aspect of life. The two regions are, however, clearly differentiated. This derives from the fact that their basic (pre-Islamic) cultures were quite different, and each followed distinctive trends of historical development. Egypt formed a world in itself, and, though brought out of cultural isolation and subject to profound cultural change through adherence to monotheistic religions, it has always displayed distinctive political and social characteristics. Yet Egypt was, viewed in its Islamic orientation, almost entirely undifferentiated, belonging wholly to Arab Islam. Regional differences, however, show themselves especially in the folk (*fallah*) culture.

The other North African regions, the Maghrib to use the Arabic term, formed another historical and cultural entity, although politically distinguished for disunity. Berbers gave this region a definite individuality. Today the majority (more than two-thirds) are Arabized, while the rest have preserved their language, especially in Morocco. Maghribi Islam is Berber Islam—the result of the Berbers' assimilation of Islamic culture, and this type of Islam is present on the borderland with Negro West Africa. In this essay no attempt will be made to trace the relations of Egypt and the Maghrib with the rest of Africa, but simply to distinguish the two regions.

Three cycles of Islamic civilization can be distinguished in West Africa. The first, the Saharan-Sahilian, characterizes more especially the Moorish tribes. The Tuareg belong to this cycle, but not the Teda, who belong to that of the Central Sudan. The Islam of this cycle is characterized by the North African form of the saint cult, a feature that was not transmitted to Negro Islam except to a limited degree (e.g. the Muridiyya). Similarly with the *tariqa-ta'ifas*, the religious brotherhoods with their multi-function *zawiyas* inseparable from the saint cult in North Africa, are different in psychological attitudes toward leaders from those of Negroes. Another characteristic, deriving from the religious apathy of nomads and particularly warrior clans, is the formation of clerical (maraboutic) clans to perform religious functions in their stead. This type of Islam has influenced the Sahilian zone, including towns like Timbuktu, and Negro slaves.

Though Islam came to West Africa through North Africans and Moors, Negro peoples have given it their own distinctive stamp. While the Saharan-Sahilian cycle belongs to the sphere of North African Islamic culture, the Islam of the Sudan displays distinctive African aspects.

Three main cycles of Sudan Islamic culture may be distinguished: West, Central, and East or Nilotic. The differences between the Western and Central cycles are so little perceptible that it is possible to speak of one West African Islamic culture, whereas the Eastern

Sudan culture is distinctly different. That there is a difference between the first two is the sort of thing we acquire by direct contact, which we claim to know by intuitive insight, but which it is difficult to formulate or work out as a distinctive pattern by means of which we may explain what we feel.

Western Sudan. Tokolor and Soninke, the first Sudanese converted to Islam, have left their mark upon it. In certain ways West Sudan clergy have had a deeper influence than those of the central cycle in spite of the excessive worship of the Law in the latter. The difference can be seen if their effect upon newly Islamized areas is contrasted; for instance, the effect of Tokolor and Mande clergy upon pagans in western Guinea and the effect of Hausa upon pagans in the northern territories of Ghana, Togo, Dahomey, and Nigeria. The primary influence upon Tokolor and Soninke was from North Africa, which established a distinctive type of Islamic consciousness and forms of observance. The agents of diffusion today are mainly Tokolor, Soninke, and other Mande teachers and traders.

Characteristics distinguishing it from the parent culture and the central cycle include a pattern of family festivals (e.g. at the eighth-day ceremony—the simultaneous pronouncing of the name, slaughtering of the victim, shaving, and, in Guinea, pounding of grain) at which the stress is on the *white* rice (or other staple food) "sacrifice," rather than upon the offering of a victim. Spirit practices follow a distinctive Mande pattern. They believe in the "crossing of the river" after death, and the place of waiting of departed spirits is called *arafo.* The cycle has its distinctive Islamic legends (e.g. the Prophet and the pig). The primary state structure is that of the village.

The Central Sudan Cycle, east of the Niger, has been subject to Islamic radiation from the Nile Valley (both Egypt and the Nilotic Sudan) as well as the middle Maghrib. The transition zone is roughly between the occupational caste system of the western cycle and the class system characteristic of the Kanuri-Hausa cycle, with its wide categories of grades and titles in the state system. Social mobility saved the peoples of the central cycle from developing any rigid caste system. Kanembu and Kanuri were the first people to be converted and gave a distinctive stamp to Chadian Islam, though they have never been active missionaries, regarding Islam as the cult of the city and aristocracy, and as a specialized occupation cult. The Songhay of the middle Niger, though so different from the Kanuri, belong to this cycle rather than midway, primarily because of the strength of the Paleo-Negritic foundation and the type of organized possessive-spirit cult which persists in flourishing, though no longer the folk cult, in spite of the disapproval of established Islamic authority. While dowry in the western cycle is given by the husband to the wife, in the central it is brought by the wife to the marriage. The city-state, with its elaborate hierarchy of functionaries, contrasts with the village-state organization of the Mande peoples before the formation of theocratic states. The failure of the attempt to found a theocracy in Hausaland was due to the power of this aristocratic state structure, which captured the clerical reformers, the Islamic religious hierarchy being incorporated into it. In the west, on the contrary, the reformers did not carry on the previous organization in any true sense, but formed a new type of state more clearly based upon the precepts of Islam.

Other West African Culture Areas (Western Guinea, Southern Sudan belt, Voltaic, and South Guinean) were not influenced by Islam until the nineteenth century. Islam spread rapidly in western Guinea, its type of Islam being derived primarily from Futa Jalon. The Voltaic peoples have remained relatively uninfluenced. In the southern Sudan belt many chiefs (e.g. Middle belt of Nigeria) have accepted it, but it has made relatively little impression upon their peoples. In the South Guinean region it has made significant gains only among the Yoruba. In many of these areas the penetration of Islamic and Western influences coincided, and this has affected their type of Islam. The interaction of the old heritage, Islamic and Western secular attitudes to life, is leading to a more secular religious attitude and outlook upon life.

The Eastern or Nilotic Sudan Cycle. The foundation so far as Islam is concerned was Eastern Hamitic, both riverain Nubians and rainland cultivators (Hamitic Negro) and nomads (Beja). Its geographical position in the Nile valley has made it a zone of interaction between Hamitic, Negro, and Arab Africa. Because Arabic spread along with Islam the Nilotic Sudan is, like the Maghrib, culturally part of the Near East as well as Africa, while the other regions of the Sudan belt (Mauritania being regarded as culturally belonging to the Maghrib) are not. This great cultural distinction is due to Arabic rather than to Islam. The penetration of Islam, late when compared with Egypt just to the north, came through the dispersion of nomadic Arab tribes in the early fourteenth century. The Arabs did not seek here, any more than in the early centuries of Islam, to consciously spread their religion, though, of course, surface Islamization went along with Arabization. Arabic became the lingua franca and then substituted itself for the languages of the sedentary cultivators (though not the northernmost Nubians and Beja nomads), but Islam claimed the souls of the people through the work of Arabized Nubians who formed an indigenous clerical class.

The conversion of the Nubians in great numbers took place especially between 1300 and 1320. Southward Islamization went along with Arabization. The widespreading of Arab nomads from Upper Egypt was mainly responsible for the Arabization of Hamitic-speaking peoples (e.g. Sha'iqiyya and Ja'liyyin), but the wholehearted adoption of Islam came after an indigenous clerical class grew up who "lit the fire of 'Abd al-Qadir" in one riverain community after another, and in particular among Nubians such as the Mahas, who migrated southward in large numbers and Arabized in the sixteenth century. These set the pattern of Nilotic Sudan Islam.

The most important aspect of this Islam was the harmonious blending of *fiqh* and *tasawwuf*, i.e. the tempering of legalism by mysticism. We do not find that rigidity (nor parallelism) which is characteristic of Muslim leaders in Northern Nigeria. The clerics were at one and the same time *fuqaha* and *fuqara*. The prevalent law school (*madhhab*) was that of Malik, though the Egyptian and Hijazi links—the principal external contacts—led to some teachers (e.g. Dushain of Arbaji) adopting the Shafi'i code. Popular religion was based on Sufism in the form mediated by personal and family *tariqa-ta'ifas* and inseparable from the cult of saints. We may note that the saint cult is characteristic of what, for want of a better term, I call Arabized Hamites, as in the Maghrib, Mauritania, and the Eastern Sudan, but not of the Negro Muslim world.[2]

The North-eastern Ethiopic Zone, the Islam of the plains people of the Eastern Horn. This is a region that embraces the greatest contrasts, not only geographically but in human diversity, cultural levels,

---

[2] The weakness of the cult of saints and of belief in their *karamat* in Negro Africa is perhaps due to the fact that belief in miracles is linked with a historical and static view of the universe and does not accord with the Negro view of a dynamic universe. The cult of ancestors is not bound up with their graves. Similarly with the religious orders. Their reduced role in Negro Africa, where they are more in the nature of an Islamic label, seems to be connected with the fact that the saint cult did not accompany their diffusion, whereas in the Nilotic Sudan it was integral.

languages, and religions. The destinies of this region have been tied indissolubly with the Red Sea much more than with the Nile Valley, and it is from Arabia that it received the imprint of Semitic languages and culture and later of Islam.

The region, from the point of view of Islamic influence, divides into three zones. (*a*) The plains where the nomadic 'Afar (Danakil) and Somali live. These are wholly Muslim and historically connected with migratory and commercial currents across the Red Sea. (*b*) The northern and central plateau region, where the Christian Ethiopian state, with deep-rooted non-African traditions, which throughout history has arrested the expansion of Muslim tribes or states and maintained its religious integrity, provides the region's only unity. The northern Galla of the plateau region (Yejju, Raya, and Wallo) are Muslim. (*c*) South-western Ethiopia, where Islam succeeded in superimposing itself upon the paganism of a group of Sidama and Macha Galla tribes.

In accordance with the varied types of peoples there are considerable variations in their apprehension of, and the forms taken by, their Islam, as, for example, between Jabarti and Galla of the highlands, the Galla-Sidama of Jimma, the Galla of the south-east, the townspeople of Harar, and the nomadic 'Afar and Somali of the plains.

The Swahili Cycle. Islam penetrated into East Africa from the Red Sea and the Indian Ocean. It gained all the Hamitic nomads of the Red Sea coast and the Eastern Horn of the last-mentioned cycle as communities, but inland south of the Somali it did not begin to penetrate until the nineteenth century and has spread largely by individual conversions. Whereas in the Sudan belt Islam claimed whole peoples and made its deepest impact upon Africans, it hardly affected the Bantu and other peoples of East Africa. Immigrants from overseas formed what were virtually closed-class communities based on settlements. These insular and coastal settlements led not to the spread of Islam among the Bantu or nomads but to the formation of a new population, the Swahili, characterized by a distinct Islamic-Bantu language and sub-culture, who stretch from Lamu to Mozambique. The Swahili so formed are not a homogeneous people. They consist of Shirazi (the inhabitants of Zanzibar and Pemba islands and a series of remnant families along the coast), Afro-Arabs who distinguish themselves on racial grounds from Africans, descendants of slaves, and settled detribalized laborers from the interior. They are a collection of different social classes, a stratified society, a cultural group, following an Islamic way of life.

The dominant Islamic influence in moulding Swahili culture came from Hadramaut (e.g. Shafi'ite in *madhhab*), an influence not only obvious in ritual and law but also in the details of *rites de passage* and superstitious usages.

Not until the end of the nineteenth century did Islam spread inland. It spread into Tanganyika in some strength, especially among the Yao and coastal tribes. A point to be stressed is that although all aspects of Islam which were adopted were those of coastal Swahili Islam, the characteristic medieval attitude to religion has not been able to establish itself. Islam in East Africa, contrary to what prevails elsewhere, still bears many of the characteristics of a foreign religion. Muslims form separate communities, and while Islam has its place in local issues, it has no wide influence upon affairs. The indigenous element that distinguishes the Islam of Tanzania is the *jando* circumcision-initiation, essentially a mainland Islamic initiation rite. The saint-cult and *tariqas* in their characteristic form are limited to the islands and coastal region.

Islam's penetration into central and south Africa is so slight that it may be ignored in this sketch. The proportion of Muslims in former French Equatorial Africa (except Chad Territory and northern Cameroons which belong to the Sudan belt) and the Congo is insignificant; while in South Africa it is confined to special groups like the colored people of Malay origin.

Bibliography

Aberle, D. F.; Cohen, A. K.; Davis, A. K.; Levy, M. J., Jr.; Sutton, F. X.
   1949   "The Functional Prerequisites of a Society," *Ethics*, 60:1:100–11.

Abraham, R. C.
   1940   *The Tiv People*. London: Crown Agents, 2d ed.
   1958   *Dictionary of Modern Yoruba*. London: University of London Press.

Adams, R.
   1960   "An Enquiry into the Nature of the Family," *Essays in the Science of Culture*, ed. by G. E. Dole and R. L. Carneiro, pp. 30–49. New York: Crowell.

Alimen, H.
   1955   *Préhistoire de l'Afrique*. Paris: N. Boubée.
   1957   *The Prehistory of Africa*, A. H. Brodrick, tr. London: Hutchinson.

Alland, Alexander, Jr.
   1971   "Human Biological Diversity in Africa." Original article, specifically prepared for this Reader.

Allen, J. G. C.
   1934   "Notes on the Customs of the Ngwa Clan."
   "Supplementary Reports on the Ngwa Clan."
   [Local Archives, Eastern Region Government, Nigeria.]

Allen, J. W. T.
   Utenzi. (n.d., n.p.)

Ames, Oakes.
   1939   *Economic Annuals and Human Culture*. Cambridge, Mass.: Botanical Museum of Harvard University.

Anderson, Edgar.
   1952   *Plants, Man and Life*. Boston: Little, Brown & Co.

Angas, G. F.
   1849   *The Kaffirs Illustrated*. London: J. Hogarth.

Annual Foreign Trade Reports for 1952–61. Department of Statistics, Sudan Government.

Antinori, O.
1868 Viaggi di O. Antinori e C. Piagga nell' Africa Centrale. *Boll. Soc. Geog. Ital.*, I:91–165.

Arbousset, J. T.
1846 *Exploratory Tour in South Africa.* (See *Narrative of an Exploratory Tour to the North-East of the Colony of the Cape of Good Hope.* Cape Town: C. Struik, 1968.)

Arkell, A. J.
1949 *Early Khartoum.* London and New York: Oxford University Press.
1953 *Shaheinab.* London: Oxford University Press.

Arkell, A. J.; Fagan, B.; and Summers, R.
1966 "The Iron Age in Sub-Saharan Africa," *Current Anthropology,* 7:4:451–84.

Asad, Talal.
1964 "The Seasonal Movements of the Kababish Arabs of Northern Kordofan," *Sudan Notes and Records,* 45:45–58.

Attwater, D.
1948 *The Christian Churches of the East.* Milwaukee: Bruce.

Awad, Mohd.
1962 "Nomadism in the Arab Lands of the Middle East," *The Problems of the Arid Zones.* Paris: UNESCO.

Baasher, Dr. Mustafa.
1962 "Range and Livestock Problems Facing the Settlement of Nomads," *The Effect of Nomadism on the Economic and Social Development of the People of the Sudan.* Khartoum, Sudan: The Philosophical Society of the Sudan.

Bailloud, G.
1959 "La préhistoire de l'Éthiopie," *Mer Rouge, Afrique Orientale,* ed. by M. Albospeyre, *et al.*, pp. 15–43. Paris: J. Peyronnet.

Barker, W. H., and Sinclair, Cecilia.
1917 *West African Folk-Tales.* London: Harrap.

Barth, F.; Cunnison, I.; and Dyson-Hudson, N.
1963 "The Settlement of Nomads as a Development Policy" (in Arabic), *Sudan Society,* No. 2.

Barth, H.
1859 *Travels and Discoveries in North and Central Africa,* 3 vols. New York: Harper and Brothers.

Bascom, W. R.
1941 "The Sanctions of Ifa Divination," *The Journal of the Royal Anthropological Institute,* 71:43–54.
1942 "Ifa Divination," *Man,* 42:21:41–43.
1944 "The Sociological Role of the Yoruba Cult Group," *American*

Anthropologist (New Series), 46:1:5–75. (Also separately issued as Memoir 63 of the American Anthropological Association.)

1955   "Verbal Art," *Journal of American Folklore,* 68:245–52.

1960   "Yoruba Concepts of the Soul," *Selected Papers of the Fifth International Congress of Anthropological and Ethnological Sciences* (1956), Philadelphia, pp. 401–10.

1961   "Odu Ifa: the Order of the Figures of Ifa," *Bulletin de l'Institut Français d'Afrique Noire,* Ser. B, 23.

Basset, H.

1920   *Essai sur la littérature des Berbères.* Alger: J. Carbonel.

Batty, Mrs. R. B.

. 1890   "Notes on the Yoruba Country," *The Journal of the Royal Anthropological Institute,* 19:160–64.

Baudin, N.

1884   *Fétichisme et Féticheurs.* Lyon (English edition, *Fetichism and Fetich Worshippers,* New York: Benziger Bros., 1885).

Baumann, H.

1935   *Lunda.* Berlin: Würfel.

1943   "Steingräber und Steinbauten in Angola," *Koloniale Völkerkunde Beiträge zur Kolonialforschung,* ed. by H. Baumann, Vol. 1, pp. 45–55. Berlin: F. Berger.

1956   "Die Frage der Steinbauten und Steingräber in Angola," *Paideuma,* 6:118–51.

Baumann, H., and Westermann, D.

1948   *Les Peuples et les Civilisations de l'Afrique.* Paris: Payot.

Baumann, O.

1894   *Durch Massailand zur Nilquelle.* Berlin: D. Reimer.

Beattie, J. H. M.

1957   "Nyoro Personal Names," *Uganda Journal,* 21:101–2.

1958   "Nyoro Marriage and Affinity," *Africa,* 28:1:1–22.

1961   "Nyoro Mortuary Rites," *Uganda Journal,* 25:1:171–83.

1964   "Bunyoro: An African Feudality?" *Journal of African History,* 5:1:24–36.

Bequin, J., *et al.*

1952   *L'Habitat au Cameroun.* Paris: Éditions de l'Union Française.

Beier, U.

1954   "The Palace of the Ogogas in Ikerre," *Nigeria,* 44:303–14.

1956   "The Egungun Cult," *Nigeria,* 51:380–92.

1958   "Gelede Masks," *Odù,* 6:5–23.

1960   *Art in Nigeria, 1960.* Cambridge: University Press.

Beiträge zur Kulturgeschichte von Ostafrika, Berlin, 1909.

Berque, J.
1959 Introduction to "Nomads and Nomadism in the Arid Zone," *International Social Science Bulletin*, 11:4:481–98.

Biarnay, S.
1917 "L'Histoire d'Haddidouan," *Étude sur les dialectes berbères du Rif*. Paris, pp. 312–18.

Binger, L. G.
1892 *Du Niger au Golfe de Guinee*, 2 vols. Paris: Hachette.

Biobaku, S. O.
1952 "An Historical Sketch of Egba Traditional Authorities," *Africa*, 22:35–49.
1956 *Ogboni, the Egba Senate*. Third International West African Conference (1949), Lagos.
1957 *The Egba and Their Neighbours, 1842–1872*. Oxford: Clarendon Press.

Bird, J.
1888 *Annals of Natal, 1495–1845*, 2 vols. Pietermaritzburg (Cape Town: C. Struik, 1965).

Bittremieux, L.
1936 *La Société Secrète des Bakhimba au Mayombe*. Bruxelles: I.R.C.B.

Boettger, J.
1958 *Die Afrikanische Haustiere*. Jena.

Bohannan, Laura
1958 "Political Aspects of Tiv Social Organization," *Tribes without Rulers*, ed. by John Middleton and David Tait, pp. 33–66. London: Routledge and Kegan Paul, Ltd.

Bohannan, L., and Bohannan, P.
1953 *The Tiv of Central Nigeria*. London: International African Institute.

Bohannan, P.
1959 "The Impact of Money on an African Subsistence Economy," *The Journal of Economic History*, 19:491–503.
1960 "Homicide Among the Tiv of Central Nigeria," *African Homicide and Suicide*, ed. by P. Bohannan. Princeton: Princeton University Press.

Boston, J. S.
1960 "Northern Ibo Masquerades," *The Journal of the Royal Anthropological Institute*, 90:1:54–65.

Bouche, P.
1885 *La Côte des Esclaves et le Dahomey, Sept Ans en Afrique Occidentale*. Paris: Plon.

Bovill, E. W.
1958 *The Golden Trade of the Moors.* London and New York: Oxford University Press.
Bowen, T. J.
1857 *Central Africa: Adventures and Missionary Labours in Several Countries in the Interior of Africa from 1849 to 1856.* Charleston (English edition, London: Cass, 1968).
Bradbury, R. E.
1957 *The Benin Kingdom.* London: International African Institute.
Brelsford, V. W.
1946 *Fishermen of the Bangweulu Swamps.* Rhodes-Livingstone Papers, No. 12.
Brightman, F. E.
1896 *Liturgies Eastern and Western.* Oxford: Clarendon Press.
Brodrick, A. H. (tr.)
1957 *The Prehistory of Africa.* London: Hutchinson.
Brown, P.
1951 "Patterns of Authority in West Africa," *Africa,* 21:261–78.
Bryant, A. T.
1905 *Zulu-English Dictionary.* Pinetown: The Mariannhill Mission Press.
1965 (orig. 1929) *Olden Times in Zululand and Natal.* Cape Town: C. Struik (1929 ed., London: Longmans Green).
Bulletin de Madagascar.
1964 "Rapport sur certaines coutumes Tsimihety," No. 214. Tananarive, Malagasy République.
Bullough, Edward.
1912 " 'Psychical Distance' as a Factor in Art and an Aesthetic Principle," *British Journal of Psychology,* 5:2:87–118.
Burton, R. F.
1863 *Abeokuta and the Cameroons Mountains: An Exploration,* 2 vols. London: Tinsley Brothers.
Busia, K. A.
1951 *The Position of the Chief in the Modern Political System of Ashanti.* London: Oxford University Press.
Caillie, R.
1830 *Travels Through Central Africa to Timbuctoo.* London: H. Colburn and R. Bentley.
Calame-Griaule, G.
1954 "Esotérisme et fabulation au Soudan," *Bulletin IFAN,* Ser. B., 16:3–4:307–21.
Callaway, H.
1870 *Religious System of the Amazulu.* Springvale, Natal: J. A. Blair.

Calonne-Beaufaict, A. de.
1921 *Azande*. Bruxelles: Lamertin.
Campbell, R.
1861 *A Pilgrimage to my Motherland*. New York: T. Hamilton.
Carlson, Lucile.
1967 "African Landscapes," *Africa's Lands and Nations* by Lucile Carlson, pp. 3–24. New York: McGraw-Hill.
Casati, Gaetano.
1891 *Ten Years in Equatoria and the Return with Emin Pasha* (tr. from orig. Italian by Hon. Mrs. J. Randolph Clay and Mr. I. Walter Savage Landor), 2 vols. London and New York: F. Warne.
Caton-Thompson, G.
1944 *The Tombs and Moon Temple of Hureidha*. London: Soc. of Antiquaries, Report No. 13.
1931 *The Zimbabwe Culture*. Oxford: Clarendon Press.
Châtelain, Héli.
1894 *Folk-Tales of Angola, Memoirs of the American Folklore Society*.
Chevalier, A.
1909 "Dans le nord de la Côte d'Ivoire," *La Géographie*, 20:25–29.
Childe, V. G.
1935 (orig. 1934) *New Light on the Most Ancient East*. London: K. Paul, Trench, and Trubner.
1942 *What Happened in History*. Harmondsworth, Middlesex: Penguin.
Christaller, J. H.
1879 *Tẅi Mmebusem, Mpensä-Ahansia Mmoaano*. Basel: Basel German Evangelical Missionary Society.
Christensen, J. B.
1954 "African Political Systems: Indirect Rule and Democratic Processes," *Phylon*, 1st quarter, 69–83.
1954 *Double Descent Among the Fanti*. New Haven: Human Relations Area Files.
1958 "The Role of Proverbs in Fante Culture," *Africa*, 28:3:232–43.
Clapperton, H.
1829 *Journal of a Second Expedition into the Interior of Africa*. London: Carey, Lea and Carey (American edition, Philadelphia).
Clark, J. D.
1954 *The Prehistoric Cultures of the Horn of Africa*. Cambridge: University Press.
1959 *The Prehistory of Southern Africa*. Harmondsworth, Middlesex: Penguin.
1961 "Sites Yielding Hominid Remains in Bed I, Olduvai Gorge," *Nature*, 189:903–4.

1962 "The Spread of Food Production in Sub-Saharan Africa," *Journal of African History,* 111:2:211–28.

1964 "The Prehistoric Origins of African Culture," *Journal of African History,* 5:2:161–83.

Clarke, J. D.

1939 "Ifa Divination," *The Journal of the Royal Anthropological Institute,* 69:235–56.

Codere, H.

1962 "Power in Rwanda," *Anthropologica,* 4:1:45–85.

Cohen, R.

1962 "Power in Complex Societies in Africa," *Anthropologica,* 4:1:5–8.

Cole, Sonia.

1963 *The Prehistory of East Africa.* New York: Macmillan (orig. Harmondsworth, Middlesex: Penguin, 1954).

Colenso, J. W.

1905 *Zulu-English Dictionary.* Pietermaritzburg.

The Collector, ed. by Wanger, Nos. 926 & 927. (n.d., n.p.)

Colonial Office.

1957 *The Indigenous Cattle of the British Dependent Territories in Africa.* London: His Majesty Stationery Office.

Colson, E.

1951 "The Plateau Tonga of Northern Rhodesia," *Seven Tribes of British Central Africa,* pp. 94–162. London: Oxford University Press.

1951 "The Role of Cattle Among the Plateau Tonga of Mazabuka District," *The Rhodes-Livingstone Journal (Human Problems in British Central Africa),* 11:10–46.

1952 "Residence and Village Stability Among the Plateau Tonga," *The Rhodes-Livingstone Journal (Human Problems in British Central Africa),* 12:48–50.

1953 "Social Control and Vengeance in Plateau Tonga Society," *Africa,* 23:3:199–211.

(n.d.) "Clans and the Joking Relationship among the Plateau Tonga," *University of California Publications in Anthropology.*

1955 "Native Cultural and Social Patterns in Contemporary Africa," *Africa Today,* by C. G. Haines, pp. 69–84. Baltimore: Johns-Hopkins Press.

Coon, C. S.

1962 *The Origin of Races.* New York: Alfred A. Knopf.

1965 *The Living Races of Man.* New York: Alfred A. Knopf.

Coon, C. S.; Garn, S. M.; and Birdsell, J. B.

1950 *Races: a Study of the Problems of Race Formation in Man.* Springfield: Thomas.

Copland, A.
1953 *What to Listen for in Music.* New York: Mentor.
Cornevin, R.
1956 *Histoire de l'Afrique, les Origines ā nos Jours.* Paris: Payot.
Coulbeaux, J. B.
1929 *Histoire politique et religieuse d'Abyssinie.* Paris: Geuthner.
Crowther, S. A.
1852 *A Grammar of the Yoruba Language.* London: Seeley.
Culver, C. A.
1941 *Musical Acoustics.* Philadelphia: The Blakiston Co.
Cunnison, I.
1960 "The Social Role of Cattle," *Sudan Journal of Vet. Science and Animal Husbandry,* Vol. I, No. 1. Khartoum, Sudan.
Czekanowski, Jan.
1924 *Wissenschaftliche Ergebnisse der Deutschen Zentral-Afrika-Expedition 1907–1908, unter Führung Adolf Friedrichs Herzog zu Mecklenburg,* Bd. 6, 2: *Forschungen in Nil-Kongo-Zwischengebiet.* Leipzig: Klinkhardt.
Dammann, Ernst.
1940 *Dichtungen in der Lamu-mundart des Suaheli.* Hamburg: Friederichsen, de Gruyter & Co.
Daoud, M.
1954 *The Liturgy of the Ethiopian Church.* Addis Ababa: Berhane Selam Printing Press.
d'Arianoff, A.
1952 *Histoire des Bagesera, souverains du Gisaka.* Bruxelles, I.R.C.B., t. 24, fasc. 3.
Dart, R. A.
1948 "The Infancy of Australopithecines," *Robert Broom Commemorative Volume,* Johannesburg, pp. 143–52.
1957 "The Osteodontokeratic Culture of *Australopithecus prometheus.*" Pretoria: Transvaal Museum, Mem. No. 10.
Davidson, Basil.
1959 *Old Africa Rediscovered.* London: Gollancz.
Davis, A. J.
1967 "Coptic Christianity," *Tarikh,* 2:1:43–51.
Deevey, E. S., *et. al.* (eds.)
1963 *Radiocarbon Measurements,* 5:37:170–72. New Haven: American Journal of Science.
Delegorgue, A.
1847 *Voyage dans l'Afrique Australe.* Paris: A. René et Cᵉ.
Denham, D., and Clapperton, H.
1826 *Narratives of Travels and Discoveries.* New York and London: J. Murray.

Dennett, R. E.
1910 *Nigerian Studies: or the Religious and Political Systems of the Yoruba.* London: Macmillan.
Destaing, E.
1911 *Étude sur le dialecte berbère des Beni Snous,* t. II. Paris.
Dieterlen, G.
1951 *Essai sur la religion Bambara.* Paris: Presses Universitaires de France.
1954 "Les rites symboliques du mariage chez les Bambara," *Zaïre,* 8:8:815–41.
1955 "Mythe et organisation sociale au Soudan français," *Journal de la Société des Africanistes,* 25:39–76.
1956 "Parenté et Mariage chez les Dogon," *Africa,* 26:2:107–48.
1957 "The Mande Creation Myth," *Africa,* 17:2:124–38.
Diké, K. O.
1956 *Trade and Politics in the Niger Delta, 1830–1885.* Oxford: Clarendon Press.
Doke, C. M.
1931 *The Lambas of Northern Rhodesia.* London: Harrap.
Douglas, M.
1954 "The Lele of Kasai," *African Worlds,* ed. by Daryll Forde, pp. 1–26. London: Oxford University Press.
Downes, R. M.
1933 *The Tiv Tribe.* Kaduna: Government Printer.
Dubois, F.
1899 *Tombouctou, la mystérieuse.* Paris: E. Flammarion.
Dupire, Marguerite.
1963 "The Position of Women in a Pastoral Society," in *Women of Tropical Africa,* ed. by Denise Paulme. London: Routledge and Kegan Paul, Ltd., pp. 53–59.
East, R. (ed. and tr.)
1939 *Agika's Story.* London: Oxford University Press.
Eisenstadt, S. N.
1963 *The Political Systems of Empires.* London and New York: Free Press of Glencoe.
Elias, T. O.
1962 (orig. 1951) *Nigerian Land, Law and Custom.* London: Routledge and Kegan Paul.
Ellis, Sir A. B.
1890 *The Ewe-Speaking Peoples of the Slave Coast of West Africa.* London: Chapman and Hall.
1894 *The Yoruba-Speaking Peoples of the Slave Coast of West Africa.* London: Chapman and Hall.

Epega, D. O.
1931 *Ifa-amona awon baba-wa.* Lagos (Eng. ed. tr. by the author, *The Mystery of the Yoruba Gods,* Lagos Printing, Nigeria, 1932).
Evans-Pritchard, E. E.
1937 *Witchcraft, Oracles and Magic Among the Azande.* London: Oxford University Press.
1940 *The Nuer.* London: Oxford University Press.
1953 "The Sacrificial Role of Cattle among the Nuer," *Africa,* 23:181–97.
1954a "A Zande Slang Language," *Man,* 54:289:185–86.
1954b "The Meaning of Sacrifice Among the Nuer," *Journal of the Royal Anthropological Institute,* 84:21–33.
1955, 1956, 1957 "Zande Historical Texts," *Sudan Notes and Records,* 36:123–45; 37:20–47; 38:74–99.
1956a "A History of the Kingdom of Gbudwe," *Zaïre,* 10:t. 1, 451–91; t. 2, 675–710, 815–60.
1956b "Zande Clan Names," *Man,* 56:62:69–71.
1956c "Zande Totems," *Man,* 56:110:107–9.
1957a "The Origin of the Ruling Clan of the Azande," *Southwestern Journal of Anthropology,* 13:322–43.
1957b "Zande Border Raids," *Africa,* 27:217–31.
1957c "Zande Warfare," *Anthropos,* 52:239–62.
1957d "The Zande Royal Court," *Zaïre,* t. 1:361–89, 493–511; t. 2: 687–713.
1957e "Zande Kings and Princes," *Anthropological Quarterly,* 30:618–90.
1958a "The Ethnic Composition of the Azande of Central Africa," *Anthropological Quarterly,* 31:95–118.
1958b "An Historical Introduction to a Study of Zande Society," *African Studies,* 17:1–15.
1959 "The Distribution of Zande Clans in the Sudan," *Man,* 59:24:21–25.
1960a "Zande Cannibalism," *The Journal of the Royal Anthropological Institute,* 90:238–58.
1960b "Zande Clans and Settlements," *Man,* 60:213:169–72.
1960c "A Contribution to the Study of Zande Culture," *Africa,* 30: 309–24.
1960d "The Organization of a Zande Kingdom," *Cahiers d'Études Africaines,* 4:5–37.
1960e "The Ethnic Origin of Zande Office-holders," *Man,* 60:141: 100–2.
1961 "Zande Clans and Totems," *Man,* 61:147:116–21.

Fagan, B. M.
1963 "The Iron Age Sequence in the Southern Province of Northern Rhodesia," *Journal of African History*, 4:2:157–77.

Fagg, B.
1956 "The Discovery of Multiple Rock Gongs in Nigeria," *African Music*, 1:3:6–9.

Fallers, Lloyd.
1963 "Equality, Modernity and Democracy in the New States," *Old Societies and New States*, ed. by Clifford Geertz, pp. 158–219. Glencoe, Illinois: The Free Press.

Farrow, S. S.
1926 *Faith, Fancies and Fetish, or Yoruba Paganism*. London: Society for the Promotion of Christian Knowledge.

Forde, C. D.
1941 *Marriage and the Family among the Yakö of Southeastern Nigeria*. London: P. Lund, Humphries and Co.

Fortes, M.
1945 *The Dynamics of Clanship Among the Tallensi*. London: Oxford University Press.
1950 "Kinship and Marriage Among the Ashanti," *African Systems of Kinship and Marriage*, ed. by A. R. Radcliffe-Brown and D. Forde, pp. 252–85. London: Oxford University Press.
1953 "The Structure of Unilineal Descent Groups," *American Anthropologist*, 55:17–41.
1959 "Descent, Filiation and Affinity: A Rejoinder to Dr. Leach," *Man*, 59:309:193–97, 331:206–12.

Fortes, M., and Evans-Pritchard, E. E.
1940 *African Political Systems*. London: Oxford University Press.

Fortes, M. and S. L.
1936 "Food in the Domestic Economy of the Tallensi," *Africa*, 9:237–76.

Foster, G.
1961 "The Dyadic Contract: A Model for the Social Structure of a Mexican Peasant Village," *American Anthropologist*, 63:6:1173–92.

Freeman, J.
1961 "On the Concept of the Kindred," *Journal of the Royal Anthropological Institute*, 91:2:192–220.

Frobenius, L.
1912 *Und Afrika sprach*, 2 vols. Leipzig (English tr., [R. Blind] *The Voice of Africa*, London: Hutchinson, 1913).
1926 *Die Atlantische Götterlehre*, Vol. 10 of *Atlantis*. Jena (French tr., [F. Gidon] *Mythologie de l'Atlantide*, Paris: Payot, 1949).

1931 *Erythräa.* Berlin: Atlantis-Verlag [1930].
1954 (orig. 1933) *Kulturgeschichte Afrikas.* Zürich: Phaiden-Verlag.
Fuze, (n.f.n.).
Abantu Abamnyama lapa Bovela Ngakona. (n.d., n.p.)
Gabriel, E., and Rathjens, C.
1956 "Die Nordsyrischen Bienenkorbhäuser," *Tribus,* Neue Folge, 4–5:237–49. Stuttgart: Linden-Museum.
Gajdusek, C.
1964 "Factors Governing the Genetics of Primitive Human Populations," *Cold Spring Harbor Symposia on Quantitative Biology,* 29:121–36.
Gamble, D. P.
1957 *The Wolof of Senegambia.* London: International African Institute.
Ganshof, F. L.
1952 *Feudalism* (tr., Philip Grierson). London and New York: Longmans, Green.
Garcia, Lt.
1955 "Moeurs et coutumes des Teda du Tou," *Bulletin de l'Institut d'Études Centrafricaines,* No. 10.
Gardiner, A. F.
1836 *A Journey to the Zoolu Country.* London: W. Crofts.
Gerth, H. H., and Mills, C. W. (eds.)
1946 *From Max Weber: Essays in Sociology.* New York: Oxford University Press.
Gielgud, Val.
1905 "Notes" in H. Marshall Hole, "Notes on the Batonga and Batshukulumbwi Tribes," *Proceedings of the Rhodesia Scientific Association,* 5:2:62–67.
Glück, Julius.
1956 "African Architecture," *Tribus,* Neue Folge, 6:65–81. Tr. by Vera C. Chimene and Marguerite Chesbrough (orig. "Afrikanische Architektur," Stuttgart: Linden-Museum).
Gluckman, M.
1949 "The Role of the Sexes in Wiko Circumcision Ceremonies," *Social Structure,* ed. by M. Fortes, pp. 145–67. Oxford: Clarendon Press.
1950 "Kinship and Marriage Among the Lozi of Northern Rhodesia and the Zulu of Natal," in *African Systems of Kinship and Marriage,* ed. by A. R. Radcliffe-Brown and D. Forde. London: Oxford University Press.
Goodenough, Ward.
1965 "Rethinking 'Status' and 'Role': Toward a General Model of

the Cultural Organization of Social Relationships," *The Relevance of Models for Social Anthropology,* ed. by M. Banton, pp. 1–24. London: Tavistock Publications.

Goodfellow, D. M.
1939 *Principles of Economic Sociology.* London: Routledge and Sons.

Goody, J.
1962 *Death, Property and the Ancestors.* Stanford: Stanford University Press.
1963 "Feudalism in Africa," *Journal of African History,* 4:1:1–18.

Gouldsbury, V. S.
1897 "Report of His Journey into the Interior of the Gold Coast," Accra, March 27, 1876. C.O. 96.119, No. 5162/s, enclosed in Gov. G. C. Strahan to Lord Carnarvon, April 30, 1876, in the Public Record Office. Cited in F. Wolfson, *Pageant of Ghana,* London: Oxford University Press, 1958.

Grandidier, A.
1908 *Histoire physique, naturelle et politique de Madagascar,* Vol. 4, tome 1., *Ethnographie de Madagascar.* Paris: L'Imprimerie nationale.

Gravel, P.
1962 *The Play for Power.* Unpublished Ph.D. dissertation.

Green, M. M.
1941 "Land Tenure in an Ibo Village," published for the London School of Economics and Political Science. *Monographs on Social Anthropology,* No. 6, pp. 1–44.

Greenberg, J. H.
1955 *Studies in African Linguistic Classification.* New Haven: Compass.
1970 "African Languages," *Collier's Encyclopedia,* I:243–47.

Griaule, M., and Dieterlen, G.
1951 *Signes graphiques soudanais.* Paris: Hermann.
1965 *Le Renard Pâle.* Paris: Institut d'ethnologie.

Grove, A. T.
1951 "Soil Erosion and Population Problems in Southeast Nigeria," *Geographic Journal,* 117:291–306.

Gulliver, P.
1951 *A Preliminary Survey of the Turkana.* Cape Town: Communications from the School of African Studies, University of Cape Town, New Series, No. 26.
1953 "The Age-set Organization of the Jie Tribe," *Journal of the Royal Anthropological Institute,* 83:147–68.
1955 *The Family Herds.* London: Routledge and Kegan Paul.
1963 *Social Control in an African Society.* New York: New York University Press.

Hailu, A. P.
1946 *Messa Etiopica detta "Degli Apostoli."* Rome: Casa Editrice degli Lazariste.

Hambley (Hambly), W. D.
1934 *The Ovimbundu of Angola.* Field Museum of Natural History, Anthropology Publication Series, 21:2:89–362.

Hamer, J. H.
1967 "Voluntary Associations as Structures of Change among the Sidamo of Southwestern Ethiopia," *Anthropological Quarterly,* 40:2: 73–91.
1970 "Sidamo Generational Class Cycles: A Political Gerontocracy," *Africa,* 40:1:50–70.

Harden, J. M.
1928 *The Anaphoras of the Ethiopic Liturgy.* London: Macmillan.

Harrison, J. E.
1948 (orig. 1913) *Ancient Art and Ritual.* London: Oxford University Press.

Hay, R. L.
1963 "Stratigraphy of Beds I through IV, Olduvai Gorge, Tanganyika," *Science,* 139:829–33.

Heinzelin, J. de.
1962 "Ishango," *Scientific American,* 206:6:105–16.

Herskovits, M. J.
1926 "The Cattle Complex in East Africa," *American Anthropologist,* 28:230–72, 361–80, 494–528, 663–64.
1938 *Dahomey: An Ancient West African Kingdom,* 2 vols. New York: J. J. Augustin.
1948 *Man and His Works.* New York: Alfred A. Knopf.
1952 "Some Problems of Land Tenure in Contemporary Africa," *Land Economics,* 28:37–45.

Hichens, W. (ed.).
1940 *Muyaka bin Haji Al-Ghassaniy.* Johannesburg: University of the Witwatersrand Press.

Hichens, W.
1939 *Inkishafi.* London: Sheldon Press.

Hiernaux, J.
1968 *La Diversité-Humaine en Afrique Subsaharienne.* Brussels: Université Libre de Bruxelles.

Hill, D.
1957 "The Origins of West African Cattle," *Ibadan,* 1:14–16.

Himmelheber, H.
1951 *Aura Poku.* Eisenach: E. Röth.

Hinawy, Mbarak Ali.
1950 *Al-Akida and Fort Jesus, Mombasa.* London: Macmillan.

Historique et Chronologie du Ruanda (anonymous, n.d., n.p.).
Holas, B.
   1952   *Les Masques Kono, Haute-Guinée Française*. Paris: Geunther.
   1957   *Les Sénoufo*. Paris: Presses Universitaires de France.
Holden, W. C.
   1866   *Past and Future of the Kaffir Races*. London: Richards.
Hornbostel, E. von.
   1928   "African Negro Music," *Africa*, 1:30–62.
Horton, R.
   1962   "Kalabari World View: An Outline and Interpretation," *Africa*, 32:197–220.
   1963   "The Kalabari *Ekine* Society: A Borderland of Religion and Art," *Africa*, 33:2:94–113.
Hughes, A. J. B., and Van Velsen, J.
   1955   "The Ndebele," in *The Shona and Ndebele of Southern Rhodesia*, by Kuper, Hughes, and Van Velsen. London: International African Institute, Ethnographic Survey of Africa.
Huntingford, G. W. B.
   1950   *Nandi Work and Culture*. London: Colonial Office.
   1953   *The Southern Nilo-Hamites*. London: International African Institute, Ethnographic Survey of Africa.
Hutchinson, J. B.
   1954   "Evidence on the Origin of the Old World Cottons," *Heredity*, 8:225–41.
Hutereau, A.
   1909   *Notes sur la vie familiale et juridique de quelques populations du Congo Belge*. Tervueren, Belgium: Musée du Congo, Annales; Ethnographie et Anthropologie, Sér. 3.
   1922   *Histoire des peuplades de l'Uele et de l'Ubangi*. Bruxelles: Goemaere.
Idowu, E. B.
   1962   *Olódùmarè: God in Yoruba Belief*. London: Longmans, Green & Co.
Immenroth, W.
   1933   *Kultur und Umwelt der Kleinwüchsigen in Afrika, Studien für Völkerkunde*, 6:1–380. Leipzig: Verlag der Werkgemeinschaft.
Isaacs, N.
   1936   *Travels and Adventures in Eastern Africa*. Cape Town: The Van Riebeeck Society.
Jackson, J.
   (n.d.)   "Intelligence Report on the Ngwa Clan, Aba Division" [Local Archives, Eastern Region Government, Nigeria].
Johnson, S.
   1921   *The History of the Yorubas*. O. Johnson, ed., Lagos.

Johnston, B. F.
1958 *The Staple Food Economies of Western Tropical Africa.*
Stanford: Stanford University Press.
Johnston, H. H.
1923 *A Comparative Study of the Bantu and Semi Bantu Languages.*
Oxford: Clarendon Press.
Jones, A. M.
1959 *Studies in African Music.* London: Oxford University Press.
Jones, W. O.
1960 (orig. 1959) *Manioc in Africa.* Stanford: Stanford University
Press.
Junker, Wilhelm.
1890–92 *Travels in Central Africa during the Years 1875–[1886].*
(tr. by A. H. Keane), 3 vols. 1875–1878, 1879–1883, 1882–1886.
London: Chapman & Hall.
Junod, H. A.
1927 *The Life of a South African Tribe.* London: Macmillan.
Kaberry, P.
1957 "Primitive States," *British Journal of Sociology,* 8:224–34.
Kagame, Alexis.
1961 *L'histoire des armées-bovines dans l'ancien Rwanda.* Bruxelles:
Académie royale des sciences d'outer-mer, Mem. n.s., t. 25, fasc. 4.
Kelly, E. J. G.
(n.d.) Supplementary Memorandum to J. Jackson's Report [Local
Archives, Eastern Region Government, Nigeria].
Kent, R.
1962 *From Madagascar to the Malagasy Republic.* New York:
Praeger.
Kenya Land Commission.
1934 Report Cmd. 4556. London: Colonial Office.
Kenyatta, Jomo.
1938 "Marriage System," in *Facing Mount Kenya,* pp. 163–85.
London: Martin Secker and Warburg, Ltd.
Kenyon, K. M.
1957 *Digging Up Jericho.* London and New York: Praeger.
Kirby, P. R.
1932 "The Recognition and Practical Use of the Harmonics of
Stretched Strings by the Bantu of South Africa," *Bantu Studies,*
6:31–46.
1934 *Musical Instruments of the Native Races of South Africa.*
London: Oxford University Press.
Kirkman, J. S.
1964 *Men and Monuments on the East African Coast.* New York:
Praeger.

Kleindienst, M. R.

1961 "Variability Within the Late Acheulian Assemblage in East Africa," *South African Archaeological Bulletin,* 16:62:35–48.

1962 "Components of the East African Acheulian Assemblage: An Analytical Approach," *Actes du IVᵉ Congrès Panafricain de Préhistoire* (Léopoldville, 1959), ed. by G. Mortelmans, pp. 81–112. Tervueren, Belgique: Musée royal de l'Afrique Centrale.

Knappert, Jan.

1966 "Some Aspects of Swahili Poetry," *Tanzania Notes and Records,* No. 66:163–70.

Krige, E. J.

1936 "The Military Organisation of the Zulus," *Social System of the Zulus.* London: Longmans, Green & Co., Ltd., pp. 261–79.

Labouret, H., and Rivet, P.

1929 *Le Royaume d'Arda et son evangélisation au XVIIᵉ siécle.* Trav. et Mém. de l'Institut d'Ethnologie. Paris: Université de Paris.

Lacger, Louis de.

1940 *Ruanda.* Namur: Grand Lacs (Kabgaye, 1959).

Lagae, C. R.

1926 *Les Azande; ou, Niam-Niam.* Bruxelles: Vromant & Co.

Lagae, C. R., and Van Den Plas, H. V.

1921 *La langue des Azande:* Vol. I, *Introduction historico-geographique.* Gand: Éditions dominicaines "Veritas," t. 1.

Lander, R. L.

1830 *Records of Captain Clapperton's Last Expedition to Africa* . . . , 2 vols. London: H. Colburn and R. Bentley.

Lander, R. L., and Lander, J.

1832 *Journal of an Expedition to Determine the Course and Termination of the Niger,* 3 vols. London: J. Saunders.

Larken, P. M.

1926 "An Account of the Zande," *Sudan Notes and Records,* 9:1–55.

1927 "Impressions of the Azande," *Sudan Notes and Records,* 10: 85–134.

Leach, E.

1962 "On Certain Unconsidered Aspects of Double Descent Systems," *Man,* 62:214:130–34.

Leakey, L. S. B.

1931 *The Stone Age Cultures of Kenya Colony.* Cambridge: University Press.

1951 *Olduvai Gorge.* Cambridge: University Press.

1958 "Recent Discoveries at Olduvai Gorge, Tanganyika," *Nature,* 181:1099–103.

1959 "A New Fossil Skull From Olduvai," *Nature,* 184:491–93.

1960 "Recent Discoveries at Olduvai Gorge," *Nature*, 188:1050–51.
1961 "New Finds at Olduvai Gorge," *Nature*, 189:649–50.
1963 "Adventures in the Search for Man," *National Geographic Magazine*, 123:132–52.

Leakey, L. S. B.; Evernden, J. F.; and Curtis, G. H.
1961 "The Age of Bed I, Olduvai Gorge, Tanganyika," *Nature*, 191:478.

Lebeuf, J. P., and Detourbet, A. M.
1950 *La Civilisation du Tchad.* Paris: Payot.

Lee, V.
1932 *Music and Its Lovers.* London: George Allen and Unwin.

Lemarchand, René.
1966 "Power and Stratification in Rwanda: A Reconsideration," *Cahiers d'Études Africaines,* 6:4:592–610.

Les Mille et Une Nuits, trad. Galland, Paris: Garnier, t. 1.

Linton, R.
1936 *The Study of Man.* New York: D. Appleton-Century Co.

Lonsdale, R. L. T.
1882 Parliamentary Papers 46, 1882 (C-3386), No. 42 (pp. 182–86). Enclosure 2. Cited in F. Wolfson, *Pageant of Ghana,* London: Oxford University Press, 1958.

Louis, Roger.
1963 *Ruanda-Urundi, 1884–1919.* Oxford: Clarendon Press.

Lounsbury, F.
1964 "The Structural Analysis of Kinship Semantics," *Proceedings of the Ninth International Congress of Linguists,* Cambridge, Mass., August 27–31, 1962, ed. by Horace G. Lunt. The Hague.

Lucas, J. O.
1948 *The Religion of the Yoruba.* Lagos: C.M.S. Bookshop.

Ludlow, W. R.
1969 (orig. 1882) *Zululand and Cetewayo.* Pretoria: The State Library.

Luschan, F. von.
1898 "Beiträge zur Ethographie des abflusslosen Gebietes in Deutsch-Ost-Afrika," *Die mittleren Hochländer des nördlichen Deutsch-Ost-Afrika,* ed. by C. W. Werther, pp. 323–85. Berlin: Paetel.

McBurney, C. B. M.
1960 *The Stone Age of Northern Africa.* Harmondsworth, Middlesex: Penguin.

McCulloch, M.
1951 *The Southern Lunda and Related Peoples.* London: International African Institute, Ethnographic Survey of Africa.
1952 *The Ovimbundu of Angola.* London: International African Institute, Ethnographic Survey of Africa.

Magnes, B.
1953 "Essai sur les institutions et la coutume des Tsimihety," *Bulletin de Madagascar,* No. 89:5–85.
Mair, L. P.
1962 *Primitive Government.* Baltimore: Penguin.
Malherbe, W. A.
[Unpublished manuscript kept at Mkar Hospital]
Mangin, Fr. Eugène.
1921 *The Mossi.* Paris: Augustin Challamel.
Manoukian, M.
1950 *Akan and Ga-Adangme Peoples of the Gold Coast.* London and New York: Oxford University Press.
1952 *The Ewe-Speaking Peoples of Togoland and the Gold Coast.* London: International African Institute.
Mansfeld, A.
1908 *Urwald-dokumente.* Berlin: D. Reimer.
Maquet, J. J.
1961 *The Premise of Inequality in Ruanda.* London: Oxford University Press.
Maquet, J. N.
1956 *Notes sur les Instruments de musique Congolais.* Mémoires n.s., Tome 6, fasc. 4, 3–71. Bruxelles: Académie Royale des Sciences Coloniales.
Marees, Pieter de.
1602 *A Description and Historical Declaration of the Golden Kingdom of Guinea, Otherwise called the Golden Coast of Myna . . .* Cited in F. Wolfson, *Pageant of Ghana,* London: Oxford University Press, 1958, pp. 55–56.
Marshall, John.
1958 "Hunting Among the Kalahari Bushmen," *Natural History,* 67:291–309, 376–95.
Mate Kole, A.
1955 "The Historical Background of Krobo Customs," *Gold Coast and Togoland Historical Society, Transactions,* 1:4:133–40.
Mattei, L.
1938 "Les Tsimihety," *Bulletin de l'Académie Malgache,* n.s., t. 21.
Maupoil, B.
1943 *La Géomancie à l'Ancienne Côte des Esclaves.* Trav. et Mém. de l'Inst. d'Ethnologie, No. 42. Université de Paris.
Meek, C. K.
1931 *A Sudanese Kingdom.* London: K. Paul, Trench, and Trubner.
Mercer, S. A. B.
1915 *The Ethiopic Liturgy.* Milwaukee: The Young Churchman.

Mercier, P.
1954 "The Fon of Dahomey," *African Worlds,* ed. by D. Forde, pp. 210–34. London: Oxford University Press.
Merriam, A. P.
1953 "African Music Re-Examined in the Light of New Materials from the Belgian Congo and Ruanda-Urundi," *Zaïre,* 7:3:245–53.
1957 *Africa South of the Sahara.* Album notes for EFL Album FE503; New York: Folkways and Service Corp.
1959a "African Music," *Continuity and Change in African Cultures,* ed. by W. R. Bascom and M. J. Herskovits. Chicago: University of Chicago Press, 49–86.
1959b "Characteristics of African Music," *Journal of the International Folk Music Council,* 11:13–19.
Metman, P.
1963 "Schizophrenia or Initiation?" *The New Morality,* Inverno, 6:23–48.
Meyer, A. S.
1956 *Emotion and Meaning in Music.* Chicago: University of Chicago Press.
Middleton, J.
1953 *The Kikuyu and Kamba of Kenya.* London: International African Institute, Ethnographic Survey of Africa.
Mihaymid, Dr.
1962 "Discussion" following Dr. El Hadji El Nagar and Dr. Taha Baasher, "Psychomedical Aspects of Nomadism in the Sudan," *The Effect of Nomadism on the Economic and Social Development of the People of the Sudan.* Philosophical Society of the Sudan.
Miller, D. C.
1934 *The Science of Musical Sounds.* New York: Macmillan.
Miner, H.
1953 *The Primitive City of Timbuctoo.* Memoirs of the American Philosophical Society, No. 32. Princeton and Philadelphia.
Moerman, M.
1965 "Ethnic Identification in a Complex Civilization: Who are the Luc?" *American Anthropologist,* 67:5:1215–30.
Molet, L.
1953 "Le boeuf dans l'Ankaizinana; son importance sociale et économique," *Mémoires de l'Institut Scientifique de Madagascar,* Ser. C, t. 2.
1956 "Démographie de l'Ankaizinana; son importance Sociale et Économique," *Mémoires de l'Institut Scientifique de Madagascar,* Ser. C, t. 3.
1959 "L'Expansion Tsimihety. Modalités et motivations des migra-

tions intérieures d'un groupe ethnique du Nord du Madagascar," *Mémoires de l'Institut Scientifique de Madagascar*, Ser. C, t. 5.

Montagu, M. F. A.

1960 *An Introduction to Physical Anthropology*. Springfield, Ill.: Thomas.

Monteil, C. V.

1905 *Soudan français. Contes soudanais*. Paris: E. Leroux.

Monteil, G.

1950 "Réflexions sur le problème des Peuls," *Journal de la Société des Africanistes*, 20:2:153–91.

Monteil, P. L.

1894 *De Saint Louis à Tripoli par le Tchad*. Paris: F. Alcan.

Morgan, W. B.

1953 "The Lower Shire Valley of Nyasaland: A Changing System of African Agriculture," *Geographic Journal*, 119:459–69.

1955 "Farming Practice, Settlement Pattern and Population Density in South-Eastern Nigeria," *Geographic Journal*, 121:320–33.

Morton-Williams, P.

1956 "The Egungun Society in South-western Yoruba Kingdoms," *Proceedings of the Third Annual Conference of the West African Institute of Social and Economic Research*. Ibadan: University College.

1960a "Yoruba Responses to the Fear of Death," *Africa*, 30:1:34–40.

1960b "The Yoruba Ogboni Cult in Oyo," *Africa*, 30:4:362–74.

1964 "An Outline of the Cosmology and Cult Organization of the Oyo Yoruba," *Africa*, 34:3:243–61.

Murdock, G. P.

1959 *Africa: Its People and Their Culture History*. New York: McGraw-Hill.

Murray, K. C.

1961 "Comment" in *The Artist in Tribal Society*, ed. by M. W. Smith. London: Routledge and K. Paul, Ltd.

Nadel, S. F.

1942 *A Black Byzantium*. London: Oxford University Press.

Napier, J. R., and Weiner, J. S.

1962 "Olduvai Gorge and Human Origins," *Antiquity*, 36:41–47.

Naroll, R.

1964 "On Ethnic Unit Classification," *Current Anthropology*, 5:283–312.

Neuhaus, G.

1935 *Maulidi* (Mauludi). Berlin.

Newns, (n.f.n.).

1942 Intelligence Report on the Kalabari Clan. [Colonial Archives, Enugu, Eastern Region, Nigeria.]

Nicholson, G. E.
1960 "The Production, History, Uses and Relationships of Cottons in Ethiopia," *Economic Botany,* 14:3:3–36.

Nketia, J. H.
1955 *Funeral Dirges of the Akan People.* Achimota Press, Ghana (1969 ed., New York: Negro Universities Press).
1957a "Organisation of Music in Adangme Society," *Universitas,* 4:1:9–11.
1957b "Possession Dances in African Societies," *Journal of the International Folk Music Council,* 9:4–9.
1958a "Traditional Music of the Ga People," *Universitas,* 3:3:76–81.
1958b "Yoruba Musicians in Accra," *Odù,* 6:35–44.
1958c "Drum Proverbs," *Voices of Ghana* (pub. by Radio Ghana), 49–53.
1959a "Drum, Dance and Song," *Atlantic,* April, 69–72.
1959b "Changing Traditions of Folk Music in Ghana," *Journal of the International Folk Music Council,* 11:31–36.
1961 "African Music," *AMSAC Newsletter,* 3:19:3–6 (January–February), 4–8 (March–April).

Noll, Ned.
1960 "Le Haut Dahomey, d'après le Lieut. Tilho," *La Géographie,* 1:402–4.

Oberg, K.
1950 "The Kingdom of Ankole in Uganda," *African Political Systems,* by M. Fortes and E. E. Evans-Pritchard. London: Oxford University Press.

Ollone, Capt. de.
1901 *De la Côte d'Ivoire au Soudan et à la Guinée.* Paris: Hachette.

Ottino, P. A.
1963 *Les Économies paysannes malgaches du Bas Mangoky.* Paris: Berger-Levrault.

Pacques, V.
1954 *Les Bambara.* Paris: Presses Universitaires de France.

Palmer, H. R.
1908 "The Kano Chronicle," *Journal of the Royal Anthropological Institute,* 38:62–65.

Park, M.
1799 *Travels in the Interior Districts of Africa,* 2 vols. London: Neunes.

Parkinson, J.
1906 "The Legend of Oro," *Man,* 6:66:103–5.

Parrinder, E. G.
1949 *West African Religion.* London: Epworth Press (rev. ed., 1961).

Paulme, D.

1940 *Organisation sociale des Dogon.* Paris.

1961 "Oral Literature and Social Behavior in Black Africa," *L'Homme,* Tome 1, No. 1:37–49. (Tr. from orig. "Littérature Orale et Comportements Sociaux en Afrique Noire," by M. Chesbrough and E. P. Skinner, 1970–71.)

Paulme, D., and Lifszyc, D.

1936 "Les animaux dans le folklore dogon," *Revue de folklore français et de folklore colonist,* 7:282–92.

Peristiany, J.

1951 "The Age-set System of the Pastoral Pokot," *Africa,* 21:188–206, 279–302.

Piaggia, Carlo.

1941 *Le memorie di Carlo Piaggia a cura di G. Alfonso Pellegrinetti.* Florence [Firenze]: Vallecchi.

Plancquaert, M.

1930 *Les Sociétés Sécrètes chez les Bayaka.* Louvain: Bibliothèque Congo.

Posnansky, M.

1962 "Some Archaeological Aspects of the Ethno-history of Uganda," *Actes du IVᵉ Congrès Panafricain de Préhistoire* (Léopoldville, 1959), pp. 375–80, G. Mortelmans, ed. Tervueren, Belgique: Musée royal de l'Afrique Centrale.

Price-Williams, D. R.

1962 "A Case Study of Ideas Concerning Disease among the Tiv," *Africa,* 32:2:123–31.

Pugh, J. C.

1952 "Rainfall Reliability in Nigeria," *Proceedings of the International Geographical Congress:* Commission on Periglacial Morphology and Section on Climatology, pp. 36–41.

Radcliffe-Brown, A. R.

1952 *Structure and Function in Primitive Society.* London: Cohen and West.

Radcliffe-Brown, A. R., and Forde, D. (eds.)

1950 *African Systems of Kinship and Marriage.* London: Oxford University Press.

Randell, J.

1962 "The Potential Development of Lands Devoted to Nomadic Pastoralism," *The Effect of Nomadism on the Economic and Social Development of the People of the Sudan.* Philosophical Society of the Sudan.

Rattray, R. S. (ed. and tr.)

1916 *Ashanti Proverbs.* Oxford: Clarendon Press.

Rattray, R. S.
1923 *Ashanti.* Oxford: Clarendon Press.
1930 *Akan and Ashanti Folk Tales.* Oxford: Clarendon Press.
Rehse, H.
1910 *Kiziba, Land und Leute.* Stuttgart: Strecker.
Reischauer, E. O.
1965 "Japanese Feudalism," *Feudalism in History,* ed. by Rushton Coulborn. Princeton: Princeton University Press. pp. 28–30.
Revue Internationale de Botanique Appliquée et Expérimentale d'Agriculture Tropicale. See articles by: A. Chevalier, 32 (1952); H. Jaques-Felix, 37 (1947); A. Walker, 32 (1952).
Richards, A. I.
1950 "Some Types of Family Structure Among the Central Bantu," *African Systems of Kinship and Marriage,* ed. by A. R. Radcliffe-Brown and D. Forde, pp. 207–51. London: Oxford University Press.
Robinson, J. T., and Mason, R. J.
1962 "Australopithecines and Artifacts at Sterkfontein," *South African Archaeological Bulletin,* 17:66:87–125.
Roscoe, J.
1911 *The Baganda.* London: Macmillan.
Roth, Ling.
1903 *Great Benin; Its Customs, Art and Honors.* Halifax, England: F. King.
Rouch, J.
1954 *Les Songhay.* Paris: Presses Universitaires de France.
Sachs, C.
1940 *The History of Musical Instruments.* New York: W. W. Norton.
1943 *The Rise of Music in the Ancient World.* New York: W. W. Norton.
Samuelson, R. C. A.
1929 *Long, Long Ago.* Durban, South Africa.
Sansom, G. B.
1931 *Japan: A Short Cultural History.* New York: The Century Co.
Sauer, C. O.
1952 *Agricultural Origins and Dispersals.* New York: American Geographical Society.
Schapera, I.
1955 *A Handbook of Tswana Law and Custom.* London: Oxford University Press.
1943 *Tribal Legislation Among the Tswana.* London School of Economics Monographs on Social Anthropology, No. 9, 1–101.
1956 "The Development of Customary Law in the Bechuanaland Protectorate," in the symposium, *The Future of Customary Law in Africa,* pp. 102–16. Leiden: Afrika-Instituut.

1957 "The Sources of Law in Tswana Tribal Courts: Legislation and Precedent," *Journal of African Law,* 1:150–62.

Schebesta, P.
1926 "Die Zimbabwe-Kultur in Afrika," *Anthropos,* 21:484–545.
1932 *Bambuti.* Leipzig: F. A. Brockhaus.
1937 *Die Bambuti-Pygmäen von Ituri.* Bruxelles: Falk.

Scheffler, H.
1966 "Ancestor Worship in Anthropology; or, Observations on Descent and Descent Groups," *Current Anthropology,* 7:5:541–51.

Schneider, D.
1965 "Some Muddles in the Models; or, How the System Really Works," *The Relevance of Models for Social Anthropology,* ed. by M. Banton. New York: Tavistock Publications.

Schneider, H. K.
1953 "The Pakot of Kenya with Special Reference to the Role of Livestock in their Subsistence Economy," Ann Arbor, University Microfilms.
1956 "The Interpretation of Pakot Visual Art," *Man,* 56:103–6.
1957 "The Subsistence Role of Cattle Among the Pakot and in East Africa," *American Anthropologist,* 59:2:278–300.

Schwab, G.
1947 *Tribes of the Liberian Hinterland.* Cambridge, Mass.: Papers of the Peabody Museum of American Archaeology and Ethnology, Harvard University, Vol. 31.

Schweinfurth, Georg.
1873 *Im herzen von Afrika* (*The Heart of Africa,* tr. by E. E. Frewer), 2 vols. Leipzig: Brockhaus (Frewer tr., 1969, Chicago: Afro-American Books).

Seashore, C. E.
1938 *Psychology of Music.* New York: McGraw-Hill.

Sempebwa, E. K. K.
1948 "Baganda Folk Songs: A Rough Classification," *The Uganda Journal,* 12:1:16–24.

Shack, W.
1966 *The Gurage.* London: Oxford University Press.

Shantz, H. L., and Marbut, C. F.
1923 *The Vegetation and Soils of Africa.* New York: American Geophysical Society, Res. Series 13, pp. 125–26.

Sheddick, V. G. J.
1953 *The Southern Sotho.* London: International African Institute, Ethnographic Survey of Africa.

Shooter, J.
1857 *The Kaffirs of Natal and the Zulu Country.* London: E. Standford.

Sicard, H. von.
1952 "Ngoma Lungundu—eine afrikanische Bundeslade," *Studia Ethnographica Upsaliensia,* 5:1–175.
"Signes des Keita," *Signes Graphiques Soudanais,* by M. Griaule and G. Dieterlen, pp. 7–86. Paris: Hermann.
Skinner, Elliott P.
1957 "An Analysis of the Political System of the Mossi," *Transactions of the New York Academy of Sciences,* 19:8:740–50, Ser. 2.
1960a "The Mossi 'Pogsioure,'" *Man,* 60:27–50:20–23.
1960b "Labor Migration and Its Relationship to Socio-Cultural Change in Mossi Society," *Africa,* 30:375–401.
1960c "Traditional and Modern Patterns of Succession to Political Office Among the Mossi of the Voltaic Republic," *Journal of Human Relations,* 8:394–406.
1961 "Intergenerational Conflict Among the Mossi: Father and Son," *Journal of Conflict Resolution,* 5:55–60.
1964 "West African Economic Systems," *Economic Transition in Africa,* ed. by M. J. Herskovits and M. Harwitz. Evanston, Illinois: Northwestern University Press, pp. 77–97.
Smend, O. von.
1907 "Eine Reise durch die Nordostecke von Togo," *Globus,* 92: 245–50, 265–69.
Smith, M. F.
1954 *Baba of Karo.* London: Faber and Faber (1959, New York).
Smith, M. G.
1957 "The Social Functions and Meaning of Hausa Praise-Singing," *Africa,* 27:1:26–43.
Smith, M. W. (ed.)
1961 *The Artist in Tribal Society.* London: Routledge and Kegan Paul, Ltd.
Snowden, J. D.
1936 *The Cultivated Races of Sorghum.* London.
Soderberg, B.
1956 "Les instruments de Musique au Bas-Congo et dans les Régions Avoisinantes," *The Ethnographic Museum of Sweden Monograph Series,* Stockholm, Pub. No. 3.
Southall, A.
1956 *Alur Society.* Cambridge: University Press.
Spencer, Joseph E.
1954 *Asia, East by South.* New York: John Wiley & Sons, Inc.
Spencer, P.
1965 *The Samburu.* Berkeley: University of California Press.
Stamp, D. S.
1953 *Africa: A Study in Tropical Development.* New York: John Wiley & Sons.

Stekelis, M.
1963 "Recent Discoveries in the Jordan Valley," *South African Journal of Science*, 59:3:77–80.

Stokes, E. T. (ed.)
1962 "Historians in Tropical Africa," *Proceedings of the Leverhulme Intercollegiate History Conference* (Salisbury, 1960). Salisbury, Southern Rhodesia.

Stuart, James.
1913 *History of the Zulu Rebellion 1906.* London: Macmillan & Co., Ltd.
1924 *uTulasizwe.* London.
(n.d.) *uKulumetule.* (n.p.)

Summers, R. F. H.
1957 *Inyanga.* Cambridge: University Press.

Sumner, C.
1957 "Du Guèze à l'amharique moderne," *Étude expérimentale de l'amharique moderne.* Montréal: Éditions Bellarmin, pp. 14–19.
1958 *The Ethiopic Liturgy.* Addis Ababa: Artistic Printing Press.
1963 "The Ethiopic Liturgy: An Analysis," *Journal of Ethiopian Studies,* 1:1:40–46.

Talbot, P. A.
1912 *In the Shadow of the Bush.* London: W. Heinemann.
1926 *The Peoples of Southern Nigeria.* London: Oxford University Press.
1932 *Tribes of the Niger Delta.* London: Cass.

Taylor, W. E. (Rev.)
1915 "Inkishafi." See Taylor's tr. in *Inkishafi* by C. H. Stigand. Cambridge: University Press.

Thornthwaite, C. W.
1948 "An Approach Toward a Rational Classification of Climate," *Geographical Review,* 38:1:55–94.

Tobias, P.
1966 "The Peoples of Africa South of the Sahara," *The Biology of Human Adaptability,* ed. by Paul Baker and J. S. Weiner, pp. 111–200. Oxford: Clarendon Press.

Torday, E., and Joyce, T. A.
1910 *Les Bushongo.* Tervueren, Belgium: Musée du Congo belge, Annales, Ethnographie et anthropologie, Ser. 4, t. 2, Sec. 2.

Tracey, H.
1948 *Chopi Musicians: Their Music, Poetry and Dance.* London: Oxford University Press.
1949 "Musical Wood," *African Music Society Newsletter,* 1:2: 17–21.

Trautmann, R.
1927 *La littérature populaire à la Côte des esclaves.* Paris: Institut d'ethnologie.
Trewartha, Glenn T.
1961 *The Earth's Problem Climates.* Madison, Wisconsin: The University of Wisconsin Press.
Trimingham, J. S.
1966 "The Phases of Islamic Expansion and Islamic Culture Zones in Africa," *Islam in Tropical Africa,* ed. by I. M. Lewis, pp. 127–43. London: Oxford University Press.
Tucker, A. N., and Bryan, M. A.
1956 *The Non-Bantu Languages of North-Eastern Africa.* London: Oxford University Press.
Turner, V. W.
1955 "The Spatial Separation of Generations in Ndembu Village Structure," *Africa,* 25:2:121–37.
Tyler, J.
1891 *Forty Years Among the Zulus.* Boston: Congregational S. S. and Pub. Soc.
Van den Plas, H. V. (See C. R. Lagae and H. V. van den Plas.)
Van Gool, D.
1953 "Puberteitsriten bij de Bayaka," *Anthropos,* 48:853–88.
Vansina, J.
1955 "Initiation Rituals of the Bushong," *Africa,* 25:2:138–52.
1962 *L'évolution du Royaume Rwanda des origines à 1900.* Bruxelles: Académie royale des sciences d'outer-mer, t. 26, fasc. 2.
Van Wing, J.
1920 *De geheime sekte van't Kimpasi.* Bruxelles: Kongobibliotheek.
Verger, P.
1957 *Notes sur le culte des Orisa et Vodun à Bahia, la Baie de Tous les Saints, au Brésil et à l'Ancienne Côte des Esclaves en Afrique.* Dakar: Mémoires de l'Institut français d'Afrique noire, No. 51.
Wachsmann, D. P. (and Trowell).
1954 *Tribal Crafts of Uganda.* London: Oxford University Press.
1957 "Comment on Nketia: Possession Dances," *Journal of the International Folk Music Council,* 9:8.
Wagner, G.
1940 "The Political Organization of the Bantu of Kavirondo," *African Political Systems,* by M. Fortes and E. E. Evans-Pritchard, pp. 197–239. London: Oxford University Press.
Wallaschek, R.
1893 *Primitive Music.* London: Longmans Green.
Ward, E. F.

1927 "Music in the Gold Coast," *Gold Coast Review,* Vol. 3 (July–December).

War Office Précis.

Washburn, S. L.
1960 "Tools and Human Evolution," *Scientific American,* 203:3:1–15.

Waterston, J. M.
1953 "Observation on the Influence of Some Ecological Factors on the Incidence of Oil Palm Diseases in Nigeria," *Journal of the West Africa Institute for Oil Palm Research,* No. 1:24–59.

Wauters, G.
1949 *L'Ésotérie des noirs dévoilée.* Bruxelles: Éditions européennes.

Weber, M.
1923 *General Economic History.* London: Allen and Unwin.

Wescott, J.
1962 "The Sculpture and Myths of Eshu-Elegba, the Yoruba Trickster: Definition and Interpretation in Yoruba Iconography," *Africa,* 32:4:324–35.

Wescott, J., and Morton-Williams, P.
1962 "The Symbolism and Ritual Context of the Yoruba *Laba Shango,*" *The Journal of the Royal Anthropological Institute,* 92:23–37.

Westermann, D.
1927 *Die Westlichen Sudansprachen.* Berlin: W. de Gruyter u. Co.

White, C. M. N.
1949 "Stratification and Modern Changes in an Ancestral Cult," *Africa,* 19:324–31.

1955 "Factors in the Social Organization of the Luvale," *African Studies,* 14:3:97–112.

1956 "The Role of Hunting and Fishing in Luvale Society," *African Studies,* 15:2:75–86.

Wieschoff, H. A.
1941 *The Zimbabwe-Monomotapa Culture.* Menasha, Wisconsin: George Banta Publishing Co.

Wilson, P.
1961 *The Social Structure of Providencia Island, Colombia.* Unpublished Ph.D. Thesis, Yale University.

1967 "Tsimihety Kinship and Descent," *Africa,* 37:2:133–53.

"Review" of M. G. Smith's "Social Stratification in Grenada," *Caribbean Quarterly,* University College of the West Indies.

Wolfson, F.
1958 *Pageant of Ghana.* London: Oxford University Press.

Wrigley, C. C.

1959 "Kimera," *Uganda Journal,* 23:1:38–43.

1960 "Speculations on the Economic Prehistory of Africa," *Journal of African History,* 1:2:189–203.

Zahan, D.

1949 "Aperçus sur la pensée théogonique des Dogon," *Cahiers Internationaux de Sociologie,* 4:113–33.

Zeuner, F. E.

1946 *Dating the Past.* London: Methuen and Co., Ltd. [4th ed., 1958].

Zinderen Bakker, E. M. Van.

1963 "Early Man and His Environments in Southern Africa: Palaeobotanical Studies," *South African Journal of Science,* 59:7:332–40.

Index